Managerial Economics

PEARSON
Education

We work with leading authors to develop the
strongest educational materials in economics,
bringing cutting-edge thinking and best learning
practice to a global market.

Under a range of well-known imprints, including
Financial Times Prentice Hall, we craft high quality
print and electronic publications which help readers
to understand and apply their content, whether
studying or at work.

To find out more about the complete range of our
publishing, please visit us on the World Wide Web at:
www.pearsoneduc.com

THIRD EDITION

Managerial Economics
An Analysis of Business Issues

Howard Davies and Pun-Lee Lam

The Hong Kong Polytechnic University

FT Prentice Hall
FINANCIAL TIMES

An imprint of **Pearson Education**
Harlow, England • London • New York • Boston • San Francisco • Toronto • Sydney • Singapore • Hong Kong
Tokyo • Seoul • Taipei • New Delhi • Cape Town • Madrid • Mexico City • Amsterdam • Munich • Paris • Milan

Pearson Education Limited
Edinburgh Gate
Harlow
Essex CM20 2JE

and Associated Companies throughout the world

Visit us on the World Wide Web at:
www.pearsoned.co.uk

———————————

First published 1989
Second edition published 1991
Third edition published 2001

ISBN 978-0-273-64628-0

British Library Cataloguing-in-Publication Data
A catalogue record for this book is available from the British Library

Library of Congress Cataloging-in-Publication Data
Davies, H. (Howard), 1951–
 Managerial economics / Howard Davies and Lam Pun-Lee.—3rd ed.
  p. cm.
 Includes bibliographical references and index.
 ISBN 0–273–64628–1 (lib. bdg.)
 1. Managerial economics. 2. Business enterprises—Finance. I. Lam, Pun-Lee. II. Title.
HD30.22.D375 2001
338.5′024′658—dc21   00–069934

ARP Impression 98

Typeset in 9.5/12.5pt Stone Serif by 35
Printed in Great Britain by Ashford Colour Press Ltd

Contents

List of figures

List of tables

Preface to the Second Edition

Managerial economics is a subject which relates very closely to more directly practical business disciplines including management accounting, marketing, and corporate strategy. Indeed, many economists would insist that in so far as these other subjects have sound theoretical foundations they are usually to be found in economics.

Nevertheless, the relationship between the different disciplines is often an uneasy one. Economic models were not originally intended to provide prescriptions for managers, and yet they have often been used for that purpose when translated into the other disciplines. To the chagrin of the economists they find that their beloved models are used for purposes for which they were never intended and are then castigated for not fulfilling those purposes well. At the same time economists have tended to sell themselves short in terms of the potential practical usefulness of the subject by insisting on a very high degree of rigour, at the expense of usefulness. Marketing analysts and corporate strategists pick out some of the key qualitative insights of the economic models, and flesh them out with a level of detail which managers can recognise, to produce a highly saleable product which the economists rather wish they had thought of themselves.

This book aims to show how managerial economic analysis can be of relevance to decision-making, without attempting to make pretentious claims for its practical application, which would not bear scrutiny. In doing so, it attempts to differentiate itself from other texts on the subject by incorporating material not usually included in managerial economics textbooks written to date. This material includes aspects of marketing, like 'the marketing mix' and decisions associated with it. It also includes an introduction to Porter's work on the structural analysis of industries, and an outline of the basic elements of corporate strategy. Linking to that analysis is a treatment of the 'scope' of the firm which introduces the transactions cost framework of analysis, and its application to the theory of the multinational enterprise.

This mix of material should make the book useful to those involved in a variety of courses. Undergraduates in business studies will find it most useful at second year level, but can also use many sections in their first year. Post-experience courses such as the Master's in Business Administration (MBA) or the Diploma in Management Studies (DMS) should also find that while the material can be used by those with no background in theoretical economics, it develops their knowledge to a level which is appropriate for a general management student at master's level.

Each chapter contains a list of self-test questions, which should assist the student in checking that they have grasped the vocabulary and some of the fundamental analytical issues. There is also a question of examination standard at the end of each chapter, for which answers have been provided at the end of the book.

Howard Davies
October 1990

Preface to the Third Edition

It has been pleasing to see healthy sales of the first two editions of this text and the basic objective of this third edition remains the same. That is to 'show how managerial economic analysis can be of relevance to decision-making, without attempting to make pretentious claims for its practical application, which would not bear scrutiny'.

In writing this edition we have drawn on our experience of using the book as a text for nearly ten years, and on the developing literature. This version is significantly different in a number of respects. First, it has been co-authored, with P-L Lam bringing his considerable experience of teaching the subject to bear. Second, as a result of that input, we have re-arranged the structure so that the material concerning the firm itself comes first, followed by a consideration of the business environment, then the analysis of business decisions before concluding with two chapters on public policy. Third, we have incorporated new material in a number of respects. There are new chapters on game theory, the economics of networks and the economics of regulation. The approach to business strategy now focuses much more closely on the contribution that has been made by economists to the analysis of strategy, first in the structure–conduct–performance tradition and then in the resource-based approach. The amount of space devoted to the issue of ownership and control, and to transaction cost analysis, has been significantly increased.

Looking over the new edition, two observations offer themselves. The first is that we have tried to extend the 'academic reach' of the material upwards a little. We believe that it is still accessible for students who have never studied economics before, or whose background is limited. At the same time we have tried to show what is happening at a more advanced level. Second, it is interesting to see that the references now include many more papers from outside Economics as narrowly defined. In Management, Marketing, Business Strategy and Finance, analysts have found it increasingly useful to draw on the conceptual frameworks put in place by economists. We find that encouraging and we hope that readers of this latest edition will appreciate that economic analysis can speak to the problems facing managers, without providing 'recipes' or 'cookbooks'.

Finally we would like to take this opportunity to thank our students for their help, our families for their forbearance and the staff at Pearson Education for their patience.

Howard Davies and Pun-Lee Lam
Hong Kong
December 2000

Publisher's acknowledgements

We are grateful to the following for permission to reproduce copyright material:

Table 3.1 based on *Economic Organization*, published by Wheatsheaf, reprinted by permission of Pearson Education Ltd. (Williamson, O. 1986); Table 4.1 from Shareholder Value and the Market in Corporate Control in OECD Countries in *Financial Market Trends*, 69, February, copyright OECD 1998 (Thompson, J. K. 1998); Figure 5.1 from Global Strategy: A Review and an Integrated Conceptual Framework in *European Journal of Marketing*, 30, 1, MCB University Press Ltd. (Zou, S. and Cavusgil, T. 1996); Table 5.1, Table 5.2 and Table 5.3 from *United Nations Conference on Trade and Development (UNCTAD) World Investment Report 1999: Foreign Direct Investment and the Challenge of Development*, United Nations, New York and Geneva, 1999; Table 8.1 from Advertising Effects in Complete Demand Systems in *Applied Economics*, Vol. 24, Taylor & Francis Ltd, *http://www.tandf.co.uk/journals* (Baye, M., Jansen, D., and Lee, J. 1992); Table 8.3 from Re-structuring the Hong Kong Gas Industry in *Energy Policy*, Vol. 24, No. 8, Elsevier Science (Lam, P.-L. 1996); Table 9.1 from *Economies of Scale in Manufacturing Industry*, University of Cambridge, Department of Applied Economics, Occasional Papers, No. 28, reprinted by permission of Cambridge University Press (Pratten, C. F. 1971); Figure 11.1 from *Competitive Strategy: Techniques for Analyzing Industries and Competitors*, The Free Press, a Division of Simon and Schuster, Inc. (Porter, M. E. 1980); Figure 12.6 from *Financial Statement Analysis*, (c) 1978, reprinted by permission of Prentice-Hall, Inc., Upper Saddle River, NJ (Foster, G. 1978); Figure 18.1 from Measurement of Business Performance in Strategy Research: A Comparison of Approaches in *Academy of Management Review*, 11 (4), Academy of Management (Venkatraman, N. and Ramanujam, V. 1986); Figure 19.1, Table 19.1 and Figure 19.5 from *Winners and Losers*, The Independent Institute (Leibowitz, S. and Margolis, S. 1999); Table 19.2 from The Economics of Networks in *International Journal of Industrial Organization*, October, Elsevier Science (Economides, E. 1996).

1 The definition and scope of managerial economics

A definition of managerial economics

Managerial economics is most easily defined as the application of economic analysis to business problems. That very general definition covers a wide variety of topics and a number of very different approaches to the subject, reflected in the range of textbooks available. Before proceeding it is useful to set them in context.

The origins and methods of managerial economic analysis

Managerial economics and microeconomics

Most of the analysis to be found in textbooks on managerial economics has its origins in theoretical microeconomics. Topics like the theory of demand, the profit-maximising model of the firm, optimal prices and advertising expenditures and the impact of market structure on firms' behaviour are all approached using the economist's standard intellectual 'tool-kit' which consists of building and testing models.

The process of model-building

The use of models is a common feature of widely different types of investigation. Engineers build scaled-down replicas of aircraft and motor-cars, or computerised simulations, in order to examine their behaviour. Meteorologists use computer models of weather patterns to make forecasts. Accountants build financial models of companies in order to examine the impact of different decisions or different external circumstances on their financial position. Economic models are just another example of this widely used technique.

The process of building and testing an economic model is described in Figure 1.1.

The first step is to establish a set of definitions and assumptions about the entity to be modelled, which could be an individual household, the market for an individual product, the national economy or an individual firm. Having established a set of assumptions, the next stage in the process is one of theoretical

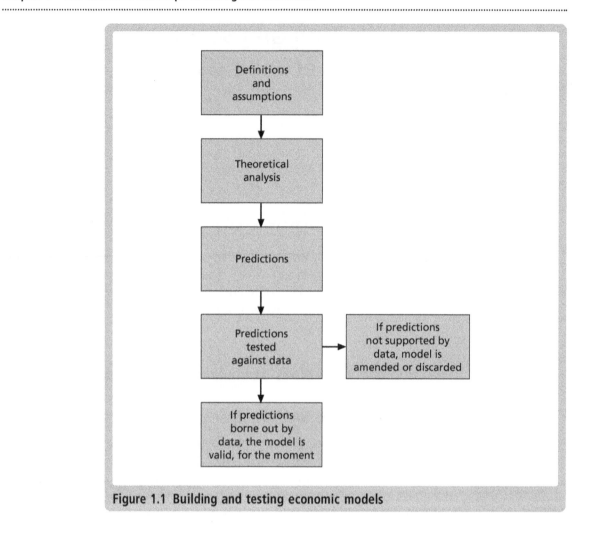

Figure 1.1 Building and testing economic models

analysis, or logical deduction, whereby the logical implications of the assumptions are followed through and identified. This can be a very difficult process, as the implications of the assumptions may be difficult to unravel and they may change dramatically with slight changes in the details of the assumptions made. As a result, this process takes up a very substantial proportion of the total effort involved and many economists specialise in this particular aspect of model-building. A brief examination of most learned journals in economics shows that a very high proportion of articles published are solely concerned with theoretical issues, unconnected with any empirical evidence. Nevertheless, despite economists' professional enjoyment of the theoretical aspects of model-building ('illicit relationships with beautiful models'), a model has little value until it has been tested against data on the actual behaviour of the entity being modelled. If a model provides a better explanation of the facts than the alternatives then it can be regarded as a useful means of explaining and predicting the behaviour that has been modelled. If it does not, the model must either be discarded or amended.

The use of economic models for decision-making purposes

It is clear that the various models explored in this book are in some sense 'about' business problems, including decisions on price and output, the scope of the firm, its structure and strategies for competition. However, that is not enough to demonstrate that the models can be used 'for' business in the improvement of decision-making. Such a claim is highly problematical, for a number of reasons. Most fundamentally, there is a wide gulf between the original aims of the microeconomic model-builders and the attempt to use their results directly for management purposes. The major objective of economic models of the firm has been to act as a building block in our understanding of how the economic system as a whole works to allocate resources. The research question being asked is 'how well or how badly does a market economy function, and what can be done to improve it?' That is a very different aim from that of assisting managers to take better decisions, and as a result there is a considerable tension between the major objectives of the models, the form they take and the attempt to use them for decision-making.

This tension is most apparent in the contrast between the 'normative' and 'positive' approaches to theory and the different types of methodology associated with each approach. A 'positive' theory is one that is concerned to explain what 'is', while a 'normative' theory is concerned with 'what ought to be'. In the positive approach to theory, which dominates mainstream economics, the main concern of theoretical analysis is to provide models that generate hypotheses that can be tested against data on the phenomenon in question. The aim is to explain what 'is'. If a model produces predictions about firms' behaviour that are testable, and if those predictions are supported by the evidence, then the model can be pronounced a success, at least until it is refuted by new evidence or supplanted by a theory that provides a more powerful explanation.

This approach to theory and model-building has a number of implications which can cause difficulties if the same models are used in a normative way to tell managers what they 'ought to do'. Most obviously, there is no need for the assumptions to be realistic. The test of a 'good' positive model is its ability to generate testable and accurate predictions by identifying the most important factors at work and excluding others. As a result, a firm as described in theory need bear no descriptive similarity to any recognisable real firm. Indeed, the whole purpose of theory is to cut through the complexities of real life in order to get to the essence of the way in which the world works. To do that successfully may demand the adoption of wholly unrealistic assumptions.

Clearly, then, given the basic aims and methods of mainstream economics, it is perfectly legitimate to construct a model of the firm that is wholly unrealistic as a description of real firms. Real firms are assumed to behave 'as if' they conform to the assumptions, and the process of deducing and testing predictions can follow from that assumption. If prediction of the firm's behaviour is the purpose of the theory, then the analysis is immune to the common lay criticism that it is unrealistic. The economist has a cast-iron defence. However, if the same models are used without amendment for the normative purposes often attributed to managerial economics, management accounting or marketing, there is much more substance to the criticism. For instance, the basic model of the firm assumes that the aim is to maximise profit and that perfect knowledge of cost and demand conditions is freely available. In that case the firm will set price and output in such a way that marginal cost and marginal revenue are equal to each other and predictions can be made on how the firm will respond to changes in costs, demand and market structure. Such a model underpins the analysis of how markets work and in general it performs very well as a predictive device. At the same time, if the aim is to help managers to maximise profit in an uncertain world, there is very little value in simply declaring that they should behave 'as if' they had perfect knowledge of cost and demand. Such an injunction is not operational and cannot be acted upon. In that sense the criticism of 'unrealism', which is often levelled at economic models, is perfectly valid if the models are used to derive prescriptions for managers to follow.

If many economic models cannot be put to direct use by managers, how can their use be justified in the context of decision-making? Is this book a waste of time and effort? There are a number of possible and powerful defences. The first is to argue that the adoption of a positive methodology, and the acceptance of an external perspective, is itself useful for decision-makers. By stepping outside their own individual circumstances managers may be able to avoid the common fault of generalising from an unrepresentative sample of one (their own experience). A second argument stresses the value of thinking logically through a problem and avoiding mistakes arising from simple logical errors. For instance, there has been a substantial debate over whether licences to provide Internet-enabled third-generation mobile phone services should be auctioned by governments. One argument made by those who oppose such auctions is that if the providing firms are required to make large payments, that will increase the price of the services they provide and thereby delay the adoption of the new technology. The basic economic analysis of the firm, set out in Chapter 2, shows this argument to be false. Payments for a licence are fixed costs that do not affect prices. The more appropriate logic is that firms estimate the profit they can make if they provide services at the most profitable price. The amount they are willing to bid for a licence is then determined by that estimate. The amount they offer for the licence is determined by the price they believe they can charge, not the other way round. Failure to understand that basic economic logic has led to a confused debate which could cost governments billions of dollars in revenue while inefficiently allocating important economic assets on the basis of dubious 'beauty contests'.

Another example of the value of simple economic logic is to be found in management accounting where a standard problem concerns whether a firm should accept an order for which the extra revenue exceeds the extra cost of meeting the order, but does not exceed the average cost as calculated using overhead cost allocation techniques. The economic model shows clearly that if the aim is to maximise profit, an order should be accepted even if average cost per unit exceeds the price per unit. A third argument in support of economic analysis is that simple but unrealistic models provide a stepping stone towards more realistic and complex versions that may provide usable normative guidelines.

Taking these arguments together, it is clear that there is considerable value in using the methods of economic analysis to examine the problems facing business decision-makers. However, it would be misleading to claim that the analysis can produce a set of normative decision rules which provide 'off-the-shelf' answers to complex business problems. It is as well to remember Lord Keynes's remark that economics is essentially a way of thinking about problems, rather than a set of solutions. This text will not show how a manager can select the 'correct' price or the right amount to spend on advertising, except in very restricted circumstances. It will indicate the factors and the forces that need to be taken into account when making those decisions, and comment on what we know about the links between theory and managerial practice.

The links between managerial economics and industrial economics

In managerial economics the emphasis is on the firm, the environment in which it finds itself, and the decisions that individual firms have to take. The relationship between managerial economics and industrial economics has changed very significantly over the last few decades. For many years industrial economics, or the economics of industrial organisation, was dominated by the *Structure–Conduct–Performance* paradigm. In that approach, the unit of analysis was the industrial sector and the key research question being addressed was 'what determines the average profitability of an industry?' The basic answer given to the question was that an industry's profitability (its performance) was determined by the conduct of the firms within it, which in turn was determined by the structure of the industry. Industry structure referred to a number of dimensions, namely:

- the level of concentration
- the height of entry barriers
- the degree of product differentiation
- the extent of vertical integration
- the extent of diversification.

Industry conduct referred to the type of behaviour engaged in by the sector's constituent firms, including:

- company objectives
- collusive versus competitive behaviour
- pricing policies
- advertising policies
- competitive strategies.

Performance referred to the outcomes achieved by the industry on average. While most emphasis was placed on profitability, other dimensions of performance included:

- growth
- productivity increases
- export performance or international competitiveness.

In most applications of the structure–conduct–performance paradigm, structure was treated as exogenous and as the cause of both conduct and performance. For instance, in a highly concentrated industry with high entry barriers it was anticipated that firms would adopt collusive policies and set high prices, hence earning high levels of profit. Conversely, in industries with low levels of concentration and free entry, firms would be forced to compete and profits would be relatively low. The most common approach to empirical work involved testing these hypotheses through cross-industry analyses where data on concentration, entry barriers and profitability were collected for a large number of industrial sectors and regression analysis was used to test for positive relationships between concentration, entry barriers and profitability.

For as long as industrial economics was dominated by the structure–conduct–performance approach its concerns were very different from those of managerial economics. The focus lay with the industry, not with the individual firm, and decisions take by individual firms received very little attention. Of course, there was some degree of overlap in that industrial economic models needed at least to refer to the way in which firms set prices, for instance, and managerial economics could not avoid considering the industrial structure within which the focal firm takes its decisions. However, the two approaches remained quite distinct.

This differentiation has been broken down to a significant extent as the 1980s saw a paradigm shift in industrial economics. In place of the structure–conduct–performance approach, 'game theory' has come to dominate the theoretical approach and detailed case studies have become the preferred form of empirical work. As game theory, explained in Chapter 13, centres upon the decisions taken by individual firms, viewed as 'players', the separation between the two branches of economics has become much less marked.

The links between managerial economics and management science

Just as managerial economics bears a relationship to industrial economics, so there are links between managerial economics and management science or the decision sciences. Management science is essentially concerned with techniques for the improvement of decision-making and hence it is essentially normative, in contrast to the positive approach adopted by mainstream economics. Mathematical techniques used in operational research like linear programming, goal programming, queuing theory and forecasting are all aspects of management science, which tends to have a heavily quantitative bias. In so far as managerial economics is often concerned with finding optimal solutions to decision problems, the boundaries between the two subjects are not clearly defined. Many textbooks on managerial economics contain sections that could quite easily be found in books on management science or quantitative methods. Nevertheless, it is important to recognise that the positive/normative distinction represents a very fundamental difference between the economist's approach to the firm and that of the management scientist. Economists build models of firm behaviour in which managers select optimal solutions to their problems. Hence they need to identify those optimal solutions and to that extent their models have an important common element with the problems addressed by management science. However, as explained above, the assumptions upon which the economic models are built need not be descriptively realistic and the primary purpose of the models is to predict how firms will behave, not to advise them what they ought to do. Economic models generally assume that managers themselves find the optimal solution, which becomes the predicted outcome. In management science, by contrast, the identification of optimal solutions is the end itself, descriptive realism represents a better specification of the problem on hand and the purpose is to tell firms what they ought to do in order to maximise some objective function. In management science it is not assumed that firms find the optimal solutions for themselves and those solutions are not used as *predictions* of company behaviour, but rather as *prescriptions* for what the firm should do to solve the problem under scrutiny.

Illustration | Economic theory and business practice – the overtaking analogy

One of the earliest contributions to the debate on the relationship between economic theory and business practice, written by Fritz Machlup in 1946, still provides one of the most vivid illustrations of the relationship between the 'unrealism' of economic theories and business practice.

Machlup drew an analogy between profit-maximising behaviour and the situation facing a motorist who is deciding whether or not to overtake on a two-lane highway. If we attempted to model the overtaking decision we would need to construct a very complex set of equations, taking into account a long list of factors including the weight, speed, power and acceleration of the vehicle being driven, the weather, the condition of the road and its gradient, plus the same information about any oncoming vehicles and a series of assumptions about the objectives and behaviour of the drivers. The model would then have to make the assumption that the overtaking driver has all of this information and it would be reasonable to conclude that the decision on whether to overtake is so complex that it cannot be taken correctly. And yet every day millions of drivers make dozens of such decisions and in the vast majority of cases those decisions are correct.

The overtaking decision may be compared with the attempt to make maximum profit. The standard model of the firm in economics assumes that decision-makers have perfect information about cost and revenue conditions, which is unrealistic. Nevertheless, that does not prove that they cannot maximise profits. Like the driver taking the decision to overtake, managers behave 'as if' they had the relevant information in which case they will behave like the profit-maximising model and that model will be a good predictor of their behaviour. The fundamental point is that a model based on unrealistic assumptions may effectively 'cut through' the complexities of an observed phenomenon to capture the most important features and thereby effectively predict behaviour.

The structure of this book

This book has been divided into four parts. Part I contains four chapters dealing with various aspects of the firm, including basic models (Chapter 2), the nature of the firm (Chapter 3), ownership and control (Chapter 4) and the multinational enterprise (Chapter 5). Part II turns to the analysis of the firm's environment, beginning with the theory of consumer behaviour and demand (Chapters 6 and 7) and methods for demand estimation and forecasting (Chapter 8). The structure of costs is examined in Chapter 9 while Chapters 10 and 11 explain formal models of market structure and Porter's five forces analysis. Chapter 12 outlines the ways in which risk and uncertainty in the environment may be taken into account. Part III examines business decisions, beginning with an introduction to game theory in Chapter 13, followed by the theory and practice of pricing decisions (Chapters 14 and 15) and non-price marketing decisions (Chapter 16). Chapter 17 examines investment decisions and Chapter 18 examines business strategy and its relationship to economics, while Chapter 19 analyses the information sector and the Internet. Part IV is concerned with public policy and the ways in which managers' decisions may be affected by government action. Chapter 20 examines policy towards competition, while Chapter 21 covers the analysis of regulated industries.

References and further reading

The overtaking analogy was set out in:

F. Machlup, 'Marginal Analysis and Empirical Research', *American Economic Review*, vol. 36, September 1946, pp. 519–54.

PART I

The firm

Business objectives and basic models of the firm

This chapter considers a number of basic models of the firm, each one based upon different assumptions about its objective. The neo-classical model is developed first and then the chapter goes on to examine some of the criticisms that have been directed at that model, and some of the alternatives that have been put forward in its place.

The neo-classical economic model of the firm

There are many different models of the firm, embodying many different assumptions, which could be described as 'economic' models. However, there is one particular version that forms the mainstream orthodox treatment of the firm, to be found in every introductory textbook and explained in more depth by Kreps (1990, chs 7 and 19). That is the 'neo-classical model of the firm'. This model centres around three basic sets of assumptions concerning the aim of the firm, and the cost and demand conditions facing it.

The assumption of profit maximisation

The first component of the neo-classical model of the firm is the assumption that the objective of the firm is to maximise profits, defined as the difference between the firm's revenues and its costs. In that form the assumption is too vaguely specified, because it makes no reference to the period of time over which profits are to be maximised. That may be resolved in one of two ways. The simplest is to see the model as a one-period or short-run model, where the firm's assumed aim is to make as much profit as possible in the short run. The short run is defined by economists as the period in which the firm is restricted to a given set of plant and equipment, and has some fixed costs which cannot be avoided even by ceasing production.

A slightly more complex version, which establishes a multi-period setting for the model, is to assume that the objective of the firm is to maximise the wealth of its shareholders, which in turn is equal to the discounted value of the expected future net cash flows into the firm. In that case, the firm can be seen as facing two interrelated kinds of decision. First, it has to take long-run or *investment decisions* on the level of capacity and the type of plant it wishes to install. Second, it has to decide upon the most profitable use of that set of plant and equipment. These short-run, *capacity utilisation*, decisions are essentially the same as those facing the firm maximising profits in the short run, and the same analysis applies.

If the profits made in each period are independent of each other, the single-period and multi-period models will be consistent with each other. However, there is a more difficult problem if the profits made in the current period could have an influence on the profits made in the future, because in that case it is possible that shareholders' wealth could be maximised by sacrificing profits in the current period. For instance, if a firm has a monopoly position, the maximum profit possible in the current period may be very large. However, if the firm uses its monopoly power to make that maximum profit, other firms may be attracted into the industry, or it might draw the attention of the anti-trust authorities. In either case, it is possible that the maximisation of shareholders' wealth will be better achieved by not taking the maximum profit available in the short run. The simple neo-classical model of the firm does not consider such complications, and it is best to interpret it as being concerned with the maximisation of short-run or single-period profits.

The assumption of profit maximisation gives the basic model of the firm a number of characteristics that distinguish it from other models. In the first place, it identifies a model that is *holistic* in the sense that, however large and complex, the firm is seen as an entity that can have objectives of its own and that can be said to take decisions. This is in marked contrast to the 'behavioural' model of the firm, where it is argued that 'only people can have objectives, organisations cannot'.

The second characteristic of the model, which also stems from the assumption of profit maximisation, is that it is an *optimising* model, where the firm is seen as attempting to achieve the best possible performance, rather than simply seeking 'feasible' performance which meets some set of minimum criteria. Again, this is in contrast to the behavioural model and to many quantitative techniques in operational research or operations management which seek to identify feasible rather than optimal solutions to problems.

Costs and output

The second component of the textbook model of the firm concerns the nature of the firm's production and the behaviour of costs, considered in more detail in Chapter 9. The firm is assumed to produce a single, perfectly divisible, standardised product for which the cost of production is known with *certainty*. In the short run, when some costs are fixed, the average cost curve will be U-shaped, as shown in Figure 2.1.

Cost per unit falls over the range A to B, as the fixed costs are spread over a larger number of units, but begins to rise beyond B as the principle of diminishing returns leads to increasing variable costs per unit.

As the textbook model is concerned with the short-run situation, it is short-run cost curves that are most relevant, and which are shown in the diagrams. The model depicts a firm that is attempting to maximise its profit with respect to a particular set of plant and equipment which has a particular short-run cost curve. If we also wish to consider long-run decisions then attention needs to

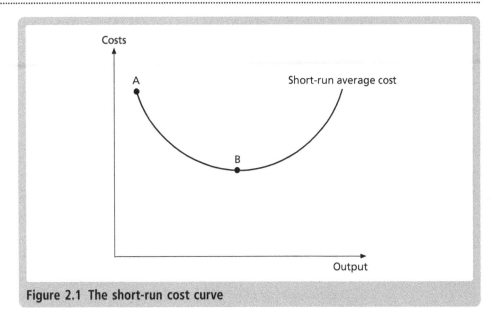

Figure 2.1 The short-run cost curve

be paid to the behaviour of costs in the long run, considered in more detail in Chapter 9.

Demand conditions

The third component of the orthodox model of the firm is the assumption that the firm has certain knowledge of the volume of output that can be sold at each price. These 'demand conditions' are considered in more detail in Chapters 6 to 8. For the purposes of this chapter it is sufficient to note that demand depends upon two sets of factors. First, it depends upon the behaviour of consumers, which determines the total demand for the product. Second, it depends upon the structure of the industry in which the firm is operating, and the behaviour of rival sellers. The simplest example to consider is that of the monopolist, where there is only one supplier of the product in question. In that case, consumer demand for the product can only be met by the single firm and there is no distinction between the total demand for the product and the demand for the individual firm. There is only one demand curve, which serves for both the firm and the industry. The precise shape of that curve depends upon the nature of the product in question, the number of consumers in the market concerned and their incomes, wealth and tastes. However, as the analysis in Chapters 6 and 7 shows, it can generally be assumed that the demand curve will slope downwards from left to right, indicating that more of the product can be sold at lower prices.

Equilibrium in the profit-maximising monopoly model

Having assumed profit maximisation and certain knowledge of cost and demand conditions, it is possible to move on to the second stage of model-building, which is to draw out the implications, or predictions, that follow from the assumptions.

The method of reasoning used to do this is essentially that of the mathematician. It is assumed that the problem has been solved, and then the conditions that must therefore hold are examined. The mathematical formulation of the model can be simply set out as follows:

Maximise $(q)

$(q) = R(q) – C(q)   where

$(q) = profit
R(q) = total revenue
C(q) = total costs
q = units of output produced and sold

Translated into words, this simply means 'maximise profit where profit is equal to revenue minus costs, and where costs and revenue each depend upon the amount of output that is sold'. Elementary calculus shows that if profit is maximised, the following conditions must hold:

Condition 1: $d\$/dq = dR/dq – dC/dq = 0$
     or $dR/dq = dC/dq$

Condition 2: $d^2R/dq^2 > d^2C/dq^2$

Restating these equations verbally, profit will be a maximum if the firm produces the level of output such that marginal revenue (dR/dq) equals marginal cost (dC/dq) and when the slope of the marginal cost curve exceeds the slope of the marginal revenue curve. This rather formal presentation of the model can be expanded upon using a diagrammatic version, shown in Figure 2.2.

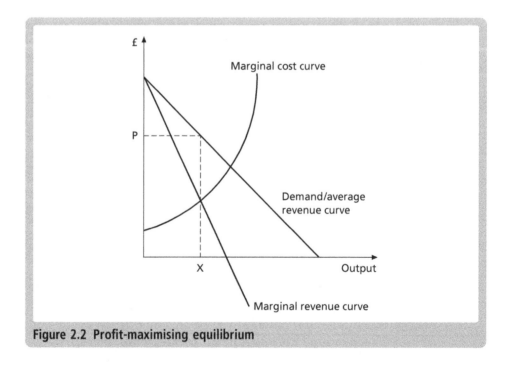

Figure 2.2 Profit-maximising equilibrium

In Figure 2.2, the profit-maximising level of output is X and the profit-maximising price is P. The reason for that is easily explained without resort to mathematics. The decision that the firm is facing concerns the level of output that should be produced and sold using the set of plant and equipment that has been installed. (The simple model always assumes that sales volume and output are equal, taking no account of the possibility of producing to stock or selling from stock.) It will pay the firm to produce any unit of output for which the extra revenue earned (marginal revenue) exceeds the extra cost (marginal cost). At level of output X all such units are being produced. If output is increased further, the additional units produced will add more to costs than to the revenues, and the level of profit will fall.

The diagram and the equations set out above identify the profit-maximising equilibrium for the firm. In the short run, under the assumptions made, the firm will produce the indicated level of output and sell it at the indicated price. If cost and demand conditions remain the same, the firm has no incentive to alter its price or output, and the firm is said to be in equilibrium.

Applications of the simple model

The model that has been developed above may be used in a number of ways. Its purpose in mainstream economic theory is essentially to predict how a firm will respond to changes in its environment. If some aspect of the environment changes, the model indicates the ways in which the firm will respond in order to move to a new equilibrium. For instance, if demand increases, both price and output will increase. If costs rise, price will rise but output will fall. Table 2.1 shows the comparative static properties of the profit-maximising model.

In addition to these 'positive' uses of the model, it may be used (with caution) for 'normative' purposes, providing prescriptions telling managers what they 'ought to do' in certain circumstances. For instance, a direct implication of the model is that a firm seeking maximum profit should produce every unit of output for which the marginal revenue exceeds marginal cost. If it is not doing so, then it is not maximising. That point may be presented as a prescription, and it is often extended in the management accounting literature into the very similar finding that firms should always agree to accept business that brings in greater *incremental revenue* than *incremental cost*. (The difference between the two is that *marginal* revenue and cost refers to the changes in total revenue and total cost when *one*

Table 2.1 The comparative static properties of the profit-maximising model

Change	Impact of the change on:	
	Price	Output
Demand increase	Increases	Increases
Demand fall	Falls	Falls
Increase in variable cost	Increases	Falls
Lump sum tax or change in fixed costs	No effect	No effect

more unit of output is produced and sold – or the rates of change of revenue and cost with output – while *incremental* revenue and cost refers to the change in total revenue and cost associated with an increase in output of any size, usually a batch or an order.)

Such prescriptions are valid, provided that the firm is attempting to maximise profit and the assumptions of the model are completely fulfilled. If they are not, however, it could be inappropriate to adopt the prescriptions without further thought.

Profits in the long run: the maximisation of shareholders' wealth

The profit-maximising model set out above is concerned with capacity utilisation and the short run. The firm has some fixed costs, arising from a given set of plant and equipment, and is concerned to make as much profit as possible, given the constraints set by that equipment. However, the firm also has to take investment decisions, which are concerned with the long run, in which no costs are fixed and when the firm is free to choose whichever set of plant and equipment it prefers.

When considering these long-run decisions it is not sufficient to characterise the firm's objective as 'profit maximisation' because profit is defined as revenue minus opportunity cost in a single period, without reference to the pattern of returns over time. It might be argued very simplistically that long-run profit maximisation consists of maximising the simple sum of profits over a number of short periods, but that would leave the unanswered question 'over how long should profits be added up?'. More significantly, such a simple addition would give the same weighting to returns occurring at different times, thereby ignoring the time-value of money (see Chapter 17 for a fuller explanation).

In order to avoid this difficulty, the long-run objective of the profit-maximising firm is said to be the maximisation of shareholders' wealth, which is achieved by maximising the value of the firm. This in turn is measured by the *present value* of the stream of expected future net cash flows accruing to the firm. The restatement of the firm's profit objective in this way allows the short run and the long run to be properly integrated. In the long run, as shown on Chapter 17, the firm decides upon the set of capital equipment to purchase by using investment appraisal techniques based upon the calculation of present values. However, these calculations themselves require estimates of the revenues and costs that are associated with each investment project, on the assumption that the equipment, once purchased, will be used to secure maximum profit. Choosing a set of capital equipment in the long run therefore requires the solution of the questions concerning revenues, costs and profits in the short run.

If the profits earned in each period, or each short run, are independent of each other, then the maximisation of profit in each period will lead to the maximisation of shareholders' wealth. However, as noted earlier in this chapter, if profits in one period depend upon profits in another, there may be a conflict between the two objectives. A firm with a monopoly position might make maximum profit in the short run by exploiting that position to the full, but in doing so it might attract entry to the industry, or anti-trust action from government, which would reduce profit in future periods. Maximising shareholders' wealth could require the sacrifice of immediate profits in order to protect their value in the longer term, depending upon the shape of the time-stream of profits, and the *discount rate* used to calculate present values. As the long-run objective, formulated in present value terms, takes account of the relative weighting to be given to profits accruing at different times, it should be given priority if such a conflict between objectives arises.

Managerial discretion models of the firm

'Managerial' criticisms of the profit-maximising model

The textbook model of the profit-maximising firm has been criticised on a number of different grounds. Perhaps the best known of these centres around the claim that it is unrealistic to assume that firms aim for maximum profits in a modern economy where ownership and control of firms lie with different groups of individuals. The pioneering work of Berle and Means (1932) in the United States demonstrated that the modern corporation was not simply a larger version of the owner-managed firm, but that ownership and control had become separated. Control lay in the hands of professional managers while ownership rested with shareholders. If the interests of shareholders and managers differ, if shareholders have relatively limited information about the performance of the firms they own, and if shareholders take relatively little interest in the firms' operations (provided that a satisfactory dividend is paid), then managers may have a good deal of 'discretion' to pursue their own objectives. This will be particularly true where firms have some degree of monopoly power and do not need to compete keenly in order to make a satisfactory level of profit. It has been suggested, therefore, that in such markets firms do not pursue profit as their major objective.

The suggestion that profit is not the objective of modern corporations has led to the search for alternative models based upon different assumptions about the firm's objective. There are many such models, but the classic examples are:

- the sales revenue maximising model, developed by Baumol (1958)
- the managerial utility maximising model (O. Williamson 1963)
- J. Williamson's integrative model (1966).

Baumol's sales revenue maximising model

Baumol's model stems from his observation that the salaries of managers, their status and other rewards often appear to be more closely linked to the size of the companies in which they work, measured by sales revenue, than to their profitability. In that case, managers may be more concerned to increase size than to increase profits, and the firm's objective will be to maximise sales revenue rather than profits.

If the assumption of profit maximisation is replaced by that of sales revenue maximisation, then a different model results. In many respects, it shares

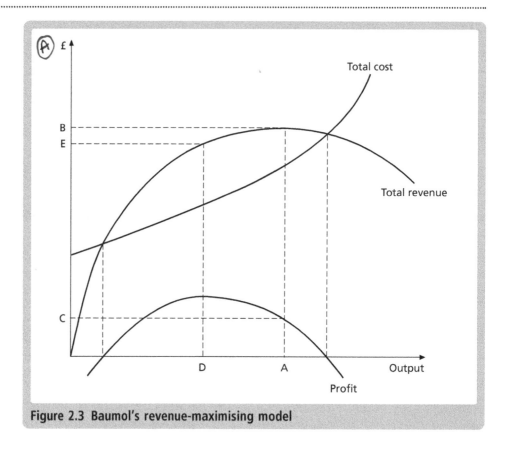

Figure 2.3 Baumol's revenue-maximising model

fundamental characteristics with the standard model, as it is also an optimising model in which a single product firm aims for a single objective, having perfect information about its cost and demand conditions. Nevertheless, the details are different, as illustrated in Figure 2.3, which sets out the basic version of the model, using total revenue, total cost and profit curves.

In Figure 2.3 the firm will choose to produce level of output A, giving total revenue B and profit C. Note that this implies a higher level of output, and therefore a lower price, than the equivalent profit-maximiser, who would produce output D and earn revenue E.

A straightforward revenue-maximiser will always produce more and charge less than a profit-maximising firm facing the same cost and demand conditions for the following reason:

- for revenue maximisation, marginal revenue = 0
- for profit maximisation, marginal revenue = marginal cost
- as marginal cost must be greater than 0, then for a profit-maximiser marginal revenue must be greater than 0
- therefore marginal revenue for a profit-maximiser must be greater than marginal revenue for a revenue-maximiser
- as marginal revenue slopes downwards to the right, equilibrium output must be higher for a revenue-maximiser than for the profit-maximiser.

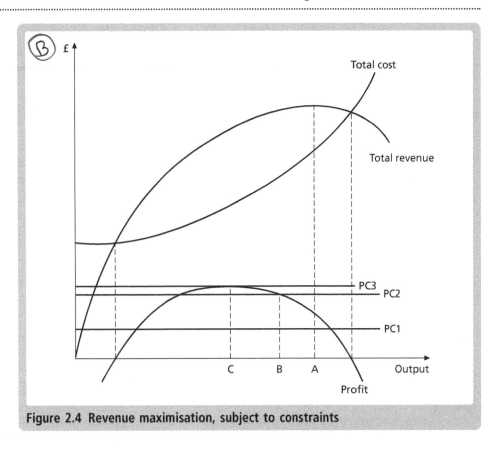

Figure 2.4 Revenue maximisation, subject to constraints

In the example shown in Figure 2.3 the sales-maximiser also makes some profit. However, this may not be enough to satisfy the shareholders, and in many cases maximising revenue may imply making losses. As a result the simple revenue-maximising model is implausible, and the model needs to be amended to include a profit constraint. Instead of simply assuming that the firm aims for maximum revenue, without regard to the implications for profit, it is assumed that the object-ive is the maximisation of sales revenue, subject to meeting a minimum profit constraint. This version is shown in Figure 2.4.

As the figure shows, there are three possible cases in this amended version of the model. The first is where the profit constraint is as shown by the line PC1. In this case the constraint does not 'bite'. At the level of output that maximises revenue, enough profit is made to satisfy the shareholders. The second case is where the profit constraint is as indicated by PC2. At the revenue-maximising level of output, insufficient profit is made to satisfy the shareholders. Hence, out-put is reduced until that constraint is met, at level of output B. The third case is where the minimum profit required to satisfy the shareholders is equal to the maximum profit that can be made, in which case the firm has to reduce its out-put to C.

In this third case, the firm behaves in exactly the same way with respect to its output and price as a profit-maximiser, despite the fact that it has set itself a different objective. This is an important point, which takes the analysis back to an argument made above in the discussion on the purpose of models. If shareholders insist upon the maximum level of profit being earned, then the profit-maximising model will provide accurate predictions of the behaviour of a firm whose management prefers to maximise sales revenue. If the purpose of the model is to predict the firm's behaviour, the fact that managers see their aim as maximising sales revenue, and not profit, is irrelevant. The firm behaves 'as if' it were a profit-maximiser.

The revenue-maximising model can be compared to the profit-maximising model with respect to its comparative static properties, which reveals both similarities and differences. If demand increases, both types of firm respond in the same way, with an increase in output and price. On the other hand, it has been shown above for a profit-maximiser that if fixed costs increase, or a lump-sum tax is imposed, price and output will not change. However, for a revenue-maximiser whose profit constraint is already biting, a lump-sum tax will reduce profits and will force the firm to lower its output and raise its price.

The managerial utility maximising model

In Baumol's sales revenue maximising model, managers' interests are tied to a single variable, with the addition of a profit constraint. Oliver Williamson's managerial utility maximising model takes account of a wider range of variables by introducing the concept of 'expense preferences', beginning with the assumption that managers attempt to maximise their own utility. The term 'expense preference' simply means that managers get satisfaction from using some of the firm's potential profits for unnecessary spending on items from which they personally benefit. Williamson identifies three major types of expense from which managers derive utility. These are:

1. *The amount that managers can spend on staff, over and above those needed to run the firm's operations (S).* This variable captures the power, prestige, status and satisfaction that managers experience from having control over larger numbers of people.
2. *Additions to managers' salaries and benefits in the form of 'perks' (M).* These include unnecessarily luxurious company cars, extravagant entertainment and clothing allowances, club subscriptions, palatial offices and similar items of expenditure. Such items may also be thought of as 'managerial slack' or 'X-inefficiency' (see below). They appear as costs to the firm, but are not necessary for the efficient conduct of its activities and are in effect coming out of profits.
3. *Discretionary profits (D).* These are after-tax profits over and above the minimum required to satisfy the shareholders. They are therefore available to the managers as a source of finance for 'pet projects' and allow the managers to invest in developing the firm in directions that suit them, enhancing their power, status and satisfaction.

Clearly there are conflicts and trade-offs between the different objectives in this model, and it is considerably more complex than those considered thus far. The detailed workings of the model require mathematics that go beyond the requirements of this text. Nevertheless, the main outlines are reasonably accessible. The basic form of the model is as follows:

$U = f(S, M, D)$ – managerial utility (U) depends upon the levels of S, M and D available to the managers

In common with the theory of consumer behaviour (see Chapter 6) it is assumed that the *principle of diminishing marginal utility* applies, so that additional increments to each of S, M and D yield smaller increments of utility to the management.

If R = revenue, C = costs and T = taxes, then:

Actual profit = $R - C - S$

Reported profit = $R - C - S - M$

If the minimum post-tax profit required by the shareholders is Z, then:

$D = R - C - S - M - T - Z$

The solution to the model requires the use of calculus in order to maximise the utility function (see the Illustration to this chapter on page 27 for an outline of the working). However, it is possible to set out a simplified version. If managerial utility is to be maximised, the last pound spent on S, M and D must yield the same marginal utility, i.e.:

$MU_S = MU_M = MU_D(1 - t)$ where t is the rate of tax on profits

This can be used to examine some of the comparative static properties of the model. If demand declines, then at every level of output D will decline. On the assumption of diminishing marginal utility, MU_D will rise, so that the equilibrium condition is no longer fulfilled. To regain equilibrium the available profits will be redistributed towards D and away from S and M. The level of output will fall. Similarly for a rise in fixed costs, or a lump-sum tax.

If the tax on profits increases, then $MU_D(1 - t)$ will fall and there will be a shift towards S and M, accompanied by increasing output.

The complexity of the Williamson model can make it difficult to examine in every detail. However, it does have an interesting application in explaining how take-overs are often followed very quickly by increases in reported profits. If the new management team exhibits a weaker preference for S and M, both of which entail unnecessary costs, they will prune these in line with their own preferences and will be able to report higher profits very quickly without too much difficulty and before altering any of the fundamentals of the business.

As in the case of the Baumol model, it should always be remembered that the logic of the utility-maximising model depends upon the management team having the discretion to earn less than maximum profits. If the minimum profit required by the shareholders is equal to the maximum possible, the managers will not have the discretion to indulge their taste for 'perks' and unnecessary staff.

J. Williamson's integrative model

Both of the models outlined above have been based around a single objective function. J. Williamson's integrative model goes one step further by combining single-period profit and sales maximisation with growth maximisation and the maximisation of the present value of future sales. All of these are shown in Figure 2.5.

The lower part of the diagram in Figure 2.5 shows total cost, revenue and profit in a single period, along with the profit constraint required in the Baumol model. The upper quadrant shows the relationship between the rate of growth and current sales revenue. Growth of sales revenue is assumed to be directly related to profits, so that growth is maximised when profits are maximised and growth is zero when profits are zero. A single-period profit-maximiser and a sales growth-maximiser will therefore both produce level of output Q_1. A single-period revenue-maximiser, subjected to the externally imposed profit constraint PC_{ext} will produce a higher level of output Q_2.

A firm that aims to maximise the present value of future sales will seek the combination of current revenue and growth rate that gives such a maximum. That can be found in Figure 2.5 by constructing 'iso-present-value' curves joining all points that have the same present value. As present value increases with both the growth rate and the current sales value, the maintenance of a constant present value requires that a higher growth rate be combined with a lower current

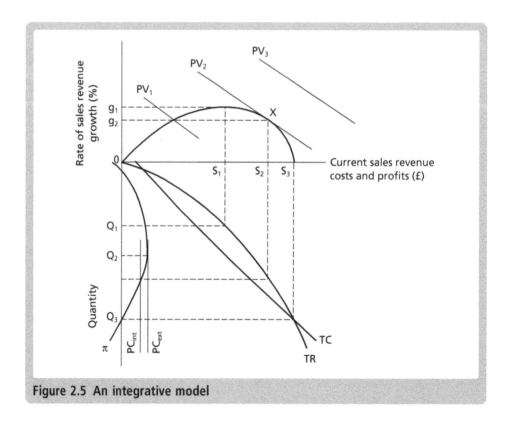

Figure 2.5 An integrative model

value of sales and vice versa. The 'iso-present-value' lines must therefore be negatively sloped as shown in the diagram by the lines PV_1 to PV_3. Higher present values are given by lines that are further away from the origin and the present value of sales is maximised at point X. That must lie to the right of the profit-maximising position, by virtue of the downward slope of the 'iso-present-value' lines, so that a firm that aims to maximise the present value of sales will always choose a level of output that exceeds that of the profit-maximiser. If the firm is to achieve its maximisation target it must grow at rate g_2, which requires the level of current profit given by the profit constraint PC_{int}, which is an internally imposed profit constraint set by the management in recognition of the need to achieve growth rate g_2.

In the diagram shown, the internally generated profit constraint is lower than that imposed externally. Maximising the present value of sales requires an output level greater than Q_2 and there is a conflict between the firm's desire for a higher level of sales and the need to meet the profit constraint. The outcome of that conflict depends upon the extent to which the managers of the firm have the discretion to pursue their own objectives when they conflict with others.

The behavioural approach to the firm

'Behavioural' criticisms of models of the firm

The 'managerial' models of the firm stem from criticism of the profit-maximising assumption, on the grounds that when ownership and control are separate, and many firms compete in relatively comfortable market structures, managers are able to direct the resources of companies towards their own ends. In many other respects the managerial models share similar characteristics with the orthodox textbook model of the firm. They are 'holistic' in the sense that the firm behaves as if it were a single entity, being capable of having objectives, even if those objectives are held by a group of managers and differ from those of the shareholders. The firm is seen as taking and implementing decisions. The models outlined above are all optimising models and it is also assumed that the firm has certain knowledge of the cost and demand conditions facing it. In effect the managerial models differ from the orthodox only in that they begin with a different assumption with respect to the firm's objective.

A more radical attack on the orthodox model of the firm, which also implies criticism of the managerial models, has been made by a group of theorists referred to as the 'behavioural school', building on seminal work by Simon (1959) and Cyert and March (1963). In this approach attention focuses on behaviour within the firm, which is not seen as a single entity but as a set of shifting coalitions among individuals, each of which has their own set of objectives. The fundamental argument is that organisations cannot have objectives, only people can, and that to perceive a firm as having an objective is an example of 'reification', confusing an abstract concept with a real entity.

In addition to rejecting the notion that a firm can have objectives, the behavioural theorists also reject the assumption that those taking decisions are perfectly informed. The assumption of certainty is abandoned and emphasis is placed on the idea that most organisations are so complex that the individuals within them have only limited information with respect to both internal and external developments.

The behavioural alternative

The behavioural model of the firm is therefore very different from either the orthodox model or the managerial models. It is not a 'holistic' model because the firm is not seen as a single entity with a single purpose. It is not an optimising model where the firm achieves the best possible performance with respect to its objective, and it is not based upon the assumption of certainty. In place of these features of the other models, it contains a number of key elements.

First, the 'firm' hardly exists, consisting of a group of individuals who form coalitions and alliances among themselves based upon common interests or characteristics, departmental loyalties or personal affinity. As a result the firm has multiple objectives which are in conflict with each other and which cannot be reconciled through a concept like the utility function, which gives a weight to each objective and allows an overall 'score' to be achieved. The accountants in a firm may wish to keep the level of stocks down in order to reduce the costs of holding them. At the same time the sales force may wish to hold a high level of stocks in order to be able to meet orders quickly. The research department may wish to employ a large number of qualified scientists, while the marketing department would prefer to spend more on advertising. Longer established employees may wish to avoid interruptions to their routine while newly employed executives may be anxious for change. Each individual will themselves have multiple objectives, arising from their personal histories, preferences and position within the firm and these multiple sets of objectives cannot be reduced to any simple overall statement that explains what the organisation as a whole is attempting to achieve.

The second major feature of the behavioural model, which distinguishes it from those outlined above, is that decision-makers exhibit 'satisficing' behaviour rather than 'optimising' behaviour. Neither the firm nor its component coalitions, nor individuals, are seen as attempting to maximise or minimise anything. Instead, each person or group has a 'satisficing' level for each of its objectives. If these levels are reached, they will not seek for more, in the short term at least, but if they are not met, action will be taken in order to remedy the problem. An important consequence of satisficing behaviour is that firms acting in this way will not keep costs down to a minimum. Instead they will exhibit 'organisational slack', incurring higher costs than are absolutely necessary.

A third feature of the behavioural model is that action within the firm takes the form of 'problem-oriented search using rules-of-thumb'. If one of the multiple objectives is not met, so that someone within the firm is dissatisfied, a search will take place for a means of meeting that objective. However, the search will be fairly narrow, relating solely to the objective that is not being met, and the firm will use rules-of-thumb to attempt to put the problem right. These rules of thumb are not arrived at through any detailed analysis, but are a function of the past experience of the firm and the people within it. For instance, if revenue falls, the firm may automatically raise its price, because that has been tried in the past and appeared to be successful.

Fourth, the aspirations of the individuals within the firm, which determine the levels of each objective with which they will be satisfied, change over time as a result of 'organisational learning'. If a firm succeeds in meeting all of its objectives for a period of time then eventually the individuals and groups will raise their aspiration levels, demanding more of whatever it is they care about. Eventually a situation will be reached where not everyone achieves 'satisficing' levels with respect to all of their objectives, at which point a problem-oriented search will take place to seek a solution to the problem. If one is found, the process of gradually increasing aspirations can continue. On the other hand, if a solution is not found despite a number of searches, aspiration levels with respect to the particular variable concerned will have to be reduced.

Clearly, the behavioural model is very different to the others that have been considered, and describes a number of very familiar features of organisational life. In many respects it is descriptively more realistic than either the orthodox or the managerial models and is attractive for that reason. However, it also has to be recognised that it has relatively limited value in addressing the questions with which managerial economics is concerned. If we consider the positive question of 'how do firms respond to changes in their environment?', the model offers little assistance because it focuses entirely within the firm. If we consider the normative question 'can we identify the decision rules that firms should follow in order to meet their objectives?', that question is not addressed either by the behavioural model. On the other hand, a firm that conforms well to the description set out by the behavioural theorists could behave in exactly the same way with respect to price and output decisions as the profit-maximising firm, or the firm described by one of the managerial models. If the shareholders are a powerful group within the firm and will only be satisfied with maximum profit, and if employees and managers are concerned for the firm's survival, the process of organisational learning may lead the firm towards profit maximisation. For the purposes of managerial economics, then, the behavioural model is of relatively limited usefulness.

The concept of X-inefficiency

A useful concept that links the behavioural model and the managerial utility model is that of *X-inefficiency*. In the standard, neo-classical, profit-maximising model it is assumed that the firm incurs the minimum cost achievable for the level of output being produced, given the set of plant and equipment that has been installed. In terms of the diagram, the firm is on its cost curve. Such a firm may be described as being 'X-efficient' or 'operationally efficient'. However, this may not be the case. A firm that is maximising managerial utility, for instance, will tend to spend more on staff and on 'perks' for the management than is necessary, in which case it may be said to be 'X-inefficient'. In terms of a diagram, it will be above its cost curve, as shown in Figure 2.6.

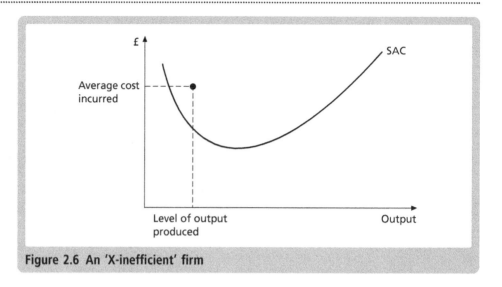

Figure 2.6 An 'X-inefficient' firm

Similarly, a firm that conforms to the behavioural model will incur higher costs than are strictly necessary and be X-inefficient, or have 'organisational slack'. Leibenstein (1966) emphasised the importance of X-inefficiency and considered the factors that are likely to encourage or discourage it. That analysis draws together a number of issues already considered above.

First, the degree of X-inefficiency will be partly determined by factors that are internal to the firm. If contracts between *principals* (the owners) and *agents* (managers and workers) are not efficient, then workers and managers will not be motivated to keep costs down, and the firm will be X-inefficient. If larger firms are more difficult to control, with a greater degree of bureaucratic rigidity, then they will also tend to be more X-inefficient.

The second set of factors that determine the degree of X-inefficiency is to be found in the external environment in which the firm operates. If the firm is forced by its environment to aim for maximum profit, it must eliminate X-inefficiency. On the other hand, if the management has the discretion to avoid profit maximisation, it will allow its costs to rise above the level that is strictly necessary. The environmental factors that lead to X-inefficiency are therefore the converse of the factors that force the firm to aim for maximum profits. If shareholdings are diffused among a large number of relatively ill-informed small shareholders, there may be little pressure from that direction. If the threat of take-over is limited, perhaps because the firm is too large to be under serious threat, or because anti-trust legislation prevents take-over, then the likelihood of X-inefficiency is correspondingly higher.

Similarly, the degree of X-inefficiency will tend to be higher as the market structure in which the firm operates is less competitive. If there are a small number of competitive rivals who are able to avoid direct competition with each other, and they are protected by barriers to entry into the industry, then there will be few penalties for slackness and X-inefficiency is correspondingly more likely to result.

In defence of the profit-maximising model

The methodological defence

The models described above have their origins in dissatisfaction with the profit-maximising model, arising from the claim that in practice firms do not attempt to maximise profits. The world is an uncertain place, where ownership and control are separate, where firms may not have a unified purpose and where they have a degree of monopoly power that cushions them from the need to maintain profits at their maximum level.

These issues are examined in more detail in Chapter 4, which deals with the relationship between ownership and control in the modern corporation. At this point, however, it is worth noting that supporters of the profit-maximising model may put forward a methodological argument in its defence. As explained in Chapter 1, the descriptive realism of an assumption is not necessarily a valid criterion on which to judge a model. If the purpose of the model is to predict, rather than to describe, then the criteria for evaluation are quite clear. First, the model must yield predictions, which is true for the profit-maximising model. Second, those predictions should be testable against the data, which is a test the model also passes. Third, the predictions should be supported by the data, which its supporters would claim is also the case. If this proposition is accepted, then the basic arguments of the managerial and behavioural schools are ill founded, because the realism of the profit-maximising assumption is irrelevant. It has been shown in Baumol's model, for instance, that a revenue-maximising firm will produce the same output and sell it at the same price as a profit-maximiser if the profit constraint is tight enough. It has also been shown that a firm that behaves as described by the behavioural model will make the same price and output decisions as a profit-maximiser if shareholders are powerful enough to insist on their right to the highest return on their investment. In both of these cases it would be descriptively inaccurate to describe the firm's objective as profit, but the profit-maximising model will predict behaviour very well.

Illustration ## Using calculus to solve Williamson's utility-maximising model

The Williamson model is relatively complex but an outline of its solution illustrates how economic models can be constructed and used. The basic problem is as follows, following Moschandreas (1994, pp. 320–1):

Maximise managerial utility = U = f(S, M, D)

Subject to $\Pi_r = \Pi_{min} + T$

Where: S = spending on staff; M = spending on managerial perquisites; D = discretionary investment spending; Π = total profit; Π_r = reported profit; Π_{min} = minimum profit required by shareholders; T = taxes, which are equal to the tax rate 't' multiplied by reported profit, i.e. $T = t\Pi_r$.

$\Pi = R(q) - C(q) - S$

Where: R = total revenue; C = total cost of production and sales; q = output.

$$\Pi_r = \rho\Pi = \rho(R(q) - C(q) - S)$$

Where: ρ = the proportion of profit that is reported.

$$M = (1 - \rho)\Pi \text{ and:}$$

$$D = \Pi_r - \Pi_{min} - T$$

It follows from these equations that:

$$M = (1 - \rho)(R(q) - C(q) - S), \text{ and:}$$

$$D = \rho(R(q) - C(q) - S) - \Pi_{min} - t\rho(R - C - S), \text{ which can be written as:}$$

$$D = \rho(1 - t)(R(q) - C(q) - S) - \Pi_{min}$$

This definition of D implies that the constraint can be ignored. Hence the problem becomes one of simple maximisation, as follows:

$$\text{Maximise } U = f[S, (1 - \rho)(R(q) - C(q) - S), \rho(1 - t)(R(q) - C(q) - S) - \Pi_{min}]$$

$$\text{Define } \delta U/\delta S = U_S; \; \delta U/\delta M = U_M; \; \delta U/\delta D = U_D$$

The decision variables are output (q), staff spending (S) and the proportion of profit to be reported (ρ). The first-order conditions for a maximum are then:

$$\delta U/\delta q = U_M(1 - \rho)(dR/dq - dC/dq) + U_D\rho(1 - t)(dR/dq - dC/dq) = 0$$

$$\delta U/\delta S = U_S + U_M(1 - \rho)(dR/dS - 1) + U_D\rho(1 - t)(dR/dS - 1) = 0$$

$$\delta U/\delta\rho = U_M(-1)(R(q) - C(q) - S) + U_D(1 - t)(R(q) - C(q) - S) = 0$$

For the first of these conditions to hold dR/dq = dC/dq, so that production decisions are made in the usual way.

From the second condition:

$$dR/dS = 1 - [U_S/(U_M(1 - \rho) + U_D\rho(1 - t)]$$

Since U_S, U_M, U_D, $1 - \rho$, and $1 - t$ are all positive, dR/dS < 1 and spending on staff is carried beyond the profit-maximising level.

From the third condition:

$$(R(q) - C(q) - S)[-U_M + U_D(1 - t)] = 0$$

Therefore, if R(q) > C(q) + S (and there is some profit) then:

$$U_M/U_D = 1 - t$$

U_M and U_D are the rates of change of utility with M and D, and their ratio is referred to as the 'marginal rate of substitution' (MRS). It indicates the rate at which a utility maximiser will exchange M for D. If the tax rate is higher so the MRS is lower, indicating that the proportion of profits that will be absorbed as managerial perquisites will be higher and the amount of discretionary investment will be lower.

Derivation of the full set of comparative static results for Williamson's model is beyond a text at this level but the exposition here should be enough to illustrate the general approach.

References and further reading

W. Baumol, 'On the Theory of Oligopoly', *Economica*, N.S. 25, 1958, pp. 187–98.

A.A. Berle and G. Means, *The Modern Corporation and Private Property*, New York, Macmillan, 1932.

R. Cyert and J. March, *Behavioural Theories of the Firm*, Englewood Cliffs, NJ, Prentice Hall, 1963.

D. Kreps, *A Course in Microeconomic Theory*, Princeton, Princeton University Press, 1990.

H. Leibenstein, 'Allocative Efficiency vs X-Efficiency', *American Economic Review*, vol. 56, 1966, pp. 392–415.

M. Moschandreas, *Business Economics*, London, Thomson, 1994.

H. Simon, 'Theories of Decision-Making in Economics and Behavioural Science', *American Economic Review*, vol. 49, June 1959, pp. 253–83.

J. Williamson, 'Profit, Growth and Sales Maximisation', *Economica*, vol. 34, February 1966, pp. 1–16.

O. Williamson, 'Managerial Discretion and Business Behaviour', *American Economic Review*, vol. 53, December 1963, pp. 147–62.

Self-test questions

1. In which of the following models will the firm incur higher costs than are necessary?

    (a) Baumol's revenue-maximising model
    (b) Williamson's managerial utility model
    (c) the behavioural model

2. Which of the following concepts are compatible with the behavioural model of the firm?

    (a) optimising
    (b) satisficing
    (c) certainty
    (d) aspiration levels
    (e) rules of thumb

3. If fixed costs rise, what will happen to the level of output in each of the following models?

    (a) profit-maximising
    (b) revenue-maximising, with a profit constraint
    (c) managerial utility maximising

4. Which firm would you expect to have the highest share price?

    (a) a profit-maximiser
    (b) a revenue-maximiser
    (c) a managerial utility maximiser

Essay question

Explain the relationship between the neo-classical theory of the firm and the concept of X-inefficiency.

3 The nature of the firm

In Chapter 2 it was taken for granted that firms exist and carry out some set of production and marketing functions. No attention was paid to why they exist or to the factors that differentiate the activities that take place *within* firms from those that take place *between* firms. This chapter turns to that issue, setting out a conceptual framework that has proved to be very powerful in the analysis of a wide range of business decisions.

Why do firms exist?

In a market economy most economic analysis is concerned with the fundamental question of how the allocation of resources is brought about by market forces. The analysis of supply and demand, for instance, explains the way in which prices act as a coordinating mechanism, answering the basic economic questions of 'what should be produced and how much?', 'how should it be produced?' and 'who gets it?' The answers to such questions are not provided by a central decision-maker, or by a single firm, but by the price mechanism, acting as a decentralised system of social organisation'. However, not all resource allocation is carried out in this way, as when a foreman or a manager in a firm orders a subordinate to move from one task to another. Coase (1937) quotes Robertson (1923) to the effect that there are 'islands of conscious power in this ocean of unconscious co-operation'. Outside the firm it is the price mechanism that coordinates the use of resources. Inside the firm, market transactions are replaced by the directives of the management. The essence of the firm, then, is that it is the super-session of the market mechanism. To put the same point in a slightly different way, the firm is 'the system of relationships which comes into existence when the direction of resources is dependent on an entrepreneur' (Coase 1937).

Having established this starting point it is possible to consider the question 'why do firms exist?' Why is the market so often superseded and what are the factors that determine this super-session?

Some simple explanations

A number of simple ideas offer themselves. The first is that individuals might prefer to be directed by other people, rather than simply taking part in abstract market transactions. Coase dismissed that explanation, although some organisational

31

psychologists might disagree. The second possibility is that some individuals may desire to exercise power over others, and would therefore be willing to pay others more than they would receive in a straightforward market transaction. That, too, can be dismissed as unlikely because it implies that those who exercise authority in firms would have to pay for the privilege, rather than being paid more than those they direct.

If these very simple explanations for the existence of the firm are rejected, a number of others may be considered. Knight (1921) argued that because there is uncertainty, some person must take the responsibility for forecasting market conditions and deciding on output and price. But the income resulting from those decisions is very uncertain and most people prefer to work for fixed or at least agreed incomes. Hence entrepreneurs take responsibility for forecasting. They accept the risks involved and pay other workers fixed wages, in return for the right to any profits. In return for the fixed wages, workers agree to accept the orders of the entrepreneur. The problem with this explanation is that a person with superior forecasting ability need not necessarily set up their own firm in order to profit from that ability. They could sell their forecasts to others. Furthermore, the entrepreneur does not need to coordinate the workers directly. The entrepreneur could simply have a contract with independent workers, guaranteeing them payment in return for the completion of certain tasks. Therefore the existence of uncertainty in itself does not require firms to be set up. Forecasters could forecast, selling that information to entrepreneurs who then set up contracts with independent workers to carry out assigned tasks.

Another approach to explaining the emergence of the firm was put forward by Alchian and Demsetz (1972). They argued that the fundamental problem lies in the 'team' nature of production, whereby many goods and services are produced by a group of people working jointly. Because it is not possible for one worker to measure the contribution of the others to the joint output, it is difficult for the team as a whole to detect whether an individual worker is shirking. If a worker does shirk, that person reaps all of the benefit from the shirking but the costs, in terms of lower output, are spread across the whole team. Hence there is a problem of *moral hazard* and an incentive to shirk in team production, which applies to all workers. Team production tends to be less efficient than it could be and that inefficiency creates an incentive for the workers to seek a solution. One possibility would be for them to appoint a monitor or overseer to observe the individual members and punish them if they do not make their best efforts. However, if the monitor is simply another worker, receiving a fixed payment in return for an unobservable level of effort, that person faces the same incentive to shirk and the problem is not solved. What would be effective (assuming that the monitor can actually gauge the effort of the other workers) is an arrangement whereby the monitor is the *residual claimant*. Ordinary workers receive a fixed level of payment and the monitor has the right to receive whatever remains of the revenue after the wages and other expenses have been paid. In that case the monitor has a clear incentive to increase output by preventing shirking and the problem is solved. If the right to the residual income can be bought and sold, then competition among rival monitors will guarantee that the monitor who can extract the largest output will own the rights, and the result will be an efficient one from society's overall point of view.

The Alchian and Demsetz explanation for the emergence of the firm is a useful one, drawing attention to the importance of asymmetric information, the moral hazard that it causes, the role of property rights and the tendency to efficiency under the right institutional conditions. However, those issues are not exclusive to the team production situation and a more general analytical framework has come to dominate explanations for why firms emerge.

Transaction cost analysis

One of the most powerful conceptual frameworks to become popular in the 1980s and 1990s has been 'transaction cost analysis' (TCA). TCA is a set of concepts and propositions that was first put forward by Ronald Coase in 1937 and has since been further developed by a number of authors, most notably Williamson (1975, 1986, 1996). While TCA has its origins in economics, it has formed the basis for studies in a wide range of other disciplines including business strategy, contract law, corporate finance, international business, marketing, political science and sociology (see Rindfleisch and Heide 1997 for an overview presented from a marketing perspective). Hence it deserves careful attention.

The 'Coasian' analysis

The key question being addressed is 'why do firms exist in market economies?' Coase suggested that the most obvious answer is that using the market involves transaction costs that might be avoided by using the firm. A transaction takes place whenever a good or a service passes from one party to another. The *direct costs* involved in making that transaction between independent parties include those that arise in respect of:

- locating buyers and sellers
- acquiring information about their availability, quality, reliability and prices
- negotiating, re-negotiating and concluding contracts
- coordinating the agreed actions of the parties
- monitoring performance with respect to fulfilment of contracts
- taking action to correct any failure to perform.

In addition to those direct costs, there are also the *opportunity costs* that arise if transacting between independent parties leads to more efficient courses of action not being taken (Masten *et al.* 1991). For instance, it may be efficient for a new piece of equipment to be purchased but that may not happen if the two parties cannot agree. Similarly, the parties to a transaction may be inappropriate for each other's requirements, they may fail to adapt properly to a changing environment or they may have to waste resources in adjusting their activities.

If two independent parties are to transact, they need to establish an agreement, a contract, which sets out the obligations of the buyer and seller. However, such contracts cannot be complete – they cannot specify what both parties will do in every possible future circumstance – because there may be thousands of such circumstances. If transaction costs are to be kept as low as possible, it would be preferable to establish long-term contracts, rather than a series of short-term contracts. However, the longer the period of the contract, the more uncertain are the purchaser's precise requirements. As a result, it will be desirable to establish a form of contract where the supplier is under an obligation to provide goods or services within certain limits, with the details left until a later date, to be decided by the buyer as their requirements become more clearly defined. Once such incomplete contracts are established, resources are directed by the authority exerted by the buyer and *a firm has come into existence.*

Another general reason for preferring internalised transactions to external ones is that internal transactions are less accessible to governments and other regulatory bodies, so that it may be profitable in some situations to internalise transactions in order to avoid taxes or controls on output.

To sum up thus far, the notion of the firm as super-session of the market mechanism leads naturally to the existence of transaction costs as the major reason for the existence of the firm. Having established that proposition, Coase went on to provide a pioneering analysis of the factors that determine the boundaries of the firm.

If there were no disadvantages to market transactions there would be no firms and all transactions would take place between individuals through markets. At the other extreme, if internalised transactions were always superior to market transactions the economy would consist of a single firm, in effect becoming centrally planned. (It can be helpful to appreciate that a firm is essentially a planned economy and a planned economy is a single firm.) As the reality lies in between these two extremes the question that remains is 'what factors determine the optimal balance between the two different types of transaction, and hence the boundaries of firms?' Coase suggested that at small firm sizes internal transactions are generally superior. However, as size or scope increases, so does the cost of organising the extra transactions until it becomes cheaper to organise the marginal transaction through the market or through the establishment of another firm. In this way the analysis of firm size and scope becomes amenable to the economist's standard marginalist tool kit.

A second factor that will set a limit to firm size will be 'managerial diseconomies of scale', whereby management makes less and less effective use of resources as the number of transactions to be handled increases. Finally, a limit might be set on firm size if larger firms have to pay more for resources than smaller firms. (It has been noted in Chapter 2, when explaining Baumol's model, that the salaries of executives may be directly correlated with firm size, with larger firms offering larger salaries. It is difficult to argue wholly convincingly that the executives of larger firms are necessarily superior to those in small or medium-sized companies.)

As a further step in the analysis, Coase identified three other factors that could cause the cost of organising additional transactions to arise. The first is an increase in the physical or geographical space over which transactions are organised. If this is the case, then any technological development that reduces the cost of organising across distance will tend to increase the size of the firm. The second factor identified is the dissimilarity of the transactions involved, an issue that is relevant to the development of the conglomerate, highly diversified, firm. The third factor is the probability of changes in the environment and in prices. If prices change rapidly then the cost of organising a transaction within the firm may rise more rapidly than the costs of organising through markets.

Coase pitched his analysis at a very general level, rather than concerning itself directly with business decisions. Nevertheless, it is easy to see that it may be applicable in more detail to a number of different choices facing the firm, particularly with respect to the level of vertical integration, the degree of diversification and the choice of overseas operation. Vertical integration is considered below, while diversification and 'multinationalisation' are considered in Chapters 4 and 5. Before turning to those issues it is useful to develop the TCA framework in more detail.

Williamson's analysis

The most powerful extension and development of TCA has been that of Williamson (1975, 1986, 1996), which sets out a general framework within which to analyse the forms that different types of transaction may take. Almost all of the studies using TCA have drawn on Williamson's version of the analysis in the attempt to explain a wide variety of phenomena (Rindfleisch and Heide 1997).

Williamson's analysis is difficult and often expressed in rather convoluted prose. It has also been extended and developed by others who express the same central ideas in slightly different ways (Milgrom and Roberts 1992, Acs and Gerlowski 1996, Besanko *et al.* 1996). However, its essence lies in bringing together two sets of concepts. The first consists of those factors that determine the cost of organising an 'arm's length' transaction between two independent parties. The second consists of a set of 'governance structures' or 'types of contracting' that are the mechanisms available for the control and coordination of the transaction. These two sets of variables are matched to show which governance structures are best suited to which set of transactional circumstances. For the purposes of prediction it is then assumed that efficiency prevails (at least in the long run) and that firms choose the type of governance structure that is best suited to the type of transaction being undertaken.

The characteristics of a transaction

A transaction takes place whenever a good or a service passes from one party to another. In the TCA framework, the relative cost of organising a transaction through different forms of governance is determined by four characteristics. These are as follows:

1. The extent to which *complete contracts* are possible (the term 'contract' refers to any agreement between parties, not only those that are formally written down).
2. The extent to which there is a threat of *opportunism* on the part of transactors.
3. The degree of *asset specificity* or *idiosyncratic investment* involved in a transaction.
4. The *frequency* with which the transaction is repeated.

These ideas require further examination in order to understand the ways in which they influence the choice of governance structure. A *complete contract* is one in which every possible future contingency is specified and the actions to be taken by both parties to the contract are also specified for every one of those contingencies. This is almost always impossible for four reasons. First, there is the existence of *uncertainty and/or complexity* with respect to the transaction. These make it difficult and expensive to identify the terms that would constitute a complete contract. Second, human beings exhibit *bounded rationality*. They do not have full information about everything, language is imprecise and there are limits to human beings' capacity to process information. Hence people are 'intendedly rational but only limitedly so'. Third, there are often *measurement problems* – difficulties in specifying and measuring the performance that is required of contractors. Fourth, there is often *asymmetric information*. That simply means that the parties to the transaction have access to different information. The differences may take the form of either 'hidden information' or 'hidden action', which lead to the problems of *adverse selection* or *moral hazard* respectively. 'Hidden information' is where at least one party to the contract has information not available to the other. 'Hidden action' is where at least one party takes actions relevant to the performance of the contract that are not observable by the other.

The difficulties associated with writing complete contracts are so fundamental that such contracts almost never exist. There is always a possibility that unforeseen events will take place and the parties will need to reach agreement on how to adapt to the new circumstances. That introduces increased negotiation costs and raises the possibility that one party might lose because of the behaviour of the other.

The difficulty of writing complete contracts would not create problems for the parties to a transaction if it were absolutely certain that they would all treat each other reasonably when unforeseen events take place. In that case the contract could state that all parties promise not to take advantage of each other in the event of unforeseen circumstances, or such a promise could be made implicitly as part of a 'gentlemen's agreement'. Whenever something happens that is not covered by the contract, the parties meet and re-negotiate, with both sides being open and truthful about everything that is relevant. However, TCA assumes that there is an additional problem, which is the threat of *opportunism*.

Opportunism is defined as 'self-interest-seeking with guile' (Williamson 1985, p. 47) and it includes lying, cheating, hiding information and breaking agreements. Opportunistic behaviour can take place both before and after a contract is agreed – it may be *ex ante* opportunism or *ex post*.

Ex ante opportunism arises when the different parties have access to different information at the time when they are negotiating the contract. For instance, each party will be better informed about their own valuation of a product or service than will their potential trading partner. As a result there will often be attempts at *strategic misrepresentation*. A buyer will try to pretend that they place a lower valuation on their potential purchase, while a seller will try to pretend that it costs more to produce than it really does.

Opportunism may also be *ex post* – it may take place after the contract has been agreed. In that situation there are two forms of behaviour that can make transacting difficult. These are *reneging* and *hold-up*. Reneging is where one of the parties to the contract does not honour it. Hold-up is where one of the parties takes advantage of the other's vulnerability, created by commitments made to meeting the contract, in order to seize a larger share of the available profits.

The combination of incomplete contracts and opportunism increases the cost of transacting between independent parties. However, it would not be important if markets were competitive and the contracting parties had nothing to lose by shifting to an alternative supplier or customer. If something went wrong with a transaction, and a mutually agreeable conclusion could not be reached, both parties could deal with someone else. Perhaps the most important characteristic of a transaction, therefore, is the extent to which it involves *idiosyncratic investment* or *asset specificity*.

Idiosyncratic investment is investment in assets whose value arises from their use in a transaction with a particular partner and whose value will be at least partly lost if the transaction does not take place. Asset specificity is the name given to the characteristic that such assets have and may be thought of as the 'value that is lost when the asset is used outside the specific setting or relationship' (Milgrom and Roberts 1992, p. 135).

Asset specificity may arise in at least five different forms. *Site specificity* is where the assets involved in a transaction are located side by side in order to reduce transport costs or achieve operating efficiencies. Steel mills make steel plates, rods and bars and they are located next to the blast furnaces that make the steel in order to conserve the energy costs of heating the materials to melting point. Factories making cans for drinks are located next to can-filling drinks plants in order to economise on inventory and transportation costs. *Physical or intellectual asset specificity* is where the assets are tailor-made for a particular usage and cannot be cheaply reconfigured for alternative uses. The jigs and fixtures used to make car bodies, for instance, and the engineering knowledge involved, are specific to a particular make and model of car. *Dedicated asset specificity* is where a firm makes an investment in general-purpose plant and equipment in order to fulfil the needs of a particular customer. In that case, the assets are not physically configured in a special way to suit the customer but they cannot be used for other customers because no such customers are currently available. *Human capital specificity* arises when individual staff members develop knowledge, skills and capabilities that have value when dealing with one particular transacting partner but which are lost if the firm deals with someone else. Finally, *brand-name specificity* arises when the value of an asset is heavily dependent upon its being using in conjunction with a particular brand name. Actors who work in a well-known soap opera will receive higher pay and other opportunities as a result of their association with that brand name and hence the value of their acting skills are brand-name specific.

Whichever form it takes, asset specificity brings about what Williamson (1985) called a 'fundamental transformation'. Before the specific investments are made, the parties to the transaction are in a 'large numbers' situation. They are free to choose among many different buyers or sellers in order to make their transaction. However, after the investment has been made they find themselves in a 'small numbers' or *bilateral monopoly* situation where they must deal with one specific exchange partner or lose the value of the idiosyncratic investments that have been made. If that partner should renege on the contract, or try to hold up the investor, the asset-specific investments will be lost. The presence of asset specificity means that opportunistic behaviour can be damaging and it makes the investor vulnerable to the actions of the other party. That vulnerability might be reduced if the investor in specific assets spends on additional monitoring of the other party's behaviour and on enforcing the contract through legal or non-legal means (a private army perhaps). However, these are all additional transaction costs that make it less attractive to deal with an independent other party.

The fourth characteristic of a transaction that needs to be taken into account is its *frequency* – the number of times it is expected to take place. If a transaction is 'one-off' it will not be efficient to devote significant resources to its coordination and control. On the other hand, if it is expected to take place many times over many years, the cost of making special arrangements for its management may be justified.

Alternative governance structures

The factors that create difficulties for transacting between independent parties through markets and contracts are the factors that make internalised transacting more attractive. Therefore it is the combination of incomplete contracts, opportunistic behaviour, asset specificity and high frequency that make coordination through managerial authority more efficient than coordination through a market. In the simplest interpretation of Williamson's analysis only two alternatives – markets and hierarchies – are considered. However, a more complete approach to the issue identifies four types of 'governance structure' which encompass a richer range of alternatives.

The first type of governance structure is *classical contracting*. In this case the identity of the two parties to the contract is irrelevant. All future contingencies are accounted for and the transaction is 'self-liquidating'. When it has been completed, neither party has any remaining obligations. This type of governance structure corresponds to the spot-market transaction in economic theory and is the way in which most personal retail transactions are governed. If a customer buys a pound of sausages or a bottle of water from a shop, that is an example of classical contracting. The contract is not written down. Neither party is concerned with the identity of the other party, the law of contract (and consumer protection legislation) takes account of any future contingencies and the transaction is completely finished when the water or sausages and the payment change hands.

The second type of governance is *neo-classical contracting*. This is used when it is not possible to account for all future possible contingencies, and therefore the agreement between two parties is recognised to be incomplete. Because of that incompleteness the contract provides some form of arbitration which allows the transaction to be completed even if there is disagreement. Contracts for large construction projects are an example of this kind of contracting. It is recognised that in the course of construction, unanticipated changes will need to be made

Table 3.1 Idiosyncratic investment, frequency and governance structures

Frequency	Extent of idiosyncratic investment		
	Low	Medium	High
Occasional	Classical contracting	Neo-classical contracting	Neo-classical contracting
Recurrent	Classical contracting	Obligational contracting	Unified governance

Source: Based on Williamson (1986).

to the design and construction of the road, bridge or building. Mechanisms are in place for the amendment of the contract and some form of arbitration is agreed to in case of conflict over the best way in which to proceed.

The third type of governance mechanism is *relational contracting*, which is even further from the classical concept of the discrete one-off transaction. Relational contracting involves links between the parties that have greater duration and complexity, where the original agreement between the parties may cease to become a point of reference, and where the relationship itself becomes the focus. The relationship may become 'a mini-society with a vast array of norms beyond those centred on the exchange and its immediate processes' (Williamson 1986). To put it more simply, the parties to a relational contract 'make it up as they go along'. Contracts of employment are an example of relational contracting. Within the general category of relational contracting, Williamson identified two variants. The first is *obligational contracting* where the transaction takes place between two independent organisations. The second is *unified governance* where the transactions are internalised within the hierarchy of a single firm.

The most appropriate form of governance for a particular transaction depends upon the four characteristics outlined above: the extent to which a complete contract can be written; the threat of opportunistic behaviour; the degree of asset specificity; and the frequency of the transaction. In so far as complete contracts never exist, there is always significant uncertainty and opportunistic behaviour is assumed to be the norm, it is asset specificity and frequency that are the most important determinants of the mode of governance to be selected. Table 3.1 shows the relationship as predicted by Williamson (1986).

As Table 3.1 shows, transactions will take place within a firm, through unified governance, when the level of idiosyncratic investment is high and when transactions take place frequently. When there is very little asset specificity, classical contracting is most appropriate and there are situations between these extremes where other forms of governance, like long-term contracts, joint ventures or strategic alliances, are the most appropriate format.

Viewed from the TCA perspective the firm may be seen as 'a set of transactions co-ordinated by managerial authority'. Alternatively it might be seen as 'a conscious, wilful effort to organise economic activity that consists of a collection of contracts when more than one party is involved' (Acs and Gerlowski 1996, p. 2). These two interpretations are only slightly different. The personnel of a firm are joined to it by contracts of employment which are relational contracts. Such contracts are incomplete, they allow the senior managers of the firm to direct those below them in the hierarchy, subject to certain limitations, and they are enforced internally by the exercise of authority. Therefore within the firm transactions are coordinated by authority, not by the market or (in detail) by the contract.

Transaction costs and the vertical boundaries of the firm

One of the most important business decisions to which TCA has been applied is the level of vertical integration, defined as the extent to which different stages of production take place within the same firm. In this case, the transactions that are internalised link the flow of output between different stages of production, from the extraction and processing of raw materials at one extreme to retail supply at the other.

It is important to recognise that all firms are vertically integrated to some extent because most stages of production can be sub-divided into increasingly smaller stages. A firm that was totally 'disintegrated' vertically would carry out a single indivisible operation and contract with independent parties for everything else. The question is not whether a firm will be vertically integrated, but what level of integration will be optimal, and what factors will encourage more or less integration to take place.

The most obvious advantages of coordinating vertically through internal transactions relate to technical economies in production, where close coordination between different stages of production can reduce costs. Bain (1968) argued that unless such technical relations are involved, there are unlikely to be substantial cost savings. The most common example used here is vertical integration in the steel industry where the direct transfer of hot metal from blast furnace to rolling mill saves considerable quantities of energy. This is a useful example, because it also shows that the fundamental issue is not technological, but lies in the disadvantages of classical or neo-classical contracting.

In principle, it would be possible for one firm to specialise in the production of molten steel, and another in the use of that steel to make sheets, rods and bars. However, to be technically efficient, the two plants would need to be located side by side in which case they would only be able to transact with each other. That would involve a very high level of site-specific investment by both parties and it would introduce the 'small numbers' problem. In order to protect their investments they would need to negotiate, draft, monitor and enforce a very detailed contract between two independent firms, which could substitute for the internal organisation of the flows of hot metal from one stage of the process to another. The provision of such a contract would be so difficult, expensive and risky that internal organisation – unified governance – is the preferred mechanism. The employees working in both the blast furnace and the rolling mill have contracts of employment which require them to follow the instructions of the same group of managers. When something unexpected happens, that group of managers can instruct workers in both facilities without having to re-negotiate a contract.

Vertical integration in the motor-car industry

TCA is expressed in rather abstract terms and it can be difficult to measure variables like asset specificity, frequency, uncertainty and the threat of opportunism. It is useful therefore to examine some examples of its application. The motor industry provides a number of classic cases.

The first example involves the relationship between General Motors and Fisher Body (Klein *et al.* 1978). In the 1920s General Motors (GM) assembled vehicles using bodies purchased from Fisher Body, which was an independent company. As motor-car technology developed, wooden bodies were replaced by metal and GM realised that, to be technically efficient, car bodies should be produced next to the assembly plant. The senior management therefore requested that Fisher Body build a new body plant adjacent to a new GM plant. However, that would involve a very high level of idiosyncratic investment in assets that were both site-specific and physical and intellectual asset-specific. If the Fisher Body plant were not used to make bodies for GM it would lose almost all of its value, partly because bodies could not be shipped to car assembly firms in other places and partly because the bodies being made were specifically designed to fit GM cars. Fisher Body executives were not prepared to meet GM's request, fearing that once they had made the investment they would be vulnerable to any demands that GM might later make – *ex post* opportunism. GM solved the problem by purchasing Fisher Body and building the body plant where it was required.

In the GM/Fisher Body case vertical integration involved two major aspects of the production process – body manufacture and vehicle assembly. Monteverde and Teece (1982) extended the analysis, noting that vehicle assembly involves bringing together thousands of components, some of which are purchased from independent suppliers and some of which are produced in-house. They hypothesised that the key determinant of the make/buy choice for components lies in the level of 'applications engineering' effort required to develop each component for use in a particular model of vehicle. Spending on such development generates specialised, non-patentable know-how that is highly specific to the particular transaction involved – there is intellectual asset and human capital specificity. It may also lead to the development of customised equipment and fixtures, adding an element of physical capital specificity. There is therefore a risk that supplier or buyer will behave opportunistically by demanding better terms at the last moment, knowing that the other party to the transaction cannot simply take their business elsewhere. In that situation (frequent transactions, high level of idiosyncratic investment), economising requires that the transactions be organised through unified governance. On the other hand, if a component does not require a high level of engineering effort specific to the vehicle manufacturer's products, there is no asset specificity, no 'small numbers' problem, and it is more efficient to source the product on the open market from independent suppliers who compete with each other.

Monteverde and Teece found a way to measure the applications engineering cost associated with 133 different motor-car components used by GM and Ford and their hypothesis was supported in that components involving higher costs were more likely to be produced in-house.

While the Monteverde and Teece study showed that TCA has significant explanatory power, its findings also showed a need for caution. The two companies studied were very different, with GM choosing in-house production of many components which were bought in by Ford. Acs and Gerlowski (1996, pp. 160–2) point out that in the early 1990s Chrysler was even less vertically integrated than Ford, having taken a deliberate decision to give outside suppliers a larger role in the vehicle production process, from design and component production to assembly. If different firms embody different capabilities, built up over decades of experience, those differences may outweigh transactional considerations. If those capabilities include the skills needed to build good relationships with suppliers so that opportunism is less of a threat, the balance of advantage between internalised and arm's length transactions may shift.

This last point draws attention back to the fact that it is the combination of incomplete contracts, asset specificity and opportunism that makes arm's length transacting difficult. Most analyses have taken opportunism for granted, making it an assumption (Rindfleisch and Heide 1997). If contracts are always incomplete, that identifies asset specificity as the main determinant of the firm/ arm's length contract decision. However, it may be inappropriate, or unnecessarily cynical, to assume that behaviour is always opportunistic. Business reputation is important to firms, because a reputation for fair dealing may help in acquiring custom. It can therefore be a powerful mechanism for preventing opportunism. That tendency is often reinforced through informal and social connections between executives, and in some cases by formal systems of experience ratings where firms pool their knowledge of dealings with suppliers and customers (Leff 1970). Even when complete contracts cannot be written or enforced, and there are valuable specific assets at risk, market transactions between independent firms may still be possible through 'obligational contracting' if the parties in question place a high value on their reputation. In industries where this effect is strong, vertical integration need not proceed as far as would otherwise be the case, because long-term relationships between firms substitute for common ownership and acceptance of the same supervisory authority.

The problems of vertical integration

TCA makes it clear that the transacting problems that arise when dealing with independent parties provide an explanation for the internalisation of many transactions, leading to vertical integration. The ability of a firm's managers to use their authority to direct employees (within the limits of their employment contracts) avoids the costs of negotiation and re-negotiation and the risk of losing value in specific assets. However, it should also be noted that internal transactions suffer from their own limitations so that the optimal choice of governance mode depends on balancing the costs and benefits of the alternatives. Williamson (1975, 1986) also extended Coase's analysis on this issue, pointing to some of the limits to internal transactions in the context of vertical integration.

The first of these is the tendency for internal sources of supply to distort procurement decisions. If a supplying division is set up within a firm, the interests of the managers responsible for that division may militate against the use of outside sources of supply, even if they should become more efficient and cost effective. It may also be difficult to make proper comparisons between the cost of purchasing a product and the cost of making it in-house because of the problems and potential arbitrariness involved in allocating overhead costs to individual products. One of the unusual features of the firm/market distinction is that it is often easier to measure the cost of a product produced by someone else and purchased on the market than to measure the cost of producing it in-house.

Even if managers have guaranteed employment there will often be loss of status attaching to association with a 'failed' operation, and they may resist attempts to close down inefficient parts of the firm. There may also be a more general resistance to change stemming from the bureaucratic nature of many organisations, and the horse-trading that takes place as managers form shifting alliances with each other in support of their own 'pet projects'. This weakness of internal organisation is closely related to the 'persistence' phenomenon, whereby existing activities in organisations tend to be continued even in preference to demonstrably superior new projects. It also involves the wasteful expenditure of resources on what Milgrom and Roberts (1992) refer to as 'influence activities' where managers spend their time on office politics, trying to influence the allocation of the firm's resources in their favour.

Another weakness of internal organisation lies in the distortion of communications between managers, who may tend to tell their supervisors or subordinates what they hope to hear, rather than the truth. If information about the firm's operations were easily checked, this tendency could be curbed through internal audit procedures. However, in many cases information is too deeply embedded in the details of operations for supervisors to be able to check its truthfulness at reasonable cost. In that case there are important information asymmetries within the firm, as well as between firms, and they may lead to inefficiencies.

Limitations of the TCA approach

The TCA approach is a flexible framework expressed at a rather abstract level, and not a set of fixed propositions. Its power lies in the fact that it can be interpreted and extended in many different directions in order to explain many different organisational phenomena. At the same time, a number of important criticisms may be noted. Most fundamentally, the central constructs that make up TCA are not directly observable, which raises fundamental problems when trying to carry out empirical research (Godfrey and Hill 1995). Milgrom and Roberts (1992, pp. 33–4) note that transaction costs can often not be identified separately from other categories of cost and that efficiency does not necessarily require that transaction costs be minimised. They also point out that there may be many different efficient solutions to a transactional problem so that the assumption of efficiency may not be a strong enough criterion for prediction. For instance, in a situation of high asset specificity, unified governance is said to be most efficient. That basic insight underpins most of the studies carried out using the TCA framework. But its validity hangs on the assumption that there is a significant threat of opportunism. If some method can be found to reduce opportunism then another form of governance could also be efficient.

This last point leads to two further criticisms. The first is that the TCA framework assumes that opportunism is universal when a whole body of literature suggests that it may be avoided. As John (1984) put it, 'refusals to honour agreements and misrepresentation of intentions cannot be taken for granted'. Ghoshal and Moran (1996) go so far as to suggest that the assumption of opportunism, and teaching TCA to students, is bad for business practice because it encourages managers to take opportunism for granted. There are mechanisms, like reputation and prior cooperation, that can reduce opportunism and rational managers will use those mechanisms. There is a very substantial literature on trust, showing that it provides an important 'cement' for many business relationships. It has also been pointed out that in many Asian cultures business transactions are based almost entirely around personal trust, with formal written agreements playing a very limited role (Whitley 1992).

TCA's adherents could argue that the assumption of opportunism is not so strong, and it may be relaxed. However, in that case TCA becomes so flexible that it leads very easily to *ex post* rationalisation. Almost any outcome can be explained in TCA terms after it has been observed, but it is more doubtful whether the prediction could have been made in advance. For instance, if Fisher Body had agreed to build the plant for GM, the decision could have been explained in TCA terms as evidence that GM and Fisher Body managers had found ways to limit the threat of opportunism, and thereby made the specific investments much less vulnerable to hold-up. When Fisher Body did not build the plant, the case is explained by maintaining the assumption of opportunism.

Finally, most economists are comfortable with the assumption that efficiency will generally be achieved in the long run. However, others are not and it should be recognised that TCA depends upon that assumption for its predictive power (though not for its prescriptions).

Illustration A diversity of applications

A useful way to illustrate the range of issues that have been addressed using transaction cost analysis is to provide diverse examples.

1. Geographical differences in the same industry: power stations and coal mines in the United States

Joskow (1988) examined the relationships between coal mines and coal-burning electricity plants in the continental United States. In the west of the country, the quality and composition of the coal varies a great deal from mine to mine. Hence the power stations that use that coal must be designed specifically for a particular type of coal. There is *physical asset specificity*. In the east of the country, coal is very homogenous. In the west, transport costs for coal are higher than in the east so that coal mines and power stations must be closer together in order to be efficient. There is a greater degree of *site specificity* in the west. The governance structures for the transaction of coal from mines to power stations reflect these differences. In the west there are many 'mine-mouth' power stations where the two facilities are located next door to each other, and these are vertically integrated. Where power stations and coal mines are not vertically integrated, supply contracts are for longer terms and are more complex in the west than in the east. The spot market for coal (classical contracting) is important in the east but not in the west.

Joskow's findings are consistent with TCA in terms of the general pattern of differences between the east and the west. However, it is also instructive to consider why there is not more vertical integration in the west, where long-run contracts are frequently used. Given the described pattern of asset specificity, and the huge expense associated with both power stations and mines, it seems surprising that contracts between independent firms are used at all. The reason given is that coal is not the only source of energy for power stations and the relative cost of different energy sources may fluctuate. Hence the electricity companies might want to switch to a different type of fuel at some time in the future if coal becomes relatively expensive. In TCA terms that means that the degree of asset specificity might become less in future as the value of the power station depends less upon its being used in conjunction with the coal mine. That explanation is satisfying but it also amounts to saying that in many cases asset specificity is too high in the short term for spot markets and short-term contracts but too low in the long term for vertical integration. As the boundaries between 'too high' and 'too low' and between 'short term' and 'long term' are not specified, it is difficult to argue convincingly that TCA would have predicted the observed pattern in advance. Once the pattern is observed it can be seen to have elements consistent with the theory. Whether the theory really passes the test of providing testable predictions in advance of observing the phenomenon is questionable.

2. Differences across similar industries world-wide: tin and aluminium

In the aluminium industry there is almost always vertical integration between the bauxite mines that produce the ore and the refineries that use it to produce the metal itself (Hennart 1988). In the tin industry, mining for tin ore and refining are carried out by independent companies (Hennart 1986). The explanation is essentially the same as that for the east/west differences in the US coal industry. Bauxite varies very significantly in its composition from one mine to another. Hence the plants that process the ore exhibit a high degree of *physical asset specificity*. They cannot function without the ore from their co-specialised mine and the ore from that mine cannot be processed elsewhere without very significant additional expense. Tin ore does not vary very much from one source to another. Neither mines nor processing plants are subject to significant asset specificity. Hence there is no 'small numbers' problem. Mines and processing plants compete for each other's business and transactions are organised on the basis of spot transactions or short-term contracts. Longer-term contracts or vertical integration is not required.

3. The choice between joint ventures and wholly owned subsidiaries

Joint ventures (JVs) are firms that are formed by a contract between two or more parent companies. They are often referred to as 'hybrid' forms of governance because they combine obligational contracting between the parents with unified governance inside the JV itself. A number of authors, including Hennart (1988, 1991), Erramilli and Rao (1993) and Hu and Chen (1993), have used the TCA framework to explain how firms choose between shared (JV) versus full control (subsidiary) forms of operation. The details of the methods used vary widely, and the chains of reasoning that link the theory with the hypotheses tested are often rather long. However, overall the results suggest that TCA can explain the choice made in many cases.

4. The information content of technology transfers

Davies (1993) used a TCA approach to compare the information content of technology transfers carried out through licensing agreements between independent companies with the information content of in-house internalised transactions. Evidence from machine tool companies in Britain, Germany and the US showed that licensing agreements tended to involve older technology and more limited packages of assistance. Licensed transfers tended to be limited to engineering knowledge, involving the 'one-off' provision of designs and drawings for complete machine tools. Internalised transfers more frequently provided for the transfer of 'team' knowledge involving marketing and management as well as engineering, and of components. Overall, the type of information and assistance provided under licensing agreements involved less important knowledge assets – reducing the risks arising from opportunism – and less physical and human capital specificity. Internalised transfers were used for strategically important knowledge and for more complex knowledge whose transfer required the development of specific skills.

5. Applications in marketing

There have been enough applications of TCA in the marketing field to justify a review in the discipline's leading journal (Rindfleisch and Heide 1997). Topics include: the choice between a direct sales force and manufacturer's representatives (Anderson 1985); manufacturer and distributor commitment to their relationship (Anderson and Weitz 1992); single or multiple vendors in the distribution of semiconductor devices (Dutta and John 1995); outsourcing of the warehousing function (Maltz 1994); perceptions of opportunism, contractual safeguards and the performance of strategic alliances (Parkhe 1993).

The application of TCA in marketing provides an illustration of the framework's flexibility. Most of the studies examined begin with reference to Williamson (1975, 1986) and make use of the same set of concepts – the TCA paradigm. At the same time, however, the relationships among the concepts are often specified in very different ways from those in the original. In particular the assumption of opportunism is often questioned and the threat of such behaviour treated as an endogenous or dependent variable.

References and further reading

Z. Acs and D. Gerlowski, *Managerial Economics and Organization*, New Jersey, Prentice Hall, 1996.

A. Alchian and R. Demsetz, 'Production, Information Costs and Economic Organization', *American Economic Review*, vol. LXII, no. 5, 1972, pp. 777–95.

E. Anderson, 'The Salesperson as Outside Agent or Employee: A Transaction Cost Analysis', *Marketing Science*, vol. 4, Summer 1985, pp. 234–54.

E. Anderson and B. Weitz, 'The Use of Pledges to Build and Sustain Commitment in Distribution Channels', *Journal of Marketing Research*, vol. 29, February 1992, pp. 18–34.

J.S. Bain, *Industrial Organization*, New York, Wiley, 1968.

D. Besanko, D. Dranove and M. Shanley, *Economics of Strategy*, New York, Wiley, 1996.

R.H. Coase, 'The Nature of the Firm', *Economica*, vol. 4, 1937, pp. 386–405.

H. Davies, 'The Information Content of Technology Transfers', *Technovation*, vol. 13, no. 2, 1993, pp. 93–100.

S. Dutta and G. John, 'Combining Lab Experiments and Industry Data in Transaction Cost Analysis: The Case of Competition as a Safeguard', *Journal of Law, Economics and Organization*, vol. 11, no. 1, 1995, pp. 87–111.

M.K. Erramilli and C.P. Rao, 'Service Firms' International Entry Mode Choice: A Modified Transaction-Cost Approach', *Journal of Marketing*, vol. 57, July 1993, pp. 19–38.

S. Ghoshal and P. Moran, 'Bad for Practice: A Critique of the Transaction Cost Theory', *Academy of Management Review*, vol. 21, no. 1, January 1996, pp. 13–48.

P. Godfrey and C. Hill, 'The Problem of Unobservables in Strategic Management Research', *Strategic Management Journal*, vol. 16, no. 7, October 1995, pp. 519–34.

J-F. Hennart, 'The Tin Industry', in M. Casson and Associates, *Multinationals and World Trade*, London, George Allen & Unwin, 1986.

J-F. Hennart, 'A Transaction Costs Theory of Equity Joint Ventures', *Strategic Management Journal*, vol. 9, 1988, pp. 361–74.

J-F. Hennart, 'Transaction Costs Theory of Joint Ventures: An Empirical Study of Japanese Subsidiaries in the United States', *Management Science*, vol. 4, April 1991, pp. 483–97.

M. Hu and H. Chen, 'Foreign Ownership in Chinese Joint Ventures: A Transaction Cost Approach', *Journal of Business Research*, vol. 26, Fall 1993, pp. 149–60.

G. John, 'An Empirical Examination of Some Antecedents of Opportunism in a Marketing Channel', *Journal of Marketing Research*, vol. 21, August 1984, pp. 278–89.

P. Joskow, 'Asset Specificity and the Structure of Vertical Relationships: Empirical Evidence', *Journal of Law, Economics and Organization*, vol. 4, no. 1, 1988, pp. 95–117.

B. Klein, R. Crawford and A. Alchian, 'Vertical Integration, Appropriable Rents and the Competitive Contracting Process', *Journal of Law and Economics*, vol. 21, 1978, pp. 297–326.

F. Knight, *Risk, Uncertainty and Profit*, Boston, Houghton Mifflin, 1921.

A. Leff, 'Contract as a Thing', *American University Law Review*, 1970.

A. Maltz, 'Outsourcing the Warehousing Function: Economic and Strategic Considerations', *Logistics and Transportation Review*, vol. 30, September 1994, pp. 245–65.

S. Masten, J. Meehan and E. Snyder, 'The Costs of Organization', *Journal of Law, Economics and Organization*, vol. 7, Spring 1991, pp. 1–25.

P. Milgrom and J. Roberts, *Economics, Organization and Management*, New Jersey, Prentice Hall, 1992.

K. Monteverde and D. Teece, 'Supplier Switching Costs and Vertical Integration in the Automobile Industry', *Bell Journal of Economics*, vol. 13, Spring 1982, pp. 206–13.

A. Parkhe, 'Strategic Alliance Structuring: A Game Theoretic and Transaction Cost Examination of Interfirm Cooperation', *Academy of Management Journal*, vol. 36, August 1993, pp. 794–829.

A. Rindfleisch and J. Heide, 'Transaction Cost Analysis: Past, Present and Future Applications', *Journal of Marketing*, vol. 61, October 1997, pp. 30–54.

D.H. Robertson, *The Control of Industry*, London, Nisbet, 1923.

R. Whitley, *Business Systems in East Asia: Markets, Firms and Societies*, London, Sage, 1992.

O. Williamson, *Markets and Hierarchies*, New York, Free Press, 1975.

O. Williamson, *The Economic Institutions of Capitalism*, London, Collier Macmillan, 1985.

O. Williamson, *Economic Organization*, Brighton, Wheatsheaf, 1986.

O. Williamson, *The Mechanisms of Governance,* New York, Oxford University Press, 1996.

Self-test questions

1. Give an example of each of the following transactions:
   (a) an infrequent transaction, involving no idiosyncratic investment
   (b) a frequent transaction involving a high level of idiosyncratic investment
   (c) an infrequent transaction involving a high level of idiosyncratic investment
   (d) an infrequent transaction involving some idiosyncratic investment

2. For each of the transactions in Question 1, identify the most appropriate form of governance structure.

3. Give an example for each of the five different types of asset specificity.

4. Which of the following components would you expect a motor-car assembler to produce in-house?
   (a) engines
   (b) electric motors for windows and windscreen wipers
   (c) wheels
   (d) bodies
   (e) light bulbs

Essay questions

Book publishers usually have their books printed by independent firms. Newspaper publishers usually print their paper themselves. Consider how transaction cost analysis might explain that difference.

4 Ownership and control, diversification and mergers

Chapter 3 has examined why firms exist, focusing on the idea that the firm is the super-session of the market, or a set of transactions that are coordinated by managerial authority, within a set of contracts. It has also explained the major factors that determine the extent of vertical integration. In this chapter attention shifts to three related questions:

1. To what extent do firms seek maximum profit when ownership and control are in the hands of different people?
2. What factors determine the extent to which a firm diversifies across different industries?
3. How and why do mergers and take-overs take place?

Do firms really try to maximise profits?

The traditional model of the firm, which underpins our understanding of the market economy, assumes that the aim of the firm is to maximise profits or shareholder value. However, it has been pointed out in Chapter 2 that the assumption of profit maximisation may be unrealistic in a world where ownership and control are in the hands of different groups of people. At the same time, it is possible to identify counter-arguments to suggest that the basic assumption is in fact more realistic than its critics might suggest. This part of the chapter assesses that debate.

Do shareholders always seek maximum profits?

Most of the debate on ownership, control and profit maximisation in the joint stock company assumes that shareholders unambiguously prefer higher profits. In that case the question 'do firms try to maximise profits?' can be re-stated as 'do senior managers behave in ways that are consistent with shareholders' interests?' However, there are situations where a shareholder may not prefer maximum profit, as Kreps (1990, p. 727) and Milgrom and Roberts (1992, p. 40) point out. For instance, if the firm has some degree of market power and a shareholder is also a customer, the shareholder may lose more from being charged higher profit-maximising prices than they gain from the enhanced value of their shareholding. This will be particularly marked if the shareholding in the firm is small but the purchases made from it are large. If a shareholder is also a supplier to a firm, they may prefer that the firm does not use that market power to maximise profits because that may entail bidding down the price paid for the supplies. If the shareholder has a diversified portfolio of shares, maximising the profit made by one firm may reduce the value of the others.

Even if a shareholder faces none of these conflicts, buying nothing from the firm, selling nothing to it and owning shares in no other firms, they may still face a penalty for profit maximisation. If the shareholder consumes a product that is complementary to an input that the firm uses, and the drive for profit leads the firm to force the price of that input downwards, demand for the input from other sources will rise, increasing demand for the complement and forcing the shareholder to pay a higher price for it!

This last example may seem rather far-fetched, given that the effects involved, and the consequent loss, are likely to be quite small. However, it illustrates the central point that, *if a firm can influence prices* and its shareholders are affected by those prices, they may prefer to sacrifice some profit and hence will not seek to maximise.

There is another reason why shareholders may not seek profit maximisation. In the long term, profit maximisation requires maximising the present value of the stream of profits made into the future. However, the valuation of that stream depends upon the relative weighting given to the future by each individual shareholder. If different shareholders have different weightings (some value income in the future more or less than others) they will give different valuations to the alternatives facing the firm and will not be able to agree on which is the maximising alternative.

Both of these conflicts disappear if the firm is a price-taker, operating in a competitive market where it cannot influence prices, and if markets are complete in the sense that a full set of competitive product, financial and insurance markets are in place. In that situation the only connection between the firm's behaviour and shareholders' well-being lies in the profits earned and hence shareholders will want to maximise those. The problem of placing different valuations on the future is also solved as there will be a market-determined 'overall' weighting of the future relative to the present, represented by the interest rate. Rational shareholders will seek to maximise profits using that weighting and those who place more value on income in the future will invest their share of the profits, while those who prefer income immediately can use financial markets to borrow.

In the discussion that follows it is generally assumed that shareholders seek profits, even though there are doubts on that issue. That is the starting point for most economic analysis and it is useful to appreciate that when economists say 'we assume' they do not mean 'we believe this to be true'. An assumption is a working hypothesis or a logical starting point which simplifies the world and allows models yielding predictions to be made. The logic is 'if shareholders do aim to maximise the value of the firm, what are the problems they face when direct control is in the hands of a separate group of managers?'

Links between ownership and control

It has been pointed out in Chapter 2 that 'managerial discretion' models of the firm, like Baumol's revenue-maximiser and Williamson's utility-maximiser, had their inspiration in the pioneering work of Berle and Means (1932) in the United States. Their key finding was that in large public corporations shareholdings were highly dispersed, with large numbers of small shareholders. As that type of shareholder has relatively little invested, they are unlikely to spend much effort monitoring the running of the company. Furthermore, their dispersion would make it difficult for them to coordinate any action against the managers. Berle and Means therefore drew the conclusion that shareholders in such firms would not be able to exert control over the managers. 'Management-controlled' firms were defined as those in which no single shareholder held more than 20 per cent and on that criterion 58 per cent of the assets of America's 200 largest firms were management controlled in 1929. An updating of that calculation for 1963 showed a rising trend, to 85 per cent (Larner 1966).

Clearly, the set of people who own a public corporation is not the same as the set of people who manage it. However, that separation between ownership and control, and the dispersed nature of shareholdings, are not enough to demonstrate that managers are able to run the company in their own interests, without regard to shareholders' objectives, for a number of reasons.

First of all, although shareholders and managers are not the same set of people, there is considerable overlap between the two. In most firms the CEO, the directors and other senior executives own shares in the company. If a large part of their income arises from the return on those shares they will have a powerful incentive to aim for maximum profit. Studies have differed on the extent to which this is the case. Cosh and Hughes (1987) reported that in the United States 33 per cent of executive directors and 21 per cent of all directors had holdings in their own companies worth more than one million pounds, the implication being that they would be motivated towards profit. Certainly, the personal wealth of many high-profile CEOs of major companies arises from their ownership of shares in the firms they manage, the granting of options to purchase stock at predetermined prices and profit-related bonuses. On the other hand, Jensen and Murphy (1990) calculated that for CEOs in the United States the additional personal wealth arising from an increase in shareholder value of $1,000 was only $3.25 which they concluded was not sufficient to align CEOs' interests with those of shareholders. Wherever the balance lies, there is a very important group of individuals who are both shareholders and senior managers, bridging the gap between ownership and control.

The concentration of ownership

Berle and Means classified firms as 'management controlled' if no single shareholder held more than 20 per cent of the voting stock. But the extent to which shareholders can exert control need not depend solely on that figure. Cubbin and Leech (1983) argued that the power of a coalition of the largest shareholders increases as it holds a larger proportion of the shares and as the remaining shares are more widely dispersed across other, smaller, shareholders. In that case it could be possible for a very small group of shareholders, each holding a relatively small proportion of the total stock, to exert effective control. The costs of forming a coalition among a small number of shareholders would not be large and many more firms would therefore be subject to effective shareholder control. Leech and Leahy (1991) applied this idea to a large sample of UK companies and concluded that in 54 per cent of cases a coalition of three shareholders or fewer could potentially wield control. Even more dramatically, they found that the patterns of shareholding were such that in only one case would a coalition need to have more than ten members in order to have control.

The influence of institutional shareholders

The argument that managers do not seek maximum profit is also based in part on the idea that shareholders are not well informed about the activities of the firms they own, and exhibit only minor concern about their performance. They are seen as being disinclined to criticise or displace the incumbent management, provided that a moderate level of dividend is paid.

In so far as shareholders are private individuals, with small shareholdings and limited time to spend monitoring their performance, this is a valid argument. However, ownership of shares is not typically spread across private individuals alone, but is frequently concentrated in the hands of financial institutions like pension funds, investment trusts, insurance companies and other similar organisations. Table 4.1 shows the figures for a number of OECD countries at the end of 1996.

As the figures show, the financial sector holds very significant proportions of corporate equity, especially in the United Kingdom, the United States and Japan. Whether this puts managers under pressure to seek shareholder value depends upon the behaviour of those institutions. It could be argued that they depend

Table 4.1 The ownership of listed corporate equity by category of shareholder – per cent at the end of 1996

	United States	Japan	Germany	France	United Kingdom	Sweden	Australia
Financial sector, of which:	46	42	30	30	68	30	37
Banks	6	15	10	7	1	1	3
Insurance companies and pension funds	28	12	12	9	50	14	25
Investment funds	12	–	8	11	8	15	–
Other financial institutions	1	15	–	3	9	–	9
Non-financial enterprises	–	27	42	19	1	11	11
Public authorities	–	1	4	2	1	8	–
Households	49	20	15	23	21	19	20
Rest of the world	5	11	9	25	9	32	32
Total	100	100	100	100	100	100	100

Source: Thompson (1998).

upon the financial performance of the firms in which they have invested in order to attract funds and to survive and make profits themselves. In that case they will be motivated to employ professional managers to monitor their investments and to use industry analysts (usually employed by their stockbrokers) to scrutinise the performance of the firms in which they have invested. Institutional shareholders are powerful and have the potential to be well informed about the firms in which they own shares. As a result they may exert considerable pressure on managers to aim for maximum profit, removing the discretion they must have if the managerial models are to apply.

The validity of this argument depends upon the actual behaviour of the financial institutions. Cosh and Hughes (1987) found that while institutional shareholders had great potential power, very few of them were prepared to use it. They believed that attempts to intervene in the running of companies they owned would be expensive and not very effective. There may be a number of reasons for that apparent lack of interest. If the financial institutions themselves are under little competitive pressure they may make only limited efforts to monitor and control the firms in which they own shares. A financial institution may become 'locked into' a firm in which it has a major financial stake, being afraid to make public any doubts it has about the firm's policies and performance for fear of seeing a fall in the share price and a weakening of the performance of its own investment portfolio.

The balance of the argument is not completely clear. However, it does appear that a significant change took place from the late 1980s onwards. Liberalisation and de-regulation of the financial services industry led to much greater competition in that sector, which in turn forced the financial institutions to pay much greater attention to the performance of the companies they own (Thompson 1998).

One interesting aspect of the debate over the role of institutional shareholders concerns the differences between the American and British systems, on the one hand, and the Japanese and German on the other. The US and UK systems may be described as 'outsider' or 'market-oriented' systems (Berglof 1990, Thompson 1998). In that type of system institutional shareholders play a limited role in monitoring and influencing the managers of the firms they own. Instead, they simply observe the share price and sell the shares of firms they think are underperforming. In Hirschman's (1970) terminology, they exert pressure by 'exit' rather than 'voice'. That contrasts with the German and Japanese approaches which are 'insider' or 'bank-oriented' systems. In Germany and Japan the banks have 'obligational' contracts with the firms they own. They are not simply concerned at arm's length with the share prices of those firms. Instead they have direct representation on the boards of the companies they own, they buy and sell shares less frequently and they are part of the 'insider' group whose 'voice' controls those firms.

The consensus judgement on the merits of the two approaches has shifted over time with the relative performance of the economies they serve. In the 1960s and 1970s it was often argued that German and Japanese financial institutions took a longer-term view of the companies in which they invested, because of their closer involvement. As a result they were more prepared to support spending on research and development and expensive entry into new markets overseas, which was seen as an advantage. The American and British systems were criticised for encouraging 'short-termism' among senior managers who were required to keep constant vigilance over their share prices which were in turn determined by short-sighted participants in the stock market. However, in the last two decades of the twentieth century both the Japanese and the German 'miracles' ground to a halt. It became clear in Japan that the cosy 'insider' relationships between banks and companies had allowed both sectors to become inefficient and mismanaged, to the point where the Japanese financial sector might easily collapse altogether. The Asian financial crisis of 1997 further emphasised the dangers of 'insider' systems, from Japan to Thailand, South Korea, Indonesia and the Philippines. Comparison with the stellar performance of the US and (to a lesser extent) the UK economy convinced the world that 'outsider' systems based on markets were a superior approach to corporate governance.

The 'market for corporate control'

Shareholders may use 'voice' to exert direct pressure on the management of a company if they believe it to be earning less profit than it could, or they could use 'exit' – selling shares in a company if they think that it is poorly managed. The existence of a market for voting shares – the market for corporate control – therefore provides a source of pressure on managers through the working of share prices.

Share prices are determined fundamentally by the amount that investors are willing to pay for them. For rational profit-seeking investors this will be equal to the present value of future profits. If a company's management is considered by the market to be using the firm's resources to make less than maximum profit, the share price will be lower than it would be if the management were more efficient. The firm and its assets will therefore be under-valued. The company will present an attractive target to 'take-over raiders', who may seek to buy up the undervalued shares, shake up or dispose of the existing management, and use the firm's resources more effectively in order to produce higher profits and a capital gain through an increase in the share price.

This form of discipline may work in two different ways. The most obvious one is where take-overs actually take place and lazy managers are displaced or disciplined by new owners with a greater concern for profits. Alternatively (see Holl 1977) the threat of possible take-over may be enough in itself to act as a disciplinary force. In either case, the ability of managers to exercise discretion over the ways in which the firm's resources are used is severely restricted.

John Thompson, Head of the Financial Affairs Division of the Organization for Economic Co-operation and Development (OECD), has argued that one of the most important structural changes in the world's economy in the 1980s and 1990s has been the emergence of increasingly efficient markets for corporate control which give shareholders a much greater ability to influence the senior managers of publicly held companies (Thompson 1998).

However, as Kreps (1990, p. 725) points out, the effectiveness of this mechanism depends upon whether under-performing firms really are threatened with take-over and whether the senior managers of 'victim' firms suffer enough loss of wealth or prestige to motivate them to avoid it through diligence and effort.

There are a number of factors that may limit the effectiveness of the take-over mechanism as a means of exerting discipline over managers (Shleifer and Vishny 1988). First, there are always information asymmetries so that a firm whose value is perceived by the market to be low may not be badly run at all. It may be well run and facing real difficulties of which the market is not aware. Rational market participants will understand this and be unsure whether a take-over is worthwhile. Second, it should be recognised that take-over will only take place if the 'raider' stands to benefit and this is not as clear as the simple analysis suggests.

In the simple analysis a victim firm is under-valued, relative to the price it would command when properly run. The raider buys it at the low price and makes a large profit when the management is improved. But consider the position of a shareholder in the victim firm. If they know that shares in a firm will be worth £50 after a take-over is successful, they will not be willing to sell their shares for less than that amount. The raider will be forced to offer that amount in order to get control. However, a take-over bid involves significant costs and therefore there will be no profit for the raider, who will therefore not bid for the firm. On this logic the threat of take-overs cannot act as an effective disciplinary mechanism.

The senior management of a raiding firm could benefit from a take-over if they accumulated a holding in the victim firm at lower prices before the take-over bid is made. In that case they could afford to pay other shareholders the full value of their shares and then benefit from the capital appreciation in their own holdings. However, the pre-bid acquisition would have to go unnoticed by the market or the raiders would be unable to purchase at the lower price. That in turn implies that the pre-bid holding would have to be quite small and the post-merger gains would therefore need to be very large in order to compensate for the cost of implementing the take-over.

There are other reasons for suspecting that the effectiveness of the take-over mechanism is limited. The managers of companies at risk of being taken over may use a variety of stratagems to defend themselves (Ricketts 1994, pp. 256–9). They may persuade their shareholders to change the company constitution so that large majority votes are needed for the approval of mergers or changes in the board of directors – *supermajority amendments*. They might issue categories of stock that carry the right to dividends but no voting rights. They might adopt a *poison pill* defence whereby existing shareholders are given the right to sell their shares to the company at high prices after a change in ownership takes place, giving the incumbent an impossible burden if the take-over should succeed. They might agree to a *green-mail* arrangement where the raider is offered a high price for the shares it has already purchased in return for abandoning the bid, or they may award themselves *golden parachutes* in the form of large severance payments following take-over. If the parachutes were very large, they would have the same effect as a poison pill, but their more usual effect would simply be to undermine the incentive properties of take-over.

Taken overall, it is clear that there are limits to the effectiveness of take-over as a mechanism for forcing senior managers to aim for maximum profit. It would be wrong to dismiss it entirely but naïve to presume that it operates with full force.

Managerial labour markets

If shareholder pressure and the market for corporate control do not force senior managers to aim for maximum profit, another possibility is that they are disciplined by managerial labour markets – the arrangements that determine whether they can find jobs and the returns they receive in those jobs (Fama 1980). If top managers' earnings are dependent upon their reputations for effectiveness, and those reputations are determined by their track records, they may be under adequate pressure to perform well. Managers' wages fall when they are associated with failure and rise when they are associated with success. In that case, there is an external pressure on managers to perform and hence they will not shirk.

The difficulty with this idea (Ricketts 1994, p. 239) is that the selection of senior managers is determined by a company's existing senior management. If those managers are not disciplined by some other mechanism to seek out the best interest of the shareholders, there is no reason to assume that they will pick the best performer. When shareholders are unable to observe their abilities, incumbent managers might even prefer to appoint incompetent new colleagues in order to make themselves appear more able.

The idea that external labour markets might exert firm discipline over senior managers is credible if managers are constantly moving from job to job, if they believe that other managers can observe any shirking and will punish them for it because they, in turn, believe that they themselves will be punished if they do not. However, such beliefs would essentially be based on 'thin air' and the proposition is not convincing. A more persuasive argument refers back to the take-over mechanisms examined above. If senior managers are aware that the market contains at least some external observers who are capable of identifying under-performance, and that those observers have an incentive to act on that information by taking the firm over and influencing appointments, then managerial labour markets may discipline managers.

Principal/agent theory

The difficulties that arise in respect of shareholders' ability to exert control over managers may be described as an example of the principal/agent problem. This arises whenever one economic actor (the principal) engages another (the agent) to carry out a task on their behalf in a situation where perfect information is not free and monitoring is costly. As the principal (the shareholders) cannot observe the level of effort that the agent (the manager) puts into the job, there is an incentive for the agent to shirk. The problem is that of *moral hazard*, defined as 'an ex post contracting situation and a source of transaction costs that occurs when one party's actions are imperfectly observable and when the incentives of the parties are imperfectly aligned' (Acs and Gerlowski 1996, p. 446). Moral hazard is a general problem whose solution lies in designing the relationship between principal and agent in a way that aligns their incentives. There are two basic ways with which it may be dealt.

The first approach to solving the moral hazard problem is *monitoring*. The principal spends more time, effort and resources in observing the agent's behaviour and punishing the agent for shirking. As noted in Chapter 3, a major difficulty with that approach is that the principal has limited time available and if the principal hires someone else as the monitor, that person is simply another agent with the same incentive to shirk. In the shareholder/manager situation, the chief executive officer (CEO) may be seen as the monitor hired to control the other managers and workers. The problem that the shareholders then face is how to monitor the monitor. By giving the CEO a share in the residual rights, through profit-related bonuses or share options, the shareholders avoid the difficulty of observing the CEO's effort. Provided that they can observe performance (profit), they can align the CEO's incentives with the objectives of the shareholders.

Ownership of shares and the granting of profit-linked bonuses and options are therefore examples of *incentive contracts*, which are the alternative to monitoring. The threat of take-over or managerial labour markets may act as another form of incentive contract whereby the CEO seeks maximum profit because they will lose their job or suffer reduced pay if they do not perform well. However, questions have been raised above concerning whether the incentives arising in these ways are actually sufficient to motivate CEOs to seek maximum profit.

Profit-maximisers or not?

The sections above have tried to establish whether managers have the discretion to use the resources of the firm in their own interests, or whether they are under sufficient pressure to put the shareholders' interests before their own. The conclusion must be mixed. On the one hand there are a variety of mechanisms that prevent managers from simply doing as they please. Indeed, if they were able to do whatever they like it is unlikely that the market economy would have proven so successful. On the other hand, both theoretical analysis and the evidence makes it unreasonable to believe that managers are tied completely to the service of their shareholders.

Overall, it seems reasonable to conclude that in many large firms the senior managers have significant room for discretion, especially in the short to medium term. However, if they use that discretion to generate excessive slack and to sacrifice significant proportions of the potential profits, there are sufficient sources of discipline to bring retribution in the longer term.

We must doubt the descriptive realism of the profit-maximisation assumption. However, that does nothing to reduce its value as the starting point for positive models of the firm. Nor does it prevent analysts from developing useful prescriptions based on the fundamental logic of the profit-maximising model. If the aim of the firm is to maximise profit, how should it behave?

New directions in the debate on ownership and control: did Berle and Means get it wrong?

Before moving on to examine diversification and mergers it is useful to consider a number of studies that have recently returned the ownership and control debate back to its beginnings. Berle and Means (1932) established a picture of the modern corporation as 'widely held', that is to say having ownership and the right to vote on major issues spread across a large number of shareholders. That image of the large firm has dominated thinking for two generations and focused attention on the issues that arise when ownership is dispersed and control is in the hands of managers. However, increased interest in the question of corporate governance (Shleifer and Vishny 1997) and the experience of the Asian financial crisis have shed doubt on the empirical validity of that image. A recent study by La Porta *et al.* (1999) examined the twenty largest firms in the world's twenty-seven richest economies. First, following Grossman and Hart (1986), they distinguished between the voting rights held by shareholders and their rights to the cash flows generated. They then focused on voting rights and attempted to distinguish between firms that are *widely held*, as in the Berle and Means image, and those that have *ultimate owners* or *controlling shareholders*. In common with Berle and Means's original approach, they used 20 per cent ownership as the cut-off point for defining a corporation as having a controlling shareholder, so that any corporation having a shareholder holding more than 20 per cent of the voting rights is said to have an ultimate owner. However, this analysis went further than Berle and Means by paying careful attention to the patterns of cross-holdings and pyramid structures whereby an ultimate owner may have both *direct voting rights* (through shares registered in their own name) and *indirect voting rights* (through shares held by entities that the ultimate owner controls). The results showed that for the twenty-seven countries as a whole, only 36 per cent of the largest firms were widely held. Thirty per cent were family controlled, 18 per cent were state controlled and the remaining 15 per cent were controlled by other types of ultimate owner, including widely held industrial or financial firms.

While the overall figures cast a general doubt on the conventional wisdom held since Berle and Means (1932), the results for individual countries show very significant variation from place to place. The proportion of widely held firms ranged from 100 per cent in the United Kingdom, 90 per cent in Japan and 80 per cent in the United States down to zero in Argentina and Mexico. Family-controlled firms ranged from 100 per cent in Mexico and 70 per cent in Hong Kong to 5 per cent in Australia and Japan. La Porta *et al.* (1999) suggest that a major reason for these differences lies in the extent to which the law in different countries provides for *anti-director rights*. Such rights are defined as 'high' when: shareholders can mail proxy votes to the firm; shareholders are not required to deposit their shares prior to a General Meeting; proportional representation of minority shareholders is allowed; an oppressed minorities mechanism is in place; less than 10 per cent ownership is needed for a shareholder to be entitled to call an Extraordinary Shareholders' Meeting; shareholders have pre-emptive rights that can only be waived by a vote of the shareholders.

If anti-director rights are high (as in rich common-law countries) there is good legal protection of minority shareholders and hence controlling shareholders will be less worried about being expropriated in case of a take-over. They will therefore be more willing to reduce their voting rights by selling shares. Certainly the data presented by La Porta *et al.* (1999) support that view overall because the proportion of widely held large companies was 48 per cent in countries with 'high' anti-director rights and only 27 per cent where anti-director rights were low. On the other hand, there were very wide variations within the two categories, with no large firms being widely held in Argentina and only 10 per cent and 15 per cent being widely held in Hong Kong and Singapore respectively, despite all three countries having a high level of anti-director rights.

Another interesting feature of these results lies in the relative importance of the family in comparison with financial institutions. While family-controlled firms made up 30 per cent of the large firms examined, only 5 per cent were controlled by widely held financial institutions. Even in the United States, where the Berle and Means image remains most applicable, 20 per cent of large publicly traded firms were family controlled. Furthermore, in these family firms typically there were no other large shareholders having sufficient voting rights to exercise restraint over the family. As La Porta *et al.* (1999, p. 505) conclude: 'Family control of firms appears to be common, significant and typically unchallenged by other equity holders.' This rediscovery of the family firm as a powerful force in most major economies has led to further work in a number of directions. Claessens *et al.* (2000) examine the situation in East Asia, providing results for nearly 3,000 corporations in nine countries. Perhaps unsurprisingly, they also find that family control is extensive, with the largest ten families in Indonesia, the Philippines and Thailand controlling half of the corporate assets in the sample. In Hong Kong and Korea the top ten families control about one-third of the corporate sector.

A major concern in East Asia, and by extension in other economies where family control is substantial, concerns the impact of 'crony capitalism' on the efficiency of the economy and on its development. When a small number of families control such a large part of the economy they have both the means and the motivation to lobby government for preferential treatment like import controls, award of public contracts and government financing, which reduce the efficiency of the economy. They may also inhibit the development of legal structures that protect other shareholders and hence reduce the efficiency of the country's investment allocation mechanisms.

These concerns over 'crony capitalism' are by no means restricted to East Asia because in western Europe as a whole, family control is actually more pronounced than in East Asia. However, as Faccio *et al.* (forthcoming) have shown, the controlling shareholders in East Asia seem to be much more able and willing to use their position to expropriate the corporation's assets. In Europe, family-held firms pay higher dividends than such firms in East Asia, suggesting that European capital markets recognise the danger of expropriation and force firms to issue higher dividends, taking the assets out of the hands of the insiders. In East Asia these mechanisms are weaker, especially in the case of loosely held groups where the linked shareholdings exceed 10 per cent but not 20 per cent. In such groups it is almost impossible to trace related transactions. That gives the controlling shareholders the ability to extract high returns for themselves from projects that yield negative returns for the corporation.

This analysis echoes the original Berle and Means concern, but in a different way. The original finding was that corporations are widely held and that, as a result, the shareholders could lose when the managers expropriated their assets in the form of unnecessary slack, over-large workforces and unnecessary perquisites for themselves. The owner-controlled firm was seen as one in which agency problems were less severe and hence efficiency was more likely to be achieved. In the new view, the Berle and Means stereotype is only typical for the United Kingdom, the United States and Japan because many corporations elsewhere are not widely held. However, these owner/family-controlled firms represent a different type of problem because the insider shareholders may be able to use their position to expropriate the assets of the others. In the better developed legal and financial systems of western Europe this effect seems to be controlled by the law's ability to protect minority shareholders and the market's ability to force insiders to pay dividends to outsiders in compensation for their vulnerability. In countries where the institutional framework is less well developed, shareholders outside the family are much more open to expropriation.

The extent of diversification

In the elementary model of the firm, the business produces a single product. However, virtually all firms in all industries are multi-product and the question is not whether to be diversified, but how far the diversification should be taken. Companies may be diversified along a very narrow spectrum of closely related activities, or they may be 'broad-spectrum diversified' or 'conglomerate', encompassing a range of activities that bear little technological or marketing connection with each other.

There are a number of factors that are important in determining the most efficient degree of diversification.

Economies of scope

Economies of scope are examined in more detail in Chapter 9. The term is used to refer to a situation where it is cheaper to combine two or more product lines in one firm, rather than producing them separately.

The key feature of economies of scope is that they are linked to the existence of inputs that are 'sharable' in the sense that, once purchased or hired for the production of one product, they are also available at little or no additional cost for the production of others. Generators for electric power and the cables and equipment needed to distribute the power are an example as they can be used for different products at the same time. Other examples are factory buildings, human capital like managerial skill or inputs like sheep and cattle which produce joint outputs (mutton and wool, beef and hides). The range of such sharable inputs is quite broad, and could extend as far as marketing skills which can be used for a variety of products, or to the ownership of distribution channels down which a variety of goods could be sent. If such sharable inputs exist there will be economies of scope. Wherever such economies exist it is to be expected that the multi-product firm will be the norm, because any firm that is not producing an appropriate range of products will be at a cost disadvantage relative to those who do.

Economies of scope undoubtedly exist and provide the rationale for diversification in many cases. However, if diversification is to be fully explained in this way, it might be expected that the different businesses involved would share either similar production technologies or similar markets. In fact, Nathanson and Cassano (1982) found that was not the case for many diversified US firms and hence it seems unlikely that the extent of diversification in practice can be fully explained in these terms.

The exploitation of specific assets

A slightly different interpretation of the economies of scope issue concerns the possession and development of specific assets that may be exploitable in a number of different activities, thereby linking different technologies and different markets. Companies may have 'core' skills or 'key capabilities' that provide the foundation for a move into a wider range of activities. Hence there may be economies of scope even if there are no shared technologies or markets in the narrow sense. Penrose (1959) noted that as firms grow, some of their assets are constantly regenerated in changing forms, which allow them to carry out new activities. Prahalad and Bettis (1986) suggested that senior managers may subscribe to a 'dominant general management logic' which allows them (or so they believe) to allocate resources well across a variety of unrelated activities.

One example of a core skill that might lead to diversification concerns research and development activity (R&D). If a firm carries out R&D successfully then it may produce new discoveries in products or processes that can be exploited outside the firm's current range of products and markets. Some of the early empirical evidence (Gort 1969) showed a distinct relationship between the level of R&D in firms and industries and the extent of diversification.

This again raises the issue that was considered in detail in Chapter 3 – the choice between an internalised transaction that takes place within the hierarchy of the firm and a transaction between independent firms, coordinated by contract. If arm's length transactions in knowledge or capabilities were superior to internalised transactions, firms having those capabilities would not become more diversified. Instead, they would sell or license their innovation or capabilities to others. If a technology is easily identified and protected, if it can be cheaply transferred to a licensee, and if competition pushes the licence fee high enough, then licensing will be preferred (Davies 1977, 1993). In that case, the ownership of technological assets will not lead to greater diversification on the part of the innovating firm. On the other hand, if it is expensive to transfer the know-how from one firm to another, and if the technological advantage is difficult to protect, the cost of an arm's length transaction will be high. As a result it will be more profitable to use the technology in-house and diversification will take place.

The general argument here is that diversification is required if a firm has any kind of specialised resource that can be used in a variety of activities at the same time and which cannot be transacted at arm's length. As with economies of scope, it is clear that at least some of the diversification that is observed in practice can be explained in this way. However, the obvious difficulty is that it can be almost impossible to verify with any certainty that some types of resource exist at all, or have real value. Pilkington's clearly expanded into diverse markets and products on the basis of their core skills in glass (Edwards and Townsend 1967). On the other hand, a group of senior managers may deem themselves to possess a particularly effective 'dominant logic' and proceed to diversify in order to use it, when in fact they possess nothing more than an inflated notion of their own abilities.

The reduction of risk and uncertainty

The issues considered above concern diversification into activities that have some connection with the firm's existing operations, either through the structure of costs, the firm's core skills, or its R&D activity. However, with the possible exception of the 'dominant logic', none of these factors is sufficient to explain the existence of the true conglomerate firm composed of a completely disparate set of activities.

One possible explanation for the existence of unrelated conglomerate firms lies in the reduction of risk and uncertainty. If the firm is viewed as a financial asset, then it is easily shown that the risk associated with it can be reduced by grouping together a number of different activities. This can happen in two ways. First, the average risk will be reduced as activities are 'pooled'. Second, risk can be reduced most effectively by combining activities whose returns are negatively correlated with each other. As a result, the diversified firm may be a more attractive prospect to suppliers of capital.

The problem with this argument is that an investor could achieve the same result, or better, by investing in a diversified portfolio of shares, or a unit trust, rather than in a diversified firm. In fact, if investors are rational and dislike risk they will already have done so. Hence a diversified firm will have no additional attraction for investors.

This last proposition is only valid when capital markets are perfect, and investors well informed. Investors might therefore rate the diversification skills of managers with inside information more highly than their own or those of investment managers. Williamson (1985), for instance, has argued that the top managers of multi-divisional conglomerates have access to better and more detailed information on investment opportunities within the firm than does the external capital market.

It might be true that the managers of a diversified firm have advantages over the capital market in respect of their knowledge on how resources should be allocated within the firm. However, as the first part of this chapter and the discussion of vertical integration in Chapter 3 have made clear, they may not use that knowledge to the benefit of the shareholders. Much of the evidence suggests that the managers of diversified firms practise a kind of 'corporate socialism' (Scharfstein 1998), shifting funds towards poorly performing divisions which 'need' them. Many diversified firms tolerate losses for much longer than specialised firms would allow (Berger and Ofek 1995). They over-invest in industries that have poor investment prospects and they under-invest where prospects are good (Lamont 1997). That tendency is particularly marked in firms whose business is spread across a range of sectors that have widely divergent investment prospects (Rajan *et al.* 1998). Berlin (1999) concludes that in diversified firms the internal capital market is not an efficient mechanism for the allocation of resources because their head offices tend to buy the cooperation of the weaker business units by shifting funds in their direction, something that the external capital market would not do.

Trends in diversification and the relationship with firm performance

The sections above have shown that some degree of diversification is necessary for efficiency but that the extent to which it is taken in practice may not be optimal. Palich *et al.* (2000) reviewed more than fifty studies of the diversification–performance linkage and confirmed a curvilinear relationship whereby performance improved as firms shifted from single-business strategies to 'related diversification' but then decreased as they diversified further into unrelated industries.

This section examines how corporate attitudes to diversification have shifted over time, partly in response to changes in the balance of power between managers and shareholders, and partly in response to its perceived performance consequences.

In the 1960s and 1970s companies generally became more diversified. However, while the typical purchaser acquired a firm that was performing better than the average for its industry, the merged firm usually suffered from deteriorating performance (Ravenscraft and Scherer 1987). It also became clear in the 1980s and 1990s that there was a 'diversification discount' whereby stock markets valued a diversified firm at approximately 15 per cent less than the sum of its component parts (Berger and Ofek 1995). It appeared in many cases that diversifying firms had not understood the markets into which they were moving, or their skills were not useful in their new settings.

As might be expected in a relatively efficient market system, stockholders and the market for corporate control responded to the diversification discount by forcing managers to restructure towards greater focus (Berger and Ofek 1997). Firms either divested themselves of earlier diversified acquisitions or they were taken over by corporate raiders who then sold off, spun off or liquidated the less related activities (Kaplan and Weisbach 1992). Stock markets responded favourably to asset sales and divestitures which reduced the degree of diversification (Berlin 1999) and, as a result, the trend towards diversification was reversed (Comment and Jarrell 1995), with the possible exception of the very largest firms in the United States (Montgomery 1994).

The evidence that the diversification of the 1960s and 1970s failed so comprehensively, when viewed with hindsight, naturally raises the question of 'why did it happen in the first place?' Two possible answers offer themselves. The first is that the economy has changed in some way so that diversification was efficient in the earlier period but became less so later. That possibility is supported by the fact that the diversification discount was not apparent in the United States during the first half of the 1970s. As financial markets were considerably less developed and considerably less competitive in the earlier period, it could be argued that internal capital markets did then have advantages over external markets. It was therefore efficient to diversify at that time but became less so as financial markets were de-regulated and liberalised in the 1980s and 1990s. That explanation is plausible, although Berlin (1999) suggests that more concrete evidence is needed before it could be regarded as wholly convincing.

The other explanation for the shift is that diversification was instigated by managers, against the interest of the shareholders, but that over time shareholders increasingly asserted their influence and replaced the diversifying management teams with new teams more intent on serving shareholder interests. Certainly Berger and Ofek (1997) found that firms that had re-focused between 1983 and 1994 were more likely to have replaced their senior managers in the preceding year. Firms whose managers hold higher proportions of the company's stock are usually more focused because in that case the managers are also shareholders and therefore more likely to seek the maximisation of shareholder value (Denis *et al.* 1997).

These alternative explanations for the shift away from conglomerates and back towards focus share a common foundation in the idea that financial markets have become significantly more efficient over the last twenty years. The consequences of the 'Big Bang' in the City of London, de-regulation, liberalisation, globalisation and increased competition extend far beyond the financial sector into the systems that monitor and control the behaviour of senior managers in non-financial corporations.

Mergers and take-overs

Firms may diversify or integrate vertically through two different routes. The first is through *internal development* and the second is through *merger* or *acquisition*. An examination of the forces that lead mergers to take place, and an analysis of their consequences, provide some additional insight into the issues that have been discussed in the earlier sections of this chapter.

Alternative forms of merger

A merger may be defined as the process by which a firm acquires resources that are already organised by another firm. If this process is uncontested, it is referred to as a merger. If the incumbent managers of the 'victim' contest the process, then it is usually referred to as a 'take-over'. In practice the distinction between mergers and take-overs is often blurred. Three types of merger may be distinguished. These are:

1. *Horizontal mergers*, between potential competitors.
2. *Vertical mergers*, between firms at different stages of the production process.
3. *Conglomerate mergers*, between firms in unrelated activities.

Mergers in a perfect world: synergy or the acquisition of market power

The simplest way to begin is to consider the situation where all managers are efficient; the market value of every firm is an accurate reflection of expected future earnings; there is no uncertainty; managers are constrained to act in the interests of shareholders; and every investor uses the same discount rate in the evaluation of future returns.

In this situation, every investor will place the same value on every company and no one will be willing to pay more for a firm than anyone else. Mergers will then only take place if the merged firm has a higher value than the sum of its parts. This could arise for two basic reasons, which are as follows.

Synergy

Synergy is a blanket term covering the general idea that 'two plus two may be greater than four'. In times of merger booms there are often rather vague claims made for the existence of synergistic effects, which amount to wishful thinking or *ex post* rationalisation. Nevertheless the effects could be real and could arise through a number of different mechanisms, many of which have been outlined in Chapter 3 and earlier sections of this chapter.

One source of synergy could be under-exploited economies of scope in production, marketing or distribution. Similarly, if there are under-exploited economies of scale, a merger may allow the combined firm to produce at lower unit cost. One of the most important sources of such scale economies is indivisible resources. If a firm has an indivisible and under-utilised management team, distribution network or set of plant and equipment, it may be able to reduce costs by applying these resources to a larger set of merged activities.

Synergy may also arise if transaction costs are reduced by replacing market transactions with internalised transactions, if there are economies in raising finance, or if the merged firm has enhanced debt capacity. If any of these factors are present, there will be real synergistic effects arising from merger and the value of the merged firm will exceed the value of its pre-merger components.

Increased market power

A horizontal merger, or a vertical merger, may give the combined firm more market power, allowing an element of monopoly profit to be made and enhancing the value of the merged firm above that of its pre-merger components. If restrictive collusive agreements between firms are outlawed, for instance, as under the UK restrictive practices legislation, mergers may take place in order to allow the same collusive arrangement to continue within a single firm. Of course, such mergers might also fall foul of the competition legislation.

In the perfect world described, mergers would only take place if synergy or market power effects really exist. Indeed, in such a perfect world all the mergers that increase the value of the firm will already have taken place so that new mergers will only arise if technologies, markets or institutions change to create hitherto unavailable opportunities. A first possible explanation for merger activity, then, is that some change in the environment has altered the most efficient configuration of the firm in such a way that the integration of previously separate organisations has become more efficient.

Mergers as the transfer of resources to more efficient managers

It has been noted above that if the market for corporate control works efficiently, the value of a firm's shares will reflect the future profits that the firm is expected to earn. If some managers are more efficient than others, companies run by them will have higher expected profits and higher valuations. Conversely, firms run by less competent or X-inefficient managers will have relatively low valuations and relatively low share prices.

In this situation a strong management team will place a higher value than the market on the assets of a firm being run by a poor management team, the presumption being that the stronger team would be able to use the same assets to make a higher level of profit. As a result, the market for corporate control will ensure that mergers are a means by which the economy's resources are concentrated in the hands of more efficient managers (Manne 1965). More efficient managers scan the market for less efficiently run firms which may be taken over, to the benefit of the shareholders.

In this view, mergers are an important mechanism for the improvement of efficiency. However, the limitations of the market for corporate control have been examined above and the implied improvement in post-merger performance is difficult to find empirically, as explained below.

Mergers as a result of stock market manipulation

In the absence of well-informed investors it is possible that mergers could take place as part of a ploy by merger promoters. In the early American merger booms, for instance, the practice of 'stock watering' was common. That involved a merger promoter planting rumours that there would be substantial gains to be had from a merger. If the rumours were believed, investors would place an unrealistically high price on the stock of a merged firm, at least until the market recognised the fallacy, by which time the merger promoter had realised a substantial profit and sold any holdings. Koutsoyannis (1982, p. 244) outlines a more sophisticated version of this technique, known as 'bootstrapping'. If a firm has a high price/earnings (P/E) ratio and acquires a firm with a lower P/E ratio by swapping shares, then if investors can be persuaded that the combined operation should be valued at the higher ratio, the share price of the combined firm will rise. It is likely, of course, that the acquired firm had a lower P/E ratio because it had more limited prospects and that eventually the higher P/E ratio will be seen by the market to have been unrealistic. However, in the short term, substantial speculative profits could be made.

Mergers as a result of valuation discrepancies

Discrepancies in valuation may arise because managers have different levels of ability and better managers value the same set of assets more highly. However, differences in the valuation of the same firm by different investors could arise in other ways. In times of economic disturbance, for instance, with rapid technological progress, shifting demand patterns and widely fluctuating share prices, there will often be genuine opportunities to exploit new synergies or sources of market power. However, in such uncertain conditions, different groups of investors may also develop different expectations about the value of the same business. Hence mergers may take place for that reason, independently of poor managers, synergies or market power. Gort (1969) suggested that this effect could account for the existence of merger 'booms'. In periods of enhanced uncertainty valuation discrepancies emerge more often and merger activity tends to be concentrated in such periods.

The performance consequences of mergers

If mergers take place in order to exploit new opportunities for synergy, to increase market power, or to strengthen management, it should be expected that the performance of merged firms will improve. However, the empirical evidence provides very limited support for that proposition. In the United States more than 35,000 corporate acquisitions were completed between 1976 and 1990 (Jensen 1993) without any clear pattern of performance improvement emerging. In some cases companies did perform better and Healy *et al.* (1992) found improvements in productivity and cash flows in a sample of the fifty largest US mergers. However, if a general pattern is to be found it is that acquisitions have a neutral to negative effect on the shareholder value of acquirors (Bradley *et al.* 1988, Berkovitch and Narayan 1993). In many cases the shareholders of the acquired firm do gain, because the 'raider' pays a premium over the market price for the 'victim'. However, those gains are not part of an overall increase in the value of the company, simply a shift in wealth from the shareholders of the acquiring firm to the shareholders of the so-called 'victim'.

These results for the United States echo earlier studies in the United Kingdom. Singh (1971) found that at least half of the firms involved in a sample of British mergers experienced decreases in profitability after the merger. Newbould (1970) showed that in many cases firms considering a merger carried out little or no analysis of their 'victim' in the pre-merger stage, and only about half of the studies even attempted to secure synergistic gains post-merger. On balance there is little evidence that mergers consistently lead to significant improvements in corporate performance.

Are mergers really for managers?

If the shareholders of the acquiring firm do not gain from a merger it is natural to consider whether the managers gain and whether mergers are another example of managerial discretion. It has been noted above that a conglomerate merger may reduce the level of risk, but that it is a relatively inefficient way of doing so for an investor, who could simply buy a more highly diversified portfolio of shares. For the managers, however, who are restricted to working in one firm at a time, the risk attached to their employment arises from the volatility of that single firm's activities. From their point of view, risk reduction through in-house diversification may be very attractive, providing for a quieter life. Mergers may also take place because firm size, or growth, is an important element in the managers' objective function, giving them status, prestige and higher benefits. In that case, it is the needs and interests of managers that determine merger activity, not those of the shareholders or the economy as a whole.

This idea that mergers are for managers has been taken further by Roll (1986) and Hayward and Hambrick (1997). They argue that many mergers take place because the CEOs of the acquiring companies suffer from *hubris*, which may be defined as 'exaggerated pride or self-confidence, often resulting in retribution'. Furthermore, because they exaggerate their own ability to improve the performance of the acquired companies, such CEOs tend to pay too much for the companies they buy and hence actually cause the poor performance that so often follows. Hayward and Hambrick (1997) test a model in which CEOs' hubris is increased by three factors: the recent success of the organisation they head; positive media coverage of the CEO; and the CEO's self-importance as measured by the size of the compensation package relative to other top executives. Each of these factors increases the premium paid for an acquired company, defined as the ratio of the price offered to the pre-bid price of the firm. That premium is then negatively related to the performance of the merged firm, post acquisition. Statistical tests of the model support all of the implied hypotheses. The premiums paid were higher when the acquiring firm had performed well recently, when the CEO had been praised by the media, and when the CEO was very highly paid relative to other executives. Higher premiums were also associated with lower shareholder returns in the period following the merger.

Clearly, the Hayward and Hambrick (1997) study points to significant managerial discretion in the acquisition process and links back to the discussion above on ownership and control. Some of the more detailed results are also interesting in that context. For instance, the study also tried to measure the extent to which the board of directors exerted vigilance over the CEO, using proxy variables. If the CEO was chairman of the board, that was interpreted as indicating a lower level of board vigilance, as was a higher proportion of internal board members. Both of those variables had a powerful 'interaction effect' on the size of the premiums paid. In other words, the positive effect of CEO hubris on acquisition premiums was stronger when the board of directors exerted less vigilance and weaker when the board had more control.

Illustration 1

Illustration 1 — The impact of hostile take-overs on managerial turnover in the United Kingdom

One of the mechanisms that may reduce managerial discretion and force top executives to seek maximum profits is the hostile take-over. A number of analysts have argued that while friendly take-overs are usually motivated by perceived synergies between the merging companies, hostile take-overs (those that are opposed by the incumbent management) are motivated by under-performance and followed by replacement of the poorly performing managers and restructuring of the firm's assets. Dahya and Powell (1998) examined this issue using a sample of ninety-two successful take-overs in the United Kingdom, thirty-eight of which were classified as 'hostile'. The results showed that target firms as a whole reported negative growth in profitability in the twelve months preceding the announcement of the bid. Those firms that were subjected to hostile take-overs reported the most dramatic decline in profitability, at 22 per cent over the preceding twelve months, compared with 13 per cent for the firms involved in friendly take-overs. The hypothesis that firms subject to hostile take-overs have been performing badly (and worse than those in friendly take-overs) is therefore supported. For the sample as a whole, 47 per cent experienced a change in the top executive category following the take-over bid compared with 16.5 per cent and 17.5 per cent three years and two years before the bid. Interestingly enough, 26 per cent saw top executive departures in the year preceding the bid, which is significantly more than the preceding years but significantly less than after the take-overs took place. It would appear that signs of trouble and the possibility of a bid lead some top executives to leave before the take-over actually materialises. For the firms involved in hostile take-overs the proportions that experienced top executive departures in the year before the bid and in the year after the take-over were much higher than for the firms involved in friendly take-overs.

Overall, these results show that hostile take-overs do involve firms that are under-performing due to poor management and they are accompanied by a relatively high degree of 'top management disciplining'. If that interpretation is correct, it suggests that the hostile take-over mechanism is an effective means by which management teams are changed and redirected towards the search for shareholder value.

Illustration 2 — Incumbent British insiders resist US-style pressure for change in Hong Kong, but for how long?

The Jardine group of companies has its origins in one of the British 'hongs' – major trading companies established in Hong Kong in the nineteenth century. Control of the company, which was established by William Jardine, a Scot, passed into the hands of the Keswick family in 1874. Having built the original business and profits around trade (most notoriously in opium) the company grew to become a well-respected pillar of the Hong Kong colonial establishment. Its generally upper-class British managers were known as 'Jardine Johnnies', newly recruited management trainees as 'cadets' and the company's place of influence in business, politics and expatriate social life was assured. By the 1970s the firm had become a major conglomerate whose activities included supermarkets, prestigious hotels, property,

▶

distribution franchises and financial services and it enjoyed a reputation as a well-run company with a solid portfolio of valuable assets.

This picture of corporate strength began to change in the 1980s. In the first year of that decade local tycoon Y-K. Pao was able to seize control of Wharf Holdings, a major Jardine company. Shortly afterwards, Hong Kong 'Superman' Li Ka-shing, noted for the brilliance of his deal-making, bought a minority share in Jardine Matheson, perhaps as part of a take-over attempt, and then sold it back to the company at a higher price in what amounted to a 'green-mail' arrangement.

Faced with these threats to their control, and a further 'attack' from local tycoons, the Jardine management, dominated by the Keswick family, took a number of steps. First, they moved the domicile of the company to Bermuda where the authorities obligingly passed 'one of the most astonishing pieces of companies legislation ever written in a British legal jurisdiction' (Pritchard 2000). The Jardine Matheson Holdings Consolidation and Amendment Act 1988 contained a number of provisions designed to block a hostile take-over, including the 'chain principle' that forces a bidder for a Jardine subsidiary to bid for the rest of the group also.

Second, the Jardine management put in place a cross-shareholding structure which effectively sealed the Keswick family's control. Under the cross-shareholding arrangement the company is organised around two major entities – Jardine Matheson Holdings (JMH) and Jardine Strategic Holdings (JSH). JMH owns 61 per cent of JSH while JSH owns 40 per cent of JMH. The Keswick family and the Weatherall family are estimated to hold around 5 per cent each (Pritchard 2000) while a management remuneration trust, with trustees appointed by the company, holds a similar amount, and stock options allocated to staff carry voting rights. Under this arrangement, resolutions supported by board members are bound to succeed, and those put forward by minority shareholders are bound to fail.

A third step to protect the company from take-over was taken in 1994/5 when the group de-listed in Hong Kong in order to ensure that it would not be subject to the city's take-over code after the hand-over to China in 1997.

While the Jardine management was constructing these defences against a hostile take-over, the business performance of the group was increasingly poor. Alone among the major corporations in Hong Kong, the company failed to make any strategic alliances with powerful interests from the Chinese mainland. Indeed, Henry Keswick described the Chinese regime to the British Parliament as 'Marxist–Leninist, thuggish, oppressive'. In an era when huge corporate growth and profits were to be had in Hong Kong port operations, telecommunications and residential property, the group took no advantage of those opportunities. An expansion into Asia was disastrously timed, coming just before the crisis in 1997, and a series of acquisitions – property in Britain, stock-broking in the United States, sugar in Hawaii, cars in Arabia (van der Kamp 2000) – proved to have been poor decisions.

As a result of this poor performance, the share price languished at a level in mid-2000 below that of 1973. With a sum-of-the-parts valuation as high as US$40 billion, but a market value of only US$11 billion, the group clearly represented a poor reward to shareholders and a potential opportunity for anyone who found the key to unlocking the potential value. This led to a dramatic sequence of events in 2000. In March of that year Alasdair Morrison, group managing director and 'taipan', was ousted, supposedly at one hour's notice. The reason for that coup against

Illustration 2

a 'Jardine Johnny' of almost thirty years' standing was apparently that he had challenged the authority of the Keswick family by suggesting an unravelling of the cross-shareholding operation (Porter 2000). Morrison was replaced as taipan by Percy Weatherall, Henry Keswick's nephew, whose appointment had been regarded as unlikely just a few months earlier on the grounds that it would be an 'unacceptable throwback to the days of nepotism' (Pritchard 2000).

While the hold of the controlling insiders seemed to be as firm as ever, the challenge to them began to gain pace. An American investor, Brandes Investment Partners of San Diego, led by managing partner Brent Woods and owning 8 per cent of JMH and 2 per cent of JSH, put six resolutions to the boards calling for the dissolution of the cross-holding. As anticipated, those resolutions were rejected, with a 75.7 per cent majority. Brandes represented 80 to 90 per cent of the independent shareholders and Woods made the case that such shareholders had no voice in decision-making and were unable to receive full value for their shares.

Although the insiders comfortably won the vote in June 2000 there were a number of signs that their position was becoming exposed. It was argued by Woods that Jardine's overlapping directors were placing themselves in a difficult personal position, practically and legally, because of the potential conflict of interest and because they were effectively voting for themselves. It has been suggested that directors of both JMH and JSH could be personally vulnerable to class-action law suits brought by shareholders for breach of fiduciary duty and that action might be brought in the United States where JMH has American Depositary Receipt shares. In addition to the pressure being brought to bear by Brandes, the opposition to Jardine's management has been joined by Brierley Investments of Singapore, whose managing director Greg Terry was a former Jardine's director involved in crafting the legal defences and hence is well informed about any possible weaknesses they might have.

In the face of this pressure, a number of the 'insider' directors were said to be wavering, either from fear of their own position or because they no longer felt able to support the anachronistic governance structure of the company. A number of well-known investment 'gurus', including Mark Mobius of Templeton Investments, began taking an interest in the issue and in the background Li Ka-shing remained a quiet observer.

It was not clear in the summer of 2000 whether the Jardine insiders would lose their grip on the company. However, the case is a useful illustration of the way in which managers owning relatively small proportions of a company can ignore shareholder value for a significant period of time by crafting safeguards for themselves. At the same time it also shows how the resulting unrealised opportunity for profit leads to very powerful long-term pressures, tending to force shareholder value back into the forefront of managers' minds.

Another fascinating aspect of the case concerns the strategy being followed by Li Ka-shing. The most obvious interpretation of his position is that he will return to make another attack on the company if its defences begin to unravel. On the other hand, some observers of the Hong Kong business scene note that Jardine represents the only competition to Li's companies in a number of fields. As Hong Kong legislators become more concerned about the high degree of monopoly power that is being exercised over some market sectors, it may suit Mr Li to have at least some competition, especially one whose senior managers are more focused on defending themselves against merger than on competing effectively.

References and further reading

Z. Acs and D. Gerlowski, *Managerial Economics and Organization*, New Jersey, Prentice Hall, 1996.

P. Berger and E. Ofek, 'Diversification's Effect on Firm Value', *Journal of Financial Economics*, vol. 37, 1995, pp. 39–65.

P. Berger and E. Ofek, 'Bustup Takeovers of Value-destroying Diversified Firms', *Journal of Finance*, vol. 51, September 1996, pp. 1175–200.

P. Berger and E. Ofek, 'Causes and Effects of Corporate Re-focusing Programs', Working Paper, New York University, August 1997.

E. Berglof, 'Capital Structure as a Mechanism of Control: A Comparison of Financial Systems', in M. Aoki *et al.* (eds) *The Firm as a Nexus of Treaties*, New York, Sage, 1990.

E. Berkovitch and M. Narayan, 'Motives for Take-overs: An Empirical Investigation', *Journal of Financial and Quantitative Analysis*, vol. 28, 1993, pp. 347–62.

A. Berle and G. Means, *The Modern Corporation and Private Property*, New York, Harcourt, Brace and World, 1932 (rev. edn 1967).

M. Berlin, 'Jack of All Trades? Product Diversification in Nonfinancial Firms', *Business Review – Federal Reserve Bank of Philadelphia*, May/June 1999, pp. 15–29.

S. Bhagat, A. Shleifer and R. Vishny, 'Hostile Take-overs in the 1980s: The Return to Corporate Specialization', *Brookings Papers on Economic Activity: Microeconomics*, 1990, pp. 1–72.

A. Bhide, 'Reversing Corporate Diversification', *Journal of Applied Corporate Finance*, vol. 3, 1990, pp. 70–81.

S. Claessens, S. Djankov and L. Lang, 'The Separation of Ownership and Control in East Asian Corporations', *Journal of Financial Economics*, October 2000.

R. Comment and G. Jarrell, 'Corporate Focus and Stock Returns', *Journal of Financial Economics*, vol. 37, 1995, pp. 67–87.

A. Cosh and A. Hughes, 'The Anatomy of Corporate Control: Directors, Shareholders and Executive Remuneration in Giant US and UK Corporations', *Cambridge Journal of Economics*, vol. 11, 1987, pp. 285–313.

J. Cubbin and D. Leech, 'The Effect of Shareholding Dispersion on the Degree of Control of British Companies: Theory and Measurement', *Economic Journal*, vol. 93, no. 2, 1983, pp. 351–69.

J. Dahya and R. Powell, 'Ownership, Managerial Turnover and Take-overs: Further UK Evidence on the Market for Corporate Control', *Multinational Finance Journal*, March 1988, pp. 63–85.

H. Davies, 'Technology Transfer Through Commercial Transactions', *Journal of Industrial Economics*, vol. 26, 1977, pp. 161–75.

H. Davies, 'The Information Content of Technology Transfers: A Transactions Cost Analysis of the Machine Tool Industry', *Technovation*, vol. 13, No. 2, March 1993, pp. 99–107.

D. Denis, D. Denis and A. Sarin,' 'Agency Problems, Equity Ownership and Corporate Diversification', *Journal of Finance*, vol. 52, March 1997, pp. 1350–60.

R. Edwards and H. Townsend, *Business Enterprise*, London, Macmillan, 1967.

M. Faccio, L. Lang and L. Young, 'Dividends and Expropriation', *American Economic Review*, forthcoming, 2001.

E. Fama, 'Agency Problems and the Theory of the Firm', *Journal of Political Economy*, vol. 88, 1980, pp. 288–307.

R. Fox, 'Agency Theory: A New Perspective', *Management Accounting*, 1984.

M. Gort, 'An Economic Disturbance Theory of Mergers', *Quarterly Journal of Economics*, vol. 83, November 1969, pp. 624–42.

S. Grossman and O. Hart, 'One Share – One Vote and the Market for Corporate Control', *Journal of Financial Economics*, vol. 20, 1986, pp. 175–202.

M. Hayward and D. Hambrick, 'Explaining the Premium Paid for Large Acquisitions: Evidence of CEO Hubris', *Administrative Science Quarterly*, vol. 42, no. 1, March 1997, pp. 103–27.

P. Healy, K. Palepu and R. Ruback, 'Does Corporate Performance Improve After Mergers?', *Journal of Financial Economics*, vol. 31, no. 2, April 1992, pp. 135–77.

A. Hirschman, *Exit, Voice and Loyalty: Responses to Decline in Firms, Organizations and States*, Cambridge, MA, Harvard University Press, 1970.

P. Holl, 'Control Type and the Market for Corporate Control in Large US Corporations', *Journal of Industrial Economics*, vol. 23, no. 4, 1977, pp. 257–72.

M. Jensen, 'The Modern Industrial Revolution, Exit and the Failure of Internal Control Systems', *Journal of Finance*, vol. 48, 1993, pp. 53–80.

M. Jensen and K. Murphy, 'CEO Incentives', *Harvard Business Review*, vol. 68, no. 3, 1990.

S. Kaplan and M. Weisbach, 'The Success of Acquisitions: Evidence from Divestitures', *Journal of Finance*, vol. 47, March 1992, pp. 107–38.

J. Kose and E. Ofek, 'Asset Sales and Increase in Focus', *Journal of Financial Economics*, vol. 37, 1995, pp. 105–26

A. Koutsoyannis, *Non-price Decisions*, London, Macmillan, 1982.

D. Kreps, *A Course in Micro-economic Theory*, Princeton, Princeton University Press, 1990.

R. La Porta, F. Lopez-de-Silanes and A. Shleifer, 'Corporate Ownership Around the World', *Journal of Finance*, vol. 54, no. 2, April 1999, pp. 471–517.

O. Lamont, 'Cash Flow and Investment: Evidence from Internal Capital Markets', *Journal of Finance*, vol. 52, March 1997, pp. 83–109.

R. Larner, 'Ownership and Control in the 200 Largest Non-financial Corporations, 1929 and 1963', *American Economic Review*, vol. 56, 1966, p. 777.

D. Leech and J. Leahy, 'Ownership Structure, Control Type Classifications and the Performance of Large British Companies', *Economic Journal*, vol. 101, no. 409, 1991, pp. 1418–37.

W. Lewellen, 'A Pure Financial Rationale for the Conglomerate Merger', *Journal of Finance, Papers and Proceedings*, vol. 26, 1971, pp. 521–37.

H. Manne, 'Mergers and the Market for Corporate Control', *Journal of Political Economy*, vol. 73, April 1965, pp. 110–20.

P. Milgrom and J. Roberts, *Economics, Organization and Management*, New Jersey, Prentice Hall, 1992.

C. Montgomery, 'Corporate Diversification', *Journal of Economic Perspectives*, vol. 8, Summer 1994, pp. 163–78.

D. Nathanson and J. Cassano, 'What Happens to Profits When a Company Diversifies?', *Wharton Magazine*, Summer 1982, pp. 19–26.

G. Newbould, *Management and Merger Activity*, Liverpool, Guthstead, 1970.

L. Palich, L. Cardinal and C. Miller, 'Curvilinearity in the Diversification–Performance Linkage: An Examination Over Three Decades of Research', *Strategic Management Journal*, February 2000, pp. 155–74.

E. Penrose, *The Theory of the Growth of the Firm*, Oxford, Blackwell, 1959.

B. Porter, 'Jardine's Taipan Removed "After Challenging the Keswick Family"', *South China Morning Post*, 23 March 2000.

C. Prahalad and R. Bettis, 'The Dominant Logic: A New Linkage Between Diversity and Performance', *Strategic Management Journal*, vol. 7, 1986, pp. 485–501.

S. Pritchard, 'Jardine's Chief May Find Hong Uncomfortably Exposed', *South China Morning Post*, 1 March 2000.

S. Pritchard, 'Venerable Hong Has Rarely Looked Cheaper', *South China Morning Post*, 24 March 2000.

S. Pritchard, 'Last Lair of a Taipan', *South China Morning Post*, 16 May 2000.

R. Rajan, H. Servaes and L. Zingales, 'The Cost of Diversity: The Diversification Discount and Inefficient Investment', Working Paper, University of Chicago, June 1998.

D. Ravenscraft and F. Scherer, *Mergers, Sell-offs and Economic Efficiency*, Brookings Institution, Washington DC, 1987.

M. Ricketts, *The Economics of Business Enterprise*, 2nd edn, Hemel Hempstead, Wheatsheaf, 1994.

R. Roll, 'The Hubris Hypothesis of Corporate Take-overs', *Journal of Business*, vol. 59, 1986, pp. 197–216.

D. Scharfstein, 'The Dark Side of Internal Capital Markets II: Evidence From Diversified Conglomerates', Working Paper 6532, National Bureau of Economic Research, January 1998.

A. Shleifer and R. Vishny, 'Value Maximization and the Acquisition Process', *Journal of Economic Perspectives*, vol. 2, no. 1, 1988, pp. 7–20.

A. Shleifer and R. Vishny, 'Take-overs in the '60s and '80s: Evidence and Implications', *Strategic Management Journal*, vol. 12, 1991, pp. 51–9.

A. Shleifer and R. Vishny, 'A Survey of Corporate Governance', *Journal of Finance*, vol. 52, 1997, pp. 737–83.

H-H. Shin and R. Stulz, 'Are Internal Capital Markets Efficient?', *Quarterly Journal of Economics*, vol. 112, May 1998, pp. 531–52.

A. Singh, *Takeovers*, Cambridge, Cambridge University Press, 1971.

J.K. Thompson, 'Shareholder Value and the Market in Corporate Control in OECD Countries', *Financial Market Trends*, no. 69, February 1998, pp. 15–38.

J. van der Kamp, 'Jardines Learns An Old Trick', *South China Morning Post*, 7 August 2000.

O. Williamson, *Economic Organization*, Brighton, Wheatsheaf, 1985.

Self-test questions

1. Explain whether each of the following will make firms *more likely* or *less likely* to adopt profit maximisation as their objective.

   (a) an anti-trust policy which forbids take-overs

   (b) powerful, well-informed shareholders

   (c) an efficient stock market

   (d) oligopolistic market conditions

   (e) stock option schemes for managers

2. Give *two* reasons that a shareholder might prefer lower profits to higher profits.

3. Describe the difference between an 'outsider' or 'market-based' financial system and an 'insider' system.

4. List *three* characteristics of a company that may lead it to pay a premium when it takes over another company.

Essay question

Discuss the view that the liberalisation of the financial sector has significantly reduced managerial discretion and improved the effectiveness of the market for corporate control.

5 The multinational enterprise

This chapter is concerned with the multinational enterprise (MNE). A brief outline of the MNE's development is followed by an examination of the ways in which economic theory has attempted to explain the pattern of multinational activity. That is followed by a brief analysis of the impact of the MNE on host and source countries, and the chapter concludes with a discussion of global corporate strategy.

The development of the multinational enterprise

A definition of the MNE

Caves (1996, p. 1) defines a multinational enterprise (MNE) as 'an enterprise that controls and manages production establishments – plants – located in at least two countries'. It might be argued that the definition should be more restrictive, perhaps by including only firms above a certain size, by excluding minority ownerships abroad or by excluding firms having operations in only two countries. On the other hand, to do so would be arbitrary and might exclude important and interesting phenomena. It could also be argued that the reference to 'plants' excludes multinationals in the service sector, which have become increasingly important (Li and Guisinger 1992). However, provided it is accepted that the term 'production establishments' extends to the production of service products, the definition is suitably broad and will be adopted for the purposes of this chapter.

The significance and pattern of multinational activity

Problems in collecting and collating statistics on a comparable basis across countries make it difficult to secure wholly satisfactory quantitative data on the activities of MNEs. Nevertheless, agencies like the European Commission, the International Monetary Fund (IMF), the Organization for Economic Co-operation and Development (OECD), the United Nations Conference on Trade and Development (UNCTAD) and the United Nations Centre for Transnational Corporations (UNCTC) all collate and report on the extent of multinational activity.

According to UNCTAD (1999) MNEs comprised more than 500,000 foreign affiliates in 1998, established by around 60,000 parent companies. The stock of

Table 5.1 Stock of inward foreign direct investment, 1998, by host region

Host region/economy	US$bn	% of total	Host region/economy	US$bn	% of total
World	4,088	100	Developing countries	1,219	29.8
Developed countries	2,785	68.1	Latin America and the Caribbean	416	10.2
Western Europe	1,571	38.4	Africa	75	1.8
European Union	1,486	36.4	Developing Europe	6	0.1
Canada	142	3.5	Asia	717	17.5
USA	875	21.4	China	261	6.4
Australia	105	2.6	The Pacific	5	0.1
Japan	30	0.7	Central and eastern Europe	83	2.0
Hong Kong	96	2.3	Russia	13	0.3

Source: UNCTAD 1999.

Table 5.2 Stock of outward foreign direct investment, 1998, by host region

Host region/economy	US$bn	% of total	Host region/economy	US$bn	% of total
World	4,117	100	Developing countries	391	9.5
Developed countries	3,714	90.2	Latin America and the Caribbean	56	1.4
Western Europe	2,165	52.6	Africa	16	0.4
European Union	1,956	47.5	Developing Europe	1	0.0
Canada	157	3.8	Asia	316	7.7
USA	994	24.1	China	22	0.5
Australia	62	1.5	The Pacific	<1	0.0
Japan	286	6.9	Central and eastern Europe	11	0.3
Hong Kong	155	3.7	Russia	7	0.2

Source: UNCTAD 1999.

foreign direct investment was valued at more than US$4,000 billion and the sales of foreign affiliates exceeded US$11,000 billion. Employment in foreign affiliates was estimated at approximately 35 million workers.

The pattern of multinational activity is illustrated in Tables 5.1 to 5.3, which show the distribution of foreign direct investment (FDI) by region and by sector.

As Table 5.1 illustrates, more than two-thirds of the world's stock of inward FDI was in the developed countries, with the United States and the European Union accounting for more than half of the total. Japan accounted for very little of the inward investment, while Hong Kong (population 6 million) was host to more FDI than the whole of Africa. Clearly, the distribution of FDI is very uneven so that countries accounting for large proportions of the world's population host

Table 5.3 Stock of inward foreign direct investment, 1997, by sector

Sector	% of total	Sector	% of total
Primary, of which:	6.3	Manufacturing, of which:	42.5
Mining, quarrying		Chemicals and chemical	
and petroleum	5.6	products	7.5
Services, of which:	48.5	Electric machinery	3.2
Finance	14.4	Food, beverages and tobacco	2.9
Trade	10.2	Basic metals	2.8
Real estate	7.3	Coke, petroleum and nuclear	2.6
Business services	1.5	Machinery and equipment	2.3

Source: UNCTAD 1999.

very small proportions of the incoming investment, and vice versa. The pattern of investment by source is even more concentrated, as Table 5.2 illustrates.

More than 90 per cent of the stock of outward FDI originated in the developed countries with the 'triad' nations of the European Union, the United States and Japan accounting for nearly 80 per cent of the total. Of the 20 per cent that did not originate in the 'triad', approximately half originated in developing nations, and almost 4 per cent came from Hong Kong.

While the manufacturing sector accounted for the larger part of FDI until the late 1980s, there has been a dramatic increase in service sector FDI.

As Table 5.3 shows, MNE activity spreads across all three major sectors of economic activity – primary, manufacturing and services. The largest proportion is now to be found in services, at almost 50 per cent of the total, while manufacturing makes up around 42 per cent, with the primary sector contributing around 6 per cent. The predominance of service sector FDI is a relatively recent phenomenon, driven to a great extent by the liberalisation of financial markets in the late 1980s and the 1990s.

An outline history of the multinational

According to Ghertman and Allen (1984) the first multinational, dating from the beginning of the nineteenth century, was the S.A. Cockerill steelworks established in Prussia in 1815. However, Dunning (1992) points out that much earlier examples of embryonic MNEs must have been found in the ancient trading cultures of China, the Middle East and the Americas, and Moore and Lewis (1998) describe Assyrian multinational business activity taking place as long ago as 2000 BC.

By the end of the fourteenth century there were 150 Italian banking firms who were truly multinational (Hawrylyshyn 1971) and the Hanseatic League of Germany was developing agriculture in Poland, sheep-rearing in Belgium and manufacturing industry in Sweden (Williams 1929). Clearly, the multinational is a long-established phenomenon that has affected the daily life of many people for millennia. Dunning (1992), however, identifies the period around 1870 with the emergence of the modern MNE, following a series of technological and organisational innovations.

As might be anticipated from the pattern of global economic development, the first modern multinationals were mostly European-based and included a number of firms that continue to be household names including British American Tobacco, Lever Brothers, Michelin and Nestlé. The geographical scope of many of these firms reflected the distribution of colonial influence and a large proportion of them were involved in backward integration into agriculture and minerals in the colonies. That provided a means of securing raw materials to be processed in the imperial homeland for sale at home or for export. While there were a number of such multinationals before the Second World War, they were largely restricted to these kinds of colonialist activity and were not a major feature of the world business scene. As Casson (1987) noted, a much more common approach to global competition, especially in the 1920s and 1930s, was the establishment of international cartels in many of the industries that later came to be dominated by MNEs.

The major period of growth for the multinationals, especially in manufacturing, was the 1950s through to the early 1970s. This wave of development was led by American firms moving into the European market where their presence became so marked that *The American Challenge* (Servan-Schreiber 1967) was seen as a serious threat to Europe's ability to achieve self-sustaining growth. European economies were said to be in danger of becoming dependent upon American firms for their higher level business functions, including R&D and marketing, and the European consumer was held to be at the mercy of American tastes and the market power of US corporations.

The American multinationals of this period had a number of characteristics which, for a time, were seen as the defining features of the post-war MNE. In the first place, they were drawn to the other major developed countries, rather than former colonies or other developing nations. Their purpose was to serve large markets like the European Community from a local base and they were involved in the production of import substitutes, rather than backward vertical integration towards sources of raw materials. Second, the development of the American MNE was strongly associated with highly concentrated and research-intensive industries which also exhibited high levels of advertising intensity and made use of large proportions of highly skilled workers. The theory of the multinational (see below) produced explanations for this pattern, and for some time multinational activity as a whole was seen as conforming to this stereotype.

In the 1970s, 1980s and 1990s it became clear that the MNE could take other forms. The emergence of the Japanese multinational, focused initially on offshore, 'export platform' activities in the newly industrialising countries, ran counter to the stereotype of the skilled labour, R&D-intensive activity associated with the American MNE. The 'American Challenge' was reversed as European firms entered the American market and European ownership of American firms became as visible as American ownership in Europe (to the chagrin of some American observers). The emergence of MNEs based in developing nations like India (Wells 1983) ran counter to the established pattern, as did the realisation that there are many quite small multinationals, and the rapid expansion of service sector FDI (Li and Guisinger 1992). This increasing heterogeneity of multinational activity led to a reassessment and recognition that the MNE could take many more forms than had hitherto been appreciated.

Economic theory and the multinational

The application of alternative perspectives

One of the most interesting features of the multinational is that it brings together a number of different, otherwise unrelated, areas of economic analysis (Caves 1996, 1998). The theory of international trade is relevant, because MNEs trade across national boundaries and it is important to understand how they impact on the location of different types of economic activity. Theories of industrial structure and behaviour are important, as MNEs are engaged in strategic actions that may affect rivals. Finally, the MNE is involved in coordinating transactions across national boundaries which raises the issue of 'internalisation' or 'markets versus hierarchies' discussed in Chapter 3. As Casson (1987) noted, the application of general theory to the specific issues raised by the MNE gives a special 'twist' to the theory in the course of the application, which makes it a particularly interesting area to explore.

The Hymer–Kindleberger proposition

The starting point for almost any exposition of the theory of the MNE is to be found in the work of Hymer and Kindleberger. Hymer's PhD dissertation of 1960 remained unpublished until 1976, but some of its central points, which drew heavily on Bain's (1956) analysis of entry barriers, were taken up by Kindleberger (1969) to begin a theoretical debate which extended the issues beyond Hymer's original insight.

Hymer's initial observation was that firms operating abroad must face some disadvantages relative to incumbents in those markets. For them to compete in such markets, they must possess some form of offsetting competitive advantage. In that case the development of the MNE might be attributed to the acquisition of quasi-monopolistic advantages by firms that then find that these advantages can be exploited for profit in overseas markets.

Such advantages could take a number of forms, and the literature on the MNE contains a good deal of debate on the issue. Caves (1971) pointed out that the advantage in question needs to be a public good within the firm, so that its use in one location does not deprive the firm of its use in another. As corporate knowledge and skills are the most obvious assets to have this characteristic, they would appear to provide the foundation for the development of the MNE. Following on from that insight, corporate knowledge and skills were often identified with, and proxied by, in-house R&D spending. Examination of the links between these variables and the extent of multinationality showed that they had substantial explanatory power in the case of American multinationals, hence the association referred to above between the MNE and technological superiority.

The possession of some form of advantage may provide a necessary condition for going abroad and competing with indigenous firms, but it cannot be a sufficient condition as there is always the option of selling or licensing the advantage to a local firm. If those firms have advantages of 'localness', that would suggest that they should be able to make more profit from the use of the advantage than the would-be MNE. If there were competition to buy the advantage, driving its price up until it was equal to the extra profits to be made, that would suggest that licensing would be more profitable than FDI (Davies 1977). The theory of the multinational therefore also has to explain why firms should choose to use their advantages themselves, rather than trade them. Hymer's suggestion was that the market for such knowledge is imperfect, so that MNEs cannot secure all of the monopoly rents accruing to their advantages by selling them. In that case there is a clear incentive to keep the transfer of the advantage in-house, and the MNE is seen as a conduit for the transfer of knowledge from one location to another. Casson (1987) noted that at this point in the analysis Hymer's theory failed to distinguish between two very different aspects of market imperfections in knowledge. The first, on which Hymer focused, arises from imperfections in market structure. If, for example, a company's products are highly differentiated and cannot be easily reproduced, the company has a quasi-monopolistic advantage which could provide the rationale for the MNE. However, there is another, conceptually quite distinct, type of imperfection which links to the work of Coase and Williamson, described in Chapter 3. That is imperfections in markets arising as a result of transaction costs and the difficulties of organising transactions between independent organisations in conditions of uncertainty.

'Internalisation' and transactions cost theory

The suggestion that the MNE could be explained through a similar set of analytical tools to that applied to vertical integration or diversification formed the basis for theoretical advances from a number of writers, most notably McManus (1972), Buckley and Casson (1976), Rugman (1981) and Casson (1982). While many of the ideas have close links with those of Coase and Williamson, they are often expressed in different ways.

Buckley and Casson's analysis, in particular, has become the foundation for further developments around the concept of 'internalisation'. In their 1976 formulation they identified five advantages that an internalised transaction can have over the market:

1. Increased ability to control and plan.
2. The opportunity for discriminatory pricing.
3. Avoidance of bilateral monopoly.
4. Reduction of uncertainty.
5. Avoidance of government intervention.

There are other factors that are also relevant to the choice between FDI and the sale or hire of an advantage through licensing or franchising. The first concerns the nature of the advantage that is being transacted. In some cases, where this consists of a patented machine, or a 'secret ingredient', it may be easy to identify the advantage and transfer it to another firm. However, in other cases a firm may not know exactly what gives it a competitive edge and it will be impossible to sell such an imprecisely defined advantage. Similarly, it may be expensive to transfer an advantage outside the bounds of the originating firm, which would make it preferable to invest, or there may not be competent local entrepreneurs to bid for the advantage. Both Rugman (1981) and Porter (1985) stressed the possible loss of control associated with selling a competitive advantage to an independent firm that might use it to become an effective competitor in future. In principle, this might be overcome through the drafting and enforcement of contracts, but that raises the major points stressed in the Williamson analysis, namely that a combination of uncertainty and opportunistic behaviour will render such modes of governance inefficient. In the multinational context transactions between independent firms will be made more difficult by distance, different legal regimes and by the lack of regular informal business contacts between the parties to the transaction, who may inhabit very different business cultures.

While internalisation has a number of advantages over markets, and foreign investment therefore tends to be favoured over licensing, it is as well to note that these advantages are not absolute. Licensing does take place on a substantial scale and in some industries (chemicals and pharmaceuticals) is a major form of activity. Buckley and Davies (1979), Telesio (1979) and Michalet and Delapierre (1976) all outlined situations where licensing will tend to be important.

Casson (1982) took up the issue of transactions costs in a rather different way, refining the internalisation theory to provide a more general explanation for FDI in industries where advantages based upon technology or product differentiation are less important. If a market transaction is to be made, there are a series of 'market-making' or 'transaction-supporting' activities that have to be carried out, each of which involves costs. These steps, taken in sequence, have been examined in Chapter 3 and consist of the following:

- contact-making
- specification and communication of details to each party
- negotiation
- monitoring, including the screening of quality
- transport of goods
- payment or avoidance of taxes
- enforcement.

These market-making services are provided by offices, showrooms and shops which could in principle simply specialise in providing these services (as do travel agents or estate agents). However, in most cases market-making is linked to the sale of the commodity itself, in order to avoid purchasers having to make two separate transactions. Furthermore, if buyers place a high level of importance on the monitoring of quality control it may pay them to integrate backwards into the production of the commodity, instead of relying upon independent market-makers to carry out the monitoring.

While Casson's analysis can be seen as an extension of the Coase and Williamson approach, it also offers a particular insight into the development of the MNE. If buyers are internationally mobile they will prefer to buy from a single market-maker, rather than deal with a different one in each location. However, the credibility and business reputation of the market-maker will depend crucially upon their ability to meet the same quality standards in each location. The incentive to integrate backwards into production will therefore be particularly strong, and a multinational is the result. Similarly, buyers may wish to place orders in one location for supply in another, which requires close liaison between branch plants in different locations. Finally, Casson's analysis can be integrated back into the Hymer–Kindleberger framework by noting that some firms may develop a competitive advantage in market-making itself, which is internationally transferable. In this case, it is that particular advantage that provides the foundation for 'going abroad'.

In terms of predictions the model suggests that MNEs will tend to be most heavily represented in market segments where high quality is most important. Two examples, which illustrate the ability of the model to explain the MNE's existence in market segments where neither technology nor product differentiation is particularly important, are to be found in the international hotel industry and in the export of tropical fruit. The major hotel chains (Dunning and McQueen 1982) do not appear to provide highly differentiated products. What they offer are international reservation systems (a market-making activity) and systems of hotel management that maintain product quality while using unskilled labour. In the banana industry two distinct sub-sectors can be distinguished. An unintegrated, market-directed trade exists, selling unbranded bananas to small retailers, on a seasonal basis. At the same time, there are multinational producers operating at the quality end of the market. These sell heavily advertised branded fruit (a market-making activity) and offer year-round supplies, delivered to retail chains through a fleet of special ships. The fruit and delivery systems are both subject to a system of quality control which allows any faults to be rectified.

The 'eclectic' framework: OLI

The 'internalisation' analysis provides a general theory in explanation of the MNE. However, whether it is complete remains the subject of debate. A closely related but slightly different approach is Dunning's 'eclectic' framework, first put forward in 1976 and often referred to as the 'OLI model'. That theory states that the extent, form and pattern of multinational activity is determined by the existence of three sets of advantages. The first, which relates back to the Hymer analysis, consists of *ownership advantages* – the 'O' in OLI. These may arise either because MNEs have assets not owned by other firms, or because their managerial hierarchies are particularly good at reducing the transactions costs associated with coordinating activities located in different countries.

The second strand in the eclectic paradigm concerns the location of production. For multinationalisation to take place, not only must firms have ownership advantages, but there must also be benefit in combining those O advantages (like management skills or technological advantages) with other inputs in the host country. There must be 'L' or *locational advantages*. Otherwise the firm would simply operate in a single location. Such L advantages could arise in a number of ways. Most obviously there will be differences in local cost and revenue conditions, arising from different levels of wages and other input prices, or barriers to trade and factor mobility. Hirsch (1976) examined this choice in terms of cost minimisation, and suggested the following inequalities as a decision rule on whether to produce at home or abroad:

Export to country B if:

$P_A + M < P_B + C$ where:

P_A, P_B = production costs in country A, country B; M = additional costs of export marketing; C = extra costs of controlling a foreign operation.

Produce in country B if:

$P_A + M > P_B + C$

Production costs, marketing costs and the costs of control will depend upon a wide variety of factors, including:

- tariffs and trade barriers
- economies of scale and scope in each market
- the costs of labour and other inputs
- government controls
- transport costs.

These incentives to shifting the location of production arise from market imperfections, without which they would cease to exist. However, even in the absence of such imperfections, MNE activity would still occur if there were L advantages arising from the transactional gains to be had from common ownership of activities in different locations. Such advantages could include spreading foreign exchange risk or political risk, protecting supplies by multiple sourcing and the opportunity to use transfer prices to redistribute gains between different tax regimes.

The third condition for international production is that it should be in the best interests of the firms having ownership advantages that they be transferred to different locations through managerial hierarchies, rather than through markets – there should be *internalisation advantages*, the 'I' of the OLI paradigm. 'Internalisation' theory thus forms one of the three central strands in the eclectic paradigm. Buckley and Casson (1985) argued that that amounts to double-counting and that the failure of intermediate product markets is itself a necessary and sufficient condition for multinationalisation to take place. Dunning (1985), on the other hand, argued to the contrary, suggesting that a distinction should be made between a firm's ability to internalise and its reasons for doing so. Wherever the balance of the argument lies, it is clear that there are close links between the eclectic paradigm and the internalisation model.

The breadth and flexibility of the 'eclectic' paradigm have led to its adoption in a wide variety of empirical studies (Dunning 1980, 1992). Agarwal and Ramaswami (1992) used it to examine the entry mode adopted by foreign investors. Beamish and Banks (1987) applied the model to joint ventures, and many textbooks in international business use it as an organising framework for at least part of their discussion. Dunning (1995) has suggested that the OLI model needs to be re-appraised so that each of its three main elements takes into account the changes brought about as the boundaries between firms, countries and markets become more 'porous'. Nevertheless, it remains in place as a very useful organising principle through which to examine the MNEs' activities.

The impact of the multinational

The debate over the multinational

The impact of the multinational on the world economy is an issue that has been hotly debated in a discussion that has substantial political overtones. On one side of the debate, the multinational and the process of globalisation have been identified with the large, monopolistic American or European corporation, seen as a vehicle for the exploitation of workers, consumers and the environment and as a threat to the independent government of smaller nations. On the other side, the multinational has been regarded with much less suspicion, as a means by which the impact of market forces may be felt on a global scale, bringing enhanced efficiency and an improved global allocation of resources. Such broad generalisations are an inadequate description of such a complex and important set of issues, and a more detailed analysis is justified.

The impact of the MNE on host economies

Multinational activity can impact on its host environment in a number of different ways, each of which merits attention. Following Hood and Young (1979) it is possible to identify four different types of effect, namely:

1. Resource transfer and technology transfer effects.
2. Trade and balance of payments effects.
3. Effects on competitive structure and performance.
4. Effects on sovereignty and local autonomy.

The transfer of resources and technology

The MNE may involve an inflow of both capital and 'technology', broadly defined, the impact of which on the host economy depends upon a number of factors. In the case of capital, an inflow adds to the resources available for host-country production and the presence of MNEs that have identified profitable opportunities may also help to mobilise domestic savings. In developing nations, which have tended to be the focus for much of the concern over the impact of the MNE, the presence of multinationals may also stimulate the provision of aid from the home country, in support of their trading activities.

On the other hand, MNEs may raise finance in the host nation or fund their expansion by re-investing profits made by local subsidiaries. They may also repatriate their profits. In that case they may not add anything to the capital stock of the host nation and might even reduce it. If the MNE does not increase the capital available to a host country it may still bring gains through an improvement in the efficiency with which the existing capital is used. If MNEs put the capital to better use than local firms, making use of technological or other advantages, there may still be an improvement through the improved productivity of the limited capital available. Nevertheless that may make it more difficult for local firms to raise capital for their own activities, which will be a disadvantage if local control of economic activity is seen as desirable for its own sake.

In practice, capital flows are not seen as a major aspect of the multinationals' activity and their contribution to net inflows is generally unimportant (Caves 1996, p. 233). A much more important set of issues concerns the transfer of technology, broadly defined to encompass all kinds of ownership advantage including managerial skills as well as narrowly technological assets like patents and product designs. Technology transfer raises a number of questions (see Davies 1979 and Dunning 1992 for reviews).

The first issue, particularly in the context of developing nations, concerns the appropriateness of the technologies transferred. In low-wage economies economic theory suggests that relatively labour-intensive techniques of production will be appropriate, both in terms of cost minimisation and employment effects. However, much of the evidence suggests that MNEs often make only limited adjustment to the techniques of production they transfer (Davies 1977), which could imply allocative inefficiency. On the other hand, there are reasons for supporting the transfer of more advanced techniques. For many commodities, labour-intensive production techniques may not be available. Standard economic theory, outlined in Chapter 9, assumes that any given technology provides an infinite range of production techniques, which is often unrealistic. Even if labour-intensive techniques are available they will usually be drawn from older technologies that are obsolete in the context of major industrial nations. The use of such methods may have an adverse impact on the quality of the product produced, even rendering it unsaleable in world markets. MNEs may also prefer machine power to humanpower because they see difficulties in recruiting and managing a labour force whose work ethos is very different from their own.

The second issue concerns the transfer of managerial skills which accompanies inward FDI. An inflow of entrepreneurial talent and better-trained managers may lead to improvements in efficiency in both the static sense of reducing costs and improving marketing activity and the dynamic sense of adjusting more quickly to changes in the environment and spotting opportunities for innovation. Dunning (1985), for instance, found that MNEs in the United Kingdom assisted in the restructuring of the economy more effectively than indigenous firms and also responded more quickly to changes in Britain's locational advantages in respect of resource endowments, thereby improving the competitiveness of the economy. Child *et al.* (2000) found that when UK firms were acquired by foreign investors, significant changes in management practice took place. The fact that managers in a multinational are able to take a global perspective through internalised flows of knowledge about the global changes in their own industry may have advantages for the economies in which they are operating.

On the negative side of the balance sheet, there may be little diffusion of improved management practices into local industry if MNEs make substantial use of expatriate managers from the home country, who remain within the MNE and eventually return to work in the home country. On the other hand, if they bring with them improved working practices and management techniques, these will involve workers, supervisors and indigenous junior managers in implementing the improved practices which may then diffuse through indigenous industry as these workers change jobs. Similarly, if local managers seek to emulate the practices of incoming MNEs in order to compete with them, new techniques may be effectively diffused. Certainly in the United Kingdom the number of seminars offered by management consultants on Japanese-inspired practices like quality circles and 'just-in-time' methods of manufacturing suggests that this has been the case. It might be argued that this could be achieved without the Japanese firms actually moving to British locations, but the effect of demonstrating that Japanese practices are transferable into other locations provides a powerful stimulus to emulation.

Trade and balance of payments effects

An inflow of MNEs may affect the balance of payments in a number of ways. If there is a capital inflow, this will improve the capital account, but that will be offset by any repatriation of profits and dividends to the source country. If the MNE is involved in producing for export, or producing import substitutes, then the current account on the balance of payments will be improved. This depends upon the extent to which value is added in the host country, an issue that has been sensitive in the case of Japanese investments into Europe and the *maquiladora* plants in Mexico. Some policy-makers have been concerned that the local content of some MNE products is very low, with 'screwdriver plants' being established which import a large proportion of the total value of the final product in the form of components produced elsewhere. These are simply assembled and packaged. Clearly such plants will do little to improve the balance of payments of host countries, but whether they should be outlawed on those grounds is a matter for debate. The more fundamental question is whether controls should be placed on firms' location and production decisions.

Balance of payments issues also raise the sensitive question of transfer pricing within MNEs. One of the possible reasons for internalising multinational transactions is that it offers a means by which a firm may divert its profit from one location to another, by manipulating the internal prices that it charges for intermediate products (Vaitsos 1974; Caves 1996, pp. 208–11). Such transfers may be worthwhile in the light of different tax regimes and fluctuating exchange rates. To take an extreme example, for instance, a firm that is making profits in the United Kingdom could transfer those profits to a tax haven by establishing a stationery supply office in the tax haven which supplies paper clips at very high prices to the UK subsidiary. Such practices would not only affect the balance of payments of the United Kingdom but would also deprive British shareholders of their legitimate share in the profits and could reduce the earnings of workers or increase prices to local consumers.

The intensity of the incentive to manipulate transfer prices depends on the differences in tax regimes from location to location, international taxation agreements and the volatility of exchange rates. In so far as governments attempt to collaborate on taxation, and exchange rates are either stable or so unstable that it becomes impossible to make sensible predictions about their behaviour, the incentive will be reduced. Nevertheless, transfer pricing raises some major questions about the global distribution of the benefits that flow from MNEs' activity.

The competitive and structural impact of the MNE

While an influx of FDI may affect competition through its impact on the rate of technological change and the adoption of new management techniques, it may also affect the conduct and performance of industry in the host economy through its impact on industrial structure. In particular, if multinational transactions are internalised in order to ensure that the MNE receives the full value of the monopoly rents accruing to its knowledge-based assets, the process of multinationalisation may in effect be a means of securing collusion by other means. As Casson (1987) put it, 'a firm that has developed a new technology can . . . only recover its costs through the exercise of monopoly power'. If MNEs are able to use their global interconnections to create additional entry barriers, this may also give them additional market power which may be a cause for concern.

MNEs may also give cause for concern if the international division of labour which they find most profitable does not accord with that which governments consider to be in the host country's best interest. For instance, in the case of the alleged 'screwdriver' plants, the parent firms find it most efficient to restrict the operations carried out at certain locations to assembly and packaging, rather than the production of components. Some host governments find that unacceptable. In a similar way, MNEs frequently prefer to keep many of their higher level functions like R&D and headquarters activity in their home location, thereby limiting indigenous technological innovation in host nations.

Effects on sovereignty and local autonomy

This last point leads naturally into one of the most contentious areas of debate concerning the impact of the MNE on host countries. The very nature of the MNE implies that it is involved in coordinating activities on a global scale through internalised transactions which are effectively out of the reach of national governments. As a result, governments may lose a substantial degree of sovereignty. Monetary policies may be side-stepped through operations in global financial markets. Fiscal policies may be avoided through transfer pricing. National governments, and local authorities within them, may find themselves competing with each other to provide financial incentives to induce MNEs to locate within their jurisdictions to the point where it is the multinational that secures the gains to be had, rather than the local economies. It may also be the case that economic development in host countries is driven by decisions taken outside those countries, thereby reducing national governments' autonomy and their ability to determine the course of events within their own national boundaries. Such considerations open up very much broader aspects of the debate, including their implications for democracy and freedom (Boddewyn 1988). In a world made increasingly economically interdependent by the operations of the MNE, the ability of any national government to pursue policies of its own choosing is heavily circumscribed.

The balance of judgement on the impact of the multinational depends heavily on the relative priorities given to their efficiency-enhancing properties versus their impact on local autonomy. In the 1960s, when the multinational was best characterised as a powerful American corporation and the global consensus was one of concern over their market power, there was much discussion of the ill effects of the MNE, especially among the political Left. In the 1980s, with the Left wielding less influence in both Britain and the United States, with the development of a wider spectrum of multinationals based in many different countries, and with the loss of sovereignty arising from other developments such as the European Union and relaxed exchange controls, the balance of judgement has shifted in favour of the multinational. The opposition to MNEs and to globalisation which manifested itself at the WTO meeting in Seattle in 1999 might signal a shift back to a less friendly judgement on FDI, but that remains to be seen.

The impact of the MNE on its home country

Converse problems: the MNE and source countries

Most of the discussion on the impact of the MNE has concerned its effects on host countries, especially developing nations. At the same time there has been some concern expressed, especially in the United States, over the impact of FDI on the source country from which the investment emanated. Much of this debate is a mirror-image of that concerning host-country impact, with doubts being expressed about the impact of such investment on the following areas:

- the balance of payments
- employment
- loss of technological advantage
- tax avoidance and loss of sovereignty.

Each of these warrants a brief consideration.

Balance of payments effects

The impact of FDI on the balance of payments of the source country is essentially the opposite of that on the host. An initial injection of capital will worsen the source country's capital account, but repatriated profits will improve the current account. Goods produced abroad may substitute for exports but expansion of the host-country economy may stimulate its demand for imports from the source. The overall balance depends upon the individual circumstances.

Employment effects

MNEs have sometimes been accused of 'exporting jobs' away from the source country and it is clear that direct job losses may arise if operations are transferred to an overseas location. On the other hand, the jobs created in foreign subsidiaries may be additional to those created at home and in activities that are not economic in the home location and could not alternatively be placed there. Outward investments may create additional demand for plant and equipment sourced from the home country, and they may lead to the expansion of headquarters and other staff needed to administer an enlarged operation. There is no fundamental reason to suppose that employment in the source country will be lower than it would otherwise be as a result of outward investment, although the mix of employment may well be different as a result of the MNE's internalised international division of labour. From an analytical economic point of view, it is also a mistake to see employment as being determined by the activities of individual firms rather than by the structure and behaviour of labour markets as a whole.

Concern has also been expressed about the impact of outward investment on wage levels. If an MNE sees a locational advantage in transferring its labour-intensive activities to a low-wage country, this may reduce the source-country demand for the types of labour involved and lower wage levels in those occupations. In effect, source-country workers have to compete in a global labour market with workers earning very much lower levels of wages. On the other hand, the demand for other types of labour is likely to increase and efficient labour markets would transfer workers from one occupation to another, leaving average wage levels higher than they would otherwise be. This point gets to the heart of much of the debate on the MNE. From one perspective the MNE is acting as a highly efficient global allocator of resources, placing each of its activities in locations where the opportunity cost is lowest. This will raise total global income, allowing increased rewards for all, at least in principle. From another perspective this process involves adjustment costs that are likely to be borne by those workers who are forced to compete in global labour markets and who, as individuals, may not be able simply to move into new roles. A British or American production worker made redundant by the transfer of manufacturing to China can hardly be expected to be impressed by the reassurance that his sacrifice has provided wages and employment in a poorer part of the world and more jobs for graduates at home.

The loss of technological lead

Just as a major advantage of FDI for a host country lies in the inflow of technological skills, so it has been argued, especially in the United States and Europe, that source countries are in danger of losing their technological advantages through transferring them to other countries (Bennett *et al.* 1999). While this is primarily an economic argument, it also has a strategic military component in that there has been concern that FDI places strategically important technologies in the hands of foreign nationals who may in turn transfer them on to potentially hostile countries. Computer technology in particular has been placed in this category, as have sophisticated machine tool systems. While the military argument may be accepted, the economic argument is much less soundly based, for reasons that reflect many of the points made above. In the short term, if a technological advantage is seen as a static 'one-off' asset, its use in a wider range of locations may reduce the returns to labour in its original location, and this may cause adjustment problems. However, technology is rarely static, and in many instances the technology that is transferred abroad is more mature, even obsolescent, in its home location. To attempt to restrict the use of technology to a particular geographical location would be to prevent the MNE from organising the most efficient global allocation of resources, thereby restricting the growth of world, as opposed to national, income. The activities of the multinational do not represent a 'zero-sum game' where the benefits and costs to host countries are exactly cancelled out by costs and benefits to the source country. The overall sum is indubitably positive, although there are costs to some.

Tax avoidance and loss of sovereignty

The problems of tax avoidance and loss of sovereignty are essentially the same for source countries as they are for host countries. The multinational's ability to be everywhere and yet be effectively out of the reach of government is one of its most interesting characteristics. Those who approve of privately driven competitive activity see this as one of the multinationals' greatest achievements and one that need not be feared as competition ensures the achievement of global social goals. Others fear the power of the multinational and its lack of accountability to any power beyond that of its shareholders and managers.

Global competition and corporate strategy

The need for an analysis of global strategy

It is clear from the first part of this chapter that substantial attention has been paid to the development of theories that are capable of explaining the existence and patterns of multinational activity. That analysis has been firmly within the basic traditions of economic analysis, being essentially 'positive' in nature, having the objective of producing testable hypotheses with respect to the patterns and effects of multinational activity.

One result of that emphasis has been that the analysis provides little normative guidance to multinational firms with respect to the implications of 'globalisation' for their business strategies, a criticism that has been made both by some of the leading economists involved (Buckley 1985) and by Porter (1986) on behalf of business strategists. In response to that weakness a literature has developed in the attempt to analyse the components that make up a 'global strategy' and the nature of the links between those components and corporate performance.

The links between economic analysis and the literature on global strategy are very similar to the links between economics and the strategy literature in general, examined in detail in Chapter 18. The discussion in this chapter, therefore, focuses solely on the 'global' dimension.

A diversity of definitions and prescriptions

The meaning of the term 'global strategy' varies so widely from one analysis to another that it has become almost impossible to define satisfactorily. One of the most influential early contributions came from Levitt (1983) who argued that improved communications, higher incomes and increasing international travel have homogenised markets across the world. In that case the most appropriate global strategy is to produce and sell standardised products world-wide, taking advantage of scale economies and locational advantages to produce those products as cheaply as possible. While Levitt's work was seminal, most other analysts have disagreed with the standardisation recommendation. Quelch and Hoff (1986) emphasised the importance of responding to local market conditions in different places. Hamel and Prahalad (1985) preferred to recommend a broad portfolio of products that are competitive because they make common use of shared technologies, brand names and distribution channels. Kogut (1985) saw the advantage lying in the flexibility that operating in different locations can provide. A firm that has multiple production locations can quickly change its sourcing if exchange rates, costs or markets shift. Bartlett and Ghoshal (1991) saw success as the ability to achieve efficiency through a global allocation of resources while simultaneously maintaining the flexibility needed to meet diverse local needs.

This diversity of views, and the consequent difficulty involved in defining 'global strategy', makes it a frustrating topic to deal with. However, Collis (1991) very usefully drew together four general postulates. The first is that a global strategy is required when there are interdependencies between a firm's competitive position in one country and its position in another. Second, a global strategy is only possible if the source of those interdependencies can be identified, whether it lies in scale economies, brand names, multinational experience or 'transnational capability'. Third, *configuration* and *coordination* (see below) must be addressed as part of the strategy; and fourth, the company's organisational structure must be aligned with its strategy.

General frameworks for the analysis of global strategy

Given the diversity and contradictions among the early recommendations made in respect of global strategy, Porter (1986) began to develop a more general and sophisticated approach by suggesting that there are two dimensions that need to be taken into account. The first of these is the *configuration* of the firm's activities – the extent to which each activity is concentrated in one location or dispersed across many. The second is the *coordination* of those activities, which may range from tight central control to a very high degree of local autonomy. According to Porter, if a firm is to develop its global strategy it must first decide on what its 'generic strategy' is to be, choosing between *cost leadership* and *differentiation*. It should then consider how different configurations and degrees of coordination can enhance that strategy. For instance, in the hard disk drive industry (Gourevitch *et al.* 2000) there is little product differentiation and the need to keep costs down is paramount. However, at the same time, there are significant high-technology and high-skill elements in the production process. Hence firms carry out production themselves in order to maintain tight control but the production process is spread across many different locations, from China to the United States (see the Illustration at the end of this chapter for more detail).

Following Porter's contribution, Yip (1989, 1992) offered an alternative framework expressed in terms of globalisation 'drivers' and 'levers'. Drivers are the external factors that make it necessary or profitable for firms to coordinate their activities across different national markets. There are five categories of driver: market factors (like homogeneity or heterogeneity of consumer needs); cost factors (like economies of scope or scale); competitive factors (like the existence of rivals who operate in multiple markets); technology factors (like the need to keep tight control of intellectual property); and environmental factors. The levers are the actions that the firm can take to derive advantage from the drivers, and there are five types of lever. These are: global market participation; product standardisation; concentration of value-adding activities; uniform marketing; and integrative competitive moves.

While the Porter and Yip approaches have both proved useful, they share a common perspective and thereby underplay an important stream of analysis. As Zou and Cavusgil (1995) point out, they both stem from the industrial organisation (IO) perspective, and the structure–conduct–performance (SCP) paradigm in particular (see Chapters 1 and 18). In that perspective good performance is seen as arising from an appropriate co-alignment or 'fit' between the firm's environment and its strategy and structure. In the Porter approach to global strategy, firms decide whether the environment is better suited to cost leadership or differentiation and then they 'match' their configuration and coordination to that strategy. In the Yip framework, the external drivers determine which levers should be applied. While the IO approach has significant explanatory power, it has been partly displaced in the general strategy literature by the *resource-based* theory (Barney 1991). According to that approach the ultimate determinant of both strategy and performance is not the fit between strategy and environment but the extent to which the firm has valuable specialised resources.

The special resources that determine profitability according to the resource-based theorists may take many different forms (Barney 1991, Porter 1991). They may be physical assets, human capital, capabilities, organisational resources like routines, procedures or even corporate cultures. If a resource is to yield extra profit in the long run it must be immobile between firms and difficult to imitate, so that other firms cannot erode its value by simply copying it. The task for the business strategist in general therefore becomes one of assembling a unique portfolio of hard-to-copy assets and the task of the global strategist lies in applying those resources in the most effective way.

While the IO and the resource-based approaches to strategy are often seen as being in opposition to each other, they both have explanatory power. Hence Zou and Cavusgil (1995) put forward an integrated conceptual framework for global strategy, shown in Figure 5.1.

As Figure 5.1 shows, the framework brings together the two competing perspectives. Global strategy determines performance and is a response to the external globalisation drivers. However, at the same time strategy is also constrained and determined by the internal organisational factors. This analysis brings together most of the central ideas that have been put forward in respect of global strategy. Levitt's (1983) product standardisation appears as one dimension of strategy. Ohmae's (1985) view that success requires a presence in all three parts of the global 'triad' – North America, Europe and Japan – appears as 'global market participation'. 'Uniform marketing' reflects a framework put forward by Samiee and Roth (1992) while 'integrated competitive moves' brings in Hamel and Prahalad (1985). 'Coordination' and 'concentration' of value-added activities reflect both

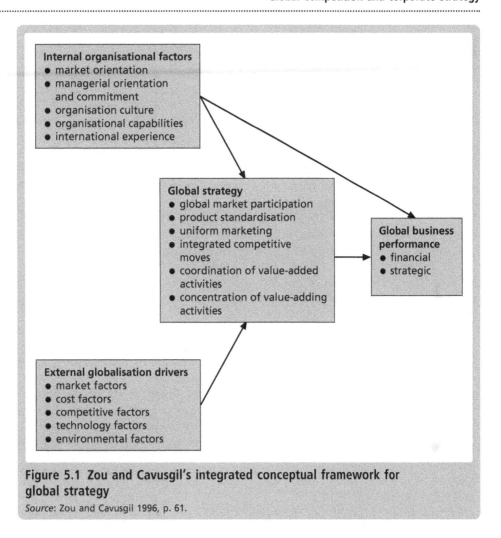

Figure 5.1 Zou and Cavusgil's integrated conceptual framework for global strategy

Source: Zou and Cavusgil 1996, p. 61.

Porter's (1986) approach and Kogut's (1985) focus on multimarket sourcing and shifting production from place to place. The globalisation 'drivers' are drawn from Yip (1989) while the internal organisational factors build on work by Amit and Schoemaker (1993), Bharadwaj *et al.* (1993), Cavusgil and Zou (1994) and Jaworski and Kohli (1993). Extending the internal factors to include culture takes account of Kotter and Hesket (1992), capabilities link to Collis (1991) and experience to Douglas and Craig (1989).

A number of observations are appropriate in the light of this long list of dimensions and the studies that have examined them. The first is that our understanding of global strategy has developed very significantly since Levitt's rather simplistic approach. The second is that managers need to recognise and pay attention to both co-alignment with the environment and the development of inimitable resources. The third is that there are so many variables involved in the determination of performance that it becomes very difficult to test as an integrated whole (see Johansson and Yip 1994 for an attempt.)

Illustration 1   Multinationals in the hotel industry

The term 'multinational enterprise' still tends to conjure up a picture of a high technology company, usually American, engaged in some form of manufacturing activity. However, that is by no means the complete picture and Dunning and McQueen (1982) provide an interesting counter-example in their study of international hotels. They use the industry in order to test the applicability of the 'eclectic' theory of the multinational, in an unusual setting.

The first strand of the eclectic theory suggests that in order to operate abroad a firm must have 'ownership-specific advantages', that is some kind of competitive advantage over local firms. In the case of the international hotel chains, there are a number of such advantages that may be identified. Hotel services are essentially an 'experience good'. The consumer can only judge the quality of the commodity being offered by actually experiencing it. In that case international hotel chains can establish an ownership-specific advantage by providing and advertising similar standards of comfort and service world-wide. The business traveller and the one-time guest (who make up the market segment in which the international hotel chains are concentrated) can experience the good in one part of the world and be informed about its quality in others. The 'brand image' of the hotel thus becomes a major asset, which cannot be reproduced by the local competition.

A second type of ownership advantage held by international hotels lies in their experience of operating superior techniques of standardised production and control, often codified in detailed instruction manuals, and in supporting those systems through well-organised staff training. As these systems take a long time to be developed and are kept as secret as possible by their owners, they constitute a type of proprietary 'know-how' or technology which is not available to the local competition.

In so far as the ownership advantages identified are all intimately connected with experience, the development of hotel chains based in different countries may depend upon the nature of the hotel industry in the home country. International hotel chains based in West Germany, for instance, own only 2 per cent of foreign-associated hotels, which is a substantial under-representation relative to West Germany's importance in international business travel. That phenomenon might be explained by the fact that the West German hotel industry is not characterised by chains of hotels, so that the experience required to run such chains overseas remained undeveloped.

If a company has ownership advantages which allow it to compete with indigenous competitors overseas it still has to decide between using these advantages in its home location (exporting the product) and transferring them overseas, combining the ownership advantage with locally available factors of production. In the case of the hotel industry, exporting is hardly an option so that servicing a market requires local 'production'. Nevertheless, hotel chains still have to decide which foreign markets to serve. As they are concentrated in the business travel market, and because they are themselves a form of MNE, it is hardly surprising that the geographical pattern of hotel chain involvement closely mirrors the world-wide distribution of FDI.

After ownership advantages and location-specific advantages, the 'eclectic' theory of the MNE refers to the advantages of 'internalisation'. If a firm has an ownership

Illustration 1

advantage, and it is most profitable to transfer that advantage to a foreign location, there remains the choice between transferring the advantage internally to another part of the company and selling it, or leasing it, to an independent company. International hotel chains are particularly interesting in this respect in that they exhibit quite complex combinations of internalised and external transactions. In some cases, MNEs in the hotel industry own their operations abroad; in others they operate leasing arrangements; in others they work through management contracts; and in yet others they have franchise agreements. The pattern of involvement exhibits noticeable differences by area and by the origin of the hotel chain. In developed countries 48 per cent of hotel rooms are in hotels owned at least in part by MNEs, while the figure for developing countries is only 18 per cent. American, French and Japanese chains appear to favour non-equity participation, while UK-based chains prefer ownership.

In most industries, ownership and control are very closely associated. If an MNE wishes to have full control of its overseas activities, it needs to own a substantial proportion of the equity. However, in the hotel industry this relationship is much less marked. In some cases, as when Arab interests purchased hotels in London, the transaction was more akin to a portfolio investment in property than to a direct investment which would provide operational control. In other cases, MNEs in the hotel industry have almost total operational control with limited or no equity participation, through the vehicle of management contracts having ten to twenty years' duration.

This phenomenon of low ownership/high control is a particularly interesting feature of the hotel industry, which may help to shed light on the whole issue of internalisation. The usual difficulties that arise from transferring ownership advantages to an independent company abroad are threefold. First, it may not be possible to transfer the ownership advantage across the boundaries between organisations. Second, there may be conflicts between the company's global interests and its local interests, which necessitate the integration of decision-making. Third, it may be difficult to fully 'appropriate' the returns accruing to an ownership advantage that has been transferred to an independent organisation. On each of these counts, the hotel industry appears to have features that ameliorate the disadvantages of contract-based control. The ownership advantages that are being transferred consist essentially of human capital in the form of experience, which can be transferred through people, supported by manuals of operating and training procedures, both of which are easily transferred to independent companies. As each hotel provides services in one particular location, there cannot be any conflict with regard to which hotel serves which location, nor can there be conflicts over which hotel specialises in which aspect of the production process. There is, therefore, little need to integrate decision-making across the chain. With respect to the appropriability problem, Dunning and McQueen (1982) argue that the economic rents arising from the ownership advantages possessed by hotel MNEs can be effectively protected by contract-based control. The use of the hotel chain's name is effectively protected, and the continuing success of the hotels depends upon its continuing involvement so that an independent firm could not simply purchase the 'know-how' and then renege on the contract.

All in all, then, the 'eclectic' theory of multinational production provides a useful framework within which to explain the pattern of MNE involvement in hotel chains.

Illustration 2 Globalisation in the hard disk drive industry

Gourevitch *et al.* (2000) provide a useful example of globalisation in their study of the hard disk drive industry. Industry revenues exceed US$30 billion and product life cycles are dramatically short, at less than eighteen months. The combination of intense competition and rapid technological change has been pushing prices down by 40 per cent per annum for more than ten years. The market is dominated by US firms which produce around 80 per cent of world output, but only 5 per cent of drives are actually assembled in the United States.

The production process for hard drives can be divided into four steps, each involving a major sub-assembly. First there are the basic electronics, including semiconductors, printed circuit boards (PCBs) and flex circuits. Second, there are the drive heads, the manufacture of which first requires highly complex wafer fabrication, followed by labour-intensive assembly operations. Third, there are the glass or aluminium media on which the data are stored and the production of which is also a high technology operation. Finally, there are the motors, largely purchased from the dominant supplier, Nippon Densan of Japan. The value chain also includes the R&D function, sales service and management.

The leading firm, Seagate, assembles all of its drives in-house, in order to retain control of the critical technologies – an internalisation advantage in terms of the 'eclectic' model. However, the production operations are remarkably dispersed in order to profit from the different locational advantages available at the company's different sites. High-tech wafer production takes place in the United States and Northern Ireland. The assembly of heads takes place in low-wage Thailand, Malaysia and the Philippines, while PCBs are assembled in Indonesia, Malaysia and Singapore. A single component may be worked on in five places before the product is complete.

These location decisions – configuration in the language of global strategy – are largely driven by the balance among the level of technical difficulty, the skill level needed and available and the cost of labour. The mix of activities generally shifts towards higher technology processes as the wage levels in a location rise. Research and development is concentrated in the United States with low-tech assembly work carried out in developing nations. However, there are a number of anomalies, perhaps because wage costs are only a small proportion of final assembly costs – 5 per cent – and because profits are very sensitive to the amount of scrap and rework that has to be done.

From the perspective of the 'eclectic' theorist, the hard disk drive industry provides an example of how ownership advantages in technology are utilised in different locations through internalised transactions. From the perspective of policymakers in the United States, Gourevitch *et al.* suggest that the industry confirms both the simple critique of globalisation – that jobs leave the United States – and the simple defence – that jobs are created through the application of the comparative advantage principle. For the theorist of global strategy, the drivers of technology and cost lead the industry to a dispersed but highly coordinated configuration in which firms use their hard-to-copy capabilities in order to dominate the competition. One case: three complementary conceptual frameworks focusing on three different sets of issues.

References and further reading

S. Agarwal and S. Ramaswami, 'Choice of Foreign Market Entry Mode, Impact of Ownership, Location and Internalization Factors', *Journal of International Business Studies*, vol. 23, 1992, pp. 1–28.

R. Amit and P. Schoemaker, 'Strategic Assets and Organizational Rent', *Strategic Management Journal*, vol. 14, January 1993, pp. 33–46.

J.S. Bain, *Barriers to New Competition*, Cambridge, MA, Harvard University Press, 1956.

J. Barney, 'Firm Resources and Sustained Competitive Advantage', *Journal of Management*, vol. 17, March 1991, pp. 99–120.

C. Bartlett and S. Ghoshal, 'Global Strategic Management: Impact on the New Frontiers of Strategy Research', *Strategic Management Journal*, vol. 12, 1991, pp. 5–16.

P. Beamish and J. Banks, 'Equity Joint Ventures and the Theory of the Multinational Enterprise', *Journal of International Business Studies*, vol. 18, 1987, pp. 1–15.

D. Bennett, X. Liu, D. Parker, F. Steward, K. Vaidya, *China and European Economic Security: Study on Medium to Long Term Impact of Technology Transfer to China*, prepared for European Commission Directorate General I, July 1999.

S. Bharadwaj, P. Varadarajan and J. Fahy, 'Sustainable Competitive Advantage in Service Industries: A Conceptual Model and Research Propositions', *Journal of Marketing*, vol. 57, no. 4, 1993, pp. 83–9.

J. Boddewyn, 'Political Aspects of MNE Theory', *Journal of International Business Studies*, vol. 19, no. 3, Fall 1988, pp. 344–63.

P.J. Buckley, 'A Critical View of Theories of the Multinational Enterprise', in P.J. Buckley and M. Casson, *The Economic Theory of the Multinational Enterprise*, London, Macmillan, 1985.

P.J. Buckley and M. Casson, *The Future of the Multinational Enterprise*, London, Macmillan, 1976.

P.J. Buckley and M. Casson, *The Economic Theory of the Multinational Enterprise*, London, Macmillan, 1985.

P.J. Buckley and H. Davies, 'Foreign Licensing in Overseas Operations: Theory and Evidence from the UK', in R.G. Hawkins and A.J. Prasad (eds) *Technology Transfer and Economic Development*, Greenwich, JAI Press, 1979.

M. Casson, 'Transaction Costs and the Theory of the Multinational Enterprise', in A.M. Rugman (ed.) *New Theories of the Multinational Enterprise*, Beckenham, Croom Helm, 1982.

M. Casson, 'Multinational Firms', in R. Clarke and T. McGuiness (eds) *The Economics of the Firm*, Oxford, Blackwell, 1987.

R. Caves, 'International Corporations: The Industrial Economics of Foreign Investment', *Economica*, vol. 38, 1971, pp. 1–27.

R. Caves, *Multinational Enterprise and Economic Analysis*, 2nd edn, Cambridge, Cambridge University Press, 1996.

R. Caves, 'Research on International Business: Problems and Prospects', *Journal of International Business Studies*, vol. 29, no. 1, First Quarter 1998, pp. 5–19.

T. Cavusgil and S. Zou, 'Marketing Strategy-Performance Relationships: An Investigation of the Empirical Link in Export Market Ventures', *Journal of Marketing*, vol. 58, no. 1, 1994, pp. 1–21.

J. Child, D. Faulkner and R. Pitkethly, 'Foreign Direct Investment in the UK 1985–1994: The Impact on Domestic Management Practice', *Journal of Management Studies*, January 2000, pp. 141–66.

D. Collis, 'A Resource-based Analysis of Global Competition: The Case of the Bearings Industry', *Strategic Management Journal*, vol. 12, 1991, pp. 49–68.

H. Davies, 'Technology Transfer through Commercial Transactions', *Journal of Industrial Economics*, vol. 26, December 1977, pp. 161–75.

H. Davies, 'Technology Transfer through the MNE', *Management Bibliographies and Reviews*, vol. 5, no. 3, 1979, pp. 203–18.

S. Douglas and C. Craig, 'Evolution of Global Marketing Strategy: Scale, Scope and Synergy', *Columbia Journal of World Business*, Autumn 1989, pp. 47–8.

J. Dunning, *US Industry in Britain*, London, Wilton House, 1976.

J. Dunning, 'Towards an Eclectic Theory of International Production: Some Empirical Tests', *Journal of International Business Studies*, vol. 11, no. 1, Spring/Summer 1980, pp. 9–31.

J. Dunning, *Multinational Enterprises, Economic Structure and International Competitiveness*, New York, Wiley, 1985.

J. Dunning, *Multinational Enterprises and the Global Economy*, Wokingham, Addison-Wesley, 1992.

J. Dunning, 'Reappraising the Eclectic Paradigm in an Age of Alliance Capitalism', *Journal of International Business Studies*, vol. 26, no. 3, Third Quarter 1995, pp. 461–92.

J. Dunning and M. McQueen, 'The Eclectic Theory of the Multinational Enterprise and the International Hotel Industry', in A. Rugman (ed.) *New Theories of the Multinational Enterprise*, Beckenham, Croom Helm, 1982.

M. Ghertman and M. Allen, *An Introduction to the Multinationals*, London, Macmillan, 1984.

I.H. Giddy and S. Young, 'Conventional and Unconventional Multinationals: Do New Forms of Multinational Enterprise Require New Theories?', in A.M. Rugman (ed.) *New Theories of the Multinational Enterprise*, Beckenham, Croom Helm, 1982.

P. Gourevitch, R. Bohn and D. McKendrick, 'Globalization of Production: Insights from the Hard Disk Drive Industry', *World Development*, vol. 28, no. 2, 2000, pp. 301–17.

G. Hamel and C. Prahalad, 'Do You Really Have A Global Strategy?', *Harvard Business Review*, vol. 63, July–August 1985, pp. 139–48.

B. Hawrylyshyn, 'The Internationalization of Firms', *Journal of World Trade Law*, vol. 5, no. 1, January/February 1971, pp. 72–82.

S. Hirsch, 'An International Trade and Investment Theory of the Firm', *Oxford Economic Papers*, vol. 28, 1976, pp. 258–70.

N. Hood and S. Young, *The Economics of Multinational Enterprise*, London, Longman, 1979.

B. Jaworski and A. Kohli, 'Market Orientation: Antecedents and Consequences', *Journal of Marketing*, vol. 57, no. 3, 1993, pp. 53–70.

J. Johansson and G. Yip, 'Exploiting Globalization Potential: US and Japanese Strategies', *Strategic Management Journal*, vol. 15, 1994, pp. 579–601.

C.P. Kindleberger, *American Business Abroad*, New Haven, Yale University Press, 1969.

B. Kogut, 'Designing Global Strategies: Comparative and Competitive Value Added Chains', *Sloan Management Review*, Autumn 1985, pp. 27–38.

J. Kotter and J. Hesket, *Corporate Culture and Performance*, New York, Free Press, 1992.

T. Levitt, 'The Globalization of Markets', *Harvard Business Review*, vol. 61, May–June 1983, pp. 92–102.

J. Li and S. Guisinger, 'The Globalization of Service Multinationals in the "Triad" Nations: Japan, Europe and North America', *Journal of International Business Studies*, vol. 23, no. 4, 1992, pp. 675–97.

J.C. McManus, 'The Theory of the International Firm', in G. Paquet (ed.) *The Multinational Firm and the Nation State*, Toronto, Collier Macmillan, 1972.

C.A. Michalet and M. Delapierre, *The Multinationalisation of French Firms*, Chicago, AIB, 1976.

K. Moore and D. Lewis, 'The First Multinationals: Assyria circa 2000 B.C.', *Management International Review*, Second Quarter 1998, pp. 95–107.

K. Ohmae, *Triad Power: The Coming Shape of Global Competition*, New York, Free Press, 1985.

M. Porter, *Competitive Advantage*, New York, Free Press, 1985.

M. Porter, 'Competition in Global Industries: A Conceptual Framework', in M. Porter (ed.) *Competition in Global Industries*, Boston, Harvard Business School Press, 1986.

M. Porter 'Towards a Dynamic Theory of Strategy', *Strategic Management Journal*, vol. 12, 1991, pp. 95–117.

J. Quelch and E. Hoff, 'Customizing Global Marketing', *Harvard Business Review*, 64, May–June 1986, pp. 59–68.

A.M. Rugman, *Inside the Multinationals*, London, Croom Helm, 1981.

S. Samiee and K. Roth, 'The Influence of Global Marketing Standardization on Performance', *Journal of Marketing*, vol. 56, no. 2, 1992, pp. 1–17.

J-J. Servan-Schreiber, *The American Challenge*, New York, Athenaeum, 1967.

P. Telesio, *Technology, Licensing and Multinational Enterprises*, New York, Praeger, 1979.

UNCTAD, *World Investment Report 1999: Foreign Direct Investment and the Challenge of Development*, New York and Geneva, United Nations, 1999.

C. Vaitsos, *Intercountry Income Distribution and Transnational Enterprises*, Oxford, Clarendon Press, 1974.

L. Wells, *Third World Multinationals*, Cambridge, MA, MIT Press, 1983.

J. Williams, 'The Theory of International Trade Reconsidered', *Economic Journal*, vol. 39, 1929, pp. 195–209.

G. Yip, 'Global Strategy . . . in a World of Nations?', *Sloan Management Review*, Autumn 1989, pp. 29–41.

G. Yip, *Total Global Strategy: Managing for Worldwide Competitive Advantage*, Englewood Cliffs, NJ, Prentice Hall, 1992.

S. Zou and T. Cavusgil, 'Global Strategy: A Review and an Integrated Conceptual Framework', *European Journal of Marketing*, vol. 30, no. 1, 1996, pp. 52–69.

Self-test questions

1. List the three components that make up the 'eclectic' model of the MNE.

2. Why do firms generally prefer FDI to licensing as a form of foreign business operation?

3. What are the possible disadvantages to an economy of hosting foreign direct investment?

4. List *five* dimensions of global strategy, as identified in Zou and Cavusgil's integrative model.

Exercise

Compare the OLI analysis of the MNE with the analysis of global strategy.

PART II
The market environment

6 Consumer behaviour

This chapter sets out the principal economic theories of consumer behaviour and examines their links with the demand curve for an industry's product.

Economic theories of consumer behaviour

Models of the firm and models of markets make extensive use of the concept of the demand curve, showing the amounts of a commodity that consumers are able and willing to purchase at different prices. In an elementary treatment of the issues it is sufficient to adopt a relatively simple approach to the demand curve. Common sense suggests that it slopes downwards, with more of a commodity being purchased at lower prices, and there is no need to look more deeply at the behaviour of the individuals and households who are responsible for the purchasing. However, 'common sense' can be a dangerous guide and such an approach leaves the demand curve without any theoretical underpinning. There is a need to model the behaviour of consumers with respect to their purchasing decisions, in order to predict how they will respond to changes in price and other variables.

A number of different economic models of consumer behaviour offer insights into the decision-making process and provide a theoretical underpinning for the central concept of the demand curve. However, they are all very different from the models of consumer behaviour that are examined in marketing and sometimes rather disappointing to students who are expecting a rich characterisation of human behaviour. In marketing, the disciplines that underlie the analysis of consumer behaviour are sociology and psychology and the typical questions addressed are: How does a consumer's socioeconomic status affect their purchasing decisions? Is it possible to identify groups of consumers who share common psychological traits and who behave in predictably different ways? What are the cognitive processes involved in choosing among alternative products? In economics, the focus is very different. The starting point lies in a definition and careful specification of what constitutes rational behaviour. Having set out that specification, its implications are deduced for the choices that a rational consumer will make. In other words, the question that is being examined is: how will a rational consumer respond to changes in price? Or, more specifically, can the existence of a downward-sloping demand curve be deduced from a set of axioms concerning rational behaviour? The economic analysis of consumer behaviour is therefore a rather dry and abstract affair, carried out with the mathematics of formal logic (see Kreps 1990, pp. 17–69 for a formal presentation). Four versions are examined here, namely:

1. Utility theory.
2. Indifference analysis.
3. Revealed preference theory.
4. The characteristics approach.

Utility theory

In the 'utility theory' approach to consumer behaviour it is assumed that every consumer aims to maximise their 'utility', which is a cardinally measurable concept, often denominated in some imaginary unit such as 'utils'. As a consumer obtains more and more units of a commodity, the number of utils gained from each successive unit declines according to the 'principle of diminishing marginal utility'. In order for the household to reach its objective of maximum utility it has to select amounts of different commodities such that, for any pair, the ratios of the marginal utilities are equal to the ratios of the prices. If that were not the case it would be possible for the household to gain more utility by shifting its spending from one commodity to another.

This analysis provides an underpinning for the demand curve and helps to predict how consumers will react to changes in prices. However, it relies upon a concept of utility that is cardinally measurable, like height, weight or temperature and which can be directly compared with prices. That is a very restrictive assumption to make and economists have attempted to consider whether it is possible to build a model of consumer behaviour that embodies the basic insights of the utility theory without having to assume that utility is cardinally measurable. The theory that results is known as *indifference analysis*. In many respects it is similar to utility theory although it also allows for a more detailed analysis of the changes that arise from an alteration in prices.

Indifference analysis

The indifference map

The starting point for indifference analysis is a number of 'axioms' about consumer preference. These are as follows:

- Preferences are *complete*. For any two bundles of commodities, a consumer either prefers one to the other or is indifferent between them.
- Preferences are *asymmetric*. If A is preferred to B, then B cannot be preferred to A.
- Preferences are *transitive*. If A is preferred to B and B is preferred to C, then A is preferred to C.

It might appear at first sight that these axioms simply state self-evidently obvious truths. However, that is not always the case and Kreps (1990, p. 20) provides an example showing that the way in which a choice is presented or 'framed' can lead A to be preferred to B when B is also preferred to A.

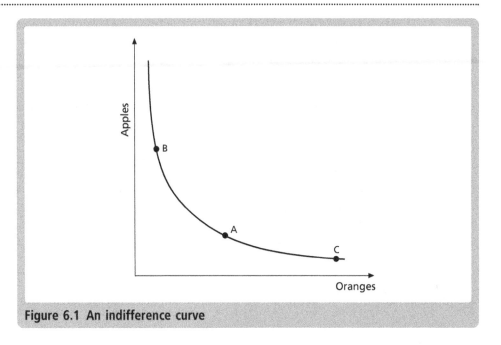

Figure 6.1 An indifference curve

In indifference analysis the consumer's aim is not to maximise cardinally measurable 'utility' but to select the preferred set of commodities from those that are available, as determined by the consumer's income. Consumers know which combinations of goods they prefer and they also know when they are indifferent between two different combinations of commodities. It will be possible, therefore, for any pair of commodities, to draw a set of *indifference curves* which show the combinations of different amounts of the two goods between which consumers are indifferent. Figure 6.1, for instance, has been arrived at by first randomly selecting a combination of apples and oranges, at point A, then considering which other combinations of apples and oranges would leave the consumer feeling equally satisfied.

The shape of an indifference curve will depend upon a number of factors. If both commodities in question are 'goods', rather than 'bads', in other words they are both commodities that consumers want, the indifference curves will slope downwards from left to right, showing that if a consumer has less of one they will require more of the other in order to remain equally satisfied.

If the basic principle behind the concept of diminishing marginal utility also holds true, so that consumers experience successively less additional satisfaction from each additional unit of a good, the indifference curves will be concave upwards, or convex to the origin, as shown in Figure 6.1.

If the consumer has a large number of apples and a small number of oranges, as at point B, they will be prepared to sacrifice quite a large number of apples (which are giving them relatively little satisfaction at the margin) for a small number of oranges (which give them a high level of satisfaction). The indifference curve will therefore be relatively steep at a point like B. On the other hand, at a point like C, where the converse is the case and the consumer has a large number of oranges and few apples, the curve will be relatively flat, showing that if they gave up a large number of oranges they would need relatively few apples in order to compensate. This is very much the same idea as the principle of diminishing marginal utility, known in the context of indifference analysis as *the diminishing marginal rate of substitution*.

Indifference analysis generally assumes that indifference curves are concave upwards like this, and also that they are smooth and continuous, implying that the goods in question are very highly divisible and that levels of satisfaction also change in a continuous fashion.

If the consumer is being faced with a choice between two 'goods', and increasing amounts of a commodity yield diminishing marginal satisfaction, indifference curves will take the general shape shown in Figure 6.1, falling from left to right and concave upwards. Their precise shape depends upon the strength of the consumer's relative preferences for the two commodities in question. If the consumer is an 'apple-lover', with a great liking for apples and a lesser liking for

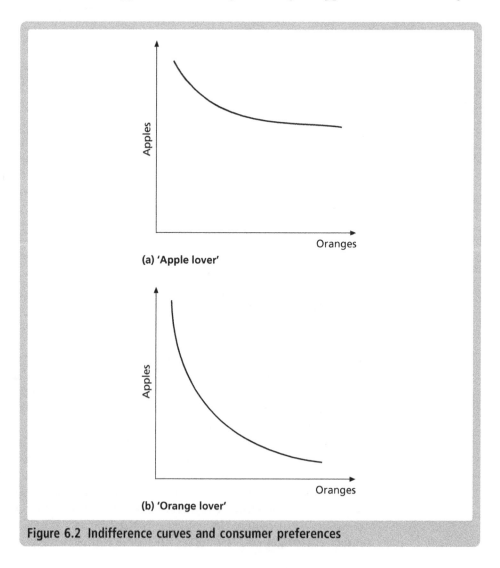

Figure 6.2 Indifference curves and consumer preferences

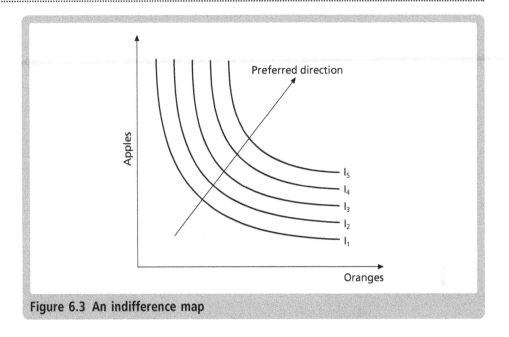

Figure 6.3 An indifference map

oranges, the curve will be relatively flat, as shown in Figure 6.2(a), because the consumer would be willing to sacrifice a large number of oranges in return for a small number of additional apples. On the other hand, if the consumer is an 'orange-lover', the curve will be relatively steep as in Figure 6.2(b).

A single indifference curve clearly embodies a great deal of information about a consumer's preferences for the commodities concerned. However, it concerns only one level of satisfaction, showing all the different combinations of apples and oranges for which the consumer is indifferent to the combination at point A. As point A was chosen at random, it is clear that there are an infinite number of indifference curves, one for every point in the space on the diagram. Figure 6.3 shows a number of indifference curves, each conforming to the general shape identified above. Clearly this can only be a selection of the total number of curves as to draw them all would involve millions of curves, completely blacking out the space.

A diagram like Figure 6.3 is known as an *indifference map* as it is a close analogy to a conventional contour map showing the height of the land above sea level.

There are two properties of an indifference map that warrant attention. The first is that curves that are further away from the origin represent higher levels of satisfaction. Consumers would prefer to move in the direction indicated by the arrow in Figure 6.3. The second property is that indifference curves cannot cross each other. If they did, as shown in Figure 6.4, a contradiction would be implied. Point X on indifference curve I_1 must indicate a higher level of satisfaction than point Y on indifference curve I_2, as it lies further from the origin. But point Z, which lies on both indifference curves, yields the same level of satisfaction as both Y and X. Clearly this cannot be the case and indifference curves cannot cross.

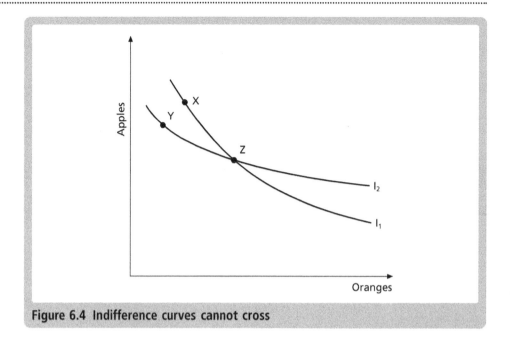

Figure 6.4 Indifference curves cannot cross

Consumer equilibrium

Having established the concept of the indifference map it is then possible to analyse the consumer's choice between alternative combinations of commodities. As the aim of the consumer is to reach the highest possible level of satisfaction, this can be represented in the analysis by noting that the consumer will choose the combination of commodities that is located on the highest possible indifference curve. However, the consumers are restricted in their choice of combinations of commodities by their income, which only allows them to purchase a limited amount of goods. The combinations of goods that consumers are able to purchase depends upon their income and the price of goods and can be represented in the diagrammatic analysis by a *budget line*, as shown in Figure 6.5.

If the consumer has an income of £100, apples cost £1 per kilo and oranges cost £2 per kilo, then the combinations of apples and oranges that the consumer can buy are given by the straight line shown in Figure 6.5. If all of the consumer's income were spent on apples, they could consume 100 kilos of apples and no oranges. Conversely, by spending all of the available income on oranges the consumer could have 50 kilos of oranges and no apples. Intermediate combinations of apples and oranges which the consumer is able to purchase are given by the straight line joining the two intercepts, which is simply the line given by the equation:

$$Y = P_A \cdot A + P_O \cdot O$$

where: Y = consumer's income
             P_A = price of apples
             P_O = price of oranges
             A = amount of apples
             O = amount of oranges

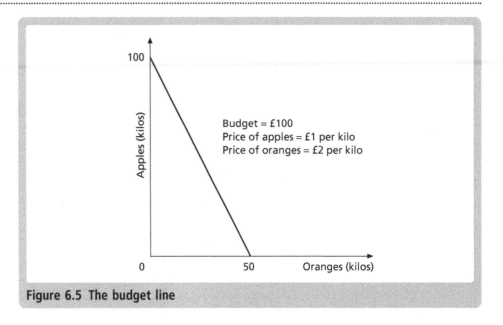

Figure 6.5 The budget line

The slope of this line, it may be noted, is equal to the ratio of the prices of the two commodities.

It is assumed that all of the consumer's income must be spent on the two goods in question, which are the only commodities available. The analysis can easily be extended to cover a larger number of goods but in that case diagrams have to be replaced by mathematical workings.

The budget line shows the combinations of goods that the consumer is able to purchase and the indifference map shows the combinations that give the highest level of satisfaction. Bringing the two together makes it possible to identify the equilibrium combination of goods, which gives the highest level of satisfaction. This is shown in Figure 6.6 at point X.

As the figure shows, at the equilibrium position the slope of the budget line, which is equal to the ratio of the prices of the two commodities, is equal to the slope of the indifference curve to which it is a tangent. That slope is the marginal rate of substitution between the two commodities in question.

Income and substitution effects

Having identified the equilibrium position for the consumer it is possible to consider how changes in prices will affect consumer behaviour and the implications of the analysis for the shape of the demand curve for commodities. Figure 6.7 shows the same initial equilibrium position as in Figure 6.6, but also illustrates the change that takes place if the price of oranges falls from £2 to £1.

The most obvious effect of the change in the price of oranges is to shift the budget line from BB to BB$_1$. As a result of that change, the optimal combination of apples and oranges shifts from X to Y.

In the example shown, more oranges are bought when their price falls (indicating a downward-sloping demand curve for oranges) and more apples are also

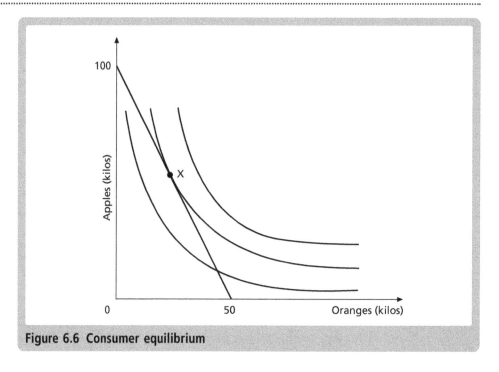

Figure 6.6 Consumer equilibrium

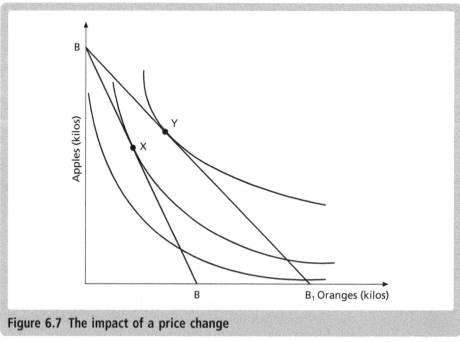

Figure 6.7 The impact of a price change

bought. This is clear enough in the specific example given, but it remains to consider whether this is a general result that must always hold, or whether it is simply a function of the particular circumstances indicated in the diagram. In order to analyse this issue effectively it is necessary to carry out a careful

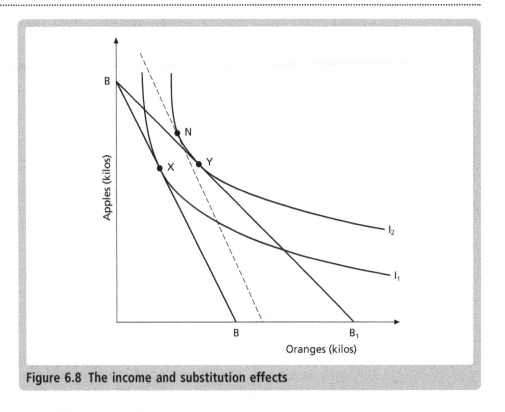

Figure 6.8 The income and substitution effects

examination of the factors involved in the shift from the original equilibrium X to the new position Y.

When the price of a good falls, leading to a change in the optimal basket of goods chosen by a rational consumer, two separate events may be said to have taken place. First, the fall in price has led to an increase in the real income of the consumer and this change in income will alter the goods that the consumer chooses to purchase. That change is known as the *income effect*. Second, the relative prices of apples and oranges have changed, which will also alter the choice of purchases. That change is known as *the substitution effect*. These two phenomena may be examined separately, by extending the diagram set out in Figure 6.7, as shown in Figure 6.8.

The overall change induced by the fall in the price of oranges is indicated by the shift from X to Y, which is known as the *price effect*. This can be subdivided into two separate components, as indicated. In order to isolate the income effect it is necessary to ask: how would the basket of goods purchased change if the consumer's real income rose by the same amount, but relative prices stayed the same? The answer can be found by recognising that the change in the consumer's real income is represented by the shift from the lower indifference curve I_1 to the higher one I_2 and that relative prices are represented by the slope of the budget line. In terms of the diagram the answer can be found by examining how the basket of goods would change if the consumer were on indifference curve I_2, enjoying the higher level of income, but relative prices were as given by the original budget line BB. This can be found simply by shifting the line BB outwards, parallel to its original position, thereby indicating the same relative prices, until it is tangential to the higher indifference curve I₂. Point N, where the two lines meet, shows the combination of goods that the consumer would purchase if their income rose sufficiently to place them on I₂ but relative prices remained unchanged. The shift from the initial equilibrium position X to N is the income effect.

The substitution effect may be found by a similar process. It may be defined as 'the change in the basket of goods that would be purchased if relative prices changed, at a constant real income'. This may be interpreted as the movement around the indifference curve I₂ from N to Y. The total 'price effect', then, may be disaggregated into its two components, the income effect changing the basket of goods from X to N and the substitution effect taking it from N to Y. Each of these may then be examined separately in order to illuminate the links between price changes and the level of demand for a good.

If the substitution effect is taken first, it is clear that its impact must always be to increase the demand for a good whose price has fallen. As indifference curves slope from left to right, with the slope decreasing to the right, then a fall in price of the commodity measured on the horizontal axis, which makes the budget line flatter, must mean that the point of equilibrium shifts to the right, as illustrated in Figure 6.9.

While the direction of the substitution effect is unambiguous and supports the notion of a downward-sloping demand curve, the income effect is much more uncertain. It is feasible that for some goods increases in income lead to less, rather than more, being bought. Such commodities are known technically as 'inferior goods': possible examples in the United Kingdom include paraffin, some types of margarine and long-distance bus travel.

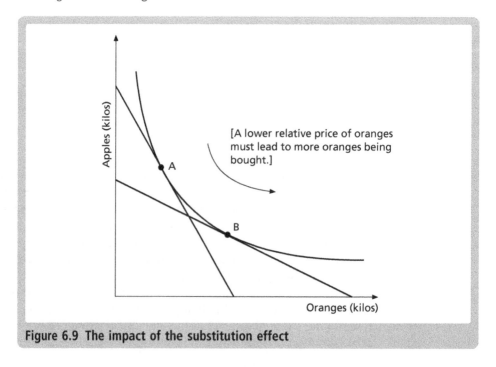

Figure 6.9 The impact of the substitution effect

In the case of inferior goods, the consumer's overall response to a fall in price depends upon the balance between the income effect and the substitution effect. If the substitution effect is larger than the negative income effect, then a lower price will lead to more of the good being bought, as in the case of normal goods. However, in the extreme case where the negative income effect is larger than the substitution effect, a fall in price will actually lead to less of the commodity being bought, rather than more, in contradiction to the downward-sloping form of the demand curve. Such goods are known as 'Giffen goods' after Sir Robert Giffen who suggested that among the very poor in the nineteenth century the demand for staple foods like bread behaved in this way. If consumers were spending a very high proportion of their income on the very cheapest food-stuffs, then a fall in their price would lead to a very substantial increase in their real income. That increase in real income could lead them to substitute other types of food for the bread that they previously relied upon, thereby reducing the demand for bread as its price fell.

Revealed preference theory

The major advantage of indifference analysis over utility theory is that it involves making a much less restrictive set of assumptions about consumers' decision processes. Instead of assuming that every consumer can assign a cardinally meas-urable utility score to every unit of every commodity consumed, it assumes that they have a consistent set of preferences and know which combinations of commodities they prefer to others. Nevertheless, it has been argued that this is still a very restrictive set of assumptions to make, and theorists have sought alternative means by which a theory of consumer behaviour may be constructed. One such alternative approach is known as *revealed preference theory*.

The starting point for revealed preference theory is the assumption that con-sumers are consistent in the way they make choices. Consistency may be said to require the fulfilment of the same two conditions that underpin indifference analysis – asymmetry and transitivity.

For any given consumer, a budget line may be constructed, in exactly the same way as for indifference analysis, as shown by the line AO in Figure 6.10.

The line shows all the different consumption possibilities facing the consumer in question. In the case of revealed preference theory no knowledge of indiffer-ence curves is assumed, so there is no way of predicting where exactly the con-sumer will choose to be on the line AO. Instead the consumers' behaviour is simply observed as a means of revealing their preferences. Imagine that the con-sumers in question choose the combination of goods indicated by point X. Now imagine that the price of oranges falls, so that there is a new budget line AO_1. As the consumers will now choose to be somewhere on the new budget line, they will choose a new combination of apples and oranges, perhaps point Z. In the example shown, point Z involves the purchase of more oranges than before, and the lower price of oranges has led to increased demand for them. The demand curve slopes downwards. However, the analysis thus far has offered no reason to suppose that this must necessarily be the case. Point Z was chosen arbitrarily,

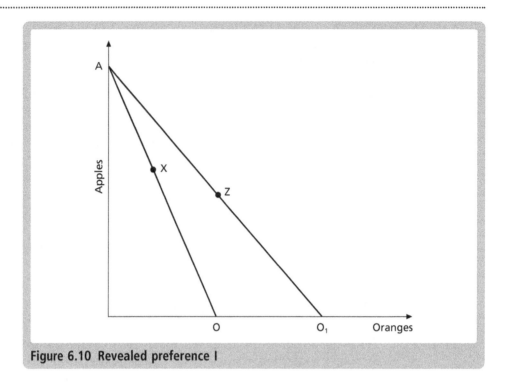

Figure 6.10 Revealed preference I

in order to illustrate the point. In the case of indifference analysis the move from one consumer's equilibrium to another was explained in terms of an income effect and a substitution effect, each of which could be seen to have certain characteristics. A similar procedure can be carried out using the assumptions of revealed preference theory, without having to assume detailed knowledge of preferences.

The example has shown a consumer moving from point X to point Z as a result of a change in price. This is the 'price effect', which may be divided into an income effect and a substitution effect. In the case of indifference analysis it was possible to isolate the substitution effect by defining 'a constant level of real income' to mean 'being on the same indifference curve', so that a movement around an indifference curve could be seen to represent a pure substitution effect, with changes in real income having been cancelled out. Clearly, this cannot be done within the framework of revealed preference theory, because no knowledge of indifference curves is assumed. However, there is an alternative way forward, which can be explained with the help of Figure 6.11.

In Figure 6.11 the thick lines and the points X and Z simply repeat the situation already described in Figure 6.10. The thin line A_1O_2 is drawn parallel to line AO_1, in order to represent the relative prices that hold after the fall in the price of oranges. It also passes through the original choice of goods at X. This line therefore shows the choices available to the consumer if their income remained at the level required to buy the original basket of goods, but the relative prices of apples and oranges were those that hold after the reduction in the price of oranges. If the consumers found themselves in this position they would choose a new combination of goods, like K for example. Without detailed knowledge

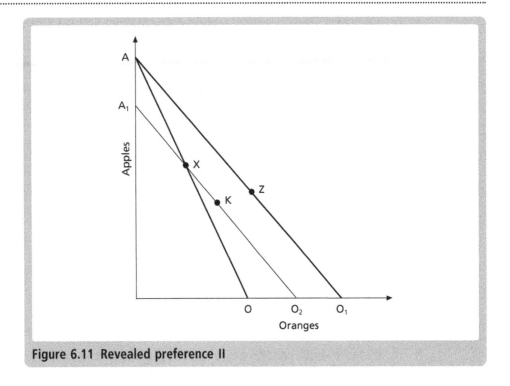

Figure 6.11 Revealed preference II

of the consumer's preferences it is not possible to predict exactly where K will be. However, on the very limited assumptions made about the consistency of consumers' choices it is certain that the point K must lie on or to the right of point X, between X and O_2. That is because the consumer's initial choice of point X indicates that it is considered superior to all the other combinations between A and X. As the combinations between A_1 and X are all inferior to those between A and X, consistency ensures that the consumer must choose to be either at X or to the right of it.

If the consumer selects point K such that it coincides with X then it could be said that there is no substitution effect. The change in relative prices leads to no change in the basket of goods selected. In this case, the whole of the shift from point X to point Z must be an income effect. On the other hand, if point K lies to the right of X (as shown) it is more difficult to unravel income and substitution effects. Certainly the move from K to Z is entirely due to the income effect, because it takes place without any change in relative prices. However, the move from X to K is a combination of substitution effect arising from changing relative prices and income effect arising from the fact that the consumer now faces a higher real income.

Revealed preference theory does not, therefore, allow a clear division of the price effect into a pure substitution effect and a pure income effect, except in the extreme case where the substitution effect is zero. What it does achieve, though, is essentially the same general conclusion as indifference analysis, without having to claim a detailed knowledge of consumers' preferences. As the consumer will never choose a point on A_1O_2 that is to the left of X, the substitution effect can never lead to less of a good being bought when its price falls. The effect must always be to increase the amount bought or, in the very extreme case, to leave it constant. The income effect may, of course, operate in either direction, as was shown in indifference analysis, and the overall effect of a price change, which determines the shape of the demand curve, depends upon the interaction of the two effects. Demand curves will slope downwards except in the case of Giffen goods where the income effect is negative and powerful enough to outweigh the substitution effect.

Managers with practical concerns may find the usefulness of an abstract exercise, like revealed preference theory, difficult to discern. Nevertheless, it has the theoretical advantage of allowing us to make at least limited general predictions about consumer behaviour without having to assume that we have detailed knowledge of consumer preferences, and it also provides a basis on which statisticians and econometricians can build empirical models of demand behaviour which could provide estimates of consumers' responses to price and income changes which would be of practical help to decision-makers.

The characteristics approach to demand

Utility theory, indifference analysis and revealed preference are all couched in terms of consumers' demand for individual commodities. An alternative approach, developed by Lancaster (1966), is to suggest that instead of demanding products, consumers demand certain 'characteristics' and that products are composed of bundles of characteristics. To take the example of motor-cars, for instance, the relevant characteristics may include speed, acceleration, safety, fuel consumption and comfort. Different models of car will be composed of different amounts of each characteristic. In the case of the oranges used in previous examples, the most important characteristics may be sweetness and juiciness. If each brand of oranges possesses these qualities in different ratios, then a consumer who purchases only one brand of oranges will only be able to consume the characteristics of sweetness and juiciness in the proportions embodied in that brand. This is illustrated in Table 6.1 and Figure 6.12.

If each brand of orange has the characteristics shown, then buying more and more oranges of a single brand will give the consumer the combinations of characteristics shown in the straight lines OA, OB and OC in Figure 6.12.

If the consumer has an income of £1,000 then they could buy 100 kilos of brand A (at point X) or 50 kilos of B (at point Y), or 33.3 kilos of C (at point Z), as shown in the diagram. By combining different amounts of the different

Table 6.1 The characteristics of different brands of oranges

Brand	Sweetness index	Juiciness index	Sweetness to juiciness ratio	Price
A	2	1	2.0	10
B	3	3	1.0	20
C	6	2	3.0	30

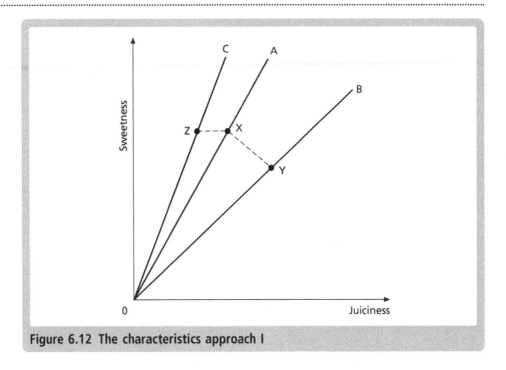

Figure 6.12 The characteristics approach I

brands the consumer can acquire different mixes of the two characteristics as given by the lines joining the points Z and X and X and Y. Points on the line ZX show the combinations of characteristics that a consumer can achieve by spending all of their income on different mixes of brand A and brand C. The line XY shows the combinations that can be had by spending all the available income on different mixes of brand A and brand B. (There is also a line between Z and Y which shows the combinations of characteristics that the consumer could acquire by spending all of their income on combinations of brand C and brand B. However, as this line lies inside the frontier set by ZXY it gives smaller amounts of both characteristics than can be had by spending the same income on the other combinations and will not therefore be chosen by a rational consumer who wants more, rather than less, of each characteristic.)

The line ZXY is rather like the budget line in indifference analysis, showing the combinations of the two characteristics that the consumer is able to purchase with their limited income, given the prices of the different brands. If the price of one of the brands falls, then the amount of it that could be purchased will rise, and the point Z, X or Y that corresponds to that brand will move outwards along the ray indicated, producing a new budget line or 'characteristics possibility frontier'. If the consumer's income rises, the whole frontier will move outwards.

As consumers have preferences for characteristics, the analysis can progress with the construction of an indifference map, with characteristics on the axes, rather than different goods. The consumer will select the combination of characteristics given by the position where the characteristics possibility frontier touches the highest possible indifference curve, as shown in position K in Figure 6.13.

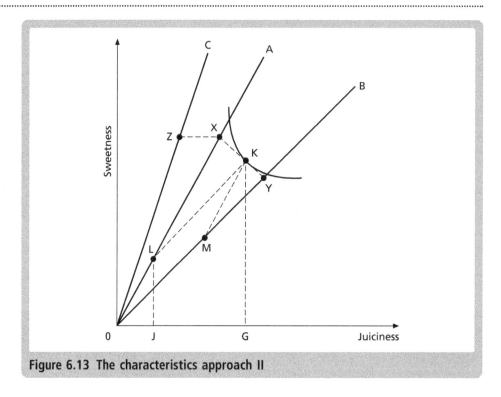

Figure 6.13 The characteristics approach II

The consumer will choose the combination of brands that gives them the indicated combination of characteristics. The precise combination of brands that achieves this can be seen with the aid of Figure 6.13.

First, a line is drawn from the point K to the ray OA, parallel to the ray OB, meeting it at point L, and a similar line is drawn from K to the ray OB, parallel to OA, meeting OB at point M as indicated by the dotted lines in Figure 6.13. The optimal brand mix at point K can then be seen to be arrived at by purchasing more and more units of A, moving along the ray OA from O to L, and then purchasing units of B, moving from L to K.

Alternatively, the brand mix can be arrived at by moving from O to M and then from M to K. It can be seen from the diagram that this is equivalent to moving from O to L, purchasing brand A and from O to M purchasing brand B. In the example shown it is apparent that the consumer will gain OJ units of juiciness from brand A and JG units of juiciness from brand B.

This framework can be used to examine the impact of changing prices upon the consumer's choice of brands, in much the same way as indifference analysis. If the price of brand A falls, the point X will move further out along the ray OA, and there is a new characteristics possibility frontier and a new equilibrium position, giving the consumer higher levels of both of the characteristics that they seek. The new combination of brands can be found as before and the impact of the price change on the demand for each brand depends upon the shapes of the indifference curves. If the price of A rises then the point X will move towards O and the characteristics frontier will move inwards until at some point the new frontier consists of a line from Z to Y, omitting X, showing that from that price onwards only combinations of C and B are efficient and brand A will not be bought at all.

The characteristics approach comes close to providing a practical tool for market researchers and for companies concerned to identify the characteristics needed for new brands. In Figure 6.13, for instance, the consumer buys a combination of two brands in order to consume sweetness and juiciness in the desired ratio available at point K. However, if a new brand were introduced having the characteristics in that desired ratio the consumer would spend all of their income on that brand.

If this approach is to be made practically useful it requires a number of extensions. In the first place, the characteristics of a brand, as seen by consumers, are not always perceived objectively. Market research may be required in order to identify the characteristics that consumers attribute to different brands. Second, different consumers may perceive the same brand as embodying characteristics in different ratios, so that the rays from the origin in Figure 6.13 have different slopes for different consumers and further research is required to measure those variations in perception. Third, if the technique is to be practically useful, consumers' preferences need to be measured, in order to provide information on their indifference curves and their preferred combinations of the subjectively perceived characteristics. Certainly, there are market research techniques that attempt to provide information on each of these issues and they might be brought together to make the characteristics approach operational. On the other hand, there is no evidence to suggest that such an approach has actually been taken up by marketing departments and it is probably more realistic simply to note its similarities with more practical aspects of market research.

Becker's revision of demand theory

Each of the analytical approaches outlined above has assumed that consumers are rational in their behaviour. The meaning of rational behaviour has been defined in each case and the implications of that behaviour explored, providing a theoretical underpinning for the demand curve. Becker (1962) provides a different framework in support of the notion that the demand curve slopes downwards, which does not rely on the assumption of rational behaviour on the part of individual consumers. Instead it rests upon statistical expectations of consumer behaviour in the aggregate. This approach can be explained with the assistance of Figure 6.14.

In Figure 6.14 the line A_1B_1 shows the original budget line facing a consumer, and point X shows the original combination of goods chosen. If the price of oranges rises, the budget line shifts to become A_1B_2. If we now consider what the position would be if the consumers experienced the price change, but suffered no decrease in their real income, this can be represented by shifting the new budget line outwards, keeping the same slope, until it just passes through the original choice point X. This gives the new line A_2B_3, which illustrates the combinations of goods available to the consumers if the new relative prices prevailed but their income were still sufficient to buy the original basket of goods. It is

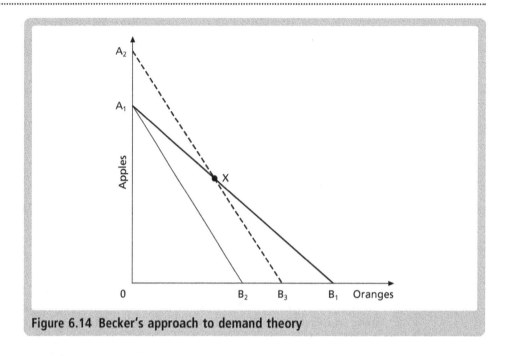

Figure 6.14 Becker's approach to demand theory

now possible to consider *the consumption opportunity set* available to the consumer in each situation. In the original situation, the consumer is able to consume any combination of the two goods in the triangle OA_1B_1. When the price of oranges rises but the consumer's income remains high enough to purchase the original basket of goods, the consumption opportunity set is given by the triangle OA_2B_3. Clearly the second set involves a greater opportunity to consume apples and a smaller opportunity to consume oranges than the original one. If rational consumers relate their decisions to the 'availability' of different products in any way, they will choose to consume more apples and less oranges than in the original situation, and the demand curve will be downward sloping.

Some of the most interesting applications of Becker's analysis are not to the rational consumers considered thus far, but to irrational consumers who buy on impulse, or inert consumers who are generally unresponsive to prices. In the case of the impulse buyer, who has no particular preferences but buys at random, it is impossible to predict where any individual consumer will choose to be. However, if a large number of independent consumers are averaged out, the average consumption will be at the mid-point of the line showing the different combinations available. In the original situation, with the combinations A_1 B_1 available, the chosen point will be the mid-point of the line, which is X. Clearly, the mid-point of the new line A_2B_3 is to the left of the point X and the analysis shows that when the price of oranges rises, the average consumer will purchase less oranges, thus indicating a downward-sloping demand curve.

In the case of the inert consumer, who tends to buy the goods they have always bought, a similar argument may be employed. Such consumers who began somewhere along the line segment A_1X will remain where they are after an income-compensated change in prices, ignoring the greater opportunities offered. However, consumers who were originally on the line segment XB_1 no longer have their original choices available to them and are forced to move leftwards, consuming less of the good whose price has risen. Again the analysis leads to the conclusion that demand curves will be downward sloping.

Limited information and conspicuous consumption

Each of the analyses above has tended to confirm the original common-sense notion that demand curves slope downwards, except in some identifiable and extreme cases. As a result the remainder of this book will use downward-sloping curves whenever a demand curve is needed. However, it is worth noting that there may be some situations where this will not be the case (apart from Giffen goods). If consumers are ill informed about the performance characteristics of a product they are purchasing, they may use the price as an indicator of quality. In that case consumers concerned to buy high quality merchandise may buy more of the same product at a higher price than at a lower price, mistakenly presuming that they are receiving a better quality product. However, for consumers to continue to behave in this way implies that they never learn and can always be seduced into parting with more of their hard-earned income than they need. If there is active competition between firms and easy entry into the industry, if there are consumer organisations and standard-setting bodies, or if consumers simply share their experiences with each other, it is difficult to argue that such behaviour will be common or long-lasting. It is certainly not a sufficiently important phenomenon to suggest that the analysis of the firm should rest upon upward-sloping demand curves, or that firms seeking profits should raise their prices in order to generate a greater volume of sales.

In addition to the case where consumers mistakenly interpret high prices as indicators of high quality, there is another situation where the demand curve for a product may slope upwards. This is where consumers take satisfaction in 'conspicuous consumption', enjoying the fact that the goods they purchase have a high price, and deriving less satisfaction from the same goods if they are available at a lower price. In this case consumers are not simply deriving utility or satisfaction from the performance characteristics of the commodity in question, and seeing the price as the sacrifice they have to make, but seeing the price itself as one of the characteristics that directly gives them satisfaction. For some types of luxury goods this is a phenomenon that should not be ignored.

The practical application of demand theory

The main purpose of the analysis set out above is to provide economists with a theoretical underpinning for their models of the firm and markets, and it would be inappropriate to expect them to have very direct practical applications for managers. Nevertheless, they do provide a starting point for the statistical analysis of demand functions which is one way in which practically useful data on the behaviour of consumers may be discovered. This, and other means of estimating demand, are considered in Chapter 8.

Illustration ## Housing in Hong Kong – prices, characteristics and *feng shui*

The 'characteristics' approach to demand can be particularly useful when examining the demand for commodities that are not homogeneous. Wong (1989) provides a good example, with an analysis of the relationships between the prices of apartments in Hong Kong and their characteristics.

In order to examine the factors at work, Wong collected data on nearly 300 recently purchased apartments in Hong Kong. For each apartment he collected data on two types of characteristics. The first concerned the attributes of the apartments themselves, which included the following variables:

- age of apartment
- net floor area
- number of bedrooms
- door facing south
- door facing north
- sunlight into bedrooms
- view of hills or greenery
- view of the sea
- households per floor
- management fees
- per cent windows facing west
- per cent windows facing south-east
- floors above ground
- subjective noise pollution.

The second type of characteristics concerned the neighbourhood in which the apartments were located. These included:

- mean age of buildings
- complaints on air pollution
- recreational facilities
- entertainment facilities
- school enrolments
- crime rate.

The prices of the apartments and their characteristics were examined by fitting 'hedonic' price equations. A computer package was used to carry out step-wise calculations of a series of multiple regression equations in which the price of the apartments was the dependent variable and their characteristics were the independent variables. As the functional form of an 'hedonic' price equation cannot be predicted from theory, various such forms were fitted including linear, log-linear and squared terms.

Examination of the results showed a number of interesting features. By far the most important explanatory variable was the net floor area of the apartments. (Newcomers to Hong Kong from the United Kingdom are often surprised by the way in which accommodation is almost universally described in terms of square footage, rather than the number of bedrooms and bathrooms, as is the practice in Britain.) This explained almost 70 per cent of the variance in housing prices. Other variables, like the age of the property, were statistically significant, but accounted for only a very small proportion of the variances. This included variables like sea views and south-facing doors which might have captured the impact of the mysterious Chinese art of *feng shui* (wind/water) which is supposed to determine the luck of those inhabiting the property. According to Wong's simplification of the immensely complicated rules of *feng shui*, a view of water should raise the value of a property and a south-facing door should reduce it, as indeed the results confirmed. On the other hand, the results confirmed that a north-facing door also reduced property values. Clearly, the subtleties of Chinese geomancy cannot be fully captured by step-wise regression.

Further examination of the equations fitted suggested that 'neighbourhood characteristics' had a statistically significant impact on prices. Property values were positively related to the mean age of buildings in the district and negatively associated with measures of noise and air pollution and the number of households per floor. However, all of these variables accounted for tiny proportions of the variance. Other neighbourhood variables, like the crime rate, were not even significant.

The evidence suggests, then, that the prices of property in Hong Kong are very largely determined by floor area, which is perhaps not surprising in a city that is said to contain some of the most densely populated areas on Earth. Such econometric analysis requires careful interpretation as the author makes clear, because 'hedonic' price equations are not direct measures of demand but 'reduced forms' which reflect the influence of both supply and demand. Nevertheless, they do provide a useful pointer to the characteristics that consumers value most and a tool for the property valuer. It is interesting to note that when Hong Kong people have emigrated to Canada, they have sometimes offended their Canadian neighbours by completely covering building plots with their dwellings. That is hardly surprising in the light of Wong's findings and suggests that the high valuation placed on floor space in Hong Kong travels with emigrants from that city to their new locations.

References and further reading

G. Becker, 'Irrational Behaviour and Economic Theory', *Journal of Political Economy*, 1962.

D. Kreps, *A Course in Microeconomic Theory*, Princeton, Princeton University Press, 1990.

K. Lancaster, 'A New Approach to Demand Theory', *Journal of Political Economy*, vol. 74, 1966, pp. 132–57.

K-F. Wong, *An Economic Analysis of Demand for Residential Housing in Hong Kong*, MPhil Dissertation, Chinese University of Hong Kong, 1989.

Self-test questions

1. Which of the following statements are correct?

   (a) the substitution effect always leads more of a good to be bought at lower prices

   (b) the income effect always leads more to be bought at lower prices

   (c) inferior goods have upward-sloping demand curves

   (d) indifference analysis involves ordinal, rather than cardinal measurement

   (e) revealed preference avoids the need for a concept of 'utility' or 'satisfaction'

2. Draw indifference maps for beer and cigarettes for consumers with the following preferences:

   (a) likes both beer and cigarettes
   (b) gets no enjoyment (or discomfort) from cigarettes, likes beer
   (c) the opposite of (b)
   (d) is made ill by both beer and cigarettes

3. Use the information in Figure 6.13 and Table 6.1 to identify:

   (a) the amount of sweetness and juiciness the consumer receives
   (b) the amount of each brand of oranges purchased

4. In Becker's approach, why will impulse buyers still tend to have downward-sloping demand curves?

   (a) because they prefer lower prices
   (b) because on the average they will tend to cluster round the mid-point of the consumption opportunity set available
   (c) because the income effect leads them to buy more

5. What assumptions are needed as a basis for the revealed preference approach?

   (a) consumers are consistent in their choices
   (b) the income and substitution effects can be separated
   (c) consumer preferences are known

Essay question

Explain why economic analysis assumes that demand curves slope downwards, using either indifference analysis or revealed preference analysis in support of your argument.

7 Demand and elasticity

This chapter examines the concepts of the demand curve and elasticity of demand, linking them to the behaviour of revenues and to the structure of the industry in question.

The market demand curve

The determinants of demand

Economic theories of consumer behaviour suggest that in general the demand curve for an industry's product will slope downwards, indicating that as the price of the product falls, consumers will choose to purchase more of it. However, the price of the product itself is only one determinant of the volume of demand. A more complete listing of the factors that may affect the demand for an individual final product includes:

- the price of the product itself (P_o)
- the price of other products, especially complements and substitutes (P_c, P_s)
- consumers' disposable incomes (Y_d)
- consumers' tastes and preferences (T)
- the level of advertising for this product (A_o)
- the level of advertising for other products, especially complements and substitutes (A_c, A_s)
- rates of interest (i)
- the availability of credit (C)
- consumers' expectations of future prices and supplies (E).

These factors may all be drawn together into a demand function, which can be written:

$$Q_d = f(P_o, P_c, P_s, Y_d, T, A_o, A_c, A_s, I, C, E)$$

As 'own-price' (P_o) is likely to be one of the most powerful influences upon demand, attention is most often focused upon the demand curve, showing the relationship between own-price and the quantity demanded. Nevertheless, it is important to remember that own-price is only one of many factors influencing demand.

The demand curve

The demand curve, like the example shown in Figure 7.1, shows the quantities of a product that will be bought at different prices, for some fixed combination of the other factors that affect demand.

The requirement that all other factors remain constant is sometimes referred to as the *ceteris paribus* assumption, that phrase being the Latin for 'other things being equal'. This is sometimes misunderstood to mean that economists believe that other things are always equal, when in reality they are clearly not. In fact, of course, the assumption implies no such thing. As the demand function shows clearly, economists are well aware that other factors like incomes, advertising and tastes may all change, affecting the level of demand. However, a diagram on a flat surface can only represent two dimensions at a time, so that a demand curve shows the links between own-price and demand, for a fixed combination of other factors. If any of those other factors should change, the demand curve will shift.

This simple distinction between movements along a demand curve and shifts of the whole curve is an important one. If not fully understood it is possible to make nonsensical, but apparently correct statements, like the following: 'demand rose, therefore prices rose which led demand to fall, then because demand fell prices fell, so that demand rose, so that prices rose . . . and so on . . .'.

The mistake in this endless sentence arises from confusion between two different types of change in demand, one involving a shift in the demand curve, and the other involving a movement along it. If the initial statement that 'demand rose' referred to an upward shift in the demand curve, then the result in a

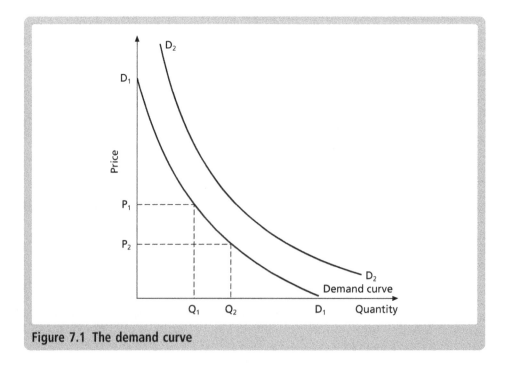

Figure 7.1 The demand curve

simple supply and demand type market would be for price to rise and a new equilibrium to be reached at the higher price. No further changes would take place. The higher price would not lead to a fall in demand because that refers to a movement along the demand curve.

In order to avoid such confusions it is only necessary to keep in mind that when own-price changes, the result is a movement along the demand curve. When any other determinant of demand changes, the demand curve shifts. In Figure 7.1, for example, the demand curve is initially as given by the line D_1D_1, the price is initially P_1 and quantity Q_1 is demanded. If the price of the product falls to P_2, demand rises to Q_2 in a movement along the curve. If, on the other hand, consumers' income increases or the price of a substitute rises, the whole curve will shift, as given by the line D_2D_2.

Concepts of elasticity

Own-price elasticity of demand

While the demand curve will generally be downward sloping, the precise extent of the slope will vary from commodity to commodity. It would be possible to use the slope of the demand curve as a measure of the responsiveness of demand to price. However, such a measure would vary with the scales being used on the price and volume axes, which is obviously unsatisfactory. A better way to measure the responsiveness of demand to changes in price is by using the concept of own-price elasticity of demand, which may be defined as:

$$\frac{\text{percentage change in quantity demanded}}{\text{percentage change in the price of the good}}$$

or

$$\frac{\text{change in quantity}}{\text{change in price}} \times \frac{\text{price}}{\text{quantity}}$$

For a downward-sloping demand curve own-price elasticity will always take negative values, as prices and quantities change in opposite directions.

Arc and point elasticities

There are two different types of own-price elasticity, known as *arc elasticity* and *point elasticity*. The term 'arc elasticity' refers to elasticity over a measurable interval along the demand curve, as in the case of the shift from point A to point B in Figure 7.2.

Referring back to the definition given above shows that there is a possible ambiguity in the calculation of elasticity of demand along the arc AB. The change in price is 2, with a plus or minus sign depending upon its direction, and the change in quantity demanded is correspondingly minus or plus 5. However, the base against which the percentage change in price and quantity is calculated differs in size with the direction of the change. If the price was originally 10 then the

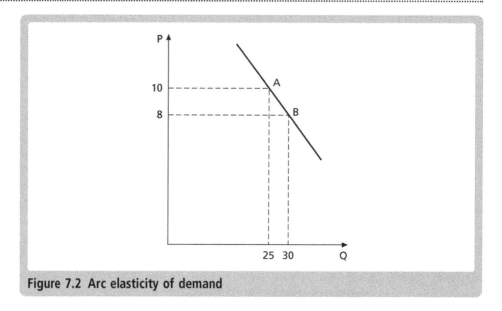

Figure 7.2 Arc elasticity of demand

original price/quantity combination is 10/25 and the value of elasticity is calculated as:

$$E_d = \frac{+5}{-2}\frac{10}{25} = -1$$

On the other hand, if the price rose from 8 to 10, moving along the curve from B to A, the calculation reads:

$$E_d = \frac{-5}{+2}\frac{8}{30} = -0.66666$$

An arc elasticity of demand takes different values for the same arc of the demand curve, depending upon the direction of the change in price and quantity. It is possible to redefine it as a form of average of the two different values, but that is not particularly helpful because the meaning of the result is unclear. It is easier to simply note that the implication of the basic definition of elasticity is that arc elasticities do quite properly take two values, depending upon the direction of the changes under consideration.

It is intuitively clear that as points A and B in Figure 7.2 come closer together, the difference between the two values for the arc elasticity will become smaller. If the distance AB is negligible then the arc has become a point and the arc elasticity is replaced by a point elasticity. This can be defined with the help of elementary calculus as:

$$E_d = \frac{dQ}{dP} \cdot \frac{P}{Q}$$

In the case of point elasticities the ambiguity with respect to the value of elasticity disappears, and it is this concept that is most frequently used in economic analysis. Figures 7.3(a) to 7.3(d) illustrate a number of different demand curves and their elasticities.

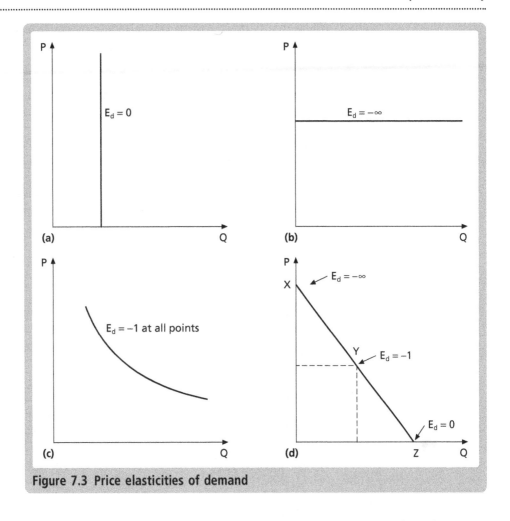

Figure 7.3 Price elasticities of demand

In Figure 7.3(a) the demand curve is a vertical line, illustrating that when price changes, quantity remains the same. In this example, elasticity is equal to zero at every point on the demand curve. In Figure 7.3(b), where the demand curve is a horizontal line, any amount of the commodity can be sold at the price of P_1, but none can be sold at a higher price, indicating an elasticity equal to infinity, at every point on the demand curve. In Figure 7.3(c) the demand curve takes the form of a rectangular hyperbola, which has the unusual property that at every point the price multiplied by the quantity is equal to the same constant. If the demand curve were this shape, elasticity of demand would be equal to –1 at every point.

Each of these three examples is unlikely to be met in practice, and it is correspondingly unlikely that elasticity of demand for a product always takes the same value. Figure 7.3(d) shows a straight-line demand curve, cutting both axes, which has more in common with most 'real-life' demand curves. As the diagram shows, and reference to the definitions confirms, elasticity of demand on this curve takes every value from zero to minus infinity along its length. At point X, where the curve meets the price axis, elasticity is equal to (minus) infinity. At point Z, where it cuts the quantity axis, elasticity is equal to zero. At the midpoint Y, elasticity takes the value –1.

The terms 'elastic demand' and 'inelastic demand' are used to describe different degrees of elasticity. If elasticity has an absolute value of less than 1, demand is said to be inelastic. If the absolute value of elasticity is greater than 1, demand is said to be elastic. In the extreme cases of elasticity being equal to zero or (minus) infinity, demand is said to be respectively infinitely inelastic or infinitely elastic. If elasticity is equal to –1, demand is said to have unitary elasticity.

Clearly, it is not usually possible to describe the demand for a product as generally elastic or inelastic, because elasticity varies at different levels of price and quantity. It is usually only possible to describe the demand for a product as elastic or inelastic, *at some particular price*. There are exceptions, as shown in Figure 7.3(a) to (c), but the demand for an industry's product is unlikely to conform to any of these in practice.

Links between elasticity and revenue

As own-price elasticity of demand measures the responsiveness of demand to changes in price, it is clear that there must be links between the extent of elasticity and the behaviour of revenues. If demand is elastic, a fall in price leads to a more than proportionate increase in the quantity demanded, as a result of which revenues will rise. Conversely, if demand is inelastic, a fall in price leads to a less than proportionate increase in the volume of demand and revenues will fall. When demand is elastic, revenues move in the opposite direction to prices. When demand is inelastic, revenues move in the same direction as prices. Figure 7.4

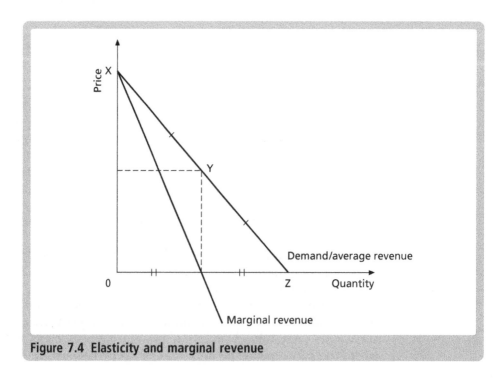

Figure 7.4 Elasticity and marginal revenue

takes this relationship one stage further, using a straight-line demand curve to illustrate the links between own-price elasticity and marginal revenue, defined as the change in revenue that takes place when one additional unit of output is sold.

The figure shows that when demand is elastic, between points X and Y, marginal revenue is positive, indicating that in order to sell one more unit of the commodity the price only has to fall by a very small proportion, so that total revenue increases. At the point Y where elasticity is equal to (−)1, marginal revenue is zero, reflecting the fact that revenue remains the same when price changes. Where demand is inelastic, between Y and Z, marginal revenue is negative, showing that in order to sell one additional unit of output the proportionate change in price is so large that revenue falls.

The determinants of own-price elasticity

The extent of own-price elasticity of demand for a product depends upon a number of factors. The most obvious of these is the existence of other commodities with similar price and performance characteristics that can act as substitutes. The closer the substitutes available, the more elastic the demand for the product will be. This also implies that the extent of elasticity will depend upon how broadly the good in question is defined. If the commodity is very broadly defined ('meat', for instance) then the closest substitutes have rather different characteristics and the demand for 'meat' will be relatively inelastic. On the other hand, if the commodity is very narrowly defined ('belly of pork', for instance) there will be a number of quite close substitutes and demand will be much more elastic.

A second factor that will determine elasticity is the proportion of the consumers' total income that is spent on the commodity in question. If a commodity absorbs a large proportion of consumers' income then a change in its price will produce a substantial income effect, which in turn will have a pronounced effect upon the level of demand. On the other hand, if a commodity absorbs only a tiny fraction of consumers' income they will be much less sensitive to changes in its price and demand for it will tend to be inelastic.

A third factor determining own-price elasticity is the period of time being taken into account. In the long run demand will tend to be more elastic than in the short run, as consumers gradually learn about price changes and devise alternative ways of meeting their needs. In the case of heating fuels, for instance, a change from coal-fired heating to gas-fired heating involves time and expense. As a result, if the relative prices of the fuels change, customers with heating systems already installed will not immediately switch energy sources but will delay the change-over until they next replace their systems. This will mean that demand is much more elastic in the long run than in the short run.

Income elasticity of demand

Own-price elasticity is the type of elasticity of demand most commonly encountered in economic theory. However, demand is also responsive to other factors and the extent of that responsiveness is measured by other variants of the elasticity concept.

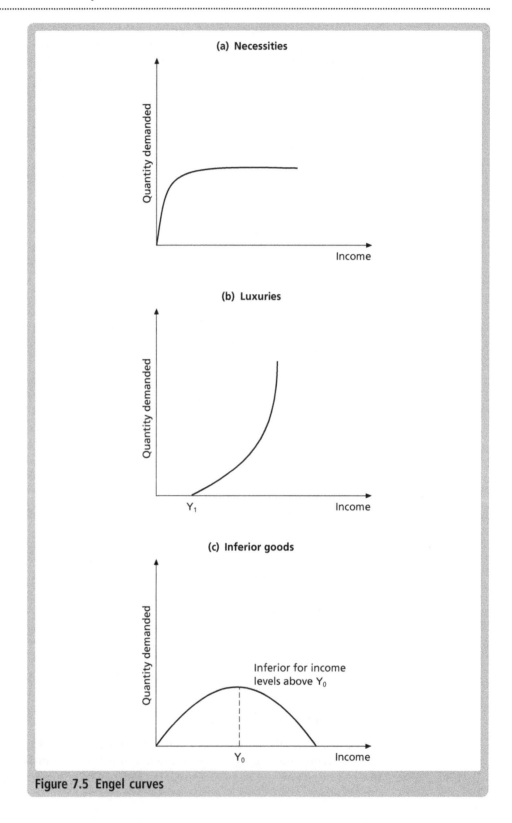

Figure 7.5 Engel curves

Income elasticity of demand is defined as:

$$E_I = \frac{\text{percentage change in quantity demanded}}{\text{percentage change in consumers' incomes}}$$

The arc income elasticity is given by:

$$E_I = \frac{\text{change in quantity demanded}}{\text{change in consumers' incomes}} \times \frac{\text{consumers' incomes}}{\text{quantity demanded}}$$

The point income elasticity is correspondingly given by:

$$e_I = \frac{dQ}{dY} \cdot \frac{Y}{Q} \qquad \text{where:}$$

$$Q = \text{quantity demanded}$$
$$Y = \text{consumers' income}$$

The size and sign of the income elasticity of demand for a product depends to a great extent upon the nature of the product in question and the level of income that consumers have reached. In the case of *necessities*, consumers will purchase a certain amount even at very low levels of income, but they will not increase their spending on these goods as their income rises. The *Engel curve*, showing the relationship between income and demand for the product, will be relatively flat, as shown in Figure 7.5(a), and income elasticity of demand will be positive but less than 1, indicating income inelasticity of demand.

In the case of *luxury goods*, little or nothing will be spent at very low levels of income, but once a threshold level has been passed, as at Y_1 in Figure 7.5(b), consumption of such goods will increase rapidly, indicating that demand is income elastic, having an income elasticity greater than 1. For *normal goods*, including both necessities and luxuries, income elasticity is positive, as consumption increases with income. For inferior goods, which have been discussed in Chapter 6, income elasticity is negative as consumers choose to purchase less of such commodities as they have higher incomes, as shown in the Engel curve in Figure 7.5(c).

Cross-price elasticities of demand

The third major category of demand elasticity is cross-price elasticity of demand, which indicates the responsiveness of the demand for a commodity to changes in the prices of other goods, the most important other goods to consider being close substitutes and complements. Cross-price elasticity between good A and good B is defined as:

$$E_x = \frac{\text{percentage change in the quantity of good A demanded}}{\text{percentage change in the price of good B}}$$

The arc cross-price elasticity is given by:

$$E_x = \frac{\text{change in quantity of A demanded}}{\text{change in price of B}} \times \frac{\text{price of B}}{\text{quantity of A}}$$

and the point cross-price elasticity by:

$$e_x = \frac{dQ_A}{dP_B} \cdot \frac{P_B}{Q_A} \qquad \text{where:}$$

$$Q_A = \text{quantity of A}$$
$$P_B = \text{price of B}$$

In the case of substitutes cross-elasticities have a positive sign, as a fall in the price of a substitute leads to a fall in demand for the product being considered. In the case of complements, cross-elasticities have a negative sign. Clearly, if there is a negligible interrelationship between the demand for two commodities the cross-elasticities between them will be zero.

This last point suggests that cross-elasticities of demand may be useful in arriving at an appropriate definition of a market and/or industry. If an industry is defined as a group of firms producing products that are close substitutes for each other, that is equivalent to saying that an industry is a group of firms producing goods that have high positive cross-elasticities of demand. If cross-elasticities could be estimated, they could be used to partition the economy into industries in an economically meaningful way.

The demand curve for an individual firm

The analysis above has been solely concerned with the market demand curve for goods, and the elasticity of that curve, which depends upon the existence of substitutes, the importance of the commodity in consumers' total spending, and upon the length of time in which consumers are able to adjust their purchasing patterns. While information on market demand is useful for individual firms they will tend to be more concerned with the demand conditions for their own individual product, rather than that for the output of the industry as a whole. That in turn depends upon the competitive structure of the industry, examined in detail in Chapters 10 and 11. A number of different cases may be distinguished.

The first, and simplest, case is where the industry is a *pure monopoly* in that there is only one firm producing the product in question, and there is no possibility of entry by other firms into the industry. In that case the demand curve for the individual firm is the market demand curve for the industry as a whole, and there are no further complications.

The second case, at the other extreme of the spectrum of market structures, is *perfect competition*, where there are a large number of firms in the industry, all producing identical variants of the product. In this case, the price will be set by the interaction of supply and demand and each individual firm will be able to sell as much as it wishes at that price, but none at higher prices. The demand curve for the individual firm will be a horizontal straight line, as shown in Figure 7.3(b).

In the case of market structures which are neither pure monopolies nor perfectly competitive, demand conditions for the individual firm will depend upon a number of factors. The first is the elasticity of market demand for the product as a whole. Clearly, if demand for the product as a whole is perfectly elastic, individual firms will be unable to sell their product at anything apart from the indicated price. The second determinant of the elasticity of demand for an individual firm is the degree of product differentiation or brand loyalty on the part of purchasers. If products are highly differentiated and purchasers are extremely loyal to a particular firm, the demand curve will be downward sloping, rather than horizontal. Each firm is essentially a 'mini-monopolist', producing a product for which there are no very close substitutes. On the other hand, if products are identical, and consumers exhibit no brand loyalty, demand curves will be horizontal lines, as no consumer will be prepared to pay more for the product of one firm than for the product of another.

The third factor that will determine the elasticity of demand for the individual firm's output will be its share of the market. If a firm has a very large market share, a reduction in its price will need to attract a substantial proportion of other firms' customers if the proportionate increase in its demand is to be large. On the other hand, a firm with a very small market share will be able to induce a large proportionate increase in its sales by attracting a relatively small proportion of its rivals' customers.

Fourth, the elasticity of demand for an individual firm's product will depend upon its rivals' reactions to its changes in price. If rivals react to a price reduction by increasing their output (and reducing their own prices), then clearly demand will be less responsive than if rivals maintain or even reduce their output. Needham (1978, p. 59) identified the following simple equation linking the various different determinants of the demand for an individual firm's product:

$$E_f = \frac{(E_m + E_s S_r)}{S_f} \quad \text{where:}$$

E_f = elasticity of demand for the firm's product
E_m = market elasticity
E_s = elasticity of rivals' supply with respect to changes in the firm's price
S_f = the firm's market share
S_r = rivals' market share

As the formula confirms, elasticity of demand for the firm's product is partly determined by rivals' reactions to its own actions, which cannot be known for certain, and which are therefore sometimes referred to as 'conjectural variation'.

A diagrammatic approach to the demand curve for a firm having rivals is known as the 'kinky demand curve' model, covered in more depth in Chapter 10. If such a firm knows that it can sell quantity Q_0 at price P, as shown in Figure 7.6, then point A is one point on the firm's demand curve. The difficult problem for the firm lies in evaluating the volume of sales at other prices, as that depends upon the reactions of its rivals. However, if the firm conjectures that its rivals will not match an increase in its price, but will match any price decreases, then demand will be highly elastic for price rises, but relatively inelastic for price reductions. The result is a kinked demand curve as shown in Figure 7.6.

If the demand curve has such a kink, the associated marginal revenue curve will have a 'dog-leg' shape, as illustrated. If the firm were to attempt to sell output greater than Q_0, it would have to reduce its price. This would lead rival firms to follow suit and even a small increase in volume sold would require a relatively substantial fall in price. As a result, marginal revenue falls dramatically for increases

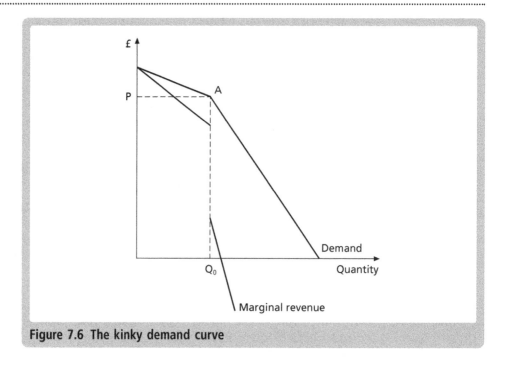

Figure 7.6 The kinky demand curve

in volume beyond Q_0. The implications of this are followed through in detail in Chapter 10, but it is clear enough from the analysis thus far that firms will be reluctant to lower prices in this situation. While the kinked demand curve approach is useful, it has become something of an historical curiosity since the analysis of firms' behaviour in situations of rivalry has come to be dominated by game theory, examined in Chapter 13.

Elasticity of demand and the power of buyers

Chapter 11 introduces the method used by Porter (1980, 1985) for structural analysis of the state of competition in an industry. One of the 'five forces' described as determining competition in that framework is the power of buyers. That power is in itself determined by two sets of factors, which determine the following:

1. The price sensitivity of buyers.
2. Their bargaining power.

Neither of these concepts are quantifiable in the Porter approach, but clearly the price sensitivity of buyers is a concept very close to that of elasticity of demand. Porter identifies the following factors as the main determinants of price sensitivity:

- *Purchases of the product as a proportion of total purchases.* If purchases of the product are an unimportant proportion of buyers' total purchases, they will tend to be relatively insensitive to price.
- *Product differences and brand identity*, which will reduce price sensitivity.

- *The impact of the product on the quality of the buyers' product or service.* If the product being sold is a key element in maintaining the quality or low cost of buyers' own product, they are unlikely to be price sensitive.
- *Customers' own profitability.* Profitable customers are said to be less price sensitive.
- *Decision-makers' incentives.* Purchasing managers within customer companies face a variety of incentives, some of which encourage them to be more price sensitive, others of which reduce the emphasis on price.

The first two of these factors have already been referred to in the section on the determinants of own-price elasticity above. The others illustrate the importance of industrial customers, as opposed to consumers. It is useful to remember that while most economic analysis focuses on the consumer as the customer, the consumer is only one type of buyer. For many firms it is the behaviour of industrial buyers that is most important.

Illustration | **Missing the demand curve – how a pricing mistake damaged Jaguar**

Harrison and Wilkes (1973) provide a good example of the losses that may be incurred by a firm that fails to give adequate consideration to the link between price and the quantity of the product that can be sold. In July 1972, Jaguar launched the XJ12 luxury sports car, having developed a product that was acknowledged to be of excellent quality and performance. The price had been set at £3,726, compared with at least £6,000 for comparable vehicles.

As might be expected, demand exceeded supply, a situation that was made worse by industrial action at the factory. By the end of 1972 there was a two-year waiting list for the product, and second-hand cars were being sold for prices that exceeded the list price by more than 40 per cent. Critics argued that by setting such a low price, which had been arrived at by estimating the cost per car at full capacity, and then adding a 'satisfactory' margin, the company was sacrificing revenue at a time when it could not afford it. Harrison and Wilkes attempted to quantify that loss, using Figure 7.7.

In Figure 7.7, the straight line shows the (unknown) demand curve for the XJ12. The price set by the company is P_0 at which price it is believed that the planned

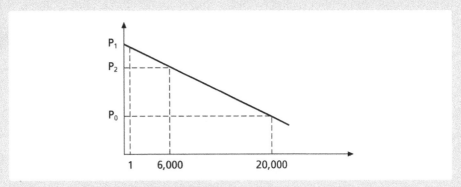

Figure 7.7 Harrison and Wilkes's analysis

output of 20,000 units could be sold. The actual quantity sold is 6,000 units. That combination of price and quantity is below the demand curve, because it is known that more cars could be sold at the current price. It is also known that one car has been sold at the higher price, P_1. The objective of the exercise is to estimate the price P_2 at which the current output of 6,000 units could be sold, in order to estimate the lost revenue arising from the pricing policy adopted.

The first stage is to make the assumption that the demand curve is linear, with intercept 'a' and slope 'b'. In that case,

$$P = a - bQ$$

As P_1 is the price at which a single unit was sold, it provides an estimate for 'a', which is therefore equal to £5,226. The slope 'b' is equal to $(P_1 - P_o)/(20,000)$, which equals 0.075. The price at which 6,000 units could be sold is therefore given by the equation:

$$P_2 = 5,226 - (0.075)(6,000) = 4,776$$

This is £1,050 more than the price that the firm actually charged, suggesting that on 6,000 units an opportunity loss of more than six million pounds was made. The loss of that revenue left the company without the funding it needed to develop new models. Jaguar had increasing difficulties in the face of competition from European luxury vehicle manufacturers (which took advantage of the British company's production problems to enter the UK market) and its market dominance was lost. Not until the company was taken over by Ford in the 1990s did it show signs of recovery.

References and further reading

R. Harrison and F.M. Wilkes, 'A Note on Jaguar's Pricing Policy', *European Journal of Marketing*, 1973.

D. Needham, *The Economics of Industrial Structure, Conduct and Performance*, London, Holt, Rinehart and Winston, 1978.

M. Porter, *Competitive Strategy*, New York, Free Press, 1980.

M. Porter, *Competitive Advantage*, New York, Free Press, 1985.

Self-test questions

1. Which of the following goods is likely to have inelastic demand with respect to price?

   (a) table salt

   (b) domestic gas

   (c) small family cars

   (d) daily newspapers

2. Which of the following goods is likely to have a negative income elasticity of demand?

   (a) bus travel

   (b) cheap margarine

   (c) expensive margarine

(d) petrol

(e) car accessories

(f) daily newspapers

3. Which of the following statements are correct?

    (a) petrol and tyres have positive cross-elasticities of demand

    (b) when demand is own-price elastic, marginal revenue is negative

    (c) the demand for food is less elastic than the demand for rice

    (d) the Engel curve for bread is vertical for most of its range

    (e) the price sensitivity of buyers is positively related to the importance of the product in their total purchases

4. If the demand curve for a product is a straight line, cutting both axes, which of the following statements are correct?

    (a) there is a price above which none of the product will be purchased

    (b) an infinite amount of the product could be given away

    (c) elasticity of demand is lower as price is higher

    (d) a rise in price above the mid-point of the curve will increase revenue

    (e) elasticity of demand is zero at the point where the curve crosses the horizontal axis

5. In an oligopolistic industry, does elasticity of demand for an individual firm's product rise or fall with:

    (a) increasing market share for the firm

    (b) decreasing market elasticity of demand

    (c) increasing rivals' cross-elasticity of supply with respect to changes in the firm's price

Essay question

Why did Jaguar set the price of the XJ12 at such a low level?

8 Estimating and forecasting demand

This chapter examines the estimation and forecasting of demand. Alternative methods of estimation are considered and the problems associated with each one examined. Attention is then directed to forecasting methods, including time-series analysis and market research techniques.

Alternative methods of estimation

It is clear that in principle the concepts of the demand curve and elasticity of demand are potentially of great significance for the process of business decision-making. However, the theoretical concepts can only be of direct practical application if reliable quantitative estimates can be made of the level of demand and of elasticity. This is a difficult task which may be approached in a number of ways. The most fundamental distinction is between *estimation*, which attempts to quantify the links between the level of demand and the other variables that determine it, and *forecasting*, which simply attempts to predict the level of demand at some future date.

Simple estimation of arc elasticity

One of the crudest ways in which the market elasticity of demand could be estimated is by observing the quantity of a product sold before and after a price change and assuming that the two known combinations of price and quantity are points on the same demand curve. In Figure 8.1, for example, if 100 units of output were sold at a price of 8 (point A) and 120 units were sold when the price fell to 6 (point B), then elasticity of demand can be directly estimated from the standard formula.

A more sophisticated version of this technique was used in a classic study by Simon (1966) which attempted to measure the price elasticity of demand for liquor in the United States (see Illustration 1 at the end of this chapter). Its advantage lies in the fact that it is very simple and estimates can be made on the basis of a single price change. The disadvantages are that adjustments have to be made to compensate for speculative building up or running down of stocks in anticipation of a price change, and there is no guarantee that the two price/output combinations that are observed lie on the same demand curve. It could quite easily be the case that both supply and demand curves shifted in the movement from A to B.

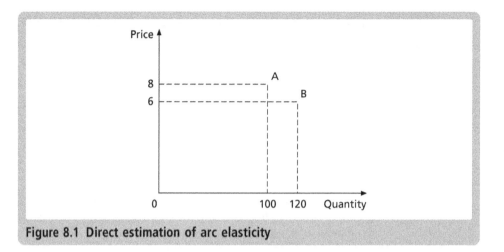

Figure 8.1 Direct estimation of arc elasticity

Econometric estimation of demand curves

The second, more sophisticated, approach to demand estimation is through 'econometrics', the statistical analysis of economic data using techniques like multiple regression, which allow empirical data on demand and its determinants to be used to estimate the coefficients of a demand function. The general form of the demand function has been set out in Chapter 7 as:

$$Q_d = f(P_o, P_c, P_s, Y_d, T, A_o, A_c, A_s, I, C, E)$$

This simply states that the quantity demanded depends upon the following:

- the price of the product itself (P_o)
- the price of other products, especially complements and substitutes (P_c, P_s)
- consumers' disposable incomes (Y_d)
- consumers' tastes and preferences (T)
- the level of advertising for this product (A_o)
- the level of advertising for other products, especially complements and substitutes (A_c, A_s)
- rates of interest (I)
- the availability of credit (C)
- consumers' expectations of future prices and supplies (E).

In the general form no particular functional relationship is specified between the dependent variable (Q_d) and the independent variables that determine it. However, if the coefficients linking the various independent variables with the level of demand are to be estimated, a particular functional form needs to be chosen. The two most common forms are the *linear demand function* and *the exponential demand function*.

The linear demand function can be written:

$$Q_d = a + b_1P_o + b_2P_c + b_3P_s + b_4Y_d + b_5T + b_6A_o + b_7A_c$$
$$+ b_8A_s + b_9I + b_{10}C + b_{11}E$$

If data are available on each of the variables, and there are sufficient observations to apply the statistical technique of multiple regression, then the coefficient for the intercept (a) and the coefficients showing the impact of each determinant upon the quantity demanded (b_1 to b_{11}) can be estimated. Once they have been estimated it is possible to predict the level of demand for any set of values for each of the determinants by simply inserting these values into the equation.

In the case of the linear specification of the demand curve, estimating the coefficients of the demand function does not provide a direct estimate of the elasticity of demand. Nevertheless, it is a simple process to calculate elasticities. The definition of own-price elasticity of demand can be written as:

$$e_d = \frac{dQ}{dP_o} \cdot \frac{P_o}{Q}$$

However, it can be seen from the demand function that:

$$\frac{dQ}{dP_o} = b_1$$

So that:

$$e_d = b_1 \cdot \frac{P_o}{Q}$$

Other elasticities, including income elasticity, cross-price elasticity and advertising elasticity, can be calculated in the same way.

The linear specification of the demand function allows the estimation of elasticity, and the own-price elasticity that is calculated as a result does change with different combinations of price and quantity, as is to be expected. However, the linear form embodies the assumption that a given change in price always has the same effect on volume, regardless of the level of price. That assumption conflicts with most economic reasoning, including theories of consumer behaviour, so that alternative specifications are often used in attempting to estimate demand.

The most popular alternative to the linear form is the exponential form, which may be written:

$$Q_d = P_o^a \cdot P_s^b \cdot P_c^c \cdot A_o^d \cdot A_s^e \cdot A_c^f \cdot Y_d^g \cdot I^h \cdot C^i \cdot E^j$$

In this form the elasticities are the exponents (the coefficients a to j) and the equation can be rewritten in a linear form by taking logarithms. This gives:

$$\log Q_d = a \log P_o + b \log P_s + c \log P_c + d \log A_o + e \log A_s$$
$$+ f \log A_c + g \log Y_d + h \log I + i \log C + j \log E$$

This equation can be estimated using the methods of multiple regression, giving direct estimates of the various different elasticities of demand. This is the most commonly used form of the demand function for the purposes of estimation, although it should be noted that it embodies an assumption that elasticities are constant, in place of the assumption in the linear form that the marginal impact of price (and the other factors) on volume is constant.

The basic principles involved in estimating the demand function are simple enough, but there are a number of very significant statistical problems involved in arriving at estimates that can be held to with any confidence. A detailed treatment of them lies beyond the scope of this book, but it is useful to note them briefly.

In the first place, the method of multiple regression does not provide an exact relationship between the level of demand and each of its determinants. It simply shows the relationship that has the 'best fit' to the data. In some cases that 'best fit' may be very poor, in which case the equation specified explains only a small proportion of the variation in the level of demand. If that is the case, the equation will have little value in estimating and predicting the level of demand.

In the second place, there may be *multicollinearity* among the independent explanatory variables. If those variables are themselves highly correlated, it will be difficult or impossible to separate out their individual influence. Third, estimated values of the individual coefficients in the demand function are only appropriate (known as *best linear unbiased estimators* – BLUEs) if a number of quite restrictive assumptions about the behaviour of the error term (the difference between the estimated level of demand given by the equation and the actual value) are valid. If they are not, then various corrections will need to be made, none of which is entirely satisfactory.

Fourth, there is what is known as the *identification problem*. If statisticians have collected a number of observations on the price of a commodity, over time, and the level of demand at each price, it is tempting to conclude that the line providing the best fit to this set of observations is the demand curve. In Figure 8.2(a) such a line is shown as ABC.

However, such a set of observations could have arisen in a number of different ways. Certainly, if it is known that the demand curve remained in the same position (indicating that none of the factors determining demand, other than price, changed over the period of observation) but the supply curve shifted, then the points traced out would identify the demand curve. On the other hand, the same set of points could have been generated by both the demand curve and the supply curve shifting, as in Figure 8.2(b), in which case the line AB does not represent the demand curve at all. It is helpful to appreciate that if neither the demand curve nor the supply curve shifted over the period of observation, the set of data recorded would consist of multiple observations of a single point on the diagram, price and quantity remaining the same at every observation.

The identification problem can be solved, subject to a range of qualifications, but the solution is complex and requires the estimation of a model made up of a number of simultaneous equations, rather than a single equation for demand. Despite their limitations, many of the attempts to estimate demand and elasticities statistically have used methods based on a single equation. In some cases, special circumstances provide justification (as in Illustration 2 at the end of this chapter). In other cases they do not and it is important to remember that standard curve-fitting techniques may 'yield results which bear little or no relationship to the actual equation being sought' (McGuigan *et al.* 1999, p. 168).

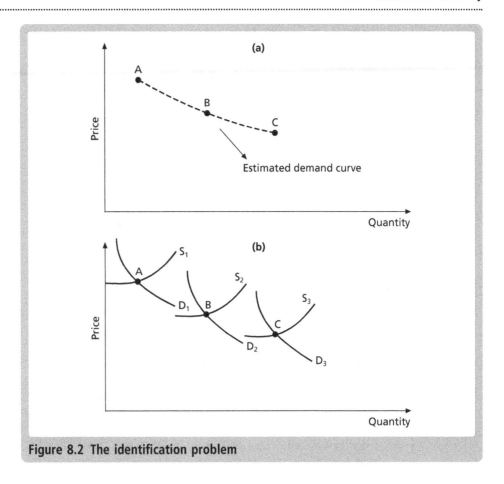

Figure 8.2 The identification problem

Some estimates of elasticity

Many analysts have attempted to estimate demand functions. In most cases, attention has focused on a very narrow range of commodities and the differences in methods used, areas covered and dates make it inappropriate to compare the estimated values across different studies. There have been a few attempts to examine a range of commodities in the same country at the same time, using the same methods, but they are now considerably out-dated. Stone (1954) produced a range of estimates for the United Kingdom over the period 1920–38 and Deaton (1975) carried out a similar exercise, also for the United Kingdom, over the period 1954–70. More recently Baye *et al.* (1992) produced estimates for a range of broadly defined commodities in the United States, shown in Table 8.1.

The figures presented in Table 8.1 accord with expectations, in that the own-price elasticities all have negative signs, and goods like transportation, alcohol and tobacco have large positive income elasticities. Most of the own-price elasticities indicate inelastic demand, which is to be expected for the relatively broad product categories identified.

Table 8.1 Estimated elasticities of demand

Product	Own-price elasticity	Advertising elasticity	Income elasticity
Transportation	−0.559	−0.027	1.787
Food	−0.672	−0.016	0.843
Alcohol and tobacco	−0.261	−0.051	1.220
Recreation	−1.094	0.078	1.067
Clothing	−0.889	0.013	1.024
Household and personal care	−0.629	−0.023	0.855

Source: Baye et al. 1992, p. 1093.

Estimates like these provide useful broad indicators of demand conditions, but the difficulties of estimation and the possibly out-dated nature of the data on which they are based require that they be treated with great caution. The very broad product categories to which many such estimates relate, and the fact that they measure market elasticity rather than firm-level elasticity, also tend to reduce their direct usefulness to companies.

In response to these limitations of the economic research on demand elasticity, marketing researchers have taken up the issue in a number of ways (Malhotra et al. 1999). Tellis (1988) carried out a useful *meta-analysis* (a quantitatively focused review) of econometric studies to date, concluding that the country in which studies are carried out has an important influence on the estimated elasticities. Dolan and Simon (1996) found that managers reported themselves to be poorly informed on the price responsiveness of their customers. In order to estimate that responsiveness, four approaches have been used. In industries having few customers, expert judgement has been the most usual approach. When customers are more numerous, researchers have used customer surveys, price experiments and the analysis of historical data as more appropriate methods. Bemmaor and Mouchoux (1991) examined the short-term effect of price promotions in grocery stores and found that *deal elasticities* – the short-term elasticities associated with 'special deal' prices – were very large, in the range of −2 to −11. They also found that there were important interaction effects between the price promotions and advertising, so that the deal elasticities were much larger when the special price deals were heavily advertised. The increasing availability of huge volumes of store-level data collected by checkout scanners has allowed estimates of store-specific price elasticities to be made, with results suggesting that these elasticities vary significantly from one store to another (Hoch et al. 1995).

While marketing researchers have paid a good deal of attention to estimating price responsiveness for narrowly defined products, their focus on the behaviour of consumers has also led them to consider the factors that determine that price responsiveness. In the Hoch et al. (1995) analysis it was found, perhaps surprisingly, that the characteristics of consumers – household size, education, home value and ethnicity – were more important in determining price responsiveness in an individual store than competitive variables like the distance of the store from its nearest competitor. As the Internet makes price comparisons much easier to carry out, it remains to be seen how that will affect the elasticity of demand for individual companies' products. The obvious hypothesis is that firm-level price elasticity will increase as the cost of searching for alternatives is reduced and the effect will be particularly marked for expensive 'big ticket' items where the potential savings are largest. However, as Malhotra *et al.* (1999) note, that remains a research opportunity to be exploited in the next few years as Internet usage expands.

Forecasting demand

The methods discussed above build upon a theoretical model of the market and the demand curve in order to estimate the way in which demand will respond to changes in price. The aim of such procedures is to quantify the causal links between the level of demand and its determinants. If the aim is more limited, being restricted to simply predicting the future volume of sales, without quantifying responsiveness to the various different determinants of demand, then a variety of other forecasting techniques may be employed.

Extrapolation and time-series analysis

One of the simplest techniques is to assume that some aspect of the past behaviour of the variable being forecast will continue to be true in the future, thereby providing the basis for the prediction. At its most elementary this includes 'naïve methods' of forecasting such as the assumption that next year's volume of sales will be equal to this year's figure, or that next year's growth of sales will be equal to this year's. A slightly more sophisticated version is to identify any trends over the recent past and then to extrapolate those trends forward into the future. Figure 8.3 illustrates the procedure.

The scatter of points in Figure 8.3 shows the level of sales in recent time-periods, and the solid line is that which provides the 'best fit' to those points, fitted either by eye or by simple linear regression. The extension of that relationship

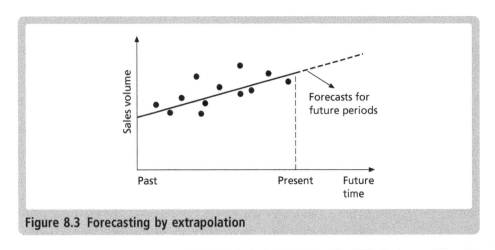

Figure 8.3 Forecasting by extrapolation

into the future, marked by the dotted line, provides the forecast of sales levels for future periods. The major weakness of such methods is that they make no reference to the causal factors that determine the volume of demand, in effect assuming that time is the only determining factor that needs to be taken into account. They also assume that the relationship between time and the variable being forecast is a very simple one consisting only of a long-term trend.

A more sophisticated type of extrapolation is *time-series analysis*, which includes a wide range of different techniques (Pecar 1993 provides a useful exposition). Perhaps the best-known of these techniques is the *decomposition method*. In this approach it is assumed that any time-series is made up of a series of components. The first component is the trend (T) showing long-run changes in the variable being considered. The second component is seasonal movement(s) within each year, and the third component is irregular movement (I), which consists of non-recurring and essentially unpredictable changes. Forecasting textbooks often also include a fourth component consisting of cyclical movement made up of regular contractions and expansions over periods of a few years, but the practical value of this component is much more doubtful. It is not at all clear whether industries really are subject to regular cyclical movements and isolating such movements from the data can involve making arbitrary judgements. Whichever model is adopted, each individual observation is assumed to be made up of these components, which may be linked additively, in which case:

$$X_t = T_t + C_t + S_t + I_t \quad \text{where:}$$

X_t = the actual observation for period t
T_t = the trend value for period t
C_t = the cyclical component for period t
S_t = the seasonal component for period t
I_t = the irregular component for period t

Alternatively the relationship between the components could be multiplicative, in which case:

$$X_t = T_t \cdot C_t \cdot S_t \cdot I_t$$

In order to use time-series analysis for forecasting, the raw data are divided up into their constituent components in a number of stages. This can be done in many different ways but a simple example can illustrate the basic features. In this example a cyclical component is not included, for the reasons outlined above.

First, the trend factor in the data is isolated, either by taking a moving average of the raw data or by fitting a straight line to the raw data using regression analysis. The new time-series that results represents the effects of the trend. If the resulting value for each time-period is subtracted from the actual observation, the differences represent the seasonal and irregular components taken together. In order to separate out the seasonal component alone, an average is taken of these 'seasonal-plus-irregular' components for each season of the year, across the full period for which data are available. As the irregular component for each season is thereby averaged out, the results provide the seasonal component, giving a value for each season. As the seasonal components should add to zero, some adjustment of the result may be needed (see the worked example below).

Once the trend and seasonal components have been identified, the construction of a forecast for any future period consists of using the regression equation to calculate the trend value for the future period in question and adding in the seasonal component for the season in question. This procedure may be made more clear by working through an example.

Stage 1: Calculate the 'trend factor'

The figures in Table 8.2 show the quarterly consumption of electricity in the United Kingdom over the period 1989–98. The purpose of the exercise is to use the data for 1989–96 to forecast consumption in each quarter of 1997 and 1998, and then to evaluate those forecasts.

Table 8.2 Electricity consumption in the United Kingdom 1989–98

Time-period	T	Consumption	Time-period	t	Consumption
1989			1994		
Q1	1	87192	Q1	21	91680
Q2	2	72192	Q2	22	75019
Q3	3	66674	Q3	23	70967
Q4	4	86069	Q4	24	86554
1990			1995		
Q1	5	92740	Q1	25	93715
Q2	6	70339	Q2	26	77556
Q3	7	67700	Q3	27	72371
Q4	8	85619	Q4	28	89727
1991			1996		
Q1	9	92613	Q1	29	97119
Q2	10	74545	Q2	30	78911
Q3	11	66721	Q3	31	75691
Q4	12	86325	Q4	32	93603
1992			1997		
Q1	13	90273	Q1	33	96295
Q2	14	73004	Q2	34	78603
Q3	15	68542	Q3	35	76511
Q4	16	86831	Q4	36	92641
1993			1998		
Q1	17	90467	Q1	37	96335
Q2	18	72696	Q2	38	81488
Q3	19	70365	Q3	39	77205
Q4	20	85998	Q4	40	91248

Source: Calculated from OECD *Energy Statistics, Monthly Series.*

A simple regression of consumption against time gives:

$$T_t = 77347 + 216t \qquad \text{where:}$$

$$T_t = \text{trend value of sales}$$
$$t = \text{time-period}$$

In this example the trend is only very slightly upwards and in fact the coefficient on time is not statistically significant and the coefficient of determination (R- square) is very low at 0.044. The variation in quarterly electricity consumption in the United Kingdom is not very well explained by the trend over time. While the UK economy grew quite strongly over 1989–96, energy-saving measures meant that electricity consumption has not exhibited a significantly rising trend. In any particular quarter the most important influence on consumption is the seasonal effect. Nevertheless, the equation can be used to calculate the trend value and thence to calculate the value of the 'seasonal plus irregular' component.

Table 8.3 Calculating the seasonal plus irregular component

t	Actual observation	Trend value	Seasonal plus irregular	T	Actual observation	Trend value	Seasonal plus irregular
1989				**1993**			
Q1	87192	77563	9628	Q1	90467	81026	9441
Q2	72192	77780	−5588	Q2	72696	81243	−8547
Q3	66674	77996	−11323	Q3	70365	81459	−11093
Q4	86069	78213	7856	Q4	85998	81675	4323
1990				**1994**			
Q1	92740	78429	14310	Q1	91680	81892	9788
Q2	70339	78645	−8307	Q2	75019	82108	−7089
Q3	67700	78862	−11162	Q3	70967	82325	−11358
Q4	85619	79078	6541	Q4	86554	82541	4013
1991				**1995**			
Q1	92613	79294	13318	Q1	93715	82757	10958
Q2	74545	79511	−4966	Q2	77556	82974	−5418
Q3	66721	79727	−13006	Q3	72371	83190	−10819
Q4	86325	79944	6381	Q4	89727	83407	6320
1992				**1996**			
Q1	90273	80161	10112	Q1	97119	83623	13496
Q2	73004	80377	−7373	Q2	78911	83839	−4928
Q3	68542	80593	−12051	Q3	75691	84056	−8365
Q4	86381	80810	5571	Q4	93603	84272	9331

Stage 2: Separate out 'seasonal plus irregular'

In the simple 'trend plus seasonal' model being used here, the relationship between the different components is as follows:

$$\text{Actual}_t = \text{Trend}_t + \text{Seasonal}_t + \text{Irregular}_t$$

Therefore:

$$\text{Actual}_t - \text{Trend}_t = \text{Seasonal}_t + \text{Irregular}_t$$

Table 8.3 shows the corresponding calculation.

Stage 3: Identify the seasonal component for each quarter

If the means for each quarter are added together, they sum to –91. However, the total of seasonal factors over a year should sum to zero, and the means are therefore adjusted by spreading the discrepancy across the four seasons. In this case the total discrepancy is very small, amounting to about 1.5 per cent of the smallest quarterly mean and it might reasonably have been ignored.

Stage 4: Make the forecast

A forecast for any future period can now be made by calculating the trend value for that period and adding in the seasonal factor. For instance, if we wished to

Table 8.4 Calculating the seasonal components

Season	Values of 'seasonal plus irregular'	Season	Values of 'seasonal plus irregular'	Season	Values of 'seasonal plus irregular'	Season	Values of 'seasonal plus irregular'
Q1		Q2		Q3		Q4	
1989	9628	1989	–5588	1989	–11323	1989	7856
1990	14310	1990	–8307	1990	–11162	1990	6541
1991	13318	1991	–4966	1991	–13006	1991	6381
1992	10112	1992	–7373	1992	–12051	1992	5571
1993	9441	1993	–8547	1993	–11093	1993	4323
1994	9788	1994	–7809	1994	–11358	1994	4013
1995	10958	1995	–5418	1995	–10819	1995	6320
1996	13496	1996	–4928	1996	–8365	1996	9331
Mean for Q1	11381	Mean for Q2	–6617	Mean for Q3	–11147	Mean for Q4	6292

Sum of the means for each season = 11381 – 6617 – 11147 + 6292 = –91

Adjust to ensure total of seasonal effects = 0 by adding 91/4 = 23 to the mean for each season

Q1 effect	11404	Q2 effect	–6594	Q3 effect	–11124	Q4 effect	6315

forecast sales volume for Quarter 4 of 1998 it is first noted that Q4 1998 is period 40. The trend value is given by the regression equation:

$$T_t = 77347 + 216t \quad \text{As } t = 40$$

$$T_{1998Q4} = 86003$$

The seasonal factor for Q4 is 6315 so that the forecast value is:

Forecast for Q4 1998 = 86003 + 6315 = 92318

As this example provides a forecast for a date whose outcome is already known, we can compare the result with the actual figure for Q4 1998, which was 91248. The discrepancy between the two figures is 1070, which is less than 1.2 per cent of the forecast figure.

It should be noted that this example adopts the simplest possible approach, which may not be the most appropriate one for the particular set of data in question. A multiplicative model, the inclusion of a cyclical factor or changing the definition of 'season' in order to interpret 'winter' as December, January and February, 'spring' as March, April and May and so on, might all alter the quality of the forecast.

Stage 5: Evaluate the forecast

After a forecast has been made, it is then possible to evaluate it, and to compare it with the forecasts made using other approaches. Pecar (1993, p. 146) identifies six criteria that a good forecast should meet:

1. *Objectivity*: the result of the forecasting process should depend entirely on the data, not on the person making the forecast. The forecast made above meets this criterion.
2. *Validity*: the forecast should approximate the time-series that is the object of interest. Calculating the correlation coefficient between the forecast and the actual data allows validity to be checked. In this case the coefficient is equal to 0.987 which is very high. Squaring the correlation coefficient gives 0.97, showing that 97 per cent of the variation in the actual data (during the period used to make the forecast) is explained by the model providing the forecast.
3. *Reliability*: the method used should produce consistent results. Repeating the analysis using different start points and checking the similarity of the resulting forecasts allows reliability to be examined. In the example here, that exercise suggests that reliability has been achieved.
4. *Accuracy*: the forecast should produce results that are close to the actual outcomes, for the period outside that used to generate the forecast. A forecast may be reliable but not accurate but it cannot be accurate and not reliable. The simplest measure of accuracy is the percentage deviation from the outcome. For the single forecast period of Q4 1998, the current forecast has been shown to be highly accurate. However, a more thorough evaluation of accuracy requires paying attention to the performance of the forecast over a longer period. This is considered below.

5. *Confidence*: there should be a high probability that we can accept the results of the forecasting exercise. It is possible that a forecast may be accurate but the confidence interval around it may be so large that it becomes inadequate for long-term forecasting. The confidence level for the current example is considered further below.

6. *Sensitivity*: the method should provide very different results when presented with data embodying very different patterns. An insensitive method will produce similar results whatever data are entered into it. Time-series analysis by decomposition is generally an acceptably sensitive method. In the case in hand, the trend is only very slight. If the method is applied to other sets of data, very different patterns emerge.

Of these criteria the most practically important is accuracy. This can be assessed using a number of different measures (Pecar 1993, pp. 146–55). The simplest is the *mean error* (ME) which is the average difference between the forecast and the actual values. This can be done for two different sets of data. First it can be done for the time-series from which the forecasting model was generated, 1989–96 in our example. For the case in hand that gives a mean error of –0.4, which is almost infinitesimally small when compared with the magnitude of each observation. However, it is not too surprising that the mean accuracy is small when calculated for the time-period used to generate the model. The results are a measure of validity rather than forecasting accuracy. What is more important is the accuracy of the model in forecasting outside the time-period that was used to generate the model. In the case in hand, for the eight quarters of 1997 and 1998, the mean error was +1060 with a range of from –1054 to +2728. If mean error is calculated as 'actual minus forecast', the positive mean error indicates that on average the actual was greater than the forecast and there was consistent under-estimation of actual consumption.

The obvious weakness of the mean error as a measure of accuracy is that its calculation adds together positive and negative errors while maintaining their sign. If a forecast produces some very large positive and some very large negative errors that are roughly equal to each other, it will have a very small mean error but it is not very accurate. The obvious adjustment to make is to replace it with the *mean absolute error* (MAE), that is to say the average error, regardless of its sign. In the example here, that is equal to 1425 for the eight quarters of the forecast period 1997 and 1998.

There are many other measures of accuracy that might be adopted. Consistent with the 'least squares' approach in regression analysis the *mean square error* (MSE) may be calculated as the sum of the squared errors divided by their number. In the example that is equal to 2,940,595. Use of this criterion penalises forecasts that have a few large errors relative to those that have a large number of consistently small errors. As the MSE is expressed in different units from the original time-series it can be difficult to assess and the MSE figure for the example looks unacceptably large. A more common approach, therefore, is to use the *root mean square error* (RMSE) which is simply the square root of the MSE, which is expressed in the same units as the original time-series. For the example that is 1714. While the RMSE uses the same units as the original time-series, in itself it is difficult to interpret – does 1714 represent a high or a low level of accuracy? Hence it is more useful to divide it by the mean of the original time-series and express the result as a percentage, known as the *variation coefficient* (V). For the electricity forecasting example this gives a result of 2.12 per cent, suggesting a very high level of accuracy. The root mean square error of the forecast for electricity consumption over the period 1997–98 is equal to slightly more than 2 per cent of the average electricity consumption over the period 1989–96.

Other measures of accuracy include the *relative root mean square error* (RRMSE), the *mean percentage error* (MPE), the *mean absolute percentage error* (MAPE), *Theil's U1 statistic* and the *correlation coefficient*. While they all have value, one of the most useful is the *error variance*, which measures the dispersion of the errors around their mean. That is linked to the MSE by the following equation (Pecar 1993, p. 153):

MSE = error variance + square of the mean error (ME)

This makes it clear that the MSE is made up of two components. The first is the variability of the errors about their mean value and the second is the extent to which the errors are biased. Calculation of the error variance also allows a confidence interval to be placed around each estimate. In the example, for instance, the variance of the errors over the eight forecast quarters was 2077777 and their standard deviation (the square root of the variance) was 1441. As a confidence interval of 1.96 standard errors on either side of the estimate will cover 95 per cent of all observations, it can be said that we can have 95 per cent confidence that an actual observation will lie in a range of 2824 on either side of the forecast value.

The fundamental limitation of time-series forecasting is that it assumes time to be the only factor determining the value of the forecast variable, and that the structure of the relationship between time and the variable – the trend and the size of the seasonal factor – will remain constant into the future. In relatively stable times and circumstances this is a reasonable assumption to make. It has been possible to forecast UK electricity consumption with a high degree of accuracy for a short period ahead. However, it will tend to break down if the variable being forecast is subject to some structural change or crisis. If the same technique is applied to the industrial consumption of electricity in Hong Kong, for instance, it proves much less successful because the opening of the Chinese mainland in the 1980s led most manufacturing operations to be shifted out of the city and into Guangdong province where labour is much cheaper.

Barometric forecasting techniques

Time-series analysis uses information about the past in order to make forecasts of the future. Barometric forecasting uses indicators of current activity in order to provide forecasts of the future. Perhaps the most common barometric technique is the use of *leading indicators*. A leading indicator is a variable whose value is known to be correlated with the future value of the variable for which a forecast is required. For instance, to take a simple example, if we wish to forecast the number of children who will be entering school for the first time in five years' time in the United Kingdom, the number of children born this year will provide a very useful leading indicator. In that example the connection between the leading indicator and the variable being forecast is very close indeed. In other cases there may be no obvious causal link between the indicator and the variable being forecast. It has been suggested, for instance, that sunspot activity is closely correlated with the business cycle (another reason perhaps for being suspicious about the value of the cyclical component!).

Given the importance to business people of being able to predict general movements in the level of economic activity, there are a large number of leading indicators that are used in the attempt to identify changes in total spending, income and employment. These include new orders for machine tools, which often rise in advance of an increase in economic activity, the length of the working week, and the performance of the Stock Exchange. A number of such general leading indicators used in the United Kingdom or the United States are as follows:

- new orders for machine tools
- average hours worked in manufacturing
- index of new business formation
- new orders for durable goods
- orders for plant and equipment
- new building starts
- changes in manufacturing inventories
- industrial materials prices
- Stock Exchange indices
- profit figures
- price to unit labour cost ratios
- increases in consumer debt.

In recent years leading indicators have been shown to be useful in a number of settings. Banking crises can be predicted from a number of macroeconomic and financial measures (Hardy and Pazarbasioglu 1999), stock prices predict investment (Aylward and Glen 2000), and a set of composite leading indicators has shown value in predicting inflation (Bikker and Kennedy 1999).

The marketing approach to demand measurement

In the simple economic model of the firm, the business being modelled produces a single product for a single market, and the amount of information required on the level of demand is relatively limited. Real companies are much more complex and require a great deal more information concerning the markets in which they operate.

Different categories of market

In the first place, distinctions may be drawn between a number of different concepts of 'the market' for a product (see any introductory marketing text for a typical marketing treatment of these concepts). The *potential market* for a product is that group of households and organisations that indicate some interest in the product on offer. However, not all of these potential purchasers will have the income needed to turn their interest into an actual purchase, and some of those who have both an interest and the necessary income will not have access to the product. The *available market* is the group of consumers who have the interest, the necessary income and access to the product. Very few companies make sales to every possible purchaser in the available market, and the *served market* is the group of households and organisations on which the company decides to focus. Finally, the *penetrated market* is those customers who actually buy the product.

This categorisation of 'the market' suggests that firms may need information on four different aspects of the market for their product. Furthermore, the firm's 'product' may also be defined at a number of different levels. Most obviously there is the distinction between the market for the industry as a whole and the market for the individual firm. However, very few firms produce a single product so that information will also be needed on the market for a product line, within that the market for a product form, and within that the market for an individual product item.

When it is also recognised that a firm needs information on different geographical markets, including local, regional, national, continental and global, and for different time-periods, perhaps simply short term, medium term and long term, then it becomes very clear that an enormous amount of information is potentially required if a firm is to be fully informed about its markets. This information may be collected in a number of different ways.

Market surveys

Perhaps the best-known form of market research is the market survey. This is not only used to forecast the level of demand for a product, but may be used for a wide range of other purposes as well, including testing buyers' reactions to different product configurations and packaging, and identifying links between purchasing behaviour and other variables, like buyers' age, sex, social status and income. If the aim is to estimate the level of demand, a sample of buyers is asked direct questions about their intentions with respect to purchasing the product within a specified future period. That information is used in conjunction with other evidence about the potential market to construct an estimate of the total volume of sales. The effectiveness of this technique depends upon a number of variables.

First, it depends upon the number of potential buyers. If the number is very large, only a small sample can be reached for a reasonable cost. It may be possible to construct a truly representative sample, in which case the results from that sample can be extrapolated in order to reach a forecast for the market as a whole. However, if the sample should contain an unknown bias, which can be difficult to avoid, the results will also be biased and could give misleading estimates. Market surveys are therefore of most use when the number of potential buyers is small so that a very high proportion of them can be questioned.

The second variable that determines the usefulness of market surveys is the clarity of buyers' intentions. If buyers themselves are vague about their own intentions they will be unable to provide useful information to the market researcher.

Other factors that will affect the cost effectiveness of market surveys are as follows:

- the cost of identifying and contacting buyers
- buyers' willingness to disclose their intentions
- buyers' propensity to carry out their intentions.

This analysis suggests that market surveys will be of most value for industrial products, for consumer durables and for other products where buyers plan their purchases in advance. Market surveys may also be useful for new products where there is no past data on sales, so that time-series analysis or estimation is not possible.

Sales force opinion

If market surveys are inappropriate, an indirect method of forecasting buyers' intentions is to survey the sales force, asking them to provide estimates of the future volume of sales. Clearly, this approach is fraught with problems as the sales force may not be fully aware of changes in the economy that may affect sales, or changes in the firm's marketing strategy. Furthermore, the sales force may have an incentive to provide biased forecasts in pursuit of their own interests. They may provide deliberate under-estimates of sales in order to be given low sales quotas which they will be able to exceed without effort, or over-estimates in order to justify their continued employment. This is an example of the principal/agent problem referred to in Chapter 4. It may be possible for the firm to devise methods that bring the interests of the firm and the interests of the sales force together, so that the sales force has an incentive to provide accurate forecasts. Bonuses could be linked to the accuracy of forecasts, for instance, or the amount spent on advertising and promotion could be linked to the forecast level of sales in order to avoid deliberate under-estimation. (This last approach could, of course, prove counter-productive if sales people deliberately over-estimate sales in order to secure greater advertising and promotion in their territories.)

While sales force opinion clearly has its drawbacks as a forecasting tool there are advantages in the method, both as a means of collecting data and as a more general instrument of good management. The sales force is closer to customers than most other groups within the firm, and may be able to spot trends first. Their knowledge is at a very detailed level with respect to different products, markets, distribution channels and individual customers, which may allow a more accurate forecast than a more aggregated approach. If the sales force is directly involved in the construction of forecasts and the setting of sales quotas they will have a better understanding of that process and will tend to exhibit greater commitment and motivation as a result.

Expert opinion

A third approach to demand forecasting is to ask experts in the field to provide their own estimates of future sales volume. Experts may include executives directly involved in the market, such as dealers, distributors and suppliers, or others whose major interest is in the forecast itself, such as stockbrokers' industry analysts, specialist marketing consultants or officers of the trade association. Various mechanisms exist for the construction of such forecasts. Most obviously, each expert could be asked independently to provide a confidential estimate and the results could be averaged. The advantage of that approach is that there is no danger that the group of experts develop a group-think mentality where their independent judgement is impaired by their desire to be seen as loyal and conforming members of the group. On the other hand, if estimates are produced entirely independently the experts have no opportunity to weigh the opinions of others or to take into account factors known to the others but not to themselves.

One well-known approach that seeks to avoid 'group-think' while allowing the experts to pool their knowledge is the Delphi technique (Rowe and Wright 1999). Each participant is asked independently to produce a forecast. Each of these forecasts, with the reasoning behind it, is then presented as feedback to each of the participants, with anonymity being maintained so that none of the experts know who is responsible for the other forecasts. Each of the experts is then asked to revise their own forecasts in the light of the forecasts and reasoning of the others, and this process is repeated until a consensus is reached. This may not always be possible if the experts disagree and will not allow their opinions to be shifted, but experience with the method suggests that the process of iteration does often lead to the convergence of the different forecasts around an agreed value. Delphi has been used to forecast demand in a variety of settings, including international tourism and the market for broad-band telecommunications (Wright 1998).

Market testing

If a product is new, or an established product is being sold in a new market or through a new distribution channel, there will be no past data to analyse. Direct questioning of buyers will be difficult as they will have only hypothetical information about the product's characteristics and neither the sales force nor the experts will have any solid basis of experience on which to base estimates of the likely demand. In this situation market testing may be the most appropriate method of collecting information. A number of different methods may be employed.

Sales-wave research involves selecting a group of consumers, supplying them with the product at no cost and then re-offering them the product and/or competitors' products at reduced prices a number of times. This allows the market researchers to measure the repeat purchase rate and to estimate the impact of different competing brands. Different groups of buyers may also be exposed to different packaging and different advertising concepts, in order to evaluate their differential effect.

Illustration 1

Simulated store techniques involve establishing a group of shoppers, showing them a number of advertising commercials, including those relating to the new product, and then giving them small amounts of money which they may spend or keep. The amounts spent on the product being investigated are noted, as is spending on competing brands. The group of shoppers are brought together to discuss their immediate reactions to the products and the reasons for their purchasing behaviour, and follow-up telephone interviews are carried out later, to establish consumers' more lasting responses.

Test marketing involves actually selling the product in a limited number of locations, while providing different marketing mixes (see Chapter 16) or different packaging, advertising or promotional concepts in order to test their effectiveness. The scale of test marketing may vary from a limited exercise in a small number of participating stores, independent of the firm's usual distribution channels, to a full-scale exercise involving whole regions.

While test marketing can provide a realistic simulation of an actual product launch and may allow the company to identify any product faults that have been overlooked, it can be expensive and may not prove an accurate means of forecasting total sales volume. The markets in which the tests take place may not be representative of the market as a whole, and general economic conditions may vary between the test marketing and the actual product launch. Perhaps most important of all, test marketing reveals the company's intentions to competitors and they may well take counter-measures, in which case the environment into which the product is launched will be substantially different to that in which the test took place, invalidating its results.

Clearly, there are no perfect solutions to the problem of demand forecasting. The choice of technique depends to a very great extent upon the particular circumstances, the cost of acquiring better information and the value of the investment put at risk if a venture should fail. If the price of failure is low there is little point in spending substantial sums on improving demand forecasts. On the other hand, if the cost of failure is high, spending on the acquisition of additional information will be well worthwhile.

Illustration 1 **Measuring the elasticity of demand for liquor – a US example**

Taxes on alcohol are a major revenue earner in many economies, which implies that the elasticity of demand for liquor is of considerable practicable importance. If elasticity is low, a tax increase will lead to large increases in tax revenue, and the tax will be largely passed on to consumers. If elasticity is high, tax revenue will be much smaller as consumers forego consumption of the product and most of the tax is absorbed by the producers.

J.L. Simon (1966) attempted to measure this important parameter, using a method that he described as 'quasi-experimental'. This consisted of a number of steps. First, monthly data were collected for the price of liquor in each of the American states. If the price changed by more than 2 per cent, then a 'price change event' was said to have taken place. (States where the production of illicit 'moonshine' liquor was important were excluded.) Second, per capita consumption of liquor was calculated for the twelve-month period that began three months before the 'price change event', and the twelve-month period that began three months after it. This gave a figure for consumption 'before' and 'after' the price change. The gap of six months was introduced in order to avoid the changes in demand that arise from consumers' attempts to stock up before a price change, and to use up those stored purchases in the period after the price change. Third, the change in consumption for the state in which the price change event took place was compared with the change in consumption in other states, taking care to exclude other states which themselves experienced price changes or sales tax changes. This provided a measure of the proportionate change in demand given by the following formula:

$$\frac{\text{Change in per capita consumption, following the price change}}{\text{Per capita consumption in comparison states, before the price change}}$$

minus

$$\frac{\text{Change in per capita consumption in comparison states}}{\text{Per capita consumption in comparison states, before the price change}}$$

Fourth, the proportionate relative change in price was estimated by calculating the actual change and comparing it with the actual change in the price of popular 'benchmark' brands. Finally, the change in quantity, as calculated above, was divided by the change in price as calculated, giving an estimate for elasticity of demand.

This process produced estimates for the different states that had a median value of –0.79, corresponding to the theoretical expectation that the demand for liquor is inelastic. The median was used as a measure of central tendency in preference to the mean in order to eliminate the influence of 'outliers' (i.e. extreme observations), and in order to avoid the conceptual problem associated with the fact that for six states elasticity was estimated to be positive, implying an upward-sloping demand curve. Indeed, the estimates for individual states varied from +0.97 to –4.35, which is a very substantial variation.

Simon's central conclusion with respect to the price elasticity of demand for liquor was that 'we may say with 0.965 probability that the mean of the population from which this sample of elasticity estimates was drawn is between –0.03 and –0.97'. If the exact value of elasticity were of crucial importance, this could hardly be said to be a very useful result. On the other hand, the key issue for policy is whether demand is elastic or inelastic. As the result suggests quite strongly that demand is inelastic, policy-makers can perhaps rest assured that liquor taxes are indeed a useful way to raise revenue, whose immediate burden falls largely on consumers.

Illustration 2 Estimating the elasticity of demand for gas in Hong Kong

In July 1995 the Consumer Council of Hong Kong (CCHK) published a report on the gas industry in the territory. That report contained annual estimates for the price elasticity of demand for town gas, manufactured by the monopolist Hong Kong and China Gas company, which varied from –1.384 in 1991 to +0.706 in 1993. However, those estimates were arrived at by the unacceptably crude process of taking the annual percentage change in quantity consumed and dividing it by

Illustration 2

the annual percentage change in price. The report also made the further error of interpreting the results to mean that electricity and liquefied petroleum gas (LPG) 'are not close substitutes for town gas with consumers having limited liability to switch in response to price changes' (CCHK 1995, p. 61). Lam (1996) pointed out that changes in consumption of town gas were caused by other factors, as well as price changes, and that it is cross-elasticity, not own-price elasticity, that determines whether or not two products are substitutes for each other.

In order to provide more appropriate estimates Lam (1996) set out the following single equation econometric model:

$$QUANTITY = \beta_0 + \beta_1 PRICE + \beta_2 INCOME + \beta_3 LPGPRICE$$
$$+ \beta_4 CLPPRICE + \beta_5 DUMMY$$

where:

QUANTITY = total sales of town gas in million megajoules (MJ)
PRICE = average price of town gas in HK$ per MJ
INCOME = gross domestic product of Hong Kong in HK$ million
LPGPRICE = list price of LPG in HK$/kg
CLPPRICE = average price of electricity charged by the China Light and Power Company in HK$/MJ
DUMMY = 0 before 1982, 1 after 1982

This equation represents the influence of the most significant factors on the demand for town gas: own-price, income and the price of substitutes. The dummy variable represents the influence of an important safety report, published in 1981, which placed severe restrictions on the storage and transportation of LPG, thereby diverting demand towards town gas. All variables were expressed as logarithms, so that the regression co-efficients β_1, β_2, β_3, β_4 represent the own-price, income and cross-price elasticities respectively. Table 8.5 sets out the results.

Table 8.5 The estimation of elasticities for town gas in Hong Kong (standard errors in parentheses)

Dependent variable = QUANTITY	Estimates for β
PRICE	–0.263 (0.587)
INCOME	1.531** (0.077)
LPGPRICE	0.059 (0.515)
CLPPRICE	–0.053 (0.202)
DUMMY	0.363** (0.084)
CONSTANT	–8.063**
R^2	0.993

** Statistically significant at the 1% level
Source: Lam (1996, p. 717).

As the results show, only INCOME and the DUMMY were significant. There appeared to be no significant cross-elasticity of demand between town gas and either electricity or LPG although the negative sign of the cross-elasticity on CLPPRICE suggested that town gas and electricity might be complements, rather than substitutes, which is credible.

While these results represent a significant improvement on the very crude estimates presented by the Consumer Council, they also illustrate the difficulties involved. The sample size (twenty-one years' data) is relatively small and multi-collinearity among the independent variables has the effect of increasing the standard errors of the estimates. There may also be an identification problem (although it may be argued that as the company has an obligation to supply whatever is demanded, that does not apply). Only with more data (which would be impossible to obtain) and more sophisticated econometric techniques involving simultaneous equations could analysts be really certain that the elasticities had been estimated with sufficient accuracy.

Illustration 3   Forecasting the demand for high definition televisions

One of the most difficult tasks facing the forecaster concerns predicting the sales of a new product, especially if that new product represents a significant innovation. Bayus (1993) examined three published reports that attempted to forecast the sales of high definition television (HDTV) sets after the introduction of the new technology.

In the early 1990s it was predicted that HDTV would be the most likely form for the new generation of television, bringing cinema quality definition and CD quality sound into the home. As sales data could not be observed, the most natural approach to forecasting lay in the use of analogy – using information on the sales history of 'similar products' to produce the forecast. The American Electronics Association (AEA) predicted sales of 11 million units by 2010, the Electronic Industries Association (EIA) predicted 13.2 million units by 2003 and the National Telecommunications Information Administration (NTIA) predicted 18.6 million units by 2008. In the light of these wide discrepancies, Bayus (1993) set out to evaluate the forecasts.

In the first step, three models were fitted to the data for twenty-seven different consumer durables. The first was a diffusion model (Bass 1969) which predicts the sales of a product using cumulative sales to date and the size of the potential market. The second was an exponential time trend model which was fitted to the trend of prices for the twenty-seven products. The third was a learning curve model (see Chapter 9) which was fitted to the data for cost per unit, capturing the way in which costs of production for each product declined over the period following its introduction. Having fitted these models, six parameters taken from their results were used to carry out an exploratory factor analysis, in order to find out whether the six were reflecting a smaller number of 'underlying' constructs. The results suggested that there were two such factors – a 'manufacturing' factor and a 'marketing' factor. The scores for these factors for the twenty-seven household appliances were then used as inputs to a cluster analysis, which identified five clusters of appliances – groups of appliances that were similar to each other but dissimilar to the members of other groups. Calculation and examination of the classification functions showed that new products could be assigned to an appropriate cluster with a reasonable degree of accuracy.

Having gone through this extraordinarily complex set of procedures Bayus (1993) then used them to evaluate the published forecasts for HDTV. By comparing those forecasts with the prior sales histories of home appliances having similar characteristics he concluded that the forecasts by the AEA implied similar coefficients in their forecasting model as those found for similar appliances. Hence that estimate was evaluated as appropriate. For the other two forecasts, the implied coefficients were inconsistent with those for similar products, and with the stated assumptions made, and hence they were judged to be inappropriate. Whether that evaluation will itself prove to be accurate will have to wait until 2010. In the meantime it is only possible to speculate on whether such a complex approach to forecast evaluation yields significant real benefits, or whether it simply satisfies academics' desire to use difficult and exotic statistical techniques.

References and further reading

A. Aylward and J. Glen 'Some International Evidence on Stock Prices as Leading Indicators of Economic Activity', *Applied Financial Economics*, February 2000, pp. 1–14.

F. Bass, 'A New Product Growth Model for Consumer Durables', *Management Science*, vol. 15, January 1969, pp. 215–27.

M. Baye, D. Jansen and J. Lee, 'Advertising Effects in Complete Demand Systems', *Applied Economics*, vol. 24, 1992, pp. 1087–96.

B. Bayus, 'High Definition Television: Assessing Demand Forecasts for a Next Generation Consumer Durable', *Management Science*, vol. 39, no. 11, November 1993, pp. 1319–33

A. Bemmaor and D. Mouchoux, 'Measuring the Short Term Effect of In-Store Promotion and Retail Advertising on Brand Sales: A Factorial Experiment', *Journal of Marketing Research*, vol. 28, May 1991, pp. 202–14.

J. Bikker and N. Kennedy, 'Composite Leading Indicators of Underlying Inflation for Seven EU Countries', *Journal of Forecasting*, July 1999, pp. 225–58.

Consumer Council of Hong Kong (CCHK), *Assessing Competition in the Domestic Water Heating and Cooking Fuel Market*, CCHK, Hong Kong, July 1995.

A. Deaton, *Models and Projections of Demand in Post-war Britain*, London, Chapman and Hall, 1975.

R. Dolan and H. Simon, *Power Pricing*, New York, Free Press, 1996.

D. Hardy and C. Pazarbasioglu, 'Determinants and Leading Indicators of Banking Crises: Further Evidence', *IMF Staff Papers*, September–December 1999, pp. 247–58.

S. Hoch, B. Kim, A. Montgomery and P. Rossi, 'Determinants of Store Level Price Elasticity', *Journal of Marketing Research*, vol. 32, February 1995, pp. 17–29.

P-L. Lam, 'Re-structuring the Hong Kong Gas Industry', *Energy Policy*, vol. 24, no. 8, 1996, pp. 713–22.

N. Malhotra, M. Peterson and S. Kleiser, 'Marketing Research: A State-of-the-art Review and Directions for the Twenty-first Century', *Journal of the Academy of Marketing Science*, vol. 27, no. 2, Spring 1999, pp. 160–83.

J. McGuigan, R. Moyer and F. Harris, *Managerial Economics: Applications, Strategy and Tactics*, Cincinnati, South-Western College Publishing, 1999.

B. Pecar, *Business Forecasting for Management*, London, McGraw-Hill, 1993.

G. Rowe and G. Wright, 'The Delphi Technique as a Forecasting Tool', *International Journal of Forecasting*, October 1999, pp. 353–75.

J.L. Simon, 'The Price Elasticity of Liquor in the US and a Simple Method of Determination', *Econometrica*, 1966.

R. Stone, *Measurement of Consumers' Expenditure and Behaviour in the United Kingdom, 1920–38*, Cambridge, Cambridge University Press, 1954.

G. Tellis, 'The Price Elasticity of Selective Demand: A Meta-Analysis of Econometric Models of Sales', *Journal of Marketing Research*, vol. 25, November 1988, pp. 331–41.

D. Wright, 'Analysis of the Market for Access to Broadband Telecommunications in the Year 2000', *Computers and Operations Research*, February 1998, pp. 127–38.

Self-test questions

1. Which of the following goods would you expect to have very low price and income elasticities of demand?

   (a) table salt

   (b) brandy

   (c) golf club membership

   (d) designer clothing

   (e) telephone calls

2. Of the goods listed in question 1 above, which would you expect to have very high income elasticities of demand?

3. Which of the following best describes a 'leading indicator'?

   (a) a variable in which changes follow changes in a variable we are trying to forecast

   (b) a variable that changes in advance of a variable we are trying to forecast

   (c) a variable that changes at the same time as one we are trying to forecast

4. The list below shows a number of goods and a number of forecasting techniques. Which technique is best suited to which good?

   (a) an industrial product with a limited potential market

   (b) a consumer good that has been on sale for many years

   (c) a new product whose full-scale launch will be very expensive

   (d) a technically very complex new product, to be sold in a very wide market

   (A) time-series analysis

   (B) expert opinion

   (C) market testing

   (D) survey of buyer' intentions

5. In which of the following situations will there be no 'identification problem'?

   (a) if it is known that neither supply nor demand curves have shifted

   (b) if it is known that both supply and demand conditions have shifted

   (c) if it is known that only the supply curve has shifted

   (d) if it is known that only the demand curve has shifted

Essay question

Explain the difference between estimation and forecasting and outline the difficulties associated with *one* method of each.

9 Production and the determination of costs

This chapter begins by setting out the basic relationships between inputs and outputs, as represented by the production function. Isoquants are then used to identify the cost-minimising combinations of inputs in both the short run and the long run, and this analysis is linked to the concept of the cost curve. The sources of scale economies and diseconomies are then analysed, paying particular attention to the problems of empirical estimation through statistical analysis, the engineering approach and the survivor technique. Having completed the analysis of scale economies, attention is then given to economies of scope and learning effects. Cost structures in the information sectors are then examined before completing the chapter with a brief examination of other 'cost drivers' and break-even analysis.

Production functions and isoquants

The production function and its properties

The starting point for the economic analysis of production and costs is to be found in the *production function*, which is simply a mathematical statement of the relationship between inputs and outputs. In its simplest and most general form the production function is usually written as follows:

$Q = f(K, L)$ where:

> Q = level of output
> K = a measure of the capital input
> L = a measure of the labour input

There are various more specific functional forms that could be taken by the production function, but one of the most useful and best known is the *Cobb–Douglas* production function, which is written:

$Q = AK^a L^b$ where:

> A = a constant
> a, b = positive fractions

The production function is assumed to have a number of properties. In the first place, both K and L are assumed to be infinitely divisible and independently variable and the function is continuous, so that output increases smoothly as either the capital input, the labour input, or both, are increased. If the level of one input, capital for instance, is kept constant and the level of the other input (labour) altered, the rate at which output changes is known as the marginal product of labour. In accordance with the *principle of diminishing returns* it is assumed that, as more and more of one factor of production is combined with fixed quantities of another, the point must eventually be reached where marginal product begins to decline.

For the specific case of the Cobb–Douglas function, simple calculus can be used to calculate the marginal product of a factor, and the slope of the marginal product curve:

$$\text{marginal product of labour (MPL)} = \frac{dQ}{dL} = bAK^aL^{b-1}$$

$$\text{slope of the marginal product curve} = \frac{dMPL}{dL} = (b-1)(b)AK^aL^{b-2}$$

As $0 < b < 1$ the slope of the marginal product curve is always negative, and it can be seen that the Cobb–Douglas function has the simple property of a marginal product curve which always slopes downwards.

If both factors of production are increased together, the impact on the level of output depends upon the returns to scale exhibited by the production function. In the case of the Cobb–Douglas example, if both capital and labour are increased by the factor 'k' it is relatively easy to calculate the increase in output:

Initial output $Q_1 = AK^aL^b$

Increased output $Q^* = A(kK)^a(kL)^b = AK^aL^bk^{a+b} = Q_1k^{a+b}$

As the equation shows, if the level of inputs increases by the factor k, the level of output increases by k^{a+b}. If $(a+b) > 1$, there are increasing returns to scale, as the increase in output is larger than the increase in inputs. If $(a+b) = 1$ there are constant returns to scale, with outputs increasing at the same rate as inputs, and if $(a+b) < 1$ there are decreasing returns to scale.

Isoquants

A production function can be represented graphically through the use of isoquants. An isoquant is a curve connecting all combinations of inputs that give the same level of output, when combined efficiently. Figure 9.1 provides some examples.

The isoquants are smooth curves, reflecting the assumption that there are continuous possibilities for substitution between one factor of production and another. They are convex to the origin or concave upwards (like indifference curves, to which they are formally equivalent) and their slope shows the rate at which one factor has to be substituted for another in order to maintain a constant level of output. This is known as the *marginal rate of technical substitution*. There is an isoquant for every possible level of output, and isoquants can never cross each other.

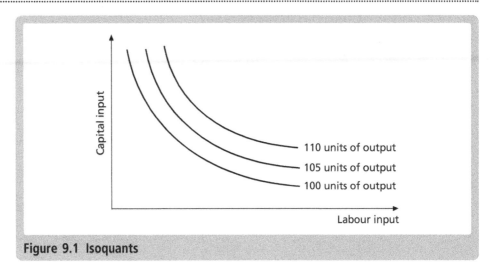

Figure 9.1 Isoquants

The figure shows isoquants labelled: 110 units of output, 105 units of output, 100 units of output, with Capital input on the vertical axis and Labour input on the horizontal axis.

If a set of isoquants were drawn for equal increments of output, the distances between the isoquants would reflect the returns to scale embodied in the production function, as shown in Figure 9.2(a) to (c).

In Figure 9.2(a), the isoquants are evenly spaced, illustrating constant returns to scale. In Figure 9.2(b) they are closer together as the distance from the origin increases, showing that there are increasing returns to scale, and in Figure 9.2(c) they are further apart, indicating decreasing returns to scale.

In the language of economic theory, a production function represents *a technology*, which encompasses all known methods of producing the commodity in question. Each point on an isoquant represents a *technique*, embodying a particular method of production, using a particular ratio of capital to labour. It is worth noting that this terminology differs from the layman's usage of the term 'technology', where it is quite in order to refer to 'a labour-intensive technology' or a 'capital-intensive technology'. In economic theory a given state of technology is deemed to encompass knowledge of a virtually infinite range of techniques.

Isoquants may be used to illustrate the way in which a firm can increase its output in the long run and the short run. In the short run, there are some fixed factors of production, represented by the capital input, and output can only be increased by using more of the variable factor, which is labour. If, in Figure 9.3, the level of capital input is fixed at K*, the short-run expansion path for output is given by the line K*B. For equal increments in output, shown by the isoquants, increasingly large increments of labour input are required, as the diagram shows, illustrating the principle of diminishing returns.

In the long run, inputs of both capital and labour can be increased in order to raise the level of output. The expansion path for output, given the use of a technique with a fixed ratio of capital to labour, will be a ray from the origin, as shown by the lines OX_1 and OX_2 in Figure 9.3. The line OX_1 indicates the use of a relatively capital-intensive technique, while OX_2 shows a more labour-intensive approach.

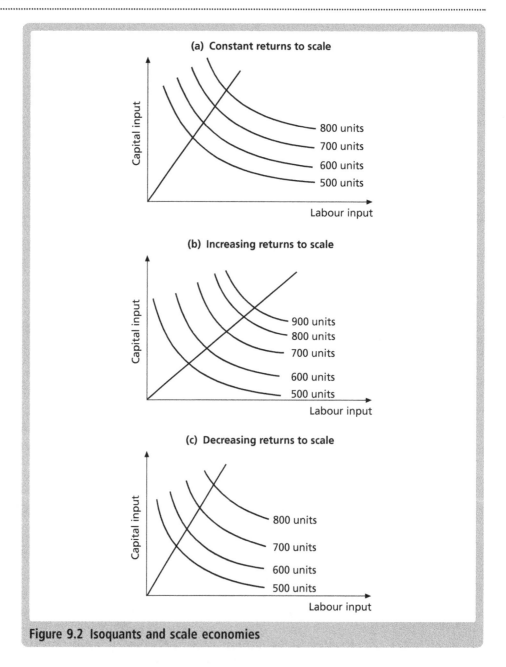

Figure 9.2 Isoquants and scale economies

Cost-minimising choice of technique

Isoquants provide a graphical means by which the cost-minimising technique of production can be identified. If the unit cost of labour is w and the unit cost of capital is r then total cost is given by the equation:

$$TC = (w)(L) + (r)(K) \qquad \text{where:}$$

$$L = \text{units of labour hired}$$
$$K = \text{units of capital hired}$$

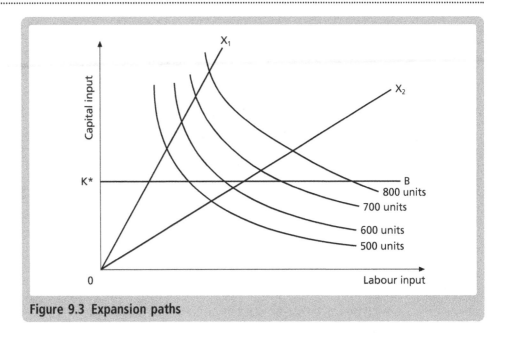

Figure 9.3 Expansion paths

If the cost-minimising method of producing Q* units of output is to be found, the problem can be stated in terms of the equations as:

Minimise TC = (w)(L) + (r)(K)

subject to Q* = f(K, L)

In terms of the diagrams the combinations of capital and labour that may be purchased for a given amount of expenditure are given by a straight line, known as an *isocost* line, whose slope is the ratio of the factor prices. Higher levels of spending have isocost lines that are further away from the origin, as shown in Figure 9.4. If level of output Q* is to be produced at minimum cost, it is necessary to find the lowest cost at which the firm can purchase a combination of capital and labour that is sufficient to produce output Q*. This can be seen in Figure 9.4, as the point where an isocost line is a tangent to the isoquant for output Q*.

It is clear from Figure 9.4 that the cost-minimising technique of production depends upon the relative prices of capital and labour. If labour is relatively expensive, the isocost lines will be relatively steep and the chosen production technique will be capital intensive. In the opposite case, if labour is cheap, the isocost lines will be relatively flat and the cost-minimising technique will be relatively labour intensive.

The diagrammatic version of the analysis can also be used to examine the condition for cost minimisation in more detail. The condition for optimality is that the slope of the isocost line should be equal to the slope of the isoquant. It can readily be seen from the diagram that the slope of the isocost line is equal to the ratio of the factor prices (w/r). The slope of the isoquant is equal to the marginal rate of substitution which is in turn equal to the ratio of the marginal product

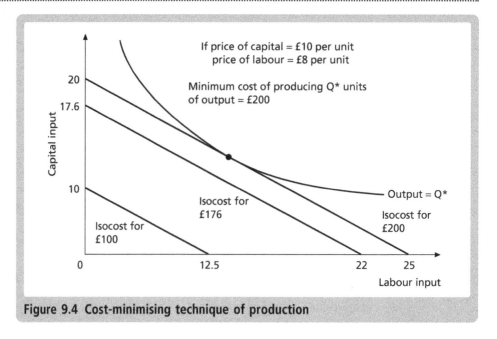

Figure 9.4 Cost-minimising technique of production

of labour to the marginal product of capital. The equilibrium condition, then, could also be written:

$$\frac{w}{r} = \frac{MP_L}{MP_K}$$

This is turn could be rewritten to give:

$$\frac{MP_L}{w} = \frac{MP_K}{r}$$

The last equation is the intuitively plausible result that cost minimisation requires the marginal productivity of the last £1 spent on labour to equal the marginal productivity of the last £1 spent on capital. If that were not the case it would be possible to shift spending from one factor to another and increase output without increasing cost.

Cost curves in the short run and the long run

From production functions to cost curves

The analysis set out above shows the amount of each factor of production that will be employed in order to achieve cost minimisation for one particular level of output, on the assumptions that the amounts of both capital and labour can be varied, but factor prices and the available technology remain constant. The resulting combination of a level of output and a figure for total cost provides one point on the firm's long-run cost curve. If the exercise were repeated for different levels of output the results would trace out a long-run total cost curve. The shape of this curve, and the long-run average cost curve, clearly depends upon the returns to scale that are represented by the production function. If there are increasing returns to scale, the long-run average cost curve will slope downwards. If there are decreasing returns to scale the long-run cost curve will slope upwards, and constant returns to scale will be reflected in a horizontal long-run cost curve.

In the short run, the level of capital input is fixed, as shown in Figure 9.3, so that costs are not arrived at by calculating the cost-minimising ratio of capital to labour as in the isocost/isoquant analysis in Figure 9.4. Returns to scale are also irrelevant as scale can only be varied in the long run. The level of cost in the short run is determined by the total cost associated with the combinations of capital and labour given by the line K*B in Figure 9.3. The determining factors for cost here are the spreading of the fixed costs across a larger number of units of output, on the one hand, and the principle of diminishing returns on the other. Fixed costs per unit fall as the level of output rises, but variable costs per unit tend to rise beyond a certain point.

Short-run cost curves

The total and average short-run cost curves implied by this analysis are shown in Figure 9.5(a) and (b). As the figure shows, fixed cost (FC) is constant, at an amount equal to K*r (the cost of using K* units of capital), yielding a downward-sloping curve for average fixed cost (AFC). Variable cost (VC) increases with a slope that first decreases (indicating decreasing marginal cost) and then increases (indicating increasing marginal cost) giving an average variable cost (AVC) curve which falls and then rises.

The combination of fixed and variable costs yields an average total cost curve (ATC) which is U-shaped and which is intersected by the marginal cost curve (MC) at its lowest point.

Long-run cost curves

In the long run the firm is free to choose whichever combination of inputs it expects to be most profitable, and in the long run the firm is essentially concerned with investment decisions. The behaviour of costs in this period depends fundamentally upon the extent to which there are economies of scale to be had from the construction of larger sets of plant and equipment.

Long-run cost curves can be constructed from a set of short-run curves. As each short-run curve shows how costs will behave when the firm has a fixed level of capital input (or is restricted to a given set of plant and equipment), the long run may be thought of as the period in which the firm chooses on which short-run cost curve to locate itself. The implication is that the long-run average cost curve is simply made up of segments of short-run cost curves. This is illustrated in Figure 9.6.

The curves SAC$_1$ to SAC$_5$ are short-run average cost curves for each of the known sets of plant and equipment in an industry where only five such sets exist. If the firm plans to produce output Q$_1$ it has a choice between SAC$_1$ and SAC$_2$, but will choose SAC$_2$ as it gives lower costs per unit. As a result, point A on SAC$_2$ is

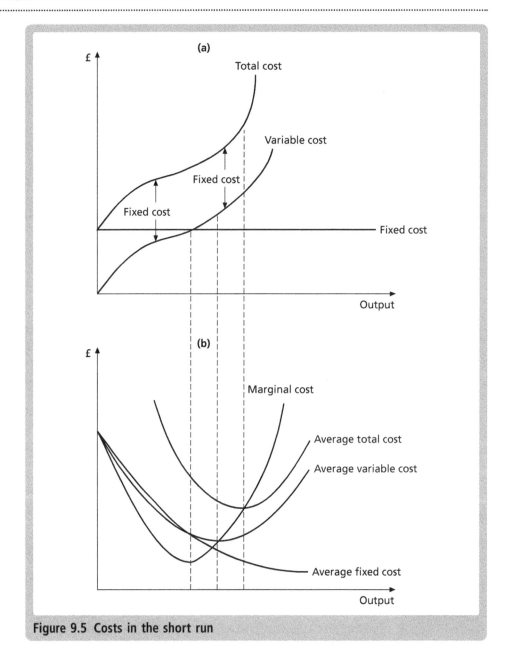

Figure 9.5 Costs in the short run

also a point on the long-run cost curve LAC. In Figure 9.6 the long-run cost curve
is indicated by the scallop-shaped heavy line.

In this example the long-run cost curve is discontinuous because, for the sake
of exposition, it has been assumed that there are only five known sets of plant
and equipment in this industry. However, as noted above, the usual assumption
is that both factors of production are infinitely divisible so that the amount of
capital used could be augmented by very small amounts, generating an almost
infinite number of different sets of plant and equipment. In that case there will

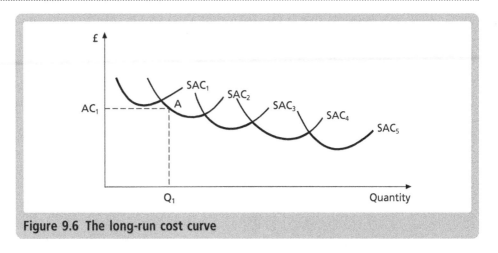

Figure 9.6 The long-run cost curve

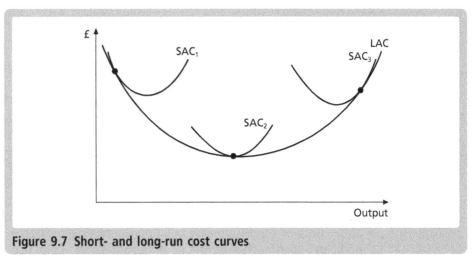

Figure 9.7 Short- and long-run cost curves

be an almost infinite number of short-run cost curves and the long-run cost curve will become smooth and continuous. Nevertheless, it is important to remember that every point on a long-run cost curve corresponds to a point on a short-run cost curve. The long-run cost curve is the 'envelope' of a set of short-run curves. Figure 9.7 shows a long-run cost curve and three of the short-run curves that underlie it.

Economies and diseconomies of scale

The sources of scale economies

The shape of the long-run cost curve is a matter of great significance for the structure and performance of an industry and has been the object of consider-able debate, both in terms of theoretical analysis and in terms of attempts to provide empirical measurements of scale effects. Theoretical analysis of scale effects suggests that both costs of production and distribution and costs of managing and controlling the enterprise need to be taken into account when considering the impact of higher levels of output on unit costs. If attention is first focused on the factors that reduce costs then it is possible to identify a number of general sources of scale economies. The first of these arises from the simple mathematics of many *production engineering relationships*. If, for example, an industrial process requires mixing or some similar activity to take place, the surface area of the tank in which the mixing is to take place increases much less rapidly than its volume. If cost depends upon the surface area but output depends upon the volume, scale economies will result as larger volumes can be processed with less than proportionate increases in cost. One classic study (Haldi and Whitcomb 1967) suggested that such factors lead to an exponential relationship between total costs and the level of output of the form:

$$TC = aQ^b \quad \text{where:}$$

$$TC = \text{total cost;} \quad Q = \text{output;} \quad a,b = \text{constants}$$

In this equation b is the scale coefficient, which is estimated to take a value around 0.6, indicating that a 100 per cent increase in output can be had for a 60 per cent increase in costs.

The second source of scale economies lies in the existence of *indivisibilities*. If some items of equipment, or some activities, have a minimum size and cannot be divided up into smaller units, operating them at less than capacity will involve a cost penalty. If a series of processes, each involving indivisibilities, are linked vertically, this effect will be magnified as efficient production will require balancing the processes against each other. For example, if a simple industrial process consists of mixing, heating and then pouring the raw material, and if mixing machines only work efficiently at three units of output per day, heating machines at five units of output per day and pouring machines at seven units per day, the plant will not reach minimum cost until output is equal to $(3 \times 5 \times 7) = 105$ units per day.

Indivisibilities are not restricted solely to aspects of production engineering, but extend into administration and management as well. The production of an invoice is an indivisible activity that may cost as much for a transaction of £1,000,000 as for one involving £10,000. A manager may be capable of overseeing a section of 100 people and the input of management may be indivisible in the sense that it is not possible to acquire smaller 'units of management' more cheaply, taking full responsibility for smaller groupings of personnel.

A third source of scale economies lies in *specialisation* and *the division of labour*. Ever since Adam Smith's observation of the pin factory in the eighteenth century it has been recognised that greater specialisation on the part of workers and machines can improve the efficiency of production as they focus on a narrower task. At smaller outputs a firm will not be able to achieve the same degree of specialisation as its volume of output will not be sufficient to utilise fully workers or machines dedicated to a relatively narrowly defined task.

Fourth, there are *stochastic economies* of scale, associated in particular with levels of inventory held and with the amounts of 'back-up' equipment that need to be provided in the event of failure. If a firm has a production process that would involve very heavy costs in the event of breakdown, it will need to have a second set of equipment on stand-by. However, if a second production line were to be installed, doubling the level of output, it would not be necessary to provide another set of back-up equipment, provided that the chance of both systems failing simultaneously is low enough to be an acceptable risk.

Sources of diseconomies

It is not in dispute that virtually every industry is subject to some degree of scale economies. It is almost impossible to think of any activity that can be carried out as cheaply at the minimum conceivable scale as at a larger one. It is also indisputable that in some industries, including motor vehicles and many parts of the chemical industry, the cost reductions attributable to larger scales of output are very substantial indeed. What is much more difficult to determine with any certainty is whether or not firms also face diseconomies of scale once their level of output expands beyond a certain size.

If attention is restricted to technological factors there is little reason to suppose that diseconomies of scale exist. There may come a level of output beyond which no further economies can be had, in which case the long-run cost curve will become flat, but none of the forces that lead to scale economies are likely to work in reverse at very high levels of output. If diseconomies of scale do exist they are attributable to managerial factors rather than technological factors. As a firm produces a higher level of output, it also becomes a larger organisation, which may become more difficult to control. Whether or not this is inevitable is the subject of debate. On the one hand, it may be argued that as an organisation becomes larger, 'control loss' inevitably begins to set in. If firms are organised in a hierarchical fashion and each individual can only function efficiently with a limited 'span of control' (the number of individuals reporting directly to them) then a larger organisation implies more layers in the hierarchy. As information travelling from the bottom of the hierarchy to its apex, and instructions passing in the other direction, have to pass through an increasing number of individuals, the opportunities for distortion, either deliberate or unintended, are increased. As the volume of detail involved in the firm's operations increases, it becomes impossible for it all to be absorbed fully by one person, and the sharing and communicating of details by a broader group is often less efficient.

If these arguments generally hold true there will be *managerial diseconomies* of scale which become more severe as the level of output increases and which may eventually outweigh the technological economies. Whether this is in fact the case remains theoretically unresolved. There clearly must be some limit to the size of firms, because otherwise the economy would consist of one single company. However, whether these limits arise as a result of diseconomies of scale, as opposed to other factors, is difficult to judge. Firms need not be organised hierarchically, in which case the arguments concerning control loss lose much of their force. On the other hand it is difficult to imagine how a firm, or part of a firm, producing a single product on a large scale could be organised in any other way. Non-hierarchical or 'organic' methods of organising firms usually require the different groupings of individuals to be involved in technologically unrelated activities, rather than coordinating the production of a single product.

Empirical evidence on scale economies

The need for empirical resolution of the theoretical problem

As the theoretical debate on the existence of diseconomies of scale remains unresolved there are a number of different shapes that the long-run cost curve might take, as set out in Figure 9.8(a) to (c).

Figure 9.8(a) shows a U-shaped long-run cost curve exhibiting diseconomies of scale beyond level of output A. Figure 9.8(b) shows a curve where economies of scale are never exhausted, so that the curve always has a downward slope. Figure 9.8(c) shows a third, commonly used form, which exhibits a downward

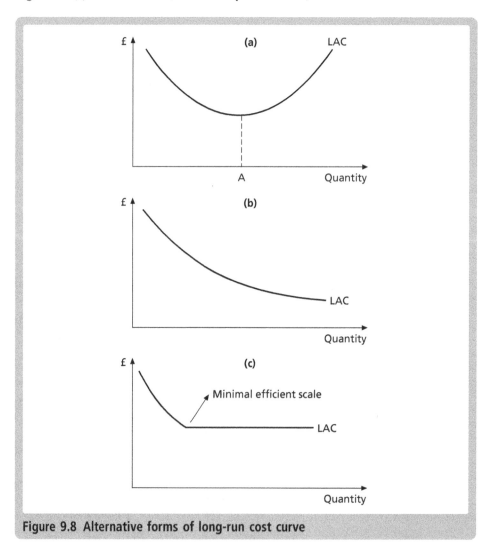

Figure 9.8 Alternative forms of long-run cost curve

slope to a point known as the *minimum efficient scale* (MES), beyond which no further scale economies are known to exist.

As theory cannot discriminate among these alternative forms of the long-run cost function it is natural to turn to the empirical evidence in an attempt to resolve the issue. Unfortunately, the difficulties of estimating the extent of scale economies in a satisfactory way are so great that it is not possible to reach an unambiguous conclusion. There are three basic ways by which empirical evidence may be sought on the shape of the long-run cost function. These are:

1. Statistical estimation.
2. The 'engineering approach'.
3. The survivor technique.

Statistical estimation of scale economies

Statistical estimation of scale economies can take two different forms. The first involves fitting a production function and the second involves directly fitting a cost function. If the production function approach is adopted, a specific mathematical form is first selected to represent the relationship between inputs and outputs. The Cobb–Douglas form is the simplest option but a more popular form in recent work has been the transcendental logarithmic production function or *translog function*. Having specified the functional form to be used, data are collected on the firms' inputs and outputs and the production function is then fitted. The extent to which there are scale economies or not can then be imputed from the coefficients estimated. For instance, if the Cobb–Douglas form has been used and (a + b) > 1, scale economies have been found. If (a + b) < 1 there are diseconomies. If cost functions are chosen, observations are collected on the costs of producing the same product in firms that are operating at different levels of output, and statistical methods used to fit equations to the data.

At first sight this direct approach to the data seems to be the most obvious appropriate way to estimate the behaviour of costs. Unfortunately, it suffers from a number of major pitfalls. In the first place, the available data on inputs, outputs and costs are often inadequate. Input data are often poorly measured and cost figures arise from accounting data that reflect accounting concepts of cost rather than the real underlying opportunity costs. Changes in the product mix introduce confusion into the measurement of output. Differences in the allocation of overheads across different products or different parts of the company affect the way in which costs are measured, as does the use of different accounting periods or different methods for the calculation of depreciation.

Even if costs could be adjusted to arrive at a commonly based estimate of the real opportunity cost and if inputs and outputs could be satisfactorily measured, there would still be a very important gap between what is being observed and the information that is being sought. The fundamental aim is to find the shape of the long-run cost curve or production function which shows *what the cost of producing each level of output would be IF each level of output were produced without X-inefficiency and with the most efficient set of plant and equipment drawn from a constant technology and at fixed factor prices.* However, firms in practice may not

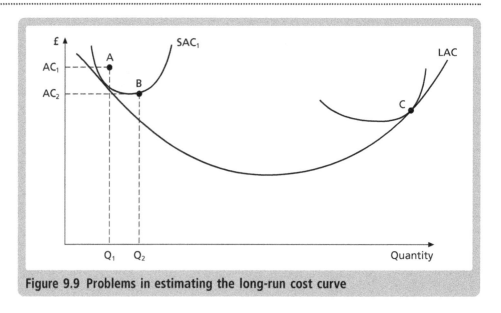

Figure 9.9 Problems in estimating the long-run cost curve

be using the best set of plant and equipment for the level of output they are producing. Differences in cost among firms may be attributed to differences in scale when in fact they are due to differences in the degree of capacity utilisation, the age of the plant or the degree of X-inefficiency. The empirical observations may be of firms that are on their short-run cost curves (or even above them), not on their long-run cost curves. Figure 9.9 illustrates this point.

In Figure 9.9 the curve LAC is the long-run cost curve whose shape is being sought, corresponding to a particular production function. The points A, B and C are observations on actual combinations of output and inputs/cost being experienced by three firms. The statistical approach would estimate a line of best-fit to these observations on the assumption that this is an estimate of the long-run cost function. However, as the diagram shows, it is no such thing. Firm A has a low level of output Q_1 and high costs because it is X-inefficient and is operating above its short-run cost curve for the level of output it is producing. Firm B has a higher output Q_2 and lower costs, but these are not attributable to scale economies as it is using the same set of plant as firm A. It is using that set of plant efficiently in the short run but has not built the most appropriate set of plant for the long-run production of Q_2. Only firm C is actually on the long-run cost curve (and the corresponding production function). Clearly, any attempt to interpret the line from A to B to C as the LAC curve is wholly misleading.

There are many other problems with statistical analysis of this type. The cost curve or production function that is sought refers to different levels of output for exactly the same product, but real firms will rarely be producing identical products. Different firms will have set up their existing capacity at different times, thereby drawing upon different states of technology, and different firms may be paying different prices for their factors of production as a result of imperfections in the markets for inputs. All of these factors reduce the usefulness of the statistical approach to the measurement of scale economies and illustrate just how difficult it can be to appeal directly to empirical evidence in an attempt to discriminate between different theories.

There is a further problem with the statistical approach, which is worth noting in view of the dispute over the existence or otherwise of diseconomies of scale. If there are such diseconomies it would be hoped that the evidence would show that beyond a certain scale of output, costs begin to rise. However, to find such evidence would imply that firms had actually built sets of plant and equipment that had higher costs than smaller and more cost-effective plants. But why should firms ever do so? It could happen by mistake but, under competitive conditions at least, a firm would never deliberately choose such a set of plant. If there are diseconomies of scale in conditions of competition it is not to be expected that firms could be observed on the rising part of the cost curve. Operating on that part of the cost curve in the long run would ensure that the firm could not survive.

Despite the limitations of the statistical approach to estimating scale economies it is possible to make acceptable estimates, at the cost of considerable analytical and statistical complexity, and with contradictory results. Forestieri (1993), for instance, reported seventy-three studies of the banking sector and twenty studies of the insurance industry. For the banking sector twenty-one studies found decreasing costs, twenty-one found a U-shaped long-run cost curve, six found some evidence for costs that rise with size, and the remainder were ambiguous. Overall the pattern of results seemed to show that scale economies in banking arise almost universally in the smaller size ranges, so that the smallest firms had higher costs than medium or large ones. However, the evidence for scale economies at larger sizes was very limited and hence the trend to larger banking groups raises serious questions for public policy. The results for the insurance sector were similarly contradictory although both Hardwick's (1997) study of the United Kingdom and McIntosh's (1998) analysis of the Canadian industry found scale economies to be important.

The engineering approach

The technological studies method, or the engineering approach, to scale economies offers an alternative means of measurement, which avoids many of the problems inherent in the statistical approach. In essence this approach involves drawing on the expertise of production engineers to design hypothetical sets of plant and equipment for the production of different levels of output. The fact that the estimates of cost are hypothetical is actually an advantage of this approach because the engineers will be able to work with the same technology for each level of output and the same factor prices.

The advantages of the engineering approach mean that the most often quoted estimates of scale economies are arrived at in this way. Nevertheless, they do embody a number of serious difficulties. The problems of reconciling accounting data with economic concepts of cost remain, as do the problems of apportioning total cost among different products in a multi-product setting. Perhaps most important of all, such estimates are clearly most accurate with respect to engineering and production aspects of cost, but much less satisfactory with respect to the costs of distribution, administration and management. Unfortunately, the focus of the debate on the existence or otherwise of diseconomies of scale hangs around the onset and impact of 'control loss' as the firm expands its scale of output. The engineering approach is therefore particularly weak on a key aspect of the evidence. As might be expected, the long-run cost curves derived from the engineering approach generally have the shape shown in Figure 9.8(c), indicating a fall in costs down to the minimum efficient scale after which costs are assumed to be constant as all known technical scale economies have been exploited and managerial diseconomies are not taken into account.

In practice it would be very expensive to calculate costs for a large number of different output levels in order to draw a smooth curve. Hence many attempts to measure scale economies in this way confine themselves to estimating just two points on the curve, the minimum efficient scale (MES), and a point corresponding to an output level at (say) 50 per cent of the MES, in order to estimate the slope of the curve and the extent of the cost penalty incurred by firms producing at below the optimal scale. It is important to note that while economies of scale may be measured in absolute terms, showing the levels of output that constitute the minimum efficient scale, it is the relationship between MES and the size of the market that is important. If it is said that there are substantial scale economies in an industry, what is meant is that the MES is large relative to the size of the market in which firms are operating. Table 9.1 shows some empirical results on MES from the classic study on British industry, expressed in this way.

As the table shows, there are some industries, including dyestuffs and machine tools, where the MES is larger than the total size of a domestic market like the United Kingdom. The implication for industrial structure, of course, is that for efficiency the domestic market can only accommodate a single producer. However, if that producer faced no competition it would be in possession of

Table 9.1 Estimated economies of scale

Product	MES as % of UK market	% increase in cost at 50% of MES
Oil refining	10	5
Dyestuffs	>100	22
Beer	3	9
Bread	1	15
Steel production	33	5–10
Cars: one model	25	6
Cars: a range	50	6
Aircraft: one type	>100	20
Machine tools: one model	>100	5
Diesel engines: one model	10	4
Footwear	0.2	2
Newspapers	30	20

Source: Reproduced by permission of the Department of Applied Economics, University of Cambridge from C.F. Pratten, *Economies of Scale in Manufacturing Industry*, CUP, 1971.

substantial undesirable monopoly power. The only resolution to that difficulty is either to control the monopolist in the domestic market or to widen the scope of the market in which competition takes place, so that there is room for more than one firm operating at minimum efficient scale.

The survivor technique

The third approach to the estimation of scale economies is known as the *survivor technique*, developed by Stigler (1958). In this method it is assumed that market forces work efficiently so that firms in the most efficient size category take an increasing share of the market, while firms in less efficient size categories take smaller market shares. The firms in an industry (or plants in some applications) are divided into size categories and the market share of each size category is observed over time in order to estimate an implied shape for the long-run cost curve. In Stigler's study of the American steel industry, the shares of the largest and smallest categories of firm both declined over time, while the shares of firms in a range of medium-sized categories grew, apparently implying a U-shaped long-run cost curve with a considerable flat range, as shown in Figure 9.10.

Unfortunately, too many assumptions have to be fulfilled if the survivor technique is to estimate the cost curve adequately. All firms must be pursuing the same set of objectives, all firms must be operating in similar environments, factor prices and technology must remain unchanged over the period of observation and market forces must work effectively, unimpeded by collusive arrangements or barriers to entry. It seems very unlikely that these conditions ever hold for a period of time long enough for differences in the market share performance of different size categories of firm to become apparent. Nevertheless, the survivor technique has been used in a variety of sectors, the best-known example being a study of the American beer industry (Elzinga 1990).

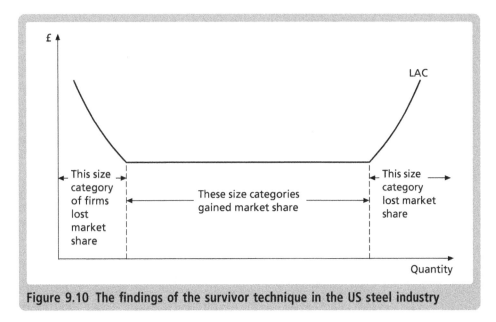

Figure 9.10 The findings of the survivor technique in the US steel industry

Economies of scope and learning effects

While the economic analysis of cost tends to focus on capacity utilisation (the short-run decision) and economies of scale (the long-run decision), there are a number of other factors that have an important influence on costs. These are economies of scope, learning effects and network effects.

Economies of scope

Economies of scope arise whenever it is more efficient to produce two (or more) products together than to produce them separately. In terms of simple equations there are economies of scope when:

$$TC(X, Y) < TC(0, X) + TC(0, Y)$$

where: $TC(X, Y)$ = total cost of jointly producing X and Y
$TC(0, X), TC(0, Y)$ = total cost of producing only X,Y

The extent of scope economies may be measured as:

$$S_c = \frac{TC(0, X) + TC(0, Y) - TC(X, Y)}{TC(X, Y)}$$

If economies of scope are present they provide the 'synergy' that has been referred to in Chapter 4 as a rationale for the merger of different activities. Such economies will exist whenever there are resources that can be shared by different activities and which cannot be sold in the marketplace. For instance, if a breakfast cereal firm has a packing line which is indivisible and whose capacity exceeds the size of the market for a single brand of cereal, there will be economies of scope in using that line to pack multiple brands. In the airline industry, economies of scope can be achieved by using 'hub-and-spoke' networks to serve a larger number of destinations at lower cost (Besanko et al. 1996, pp. 185–6). In the railway industry, passengers and freight are served by using the same set of tracks and signalling equipment.

If economies of scope are to exist, the shared resources in question must be either 'spare' (under-utilised by other activities) or a 'public good' within the firm (their use in one activity does not make them unavailable for others). The latter characteristic suggests that knowledge may be a particularly important source of scope economies and it is certainly the case that knowledge 'spill-overs' from one project to another lead to economies of scope in research and development (Henderson and Cockburn 1994). The same logic underlies the more general suggestion that firms should 'leverage their core competences' (Prahalad and Hamel 1990) or 'compete on capabilities' (Stalk et al. 1992). At the same time it may be prudent to appreciate that scope economies based upon such intangibles may be illusory, as witness the generally poor performance of the diversified firm, examined in Chapter 4.

Economies of scope lead to multi-product firms, which render the analysis of costs much more difficult (Bailey and Friedlander 1982). All of the diagrams in this chapter thus far have implicitly assumed that the firm depicted produces a single product. An expansion of output represents an increase in the output of that sole product. However, if the firm is producing a range of outputs, there is no uniquely correct way to aggregate those different products together. Hence 'total output' in volume terms becomes meaningless, as does the concept of an overall average cost curve (although the marginal cost of each individual product remains meaningful and useful). The concept of scale economies also requires some adjustment. If a firm increases its total output while maintaining the same output mix, it may be said to be expanding along a 'ray' (see Moschandreas 1994, p. 151 for a diagrammatic explanation). The way in which costs change as the firm expands in that way may be referred to as *ray returns to scale*. If increasing output with the same product mix leads to lower cost per unit of all outputs then there are said to be *ray economies of scale*. In the multi-product situation there are therefore two distinct forms of scale economies – ray economies and *product-specific economies* which arise when the output of a single product is increased, keeping the others constant. Some studies have attempted to determine both ray and product-specific economies of scale, including some of the financial service work reviewed by Forestieri (1993) and Smet and Nonneman's unusual 1998 study of all Flemish secondary schools. The latter study's results suggested that ray economies were very significant for secondary schools but product-specific economies were not.

Learning effects

Economies of scale arise when the rate of output increases and economies of scope arise when the product range is widened. *Learning effects* occur as the total cumulative output to date increases and firms 'learn by doing' how to be more efficient. If learning effects are present, the unit cost of production will decrease over time even if the same set of plant and equipment, embodying the same technology, is used at the same degree of capacity utilisation. Such effects have been recognised as important since before the Second World War. They were extensively analysed by British and American productivity teams during that war, which enabled significant increases in the supply of armaments and ships, and they have continued to attract attention. Arrow (1962) wrote the classic paper on the subject while the Boston Consulting Group (1970) made the concept of the *learning curve*, sometimes referred to as the *experience curve*, the centrepiece of their approach to business strategy. Hayes and Wheelwright's 1984 investigation of American industry found many cases where a doubling of cumulative output led to unit cost reductions in the order of 20–30 per cent and the estimation of learning effects has become a standard part of the efficiency consultant's intellectual tool-kit. As might be anticipated, learning effects appear to be particularly important when highly complex products like aircraft (Frischtak 1994) or motor vehicles are involved, or where production processes are complex, as in the chemical industry (Lieberman 1984).

In terms of the diagrammatic treatment of costs, the implication of learning effects is that each short-run and long-run cost curve must refer to a particular level of cumulative output to date. As output and learning accumulate, the set of short- and long-run curves shifts downwards, as shown in Figure 9.11.

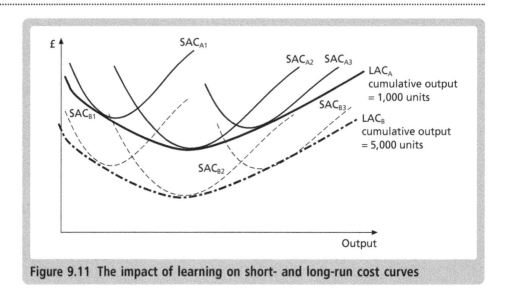

Figure 9.11 The impact of learning on short- and long-run cost curves

Costs in the information industries

Chapter 19 examines the economics of the information industries in detail. That analysis points out that the structure of costs in these industries is unusual in three ways. First, for many information products, like books, music tracks, software packages and CD-ROMs, almost all of the costs involved are fixed costs. Once a piece of software has been designed and written, the marginal cost of reproducing it is close to zero. Second, for most of these products there are no natural limits to capacity. Output can be 'scaled up' very quickly to an almost infinite level. Third, not only are most of the costs fixed costs, they are also *sunk costs*.

The distinction between fixed costs and sunk costs is an important one. A fixed cost is one that does not vary with the level of output. A sunk cost is one that is not recoverable. If a firm invests in a factory, the costs involved are fixed costs in respect of the output produced by that factory. However, they are not completely sunk because if the firm chooses to close down, it can sell the factory and recover most of its outlay. The 'first-copy' costs associated with producing a suite of software, a video or a music track are fixed costs but they are also sunk costs because if the product does not sell they are not recoverable. In the information industries there are usually two kinds of sunk cost. One is the 'first-copy' costs and the second is the marketing costs which rise in the attempt to attract customers and generate customer loyalty. These make up a significant proportion of the total costs incurred and they may be very large indeed in absolute terms. The high-profile fashion 'e-tailer' Boo.com spent millions of pounds before eventually collapsing in the summer of 2000.

The implications of sunk costs have only recently been explored in depth. Baumol *et al.* (1982) noted that sunk costs form a major barrier to entry because they increase the cost of exit. Firms may be reluctant to enter an industry if there is a high level of sunk cost because failure would lead to higher losses. Sutton (1991, 1999) uses game theory to show that if spending on sunk costs like advertising or R&D has a powerful effect in attracting customers – the so-called 'high alpha' industries – then concentration will tend to be higher as the bigger spenders attract proportionately more customers. If the information sectors are 'high alpha' industries then an escalation of spending on sunk 'first-copy' and advertising costs will be rewarded with greater market share.

Other 'cost drivers'

The analyses presented above have suggested that costs are determined by five factors. First, in the short run, there is the level of *capacity utilisation*. Second, in the long run, there are *economies of scale*. Third, there is the degree of *X-efficiency*, which determines whether firms are on their cost curves or above them. Fourth, there are *economies of scope*, and fifth, there are *learning effects*.

These five 'cost drivers' are given the most extensive treatment in economic analysis. However, as Porter (1985) points out, there are a number of others. Cost reductions may be had by *coordinating linkages* between other activities taking place within the firm, like advertising and direct sales, or production and maintenance. There may be transactional efficiencies to be had by increasing the degree of *vertical integration* within the firm, moving closer to the final customer (forward vertical integration) or to sources of supply (backwards vertical integration). Alternatively some of these gains could be had by *cooperation with suppliers and distribution channels*, rather than by undertaking these activities within the firm. Porter cites the example, for instance, of a confectioner arranging with the supplier to have chocolate delivered in bulk as liquid, rather than in solid blocks, thereby reducing costs for both the confectioner and the supplier.

Costs will also be affected by *timing* within the business cycle or timing with respect to other firms' actions. The purchase of major items of capital equipment may be heavily influenced by the level of demand and capacity utilisation in the supplying industries, where highly advantageous deals may be had if suppliers are suffering from a lack of orders and over-capacity. There may be *first-mover cost advantages* to be had by being the first to undertake an activity, especially if there are substantial learning effects, which a first-mover will begin to gain from before late-comers. On the other hand, in some situations there may be *late-mover cost advantages*, as in situations where the technology is developing very rapidly and first movers may have invested heavily in technology that has become out-dated.

Costs may also be affected by *geographical location* when factor prices, tax regimes and government incentives vary from place to place, and by *institutional factors* like unionisation, tariffs and local content rules. Finally, it should be noted that costs will also depend upon a very wide range of the *firm's discretionary policies*, like the nature and design of the product being produced, the level of service provided to customers, delivery dates achieved, the form of distribution, the nature of the technology and raw materials produced and the full package of human resources policies adopted on pay, training, incentive schemes and employee benefits.

This last section has made it clear that a full listing of the determinants of cost would be very long indeed and that the most important factors will vary from industry to industry and firm to firm. A business that hopes to be successful will need to think very carefully about which cost drivers are the most important in its own particular case in order to concentrate its efforts on keeping cost as low as possible, commensurate with implementing its overall company strategy.

Linear cost functions and break-even analysis

Linear cost functions

The cost functions considered above are all curvilinear in form, following the underlying economic principles embodied in the production function and economic concepts like the principle of diminishing returns. Many, perhaps most, economists would argue that these are the most appropriate forms for cost curves to take. However, many decision-making techniques for business, including many used by management accountants, are set out in terms of cost functions that are linear with respect to average variable costs. The theoretical foundations for such cost functions are somewhat shaky as they must imply an underlying production function that has some rather unlikely characteristics (see Dorward 1987 for an explanation of this point). Nevertheless, as they are often used in standard costing and in break-even analysis it is useful to examine them.

The typical form of a linear cost function is set out in Figure 9.12, which shows both total costs and costs per unit, in the short run.

As the figure shows, average variable costs are assumed to be constant, which implies that marginal cost is equal to average variable cost. As total fixed costs are constant, so that fixed costs per unit decline, the resulting unit cost function (ATC) is downward sloping over the whole of its range. Management accountants who use such functions but recognise their theoretical limitations often qualify them by noting that the linearity is only assumed to apply within a range of the cost curve, but that the range in question is the relevant one for the purposes on hand.

Break-even analysis

Perhaps the most common use of linear cost functions of the type outlined above is in *break-even analysis*, which shows how to identify the level of output and sales volume at which the firm 'breaks even', with revenues being sufficient to cover all of its costs. Three equivalent approaches are used to solve break-even problems, known as the following:

1. The graphical method.
2. The equation method.
3. The contribution margin method.

The graphical method is set out in Figure 9.13.

The horizontal axis depicts the level of output and the vertical axis shows revenues and costs. Total revenues are drawn as a straight line, showing the

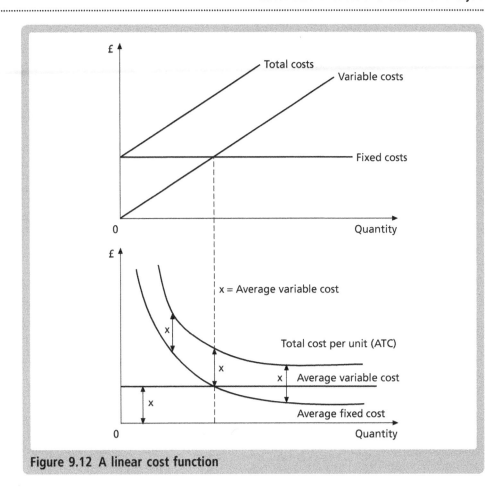

Figure 9.12 A linear cost function

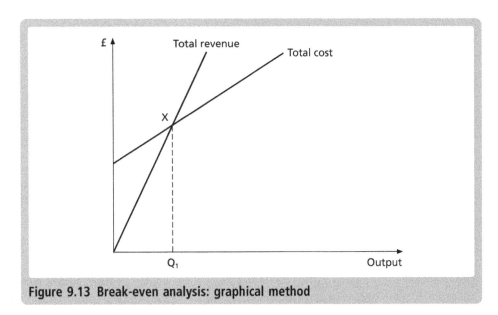

Figure 9.13 Break-even analysis: graphical method

revenues that will be earned at different levels of output if the same price is charged. Total costs are as shown in Figure 9.12 above. For each level of output profits or losses are indicated by the vertical distance between the total revenue function and the total cost function, which is equal to zero at the break-even point X, which corresponds to level of output Q_1.

Break-even analysis of this type can be used to calculate the level of sales that must be achieved in order to avoid losses, or to calculate the margin of safety that exists between the break-even point and the firm's actual or expected level of sales. The margin of safety may be defined as:

Margin of safety = Actual sales revenue − Break-even sales revenue

Management accountants sometimes take the analysis a stage further to calculate the margin of safety ratio, defined as:

$$\text{Margin of safety ratio} = \frac{\text{Margin of safety}}{\text{Actual sales}}$$

Exactly the same results may be arrived at through the *equation method*, which begins by noting that:

Profit = Sales revenue − Variable costs − Fixed costs

As, in this model:

Sales revenue = Price × Volume
Variable cost = Variable cost per unit volume
Fixed cost = a constant

and break-even volume is where:

Profit = 0

Break-even volume is where:

0 = (Price × Volume) − (Variable cost per unit × Volume) − Fixed cost

This last equation can be rearranged to give:

$$\text{Break-even volume} = \frac{\text{Fixed cost}}{\text{Price} - \text{Variable cost per unit}}$$

Provided that each of the variables in the equation is known, break-even volume is easily calculated.

It may be noted that the expression on the bottom of the right-hand side of the above equation represents 'contribution per unit of output' or 'contribution margin'. The contribution margin approach to break-even analysis consists simply of rewriting the equation in the following form:

$$\text{Break-even volume} = \frac{\text{Fixed costs}}{\text{Contribution margin}}$$

In addition to calculating break-even volumes, the method may be used to calculate the sales volume required to generate a target level of profit. All that is required is to add the target level of profit to fixed costs in the last equation, to give:

$$\text{Volume required to give target profit} = \frac{\text{Fixed costs} + \text{Target profit}}{\text{Contribution margin}}$$

A comparison of the break-even model and the standard economic model

Having set out the standard economic model of the firm in Chapter 3, and the break-even model above, it is useful briefly to compare the two, shown together in Figure 9.14(a) and (b).

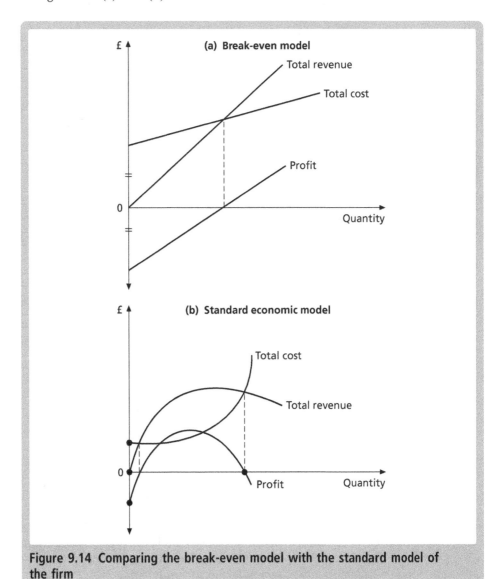

Figure 9.14 Comparing the break-even model with the standard model of the firm

A number of differences become immediately apparent. In the first place, the economic model is an optimising model, which identifies the profit- and contribution-maximising level of output and price. The break-even model shows no optimum as the levels of profit and contribution simply increase with the level of output. That does not imply that accountants using the break-even model believe that higher levels of sales always imply greater profits. The purposes of the model are different. The aim of the economic model is to predict the levels of output and price that profit-maximising firms will choose to produce. The aim of the break-even analysis is to examine cost and revenue relationships within a narrow range of output in order to assist in the planning and control of business activity and in particular with short-term profit planning.

In the break-even model price is an exogenous variable, rather than one for which the analysis provides a solution. Clearly, if the price of the good is increased, the break-even level of output will be reduced. However, that cannot be taken as a recommendation that prices should always be increased because at higher prices the level of output that can be sold will tend to be lower. Break-even analysis can be useful in assisting managers to consider likely profit levels at different prices, but only if they are sensitive to the fundamental concept of elasticity of demand.

Illustration 1 Scale economies in industrial plants – a classic study

Haldi and Whitcomb (1967) use data from the engineering literature in North America and Europe to estimate the extent of scale economies in production. They collected data on three different sources of cost, which were as follows:

1. Individual units of industrial equipment.
2. Initial investment in plant and equipment.
3. Operating costs, made up of labour, raw materials and utilities.

In respect of units of industrial equipment they used data on cost and capacity to fit a least-squares line derived from the following equation:

$C = aX^b$ where:

C = cost
X = capacity

Fitting the equation for nearly 700 types of equipment, including containers, pipes, reaction vessels and mining machinery, gave estimates of 'b' for each type, which are summarised in Table 9.2.

As Table 9.2 shows, 94.3 per cent of the estimates had a value of less than 1, implying that as capacity increased, costs rose less than proportionately and there were economies of scale.

The evidence that there are economies of scale for individual items of equipment suggests strongly that there are scale economies for complete systems, but it is not conclusive proof. In order to investigate further, Haldi and Whitcomb took data on construction costs and capacity for the plants required to produce 221 products calculated by cost engineers, and summarised the findings with respect to the estimates of 'b'. The results are set out in Table 9.3.

Illustration 1

Table 9.2 Estimates of 'b' for industrial equipment

Range of values	Number of estimates	% of estimates
0–0.49	176	25.6
0.50–0.79	442	64.3
0.80–0.99	90	13.1
1.00+	39	5.7

Adapted from: Haldi and Whitcomb (1967).

Table 9.3 Estimates of 'b' for plant investment costs

Products	<0.4	0.4–0.59	0.6–0.9	1.00+	No. of estimates
Cement			2	1	3
Fertiliser			5	1	6
Gases	4	9	29	3	45
Industrial chemicals		5	36	1	42
Plastics			3		3
Rubber			6	2	8
Misc. chemicals	3		4	1	8
Desalination			5	1	6
Electric power		8	7		15
Petroleum products		11	45	1	57
Aluminium			12	3	15
Pulp and paper			5	1	6
Shipping			1		1
Other	2	1	3		6
Totals	9	34	163	15	221
%	4.1	15.4	73.7	6.8	100.0

Table 9.4 Estimates of 'b' for operating and labour costs

Value of 'b'	Total operating costs		Labour cost only	
	No. of estimates	%	No. of estimates	%
0–0.4	4	12.5	37	71.2
0.40–0.69	9	28.1	14	26.9
0.70–0.99	19	59.4	1	1.9
1.00+	0	0.0	0	0.0
Total	32	100.0	52	100.0

Again, the evidence in support of scale economies in production is substantial, with a median value of 'b' equal to 0.73 and only 6.8 per cent of the estimates being in excess of 1.00.

The third aspect of cost investigated in this study was operating costs, defined as in-plant production costs, excluding depreciation and payments on capital. The results are shown in Table 9.4, using the same approach, and distinguishing between total operating cost and labour cost only.

▶

These results very strongly suggest that it is labour costs in particular that exhibit substantial scale economies. More detailed examination of the individual studies from which Table 9.4 was drawn point to limited scale economies in respect of the usage of raw materials and utilities, but significantly increasing returns to scale in respect of operating labour, supervision and management costs, and maintenance.

The major conclusions of the Haldi and Whitcomb study were that initial investment costs exhibit scale economies up to the largest plants observed in industrial countries, and that operating expenses for labour, supervision and maintenance also show increasing returns to scale, but that usage of raw materials and utilities offer few opportunities for the exploitation of economies.

Illustration 2   Scale economies in the service sector – the case of life assurance in the United Kingdom

Hardwick (1993) provides an analysis of cost economies in the UK life assurance industry that is not dependent upon the detailed technicalities of statistical cost-fitting and which goes further than the statistical analyses in that it attempts to identify the sources of the economies that are found to be available.

The statistical analyses have tended to suggest that in the insurance industry there are increasing returns to scale, at least over some range of output. However, most studies have treated insurance companies as single-product firms (often using premium income as a measure of output) and only a few have therefore addressed the issue of economies of scope.

In order to circumvent the problems associated with fitting cost functions this study used a simple survey approach to identify the views of senior executives in the industry. Each executive was asked his views on the following issues:

- What is the most cost-efficient size for a life insurance company?
- What are the sources of scale economies?
- To what extent are there economies of scope in the life insurance sector?
- Which resources might be shared in order to achieve economies of scope in providing different life insurance products?
- What are the reasons for diversification among life insurance firms?
- Will the number of independent life insurers rise, fall or remain the same over the next few years?

Nearly all executives believed that life insurance firms needed premium income of more than £500 million to be efficient and 62 per cent believed that more than £1 billion was required. While a few of the executives from smaller firms tended to believe that the efficient size was smaller, that was not a general pattern.

With respect to the sources of scale economies, executives most often saw improved efficiency in computing services as important, followed by better name awareness, more effective advertising and the ability to pay lower prices for equipment and vehicles. Only a small minority (23 per cent) believed that unit costs could be lowered by offering a wider variety of services. A number of them also saw the administrative burdens arising from legislation as a major problem for small firms, along with small firms' inability to benefit from direct sales forces.

Having established that executives perceived scale economies to be significant, the survey also asked them to comment on the prospect of diseconomies at higher levels of output. A large majority of them (80 per cent) supported the view that large companies suffer from increased monitoring and control costs because of their necessarily more complex organisational structures. They also felt that the costs involved in diversification have disadvantaged the larger companies in recent years.

Despite their reservations about diversification in general, the insurance executives perceived significant economies of scope, agreeing that it would be less costly for one company to provide two or more services than for each to be provided by a specialist. Those economies were felt to arise from sharing computer hardware and expertise in management and marketing. Consistent with their overall view that economies of scope and scale are significant in the life insurance industry, the unanimous belief among the respondents was that the number of independent firms in the industry would decline over the next few years.

References and further reading

K. Arrow, 'The Economic Implications of Learning by Doing', *Review of Economic Studies*, vol. 29, April 1962, pp. 155–73.

E. Bailey and A. Friedlander, 'Market Structure and Multiproduct Industries', *Journal of Economic Literature*, vol. XX, 1982, pp. 1024–48.

W. Baumol, J. Panzar and R. Willig, *Contestable Markets and the Theory of Industry Structure*, New York, Harcourt, Brace Jovanovich, 1982.

D. Besanko, D. Dranove and M. Shanley, *Economics of Strategy*, New York, John Wiley, 1996.

Boston Consulting Group, *Perspectives on Experience*, Boston, Boston Consulting Group, 1970.

N. Dorward, *The Pricing Decision: Economic Theory and Business Practice*, London, Harper Row, 1987.

K. Elzinga, 'The Beer Industry' in W. Adams (ed.) *The Structure of American Industry*, 8th edn, New York, Macmillan, 1990.

G. Forestieri, 'Economies of Scale and Scope in the Financial Services Industry: A Review of the Recent Literature' in OECD, *Financial Conglomerates*, Paris, 1993, pp. 63–124.

C. Frischtak, 'Learning and Technical Progress in the Commuter Aircraft Industry: An Analysis of Embracer's Experience', *Research Policy*, September 1994, pp. 601–14.

D. Gropper, 'An Empirical Investigation of Changes in Scale Economies for the Commercial Banking Firm, 1979–1986', *Journal of Money, Credit and Banking*, vol. 23, no. 4, November 1991, pp. 718–27.

J. Haldi and D. Whitcomb, 'Economies of Scale in Industrial Plants', *Journal of Political Economy*, vol. 75, no. 4, August 1967, pp. 373–85.

P. Hardwick, 'Cost Economies in the Life Assurance Industry', *The Service Industries Journal*, October 1993, pp. 240–7.

P. Hardwick, 'Measuring Cost Inefficiency in the UK Life Industry', *Applied Financial Economics*, February 1997, pp. 37–44.

R. Hayes and S. Wheelwright, *Restoring Our Competitive Edge*, New York, Wiley, 1984.

R. Henderson and I. Cockburn, 'Scale, Scope and Spillovers: Research Strategy and Research Productivity in the Pharmaceutical Industry', Massachusetts Institute of Technology Working Paper, 1994.

M. Lieberman, 'The Learning Curve and Pricing in the Chemical Processing Industries', *RAND Journal of Economics*, vol. 15, Summer 1984, pp. 213–28.

J. McIntosh, 'Scale Efficiency in a Dynamic Model of Canadian Insurance Companies', *Journal of Risk and Insurance*, June 1998, pp. 303–17.

M. Moschandreas, *Business Economics*, London, Thomson, 1994.

M. Porter, *Competitive Advantage*, New York, Free Press, 1985.

C. Prahalad and G. Hamel, 'The Core Competence of the Corporation', *Harvard Business Review*, May–June 1990, pp. 79–91.

C.F. Pratten, *Economies of Scale in Manufacturing Industry*, University of Cambridge, Department of Applied Economics, Occasional Papers No. 28, Cambridge University Press, 1971.

M. Smet and W. Nonneman, 'Economies of Scale and Scope in Flemish Secondary Schools', *Applied Economics*, September 1998, pp. 1251–8.

G. Stalk, P. Evans and L. Shulman, 'Competing on Capabilities: The New Rules of Corporate Strategy', *Harvard Business Review*, March–April 1992, pp. 57–69.

G.J. Stigler, 'The Economies of Scale', *Journal of Law and Economics*, vol. 1, October 1958, pp. 54–71.

J. Sutton, *Sunk Costs and Market Structure*, Cambridge, MA, MIT Press, 1991.

J. Sutton, *Technology and Market Structure*, Cambridge, MA, MIT Press, 1999.

Self-test questions

1. Which of the following statements are correct?

(a) an isoquant shows economies of scale

(b) an isoquant shows the different techniques that can be used to produce a fixed quantity of a product

(c) a technology may be described as 'labour intensive' or 'capital intensive'

(d) a given set of plant and equipment may exhibit economies of scale

(e) if a large firm is experiencing higher costs per unit than a small firm, this means that there are diseconomies of scale

2. If a firm has selected the cost-minimising technique of production, which of the following conditions must hold?

(a) the isocost line is a tangent to the isoquant

(b) the extra output per extra dollar spent on labour must equal the extra output per extra dollar spent on capital

(c) the ratio of the factor prices must equal the ratio of the marginal products of the factors

(d) a higher level of spending cannot lead to a higher level of output

(e) the same output cannot be produced with less labour or less capital

3. Which of the following factors leads the short-run cost curve to rise beyond a certain level of output?

(a) diseconomies of scale

(b) diseconomies of capacity utilisation

(c) the principle of diminishing returns

(d) reduced availability of inputs

(e) higher input prices

4. What *exactly* does a long-run average cost curve show?

5. The Business School is organising a conference, at a fee of £50 per delegate. Speakers will cost £500 and the cost of catering and conference materials is £10 per delegate. It is anticipated that forty delegates will attend.

   (a) Use the contribution margin approach to calculate the break-even number of delegates.

   (b) If the management of the Business School demands that at least £500 profit be made on any conference, calculate the required number of delegates.

Essay question

'Accountants' use of break-even models ignores the important factors of diminishing returns and elasticity of demand.' Explain this statement and consider the uses to which break-even analysis may legitimately be put.

10 Models of market structure

This chapter examines a number of formal economic models of market structure, covering the cases of perfect competition, monopoly, monopolistic competition and oligopoly.

The analysis of market structure

Having discussed the firm's objectives in Chapters 2 and 4, and having examined demand and cost conditions in Chapters 6 to 9, attention can turn to the actions that will lead those objectives to be achieved. This cannot be done without reference to the structure of the industry, because that structure determines the relationship between a firm and its competitors. Hence an important starting point for the analysis of pricing and other aspects of competitive behaviour is a careful appraisal of the structure of each industry in which the firm is involved.

This analysis can be approached in a number of ways. In the first place, formal textbook economic analysis identifies a number of different 'ideal types' of market structure for which rigorous models can be developed. These market structures are known as the following:

- perfect competition
- monopoly
- monopolistic competition
- oligopoly.

Careful examination of these models illustrates the importance of a number of economic forces that shape the competitive environment in which firms operate. However, they are restricted to a number of relatively simple market structures, and they do not cover every dimension that might be considered. As a result, it is useful to go beyond them to a less rigorous, but more complete, approach to the analysis of competitive structure, known as the 'five forces' approach, developed at the Harvard Business School by Professor Michael Porter. This chapter examines the formal textbook models of market structure. Chapter 11 introduces the 'five forces' approach.

Perfect competition

The conditions for perfect competition

Perfect competition is a relatively simple form of market structure in which a number of conditions are met. These are as follows:

- a large number of small buyers and sellers, none of whom is large enough to affect the market price by their actions (this assumption implies that scale economies are insignificant – otherwise, large firms would come to dominate the industry)
- free entry to the industry, so that any firms wishing to compete with the existing firms can do so on equal terms
- identical products
- profit-maximising behaviour on the part of all firms
- perfect mobility of factors of production
- perfect knowledge of market opportunities.

Short-run equilibrium in perfect competition

In the perfectly competitive situation the price at which every firm must sell its output is set by the market forces of supply and demand. Each individual firm will be able to sell as much as it chooses at the market price, but it will not be able to sell anything at all at a higher price. That is because its competitors are producing identical products and selling them at the market price to consumers who are well informed of the prices being asked by every firm. Figure 10.1 shows the short-run situation for both an individual firm and for the industry as a whole.

As the diagram shows, the forces of supply and demand determine a price of P and a total industry output of Q. Each individual firm has a demand curve which is a horizontal line PP, showing that it can sell any amount at the price P, but none at higher prices.

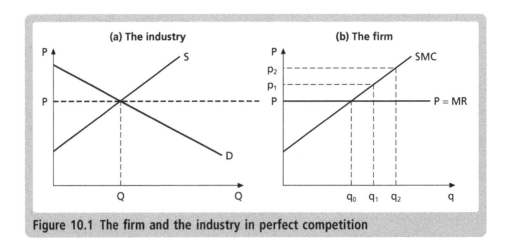

Figure 10.1 The firm and the industry in perfect competition

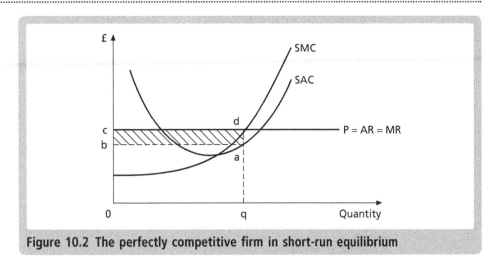

Figure 10.2 The perfectly competitive firm in short-run equilibrium

Because the demand curve is horizontal the marginal revenue curve, which shows the additional revenue earned when one more unit of output is sold, is given by the same horizontal line. When the firm sells one more unit of output, the amount it receives for it is the price P, which is also the addition to revenue.

As each firm is a profit-maximiser it will produce the level of output given by q_0 in the diagram, which is the output at which the marginal revenue is just equal to marginal cost. If the firm were to produce more than q_0 then it would be producing units of output for which the marginal cost is more than the marginal revenue, which would reduce profit. On the other hand, if it produces less than q_0 then it is failing to produce some units of output for which the marginal revenue exceeds the marginal cost, which would add to profit.

As the industry is no more than the sum of the individual firms, it is clear that the industry's output Q must equal the sum of the outputs of the individual firms. This simple point also helps in understanding the nature of the supply curve. It can be seen from the diagram for the firm that at price P the firm chooses to supply output q_0 because that is the ouput that yields most profit. If the price rose to P_1 the firm would choose to increase its output to q_1, and if the price rose further to P_2 the firm would increase output to q_2. The firm's marginal cost curve traces out the levels of output that the firm would choose to supply at each price. In other words, the marginal cost curve for the firm is the same thing as the firm's supply curve. The supply curve for the industry as a whole is simply the horizontal sum of the marginal cost curves for the individual firms.

Figure 10.1 shows only the marginal cost curve for the individual firm, in order to be as clear as possible. However, a more complete picture requires the inclusion of the average cost curve, in order to examine the level of profits being made. This is shown in Figure 10.2.

In the diagram as shown, the individual firms are making 'economic profits' or 'supernormal profits', because the average cost of producing output q is less than the price P, set by the market. The amount of profit earned is shown by the shaded area abcd and consists of the profit margin bc multiplied by the number of units sold.

Equilibrium in the long run

Up to this point the analysis has been of short-run behaviour. Each firm has a given set of plant and equipment, involving it in some fixed costs. New firms cannot enter the industry because to do so would require them to set up new plants, which is not possible in the short run. In the long run, however, such profits would attract new firms into the industry. In that case, the additional competition would push the price downwards and eventually eliminate the profits being made. In terms of Figure 10.1, new entry will move the supply curve to the right as more firms set up and their marginal cost curves contribute to the supply curve.

In order to identify where the industry's price must settle in the long run, it is necessary to examine the long-run cost curves for the individual firms. Each firm must have the same long-run cost curve, because they all have access to the same technology and the same prices of inputs. Figure 10.3 shows such a curve.

If the price were to settle at P_a, firms could continue to make supernormal profits by producing outputs anywhere between q_x and q_y. In that case, entry would continue to take place and the price would be pushed downwards. Clearly, P_a is too high to be the price at which the industry eventually settles. Similarly, P_b is too low to be the long-run equilibrium price, because if the price should fall to that level, no firm could make a profit at all, many would leave the industry and the price would rise. This argument makes it clear that in a perfectly competitive industry, the price must settle in the long run at P_L.

The long-run outcome of a perfectly competitive industry, then, is that the price is forced down to the level of the lowest possible average cost. Each firm uses the set of plant and equipment that gives least cost production and operates it at the most efficient level of output.

The working of a perfectly competitive industry is determined by its structure. The production of identical products by a large number of small firms, coupled

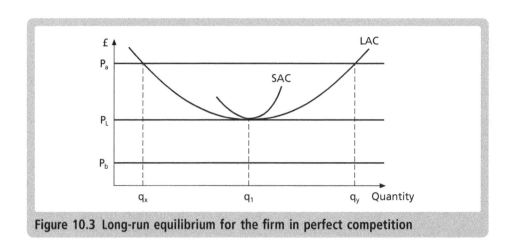

Figure 10.3 Long-run equilibrium for the firm in perfect competition

with perfect knowledge on the part of consumers, ensures that each firm has a horizontal demand curve. Freedom of entry ensures that if supernormal profits are made in the short run they will be competed away in the long run by new entry. Provided economies of scale are limited, so that the industry contains a large number of small firms, all producing at the bottom point on their long-run cost curve, a long-run equilibrium will be established and maintained until the external environment changes.

Perfect competition and 'rivalry'

In this type of market structure, the firm has very little opportunity to act for itself, and very few decisions to make. The price is set by the market, and the firm is a 'price-taker'. There is no reason to advertise because the firms are all producing exactly the same product and customers know them to be identical. The only decision the firm has to take in the short run is on the level of output. In the long run it has also to ensure that it has built the lowest cost plant, or it cannot survive. The firm is not even able to determine its own objectives because unless it makes maximum profit it will make a loss and will cease to survive.

In perfect competition the industry is 'competitive' in the sense that its structure drives prices down to the level of lowest cost, not in the sense that firms are intense rivals for each other. Indeed, in such an industry there is no rivalry at all between individual firms because each firm is very small, being faced by anonymous market forces, rather than by identifiable rival firms. In perfect competition firms could not be said to have strategies. They simply take limited decisions under very powerful pressure from market forces.

Perfect competition and social optimality

Perfect competition is often regarded as a socially optimal form of market structure, for a number of reasons. In the first place, every firm is forced by market pressures to build the least cost set of plant and equipment and to operate it at its optimal level of output, so that cost per unit is at the lowest possible level. Second, no supernormal profits can be earned, except in the short run. Third, and most important from an economic point of view, price is equal to marginal cost. This is most important because price equal to marginal cost is the condition required for the maximisation of social welfare. This can be seen using the diagram set out in Figure 10.4.

Maximisation of social welfare requires that the level of output produced is that which gives the greatest net benefit to the economy. Net benefit consists of the difference between the benefits consumers receive from having the commodity and the costs incurred in its production. If this apparently vague idea is to be given meaning, some method has to be found to measure the benefits received by consumers. This can be done quite simply if we accept three basic axioms about consumer behaviour. These are as follows:

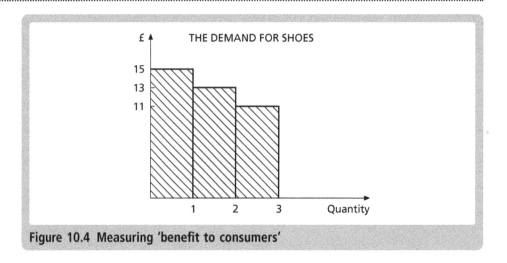

Figure 10.4 Measuring 'benefit to consumers'

1. Consumers are rational.
2. Consumers are self-interested.
3. Each individual consumer is the only valid judge of their own welfare.

If these axioms are adopted then the benefit that a consumer receives from having different amounts of a commodity is measured by the amount that they are willing to pay for them. If consumers are willing to pay a maximum of £10 for a pair of shoes, and they are rational and self-interested, that £10 is a direct measure of the sacrifice they are prepared to make in return for the shoes and an indirect measure of the benefit they expect to get from having the shoes.

Once this idea has been established it becomes relatively easy to measure the benefit to consumers from having different amounts of a commodity, because the demand curve shows how much individuals are prepared to pay for those different amounts. Figure 10.4 shows, for instance, that someone is willing to pay £15 for the first pair of shoes on the market. The total benefit from having one pair of shoes, then, is equal to £15. If the second pair of shoes will only be sold when the price falls to £13, and the third pair when the price has fallen to £11, then the total benefit of three pairs of shoes is equal to £15 + £13 + £11 = £39.

In general, the benefit to consumers from producing quantity Q of a commodity is given by the area under the demand curve at Q, as shown in Figure 10.5(a).

In a similar way, the avoidable costs of producing a commodity can be calculated by adding up the marginal costs of producing each successive unit, thereby measuring the costs of producing quantity Q by the area under the marginal cost curve, as shown in Figure 10.5(b).

Bringing the measure of the benefits and the costs together, in a simple form of cost–benefit analysis, it can be readily seen that the maximum net benefit is received at output Q_o and price P. However, it has already been noted that under perfect competition the marginal cost curve for the industry and the supply curve are the same. In other words, in perfect competition, the industry automatically produces the level of output that maximises social welfare.

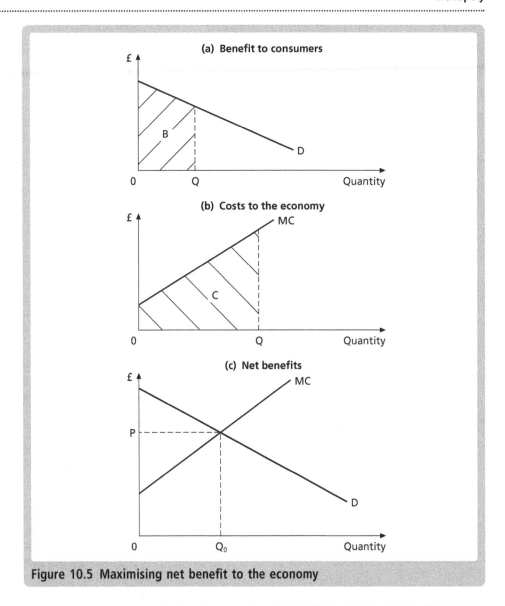

Figure 10.5 Maximising net benefit to the economy

Monopoly

Profit-maximising equilibrium in 'pure monopoly'

Monopoly is a form of market structure in which the pressures imposed on the perfectly competitive firm are absent. For an industry to be a 'pure monopoly' it must contain just one firm and there must be no possibility of entry.

In this type of market structure the firm and its management have very much more discretion to decide on both their objectives and their actions. They may decide to opt for an objective other than profit maximisation, as discussed in Chapters 2 and 4. However, textbook models of monopoly assume as a starting point that the aim of the monopolist, like the perfect competitor, is to make

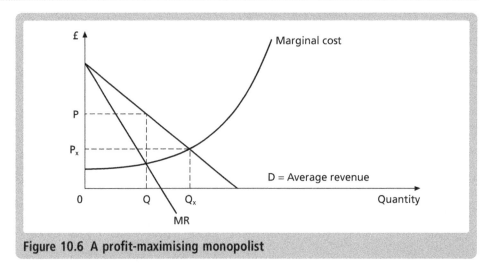

Figure 10.6 A profit-maximising monopolist

maximum profit. For the pure monopoly, the analysis is relatively simple. Figure 10.6 shows the diagram for a profit-maximising monopolist in the short run.

As there is only one firm in the industry, the demand curve for a monopolist is the same as the demand curve for the industry as a whole. It slopes downwards from left to right and, as a result, the marginal revenue curve lies below it. (This is because in monopoly the firm has to lower the price in order to sell more output, so that the extra revenue received from selling one more unit is less than the price for that unit.)

The profit-maximising monopolist will produce output Q, where marginal cost equals marginal revenue, and must sell it at price P. Provided that cost and demand conditions are favourable, supernormal profits will be made and the lack of competition from other firms or new entrants will mean that those profits can be maintained indefinitely. In the long run all the firm has to do is to consider whether there is a different set of plant and equipment that would allow it to make an even higher level of profit than that which it is making from its current capacity. If there is, then in the long run the monopolist will build that more profitable set of plant and equipment. If not, the monopolist will simply keep on replacing the current set of plant and equipment when it becomes worn out.

It is worth noting that a monopolist does not necessarily make supernormal profits. If a firm has a monopoly in a product that consumers do not want at all, or that is so expensive to produce that consumers are not willing to pay a price high enough to cover the cost, then it will not be able to make profits. What is important about monopoly is that if the firm is in a position to make profits, those profits will not be eroded away by competition.

Monopoly and the misallocation of resources

Although a firm and its shareholders will find a monopoly position highly attractive, the existence of monopoly is often regarded as socially undesirable, for a number of reasons. In the first place, the firm is not forced to set up the configuration of plant and equipment that has the lowest possible cost. In the second place, earning monopoly profit is often regarded as an 'unfair' and undesirable outcome that should be prevented. Third, and most important from an economic point of view, price in a monopoly is not equal to marginal cost. It can be seen from Figure 10.6 that the optimal level of output from society's point of view is Q_x, sold at P_x. However, the monopolist produces less, at output Q, and sells it at a higher price P. If an industry is a monopoly, there is said to be a misallocation of resources. This problem of resource misallocation under monopoly forms an important aspect of the rationale for anti-monopoly or anti-trust policy, discussed in more detail in Chapter 20.

Monopolistic competition

Equilibrium in monopolistic competition

A third form of market structure is known as 'monopolistic competition'. This type of industry resembles perfect competition in that it contains a large number of small firms and there is free entry to the industry in the long run. However, in monopolistic competition, there is some degree of product differentiation in that each firm produces a slightly different product, each of which is preferred to the others by some consumers. In this type of market structure each firm will have a downward-sloping demand curve, being a 'mini-monopolist' with respect to its own particular variant of the industry's product. The diagram that shows the firm's price and output in the short run will look exactly like Figure 10.6, illustrating monopoly, with the qualification that there is no longer an industry demand curve.

In the short run, as in perfect competition, firms may make supernormal profits. However, if they do, new entrants will be attracted into the industry, each firm will lose some of its customers to the new entrants and eventually the supernormal profits will be competed away. Figure 10.7 shows the position that firms in the industry will reach in the long run.

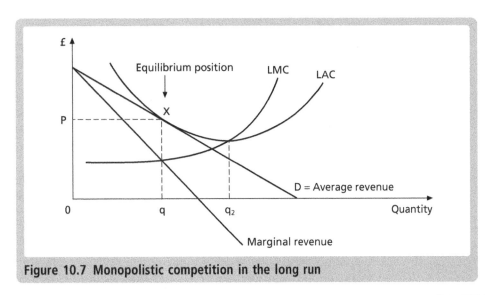

Figure 10.7 Monopolistic competition in the long run

This result is sometimes known as the 'tangency solution', because the individual firm reaches a position where its demand curve is at a tangent to its long-run average cost curve. The firm must find itself in this position because if the demand curve were any higher, supernormal profits could be made and further entry would take place. On the other hand, if the curve were any lower, losses would be made and firms would leave the industry, moving the remaining firms' demand curves upwards.

Monopolistic competition and the allocation of resources

Just as the outcome of perfect competition and monopoly can be evaluated from a social point of view, so it is possible to consider the outcome of monopolistic competition. In the long run, supernormal profits are not earned so that the charge of 'unfairness' does not arise. On the other hand, price does not equal marginal cost so that there is a misallocation of resources in that sense. Furthermore, as Figure 10.7 makes clear, each firm will not use the lowest cost set of plant and equipment. As the equilibrium is established where a sloping demand curve is tangential to the long-run average cost curve, the equilibrium level of output is one where not all economies of scale have been exploited. If each firm set up the plant and equipment designed to produce level of output q_2, costs per unit would be considerably lower. A major effect of introducing product differentiation is to reduce efficiency as each firm fails to take the maximum advantage of economies of scale. This finding is sometimes referred to as the *excess capacity theorem*. On the other hand, it must be remembered that consumers are able to choose from a wide variety of different product variations. If consumers value these differences there will be compensating gains so that an overall judgement on the allocative efficiency of an industry under monopolistic competition is difficult to reach.

While the analysis set out above outlines the basic features of monopolistic competition it is also important to point out some difficulties with the model. In particular, it is difficult to be clear on the question of which firm is illustrated in the diagram. In the case of perfect competition there is no difficulty in showing a diagram for 'the' individual firm, because all firms are producing the same products, using the same technology and facing the same prices of inputs. As a result, firms all have the same cost curves in the long run. In monopolistic competition, however, each firm is producing a different product which would seem to imply that each firm has a different cost and demand curve. If that is the case, every firm is in a different position and a single diagram cannot illustrate every case. This problem was avoided by the originator of the model (Chamberlin 1933) by adopting the 'heroic assumptions' that every firm has the same cost and demand curve, despite producing different products, and that when new entry takes place the new firms attract customers in equal proportions from all the existing firms. Unfortunately these assumptions are so restrictive and at odds with the existence of product differentiation that serious doubt is cast on the model's theoretical consistency. Leading economists differ on the value of the monopolistic competition model. Kreps (1990, p. 344) includes it in his postgraduate text only because of its presence 'in most lower level texts'. On the other hand, a general equilibrium version developed by Dixit and Stiglitz (1977) has proved to be useful in extending economic analysis into new areas. Helpman and Krugman (1985) used it to examine monopolistic competition in international trade. Masahita *et al.* (1999) use it as the starting point for a path-breaking analysis of the spatial economy, while noting (p. 6) that 'to someone not familiar with the exigencies of economic modelling the popularity of the Dixit–Stiglitz model might seem baffling'.

Oligopoly

Alternative forms of oligopoly

The term 'oligopoly' refers to an industry in which there are only a few firms. The important characteristic of an oligopolistic industry is that the firms within it are *interdependent* upon each other, so that the actions of one company have a noticeable impact on the others. The existence of that interdependence means that the oligopoly situation is much more complex than the other market structures and much more difficult to model. It also means that in oligopoly firms are centrally concerned with their competitive strategies and may be seen as rival players in a very complex game. For that reason the modern analysis of oligopoly is dominated by game theory, examined in Chapter 13. This chapter is confined to a simpler approach which pre-dates the game theoretic revolution.

Unlike perfect competition and pure monopoly, which are tightly defined market structures, in which outcomes can be easily modelled, oligopolies may vary in a number of ways. First, they may differ with respect to the *number of firms*, which may vary from two in a *duopoly* up to a dozen or more. Second, oligopolies may vary with respect to the *extent of product differentiation*. At one extreme, sometimes referred to as 'pure oligopoly', the firms may all produce identical products. At the other extreme they may produce highly differentiated products. Third, oligopolies vary with respect to the *condition of entry*. At one extreme, entry to an oligopoly may be completely 'blockaded' so that competition concerns only the incumbent firms. At the other extreme, entry may be completely free so that potential competition from new entrants is a key determinant of the incumbent firms' behaviour.

As there is such a wide variety of different types of oligopoly it is not possible to set out a single rigorous analysis that will cover all possible cases. What can be done is to examine a number of different possible outcomes and to consider the factors that make each one more or less likely to occur.

Explicit collusion or cartelisation

If firms are interdependent upon each other, and recognise that interdependence, one possible outcome of the situation is that they join together and behave as a monopolist. In that way they are able to make the maximum profit possible and avoid the costs of competing with each other. Price and quantity will be set as illustrated in Figure 10.6 above.

The formation of a cartel in this way is such an obvious strategy for firms to adopt, and the advantages to them so substantial, that it is tempting to conclude that this is the usual outcome of oligopoly. Fortunately for consumers there are a number of other factors that have to be taken into account. The first of these is the law on competition (see Chapter 20). The governments of most industrial nations subscribe to the view that monopoly is harmful and have legislation that makes cartels illegal.

Even if cartels were not illegal there are a number of forces at work that make their establishment and maintenance difficult to achieve. In the first place, a group of rivals who set out to cartelise their industry have to come to an agreement on the price to be set in order to make maximum profit. Having taken a decision on the price to be set, the members of the cartel have to decide how much output can be sold at that price and to allocate production quotas for each member. If this is not done the cartel may produce more output than can be sold at the agreed price. Output will remain unsold and stocks will pile up, exerting downward pressure on the price. The negotiation of quotas is an extremely difficult issue because precise information about demand conditions is rarely available so that the level of output that corresponds to the profit-maximising price is not known with certainty. Once an estimate has been made of the total amount to be produced, that total has to be divided among the members. This is particularly sensitive because the division of output determines the distribution of profit. It may be the case that the members are simply unable to agree on quotas and the cartel collapses before it can be put into effect.

Even if a cartel is able to negotiate production quotas there continues to be a tendency for the arrangements to collapse as a result of cheating or suspected cheating on the part of members. Every member of a cartel faces a powerful incentive to cheat on the others by charging a price that is a little way below that agreed, thereby attracting a very high level of demand. As every member is in the same position, and every member knows it, there will tend to be a high level of suspicion among the firms who make up the cartel. If one firm is suspected of cheating, the others will follow suit by cutting their prices and the cartel will have collapsed.

The key factor in this situation is the extent to which the rival firms are well informed about each other (Fraas and Greer 1977). If they are very well informed, cheating will be identified immediately, the response will be immediate, and the gains to cheating will be non-existent. As a result, it is likely that in this situation the cartel will hold together as none of the members thinks it worthwhile to cheat. On the other hand, if firms are poorly informed about each other, cheating will be difficult to identify, the incentive to cheat will be greater and the cartel is more likely to collapse.

This analysis suggests a number of variables that will determine the likely success of a cartel, each of which affects the extent to which firms are well informed about each other.

● *The number of firms.* If an industry contains a very small number of firms they will be able to monitor each other's activities at relatively low cost, thereby deterring cheating.

- *Product differentiation*. If firms produce very similar products they will be well informed about their rivals' cost and demand conditions, simply by being well informed about themselves. Cheating will be deterred. If there is a high degree of product differentiation, or if products are non-standardised, it will be much more difficult for firms to keep themselves in touch with the activities of others, and the differences between products will make it extremely difficult to set monopoly prices, taking into account the cost variation between different firms' brands.
- *Publication of prices*. If prices are published, firms will find it much easier to monitor each other's activities than if prices are kept confidential.
- *Slow rates of technological progress*. If technological progress is rapid, the industry will experience a much greater degree of uncertainty and instability than if companies are all using an established, mature set of techniques that develop only slowly. As a result, cartelisation is much more difficult in conditions of rapid technological change.
- *The existence of a trade association*. If there is an active trade association in an industry, this can provide an effective channel of communication between firms, thereby assisting in the process of cartelisation. Trade associations may also be able to exert some degree of discipline over firms that do not conform by denying them access to the association's facilities, or by more subtle means such as failing to elect them to prestigious posts or even social ostracism.

If the conditions are favourable, firms in an industry may be able to establish a cartel, negotiate prices and output quotas, and maintain orderly behaviour. In that case it will be possible for supernormal profits to be earned, in the short run at least. In the longer term there are a number of other forces that will tend to break down the cartel's power.

The first of these forces is the threat of new entry. If a cartel is successful in raising the price and increasing profits for its members, this immediately creates an incentive for other firms to enter the industry. This need not matter if entry is 'blockaded', so that new firms are absolutely unable to enter. However, totally blockaded entry is a relatively rare phenomenon and cartels in most industries are subject to breakdown in the long run as a result of the cartel's success leading to new entry. It is possible, of course, that new entrants join the cartel but that would increase the number of firms and reduce the cartel's manageability. As long as a cartel uses its power to earn supernormal profits there will be market forces working to break down that cartel.

The second factor that works to eliminate the power of a cartel in the long run is the search for substitutes. If the price of the product produced by the cartel increases, this creates an incentive for users of the product to seek alternatives, and for other firms to invent and produce such substitutes. While this may take some time its eventual effect will be to reduce the demand for the cartel's product and make it more elastic, thereby reducing the cartel's ability to charge high prices and make large profits.

Perhaps the most important example of a cartel is the Organisation of Petroleum Exporting Countries (OPEC), whose history provides a graphic illustration of the issues raised by cartels. When OPEC raised the price of oil in the early 1970s this immediately encouraged other countries to begin searching for their own sources. At the oil prices that held in the 1960s it was not commercially sensible to search for oil in difficult environments like the North Sea, because the cost of exploration and recovery could not be justified by the value of any oil that might be found. However, once the oil price rose, the economics of oil exploration changed dramatically, so that it became worthwhile for a number of countries to begin searching for oil in order to enter the industry themselves. As a result, OPEC members' share of the oil industry declined, reducing its capacity to act effectively as a cartel.

In addition to the pressures caused by new entry, the oil industry has been affected by the drive to find substitutes for its products. In some cases these substitutes are relatively direct, as in the use of ethyl alcohol as a fuel for cars. In other cases the substitutes may involve quite different products from those produced by the cartel. Better insulation for housing, for instance, or car engines with improved fuel consumption both provide indirect substitutes for oil.

To summarise with respect to cartels, then, there are a variety of market forces that tend to break them down, especially in the long run. These forces may take a considerable time to have their full effect, allowing a cartel to make substantial profit for that time, but unless governments place legal barriers in the way of potential entrants, it is to be expected that in most cases cartels contain the seeds of their own destruction.

'Price leadership' and tacit collusion

A cartel is an example of explicit collusion, where the firms involved are parties to an agreement to reduce output and raise prices to the monopoly level, in order to make maximum joint profits. In many countries such arrangements are illegal and firms risk the penalties set by law if they become involved in them. As a result, firms may not wish to become involved in explicitly collusive arrangements like cartels. However, there are other forms of unspoken or tacit collusion that firms may develop. These do not necessarily involve any form of conspiracy on the part of the firms involved; they simply stem from the recognition of interdependence among rivals and of the costs that may be involved if rivalry becomes too intense.

One of the most important forms of tacit collusion is known as *price leadership* (Markham 1951, Roy *et al.* 1994, Nagle and Holden 1995). In this situation, one of the firms in the industry adopts the role of price leader, setting a price that is followed by the others. If the firms are all producing identical products then the followers set the same price as the leader. If products are differentiated the followers use the leader's price as a benchmark and adjust their own prices upwards or downwards according to the different quality and cost of production of their particular product variants. In this way the firms in the industry can establish what is sometimes termed 'orderly' competition among themselves. In the language of the corporate strategist (Porter 1985), they behave as 'good competitors' for each other.

If price leadership is to be established, the leader must have a powerful position in the industry, in order to be able to offer an unspoken threat of punishment to any firm that fails to act as a follower. The most obvious such punishment would be to push the price down so far that the offending firm cannot survive. That implies that the price leader needs to be the lowest-cost producer in the industry, and to have substantial market share and production capacity in order for the threat to be credible.

Price wars and an elementary application of the theory of games

While cartels and tacit collusion are two possible outcomes in the oligopoly situation, competition between rivals is not always so comfortable. There are situations in which rivalry between the firms in a concentrated industry becomes so intense that a 'price war' breaks out, with prices being cut until they may even fall below marginal cost as each firm strives desperately to keep its market share. Clearly, such an outcome is not in the interests of any firm, but the structure of an oligopoly may create incentives that lead to the outbreak of price wars.

In order to understand how such a situation can arise it is useful to introduce some basic elements of game theory, in advance of a more thorough treatment in Chapter 13. This technique was originally developed during the Second World War in order to assist military strategists. Nevertheless, it is also particularly relevant to oligopoly because it concerns the behaviour of interdependent rival players, each of which has a choice of moves, the outcomes of which depend heavily upon the actions of the others.

The basic application of game theory to oligopoly can be shown in a simplified example, where we consider an industry that contains only two firms, both producing an identical product, and both firms are trying to decide between setting a high price or a low price. The results of the alternative pricing policies can be set out in a simple pay-off matrix, illustrated in Figure 10.8.

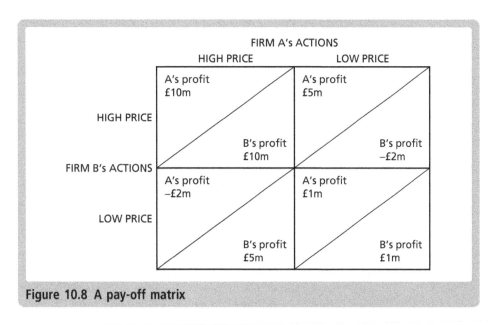

Figure 10.8 A pay-off matrix

The matrix shows the profits made by each firm, for each combination of its own decision on price and that of the other firm. As the matrix shows, if both firms decided together to opt for a high price, that would give them both very substantial profits. However, if one firm sets a high price and the other one a low price, the high-price firm loses all of its customers to the other firm. In that event the high-price firm makes substantial losses and may even go out of business, while the low-price firm makes substantial profits.

Consider the decision facing each firm trying to decide upon its price. Each has a choice between a high price and a low price, but the outcome depends upon what the other firm does. How can the firm decide? Each firm is in a situation of uncertainty, with the results of its decisions depending upon the 'state of nature' that prevails after the decision has been taken. One possible strategy in that situation is to adopt the maximin decision criterion, choosing between a high price and a low price by selecting the option that guarantees that the worst possible outcome is avoided. In that case, each firm will consider the alternatives and will then opt for the low price, in order to avoid the possibility of being undercut by its rival. However, both firms face the same situation and will tend to apply the same logic to it. As a result, both firms select a low price, the opportunity to make a higher level of profit is lost, and a price war has broken out.

Just as in the case of collusion, the key to the rivals' problem lies in the information they have about each other and the degree of trust they share. If they are well informed about each other, and trust each other not to cheat, then the price war situation can be avoided by both firms charging the joint monopoly price. On the other hand, if they do not trust each other, then fear of rivals' reactions will drive both firms to a very low price.

The example given above illustrates that, in the language of game theory, oligopoly is not generally a zero-sum game. A zero-sum game is a situation where the winner's gains are exactly equal to the loser's losses. If two gamblers bet each other £1,000 on the toss of a coin, that constitutes a zero-sum game. No matter what the outcome, the gains to one player are exactly equal to the losses incurred by the other. In the case of oligopoly it is possible for both players to gain (if they set a monopoly price) or both to lose (if they become involved in a price war).

Price stability and the kinky demand curve model

The analysis of oligopoly would be incomplete without reference to the *kinky demand curve* model, which was the standard approach to oligopoly before the game theoretic revolution. This is a simple model of the individual firm in oligopoly which brings together a number of issues already discussed, in the marginal cost and marginal revenue framework which has been used to analyse firms in other market structures. The model is set out in Figure 10.9.

The starting point for this model is the assumption that firms in the industry have found some way of establishing a price (perhaps through collusion or price leadership) and each firm knows the level of output that it can sell at that price. This position is indicated in the diagram by P_{est} and Q_{est}.

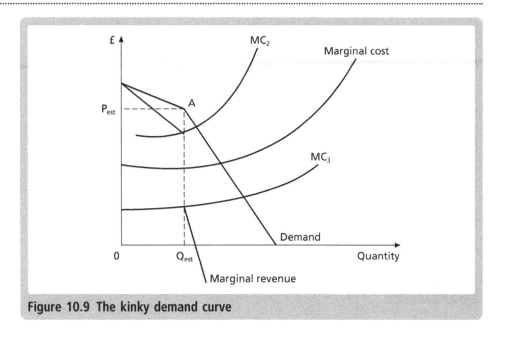

Figure 10.9 The kinky demand curve

While the firm in the diagram knows how much it can sell at the established price, the amounts that it can sell at higher or lower prices are less clear and depend upon the reaction of the firm's rivals. The firm cannot know these for certain, but can at least make guesses as to the likely responses. If the firm raises its price, it guesses that its rivals will not follow suit. As a result, price rises will imply the loss of a substantial proportion of the firm's customers, and the demand curve for prices above P_{est} will be highly elastic. On the other hand, if the firm lowers its price, its guess with respect to its rivals' reactions is that they will follow its example and also lower their prices. As a result the demand curve for price reductions is highly inelastic, as shown in the diagram.

The demand curve that results from this analysis has a 'kink' in it, as shown. Following from that, the marginal revenue curve has an even more pronounced discontinuity, taking the form of a 'dog-leg' shape, also as shown. This follows directly from the behaviour of demand. If the firm wishes to sell more than Q_{est} it has to lower the price, but if it does so then its rivals will also cut their prices so that a small increase in demand for the firm's product will require a proportionately large fall in price. As a result the additional revenue earned from an additional unit of output sold will be very small or even negative.

If the oligopolist is a profit-maximiser, it will operate at the point where marginal cost equals marginal revenue, which corresponds to output Q_{est} in the diagram. That provides very little useful information because the firm started from that position. What is useful and interesting about the model is that the same price and quantity will continue to be chosen by the firm, even if marginal costs vary quite substantially. In the example shown, marginal cost could rise as high as MC_2 or as low as MC_3 without the firm choosing to change its price. Similar considerations apply to increases in demand. If the demand curve shifts to the right, the kink remaining at the same level of price, the firm will choose to increase its output, but the price chosen will remain the same for quite substantial changes in demand.

The kinky demand curve model does not provide a prediction about the level of price that will be reached in an oligopoly situation. What it does predict is that once a price has been established it will tend to be stable in the face of changing costs and demand conditions, within limits. That is a very different prediction from those arising from the other models of market structure that have been discussed. In perfect competition, monopoly or monopolistic competition, changes in cost or demand will lead to changes in price. The reason for the difference, of course, stems from the importance of rivalry in oligopoly and each firm's fears of adverse reactions on the part of competitors. Having once found a price that can be sustained, oligopolists are wary of disturbing the delicate equilibrium by changing prices. If they do so, they might find rivals reacting adversely, to the detriment of their profitability.

Illustration 1 Price collusion and market structure

One of the key findings with respect to oligopoly is that when an industry's output is concentrated in the hands of a small number of firms there is a significant probability that the firms involved will join together to form a cartel. However, the theory does not indicate exactly how small the number of firms has to be for cartel formation to take place, nor does it identify the other factors that make price-fixing easier or more difficult. Fraas and Greer (1977) provide an empirical study of this issue.

The starting point for their analysis lay in data from the US Department of Justice over the period 1910–72, which yielded a sample of 606 cases of price-fixing. Each case was assigned to an industrial category and a range of characteristics was identified.

The theoretical analysis that underlay the study's methodology began with the observation that explicit price collusion will only take place when it is both possible and necessary. When the conditions for collusion are highly adverse, price-fixing will be impossible and will not take place. At the other extreme, when conditions for collusion are very highly favourable, price-fixing can take place without the need for explicit collusion, which becomes unnecessary.

This basic idea can be used to establish a number of empirically testable hypotheses. For instance, if there is an inverse relationship between the ease of collusion and the number of firms involved, then the numbers involved in all conspiracy cases (whether explicit or implicit) would have a lower central tendency (whether mean, median or mode) than the frequency distribution of the number of firms in industries in general. Furthermore, the distribution for explicit cases of collusion would have an inverted U-shape, not simply because the general distribution has such a shape but because the rising part of the curve reflects the changing trade-off between tacit and explicit collusion. When there are a very small number of firms in an industry, implicit collusion will be easily achieved, so that very few cases of explicit collusion will be identified. As the number of firms increases, it becomes more difficult to collude so that explicit, and hence observable, collusion is necessary and the curve is steeply positively sloped. Once the number of firms rises beyond a certain level, collusion becomes much more difficult and is rarely

Illustration 1

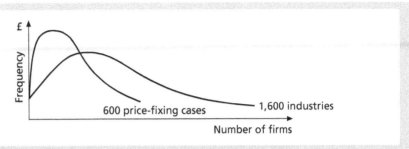

Figure 10.10 Frequency distributions for 1,600 industries and 600 price-fixing cases

Table 10.1 Median number of firms involved in price-fixing agreements having different characteristics

Sample	Median
All price-fixing agreements	8
Trade associations involved	16
International scope	5
Bid rigging	6
Patents involved	6
Resale price maintenance	12
Market allocations	7
Single sales agent	16
Coercion	10

Adapted from: Fraas and Greer (1977).

practised, so that the curve becomes negatively sloped and steeper than the distribution for firms in general. Figure 10.10 illustrates this point in a simplified form.

As Figure 10.10 shows, the distribution for price-fixing cases bears the predicted relationship to the distribution for industries.

Having compared these two distributions, the basic method may be extended by making other comparisons. If some particular structural factor (like the existence of a trade association, for instance) is thought to make price-fixing easier, then price-fixing arrangements will be able to take place when there are more firms, if that structural factor is present. Such hypotheses can therefore be tested by dividing the sample of price-fixing cases into a series of sub-samples, each associated with different structural characteristics, and examining their means, medians and modes. Table 10.1 shows Fraas and Greer's main results.

As Table 10.1 shows, the median number of firms involved in price-fixing arrangements was higher in the presence of trade associations, resale price maintenance agreements, single sales agents and coercion, indicating that these factors make collusion easier to arrange, while the involvement of international scope, bid rigging or patents make collusion more difficult.

Table 10.1 offers only a crude test of the various hypotheses because each of the sub-samples contains agreements having a number of different characteristics. Within the sub-sample of collusions involving trade associations, for instance, there are also agreements that involve patents. Fraas and Greer therefore devised a series of more sophisticated tests, using more homogeneous sub-samples and different reference groups, in order to use the same basic empirical technique.

The eventual conclusion drawn was that the data supports the belief that tacit collusion, which is difficult to 'reach' under the law, is only possible with a very small number of firms and an uncomplicated market environment. As the number of firms increases, price conspiracies are forced to adopt more elaborate and explicit cooperative arrangements which are increasingly 'reachable'. The implication for public policy is that only a slight degree of industrial reorganisation would be needed to secure an industrial structure in which tacit collusion was extremely difficult. To be more specific, Fraas and Greer suggest that competition, rather than collusion, will be the norm, provided that there are twelve or more firms in a sector and the law against explicit price-fixing arrangements is enforced.

Illustration 2 Monopolistic competition and international trade

The standard theory of international trade is based around the 'factor proportions' proposition, stating that each country will specialise in and export those goods that make most intensive use of the resource that the country has in relative abundance. Countries that are well endowed with labour relative to capital will export labour-intensive goods, and vice versa. The result of trade will be an improvement in the world-wide allocation of resources, known as the *gains from trade*.

One problem with that approach is that it only explains *inter-industry* trade, where each country produces and trades different commodities (China exports toys while the United States and Germany export machine tools). It does not help to explain the very large proportion of total trade that is *intra-industry* – the exchange of similar products between countries that have similar factor endowments. Nor does it show that there are gains from such trade. Helpman and Krugman (1985) took the unusual step of applying the microeconomic theory of monopolistic competition to this problem in international trade theory.

The starting point is with a very simple two-country world in which the two countries both have the same number of workers and consumers. Initially there is *autarky* (no trade between the two countries) and it can be shown, using a simplified version of the Dixit and Stiglitz (1977) model (Shy 1995, pp. 143–8), that in each country there will be a finite number of different brands produced. The price of each brand will equal its average cost, and will also equal twice its marginal cost. The quantity produced by each firm will be equal to its fixed cost divided by its marginal cost and the number of brands will increase as fixed cost is smaller and decrease as fixed cost is larger.

If free trade between the two countries is then introduced, the number of workers and consumers doubles. That has no effect on the price of each brand or the equilibrium level of output of each brand. However, the number of brands available to consumers in each country will double. Each country will consume half of the world's production. Because the number of brands has increased, total welfare in each country increases, demonstrating that under monopolistic competition free trade improves the allocation of resources. Hence the basic economic insight arising from the theory of comparative advantage, which applies to inter-industry trade, also applies to intra-industry trade. There are gains from trade in both cases.

References and further reading

E. Chamberlin, *The Theory of Monopolistic Competition*, Cambridge, MA, Harvard University Press, 1933.

A. Dixit and J. Stiglitz, 'Monopolistic Competition and Optimum Product Diversity', *American Economic Review*, vol. 67, no. 3, 1977, pp. 297–308.

A.G. Fraas and D.F. Greer, 'Market Structure and Price Collusion: An Empirical Analysis', *Journal of Industrial Economics*, vol. XXVI, September 1977, pp. 31, 34.

E. Helpman and P. Krugman, *Market Structure and Foreign Trade*, Cambridge, MA, MIT Press, 1985.

D. Kreps, *A Course in Microeconomic Theory*, Princeton, Princeton University Press, 1990.

J.W. Markham, 'The Nature and Significance of Price Leadership', *American Economic Review*, vol. 4, December 1951, pp. 891–905.

F. Masahita, P. Krugman and A. Venables, *The Spatial Economoy: Cities, Regions and International Trade*, Cambridge, MA, MIT Press, 1999.

T. Nagle and R. Holden, *The Strategy and Tactics of Pricing*, Englewood Cliffs, NJ, Prentice Hall, 1995.

M. Porter, *Competitive Advantage*, New York, Free Press, 1985.

A. Roy, D. Hanssens and J. Raju, 'Competitive Pricing by a Price Leader', *Management Science*, vol. 40, no. 7, July 1994, pp. 809–23.

O. Shy, *Industrial Organization: Theory and Applications*, Cambridge, MA, MIT Press, 1995.

Self-test questions

1. Which of the following characteristics are shared by perfect competition and monopolistic competition?

   (a) large number of small firms
   (b) free entry to the industry
   (c) identical products
   (d) perfect knowledge of market opportunities

2. Which of the following statements are correct?

   (a) a profit-maximising monopolist will always produce on the elastic portion of its demand curve
   (b) a monopolist will always make supernormal profits
   (c) oligopolists frequently alter their prices
   (d) monopolistic competition gives economic efficiency
   (e) perfect competitors are 'price-makers'

3. Which of the following factors will make the maintenance of a cartel more difficult?

   (a) rapid technical progress
   (b) production of identical products
   (c) a relatively large number of firms
   (d) the invention of substitutes for the cartel's product
   (e) a well-organised trade association

4. Which of the following statements are correct?

(a) in long-run equilibrium in monopolistic competition, price equals average cost

(b) in monopoly, price is greater than marginal cost

(c) in oligopoly, entry cannot take place

(d) in perfect competition, there cannot be substantial economies of scale

(e) free entry ensures that price cannot remain above average cost in the long run

Essay question

Explain the statement that perfect competition gives an optimal allocation of resources but that the existence of scale economies may make perfect competition impossible.

11 The 'five forces' approach to competitive structure

This chapter builds upon the formal models of competitive structure, outlined in Chapter 10, to introduce the more general 'five forces' approach to the structural analysis of industries. Each of the five forces is considered in turn and the analysis is applied to two very different industries, in order to illustrate its use in practice.

The structural analysis of competition

The limits of standard economic models of market structure

The relatively formal textbook analysis of market structures points to the importance of certain dimensions of market structure. In perfect competition and monopolistic competition, for instance, freedom of entry is the major force that eliminates supernormal profits in the long run. On the other hand, in the case of pure monopoly, the impossibility of entry ensures that super-profits can be made forever. Clearly, the condition of entry is a key variable in deciding how attractive an industry is for the firms in it.

The textbook models also illustrate the importance of rivalry between existing firms, the extent of product differentiation and the threat of substitutes. However, there are a number of important gaps in the textbook analyses. The first is that they pay no attention at all to the possibility of market power on the part of the firm's customers or their suppliers, which are important features in many industries. The second is that they pay no attention to the factors that determine the key dimensions of market structure. Entry, for instance, is said to be entirely free or entirely blockaded without any consideration of the factors that make it so. Rivalry exists in oligopoly, but not in any of the other market structures, and the models pay no attention to the factors that determine the intensity of that rivalry.

In order to fill these gaps left by the textbook analyses of market structure, corporate strategists have developed more thorough approaches to the characterisation of market structures, which recognise many more types of structure than the four considered in Chapter 10, and which attempt to identify the determining factors for each dimension of competitive structure.

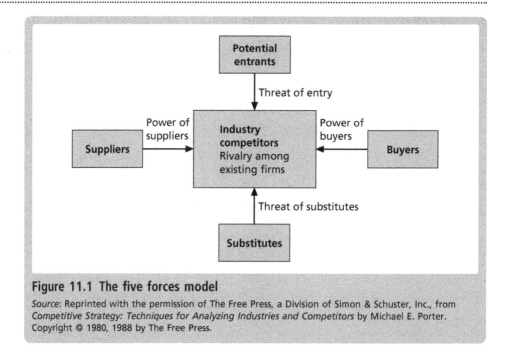

Figure 11.1 The five forces model

Source: Reprinted with the permission of The Free Press, a Division of Simon & Schuster, Inc., from *Competitive Strategy: Techniques for Analyzing Industries and Competitors* by Michael E. Porter. Copyright © 1980, 1988 by The Free Press.

An outline of the 'five forces' model

Perhaps the best-known approach of this type is the 'five forces' approach to the structural analysis of industries, developed by Michael Porter at the Harvard Business School (Porter 1980). This approach is set out schematically in Figure 11.1.

According to the 'five forces' approach, the structure of competition in an industry can be described in terms of five major 'forces':

1. The intensity of rivalry among existing firms.
2. The threat of entry.
3. The threat of substitutes.
4. The power of buyers.
5. The power of suppliers.

Each of the five forces is in turn determined by a number of different factors, which themselves need to be considered in order to build up a full picture of competition in an individual industry. The interaction of the five forces taken together determine how attractive the industry is to the firms within it.

The 'five forces' model is more complete than the set of textbook models, but it is also much less rigorous. It allows for dozens of different types of market structure but does not provide absolutely clear predictions with regard to the outcome of those structures. Indeed, its value lies not in providing predictions for every conceivable type of industry, but rather in giving executives a thorough checklist that they can use to identify the most important features of competition in their own industry. Those salient features provide a starting point from which firms can begin to develop a competitive strategy (see Chapter 18).

A clear understanding of the 'five forces' model requires a brief explanation of the factors that determine each of the five forces. When carried out in the abstract this can be a laborious process, as there are more than thirty different factors that have to be taken into account. Nevertheless, they all require some preliminary consideration if they are to be understood. Once that basic understanding has been acquired, it is possible to apply the analysis to particular cases, at which point its value becomes clearer as in most industries many of the factors listed are relatively unimportant. Once these have been identified, management's attention can focus upon those key factors that are salient.

In order to illustrate the application of the technique, each of the five forces is considered in general below, and then applied to two very different industries. The first is the industry producing touring caravans in England. Touring caravans are light mobile homes ('trailers' in American English), which are towed behind cars and provide a mobile form of accommodation for holidays or weekends. The second industry is the global industry producing an important chemical feedstock for other chemical industries. The actual name of the chemical concerned has been changed and it is referred to simply as 'feedstock'.

The intensity of rivalry among existing competitors

The *intensity of rivalry* or *competitive intensity* among firms is not a variable that features directly in economic analysis. Nevertheless, it is clear that in some industries rivalry is intense, even 'cut-throat', while in others relations between firms are 'gentlemanly', or 'polite' or 'orderly'. The Porter analysis identifies the factors that determine the degree of rivalry as follows.

Industry growth

Industry growth is a key factor. If growth of the industry as a whole is rapid, each firm will be able to grow without needing to take market share away from its rivals and managerial time will be devoted to keeping up with industry growth, rather than attacking rivals. As a result, rivalry will be less intense in rapidly growing industries. On the other hand, if an industry is growing slowly or declining, growth for one firm can only be at the expense of others and rivalry will be intense.

In touring caravans, the industry has seen a decline in output during the 1980s and 1990s, leading to intense rivalry. In feedstock production, industry growth has been positive, but less than the growth in world GNP, indicating substantial rivalry.

High fixed costs or storage costs

If these costs are high, failure to maintain the volume of sales may cause a dramatic increase in costs and loss of profits. As a result, firms will be very concerned to maintain the volume of sales and will tend to cut prices if they feel there is any danger of reducing sales volume. Rivalry will therefore tend to be directly related to the importance of these costs.

In touring caravans fixed costs are not very large, but storage costs can become prohibitive if production is not sold. In feedstock production the fixed costs of plant are enormous, running into tens of millions of pounds.

Intermittent over-capacity

If an industry experiences periods of over-capacity, either because demand fluctuates or because economies of scale require that additions to capacity are very large, rivalry will tend to become more intense. In touring caravans volatile demand often causes over-capacity. In feedstock production additions to capacity have to be very large indeed, which can cause similar problems, though for different reasons.

Product differences, brand identity and switching costs for customers

If an industry's products are identical and there is no brand identity, and customers can change from one supplier to another without incurring costs, then customers will be very sensitive to price and the demand for each firm's product will be very highly elastic, as in perfect competition. A firm that charges a low price will gain customers very substantially, and a firm that charges a high price will lose heavily. In this situation rivalry will tend to be intense. At the other extreme, if all firms produce substantially different products, with strong brand identities, and customers incur high costs in switching from one supplier to another, then demand for each firm's output will be much less elastic. Customers have preferences and brand loyalties so that rivalry will be much less intense.

Feedstock is a 'commodity chemical', being produced to an international standard, so that every firm's output is identical, provided it meets that standard. In touring caravans there are product differences and a degree of brand identity which firms attempt to reinforce. However, it is not clear how far this allows firms to create buyer loyalty.

The number of firms and their relative size

If the number of firms producing close substitutes is relatively large, it will be difficult for them to monitor each other's activities and there will be a danger that some firms believe that they can make competitive moves without being noticed. As a result rivalry will tend to be intense. A smaller number of firms will lead to less rivalry. However, if firms in an industry are of the same size that too will tend to intensify rivalry as the outcome of a competitive contest will be unclear and bold managements may be tempted to embark upon aggressive moves towards their rivals. The intensity of rivalry is likely to be lowest in an industry with a relatively small number of firms, one of which is more powerful than the others, and therefore able to ensure 'orderly' competition through mechanisms like price leadership.

In touring caravans there is a market leader who is substantially bigger than the other firms, a second tier of five or six medium-sized firms and several dozen smaller firms. 'Orderly' competition is very difficult to maintain. In feedstock production there are only about six producers world-wide. One of these has more 'free capacity' than the others (i.e. capacity whose output is not directly committed to its own plants) and it is able to exert price leadership.

Diversity of competitors

If rivals within an industry share objectives and goals and have similar 'corporate cultures' and relationships with their parent companies, then they will tend to think in similar ways, be able to predict how each other will respond and agree on an implicit set of 'rules of the game'. On the other hand, if they do not, rivalry will tend to be more intense. An industry that contains foreign competitors, or both large corporations and owner-managers, will therefore tend to have a higher intensity of rivalry.

This variable can be difficult to assess for many industries. In both caravans and feedstock the rivals seem to be similar, although the industries are radically different. In the small caravan companies executives move from firm to firm, and many are located in the same part of the country, creating a common outlook. In feedstock, the players are all global chemical companies.

Corporate stakes

Rivalry will tend to be more intense if success in the industry is of particular importance for the firms involved, either because of its potential contribution to their profits, or because it has some strategic value to them. Caravan companies are generally single-product independent firms, totally dependent upon the caravan industry for their survival. Feedstock producers are all involved in a much wider range of products, although in some cases feedstock is a major contributor to group profits.

High exit barriers

If leaving the industry entails incurring high costs then firms will be anxious to remain in the industry and rivalry will tend to be intense. The costs of leaving may include financial costs like redundancy payments or the loss in value of highly specialised assets, but may also include psychic costs like executives' unwillingness to abandon a business, or loss of goodwill from government if unemployment is caused.

The caravan industry is one in which exit barriers are very low, and exit is common. In feedstock production, exit would render tens of millions of pounds' worth of capacity valueless.

(a) Touring caravans in the UK

Determinant	Low rivalry		High rivalry
Industry growth			★
Fixed/storage costs		★	
Intermittent over-capacity			★
Product differences	★		
Brand identity	★		
Switching costs for consumers			★
Concentration/balance		★	
Diversity of competitors	★		
Corporate stakes			★
Exit barriers	★		

Overall judgement on the intensity of rivalry: *Very intense rivalry*

(b) Feedstock production

Determinant	Low rivalry		High rivalry
Industry growth	★		
Fixed/storage costs			★
Intermittent over-capacity		★	
Product differences			★
Brand identity			★
Switching costs for consumers			★
Concentration/balance	★		
Diversity of competitors	★		
Corporate stakes	★		
Exit barriers			★

Overall judgement on the intensity of rivalry: *Very intense rivalry but the importance of market leadership as a stabilising factor should be noted*

Figure 11.2 The intensity of rivalry in two industries

Summarising the intensity of rivalry

Taken together, the factors listed above determine the extent of rivalry. As each of them represents a different dimension they cannot be measured and added together to give an overall 'index of rivalry'. However, it is possible to consider whether the impact of each factor will tend to lead to relatively high or relatively low intensity of rivalry and then to attempt an overall aggregation using judgement. Figure 11.2 summarises the position for the touring caravan and feedstock industries and attempts an overall judgement.

The threat of new entry

The second of the five forces is the threat of new entrants, whose importance is determined by the height of 'barriers to entry'. If entry barriers are very high, the existing firms in the industry do not need to concern themselves unduly with the possibility that high prices and profits may attract competition from new entrants. On the other hand, if entry barriers are low, entry may take place with ease whenever the incumbent firms in an industry make substantial profits. The pioneering work on entry barriers is that of Bain (1956). Chapter 14 considers ways in which firms may set prices in order to deter entrants. The determinants of entry barriers may be considered in turn.

Economies of scale

If there are substantial economies of scale, a firm that is considering entering the industry must either build a large market share immediately, in order to achieve the scale required to keep costs down, or suffer higher costs than the incumbent firms. As a result, scale economies are a key source of entry barriers. It is important to remember that such economies are not limited to production activities. There may be important scale effects in almost any business activity, including R&D, marketing and distribution.

In the feedstock industry, economies of scale in both production and R&D are an absolutely central feature of the industry's economics. In touring caravans, by contrast, scale economies are relatively insignificant, as indicated by the continued survival of some very small firms.

Product differentiation and brand loyalty

If existing firms have successfully developed buyer loyalty to their products, a new entrant may have to make expensive and risky investments in advertising and promotion in order to overcome that loyalty. If entry should fail, those investments become worthless.

In feedstock there is no product differentiation at all. In caravans there is some differentiation but the real extent of consumer loyalty to individual brands is not clear.

Capital requirements

In some industries, very large amounts of capital have to be acquired if entry is to take place. While these may be available if capital markets work well, entry will often be regarded as a risky venture and investors will require high returns in order to persuade them to take that risk.

In feedstock production capital requirements are very high indeed and form a major entry barrier. In caravans they are insignificant.

Switching costs for buyers

If customers have to face additional costs in switching from one supplier to another, they will be unwilling to change suppliers and it will be difficult for a new entrant to be successful, without a heavy investment to help customers overcome those switching costs. Switching costs are not significant for either caravan or feedstock buyers.

Access to distribution channels

A new entrant must establish its own distribution channels, persuading whole-salers and retailers to stock and display its product alongside, or in preference to, the products of existing firms. If the incumbent firms have well-established relationships with the distribution channels it may be difficult or expensive for a new entrant to gain access to them. This factor is of some significance in the caravan industry, but is not relevant for feedstock.

Absolute cost advantages

One of the most general sources of entry barriers is the existence of absolute cost advantages, whereby incumbent firms have lower costs than entrants. If there are such advantages, existing firms will always have the ability to cut their prices to a level at which new entrants cannot survive, which will provide a major dis-incentive to entry (see Chapter 14 for details). The possible sources of absolute cost advantages include:

- *Proprietary technology.* If a firm has a product or a process that is protected by a patent, or by secrecy, new entrants will not be able to copy that product or process and will be at a disadvantage.
- *Access to inputs.* Existing firms may have access to inputs on favourable terms.
- *Proprietary learning effects.* As firms gain experience in an industry, they are usually able to reduce their costs as a result of 'learning effects'. If these effects are 'proprietary' and a new firm cannot acquire them simply by hiring executives from the existing firms, then an entrant will be at a disadvantage until it has had time to learn for itself, by which time the longer-established firms may have benefited from additional learning, staying one step ahead of the entrant.
- *Favourable locations.* For some activities there are only a limited number of suitable locations. If these are all occupied by existing firms, new entry will be extremely difficult.

In feedstock production absolute cost advantages are a crucial aspect of the industry's competitive structure. The market leader has a proprietary technology that it controls; learning effects are important and are consciously pursued through R&D. Locations next to sources of raw materials, which are relatively few, are important in securing low costs. In touring caravans existing firms have few, if any, cost advantages over entrants.

Expected retaliation

In many industries the reaction of the established firms to new entry is a key factor determining the entrant's success. If they are accommodating, an entrant has a greater chance of success. On the other hand, if they retaliate aggressively through price-cutting or promotional campaigns, the entrant will only be able to survive if it has some very strong advantages to compensate for its inexperi-ence in the industry. As a result the threat of retaliation will in itself present an important barrier to entry. In caravans the threat of retaliation is relatively empty. In feedstock production it is very important indeed.

Government policy

In some industries, in some countries, government policy sets up barriers to entry. At the extreme these involve industrial licensing, where a firm has to have government permission before setting up in an industry. In other cases the barriers to entry established by government policy may be more subtle and are often unintended. For instance, if a government imposes strict health and safety legislation on an industry, this may increase the capital requirements needed to enter and thereby raise entry barriers.

Summarising the threat of entry

The factors that determine the threat of entry cannot simply be summed in order to provide a measure of the overall threat. However, it is possible to attach subjective values to each of the determining factors, and to summarise the overall position. Figure 11.3 shows the results for the two industries under consideration.

(a) Touring caravans in the UK

Determinant	Low threat		High threat
Economies of scale			★
Product differentiation			★
Switching costs for buyers			★
Capital requirements			★
Access to distribution		★	
Absolute cost advantages			
Proprietary products/processes			★
Access to inputs			★
Proprietary learning effects			★
Government policy			★
Expected retaliation			★

Overall estimate of the threat of entry: *Very high threat of entry*

(b) Feedstock in the global market

Determinant	Low threat		High threat
Economies of scale	★		
Product differentiation			★
Switching costs for buyers		★	
Capital requirements	★		
Access to distribution		★	
Absolute cost advantages			
Proprietary products/processes	★		
Access to inputs	★		
Proprietary learning effects	★		
Government policy	★		
Expected retaliation	★		

Overall estimate of the threat of entry: *Very low threat of entry*

Figure 11.3 The threat of entry

The threat of substitutes

If substitutes are available for the industry's products, customers will be able to switch to those substitutes if the existing firms attempt to charge high prices. The threat of substitutes is therefore an important market force setting limits upon the prices that firms are able to charge. The importance of this threat depends upon three factors, each of which can be considered briefly.

The relative price and performance of substitutes

If substitutes are available which offer similar performance at the same level of price, then the threat of substitution is very strong. On the other hand, if substitutes are more expensive and offer inferior performance, the threat is much weaker.

In the case of touring caravans the only threat of substitutes comes from tents on the one hand and motorised caravans on the other. Neither offers comparable price and performance. In the case of feedstock, a number of the products derived from feedstock could be substituted for, but the product is an input into such a wide range of production processes that outright substitution on any scale is unlikely and the threat from substitutes limited, given current price/performance characteristics.

Switching costs for customers

This factor has been referred to above as a source of entry barriers, and it also determines the threat of substitutes. In the case of feedstock, customers would incur little cost in switching from one supplier of feedstock to another. However, they would incur very substantial costs indeed if they should attempt to switch from a feedstock-based process to a different one. The threat of substitutes is therefore limited. Caravan users who decide to switch to tents or motor-homes face insignificant switching costs.

Buyers' propensity to substitute

If customers put relatively little effort into searching for substitutes and are disinclined to change suppliers, the threat of substitution is correspondingly reduced. Very little is known with certainty about this factor for either industry under consideration. However, both feedstock and caravans represent major purchases for the firms and families that buy them, which suggests that the propensity to substitute, given an incentive to do so, is likely to be high.

Summarising the threat of substitutes

Figure 11.4 summarises the extent of the threat of substitutes for the feedstock and caravan industries.

(a) Touring caravans

Determinant	Low threat	High threat
Price/performance of substitutes	★	
Switching costs for buyers		★
Buyers' propensity to substitute		★?

Overall importance of the threat from substitutes: *Difficult to judge*

(b) Feedstock

Determinant	Low threat	High threat
Price/performance of substitutes	★	
Switching costs for buyers	★	
Buyers propensity to substitute		★?

Overall importance of the threat from substitutes: *Important in the longer term for some end-uses but not all*

Figure 11.4 Threat of substitutes

The power of buyers

The power of buyers depends upon two general factors. The first is the extent of their price sensitivity and the second is their bargaining leverage, each of which can be considered in turn.

Price sensitivity

Price sensitivity is essentially the same concept as elasticity of demand, although in the Porter analysis no attempt is made to express it quantitatively. Price sensitivity is a function of the following:

● *Purchases from the industry as a proportion of total purchases*. If the industry's product makes up an unimportant proportion of users' total purchases, they will tend to be relatively insensitive to its price, as it will have little impact upon their costs. On the other hand, if a product makes up a considerable portion of buyers' total purchases they will be highly conscious of its price and concerned to see it as low as possible. In caravans, a purchase is a major investment for a customer, who is likely to be price sensitive. In feedstock there are wide variations from buyer to buyer which makes generalisation difficult.

● *Product differences and brand identity*. Both of these will reduce price sensitivity. There are no such differences in the case of feedstock. In caravans there are some, though not on the scale associated with motor-cars, for example.

● *The impact of the industry's product on the quality of the customer's product or service*. If the industry's product is a key element in maintaining the quality of the customer's own product, they are unlikely to be price sensitive. This factor is irrelevant in caravans. In feedstock it varies with the end use.

- *Customers' own profitability*. Highly profitable customers are likely to be less price sensitive, which will reduce the price sensitivity of feedstock. This factor is not directly relevant to caravans where the purchasers are consumers, rather than other firms.
- *Decision-makers' incentives*. Managers responsible for purchasing may face a variety of different incentives, some of which encourage them to be highly price sensitive, some of which encourage them to place a greater premium upon other factors like delivery and quality. For caravans this is not a relevant issue. In feedstock, managers responsible for purchasing need to be assured that deliveries will be guaranteed and that international quality standards are met, but are then likely to have an incentive to seek the lowest prices.

Bargaining leverage

The extent to which buyers can exert bargaining leverage also depends upon a fairly extensive list of factors, as listed below:

- *Buyer concentration and buyer volume*. The more concentrated buyers are, and the greater volume they purchase, the more leverage they will be able to exert. Caravan buyers are not concentrated and do not purchase in volume, giving them limited leverage. In feedstock, buyers are more concentrated and purchase in greater volumes but the very wide range of end uses for the product limits buyers' power.
- *Buyer switching costs*. If switching costs for buyers are high, they will be less able to exert leverage over their suppliers, as the threat that they will take their business elsewhere will have limited credibility. Caravan buyers can easily switch to another supplier, as can users of feedstock.
- *Buyer information*. Well-informed buyers will be better able to exert leverage. Both caravan buyers and feedstock purchasers are well informed about product characteristics and prices.
- *Threat of backward vertical integration by buyers*. If buyers are able effectively to threaten to enter the industry, by backward integration, they will be able to exert powerful leverage. There is little threat of backward integration in either industry being considered. Caravan buyers are unlikely to set up in production. In the case of feedstock, users have become less, rather than more, vertically integrated in recent years.
- *The existence of substitutes*. If there are close substitutes for an industry's product, buyers will have substantial bargaining leverage. There are no close substitutes for either caravans or feedstock.

Summarising the power of buyers

Figure 11.5 shows the summary diagram for the determinants of buyer power.

(a) Touring caravans

Determinant	Weak buyers	Strong buyers
Price sensitivity:		
Price/total purchases		★
Product differences	★	
Brand identity	★	
Impact on buyers' quality	not applicable	
Buyer profits	not applicable	
Decision-makers' incentives	not applicable	
Bargaining leverage:		
Buyer concentration	★	
Buyer volume	★	
Buyer switching costs		★
Buyer information		★
Ability to integrate backwards	★	
Existence of substitutes	★	

Overall judgement on buyer power: *Buyers are price sensitive in some segments but have limited bargaining power*

(b) Feedstock

Determinant	Weak buyers	Strong buyers
Price sensitivity:		
Price/total purchases	★	
Product differences		★
Brand identity		★
Impact on buyers' quality		★
Buyer profits	★	
Decision-makers' incentives	?	
Bargaining leverage:		
Buyer concentration	★	
Buyer volume	★	
Buyer switching costs		★
Buyer information		★
Ability to integrate backwards	★	
Existence of substitutes	★	

Overall judgement on buyer power: *Buyers are price sensitive in some segments but have limited bargaining power*

Figure 11.5 The power of buyers

The power of suppliers

The last of the five forces to be considered is the power of suppliers, determined by the following factors.

Differentiation of inputs

If firms in an industry are dependent upon the particular variants of an input produced by individual suppliers, those suppliers will be relatively powerful. Neither of these factors is significant in caravans or feedstock.

Switching costs of transferring to alternative suppliers

If these are high, suppliers will be relatively powerful as firms face costs in transferring to competing suppliers. This is not a significant factor in the caravan industry but is very important indeed in the production of feedstock where the cost of switching to a different supplier of the raw materials (mainly natural gas) is prohibitively high.

Availability of substitute inputs

If substitute inputs are available, supplier power will be reduced. In caravans this can be easily done. In feedstock production the use of substitute inputs would require a completely new technique of production, involving very high levels of investment in new plant and equipment.

Supplier concentration

Higher levels of concentration among suppliers will tend to enhance their power, particularly if suppliers are more concentrated than buyers. Suppliers to caravan firms are not concentrated. Suppliers of the major inputs to feedstock production are very highly concentrated, especially in the case of natural gas where there is only one supplier in each country.

The importance of volume to suppliers

If suppliers are dependent for their survival or profits on maintaining large volumes of sales, they will tend to have more limited bargaining power. Suppliers to the caravan and feedstock industries are not substantially dependent for their sales volume upon sales to those industries and are not thereby weakened.

Cost relative to the purchasing industry's total costs

If the cost of inputs purchased from a particular supplier industry is an important part of the industry's total costs, suppliers will find it harder to exert leverage. On the other hand, if a supplier industry supplies inputs that are only a small proportion of the users' total costs, it will find it much easier to secure higher prices. In caravans, purchases of inputs are spread across a wide range of supplying industries. In the production of feedstock purchases of gas and a small number of other bulk inputs account for a high proportion of total variable costs.

The impact of inputs on costs or differentiation

Supplier power will also depend upon the importance of inputs in the users' ability to maintain low costs or to differentiate the product. If the quality of inputs, or their cost, is an important determinant of the industry's ability to compete, then suppliers will have substantial bargaining power.

This factor is unimportant in caravans. In feedstock production companies need to have supplies at particular locations, which gives suppliers at those locations considerable power.

The threat of forward integration by suppliers

If forward integration into the industry by suppliers is easy to achieve then suppliers will have considerable bargaining power. Any attempt on the part of firms in the industry to secure lower input prices could be met by suppliers establishing production facilities for themselves. In both caravans and feedstock this is unlikely. In the case of caravans, input suppliers have very different skills and competences from those required to assemble caravans. In the case of feedstock, suppliers of gas and other bulk inputs might be able to integrate forwards but the barriers to entry are so substantial that this is not seen as an immediate threat.

Summarising the extent of suppliers' power

Figure 11.6 summarises the determinants of supplier power in the two industries being examined.

Conclusions to be drawn from the 'five forces' approach

As this chapter has indicated, application of the 'five forces' technique requires quite substantial research into the industry in question, the analysis of a wide range of factors and the exercise of judgement in attempting to aggregate the different determinants of each force. However, once the analysis is complete, it is possible to focus on the most important aspects of competition for the industry in question, paying less attention to less important features. It should also be possible to assess the overall 'attractiveness' of the industry from the point of view of a firm within it.

In the case of touring caravans in the United Kingdom the analysis suggests that the important forces are rivalry among incumbents, which is intense, and the threat of entry, which is very powerful. In that case, the industry can be seen to be rather unattractive, a judgement that seems to be confirmed by the number of bankruptcies in the industry, the relatively low level of profitability, and the lack of interest shown in the industry by large conglomerates.

In the case of feedstock the picture is very different. Rivalry among incumbents is judged to be high, but the existence of a market leader does much to generate orderly competition. The threat of entry is insignificant, as is the threat of substitution. Supplier power is balanced by the industry's importance as a customer. Buyers have limited power. Clearly, this industry is a much more attractive prospect, as witness the substantial profits made by the incumbents.

Porter's 'five forces' model takes the traditional structure–conduct–performance approach in a new and different direction. The original intention of the S–C–P

(a) Touring caravans

Determinant	Low supplier power		High supplier power
Differentiation of inputs	★		
Switching costs	★		
Substitute inputs	★		
Supplier concentration			★
Importance of volume to supplier			★
Costs relative to total purchases		★	
Impact of inputs on cost/performance		★	
Threat of forward integration	★		

Overall judgement on power of suppliers: *Limited*

(b) Feedstock

Determinant	Low supplier power		High supplier power
Differentiation of inputs	★		
Switching costs			★
Substitute inputs			★
Supplier concentration			★ (gas)
Importance of volume to supplier	★ (gas)		
Costs relative to total purchases	★		
Impact of inputs on cost/performance		★	
Threat of forward integration	★		

Overall judgement on power of suppliers: *Gas suppliers have power, balanced by their need to maintain the volume of sales to feedstock producers*

Figure 11.6 The power of suppliers

theorists was entirely positive in nature. They aimed to predict how an industry's structure would affect the average performance of the firms within it. From that perspective, performance is determined by structure, rather than by the actions of the firms. However, Porter took the same basic framework and applied it in a different way. The 'five forces' analysis is a tool that executives can use to identify the key features of an industry, so that they can act on those features. Performance is not simply determined by the external environment, but by managers' ability to identify attractive sectors and market segments into which they may enter. Chapter 18 considers this contribution to the analysis of business strategy in more depth.

Illustration Carrying out a structural analysis of an industry

If the 'five forces' analysis is to be carried out effectively, a substantial volume of information on the industry must be collected. Porter (1980) offers some useful guidance on how to set about such analysis.

The first stage is to develop a framework for systematically collecting raw data by establishing a general overview. That consists of first identifying the leading firms in the industry, then searching for broadly based industry studies which may already have been completed, and reading the annual reports from the leading companies. A rapid perusal of those reports for a ten- or fifteen-year period, paying particular attention to the president's letter, will often highlight key factors in the industry's development.

Porter then suggests that the researcher should quickly become involved in fieldwork, through interviews, before trying to exhaust the published information. Rapid engagement with the industry's practitioners allows field research and library research to feed on each other. Interviewees are often aware of obscure but useful published material on the industry and are able to comment on the value of other published material, much of which may have become out-dated and useless.

As the work proceeds, Porter argues that the researcher's morale tends to go through a U-shaped cycle. An initial euphoria at grasping the basics of the industry is followed by confusion and panic as mounds of information accumulate and the sector comes to seem impossibly complex, followed by growing confidence as at last the pieces come together to form a coherent whole.

Published sources for the analysis of an industry vary in quality and quantity. If the industry is large, long established and subject to little change, then it tends to be well documented. In other cases, it may not be. In either case, two principles are important. The first is to comb published sources for other published sources, and for the names of key informants who should be interviewed. The second is to keep a careful bibliography, including the citation of sources for each item. The published material itself may be found in a number of sources, including:

- libraries
- trade associations
- market intelligence companies
- trade magazines
- business press
- company directories
- government censuses, samples and regular statistical series
- company documents, especially for publicly quoted companies.

Field data may be gathered from various sources and again it is useful to have a systematic framework within which to approach the various sources. In particular it is important to recognise that informants will exhibit varying degrees of sensitivity and nervousness about divulging their knowledge.

Porter identifies four basic categories of informant. The first are observers who have little direct stake in the industry and little reason to be sensitive about disclosing their knowledge and opinions. Such sources include international

▶

organisations, government bodies, consumer groups and the financial community, standard-setting organisations, unions, Chambers of Commerce and the press. The second category of informant works within the service organisations associated with an industry. These include the trade associations, consultants, auditors, banks and advertising agencies. In so far as these organisations have a stake in the industry they may have a degree of sensitivity to the industrial researcher but as their stake is not usually identified with an individual firm, they can often provide fairly object-ive comment on the key players. A similar group of observers may be found in the industry's suppliers, distributors and customers, some of whom may have had direct business dealings with a number of the industry's incumbents, providing them with some key insights.

Finally, and most obviously, there are the informants within the industry itself, whose direct stake may make them the most sensitive. Some of these sources will be best qualified to provide information on their own company alone, but others will also have information concerning their competitors. Market researchers and sales staff, R&D staff and engineers, servicing departments and purchasing departments – all of these have day-to-day contact with a range of useful sources and can pro-vide intelligence on a range of industry participants. This group of informants also includes former employees, although their testimony needs sensitive interpretation in the light of their reasons for leaving and their attitude towards their former company.

When approaching this mass of potential informants, it makes sense for the researcher to begin with those that do not have a direct stake in the industry, moving on to those who are more sensitive after a good general picture has been drawn up, and enough personal contacts made to give the researcher the credibility needed to secure trust. If the research process is to be successful, Porter recommends a number of practical hints:

- Make contact by telephone, rather than by letter. A telephone request for an interview is more personal and more difficult to 'shelve' than a letter.
- Allow plenty of 'lead time' when organising interview trips.
- Offer the interviewee some form of 'quid pro quo' in the form of sharing general observations, or providing a copy of the final report, where possible.
- Be clear and honest about the purpose of the research and the affiliation of the researcher.
- Persevere. Remember that an interview becomes a personal interaction and even the most unenthusiastic informant may become very helpful once the interview has begun.
- Display a good knowledge of the industry, in order to maintain credibility.
- Interview in teams of two, if possible, so that one person can keep good notes while the other engages the attention of the interviewee.
- Be careful not to ask questions in such a way as to prejudge the answer that will be given.
- Observe the informants' surroundings for clues, as well as the things they say.
- Build a relationship with the informant.
- Attempt to build in some informal activity as part of the meeting. A trip around the plant, or having lunch, may lead to the disclosure of information that would not be forthcoming in the formal setting of an interview.

- Make it clear that proprietary information is not required. If some of the questions are quantitative in nature, and might be sensitive, phrase them in terms of 'ball-park' figures or relatively wide ranges.
- Get further leads from each interview.
- Remember that the telephone interview can be very productive, especially if the questions are tightly focused, and addressed to informants who are not likely to be sensitive with respect to their content.

If these 'practical tips' are followed, the process of carrying out an industry analysis is much more likely to be successful.

References and further reading

J.S. Bain, *Barriers to New Competition*, Cambridge, MA, Harvard University Press, 1956.
M. Porter, *Competitive Strategy: Techniques for Analysing Industries and Competitors*, New York, Free Press, 1980.

Self-test questions

1. Which of the following 'five forces' analyses best fits a perfectly competitive industry?

   (a) intense rivalry among existing firms, low threat of entry, low buyer power, low threat of substitutes, high supplier power
   (b) limited rivalry among existing firms, high threat of entry, low buyer power, low supplier power, low threat of substitutes
   (c) intense rivalry among existing firms, high threat of entry, high buyer power, high threat of substitutes, high supplier power
   (d) no rivalry, no threat of entry, no buyer power, no supplier power, no threat of substitutes

2. Which of the industries described in Question 1 above will be the most attractive to incumbent firms?

3. Which of the following factors is a determinant of both rivalry among incumbents and the threat of entry?

   (a) absolute cost advantages
   (b) product differences
   (c) brand identity
   (d) scale economies
   (e) switching costs for customers

4. Which of the following would you expect to observe in the UK touring caravan industry, given the analysis of its structure set out above?

   (a) high profits
   (b) frequent entry and exit to and from the industry
   (c) ownership in the hands of large enterprises
   (d) rapid technological progress

5. Which of the following will tend to make rivalry among existing firms less intense?
   (a) rapid growth in the industry
   (b) a low ratio of fixed costs to value added
   (c) high exit barriers
   (d) existence of a price leader

Essay question

Compare the 'five forces' analysis of competitive structure with the textbook approach to perfect competition, monopoly and oligopoly. Pay particular attention to the aims of the different approaches and to their overlaps.

12 Risk and uncertainty

This chapter introduces the problem of imperfect information. Techniques for decision-making in the presence of risk and uncertainty are outlined and the chapter then goes on to consider the broader implications of uncertainty for the analysis of the firm.

Alternative states of information

Three alternative 'states of information' may be identified. The first is *certainty*, where the decision-maker is perfectly informed in advance about the outcome of their decisions. For each decision there is only one possible outcome, which is known to the decision-maker. Realistic examples are difficult to find, but it is important to remember that the simple model of the firm, outlined in Chapter 2, is based on the assumption that the firm has certain knowledge of its cost and demand conditions.

The second state of information is known as *risk*. In this situation a decision may have more than one possible outcome, so that certainty no longer exists. However, the decision-maker is aware of all possible outcomes and knows the probability of each one occurring.

The third state of information is that of *uncertainty*. In this situation a decision may have more than one outcome and the decision-maker does not know the precise nature of these outcomes, nor can they objectively assign a probability to the outcomes.

Various techniques exist to assist decision-making in conditions of risk or uncertainty, which may be considered in turn.

Techniques for decision-making in risky conditions

The use of expected monetary values

If a decision-maker knows the possible outcomes that may result from a decision, and can assign probabilities to each of those outcomes, then expected monetary values may be substituted for certain values in choosing between alternative courses of action.

The expected monetary value (EMV) of a particular course of action may be defined as:

$$EMV = \sum p_i V_i \quad \text{where:}$$

p_i = the probability of the i'th outcome
V_i = the value of the i'th outcome

and $\quad \sum p_i = 1$

Expressed in words, the EMV is equal to the weighted sum of the possible outcomes, when each outcome is weighted by its probability, and all possible outcomes are taken into account.

To take an example, an ice-cream shop may know that its takings vary with the weather, which may be sunny (with a probability (p) of 0.2) or cloudy (p = 0.4), or raining (p = 0.4). In this case, the EMV is calculated as shown below:

Weather conditions	Probability	Takings
Sunny	0.2	£500
Cloudy	0.4	£300
Raining	0.4	£100

Expected monetary value = £500(0.2) + £300(0.4) + £100(0.4) = £260

In the example given here there are only three possible weather conditions and three probabilities, which sum to 1. This is known as a *discrete probability distribution*, shown diagrammatically in Figure 12.1.

As Figure 12.1 indicates, there are no weather conditions between those specified, and no level of takings possible apart from those given. A slightly more difficult case is where there is a *continuous probability distribution*, as shown in Figure 12.2.

If the takings of the ice-cream shop can take a very wide range of values, the graph of takings against probabilities will be a smooth curve, rather than a set of discrete points. There are a wide variety of such distributions, and a detailed analysis of them lies outside the scope of this chapter. However, if the distribution

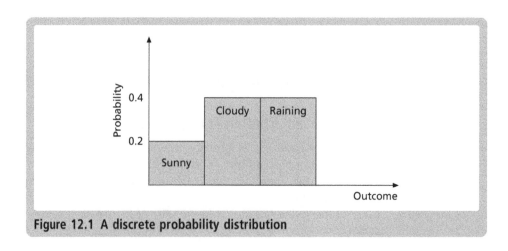

Figure 12.1 A discrete probability distribution

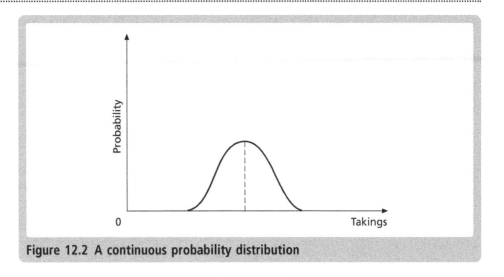

Figure 12.2 A continuous probability distribution

of ice-cream shop takings is characterised by the *normal distribution*, then the EMV of the takings is given by the mean of the distribution.

The limitations of expected values

If expected monetary values are used as the decision criterion, then a rational decision-maker deciding between two alternatives will always choose the course of action that yields the highest EMV. However, while this may appear an intuitively sensible way in which to take decisions, a number of examples show that its application can lead to a number of quite clearly nonsensical conclusions. Consider first a person's decision to insure their house against destruction by fire. If the house has a value of £100,000 and the probability of it burning down in a year is one in ten thousand (0.0001) then the expected value of the loss is £10. A decision-maker employing the expected value approach would be willing to pay £10 for insurance, but no more. However, it seems intuitively quite clear that many rational people would be willing to pay much more than £10, in order to be absolutely certain that they will never be faced with the prospect of having to lose their house without recompense. In some sense, people 'care' more about the possible loss of £100,000 than they do about the certain insurance cost of £10. The same point can be made through another example. Imagine that a rational person is asked to take part in a game with another player which consists of tossing a coin for a stake of £1. If the coin lands with 'heads' up there is a gain of £1. If it lands 'tails' up, there is a loss of £1. Provided that the coin is a fair one, so that 'heads' and 'tails' are equally likely, the expected value of this game is equal to:

$$0.5(£1) - 0.5(£1) = 0$$

A person using the EMV criterion would be absolutely indifferent to whether they played the game or not. The slightest inducement to play (a bribe of one penny, for instance) would be sufficient to encourage them to take part. When the stake involved is very small, this analysis seems intuitively quite acceptable.

However, the expected monetary value of the game remains exactly the same as the stakes rise. If the stakes were £1,000,000 the expected value would still be zero and a bribe of one penny would still be sufficient to encourage a rational person, using EMVs as the basis for the decision, to take part. This seems intuitively much less plausible, as it seems highly unlikely that a rational individual would be prepared to risk losing £1,000,000, even if that possibility were offset by the equally likely prospect of winning £1,000,000. In everyday language it seems sensible to suppose that most people would 'care' more about the prospective loss than the prospective gain.

A third example, known as the 'St Petersburg Paradox', makes the same point in an even more dramatic way. Consider the situation where a coin is tossed and a payment is made to the player, depending upon which toss of the coin first comes up 'heads'. If it comes up the first time, the payment is £2. If it does not come up until the second toss, the payment is $£2^2 = £4$, and if it does not come up until the nth toss, the payment is £2n. How much would a rational person be willing to pay to take part in this game? The expected monetary value of the game is given by:

$$EMV = 0.5(2) + 0.5^2(2^2) + 0.5^3(2^3) + \ldots + 0.5^n(2^n) + \ldots$$
$$= 1 + 1 + 1 + \ldots + 1 \ldots$$
$$= \text{infinity}$$

In other words, the EMV is infinity, and a person using the EMV as a means of decision-making would be willing to pay everything they have to take part in the game.

These examples illustrate a major problem with EMVs as a means of taking decisions. Individuals will not accept fair bets involving large amounts of money because they 'care' more about the possibility of loss than they do about the possibility of an equal gain. In the language of economic analysis, the 'utility' lost as a result of losing £100 may be more than the utility gained by winning £100.

Utility and attitudes to risk

The analysis above suggests that EMV has serious limitations as a criterion on which to base decisions. It seems intuitively likely that the value, or 'utility', placed on a loss of £100 by a rational individual may well exceed the utility arising from a gain of £100. That suggests that an explicit examination of the links between utility and income may help to provide an alternative means of assessing decisions in situations of risk. Figure 12.3 shows three different possible relationships between an individual's level of income and the utility they experience as a result of having that income. Each can be seen to illustrate different attitudes to risk on the part of the individual concerned.

In Figure 12.3(a), the curve linking utility and income becomes less and less steep at higher levels of income, indicating decreasing marginal utility of income. If such an individual is at level of income A, which gives them utility X, and is considering whether or not to accept a fair bet with a 50/50 probability of either increasing

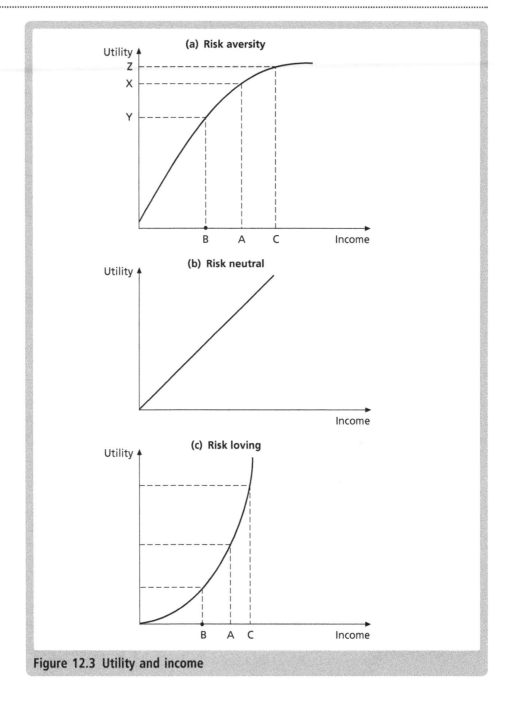

Figure 12.3 Utility and income

their income to C or reducing it by an equal amount to B, they will consider the impact on their utility. If their income is reduced to B, their utility falls to Y. On the other hand, if their income is increased to C, their utility rises to Z. However, as Figure 12.3(a) clearly shows, the decrease from X to Y is substantially larger than the increase from X to Z. If these are equally likely, as in the example given, the individual in question will not accept the bet offered.

The type of behaviour illustrated in Figure 12.3(a) is known as *risk-averse* behaviour, and it is frequently assumed that most individuals and companies behave in this way, as implied in the examples considered in the section above. Nevertheless, an individual or a firm's attitude to risk depends essentially upon their personal preferences, or the preferences of their shareholders, and not everyone may be risk averse. Figures 12.3(b) and 12.3(c) illustrate the relationship between utility and income for individuals who have different attitudes to risk. In Figure 12.3(b) the link between utility and income is drawn as a straight line. In this case, the individual places exactly the same value on a loss as on a gain of the same monetary value, and is described as *risk neutral*. For individuals whose preferences conform to this relationship, EMVs are an appropriate reflection of their decision-making. It can be seen, then, that EMVs represent a special case within the general framework of varying attitudes to risk.

Figure 12.3(c) illustrates the relationship between income and utility for a *risk lover*. For this individual the utility attaching to the gain in income from A to C is clearly larger than that arising from the loss from A to B. Such an individual will accept fair bets, even for large amounts.

In each of the examples given above the criterion of EMV has been replaced by that of expected utility (EU). Instead of choosing whichever course of action offers the highest EMV, the decision-maker chooses that which gives the highest EU, where:

$$EU = \Sigma p_i U_i \quad \text{where:}$$

p_i = probability of the i'th outcome
U_i = utility of the i'th outcome

and $\quad \Sigma p_i = 1$

The adoption of the expected utility criterion provides a means by which different attitudes to risk can be taken into account when modelling decisions. However, it can be difficult to use it in a normative way, as a prescription and a practical tool, rather than as a means of predicting firms' behaviour in a general way. That is because it involves estimating the relationship between utility and income for a particular decision-maker (or for the shareholders on whose behalf they are taking decisions, which adds to the difficulties).

One approach to solving this problem is to use what are known as *standard gamble comparisons*. This procedure can be set out as a series of steps. First, utility values are assigned to two different money values. As utility has no obvious unit of measurement this can be entirely arbitrary, provided that the larger money value is assigned the higher utility value. For example, let a money value of £0 yield a utility of 0 and a money value of £100,000 yield a utility value of 1.

The aim is now to find the utility values of monetary amounts between £0 and £100,000 for a particular decision-maker. Imagine that the aim is to find a utility value for £50,000. In this case, the decision-maker is asked to consider the choice between: (a) receiving a certain £50,000; and (b) taking part in a lottery whose outcome will be either a gain of £100,000, with probability P, or a gain of zero, with probability (1 − P).

At very low values of P, the decision-maker will prefer the certain £50,000, but at some higher value they will change their view and will prefer to take part in the lottery. Clearly, a knowledge of that value sheds light on the individual's attitude to risk, which can be used to solve the problem in hand. If, for instance, the decision-maker in question becomes indifferent between the two alternatives at a probability of 0.6 then it can be inferred that at that value the utilities attaching to the certain £50,000 and the risky '£100,000 or £0' are the same. Therefore:

$$U(£50,000) = 0.6(U(£100,000)) + 0.4(U(£0))$$

But we have assigned values to the utility arising from £100,000 and £0, and can therefore evaluate the equation given, on the same scale.

$$U(£50,000) = 0.6(1) + 0.4(0) = 0.6$$

This exercise could be repeated to find the value of utility attaching to any amount between £0 and £100,000.

If the aim is to identify the value of utility (or dis-utility) attaching to losses, rather than gains, the technique can be used in a similar way. In order to evaluate the utility loss arising from a monetary loss of £60,000, the decision-maker is asked to choose between a certain pay-off of £0 (whose utility has been assigned a value of zero) and a lottery involving probability P of losing £60,000 and probability $(1 - P)$ of gaining £100,000 (whose utility has been assigned a value of 1). Once the value of P, at which the decision-maker is indifferent, is known, then the utility value of losing £60,000 is the only unknown remaining in the equation, which can therefore be solved. For example, if the decision-maker declares themselves to be indifferent between £0 and the lottery when $P = 0.1$, then:

$$U(£0) = 0.1(U(-£60,000)) + 0.9(U(£100,000))$$

or

$$0 = 0.1(U(-£60,000)) + 0.9(1)$$

therefore

$$U(-£60,000) = -9$$

This method of estimating utilities suffers from the fact that it relies upon the decision-maker's ability to answer hypothetical questions in the same way in which they would answer real ones. Nevertheless, it offers a means of making the analysis operational.

Indifference curves and attitudes to risk

The analysis above shows how attitudes to risk are reflected in different relationships between utility and income. However, it does not provide a direct measure of the riskiness of any particular course of action. The most common measure of the riskiness of an action, or the risk associated with a particular financial asset (a share, a portfolio of shares, or a foreign currency, for instance), is the *standard deviation* of the returns accruing to it.

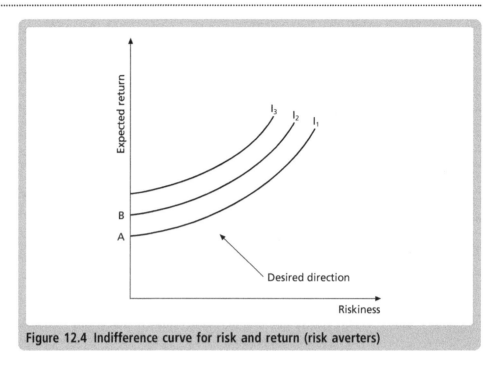

Figure 12.4 Indifference curve for risk and return (risk averters)

When considering choices between alternative courses of action, decision-makers may be thought of as deciding on different combinations of return on the one hand, measured by the expected value of the returns, and risk on the other, measured by the standard deviation of those returns. In this case, indifference curves can be drawn up, showing the different combinations of risk and return that will leave an individual equally satisfied. If individuals are assumed to be risk averse, which is the assumption generally made, then the indifference curves will be as shown in Figure 12.4, rising from left to right, with the more desirable combinations being as indicated by the arrow, having higher returns and lower risk.

The extent of an individual's risk aversion will be reflected in the slopes of the indifference curves. An individual who is very highly risk averse will be prepared to sacrifice a large amount of return in order to secure a small reduction in risk and will therefore have relatively steep indifference curves, relative to one who is only slightly risk averse. (A risk-neutral individual will have horizontal indifference curves. For a risk lover, for whom both risk and return are desirable characteristics, the curves will slope downwards from left to right, rather than in the other direction.)

The concept of the certainty equivalent

The most important applications of the 'risk versus return' (or mean/variance) indifference analysis concern the construction of portfolios of financial assets and therefore lie beyond the scope of this chapter or this book. However, there is one useful concept that should be noted, which is that of the *certainty equivalent*

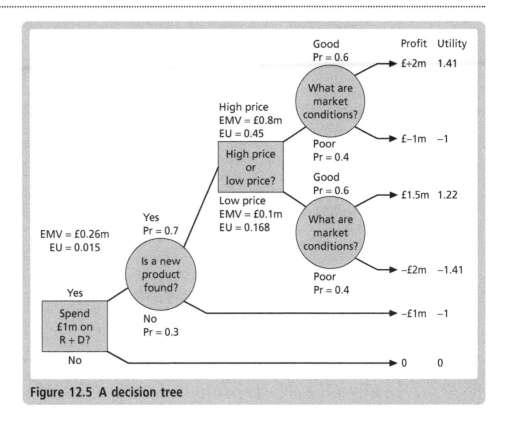

Figure 12.5 A decision tree

of a course of action involving risk. This is defined as the sum of money, available with certainty, that would leave the decision-maker as satisfied as if they had undertaken the risky action. This may be interpreted, in terms of the indifference curves, as the vertical intercept of the curve that includes the course of action concerned. In Figure 12.4, for instance, £A is the certainty equivalent of any combination of risk and return in the indifference curve I₁ and £B is the certainty equivalent of any combination on curve I₂.

The use of decision trees

Another well-known technique that can be helpful in analysing situations involving risk is the use of 'decision trees'. These are particularly useful when a number of related decisions need to be made in sequence and where the outcome of each decision depends upon the response of the environment. Figure 12.5 shows the decision tree concerning the possible development and launch of a new product, which entails two decisions. The first is whether or not to spend £1m on R&D in pursuit of the new product. The second, which only arises if the new product is successfully developed, concerns the choice between a product launch at a high price or a low price.

Decisions, or choices, are represented by square boxes, or 'decision nodes', while outcomes determined by the environment, or 'chance nodes', are represented by circles.

Working from the left, in order to set out the decision process, the first decision that has to be taken is whether to spend £1m on R&D. If the answer to this question is no, the monetary value of the exercise is zero, as shown in the lowest branch of the decision tree. If the answer is yes, the next question is whether a new product is found, which depends upon factors in the environment outside the control of the firm. The chance node shows that there is a probability of 0.7 that a new product is found, 0.3 that it is not. If no new product is found, the £1m has been wasted and the monetary value of the activity is –£1m. On the other hand, if a new product is found, the firm then has to decide whether to launch it with a high price or a low price. Whichever decision is taken, there is a range of possible outcomes, depending upon the economic circumstances of the time. Each of these is shown as an eventual profit, and the probability of that profit.

Decision trees of this kind may be used in conjunction with either the expected monetary value (EMV) or expected utility (EU) criteria. In either case, the basic method involves working backward through the decision tree from right to left. For each of the possible routes through the tree a monetary value, or utility, is calculated, as shown. Each of these is then worked back to the next chance node, and an EMV or EU calculated at that point. In the example shown, for instance, if the product is launched at a high price, the expected profits are equal to £0.8m. If it is launched at a low price, the expected profits are £0.1m. As the expected profits arising from a high price exceed those for a low price, this is the decision that will be taken, if the choice is made on the EMV criterion. If the search for a new product is successful, it will be launched at a high price, with expected profits of £0.8m. However, this will only be possible if the search for a new product has been successful, which itself has a probability of 0.7. If the decision is taken to spend £1m on R&D, then the expected value (in £m) is:

$$\text{EMV} = 0.7(0.8) + 0.3(-1) = 0.26$$

As the expected EMV is positive, the firm should decide to make the investment in R&D, if EMV is the criterion to be adopted, which implies risk neutrality.

If the firm is risk averse, which is the usual assumption with respect to attitudes to risk, the same process can be gone through using expected utilities (EUs) rather than EMVs. This requires some knowledge of the firm's utility function. In the example shown in Figure 12.5 it has been assumed that for this firm utility is equal to the square root of the monetary return, for gains, and minus the square root of the absolute value of any losses (i.e. $U(-100) = -10$). In that case, reworking the example, the EU if the product is launched at a high price is 0.45, but if it is launched at a low price, EU is equal to 0.168. The choice of price remains the same and the EU if the product is launched is equal to 0.45. The EU of spending the £1m on R&D is given by:

$$\text{EU} = 0.7(0.45) - 0.3(1) = 0.015$$

In the example given the EU criterion yields the same decision as EMV. However, it can be seen that if the degree of risk aversion were higher then both the decision on price and the decision on whether to proceed with the R&D project could alter.

Alternative types of probabilities

A situation of risk is one where the probabilities of different outcomes are known to the decision-maker. There are a number of different ways in which such probabilities might be arrived at.

A first useful distinction is between probabilities that are calculated or known *a priori* and those that are only known *a posteriori*. An *a priori* probability is one that can be calculated through prior knowledge. For instance, if a coin has two sides and is fair, it is known that the probability of it landing on either side is 0.5. *A posteriori* probabilities are only known after a sample of events has occurred and the frequency of each outcome is known. For instance, if it has rained on ten out of every thirty days in June for the past twenty years, the a posteriori probability of it raining on a day in June may be said to be 0.333.

Both a priori and a posteriori probabilities may also be described as 'objective' probabilities in that they arise from an agreed analysis of fundamental principles or from observation of past events. The effective use of many statistical techniques depends upon such probabilities being available. However, many business decisions are non-repetitive and unique, so that objective probabilities are not available. If the environment is changing then a probability drawn from past experience may no longer be applicable. In that case, resort has to be made to 'subjective' probabilities, based upon the decision-maker's own expectations, preferences, experience and judgement about the future. Such preferences may be quantified by asking the decision-maker to make comparisons between the real-world problem being considered and a hypothetical gamble whose objective probabilities are known. This can provide some assistance in allowing a probability to be estimated but it is clear that different individuals in an organisation may ascribe different probabilities to the same outcome, or that the same individual may arrive at different probabilities for the same outcome if asked at different times. As different individuals in a firm will all have slightly different information relevant to the decision, and as it is possible that no single individual has all the relevant information, the use of subjective probabilities can be a dangerous guide to decision-making.

If satisfactory probabilities cannot be ascribed to outcomes, or if the possible outcomes are not even known, then the situation is not one of risk, but of uncertainty.

The expected value of information

It is clear from the discussion above that information is valuable and that a firm may wish to improve its knowledge of a particular situation by gathering additional information. However, in order to do so cost-effectively, decision-makers need to know the value of acquiring additional information, in order to judge how much additional expenditure is worthwhile. Two different cases may be identified. The first is where it is possible to acquire perfect information about the future and the second is the more general case where it is only possible to secure imperfect revelation of which future states of nature will occur.

Table 12.1 A bank lending decision

Alternative	Alternative Outcomes	
	Firm defaults: Pr = 0.2	No default: Pr = 0.8
Lend to firm	$900,000	$1,100,000
Buy government stock	$1,070,000	$1,070,000

Source: Foster (1978), p. 6.

If it were possible to acquire perfect *advance state revelation* then the expected value of that perfect information could be measured as the difference between the expected value of future actions, given the information currently available, and the expected value of future actions, given that perfect advance state revelation had been acquired. Foster (1978) used the example of a bank that is deciding whether to make a $1 million loan at 10 per cent to a company that might default, or whether to use the same funds to purchase risk-free government securities at 7 per cent. If the loan is made to the firm, and it does not default, the bank's wealth in respect of the action is valued at $1.1 million. If the firm defaults, the bank's wealth is reduced to $900,000. If risk-free government securities are purchased, the bank's wealth is valued at $1.07 million with certainty. It is estimated that the probability of the firm defaulting is equal to 0.2. Table 12.1 sets out this basic information in tabular form.

If a decision is made on the basis of the information currently available, the bank will compare the EMVs of the two alternative courses of action, using the method outlined above. This gives the following calculation:

Expected value if the loan is made to the firm:

$$EV = (0.8)(1,100,000) + (0.2)(900,000) = 1,060,000$$

Expected value of a risk-free investment in government stock:

$$EV = 1,070,000$$

As the action with the highest expected value is investment in government stock, that is the option that will be taken up and the expected value of the action, with the information currently available, is equal to 1,070,000.

If it now proves possible for the bank to acquire perfect state revelation so that it will know for certain whether the firm will default or not, the situation changes. In this case, whichever outcome occurs, the bank will have been able to choose the optimal action. If it is discovered that the firm will default, the bank will choose to invest in government stock. If it is discovered that the firm will not default, the bank will choose to make the loan.

In order to calculate the expected value in this case, it is noted that the probability of default is 0.2 and that if default takes place, the bank will have invested in government stock. The probability of the firm not defaulting is 0.8, in which case the firm will have made the loan. This gives the expected value of the bank's wealth when it has the necessary information as:

$$EV = 0.8(\$1.1m) + 0.2(\$1.07m) = \$1.094m$$

This can be compared with the expected value of the optimal action in the situation where the bank has not acquired perfect information about the future, which has been calculated above as $1.07 million. The difference between the two values, $24,000, is the *expected value of perfect information (EVPI)*.

The circumstances under which perfect information about the future is available are very rare indeed and in most cases the purchase of additional information will not provide absolutely certain advance state revelation. Nevertheless, the calculation of EVPI is still a useful tool in such situations because it provides an upper limit to the value of additional information that might be collected. The first step that should be taken when considering the purchase of additional information is to consider whether the cost of acquiring it exceeds the EVPI. If it does, the information should not be acquired as its expected value could not possibly exceed that of perfect information.

If the cost of acquiring additional information is less than the EVPI then it may be worth acquiring that information. The basic principle involved in placing a value on the extra information is essentially the same as that involved in calculating EVPI. The value of the information is equal to the difference between the expected value given currently available information and the expected value with the additional information that has been acquired. This can be difficult to calculate in practice (see Foster 1978, pp. 8–13, for an example which is a continuation of the bank loan problem considered here), but the principle is clear enough.

Techniques for coping with uncertainty

The problems considered above have all related to situations of risk, where the probabilities of different outcomes are known. If probabilities are not known, the situation is one of uncertainty, rather than risk, and the techniques outlined above cannot be applied. Nevertheless, there are a number of different strategies that may be adopted in order to make decisions on rational criteria.

The minimax criterion

A firm making a decision may be characterised as choosing between alternative courses of action, whose outcomes depend upon which 'state of nature' happens to be in force at the time of the action. In a situation of uncertainty the probabilities of the different states of nature are not known. In order to begin analysing the problem a 'pay-off matrix' may be constructed, as shown in Table 12.2.

Table 12.2 A pay-off matrix

Actions	States of nature		
	A	B	C
1	20	40	180
2	−40	100	220
3	60	70	90

Each cell in the matrix shows the pay-off, which could be in terms of monetary values or utilities, for the given course of action, given the state of nature indicated.

If the minimax criterion is adopted, the decision-maker examines the worst pay-off for each action and then chooses the action for which the worst pay-off is highest. In the example given in Table 12.2 the worst pay-offs are as follows:

- action 1: 20
- action 2: −40
- action 3: 60.

In this example, action 3 is selected, guaranteeing that the lowest pay-off that will be received is 60.

The minimax rule ensures that the worst possible outcomes are avoided and may be described as a pessimistic, conservative or highly risk-averse strategy. The obvious difficulty is that it ignores the higher value pay-offs which may imply foregoing some possibly very large gains.

The minimax regret criterion

In the case of the minimax regret criterion the decision-maker considers the extent of the sacrifice made if a particular state of nature occurred but the best action for that state of nature was not chosen. In the example shown in Table 12.2 for state of nature A, action 1 involves a 'regret' of 40, action 2 a 'regret' of 100 and action 3 a 'regret' of 0. Table 12.3 shows a complete 'regret matrix' for all actions and states of nature.

Having set out the regret matrix, the action is chosen for which the largest regret is a minimum, leading to the choice of action 1. Such a strategy ensures that the maximum regret is not experienced, and is also a relatively pessimistic basis on which to make a decision.

As in the case of the minimax criterion, a major criticism of this technique is that it only makes use of a very limited amount of the information that is available, ignoring everything else. Actions that are rejected may have much smaller regrets than the one that is chosen, apart from their largest regrets. It is also possible that use of this approach could lead to inconsistent decisions in that if an action is chosen from a group of alternatives and then one of the rejected actions is deleted from the options, a different action may now be chosen, despite the fact that the original 'best' option is still available.

Table 12.3 A regret matrix

Actions	A	B	C	Largest regret
1	40	60	40	60
2	100	0	0	100
3	0	30	130	130

The maximax criterion

This criterion is the opposite of the minimax criterion in that the best outcomes of each action are identified, and then the action is selected for which the best outcome is largest. In the case set out in Table 12.2, this would lead to the choice of action 2. This is clearly an 'optimistic' criterion to use in that it selects the action that provides a possibility of making the highest possible return. As in the case of the other criteria considered, its main failing is that it only takes a limited amount of the available information into account. The action that offers a prospect of the highest possible return may also be the one that offers the prospect of the largest possible loss (as in the example shown), but this is ignored.

The Hurwicz 'alpha' criterion

The Hurwicz approach is an attempt to use more of the information available by constructing an index (the 'alpha index') for each action, which takes into account both the best and worst outcomes and the extent to which the decision-maker wishes to adopt a pessimistic or optimistic posture.

The index is defined in the following way for each action:

$$I_i = al_i + (1 - a)L_i \quad \text{where:}$$

I_i = the index for action i
a = an optimism/pessimism index
l_i = the lowest pay-off for action i
L_i = the highest pay-off for action i

The action that has the largest alpha index is the one selected. The optimism/pessimism index may vary from between 0 and 1 and may be estimated by increasing the value of 'x' within that range for the situation shown in Table 12.4 until the decision-maker is indifferent between the two actions.

A very pessimistic decision-maker will be indifferent between the two actions at a very low value for 'x' (they will be quite happy with a small certain gain compared with the prospect of either 0 or 1, because their pessimism leads them to suspect that the outcome of action 1 would be zero). On the other hand a very optimistic decision-maker, who suspects that the outcome of action 1 is likely to be 1, will only be equally content with a certain amount that is almost as large as 1.

Once the value of 'x' has been estimated, through direct questioning of the decision-maker, it is assumed that as the decision-maker is indifferent between

Table 12.4 Estimating the optimism/pessimism index

| Actions | States of nature | |
	A	B
1	0	1
2	X	x

action 1 and action 2, they both have the same alpha index. From the formula given, action 1 has an index of (1 − a) and action 2 has an index of 'x'. It follows, therefore, that:

(1 − a) = x

and the value of 'a' can be calculated from the known value of 'x', arrived at by experiment.

It should be noted that if 'x' has a value of 1, so that 'a' takes the value of 0, this indicates that the decision-maker is very highly optimistic, and the alpha-index criterion is exactly the same as the maximax criterion. Similarly, if the decision-maker is highly pessimistic, so that 'a' takes the value of 1, the alpha-index criterion is equivalent to using the minimax approach. The Hurwicz technique therefore has the rather elegant property of encompassing minimax and maximax as special cases, each at a different end of a spectrum that may vary from highly optimistic to highly pessimistic. As the technique also makes use of more information than either maximax or minimax, it may be said to be superior to either of them in that respect. Nevertheless, like those other techniques, it also wastes some of the available information concerning the possible outcomes of actions, using only that for the best and the worst outcomes.

Combinations of different strategies

There is no reason to suppose, of course, that firms do, or must, adopt any single criterion in taking decisions under uncertainty. They may adopt different strategies on different occasions, or may consciously combine different strategies in order to 'spread the risk' associated with any single approach.

The broader implications of uncertainty for the theory of the firm

While techniques to assist decision-making under uncertainty are potentially useful, they are clearly very limited and there is a danger that they may obscure the fact that the existence of uncertainty has very profound implications for the theory of the firm.

Uncertainty and 'bounded rationality'

If a firm is operating in a situation of uncertainty its ability to act rationally is limited because of its lack of information. The 'hyper-rational' firm represented by the neo-classical model, in which the firm has perfectly accurate knowledge of its cost and demand conditions, has to be replaced by a model in which decision-makers exhibit 'bounded rationality'. That is not to imply that they are simply irrational. Instead they are 'intendedly rational, but only limitedly so', to quote Simon's phrase (Simon 1959). Each decision-maker attempts to seek rational answers to their problems in the context of their limited knowledge and experience. Instead of 'optimising', as in the neo-classical model, decision-makers 'satisfice' as in the behavioural model of the firm. Instead of immediately identifying the appropriate course of action, or solution to a problem, actions and solutions are arrived at through a process of searching through sequences of possible alternatives, using past experience and rules-of-thumb as guidelines.

Clearly, the concept of 'bounded rationality', which is important in situations of uncertainty, leads away from the orthodox picture of the firm as a fully informed optimiser, and suggests the usefulness of a much more behavioural approach.

Uncertainty and transactions costs

Another implication of uncertainty, which has been examined in Chapter 3, is that it makes it difficult and expensive to draw up complete contracts between individuals. If all future contingencies are known, then a contract between two individuals could specify how each should behave in the event of each contingency, and the contract could be enforced by law. However, as Williamson (1986) points out, if the future possibilities are not all known, contracts will have to be incomplete and there is a difficulty in deciding how to resolve any conflicts that may arise in an unforeseen situation. This need not matter if all parties to all contracts behave without guile towards each other, because in that situation a contract may be thought of as 'a promise, rather than a plan' and each party could agree not to take advantage of the other in unforeseen situations. Unfortunately, in a situation of uncertainty some parties to incomplete contracts may behave 'opportunistically', taking advantage of circumstances to the disadvantage of their partners to the contract.

This is fundamentally important because it reaches to the heart of the question 'what is the firm?', and is important for the understanding of such apparently different phenomena as vertical integration, licensing agreements and the existence of the multinational enterprise (see Chapters 3 and 5). If contracts between individuals could always effectively and cheaply bring about transactions there would be no need for firms to even exist. All economic activity could be organised through contracts between individuals or households. Only when some transactions are organised by management authority, instead of the market mechanism, does a firm come into being. If there were complete certainty, or even just risk, then market transactions organised through complete contracts could cheaply coordinate economic activity. Only when there is uncertainty is a substitute for market transactions required and the firm has a role to play.

Kay (1984) made a similar point in a particularly graphic way by noting that most real-world firms are organised into functional departments, usually including production, marketing, finance and R&D. However, if perfect knowledge were actually available, and there were no information problems, none of these departments would be needed. Marketing departments only exist because consumers are not perfectly informed of the firm's products, their characteristics and their prices. Finance departments are only needed because the firm does not have perfect access to financial information. R&D is only required because perfect technological information is not available. Production departments would continue to exist, but they would only need capital and direct labour because the functions of foremen, managers, clerks and typists would not be needed.

Furthermore, only one category of labour would exist, because the basic difference between different types of labour is informational in that each type of labour – manager, welder, fitter, electrician – is distinguished from the others by the information that each has with respect to their own specialist function. In a world of perfect information where everyone has access to the all the knowledge required, every worker would be able to fulfil any function.

Uncertainty, entrepreneurship and innovation

Textbook models of the firm, which assume certainty or risk, present the firm as a relatively passive entity, having an objective and responding to an environment that is given and over which it has no control. Cost conditions are determined by factor prices and the state of technology and demand conditions are determined by consumers' preferences, which are internal to themselves. The firm has no capacity to change the world in which it operates. A very different way in which to characterise the firm, often associated with the 'Austrian view' on competition (see Chapter 20), is as a much more active participant in the world, changing and creating its own environment through its actions. In this view of the firm, uncertainty is the most important characteristic of the environment. Innovation is the means by which dynamic firms are constantly producing new technologies and developing new consumer needs in order to give themselves at least temporary monopoly positions, which other firms then proceed to attempt to break down by either entering the market or themselves producing hitherto unknown substitutes. In this view of the world profit is essentially a reward for taking the risks associated with innovation, which provides a (temporary) monopoly position. The entrepreneur plays a significant role in creating and changing the environment in which they operate, going far beyond the optimal responses to exogenous changes in the environment which are depicted in textbook economic models. Innovation is the key feature of firms' behaviour and that process of technological change is both a cause of, and a response to, uncertainty.

Illustration   **Betting on butter – Sainsbury's profits from the careful analysis of a risky decision**

Bunn and Thomas (1977) provide an excellent example of the way in which technique can be combined with flair to help a company think its way through a real-life decision involving uncertainty. At the time in question, butter imports were subject to a quota system, which provided substantial incentives to butter smuggling. Smugglers would attempt to disguise a load of butter as 'sweetfat', which has a similar density, by misrepresenting it in the paperwork and including some sweetfat in the load, in case of inspection.

The customs authorities intercepted such a load and then offered it for sale to retailers, one of which was J. Sainsbury Ltd. The sale was to be made by tender, with each prospective purchaser making a confidential bid, the sale being made to the highest bidder. The problem for Sainsbury's was to decide how much to offer

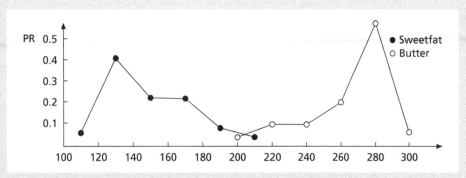

Figure 12.6 Probability distributions for butter and sweetfat prices

for the load, given that its butter content was unknown, the prices of butter and sweetfat at the time of delivery were unknown, and the prices that would be offered by the competition were unknown.

The starting point was to estimate the value of the consignment, which depended on the future prices of butter and sweetfat, and the ratio of butter to sweetfat in the load. For the prices of butter and sweetfat, the company used its market experience to estimate subjective probability distributions, shown in Figure 12.6.

A similar approach was used to estimate the proportion of butter in the load. The customs authorities provided Sainsbury's with a random selection of ten cases from the freezer, eight of which contained butter. That random sample could have been used in conjunction with the binomial distribution, in order to find a probability distribution for the proportion of butter in the load, and such a distribution was calculated. However, Sainsbury's buyer preferred to adjust that distribution in the light of a subjective 'hunch', based on 'second-guessing' the way in which the smugglers would have packed sweetfat around the butter in the hold of the ship. Having arrived at this adjusted probability distribution for the ratio of butter to sweetfat, Sainsbury's were able to calculate the probability distribution of value per ton, and the expected value per ton, which was estimated at £233. Subtracting £8 per ton for administrative expenses left £225 per ton as the net value per ton. The buyer then had to decide how much to bid, given that other firms had also been invited to tender. The starting point in this respect was the assumption that other firms would place the same value on the load as Sainsbury's had. Then it was assumed that competitors would expect to make a margin of around 20 per cent, which provided a base-line estimate of other companies' bids of £185.

This base-line figure needed adjustment in two respects. First, other firms may have placed a different value on the load, and second, other firms may have tried to 'second-guess' Sainsbury's by making their own estimate of what Sainsbury's would bid, and then raising their own bid slightly above that estimate. Sainsbury's buyer made subjective estimates of the probability distribution for each of these factors. Combining them gave a probability distribution for the average competitor's bid, shown in Table 12.5.

If Sainsbury's were to win the tender they had to make a bid that did not simply beat the average bid, but beat all offers made. As the number of competitors was expected to be around three, the probability of that happening was calculated, using the Poisson distribution, to be $e^{(-3p)}$, where p is the probability of an average

▶

Table 12.5 Probability distribution for the average competitors' bid

Price bid (x)	180	185	190	195	200	205	210	215
Probability (Pr)	0.025	0.110	0.300	0.245	0.185	0.100	0.030	0.005
Cumulative probability that competitors' bid is less than x	0.025	0.135	0.435	0.680	0.865	0.965	0.995	1.00

Table 12.6 Expected profit at each price bid

Price bid	190	195	200	205	210
Probability that a competitor bids higher	0.565	0.320	0.135	0.035	0.005
Probability of winning	0.19	0.39	0.77	0.90	0.99
Profit per ton	35.0	30.0	25.0	20.0	15.0
Expected profit per ton	6.6	11.7	19.2	18.0	14.8

competitor bidding higher. That in turn is given for each bid price in Table 12.5 by subtracting the cumulative probability in the bottom row from 1.

Taking this information together, it is possible to construct a table showing the expected profit per ton at each price bid by Sainsbury's. This is shown in Table 12.6.

In the light of the figures given, Sainsbury's bid of £203 per ton won the contract, and made an actual profit of £40 per ton. By combining market experience with simple statistical reasoning the firm was able to structure its thinking through a complex problem in order to provide a reasoned solution to its dilemma.

References and further reading

P. Bernstein, *Against the Gods: The Remarkable Story of Risk*, New York, John Wiley, 1996.

D. Bunn and H. Thomas, 'J. Sainsbury and the Haul of Contraband Butter', in G. Kaufman and H. Thomas (eds) *Modern Decision Analysis*, Harmondsworth, Penguin, 1977.

G. Foster, *Financial Statement Analysis*, Englewood Cliffs, NJ, Prentice Hall, 1978.

N. Kay, *The Emergent Firm*, London, Macmillan, 1984.

W.D. Reekie and J.N. Crook, *Managerial Economics*, Oxford, Philip Allan, 1982.

H. Simon, 'Theories of Decision-Making in Economics and Behavioural Science', *American Economic Review*, vol. 49, 1959, pp. 971–5.

O. Williamson, *Economic Organisation*, Brighton, Wheatsheaf, 1986.

Self-test questions

1. Which of the following is a situation of risk?

   (a) gambling on the toss of a coin

   (b) launching a wholly new product

   (c) lending to a firm with an established record

2. Mr X knows that the probability of his house burning down is one in a thousand. His house is worth £100,000 and he willingly pays an insurance premium of £200 per year. Which of the following best describes his attitude to risk?

   (a) risk neutral
   (b) risk loving
   (c) risk averse

3. Draw a graph with risk on the horizontal axis and return on the vertical axis. What shape will the indifference curves for a risk-neutral individual be?

   (a) vertical lines
   (b) horizontal lines
   (c) downward sloping

4. Which of the following strategies for decision-making under uncertainty would be adopted by a very optimistic decision-maker?

   (a) minimax
   (b) maximax
   (c) minimax regret

5. Which of the following best describes the phenomenon of 'bounded rationality'?

   (a) decision-makers evaluate all possible options
   (b) decision-makers evaluate those options of which they are aware
   (c) decision-makers consider only one possible option

Essay question

Distinguish between certainty, risk and uncertainty, and explain how utility theory might be used to assist decision-making in the presence of risk.

PART III
Business decisions

Game theory and its applications

This chapter introduces the basic elements of game theory and applies them to three issues: collusion; the form of competition in oligopoly; and entry deterrence.

Introduction: game theory brings managerial economics and industrial economics together

Managerial economics has been defined in Chapter 1 as 'the application of economic analysis to business problems'. That definition differentiates the subject very clearly from the 'old' industrial economics which is often described as the 'structure–conduct–performance' (SCP) approach. In the SCP paradigm the variable being explained is the 'performance' of an industry, usually interpreted as the avera   ability of its member firms. That is determined by the 'conduct' of those firms – the   the products they motional activities the   structure'. The 'old' industria   draws to a great exten   simple textbook models of competition and monopoly. It suggests that the average profitability of an industry is determined by the market power of the incumbent firms (often proxied by the level of concentration in the industry), the height of entry barriers and the degree of product differentiation. If an industry is highly concentrated, has significant barriers to entry and a highly differentiated product, the SCP approach predicts that its incumbents will earn relatively high rates of profit. Porter's (1980) analysis of competitive structure (see Chapter 11), in which the 'attractiveness' of an industry for its incumbents is determined by the 'five forces', is a loose and informal version of the 'old' industrial economics.

This 'old' industrial economics is clearly separate and different from managerial economics because it pays very little attention to the decisions taken by firms. The unit of analysis is the industry, whose average performance is determined by its structure, which is exogenously determined. Firms are assumed, for the most part, to be profit-maximisers and to take whatever decisions are required to make the maximum profits offered by the structure in which they find themselves. Decisions on price, for instance, will be affected by elasticity of demand, which is determined by the number of firms in the industry. While that level of analysis requires some passing attention to be paid to pricing decisions (conduct), the focus of attention is on the link between structure (the number of firms) and performance (profitability or price–cost margins).

This separation between managerial economics and industrial economics has been broken down by a radical change in industrial economics, whereby game theory has become the central tool of analysis. In the 'new' industrial economics attention is focused on the oligopoly situation, where a small number of firms recognise their interdependence and take decisions in the light of that interdependence. The most important consequence of that change is that decisions taken by individual firms have become the centre of theoretical attention and case studies involving small groups of rivals operating in the same sector have replaced cross-sector regressions as the dominant form of empirical enquiry. As a result, the 'new' industrial economics does involve the application of economic analysis to business decisions and a textbook on managerial economics would be incomplete if it did not recognise and try to explain some of these developments. The purpose of this chapter, therefore, is to introduce the central concepts of game theory and their application to a number of business decisions.

Some basic concepts in game theory

Game theory is difficult for the reader who approaches it from basic economics, for a number of reasons. First, it is a good example of a 'paradigm shift' in that a whole new set of concepts is required. Second, there are a bewildering variety of different types of game that may be analysed. Third, a formal treatment of the issues involved, like that in Fudenberg and Tirole's (1991) classic text, requires considerable mathematical expertise at graduate level. Fourth, the chains of reasoning required in a more informal approach are often lengthy and convoluted, involving arguments like 'I will do what is best for me in the light of what I think I know you think you know about what I think I know about you'! Fifth, the same theoretical analysis may often be applied to practical issues as widely different as the arms race, entry to an industry and children's games, which can make it difficult to maintain a clear perspective on the link between the theory and the empirical universe.

Fortunately, the spread of game theory across social science, from economics to politics and business strategy, has led to a market demand that it be made more accessible to the non-specialist. Hence a number of excellent non-mathematical texts have emerged. Dixit and Nalebuff (1991) has been an international bestseller among managers. Dixit and Skeath (1999) provides a thorough introduction suitable for a complete course on the subject and many intermediate-level economics textbooks now have a section on game theory. Varian (1993, ch. 27), for instance, provides a relatively undemanding introduction while Kreps (1990b, Part III) is more difficult.

A single chapter in this text cannot hope to equip the reader with a working knowledge of game theory. However, it is possible to introduce the basic concepts and to give some illustrations of their application.

Different types of game

The essence of a game is *interdependence* among 'players'. Any situation where a person or organisation takes actions that affect others, where the others are aware of that effect, and where the others may act and have an effect on the original person or organisation, may be described as a game. Within this very broad class of situations, games may be categorised in a number of ways. A first distinction can be made between *cooperative games* and *non-cooperative games*. Unfortunately for the use of the English language a non-cooperative game is not one in which there is never any cooperation. In fact many economic applications of non-cooperative game theory concern situations where firms do cooperate. A non-cooperative game is simply one in which the players follow their own self-interest, and choose their strategies separately, within a set of rules. In that context they may choose to cooperate, but they do so because they have each decided independently that it is in their own interest. It is the theory of non-cooperative games that has become the most important tool for economists.

A second distinction is that between a *zero-sum game* (also known as a *constant-sum game*) and a *non-zero-sum game* (also known as a *variable-sum game*). In a zero-sum game the interests of the players are diametrically opposed to each other. If one player wins amount A, the other loses exactly the same amount. In a non-zero-sum game the gains and losses are not equal. Both players may gain, both may lose and the gains and losses need not sum to zero. This very basic distinction is important and often overlooked, leading to confusion in the public debate over economic issues. For instance, when business people and politicians become concerned about the 'competitiveness' of their industry or nation's trade, they often express the debate in terms of a zero-sum game in which one country wins and another loses in diametric opposition. That is appropriate for the firms involved as they battle over market share. However, the economics of international trade makes it clear that trade between nations is not a zero-sum game. If it is properly understood that two nations trading with each other both gain, then many of the concerns over a country's 'competitiveness' are seen to be spurious.

A third distinction is between games that are *sequential* and those that are *simultaneous*. When a game is sequential, each player moves in turn and each player is aware of the moves that have been taken previously. The question each player is trying to answer is 'what should I do, given what my opponent has done and given what my opponent will do when they know how I have moved?' When a game is simultaneous, each player may be thought of as moving at the same time. However, timing itself is not the key feature of simultaneous games and the moves need not take place at the same moment. What really defines a simultaneous game is the fact that each player moves without knowing what the other has done. In that case the question asked is 'what should I do, given that I do not know what my opponent will do and my opponent does not know what I will do?'

A fourth important distinction is between games that are *repeated* and those that are *one-off*. Games that are repeated may be repeated an *infinite* number of times, a *finite but known* number of times, or an *unknown* number of times. In a one-off game the players need only concern themselves about the gains and losses arising from a single round. If games are repeated then each player needs to consider the impact of their actions in each round on the future. This can make a very important difference to the way in which a game is played, as is shown below.

A fifth distinction is between games where the pay-offs to the players are *discrete* amounts of profit (or utility) and those where the pay-offs are *continuous*, and a sixth is between games of *complete information*, where all players are aware of all circumstances, and games of *incomplete information*, or *information asymmetry*, where players have different information available to them.

In addition to these distinctions there are a number of broad classes of game which share common features. These include *prisoner's dilemma* games, *assurance* games and *chicken* games, games involving *strategic moves, evolutionary games* and a host of others.

Representing and solving games

In the face of this complexity a useful way to proceed is by taking some examples from within managerial economics and working through them. However, before doing that it is first necessary to consider how a game may be represented in order to analyse and solve it.

There are two basic ways in which a game may be represented. The first is known as the *strategic form*. Table 13.1 gives an example.

In the example shown, two firms are considering whether to set high prices or low prices. If they collude and both set a high price, they will earn profits of 100 each, giving an overall total of 200. If they both set a low price, they will both make profits of 50. However, if one of them sets a high price and the other one sets a low price, the firm setting the low price will earn 120 and the firm setting a high price will make a loss of 20.

This form of representation is most naturally suited to simultaneous games, where each player must move without knowing what the other has done. If a game is sequential, each player moving in turn, then the most natural way to represent it is in *the extensive form*. Figure 13.1 shows the same game in this form, with Company B making the first move on price.

If the firms in this game do in fact take their decisions in turn, with Company B going first, the game is sequential. In that case, the firms' behaviour can be determined by using a method known as *rollback* or *backward induction*. That involves starting with the terminal nodes – the final outcomes – and working backwards.

Table 13.1 A simultaneous game in strategic form: the pay-off matrix

		Company A's actions	
		High price	Low price
Company B's	High price	100$_A$, 100$_B$	120$_A$, −20$_B$
actions	Low price	−20$_A$, 120$_B$	50$_A$, 50$_B$

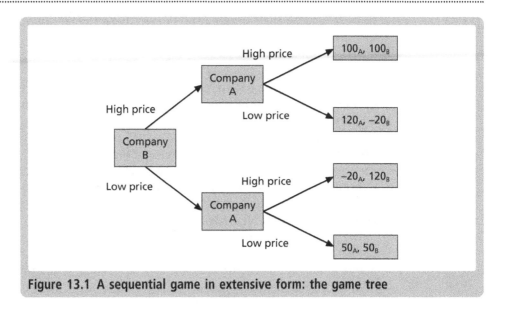

Figure 13.1 A sequential game in extensive form: the game tree

In the example shown, beginning at the top right, we can see that if Company B originally set a high price then A can earn either 100 by setting a high price or 120 by setting a low price. Assuming that A's objective is to maximise its own profit and not to inflict losses on B, then A will choose a low price. A will not take the high price option and it can be ruled out in this situation. In the language of game theory, the branch of the game tree representing a high price by A (when B has chosen a high price) can be *pruned*.

If Company B originally set a low price, then Company A can earn either 50, by setting a low price, or –20 by setting a high price. Clearly, it will choose a low price and the branch representing a high price by A (when B has set a low price) can be pruned.

The situation facing Company B is now much clearer. If B sets a high price, Company A will set a low price and B will earn –20. If B sets a low price, A will also set a low price and B will earn just 50. Choosing between –20 and 50 is straightforward enough and hence B will choose a low price. Company A will therefore also choose a low price and the equilibrium is low price/low price and 50 profit for both firms. In this example, the same outcome will occur if the order of play is reversed and Company A makes the first decision.

The same situation may also be looked at as a simultaneous game, in which case each firm must set a price in ignorance of the price set by the other. In that situation, backward induction cannot be used to solve the game and find the equilibrium. The first step, therefore, is to search for a *dominant strategy*, defined as one that outperforms the others, no matter what the opposing player does. For Company A a low price is better than a high price if B sets a high price and a low price is also better than a high price if B sets a low price. Whichever price B sets, Company A is better off if it chooses a low price. Hence low price is a dominant strategy for A. As exactly the same logic applies to Company B, setting a low price is also a dominant strategy for that firm. As it is rational for both firms to choose their dominant strategies then the equilibrium for the game is low price/low price with total profits equal to 100.

This example illustrates a very important type of game known as the *prisoner's dilemma*. In such games each player can choose between a *cooperative strategy* and a *defecting strategy* (also known as a *cheating strategy*). In the example above, setting a high price is the cooperative strategy and setting a low price is the defecting strategy. If both players choose the cooperative strategy and set high prices, joint profit will be maximised at 200. Clearly that is the preferred outcome for both firms. However, as we have seen, this does not occur. In any game with the same structure of pay-offs, both players have dominant strategies which involve defection and the equilibrium that arises from the selection of these strategies is inferior *for both players* when compared with the non-equilibrium where both cooperate and both set a high price.

The prisoner's dilemma, and its possible resolution, is considered in more detail below. However, before taking it further, it is useful to build on the example above to explain a few more of the central ideas in game theory.

In both versions of the pricing example given above we found an equilibrium, first by using rollback in the sequential version and then by looking for a dominant strategy in the simultaneous version. In both cases the equilibrium was found by assuming that each player will choose the action that is the best response to the actions of the other player. This is the concept of the *Nash equilibrium*, defined as 'a configuration of strategies, one for each player, such that each player's strategy is best for her, given that all other players are playing their equilibrium strategies' (Dixit and Skeath 1999, p. 82). If a Nash equilibrium is reached, then no player would want to change strategies when they know what their rival has done. A brief examination of the pricing example shows that this is the case. When Company A knows that Company B has set a low price, Company A would not wish to change to a high price and the same can be said for Company B.

The concept of the Nash equilibrium is a very powerful one, although it does not help to solve all games. In order to use it, it is necessary to have a method by which to identify equilibrium configurations of strategy. At this point two different kinds of strategy need to be distinguished. The first is the *pure strategy*. This is where the move made by the player is specified with certainty. In the pricing example the two firms decide on either a high price or a low price and there is no uncertainty about which they will choose in each set of circumstances. The second type of strategy is the *mixed strategy*. In this case the player does not choose a move with certainty but selects randomly from the available set of moves with some specific probability. In the pricing example Company A might decide to set a high price with a 70 per cent probability and a low price with 30 per cent probability. It might seem irrational for a firm to leave its own actions to chance, but mixed strategies are important for two reasons. First, there can be practical advantages in behaving unpredictably, and second, there are many situations where the only Nash equilibria to be found require mixed strategies.

If we restrict our attention to pure strategies, for the sake of simplicity, then the search for Nash equilibria can proceed in a number of steps. The first is to examine the game for dominant strategies. If there is a dominant strategy for both players, as in the prisoner's dilemma, those strategies will be adopted

Table 13.2 No dominant strategies: eliminate dominated strategies

		Company A's actions		
		High price	Medium price	Low price
Company B's actions	High price	100_A, 100_B	120_A, 65_B	60_A, 65_B
	Medium price	65_A, 120_B	80_A, 80_B	60_A, 55_B
	Low price	65_A, 60_B	55_A, 60_B	50_A, 50_B

and the game is easily solved. If one of the players has a dominant strategy but the other one does not then the solution is still relatively simple. It can be assumed that the dominant strategy will be adopted by the player who has one and the other player can then respond with the move that is best for them, given the choice made by their rival.

In the presence of dominant strategies, the Nash equilibrium is easily found. However, if the players' choice is restricted to pure strategies there may be no dominant strategies, in which case further steps are required in the search for a solution. One approach is to identify *dominated strategies* and eliminate them. As the term implies, a dominated strategy is one that will never be chosen because there is always another strategy that is preferable, whatever move the opposing player makes. If there are only two choices to be made by each player, as in our example, this does not make any difference to the analysis because if one strategy is dominant the other must be dominated. However, if there are three or more choices available to each player it is possible that some of a player's strategies may be dominated but that they do not have one overall dominant strategy. Table 13.2 extends the pricing example to include the possibility of a 'medium' level price for both firms. The situation depicted, following Dixit and Skeath (1999, p. 91), corresponds to one where both companies have a number of loyal customers (they live nearby) who will buy from their favoured firm at all three prices. In addition to those loyal customers there are price-conscious 'floating buyers' who will buy at the lowest price and whose custom will be divided equally between A and B if they charge the same price. In this situation, joint profit is maximised if they both charge a high price and minimised if they both charge a low price. If one firm charges a low price while the other does not, the low-price firm will attract all of the floating customers but will be earning less from the loyal ones than it might with a higher price. If one firm charges a medium price and the other one a high price, the medium pricer attracts all the floating customers and also makes a medium profit margin from their loyal customers, while the high pricer attracts none of the floating customers but earns a large margin from their loyal clients.

Examination of Table 13.2 shows that for Company A a medium price is preferred when B sets a high price or a medium price but a high price is preferred when B sets a low price. Similarly for B. If A chooses a high price or a medium price, B prefers a medium price. However, if A chooses a low price, B prefers a high price. While neither firm has a *dominant* strategy they both have a *dominated* strategy because they will never choose a low price. Hence the low price row and the low price column can be deleted and the search can continue for dominant or dominated strategies. In this new situation the medium price strategy is dominant for both firms, and hence the high price is dominated. The solution is therefore medium/medium pricing, which is the Nash equilibrium for this game.

In the example given, the successive elimination of dominated strategies leads to an equilibrium. However, that will not always be successful and two other approaches may be called upon. If the game in question is zero sum the *minimax* criterion may be used (see Chapter 12). That involves examining each strategy and finding the worst outcome associated with each one. A strategy is then selected by choosing the one for which the worst outcome is the 'least worst'. That approach amounts to making the pessimistic assumption that the other player will adopt whichever strategy will lead to the worst result for the decision-maker. In the case of the zero-sum game that is reasonable because the worst result for the decision-maker is also the best result for the other player. However, if the game is not zero-sum, minimax may not identify the equilibrium output because a player may not try to select the strategy that does its rival the least good/most harm. In the game shown in Table 13.1 adoption of the minimax strategy by both players leads to the same result as that arrived at by looking for dominant strategies. However, in the example shown in Table 13.2 adoption of the minimax strategy leads to the high price/high price combination, which is not a Nash equilibrium, as has been shown. If either firm adopts a high price the other can improve its profits by adopting a medium price and hence the minimax approach does not find an equilibrium.

If none of the techniques identified thus far is able to find a Nash equilibrium it may be necessary to fall back on the less sophisticated approach of *cell-by-cell inspection*. As its name implies, that simply involves examining each cell in the matrix in order to establish whether either player would wish to move away from that cell, given what the other player has done. In Table 13.2, the medium/medium price cell is a Nash equilibrium because if A sets a medium price, B also prefers a medium price and vice versa. The A high/B low price cell is clearly not a Nash equilibrium because if A set a high price, B would prefer a medium price, and if B set a high price, A would prefer a medium price.

Cell-by-cell inspection may be cumbersome but it will always identify Nash equilibria, if they exist, and computer software is now available to carry out the searching automatically. However, there is no guarantee that a Nash equilibrium does exist in pure strategies, or that there is only one. The Nash equilibrium concept is powerful but not always powerful enough to solve a game.

Applications of game theory I: price collusion

In the simple game illustrated in Table 13.1 two firms are trying to decide between high prices and low prices in a prisoner's dilemma game. In that example, both firms choose a low price and hence they both lose an opportunity to make significantly higher profits. Given that the senior managers in both firms will be aware of this problem it naturally raises the question of how they might escape the sub-optimal equilibrium and set up a situation where both can gain. In terms of game theory the question is whether an equilibrium involving cooperative strategies can be secured, to replace the defecting strategies that are indicated in the initial situation. Three approaches to this problem offer themselves. These are: repetition; penalties and rewards; and leadership.

Repetition as a solution to the collusion problem

The first approach is to recognise that Table 13.1 represents a *one-off* game, which is unrealistic. Most firms expect to keep on playing games with their rivals for some time into the future. Hence a first step is to reconsider the game as one that is repeated into the future.

If we return to the game shown in Table 13.1 we can first imagine that the two companies do find some way to cooperate, in which case they make joint profits of 200, 100 for each firm. If either one of them defects, the defector will increase profit to 120. However, that will end the cooperation because the other will make losses and will therefore also defect, returning to the low price/low price equilibrium. In each of the subsequent weeks both firms will make 50 profit instead of 100. Hence, if the game is repeated, the stream of future pay-offs to the cooperative strategy is 100, 100, 100 . . . into the future while the stream of pay-offs to initial cooperation followed by defection is 100, 120, 50, 50, 50 . . . into the future. As the returns to maintaining cooperation are clearly higher (unless returns from the third period onwards are so heavily discounted as to have almost no value) there is an incentive to cooperate and repeating the game may allow both firms to escape from the prisoner's dilemma.

This is a key insight but at this point the analysis becomes more complicated. If the game is repeated a fixed and known number of times, the players need to consider the complete scenario for the sequential game, using rollback to decide which price to charge each time. But this has a strange effect on the result. In the last round of the game there is no incentive for either player to cooperate, because there is no future punishment. The dominant strategy for both players in that round of the game is to cheat. In that case, there is no point in considering the future in the penultimate week and hence both will choose to cheat then as well. That applies to every round of the game so that the cooperation 'unravels' right back to the initial period. The prisoner's dilemma has not been solved, after all!

While the logic of rollback predicts that cooperation will not be established in prisoner's dilemma games of known length, intuition and a good deal of evidence suggest that this prediction is not always accurate and further analysis is required. Nevertheless, the basic insight is important and valid. It also suggests that if a game is repeated an infinite number of times then cooperation may be secured.

If a game is to be repeated an infinite number of times, there is no known end to it. As before, players can adjust their strategies according to the behaviour of their rivals in previous rounds, and all players know this. Strategies that change according to the behaviour of rivals are known as *contingent strategies*, and strategies that involve cooperating until the rival defects and then punishing the rival for that defection are known as *trigger strategies* – they are triggered by defection. The most unforgiving trigger strategy is the *grim strategy*, which is where a player cooperates until the rival defects, after which the player defects/refuses to cooperate for every subsequent round of the game. The problem with the grim strategy is that it is too unforgiving. If a rival cheated by mistake, for instance, the possibility of cooperation and higher profits is gone forever. A more forgiving and interesting strategy is *tit-for-tat* which is where each player cooperates if their rival cooperated in the last round and defects if they defected in the last round. In the tit-for-tat strategy a rival who defects is only punished for as long as they do so. If they begin to cooperate, that change in their behaviour is rewarded with reciprocal cooperation.

If we return to the example in order to examine the tit-for-tat strategy we can see that if one player defects from the cooperative situation it will gain 20 in profit (120 instead of 100) for that round but it will lose 50 relative to cooperation in the subsequent round (from 100 to 50) and profits will stay at 50 if it continues to defect. Permanent defection would only be worthwhile if the immediate gain is valued more highly than the subsequent stream of lost profits. As the loss of profits goes on forever, permanent defection is only preferable to permanent cooperation if an income stream of 120, 50, 50, 50 . . . 50 is preferred to a stream of 100, 100, 100 . . . 100. That could only be the case if returns after the first period were discounted so heavily as to be almost worthless. Hence the adoption of tit-for-tat will make permanent cheating unprofitable and hence will partially help rivals escape the prisoner's dilemma.

While permanent cheating is prevented by the adoption of tit-for-tat there remains the possibility of cheating for just one round and then returning to cooperation. If one of the rivals adopts that approach, its stream of profits will be 120 for the period of cheating, 50 for the following period of punishment then 100, 100 . . . for the remainder of the game. If that is preferred to a constant income of 100, 100 . . . it will be chosen. However, with a discount rate of 'r', choosing to cheat requires that:

$$120 + 50/(1 + r) > 100 + 100/(1 + r)$$

Only if the discount rate is greater than 150 per cent per time taken for one round of the game will it pay to cheat just once in the face of the tit-for-tat strategy. At any lower rate tit-for-tat allows firms to escape the prisoner's dilemma.

The logic described here can be extended to cover games of unknown length by noting that instead of the game going on forever, players simply know that there is some probability of a further round each time. In that case, when discounting future payments the discounting factor is not $1/(1+r)$ for a single period but $p/(1+r)$ where 'p' is the probability of a further round. Common sense and intuition suggest that if future rounds may not take place, the disincentives to cheat will be weaker. That is correct as the examples show. If the discount rate is 10 per cent and the game goes on forever, then the next round's profits are discounted by $1/1.1 = 0.909$. However, if there is only a 50 per cent chance that future rounds will take place, then the next round's profits are discounted by $0.5/1.1 = 0.45$. Rearranging this in terms of an 'effective discount rate' (edr, where $1/(1+edr) =$ the discounted value $= 0.45$) shows that the discount rate of 10 per cent that applies to the infinitely repeated game becomes 122 per cent if there is only a 50 per cent chance of a further round. At such high rates, cheating may once again become worthwhile.

Penalties and rewards as solutions to the collusion problem: the price-matching example

The problem of establishing cooperation might also be solved by the imposition of penalties or rewards upon the parties. If the cheating player suffers some penalty then the structure of the pay-offs will be changed and that new structure may lead to an equilibrium involving cooperation. This idea leads to a particularly interesting insight in the case of collusive pricing. One way in which firms may introduce such a penalty is by advertising that they will match the prices offered by their rivals. At first sight, that may appear to be evidence of intense competition among the rivals and a benefit to consumers. However, by charging a high price and advertising publicly that they will match any price charged by rivals, companies are introducing a third pricing option as shown in Table 13.3.

Table 13.3 Price-matching maintains higher prices (weakly dominated strategies are shaded)

		Company A's actions		
		High price	Low price	Advertising a high price but promising to match rival's advertised price
Company B's actions	High price	$100_A, 100_B$	$120_A, -20_B$	$100_A, 100_B$
	Low price	$-20_A, 120_B$	$50_A, 50_B$	$50_A, 50_B$
	Advertising a high price but promising to match rival's advertised price	$100_A, 100_B$	$50_A, 50_B$	$100_A, 100_B$

Searching Table 13.3 for dominant or dominated strategies shows that if A chooses a high price, B will prefer a low price. If A chooses a low price, B will prefer either a low price or matching to a high price. If A chooses the matching strategy, B will choose either a high price or a matching strategy. Hence the high-price strategy is *weakly dominated* by the matching strategy. High price is either rejected or has equal standing with another strategy. The same logic applies to Company B and hence the high-price strategy can be eliminated.

If the high-price strategy is eliminated, the game can be re-examined and it consists of the unshaded cells in Table 13.3. If A chooses a low price, B will be indifferent between setting a low price and adopting the matching strategy. If A chooses matching, then B will definitely prefer matching. The low-price strategy is weakly dominated and the Nash equilibrium is where both firms choose the matching strategy. The overall outcome is that both sell at the advertised price, which is high, while promising to match price cuts which never take place. The apparently competitive practice of offering to match rivals' price cuts is in fact a means by which high prices can be maintained!

In this example, the penalties that are imposed for 'cheating' are imposed by the players themselves and their effect is in the players' interest. However, penalties or rewards could be imposed by third parties, with a variety of effects. If consumers realise that the 'price-matching' promise is essentially a trick that leads them to pay higher prices, they may invoke the law on competition to prevent such promises being made. In that case, the pay-off matrix in Table 13.3 must be adjusted to take account of the costs of legal action if the price-matching strategy is challenged in court. In other cases the penalties imposed by third parties could improve the outcomes for the players. For instance, if the industry in question has a trade association that punishes members who break the implicit agreement to charge high prices, then all members will face improved incentives to cooperate.

Leadership as a solution to the problem of collusive pricing

A third approach to solving the problem may arise if one of the players faces much larger pay-offs than the other. In that case the 'larger' player may exercise 'leadership'. This is illustrated in Table 13.4 which is an amended version of Table 13.1.

In the game as shown, the dominant strategy for A is low price. However, the dominant strategy for B is now high price. The Nash equilibrium is the shaded cell in the pay-off matrix and the prisoner's dilemma has disappeared.

In the example shown, the analysis can be taken further. At the Nash equilibrium total profit is equal to 240. However, if the high price/high price solution could be obtained, total profits would rise to 400 and B's alone would be 300. In that case, B could offer a side payment to A, in return for A's agreement to set a high price. At the high/high combination A has a profit of 100, compared with 120 at the Nash equilibrium and A would therefore be willing to charge the higher price, provided a payment of 20 or more was offered. As B gains 180 by the move to high/high he will be prepared to offer up to that figure and the two firms can bargain with each other to reach a figure between these two limits.

The common-sense explanation for this result is simply that the largest player has most to gain from a cooperative result, and the most to lose from cheating. Hence, such a leader will adopt the cooperative strategy even if others cheat and may be able to pay the others in order to secure their cooperation. The most obvious and important real-life example is the behaviour of Saudi Arabia in the world market for oil. The Saudis are the largest player, and hence they gain most from high world oil prices and lose most from low prices. If smaller maverick

Table 13.4 Leadership as a solution

		Company A's actions	
		High price	Low price
Company B's actions	High price	100$_A$, 300$_B$	120$_A$, 120$_B$
	Low price	−20$_A$, 280$_B$	50$_A$, 50$_B$

oil producers, like Libya, break out of the cooperation and increase oil output beyond their OPEC quota, the Saudis reduce their own output in order to maintain the high price. If they simply maintained production, world prices would fall and the Saudis' losses would be greater than those they suffer by reducing their output.

To sum up on the problem of enforcing price collusion: in a simple one-off game a pair of firms choosing between high and low prices will tend to both charge low prices, to their mutual detriment. If the game is repeated they may escape from that dilemma but that in turn depends upon how often the game is repeated and how the participants value the future relative to the present. There are two other ways in which the dilemma may be escaped. The first involves the imposition of penalties or rewards on the players, which alters the incentives facing them. The second arises if one of the players is larger than the other in which case that player gains more from cooperation and loses more from cheating, to the point where it pays the 'leader' to adopt a cooperative strategy, whatever its rival does, and it may also pay the leader to 'bribe' its rival into cooperating.

Applications of game theory II: Cournot, Bertrand and von Stackelberg competition

Although game theory did not dominate the economic analysis of industrial organisation until the 1980s and 1990s, its application to oligopoly can be traced back to 1838. In that year Antoine Augustin Cournot proposed a solution to the problem of oligopoly which is now recognised to be the same as a Nash equilibrium. For many years, his model, and those of Bertrand (1883) and von Stackelberg (1934) were largely regarded as historical curiosities. However, the rise of game theory brought them back into prominence as the basis for a wide range of analyses and hence they merit an introduction here.

Cournot's model is a simultaneous game that can be most easily explained with a set of simple equations. An industry contains two firms, producing identical products. For simplicity, the demand curve for the industry is assumed to be a straight line, having the equation:

$P = a - bQ,$ where: P = price;

Q = industry output

$= Q_1 + Q_2$: $Q_{1,2,}$ = output of $Firm_{1,2}$

Total cost for each firm is given by:

$TC_{1,2} = F + cQ_{1,2}$: F = fixed cost; c = marginal cost.

(It is assumed here that both firms have the same cost functions, but that can easily be changed.)

Profit for Firm 1 is then given by:

$Profit_1 = Revenue_1 - Cost_1 = Q_1[a - b(Q_1 + Q_2)] - (F + cQ_1)$

or:

$Profit_1 = aQ_1 - bQ_1^2 - bQ_1Q_2 - F - cQ_1$

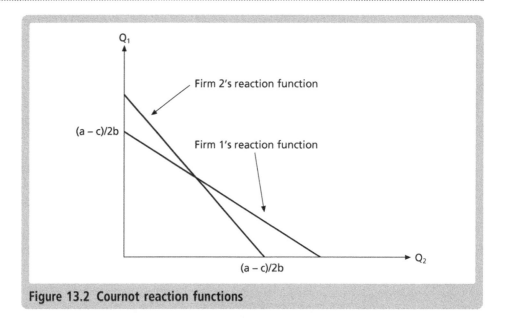

Figure 13.2 Cournot reaction functions

And profit for Firm 2 is:

$$\text{Profit}_2 = aQ_2 - bQ_2^2 - bQ_1Q_2 - F - cQ_2$$

Each firm maximises its profits by choosing the level of output at which marginal profit is equal to zero. Differentiating Firm 1's profit functions with respect to Firm 1's output gives:

$$\text{Marginal profit}_1 = a - 2bQ_1 - bQ_2 - c = 0, \text{ when profit is maximized.}$$

or:

$$Q_1 = (a - c - bQ_2)/2b$$

Similarly, for Firm 2 to maximise its profit:

$$Q_2 = (a - c - bQ_1)/2b$$

These two equations show that the quantity that each firm should produce in order to maximise its profits depends upon the quantity produced by the other firm. For instance, if Firm 2 produced zero output it would pay Firm 1 to produce $Q_1 = (a - c)/2b$ (which is also the monopoly output, as it should be). These equations are known as *reaction functions* or *best-response functions*. If each firm produces output according to its reaction function the result is a Nash equilibrium, known in this case as a Cournot–Nash equilibrium. In terms of a diagram, the equilibrium is where the two reaction functions cross, as shown in Figure 13.2. In terms of the equations given above, both firms will produce output equal to $(a - c)/3b$ and total industry output is $2(a - c)/3b$. The price will be the same for both firms, and equal to the market-clearing price for the total quantity produced.

This Cournot–Nash equilibrium is the starting point for many modern game-theoretic models, having become the analytical workhorse of much industrial economics and the basis for many studies in marketing. In common-sense terms it represents a situation where each firm adjusts its own output according to the other's. An alternative approach is that of Bertrand, who suggested that instead of adjusting the quantity of output, firms instead adjust their prices. At first sight, that might seem like a minor difference between the two models. However, where products are identical, the Bertrand model incorporates a major discontinuity because if one firm chooses a higher price, it will lose all of its customers to its rival. Because of this feature, in the Bertrand model both firms have an incentive to under-cut their rival's prices by a tiny margin. The resulting competition drives prices down to marginal cost and output is equal to that in a competitive equilibrium.

This difference between the Bertrand and Cournot models illustrates one of the salient features and central weaknesses of the game-theoretic approach. That is that changing the unobservable 'protocols' – the rules under which firms operate – leads to radically different results. Shy (1995) suggests that both Bertrand and Cournot games may be needed to understand different markets but offers no advice on how the selection might be made.

A third version of the basic game theory approach to oligopoly is to be found in von Stackelberg's (1934) leader–follower model. In this case, the game being played is sequential rather than simultaneous. One firm, the leader, first decides on a quantity to produce. Then the other firm, the follower, chooses how much to produce in the light of its observations of the leader's output. The solution of this game can be found, as for any sequential game, by working backwards. The follower's decision will be given by its reaction function. As the leader (Firm 1 here) knows that the follower (Firm 2) will set its quantity in that way, the leader can simply substitute the follower's reaction function for Q_2 in its own profit function. Hence the leader's profit depends only upon its own quantity and its profit function becomes:

$$\text{Profit}_1 = Q_1[a - b(Q_1 + Q_2)] - (F + cQ_1)$$
$$= Q_1[a - b(Q_1 + \{(a - c - bQ_1)/2b\})] - (F + cQ_1)$$

Maximising this profit function gives the leader's quantity as:

$$Q_1 = (a - c)/2b$$

The follower's quantity can then be found from its own reaction function, so that:

$$Q_2 = (a - c - bQ_1)/2b = (a - c - b[a - c]/2b)/2b$$

While these models may seem too abstract to be directly applicable in real markets, they have formed the basis for a significant stream of research on pricing, particularly in the marketing literature. Roy *et al.* (1994), for instance, examined the US motor industry and found evidence that General Motors and Ford followed a pattern of pricing that was best predicted by the leader–follower model (see the Illustration in Chapter 15).

Applications of game theory III: entry deterrence

A third area in which game theory has been applied concerns the conditions under which firms will enter an industry, and the conditions under which incumbent firms can deter entry by taking strategic actions of their own. That topic alone has generated so many studies, reviewed by Wilson (1992), that Ghemawat (1997, p. 2) has suggested that at least one leading academic journal should be re-named *The Journal of Entry Deterrence*!

A key idea being explored here is that incumbent firms can protect themselves from entry by threatening some kind of 'retaliation' after entry takes place. Most obviously, they can threaten to increase their output and lower their price if entry takes place, making it unprofitable for the potential entrant and hence deterring them from entry. However, that threat will not be effective unless it is credible. In order to make it credible the incumbent must have the ability to increase output beyond the pre-entry level and therefore it may need to build more capacity than it actually intends to use. Shy (1995) provides an extension of Spence's (1977) original analysis, showing that an incumbent firm can prevent entry by irreversibly committing resources to excess productive capacity, while continuing to charge monopoly prices.

While that idea seems intuitively sound, further game theory also shows that it is too simple. Investment in spare capacity will only deter entry if it is rational for the incumbent to carry out its threat of price war when entry takes place. That in turn will only be the case if the profits made through fighting off entry through price war are larger than the profits made by accommodating the entrant. But a path-breaking paper by Dixit (1980) used game theory to show that, in at least one set of circumstances, it would be irrational for incumbents to behave in that way. In that case, a rational potential entrant could predict that a rational incumbent would not try to fight them off and the entrant would not therefore be deterred. The implication is that a rational incumbent would not invest in excess capacity in order to deter entry. Figure 13.3 shows a simple game that illustrates the issue.

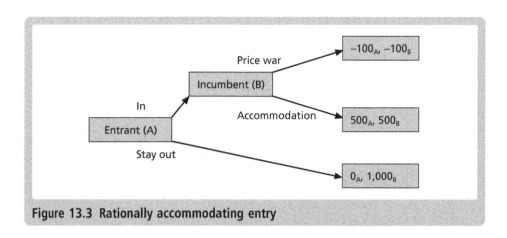

Figure 13.3 Rationally accommodating entry

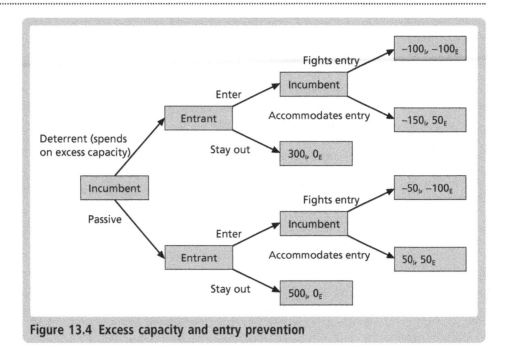

Figure 13.4 Excess capacity and entry prevention

If the incumbent threatens to set off a price war, should entry take place, the entrant is faced with the prospect of making a loss of 100. It might be expected, therefore, that the incumbent will be deterred from entering. However, if entry did take place it would be more rational for the incumbent to accommodate the entrant, sharing the market and the profits. In that case the incumbent would make a profit of 500, as opposed to the loss of 100 which would be earned if it set off a price war. Hence the entrant knows that the incumbent will not spark off a price war. The threat is not credible. The outcome will be that entry takes place and the incumbent accommodates the entrant.

The limitation of the game shown in Figure 13.3 is that it takes no explicit account of the effect that the incumbent's spending on spare capacity will have on its profits in the event that entry takes place and it accommodates entry. If a firm does invest in excess capacity it is creating a situation where its unit costs would be higher if its volume is lower (McGuigan *et al.* 1999, p. 566). Hence it may earn even less profit by accommodating entry than by fighting off the entrant. Figure 13.4 provides an example.

Adopting the backward induction approach to solving the game, the top right-hand corner of Figure 13.4 is examined first. If the entrant has decided to enter, the incumbent has a choice between fighting, in which case it will make a loss of 100, and accommodating, in which case the rise in unit costs caused by lower capacity utilisation will increase the loss to 150. The commitment made to the excess capacity ensures that the incumbent will choose to fight. The entrant knows that the incumbent will fight if entry takes place. Hence the entrant is choosing between entering (in which case its profit is –100) and staying out (profit = 0). The entrant will therefore choose not to enter. Continuing back along the tree, the incumbent now knows that if it spends enough on excess capacity, the result will be profits of 300.

Moving to the lower part of the decision tree, and starting at the right-hand side, it is clear that if the potential entrant has decided to enter, the incumbent has a choice between fighting (making the loss of 100) and accommodating, in which case profit is equal to 50. The incumbent would therefore choose to accommodate. When deciding whether to enter, the entrant is deciding between a positive profit of 50 and a profit of zero. Hence the entrant will enter.

The analysis of the game is now almost complete. If the incumbent takes a passive stance, the result will be that it makes a profit of 50. If the incumbent spends on commitment, it makes a profit of 300. Hence, it chooses to install the excess capacity and entry is deterred.

Overall, the incumbent will choose to make the commitment if the profits to be made from having a monopoly position (while incurring the costs of the excess capacity – 300 in this case) exceed the profits to be made by accommodation (50 in this case). At the same time, it should be remembered that the game only works out in this way if the profit made when the entrant enters and the incumbent accommodates but the incumbent has made a commitment (–150) represents a greater loss than that which arises from fighting the entrant (–100). The commitment to excess capacity must make it more profitable to fight than to accommodate.

As might be expected, the analysis becomes increasingly complex when the game is extended beyond a single post-entry period, when differentiated products are taken into account, when the players have imperfect information about each other's situation and when there is more than one potential entrant. Given the wide variety of situations open for analysis, it is perhaps unsurprising that relatively few clear-cut conclusions have emerged. As in many applications of game theory, the results are very sensitive to the precise specifications – the protocols – of the games, which may in practice be unobservable. This last point is returned to later.

Applications of game theory IV: how involving the government can give firms a strategic advantage in international competition

Chapters 20 and 21 of this text are concerned with the ways in which governments may intervene in markets by regulating industries or by attempting to enforce competition, and the ways in which firms may respond to those actions. While such intervention is often intended to prevent firms from acting as they would prefer, governments may also act to help companies achieve their objectives, especially if they are in competition with firms in other countries. Game theory can help to illustrate how government assistance to an industry may ensure that it secures international dominance, and why executives may rationally spend large amounts of time and effort trying to influence government in that direction.

Consider, for instance, the rivalry between Boeing and Airbus for the development of a 'super-jumbo' aircraft for the passenger market. The key feature of that market is that the development costs for such an aeroplane are so enormous, relative to the likely value of sales, that if both companies develop their own version, no profits can be made. The game is shown in Table 13.5.

In the game as shown, Boeing will prefer to develop the super-jumbo if Airbus stays out and stay out if Airbus develops. Exactly the same logic applies to Airbus. Neither firm has a dominant strategy and there are two Nash equilibria. The first is where Boeing stays out and Airbus develops the new aeroplane and the second is where Airbus stays out and Boeing takes the market. Hence the outcome is indeterminate – one of game theory's problems. However, if either government decides to subsidise its champion, the structure of the game changes in a very significant way. Consider the case where the American government decides to pay Boeing 110 in order to help its product development effort. In that case the new game is as in Table 13.6.

In this game, if Airbus decides to develop, Boeing will also choose to develop, because the profit of 10 that it makes in that case is better than the profit of zero that would be earned by staying out. If Airbus decides to stay out, Boeing will also choose to develop. Hence 'develop super-jumbo' becomes a dominant strategy for Boeing. In that case, Airbus knows that Boeing will develop the new aeroplane, whatever its own decision, and Airbus managers need only concern themselves with the pay-offs for that situation. They face the choice between losses of 100 if they develop and losses of zero if they stay out, hence they stay out. Boeing develops the aeroplane and makes a profit of 610 (which incidentally would allow it to pay back the subsidy to the government and still make a large profit). Unlike the previous game, this one has a unique Nash equilibrium in which Boeing develops the super-jumbo and Airbus does not. By subsidising product development the US government secures a dominant position for its aircraft industry.

Table 13.5 Boeing and Airbus produce a super-jumbo: no government intervention

		Airbus	
		Develop super-jumbo	Stay out
Boeing	Develop super-jumbo	-100_A, -100_B	0_A, 500_B
	Stay out	500_A,　0_B	0_A,　0_B

Table 13.6 Boeing and Airbus produce a super-jumbo: Boeing is subsidised by the US government

		Airbus	
		Develop super-jumbo	Stay out
Boeing	Develop super-jumbo	-100_A, 10_B	0_A, 610_B
	Stay out	500_A, 0_B	0_A,　0_B

The super-jumbo example is drawn from Krugman's (1986) analysis of 'strategic trade policy'. While that takes the discussion outside the strict bounds of managerial economics it illustrates how managers may secure important strategic gains for their companies by enlisting the support of their governments.

An evaluation of game theory: how much can it contribute to the understanding of business decisions?

Game theory undoubtedly provides a powerful tool for the analysis of situations that involve interdependence. Without it, it is impossible to examine the oligopoly situation with a satisfactory level of rigour and we are left with the models of perfect competition and monopoly on the one hand, and Porter's rather loose and indeterminate 'five forces' analysis on the other. At the same time, the contribution made by game theory remains problematical for a number of reasons. Kreps (1990b) identifies four key difficulties.

The first problem with game theory is that the outcome of any particular game is very sensitive to the details of its protocol. If a prediction is to be made there must be very clear and precise 'rules of the game' – the order in which the players make moves, the basis on which they take decisions, the extent of their information about each other and every other parameter that might be introduced. However, in real market situations it may be impossible to identify those protocols, leaving the analyst with no clear starting point.

The second problem is that for many of the games that are important in economics there are a number of different equilibria and the analysis offers no way to choose between them. Even in a simple example like the Airbus/Boeing case shown in Table 13.5 there are two equilibria (out of only four possible situations) and deciding which is most likely to occur requires looking outside game theory altogether. When games become complex enough to reflect many issues of real practical interest it may be a large task just to find all the equilibria, after which no further conclusion can be drawn. In order to cope with that difficulty analysts have often turned to highly detailed case studies of individual industries in order to 'supply a direct take on the practical importance of game theory in general' (Ghemawat 1997, p. 11). However, those studies often seem to reverse the usual process of research. Instead of beginning with theory, using it to make predictions and then testing those predictions, many of these studies begin with the facts about an industry's history and then proceed by trying to fit game-theoretic explanations to those facts. Ghemawat's (1997) theoretical analysis of process innovation in the steel industry, for example, begins by noting that 'the pattern of adoption of thin-slab casting might be rationalised game-theoretically in at least half a dozen ways' (p. 151). As Saloner (1991, p. 129) put it, 'the degree of modelling discretion is so significant that a model can be devised to explain almost any fact'.

The problem is compounded by the fact that in many games that have multiple equilibria there is in fact a solution because in some way the players 'know' what to do (see Kreps 1990b, pp. 100–2). Their past experiences and general sense of how people behave lead them to select one of the multiple equilibria in a way that is predictable but not predicted by formal game theory. In other words, 'common sense' sometimes performs better, which is hardly comforting to anyone who has struggled to master the complexities and difficulties of the theory.

The third problem that Kreps identifies concerns *equilibrium refinements*. These are strengthenings of the requirement that behaviour constitutes a Nash equilibrium, i.e. additional conditions that can be used to find an outcome. One example of such strengthening is backward induction and another is the requirement, in the context of Figure 13.3, that a player should not make incredible threats. In the case of backward induction, as in Figure 13.1 for example, it is assumed that Company B makes its move on the understanding that it 'knows' what Company A will do. But what happens if Company A does not make the expected move? In many games a solution can only be found if any unexpected behaviour is followed by a return to 'business as usual' where players continue to believe that their rivals will behave as expected, despite the existence of evidence to the contrary. This problem has led game theorists to try to build 'complete theories' which do not rule out any actions at all, but instead assume that those actions that are not part of an equilibrium are very unlikely, rather than ruled out entirely. Such refinements necessarily add to the complexity of the analysis and go beyond the scope of this simple outline (see Kreps 1990b, pp. 114–28 for an exposition).

The fourth problem facing game theory is related to the first. The outcome of most games is very sensitive to the protocols involved – the rules of the game. In that case it is important to know where those rules came from. However, game theory tends to take the rules for granted, treating them as exogenously determined. Hence the most important determinants of the outcome go unexplained. As different rules lead to different outcomes it is also possible, even likely, that mechanisms exist that link the two. In particular there may be mechanisms that favour the establishment of rules that lead to outcomes that the players prefer. Unfortunately, such mechanisms are not well understood. Kreps (1990b, pp. 129–32) illustrates this with an example that relates back to the discussion above. General Electric (GE) and Westinghouse were engaged in duopoly competition to supply very large turbine generators, where there was little fear of entry. The obvious expected outcome was collusion, as the two firms found ways in which to escape the prisoner's dilemma. However, at first this did not happen. The reason for this was that negotiations between the firms and their customers were carried out in secret. Hence, neither firm had the information needed to know if its rival was violating an implicit cartel agreement. That situation was altered dramatically when GE put in place a number of procedures that changed the protocols of the game. Most significantly, the company offered 'price protection' to its customers by promising that if it lowered its prices relative to a 'book price' for one customer, it would pay back similar discounts to other customers who had purchased in the last few months. The effect of that was to force GE to publish its prices, which made collusion much easier, and to make it expensive for GE to offer discounts. Hence Westinghouse soon adopted a similar approach to pricing. Both firms set relatively high prices and made significant collusive profits until the US government took action against them.

Viewed from one perspective, the GE/Westinghouse example simply confirms the economic analysis of collusion, which shows that it will be easy when firms are well informed about each other's actions and difficult when they are not. GE simply acted on that analysis and changed the rules to improve the rivals' mutual knowledge. However, as Kreps (1990b) points out, that begs the question of why GE (or Westinghouse) did not change the rules earlier. Unless we attribute it to an earlier ignorance of the economics, which was corrected by their senior executives attending the appropriate classes, we are left with no understanding of why the new rules were put into place at that particular time.

Overall, then, the contribution of game theory to the understanding of business issues remains problematical. While significant insights have been gained, there are just too many games, with too many potential solutions, from which to choose.

Illustration Auctions, bidding and selling the airwaves

Another area of business where game theory can help to advance understanding is bidding strategy and auction design (Dixit and Skeath, 1999, ch. 15). Auctions can take a number of forms. In *sealed-bid* auctions, bidders are not allowed to know what bids have been made until the auction results are announced. *Open-outcry* bidding involves making bids in public. *English auctions* are *ascending auctions* in that an auctioneer begins at a low price and calls out successively high prices until the highest bidder is found. *Dutch auctions* are *descending auctions* where the auctioneer begins at a high price that is gradually reduced until a buyer is found.

The price paid by a buyer at auction may also be arrived at in different ways. The simplest and most common approach is the *first-price* auction where the highest bidder pays the amount they bid. An alternative, which has some very useful characteristics, is the *second-price* auction where the highest bidder wins, but pays the price equal to that offered by the second-highest bidder.

The central difficulty arising in respect of auctions is that the participants do not know the valuation placed by others on the object for sale. That happens for two different reasons. In *objective value* or *common value* auctions the item for sale has the same value for all bidders but their estimates of that value are imprecise. For instance, no one knows exactly how much profit can be made from third-generation (3G) mobile phones. In *subjective value* auctions – film star memorabilia for instance – the object for sale has different value for different bidders.

These informational problems create a number of difficulties for both buyers and sellers. The best-known problem for buyers is known as the *winner's curse*. If we consider an objective value auction where buyers do not know the value of the asset offered for sale, the bidder who offers most is likely to have bid too much. The 'winner' wins because his valuation of the asset is higher than anyone else's and therefore likely to exceed the true value. It has already been noted in Chapter 4 that corporate raiders often pay too much for the firms they buy, and that may be due in part to the winner's curse. Clearly, firms that enter objective value auctions need to recognise the dangers they face and shade down their bids in order to reduce the potential losses arising from the winner's curse, which may be substantial (Thaler 1988).

In the case of subjective value auctions, bidders will hope to hide their true valuation in order to win with bids that are 'shaded' downwards. However, sellers naturally prefer bids that are not shaded but which do reflect the true valuation placed on the object by buyers. This is where auction design, based on game-theoretic foundations, can be very useful. Bidders can be encouraged to reveal their true valuation by adopting *a second-price sealed-bid* auction where the highest bidder buys the object for the bid made by the second-highest bidder. In that situation it is never sensible for a buyer to bid higher or lower than their own valuation. If a buyer bids higher than their own valuation, there are three possible scenarios.

1. *A rival bids less than the buyer's own valuation.* In this case, the buyer wins and pays less than their own valuation, making a profit equal to the difference. But the outcome would have been the same if the buyer had made a bid exactly equal to the valuation. In this scenario no purpose is served by bidding beyond true valuation.
2. *A rival bids an amount that is more than the buyer's true valuation but less than the higher bid made.* In that case, the buyer wins the auction but pays more for the object than it is worth to them and thereby loses. A bid just equal to the true valuation would prevent that from happening.
3. *A rival bids more for the object.* In that case the buyer does not win the auction. However, that outcome would also have resulted if the buyer had bid their true valuation. Again, no purpose is served by bidding beyond that valuation.

There is clearly no purpose in bidding above the true valuation because that either leads to the same or worse outcomes. Bidding above valuation is *dominated* by bidding at valuation. Nor is it worth shading the bid and offering less than true valuation, because again there are three possible scenarios.

1. *A rival bids less than the buyer.* In that case the buyer wins the auction and buys the object for an amount equal to the rival's bid. But the same result would arise if the buyer bid equal to their valuation.
2. *A rival bids an amount that is more than the buyer's bid but less than the buyer's valuation.* In this case the rival gets the object for an amount that is equal to the buyer's bid. But if the buyer had bid equal to their valuation, they would not have lost the object and would have bought it for less than valuation. Hence making a bid equal to valuation is superior in this situation.
3. *A rival bids more than the buyer's valuation.* In that case the buyer does not get the object but would not have won even if they had bid their true valuation.

This analysis shows that making a bid equal to the true valuation is a dominant strategy for buyers in a *second-price sealed-bid auction.* More generally, the design of the auction may have an important influence on its outcome, encouraging or discouraging bidders from disclosing their true valuations.

▶

One of the most significant examples illustrating the importance of auction design is to be found in the experience of those countries that have auctioned licences for mobile phone networks and broadcast licences. New Zealand and Australia were the first countries to experiment with this approach. They both experienced significant difficulties, including a comic episode in New Zealand when a student bid NZ$1 and paid nothing for a television licence because no one bid against him and there was no reserve price (McMillan 1994). Governments and auction theorists learned from these early trials and the period 1997–2000 saw licence auctions for radio spectrum in a number of countries, including the United States, the United Kingdom, the Netherlands, Germany and Italy. Those auctions led to widely differing outcomes, examined by Klemperer (2000).

A first issue that arises concerns the possibility of tacit collusion among bidders. In an ascending auction, bidders may use the early stages to send signals to rivals about who should buy which of the licences for sale. In the United States, for instance, one of the competing bidders for a licence in Rochester made a number of high bids in other areas which ended in '378', which happened to be the licence number for Rochester. Rivals interpreted this as a signal that the company would punish anyone else who bid for Rochester and they pulled out (Crampton and Schwartz 2000). Overall, that spectrum auction raised less than $14m when it had been expected to raise $1,800m. In Germany in 1999 Mannesmann put in a low bid for five licences and a slightly lower one for the other five, which rival T-Mobil understood to mean that it should bid slightly higher for the latter five but not challenge Mannesmann for the first five.

Another difficulty for auction design lies in inducing enough bidders to take part. If one firm is a clear 'favourite' because the licence (or any other asset) is worth more to it than to others, others will not enter the auction. Even if they do enter, they will be aware of the winner's curse problem and unwilling to bid higher than the favourite, who will be able to buy the licence at less than its value. Strong bidders know the value of their position and tend to reinforce it by emphasising that only they can pay the highest price and still make profits.

Although the ascending auction has these disadvantages over the first-price sealed bid approach, it nevertheless allows bidders to learn about others' valuations, improving the information that goes into securing the final price and it can therefore improve the funds raised. The experience of the UK and Netherlands 3G mobile phone licences shows how the context can be important. In the UK case, the government originally intended to auction four 3G licences. As there were already four incumbent operators, who would be natural 'favourites', the auction designers were concerned that a straightforward ascending auction would deter entrants and give the incumbents a windfall. It was therefore proposed to have an 'Anglo-Dutch' auction where an ascending auction would take place until just five bidders remained. At that point the remaining bidders would be required to make sealed bids, not lower the current price level. However, it later became possible to auction five licences. As no bidder was allowed to win more than one licence, and there were only four incumbents, at least one licence would go to a new entrant. Hence the problems of collusion and entry deterrence were mimimised by the context. An ascending auction was used, there were nine entrants and a record-breaking £22.5 billion was raised.

In the Netherlands, the ascending auction was also used, but there were only five licences and five incumbents. Strong firms from other countries opted for partnerships with the local incumbents, instead of bidding on their own account. Only one new entrant attempted to bid and soon dropped out. The auction raised £1.65 billion instead of the £6 billion that had been expected.

A further aspect of auction design concerns the structure of the industry that will be created after the auction has been completed, and governments' concern to avoid very high levels of concentration. In the German case, twelve blocks of spectrum were auctioned, from which bidders could create licences of two or three blocks. Hence, if four large firms each bought three blocks the resulting industry would be much more highly concentrated than if six firms each bought two. What actually happened in the German case was rather strange. Seven bidders participated, one of which looked relatively weak and dropped out early in the bidding. That left six bidders and two obvious ways forward for the dominant firms – Deutsche Telekom and Vodafone-Mannesmann. The first was that they could have pushed the price up further to make the weaker rivals quit, which would have given the government high revenues but left the industry highly concentrated with the two leaders dominant. The second was that they could have directed all six remaining firms to bid for only two blocks each in the next round, keeping the price low but yielding a less concentrated industry. In the event, the dominant firms behaved in a very odd way. Vodafone-Mannesmann appeared to be using the final digits of its bids to signal to Deutsche Telekom that it wished to end the auction earlier. However, Deutsche Telekom ignored the signal and continued with the process. They pushed the price up to almost UK levels but then stopped before pushing any of the weaker firms out. The government received 98 per cent of the UK revenues per capita and also secured an unconcentrated industry, gaining in both directions. Klemperer (2000) likens Deutsche Telekom's behaviour to that of someone who queues for something but then quits in frustration just as they reach the head of the line. The assumption of rationality is not always adhered to even when billions of dollars are at stake.

Auction theory represents one of the more complex applications of game theory, as this illustration has intimated. Nevertheless, the vast amounts of money involved justify an extensive modelling effort because, as Klemperer (2000, p. 22) puts it: 'in auction design, the devil is in the details.'

References and further reading

J. Bertrand, 'Reviews of *Théories Mathématique de la Richesse Sociale* by Leon Walras; and of *Recherches sur les Principes Mathématiques de la Théorie des Richesses* by Augustin Cournot', *Journal des Savants*, vol. 67, 1883, pp. 499–508.

A. Cournot, *Researches into the Mathematical Principles of the Theory of Wealth*, trans. Nathaniel Bacon, New York, Macmillan, [1838] 1929.

P. Crampton and J. Schwartz, 'Collusive Bidding: Lessons from the FCC Spectrum Auctions', *Journal of Regulatory Economics*, vol. 17, no. 3, May 2000, pp. 229–52.

A. Dixit, 'The Role of Investment in Entry Deterrence', *Economic Journal*, vol. 90, 1980, pp. 95–106.

A. Dixit and S. Nalebuff, *Thinking Strategically*, New York, W.W. Norton, 1991.

A. Dixit and S. Skeath, *Games of Strategy*, New York, W.W. Norton, 1999.

D. Fudenberg and J. Tirole, *Game Theory*, Cambridge, MA, MIT Press, 1991.

P. Ghemawat, *Games Businesses Play: Cases and Models*, Cambridge, MA, MIT Press, 1997.

P. Klemperer, 'What Really Matters in Auction Design', Working Paper, Nuffield College Oxford, September 2000.

D. Kreps, *A Course in Micro-economic Theory*, Princeton, Princeton University Press, 1990a.

D. Kreps, *Game Theory and Economic Modelling*, Oxford, Clarendon Press, 1990b.

P. Krugman, *Strategic Trade Policy and the New International Economics*, Cambridge, MA, MIT Press, 1986.

J. McGuigan, R. Moyer and F. Harris, *Managerial Economics: Applications, Strategy and Tactics*, Cincinnati, OH, South-Western College Publishing, 1999.

J. McMillan, 'Selling Spectrum Rights', *Journal of Economic Perspectives*, vol. 8, 1994, pp. 145–62.

M. Porter, *Competitive Strategy: Techniques for Analysing Industries and Competitors*, New York, Free Press, 1980.

A. Roy, D. Hanssens and J. Raju, 'Competitive Pricing by a Price Leader', *Management Science*, vol. 40, no. 7, July 1994, pp. 809–23.

G. Saloner, 'Modeling, Game Theory and Strategic Management', *Strategic Management Journal*, vol. 12, 1991, pp. 119–36.

O. Shy, *Industrial Organisation: Theory and Applications*, Cambridge, MA, MIT Press, 1995.

M. Spence, 'Entry, Capacity, Investment and Oligopolistic Pricing', *Bell Journal of Economics*, vol. 8, 1977, pp. 534–44.

R. Thaler, 'Anomalies: The Winner's Curse', *Journal of Economic Perspectives*, vol. 2, no. 1, Winter 1988, pp. 191–201.

H. Varian, *Intermediate Microeconomics: A Modern Approach*, New York, W.W. Norton, 1993.

H. von Stackelberg, *Marktform und Gleichgewicht* (Market Structure and Equilibrium), Vienna, Springer-Verlag, 1934.

R. Wilson, 'Strategic Models of Entry Deterrence', in R. Aumann and S. Hart (eds) *Handbook of Game Theory*, Amsterdam, North-Holland, 1992.

Self-test questions

1. Explain the following terms:

    (a) zero-sum game
    (b) simultaneous game
    (c) prisoner's dilemma
    (d) Nash equilibrium
    (e) dominated strategy
    (f) pure strategy

2. Re-write the Airbus/Boeing game described in Table 13.5 as a sequential game and comment on its outcome.

3. Give a non-mathematical explanation of the difference between Bertrand, Cournot and von Stackelberg solutions to the duopoly problem.

4. In isolated rural communities the sale of land is often carried out on the basis of a handshake, without benefit of lawyers or written contracts. How does game theory help to explain that phenomenon?

5. Why is the grim strategy too grim?

Essay question

Identify the key features of game theory and evaluate its contribution to our understanding of business decisions.

14 Pricing in theory

This chapter examines theoretical aspects of the pricing decision, including the predictions derived from the simple economic model of the firm, the links between pricing and market structure and the problem of pricing to deter entry. Attention is also paid to the practice of price discrimination and the relationship between pricing and the concept of the product life cycle.

Price in the simple economic model of the firm

The basic rules for optimal pricing

The simple model of the profit-maximising firm, developed in Chapter 2 and extended in Chapter 10, is one in which price and quantity are the only decision variables. The nature of the product is given, there is assumed to be no spending on promotion or advertising, and no attention is given to the question of distribution channels. In terms of the 'marketing mix', popularised by McCarthy (1960) as the 'four Ps – Product, Price, Place and Promotion', only one of the Ps is taken into account.

In this model of the firm, the rule for profit maximisation is simple. The firm should produce the level of output such that marginal cost = marginal revenue (the first-order condition) and the slope of the marginal cost curve is greater than the slope of the marginal revenue curve (the second-order condition). The price that should be charged is then derived from the profit-maximising quantity, being the price at which that quantity can be sold.

Price can be made to feature more explicitly in the model by re-writing the first-order condition (MC = MR), to give:

$$\frac{P - MC}{P} = \frac{1}{-E_d} \quad \text{where:}$$

$$P = \text{price}$$
$$MC = \text{marginal cost}$$
$$E_d = \text{elasticity of demand}$$

See p. 312 for the working

As this condition makes clear, the margin between price and marginal cost is essentially a function of *elasticity of demand*. If demand is infinitely elastic, being equal to infinity, the profit-maximising price will be equal to marginal cost. As demand is less and less elastic, so the margin between price and marginal cost will be larger.

While the equation given shows the links between price, cost and elasticity, it only provides a practical prescription for setting price if both marginal cost and elasticity are constant over a wide range of output. In that case, their values may be simply inserted into the equation to give the profit-maximising price. If they are not, which the analysis of preceding chapters has suggested is almost certainly the case, the equation can only be applied by identifying the profit-maximising level of output first, then identifying marginal cost and elasticity at that level of output, and then solving for price. A number of commentators, including Gabor (1977), have suggested that this renders the model useless for any practical purposes.

Another specification of the basic model which can be used to shed light on the profit-maximising price involves restating the cost conditions in terms of an average cost function, giving:

$$\text{Total cost} = AC(q)q \qquad \text{where:}$$

$$AC = \text{average cost}$$
$$q = \text{output}$$

In that case, the basic profit-maximising equation is as follows:

$$\text{Profit} = \text{Total revenue} - \text{Total cost}$$
$$= P(q) \cdot q - AC(q) \cdot q$$

The first-order condition for profit-maximisation can then be written:

$$\text{Price} = AC + \frac{q \cdot dAC}{dq} - \frac{dP}{dq}$$

This approach has the advantage of expressing the optimal price in terms of average cost plus a margin, which corresponds with much of the evidence on business practice (see Chapter 15). On the other hand, if it is viewed as a decision rule for managers, or as a prescription, it suffers from the same disadvantages as the previous formulation. It cannot be applied until the profit-maximising level of output is known, along with the values of dAC/dq and dp/dq at that level of output.

It should be clear, then, that the basic model of the firm does not produce a set of simple formulae that allow a manager to set a profit-maximising price. Dorward (1987) quoted Nagle (1984), to the effect that: '[marketers] are soon disillusioned if they turn to economics for practical solutions to pricing problems . . . the role of economics is not to price products, but to explain the economic principles to which successful pricing strategies will conform'.

Before turning to examine some of the more complex issues raised by the problem of pricing, it is useful to consider the links between the determination of price and the type of market structure in which firms find themselves. As these market structures have been considered in Chapter 10, the coverage in this chapter is brief, being focused entirely on pricing.

Pricing and market structures

Pricing under perfect competition

In a perfectly competitive industry, as outlined in Chapter 10, the firm does not take a pricing decision. Price is set by the interaction of supply and demand, the individual firm is too small to have any impact on the market price, and firms are known as *price-takers*. Each firm simply accepts the price set by the market and takes a decision on the level of output that maximises profit, given the market price. As each individual firm faces a demand curve that is infinitely elastic, profit-maximising behaviour on the part of each firm requires that price (which equals marginal revenue in this case) will be equal to marginal cost, at the profit-maximising level of output. If firms are able to make supernormal profits at the prevailing price then in the long run entry will take place and the price will be forced down by market pressures until the supernormal profits are eliminated.

Pricing under monopoly

A monopolist is not a price-taker, but a *price-maker*, in the sense that the price it sets is not predetermined by external market forces. That is not to say that a monopolist has complete freedom with respect to price. In order to achieve maximum profit the optimal combination of price and quantity has to be chosen by selecting the level of output at which marginal cost equals marginal revenue and then adopting the market-clearing price for that level of output. This is illustrated in Figure 14.1, which is simply a reproduction of Figure 10.6.

As the figure shows, the profit-maximising level of output is Q and the profit-maximising price is P. A limit is set to the level of price by the buyers' ability to go without the industry's product, which in turn decides the elasticity of demand and the optimal price.

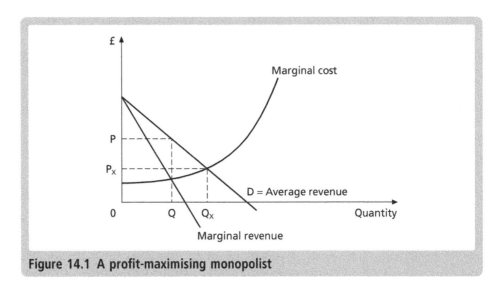

Figure 14.1 A profit-maximising monopolist

The textbook model of monopoly focuses attention on the short term, and by assumption the firm faces no threat of entry in the long term. As a result there are no long-term forces tending to eliminate any supernormal profits by forcing the price downwards. The only difference between the short run and the long run is that in the long run the firm can consider whether it has the most profitable set of plant and equipment, given the available technology and the demand curve facing it. If it does, then in the long run it will simply keep on replacing that set of plant and equipment. Cost and demand conditions will remain as shown in Figure 14.1, as will the profit-maximising price and output. If there is an alternative set of plant and equipment that would allow greater profits, that set will be built in the long run and there will be a new profit-maximising level of output and price corresponding to the cost conditions associated with the new plant.

As the textbook model of monopoly involves a firm that is protected from entry by assumption, there is no possibility that the threat of entry may be affected by the price set and the profits made. In that case simple profit maximisation will take place and, no matter how large the resulting profits, new firms cannot establish a foothold in the industry. Such a situation may arise if entry to the industry is absolutely blockaded by legal restrictions or some other absolute barrier. However, in many other situations the barriers to entry are not absolute and a monopoly firm may have to pay attention to the impact of its price and profits upon the behaviour of potential entrants. Earning maximum profit in the short run might encourage entry to take place in the long run and thereby erode the firm's monopoly position. The relationship between pricing and entry is considered further in the section on pricing and rivalry in oligopoly below.

Pricing in monopolistic competition

As shown in Chapter 10, monopolistic competition contains elements of both perfect competition and monopoly. Each firm has a downward-sloping demand curve, arising from the production of differentiated products, so that in the short run the position of an individual firm is very much like that of a monopolist. Each business is a 'price-maker' for its own variant of the product, rather than a 'price-taker', setting a price that corresponds to the profit-maximising level of output. In the long run, the existence of supernormal profits will attract new entry into the industry. That will reduce the demand for each firm's product and eliminate superprofits by forcing each firm to set a price that is equal to average cost of production at a point of tangency between the firm's demand curve and its long-run average cost curve (as shown above in Figure 10.7).

Pricing and rivalry in oligopoly

The most complex form of market structure considered in Chapter 10 was oligopoly, a generic term used for many different types of industrial structure having the common feature of consisting of just a few firms, each of which is interdependent upon the others.

The analysis of pricing under oligopoly may be approached in a number of different ways. Chapter 10 outlined a number of broadly defined possible outcomes for the oligopoly situation, including cartelisation, price war and the 'kinky demand curve' solution. Chapter 13 introduced the game-theoretic approach, including Cournot, Bertrand and von Stackelberg competition. In the last two decades, the latter approach has come to dominate oligopoly theory. Nevertheless there is still value in an integrated non-game-theoretic approach provided by Dorward (1987), using a simple mathematical framework.

The starting point is with the case where all firms produce identical products. In that case, the demand curve can be written:

$p = p(Q)$ where:

p = price
Q = total output of all firms = $\sum q_i$
q_i = output of the i'th firm

The profit function for an individual firm is then given by:

$\$_i = p(Q) \cdot q_i - C_i(q_i)$ where:

$C_i(q_i)$ = total cost of q_i

and the condition for profit maximisation is:

$$\frac{d\$_i}{dq_i} = p + q_i \cdot \frac{dp}{dQ} \cdot \frac{dQ}{dq_i} - \frac{dC_i}{dq_i} = 0$$

The most important term in this last equation is dQ/dq_i which illustrates the importance of the links between changes in the i'th firm's output and changes in the outputs of the other firms and the industry as a whole. If the i'th firm increases its output by one unit, and the other firms do not respond to that change, then clearly:

$$\frac{dQ}{dq_i} = 1$$

On the other hand, if the other firms respond to the unit increase in output by raising their own outputs by 'a' units, then:

$$\frac{dQ}{dq_i} = 1 + a$$

The term 'a' is a measure of rivals' reactions. As the individual firm can only conjecture about the reactions of its rivals, 'a' may also be described as a measure of *conjectural variation*, as perceived by that firm.

Just as the simple profit-maximising condition (MC = MR) can be rewritten to give:

$$\frac{P - MC}{P} = \frac{1}{-E_d}$$

the more complex oligopoly version can be rewritten to give:

$$\frac{P - MC_i}{P} = (-)\frac{s_i(1 + a)}{E_d}$$ where:

s_i = market share, firm i
a = conjectural variation
E_d = market elasticity

Examination of this model shows that it encompasses both perfect competition (s_i and 'a' both equal to zero) and monopoly (s_i equal to 1 and 'a' equal to zero) as special cases. In the oligopoly case, where 'a' is non-zero, the firm's pricing behaviour depends upon the sign and size of the conjectural variation. If 'a' is positive and large, indicating that other firms increase their output substantially when the firm under examination attempts to increase its own output (which implies lowering its price), then clearly demand for the individual firm's product will be very inelastic and the corresponding margin between marginal cost and the optimal price will be large. In the opposite case, if rival firms were to respond to an increase in output by reducing their own output, demand for the firm in question would be highly elastic (a reduction in price would lead to a large increase in demand as other firms reduce their output) and the optimal price/marginal cost margin would be lower.

The model set out above illustrates the importance of rivals' reactions for the optimal price in conditions of oligopoly. It can also be linked back to the more qualitative discussion of oligopoly in Chapter 10. In the case of collusion, for instance, if each firm conjectures that its partners in the joint monopoly will act in such a way as to maintain stable market shares then:

$$a = \frac{1 - s_i}{s_i}$$

This reduces the equation given above to:

$$\frac{P - MC_i}{P} = \frac{1}{-E_d}$$

which is exactly the same as in monopoly.

In the case of the kinky demand curve model, 'a' takes different values for price rises (output reductions) and price falls (output increases.) If the individual firm attempts to increase its output by lowering the price, the assumption is that its rivals will also lower price and increase output so that 'a' is positive. If the firm raises its price, thereby lowering its output, the assumption is that rivals leave their price at the initial level and increase their output, so that 'a' is negative. As 'a' takes multiple values around the existing price level, this makes the solution indeterminate, which brings the analysis back to the basic objection to the kinky demand curve theory, which is that it does not provide a prediction for the price level, but rather suggests that in oligopoly prices will tend to be stable.

This approach has been largely superseded in the literature by the game theory approach but it has also been extended in a number of directions to cover the case of differentiated products (Cubbin 1983) and price leadership (Waterson 1984).

Entry conditions and pricing

The analysis set out above has been placed in a short-run framework where firms pay no attention to the impact of their price-setting upon the entry of other firms into the industry or market segment in which they are operating.

Nevertheless, the models of perfect competition and monopolistic competition make it clear that the threat of entry is a major determinant of price in the longer run and some attention needs to be given to the links between barriers to entry and pricing. Again, the advent of game theory has changed the way in which theoreticians have addressed the issue (see Chapter 13), but again, there is still value in examining the earlier approaches and some of their limitations.

The condition of entry

Entry barriers may be defined as advantages held by incumbent firms over potential entrants. In some situations these barriers may be absolute, so that new firms cannot enter the industry, no matter how high a price is being charged by the incumbents. In that case, following the seminal work of Bain (1956) the condition of entry is said to be *blockaded*. This is the condition of entry that is assumed in the pure monopoly model.

In other situations the condition of entry may be defined as *easy* if new firms are able to enter profitably when prices are set only slightly above costs by incumbents. Entry is *ineffectively impeded* when pricing low enough to prevent entry is less profitable than maximising profit and allowing entry. *Effectively impeded* is where it is more profitable in the long run to price at a level where no entry will occur.

If the basic links between barriers to entry and pricing are to be understood, three issues need to be addressed. The first concerns the sources of entry barriers, the second concerns the determination of the entry-deterring price and the third concerns the factors that determine whether profit-maximising firms will choose to charge such a price.

The sources of entry barriers

In addition to legal barriers to entry, which may be erected by governments, Bain (1956) identified three major sources of entry barriers, each of which has been referred to above in Porter's 'five forces' analysis of competition. These are:

1. Absolute cost advantages.
2. Economies of scale.
3. Product differentiation.

Absolute cost advantages may arise when incumbent firms have exclusive or low-cost access to resources needed in the industry, a proprietary technology not available to entrants, a favourable location or access to learning effects as a result of their longer experience in the industry. If incumbent firms do have such advantages they will be able to make profits at prices that are lower than potential entrants' costs, in which case entry can be deterred by setting prices appropriately. *Economies of scale* have been discussed in some detail in Chapter 9. They arise mainly from the existence of indivisibilities and the advantages of specialisation in both production and management. If there are substantial scale economies then potential entrants will face a difficult dilemma. In order to enter the industry they must either produce at a lower volume than the incumbent firms, in which case they will suffer an important cost penalty, or they must establish a plant having very large scale, in which case they will have to secure a very large market share very quickly in order to avoid heavy losses.

Product differentiation will provide a barrier to entry if buyers have well-established preferences for the products of the incumbent firms. However, it seems reasonable to assume that new entrants can overcome these preferences through their own promotional spending. In that case entry barriers attributed to product differentiation will only arise if new entrants have to spend more on promotion and advertising for the same volume of sales than the incumbent firms. Given the inertia of buyers and the time lags involved in building an effective brand image this is probably a reasonable assumption to make. However, it does suggest that entry barriers attributable to product differentiation are simply a special case of absolute cost advantages. Sutton's recent work on endogenous sunk costs has shed further light on this issue, showing that in some industries an escalation of spending on R&D or advertising leads to greater concentration (Sutton 1996, 1999).

Identifying the limit price

The *limit price* or *entry-deterring price* may be defined as the highest price that can be charged by incumbent firms without inducing new entry into the industry. As a potential entrant will choose to enter the industry if it is able to earn at least normal profits, then entry will take place in any situation where a potential entrant's demand curve lies above its cost curve, for some level of output. The determination of the limit price therefore depends heavily upon the location of the entrant's expected demand curve. This in turn depends upon the entrant's expectations about the response of the incumbent firms to its arrival in the industry.

The traditional (pre-game theory) analysis of entry prevention strategy (Moschandreas 1994, pp. 252–6) is based around a model known as the Bain–Sylos-Labini–Modigliani model. That centres on an assumption known as the 'Sylos postulate' after Paulo Sylos-Labini (1962). That is the assumption that potential entrants assume that existing firms will maintain their output constant when entry takes place, and the incumbent firms know this to be the case.

If the Sylos postulate holds true, a potential entrant to an industry producing an undifferentiated product will be faced with a demand curve that is the segment of the industry demand curve lying to the right of the post-entry level of output produced by the incumbent firms. This is shown in Figure 14.2.

The curve D_{Ind} shows the market demand curve for the product. If existing firms produce a pre-entry quantity Q_1 then at price P_1 they satisfy the entire market demand, so that the demand for the additional output supplied by an entrant is equal to zero at price P_1. If the entrant (and the incumbents) lowered the price to P_2 total demand would rise to Q_2. If the incumbent firms are expected to behave according to the Sylos postulate and maintain their output at Q_1 this would leave $(Q_2 - Q_1)$ units of output as the demand for the output of the new entrant, and the post-entry demand curve for the entrant is given

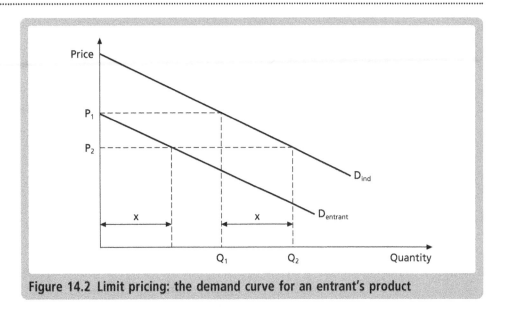

Figure 14.2 Limit pricing: the demand curve for an entrant's product

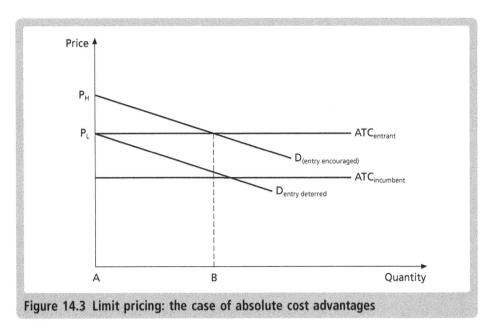

Figure 14.3 Limit pricing: the case of absolute cost advantages

by the line $D_{entrant}$. The position of the entrant's demand curve is determined by the pre-entry price and output of the incumbent firms.

This analysis allows the limit price to be determined for the two different types of entry barrier – absolute cost advantages and scale economies. Figure 14.3 illustrates the position in the case of absolute cost advantages.

If incumbent firms have average cost curves given by the line $ATC_{incumbent}$ and the potential entrant has a cost curve given by $ATC_{entrant}$ then the entrant will expect to be able to make a profit if the incumbent firms set a price higher than

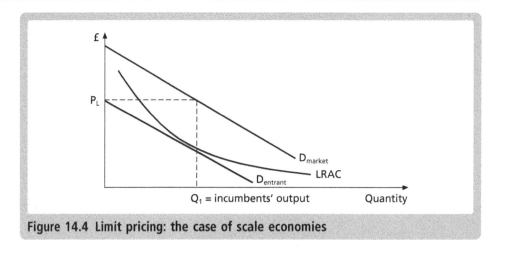

Figure 14.4 Limit pricing: the case of scale economies

P_L. If they set a price of P_H, for instance, the entrant's demand curve will be given by $D_{(entry\ encouraged)}$ which lies above its cost curve at levels of output between A and B and entry will take place. However, if incumbent firms set a price just equal to P_L, the entrant's demand curve will be as given by $D_{(entry\ deterred)}$ and there is no level of output at which the entrant can make a profit.

The case of scale economies can be examined in a similar fashion, shown in Figure 14.4. The line LRAC indicates the long-run average cost curve facing both entrants and incumbent firms, which embodies substantial economies of scale.

In this case, it is clear that the maximum price that can be charged without inducing entry is again indicated by P_L. At that price, the demand curve for the entrant, $D_{entrant}$, which is parallel to the demand curve for the market as a whole, D_{market}, is just below the cost curve LRAC, leaving no level of output at which price exceeds cost per unit for the entrant.

If the Sylos postulate is accepted as an appropriate starting point it is relatively easy to identify the limit price. That is because in that case the pre-entry level of output produced by the incumbent firms provides a direct measure of the post-entry level of output, the two being equal by assumption. However, the suggestion that incumbent firms leave their output constant in the face of entry and let potential entrants know that they will do so seems very restrictive. As Pashigian (1968) and Wenders (1971) made clear, it would be more profitable in an oligopolistic situation for the incumbents to set a joint monopoly price, which will be higher than the limit prices indicated above, but threaten to increase their output and cut that price if other firms should try to enter. Provided that the threat of increased output and price-cutting is a credible one (see the discussion in Chapter 13) it will be sufficient to deter entry without the incumbent firms having to set a price at the entry-deterring level.

It would appear then that the Sylos assumption, whereby incumbent firms will not increase their output in the face of entry, and entrants know that to be the case, is only tenable under oligopoly if the incumbent firms lack the capacity to increase output or if they face higher costs and the loss of their advantage if they attempt to increase output. The assumption will be more tenable in atomistic conditions of either perfect or monopolistic competition where there are too many firms for individual incumbents to react directly to entry.

The other major weakness of the Sylos postulate is the implicit presumption that entrants and incumbents produce identical products, so that buyers can have no preference for an entrant's product over an incumbent's. If that presumption is relaxed then an entrant who offers a product variant that is particularly attractive to buyers may be able to draw customers away from the incumbent firms. If they attempt to maintain their output at pre-entry levels they will simply be unable to sell all of that output, and the entrant may be able to make profits even if the incumbent firms charge very low prices. However, as soon as product differentiation is introduced into the model it is no longer possible to identify a market demand curve or the demand curve for an entrant, given the incumbent's output. Hence the whole analytical approach must be abandoned.

Limit pricing versus short-run profits

Even if the limit price can be identified, which is difficult unless products are identical and the Sylos postulate holds, there is no guarantee that firms will choose to set such a price. They may prefer to charge a higher profit-maximising price and make larger profits in the short run, accepting that this will induce entry and reduce profits in the longer run. Figure 14.5 compares the time-profile of profits for the two different strategies.

As the figure shows, short-run profit maximisation leads to a higher level of profit in the short run, but this is eroded over time as entry takes place. Limit pricing leads to a lower level of profit in the short term, but profits are not eroded over time to such an extent. If firms are attempting to maximise the present value of future profits the choice between the two strategies will depend upon which yields the higher discounted cash flow, which in turn depends upon three

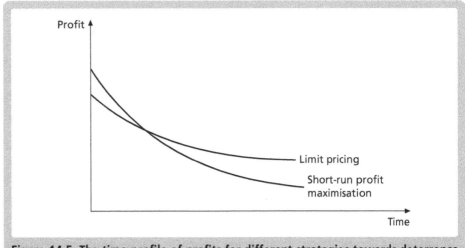

Figure 14.5 The time-profile of profits for different strategies towards deterrence of entry

factors. First, there is the difference between the profits that can be made in the short run by not setting the limit price and the profits that would be earned at that price. Clearly, as this is larger, so is the incentive to opt for short-run profit maximisation. The second factor is the speed with which entry can take place. If this is very rapid the extra profits made from short-run profit maximisation will be short lived and limit pricing will be favoured. Finally, the decision will depend upon the discount rate applied. As this is larger, the more will firms value present as opposed to future profits, and the more likely they are to choose the option of short-run profit maximisation.

In practice, incumbent firms considering their strategy with respect to potential entrants do not have a simple choice between limit pricing and short-run profit maximisation. They are also able to choose a range of intermediate prices, which may affect the rate at which entry and the erosion of profits takes place. Gaskins (1971), for instance, explored a model in which entry and the erosion of profit takes place more quickly if the incumbent firms choose a price that is substantially above the limit price and more slowly as it is closer to the limit price. Such complex dynamic models lie beyond the scope of this text but they do offer some explanatory value.

Price discrimination

Definition and necessary conditions

The analysis set out above has considered various characteristics of the price that will be set for a product, on the implicit assumption that every unit of output is sold at the same price. However, in the monopoly case, firms may find it both feasible and profitable to sell the same product at different prices in different markets, thereby practising price discrimination.

As a matter of definition it is important to note that the sale of the same product at different prices is not in itself enough to demonstrate that price discrimination is taking place. The differences in price may be attributable to differences in the costs involved in servicing the different markets. If buyers in a distant market are charged a higher price for a product, this may indicate that transport costs are higher, not that price discrimination is taking place. True price discrimination involves charging different net prices in different markets, the net price being the actual price corrected for cost differences.

For price discrimination to take place two conditions must be met. First, the total market for the product must be divisible into sub-markets that have different price elasticities of demand. Second, those sub-markets must be separated, so that a purchaser in one market cannot resell to a buyer in another. If these conditions do not hold then price differences would either be unprofitable (if elasticities were the same in all markets) or impossible (if arbitrage between one market and another meant that no buyer need pay the higher price because arbitrageurs buy in the low price market and then offer the product for resale in the high price market).

Third-degree price discrimination

Three forms of price discrimination are possible. The first is where the total market is divided up into a number of sub-markets, each containing a number of buyers, who will all be charged the same price set for that sub-market. This is known as *third-degree price discrimination*.

Sub-markets may be separated in a number of ways. Most obviously, there may be different geographical markets in which separate prices can be charged. However, it may also be possible to segment the market by age, by social status or by a wide range of other variables. In the case of rail travel in Britain, for instance, several different types of market segmentation are employed. The use of Student Railcards and Old Persons Railcards allows segmentation by age. Family Railcards (giving discounts only when a party of travellers includes children) allow segmentation by social position (and also by the purpose of the journeys being made). The distinction between First and Second Class travel also allows segmentation by income (or by the purpose of the journey).

For goods that cannot be stored at reasonable cost, segmentation through timing may be possible. In the case of telephone calls or electricity or journeys, for instance, it is not possible to purchase the good for one time-period and then use it at another. As a result, suppliers will be able to charge different prices at different times without arbitrage taking place. If elasticities of demand differ at different times it will be profitable as well as feasible to introduce price discrimination in the form of peak and off-peak pricing.

Figure 14.6 provides a formal graphical analysis of third-degree discrimination for the case where the firm is selling in two sub-markets, within each of which a common price must be charged.

In Figure 14.6(a) the demand curve D_1 indicates demand in the first sub-market and D_2 indicates demand in the second sub-market. Each has its own marginal revenue curve as indicated by MR_1 and MR_2. If the two markets are aggregated to give the firm's overall demand and marginal revenue curves the result is given by the lines $D = D_1 + D_2$ and $MR = MR_1 + MR_2$. In Figure 14.6(b) the firm's marginal cost curve is added to the diagram, showing that the profit-maximising level of total output is Q. The distribution of this total output across the two sub-markets can be seen by recognising that in each sub-market profit is maximised when marginal revenue in that market equals the marginal cost of supplying that market. As it is assumed in this simple case that the marginal cost of supplying the same unit to either market is the same, this implies that for profit-maximisation in each market:

$$MR_1 = MR_2 = MC$$

As marginal cost at the profit-maximising total output is equal to 25 it can readily be seen from the diagram that this equates to MR_1 at level of output 30 and MR_2 at level of output 50, which are the levels of output to be sold in each sub-market. The prices to be charged in each sub-market can then be read off from their respective demand curves, showing that a price of P_1 will be charged in the first market and P_2 in the second.

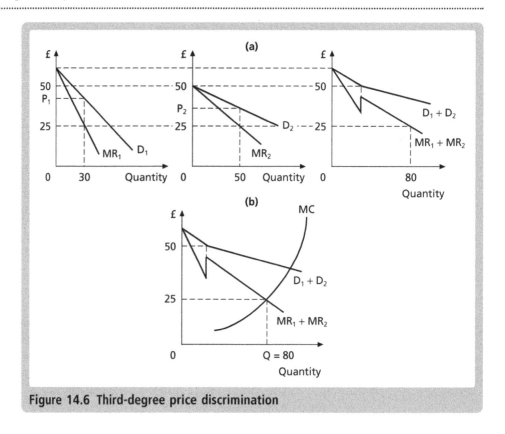

Figure 14.6 Third-degree price discrimination

First-degree price discrimination

The second form of price discrimination is known as first-degree price discrimination which is where every buyer of the firm's product can be charged a different price. In this case there is a separate market for each unit of output sold so that the supplier can extract the maximum amount that each buyer is willing to pay for each unit sold. This form of discrimination is feasible in situations where the product sold can only be used by the individual buyer, a situation that most obviously presents itself in the service industries. In the case of legal, medical, personal or financial services the product is 'customised' to the circumstances of the individual purchaser. It cannot be sold to another purchaser and first-degree price discrimination is therefore possible. Figure 14.7 provides a graphical analysis for the case of first-degree discrimination, which is considerably simpler than that for third-degree discrimination.

The curve MC indicates the firm's marginal cost curve. The curve DD shows the firm's demand curve. If first-degree price discrimination is possible then the buyer of each unit will be forced to pay the maximum price that they are willing to pay for that unit, so that the demand curve will also indicate the firm's marginal revenue. A profit-maximising firm will produce the level of output indicated by Q, and will charge a different price for each unit of output.

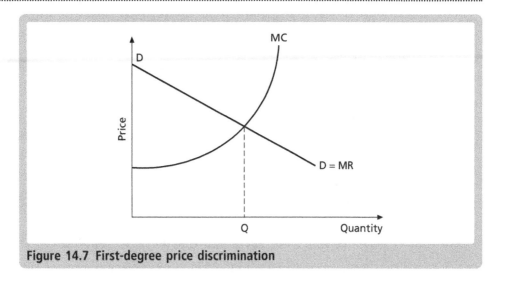

Figure 14.7 First-degree price discrimination

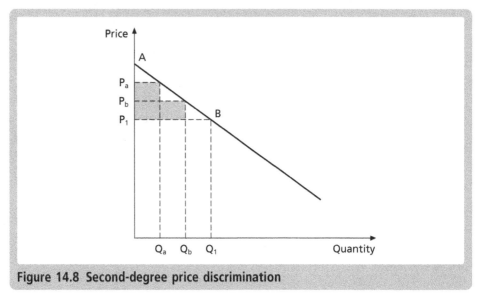

Figure 14.8 Second-degree price discrimination

Second-degree price discrimination

While third- and first-degree price discrimination receive most attention in the textbooks, second-degree discrimination also merits attention. This is where customers are charged one price for the first block of units they consume, then a lower price for the next block and so on. For that reason second-degree price discrimination is also referred to as the 'block tariff' approach. Figure 14.8 explains the situation.

Figure 14.8 shows the overall demand curve for the product. If a uniform price P_1 is charged, quantity Q_1 will be consumed. Revenue to the firm will be P_1Q_1 and consumer surplus will be the area AP_1B. However, if the first Q_a units can be sold at price P_a, the next block of $(Q_b - Q_a)$ units at P_b, and the next block of $(Q_l - Q_b)$ at price P_1, the total revenue to the firm will be increased by the shaded area shown in the diagram. Some, though not all, of the consumer surplus is transferred to the firm.

Block tariff pricing raises a number of further issues (Hay and Morris 1991; Moschandreas 1994, p. 227). One of these is common to all aspects of pricing in that it can be difficult to achieve revenue-maximising block pricing because of limited information about consumer demand. The other concerns the equity of a pricing method that may extract nearly all of the consumer surplus from poor consumers, while leaving rich consumers with large proportions of theirs.

Pricing and the product life cycle

The product life cycle and elasticity of demand

The standard analysis of pricing embodies a static view of the demand for a product. The volume that can be sold is determined by the factors discussed in Chapter 7. Unless any of these factors change, demand is assumed to remain constant, so that time itself has no influence upon the level of demand for a product. However, marketing analysts frequently find it useful to introduce the concept of the product life cycle into the discussion of pricing and marketing strategies.

The product life cycle hypothesis is the assertion that products have limited lives and that in the course of those lives they pass through a series of distinct stages. Figure 14.9 shows a typical product life cycle (PLC).

As Figure 14.9 shows, the first stage in the PLC is the *introductory period* when potential buyers are hardly aware of the product. At this stage in the product's life, sales volume is low and demand is price inelastic. The marketing department is likely to concentrate its effort on promotion of the new product, rather than

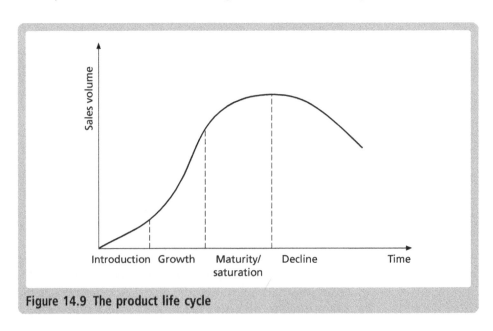

Figure 14.9 The product life cycle

on pricing it, but application of the simple pricing model suggests that a sub-stantial margin should be charged over marginal cost, if the aim is to make maximum profit.

The second stage of the PLC is the *growth phase*, when buyers become more aware of the product and sales grow rapidly. As competitors will also have had sufficient time to enter the market, demand will have become more price elastic, implying that the optimal price involves a smaller margin over costs.

The third stage is that of *maturity* or *saturation* when the growth of sales slows down, eventually to zero. Customers are well informed about the product and experienced in its use and competitors are well versed in the production of sub-stitutes, leading to an increase in the elasticity of demand, and a further reduc-tion in the optimal margin between price and marginal cost.

The fourth and final stage is that of *decline*, arising from changes in buyers' tastes or requirements, increasing competition, or technological progress. In this phase, sales volume declines, competition among incumbent firms is fierce and demand is highly price elastic, leading to very narrow margins between cost and price.

It is possible to identify a relatively simple relationship between the different stages of the PLC and the optimal level of price, the two being linked by the gradually increasing elasticity of demand over time. However, both the theoretical rationale and the practical usefulness of the PLC concept are open to debate.

At the theoretical level it is possible to provide a justification of the S-shaped PLC as a logical consequence of the way in which innovations are diffused through a population of potential users and some empirical studies have found evidence to support the hypothesis for some product categories. On the other hand, other observers (Swan and Rink 1982) have identified PLCs that have very different shapes, robbing the concept of the generality that is supposed to be its great strength.

While the development of a product through the various stages of the cycle is usually presented as an inevitable result of forces beyond the control of the firm, it is clear that some factors, like the extent of buyer awareness or the entry of competing firms into the market, are *endogenous*. That is to say that they are at least partly dependent upon the firm's own actions, such as its spending on promotion and its decision on whether to set entry-forestalling prices. It may be possible, therefore, for a firm to alter the development of the product cycle through its own actions, thereby rendering valueless any prescriptions based upon the inevitability of the transition from one phase to another.

At the practical level, there are a range of problems. The form and timing of the PLC may vary widely with the level of aggregation at which it is applied, so that the life cycle of a broad product category will generally be much longer than that of a product form or an individual brand. There is a real danger that if managers have been persuaded of the existence of the product cycle they may act on that belief in ways that reduce the firm's profits and simultaneously confirm the managers' mistaken confidence in the usefulness of the PLC as a forecasting tool. For instance, if sales of a product have been growing for some time, believers in the PLC will be expecting a slowdown in sales as maturity is reached. When that point is reached they will reduce the level of promotion and advertising for the product, and reduce its price, on the grounds that these are the appropriate actions for a product that is in maturity and is about to decline. However, those actions in themselves may lead to the fulfilment of the prediction. Price-cutting may stimulate retaliation from competitors and the reduction in promotion will erode buyer loyalty and alter buyers' perceptions of the product. As a result, a product that might have yielded healthy profits for a number of years goes into decline, not as a consequence of real changes in the environment but because the decision-makers had an inappropriate faith in the PLC hypothesis.

Pricing new products

Another issue in the analysis of price, which brings together aspects of the basic pricing model, the PLC and price discrimination, is the question of pricing new products. The best-known contribution to this topic, frequently quoted in both the economic and marketing literature on pricing, is that of Dean (1969), who drew a distinction between two basic strategies for pricing new products.

The first approach is known as a *skimming strategy*. In this case the firm sets an initially high price for the product, deliberately selling it to a relatively select group of users who are prepared to pay a high price. As the product moves through its life cycle and imitation takes place, price can be gradually reduced as demand becomes more elastic until the margin between price and cost is much lower.

The alternative strategy is known as a *penetration strategy*. This involves setting a low price at the outset, in order to build a relatively large market quickly. Various commentators, including Dean (1969) and Kotler (1984), have identified the conditions that determine the choice between the alternative strategies. Skimming is recommended when there are sufficient buyers prepared to pay a high price, when demand is price inelastic, when a high price will not attract rapid entry, and when the cost penalty for operating at relatively low volume is small. Penetration is recommended when demand is price elastic, when new firms can enter quickly if attracted by high price and when there are cost advantages to be had by operating at higher volumes of output.

It might be argued that this analysis of the choice between skimming and penetration pricing is nothing more than a restatement of the basic pricing model, which predicts a high price when demand is inelastic (skimming) and a low price when demand is elastic (penetration). On the other hand, the discussion of the choice between the two approaches does allow the introduction of more sophisticated considerations. In the case of skimming it is often argued that if there is great uncertainty about the level of demand and buyers are hostile to price increases, then such a policy will have an additional advantage in that setting an initially high price is a safe way to test the market. If it should prove too high, the price can be lowered without incurring adverse reactions from buyers. To begin with a low price and attempt to raise it later would be more difficult.

It is also argued that when the market contains identifiable groups of buyers having different elasticities of demand a policy of skimming provides a means by which the firm can practise price discrimination over time (Phlips 1983). If some groups of buyers ('early adopters' in the marketing literature) are prepared to pay a higher price in order to acquire the product earlier then it will be possible to set prices over time so that the segments that are prepared to pay the highest prices are served first. Prices can then be lowered sequentially in order to bring groups of users with progressively higher elasticities into the market.

The theoretical analysis presented here appears to suggest that a policy of skimming prices has a great deal to recommend it, being consistent with the basic model of pricing, the progressive increase in the (absolute) value of elasticity of demand over the product life cycle, and the exploitation of profitable opportunities for price discrimination. Certainly there is evidence that firms in a number of industries, including pharmaceuticals (Reekie 1978), adopt this approach. However, the conditions under which penetration pricing is to be preferred do prevail in some circumstances and the evidence does not provide universal support for the conventional view with respect to the profitability of high initial prices, followed by a programme of reductions. Dorward (1987) quotes Simon's (1979) finding for some consumer goods that price elasticities were high in the early stages of the PLC, falling in maturity and then rising again in the decline stage. Such a pattern would imply a policy of low initial prices, followed by a price rise, followed by a fall in the closing stages of the product's life. Jeuland and Dolan (1982) modelled a wide variety of different circumstances and found that optimal price paths could vary widely, from conventional skimming strategies to a policy of low initial prices followed by continuous price increases. Clearly, the choice of pricing strategy becomes a very complex matter when dynamic considerations are taken into account.

Illustration · Price elasticity and the life cycle of brands

Various authors have put forward hypotheses concerning the changes that take place in the price elasticity of demand for a product over its life cycle. This text has argued that elasticity simply rises through each of the stages. Mickwitz (1959) and Kotler (1971) suggested that elasticity increases over the first three stages (introduction, growth and maturity), but falls in the fourth (decline), while Parsons (1975) seemed to argue somewhat inconsistently that elasticities decline over time, but are high in maturity.

Simon (1979) pointed out that throughout these analyses there is a degree of confusion on whether the life cycles in question refer to products, as implied by the term 'product life cycle', or brands. In order to overcome this confusion, he provided an empirical analysis of the brand life cycle. The starting point lay in data for forty-three brands, twenty-eight of which were pharmaceuticals and fifteen were detergents. A statistical model was then developed, having the general form:

$$q_{i,t} = A_{i,t} + B_{i,t} + C_{i,t} + U_{i,t} \quad \text{where:}$$

$q_{i,t}$ = no. of units sold
$A_{i,t}$ = non-price effects
$B_{i,t}$ = the impact of own price on sales
$C_{i,t}$ = sales response to price differentials between brands
$U_{i,t}$ = error term

▶

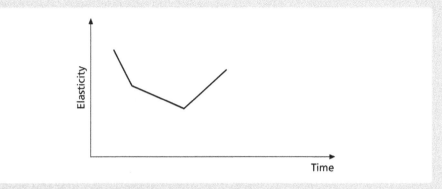

Figure 14.10 Elasticity and the brand life cycle

Various different equations were developed to represent each of the A, B and C effects, giving twenty to twenty-five different estimating equations. Each of these was fitted for each brand, giving a total of around 5,000 regressions to be computed. The equations that provided the best fits were then selected for interpretation. Examination of the best-fit equations revealed that the own-price term $B_{i,t}$ was not significant for any products, but the $A_{i,t}$ terms, which represented the carryover and obsolescence effects, and the $C_{i,t}$ terms, representing competitive price effects, were well represented. Having estimated the regression equations, the actual values for prices and quantities were inserted, in order to calculate the value of elasticity and its growth rate, for each brand. This produced a number of findings.

With respect to the values of elasticity there were two major conclusions. First, as might be expected, the pharmaceutical brands exhibited much more inelastic demand than the detergents. Second, there was a clear pattern in the values of elasticity over the different stages of the life cycle, as shown in Figure 14.10.

As Figure 14.10 shows, elasticity fell successively from introduction to growth and to maturity, but then rose again in decline.

The results with respect to the pattern of elasticity growth across the different life cycle stages was also highly uniform for all of the brands. During the growth stage of the life cycle elasticity decreased, while during the decline stage elasticity increased. For the maturity stage, the results were less clear, with elasticity for some brands rising and for others falling. However, although the sign of the elasticity growth rate varied from brand to brand in the maturity stage its size was uniformly smaller than in either growth or decline.

Simon's results clearly have implications for the optimal pricing strategy to be practised over the brand life cycle. If elasticity is relatively high during introduction and growth, then the optimal price mark-up in those stages is low, indicating a 'penetration' strategy for the pricing of new brands. As elasticity falls in maturity, so the mark-up should rise in that stage, falling again in decline, as elasticity rises again.

References and further reading

J.S. Bain, *Barriers to New Competition*, Cambridge, Harvard University Press, 1956.

J. Cubbin, 'Apparent Collusion and Conjectural Variations in Differentiated Oligopoly', *International Journal of Industrial Organisation*, 1983.

J. Dean, 'Pricing Pioneer Products', *Journal of Industrial Economics*, vol. XVII, no. 3, July 1969, pp. 165–79.

N. Dorward, *The Pricing Decision: Economic Theory and Business Practice*, London, Harper and Row, 1987.

A. Gabor, *Pricing: Principles and Practices*, London, Heinemann, 1977.

D.W. Gaskins, 'Dynamic Limit Pricing: Optimal Pricing Under the Threat of Entry', *Journal of Economic Theory*, vol. 3, September 1971, pp. 306–22.

D. Hay and D. Morris, *Industrial Economics and Organization: Theory and Practice*, 2nd edn, Oxford, Oxford University Press, 1991.

A.P. Jeuland and R.J. Dolan, 'An Aspect of New Product Planning: Dynamic Pricing', in A. Zoltners (ed.) *Marketing Planning Models*, TIMS, 1982.

P. Kotler, 'Competitive Marketing Strategies for New Product Marketing over the Life Cycle', *Management Science*, vol. 12, December 1971.

P. Kotler, *Marketing Management*, Englewood Cliffs, NJ, Prentice Hall, 1984.

E.J. McCarthy, *Basic Marketing: A Managerial Approach*, Homewood, IL, Richard D. Irwin, 1960.

G. Mickwitz, *Marketing and Competition*, Helsingfors, Centraltrykeriat, 1959.

M. Moschandreas, *Business Economics*, London, International Thomson Business Press, 1994.

T. Nagle, 'Economic Foundations for Pricing', *Journal of Business*, 1984.

L.J. Parsons, 'The Product Life Cycle and Time-Varying Advertising Elasticities', *Journal of Marketing Research*, vol. 12, August 1975, pp. 476–800.

P. Pashigian, 'Limit Price and the Market Share of the Leading Firm', *Journal of Industrial Economics*, vol. 16, no. 3, July 1968, pp. 165–77.

L. Phlips, *The Economics of Price Discrimination*, Cambridge, Cambridge University Press, 1983.

R. Polli and V. Cook, 'Validity of the Product Life Cycle', *Journal of Business*, 1969.

W.D. Reekie, 'Price and Quality Competition in the United States Drug Industry', *Journal of Industrial Economics*, vol. 26, March 1978, pp. 223–37.

E.M. Rogers, *Diffusion of Innovations*, New York, Free Press, 1962.

H. Simon, 'Dynamics of Price Elasticity and Brand Life Cycles: An Empirical Study', *Journal of Marketing Research*, 1979.

J.E. Swan and D.R. Rink, 'Fitting Marketing Strategy to Varying Product Life Cycles', *Business Horizons*, 1982.

J. Sutton, *Sunk Costs and Market Structure*, Cambridge, Mass., MIT Press, 1996.

J. Sutton, *Technology and Market Structure*, Cambridge, Mass., MIT Press, 1999.

P. Sylos-Labini, *Oligopoly and Technical Progress*, Cambridge, MA, Harvard University Press, 1962.

M. Waterson, *Economic Theory of the Industry*, Cambridge, Cambridge University Press, 1984.

J.T. Wenders, 'Excess Capacity as a Barrier to Entry', *Journal of Industrial Economics*, vol. 20, November 1971, pp. 14–19.

Self-test questions

1. Which of the following are required if the simple model of the firm is to be used directly to set the price of a product?
   (a) constant marginal costs
   (b) constant average costs
   (c) scale economies
   (d) constant elasticity of demand
   (e) inelastic demand

2. Set out the equation that links price to marginal cost, market share and conjectural variation.

3. List the major sources of entry barriers and define the term 'limit price'.

4. Set out the conditions required for price discrimination, and the difference between first-, second- and third-degree discrimination.

5. List three factors that will make a 'skimming' approach to pricing the most appropriate strategy.

Essay question

Consider the issues raised when setting prices for the following products:

(a) a new major dictionary
(b) a telephone call
(c) a garden spade

Appendix: Reworking the MC = MR condition

$$TR = P \cdot Q$$

$$MR = \frac{dTR}{dQ} = P \cdot \frac{dQ}{dQ} + Q \cdot \frac{dP}{dQ} = P + Q \cdot \frac{dP}{dQ}$$

$$E_d = \frac{dQ}{dP} \cdot \frac{P}{Q} \qquad \text{Therefore} \qquad \frac{dQ}{dP} = E_d \cdot \frac{Q}{P}$$

$$\frac{dP}{dQ} = \frac{P}{E_d \cdot Q}$$

$$MR = P + Q \cdot \frac{P}{E_d \cdot Q} = P + \frac{P}{E_d} = P\left(1 + \frac{1}{E_d}\right)$$

$$MR = MC = P\left(1 + \frac{1}{E_d}\right), \ P - MC = \frac{-P}{E_d}, \frac{P - MC}{P} = \frac{-1}{E_d}$$

15 Pricing in practice, transfer pricing and pricing for public enterprise

This chapter builds on the analysis in Chapter 14 to consider three further issues concerning the setting of prices. The first concerns the evidence on pricing in practice for private firms, the second concerns the establishment of prices for internal transfers and the third covers pricing in public enterprise.

Pricing in practice

Having outlined the major theoretical issues raised by the pricing of products for sale by the private sector, it is possible to consider the relationship between the theory of optimal pricing and the evidence on the ways in which firms take pricing decisions in practice. This is potentially difficult because it has been pointed out in Chapter 14 that economic analysis does not provide directly applicable practical solutions to pricing problems, but rather outlines the principles to which optimal solutions must adhere. It is not therefore to be expected that companies' pricing policies and methods correspond in any direct way to the prescriptions of the optimising models. The links between the theory and the practice have to be examined in a different way.

In order to examine pricing in practice this part of the chapter directs attention towards two major issues. The first can be described as pricing objectives and the second as pricing methods.

Pricing objectives

If the objective of the firm is to maximise profits then pricing may be regarded as one of the issues on which optimal decisions have to be taken in order to reach the objective set. In that case the objective of pricing is the maximisation of profit and there is little to be gained by considering the separate and independent objectives of the pricing process. Nevertheless, a number of classic and important pieces of business research (Lanzillotti 1958, Weston 1972) addressed the specific question of pricing objectives and they merit brief consideration. Two issues in particular are worth exploring. The first concerns companies' perceived objectives for pricing and the second concerns the extent to which these perceived objectives are consistent with profit maximisation as the fundamental objective.

The most common objective for pricing, referred to by approximately half of the American companies interviewed by Lanzillotti (1958) and two-thirds of British companies surveyed by Shipley (1981) was the achievement of *a target rate of return*. Clearly, if this target rate of return is equivalent to the maximum return achievable, then there is no conflict between the stated objective for pricing and the hypothesis of short-term profit maximisation. Alternatively, if the target rate of return is less than the maximum achievable, but is set at a level designed to deter entry into the industry, then its use could be seen as an aspect of long-term profit maximisation, taking account of the threat of entry. It could be argued, then, that there is no conflict between the establishment of a target rate of return as an objective for pricing and the assumption that the firm's basic aim is to maximise profits. However, as Dorward (1987) pointed out, if a target return is used as the basis for a pricing method, rather than as a statement of the pricing objective, the results may be in conflict with profit maximisation.

While target rates of return, or other profit-related objectives, are commonly cited as the most important objectives for pricing, research suggests three other aims towards which pricing policies are directed. The first is the achievement of a *target market share*. Webster (1981) found that many marketing managers have market share maintenance as their major objective, echoing an earlier study by Fruhan (1972). Roy *et al.* (1994) used pre-set sales targets as the starting point for modelling behaviour in the US motor industry, while Urbany and Dickson (1994) provided evidence that managers have a preference for volume-oriented pricing over a profit-oriented approach.

Whether this is consistent with profit maximisation depends upon the particular target that is set. Firms may seek larger market shares than are consistent with maximum profits, for the 'managerial' reasons that have been outlined in Chapter 4, or they may set a market share target that is consistent with maximum profit. In the latter case the target is simply a managerial tool which can assist with the achievement of the more fundamental objective.

The second alternative pricing objective is the *stabilisation of output and price*. Some firms attempt to set price with the aim of maintaining full order books, in order to avoid expensive fluctuations in output and painful changes in the size of the workforce. For instance, Harrison and Wilkes (1973) found that maintenance of production was a major objective for Jaguar when pricing the XJ12 luxury sports car. If fluctuations in output or price are expensive to manage, or if they deter buyers, then their avoidance is compatible with long-run profit maximisation. On the other hand there must be a suspicion that the fundamental reasons for desiring stability have their basis in managers' desire for a quiet life, rather than in serving the shareholders.

The third objective for pricing, which is often referred to in the textbooks, consists of *meeting or matching the competition*. Whether this can legitimately be described as an objective for pricing is open to question. It is perhaps better to see it as a description of a method of setting a price. However, if all firms in an industry set prices by matching the competition the logic of price-setting is confusing and circular as each firm sets prices with reference to those set by the others which in turn are set with reference to those set by others, and so on. Such a situation could only be resolved if prices are either set by market forces, as in perfect competition, or set by a price leader, who is followed by the others.

Pricing methods I: the prevalence of cost-plus pricing

Having considered the question of pricing objectives, it is possible to examine the procedures that firms use in practice to set prices and to consider the links between these methods and the economic models of optimal pricing.

By far the most common pricing method adopted in practice is to calculate the average direct cost of production for a product and then to add a margin for overheads and a further margin for profits, thereby arriving at a *full-cost-plus price*. This procedure was first brought to the attention of academic economists by a group of researchers at Oxford, reported by Hall and Hitch (1939) and their finding has since been confirmed by most other studies of pricing practice (Skinner 1970, Atkin and Skinner 1975, Govindarajan and Anthony 1983, Nagle and Holden 1995, Sim and Sudit 1995).

Pricing on a cost-plus basis does not correspond to price-setting as described in the standard profit-maximising model and some of the economists who drew attention to the prevalence of cost-plus pricing, including Hall and Hitch (1939), Andrews (1949) and Barback (1964) misinterpreted their results. They fell into the trap of believing that because firms did not explicitly adopt marginal cost and marginal revenue methods, the marginalist models had necessarily failed in their purpose. However, that conclusion was erroneous, for a number of reasons.

In the first place, it is not the purpose of the economic model to provide either a description of real firms or a simple prescription for setting prices. The model simply shows the conditions that must hold if firms have set profit-maximising prices. They are intended to predict those prices, not to show how they were arrived at. There is no reason to suppose, therefore, that a description of price-setting procedures in firms will show price-setters referring to marginal costs and marginal revenues. It is perfectly possible for firms to arrive at profit-maximising prices through procedures that they describe as cost-plus.

This point can be seen most clearly in a simple example which allows the reconciliation of the two different approaches. The profit-maximising condition may be written in the following form:

$$\frac{P - MC}{P} = \frac{1}{-E_d}$$

which is simply rewritten as:

$$P = MC \cdot \frac{(E_d)}{(E_d - 1)}$$

If average variable cost (AVC) is constant then it equals marginal cost (MC) and the equation can be rewritten:

$$P = AVC \cdot \frac{(E_d)}{(E_d - 1)}$$

As the value of elasticity of demand must exceed 1, the expression in brackets also exceeds 1, and may be interpreted as a mark-up. For instance, if elasticity has a value of 3, the price (P) will equal 150 per cent of the AVC. Provided that elasticity of demand is constant, adding a mark-up of 50 per cent to AVC will give the profit-maximising price.

This example has restricted validity because it can only be applied in the very simple case when both AVC and E_d are constant. Nevertheless, it provides a formal demonstration that cost-plus procedures can in principle lead to profit-maximising prices. While the relationship between the two is rarely so simple, an examination of the details of cost-based pricing procedures shows that many of the important influences identified in the theoretical model of pricing do have an influence on the prices set by firms, even when the process is described as simple 'cost-plus'.

The method of cost-plus pricing involves two basic steps. The first is to identify the unit cost which is to form the basis of the pricing calculation and the second is to identify the margin which is to be added to that cost figure in order to determine the price.

At first sight both the cost and the margin appear to be objective factors, easily subject to mechanical calculation. However, closer examination makes it clear that this is not the case. The estimation of cost per unit for an individual product depends heavily on the accounting procedures that are used to allocate overhead costs across the different products produced. Cost per unit also depends upon the level of output being produced, which introduces a problem of *circularity*. If the level of cost is sensitive to the level of output then a firm needs to know the level of output it is likely to produce before it can calculate the cost per unit, on which to base the price. On the other hand, the level of output that it can sell depends upon the price. In this case the firm needs to know the price it intends to charge, in order to know the level of output it will produce, in order to calculate the cost, in order to set the price! Clearly, if the firm is to set price on the basis of cost per unit it will have to make its own series of assumptions about costs, which introduces a good deal of flexibility into the apparently objective measure of unit cost.

In fact, the evidence on cost-plus pricing suggests that firms allow the measure of cost that they use to be adjusted in the light of market forces, in ways that suggest that the resulting prices may be perfectly consistent with those predicted by the marginalist analysis. When defining cost for pricing purposes, firms usually rely upon the accounting concept of *standard costs*, which involves assuming some 'normal' level of output and then applying standard budgeted labour and materials costs per unit of output, augmented by an allocation of overheads to each product. This process involves a good deal of informal discussion within the firm, which provides plenty of opportunity for firms to take market conditions into account, as Edwards (1952) found. When Fog (1960) invest-igated pricing in Danish industry he found that firms nearly always described cost-based procedures, but that demand-side influences crept into the estimation of costs. In the case of one firm, for instance, cost per unit was calculated on the assumption that the firm would be operating at full capacity when no one expected that to be the case, and actual costs were expected to be substantially higher. When questioned on why it adopted this apparently very odd procedure, the firm replied 'for competitive reasons'. In other words, it was recognised that the price that would be arrived at by using actual costs would be higher than the market would bear, so the firm adjusted its estimate of costs downwards in order to arrive at a price that was consistent with market conditions. One observer (Smyth 1967) suggested that instead of referring to 'cost-plus pricing' methods, it would be more accurate to label them a 'price-minus theory of cost'.

Similar considerations apply to the size of the margin that is added to the unit cost figure in order to arrive at a price. The early studies, which 'discovered' the phenomenon of full-cost pricing, noted that firms made a 'conventional addition (frequently ten per cent)' (Hall and Hitch, 1939, p. 19) to the cost figure, in order to arrive at the final price. However, the evidence also shows that such a figure is by no means standard across industries, and that firms adjust the size of the margin in the light of the demand conditions and the competition facing them.

If firms simply calculated a figure for cost per unit, using some objective method of measurement, and then added a predetermined margin, it could be said that prices are entirely cost-based and the marginalist model would only predict pricing behaviour with any accuracy when elasticity of demand and average cost are constant, and the margin is related to elasticity as shown in the example above. In other cases, such a procedure would lead to the setting of sub-optimal prices. There are undoubtedly cases where this occurs and firms lose profits as a result, as witness Jaguar's pricing policy in the 1970s (Harrison and Wilkes 1973). However, such behaviour is inconsistent with the drive for profits. The balance of the evidence shows that most firms do use a full-cost-plus figure as a benchmark in the pricing process. However, they allow that figure to be adjusted in the light of market conditions, and the advice of the marketing department, in order to reach a final result that better serves to meet the firm's objectives. Much of the evidence also suggests that firms regard price as only one aspect of the marketing mix, whose determination cannot be separated from the determination of product quality, advertising, packaging, promotion, service and product development.

Pricing methods II: other approaches to pricing

In addition to the full-cost-plus approach to pricing, managerial economists have identified a number of other approaches that merit a brief outline. The first of these is *target return pricing*, which can be linked to the pursuit of a target rate of return on capital as a pricing objective. In order to link the target rate of return and the price, a firm first calculates the total profit required, which is given by the simple formula:

Required profit = aK   where:

$$a = \text{target rate of return}$$
$$K = \text{capital employed}$$

The margin to be charged over unit cost can then be arrived at by dividing the total profit required by the expected, or budgeted, level of output, to give:

$$m = \frac{aK}{Q_b} \quad \text{where:}$$

$$m = \text{the margin}$$
$$Q_b = \text{budgeted level of output}$$

Firms using this approach are reported to do so because they wish to take a long-run view of pricing and because they wish to prevent short-term cyclical influences from leading to erratic price changes (Lanzillotti 1958). As a result, it can be shown to be inconsistent with short-run profit maximisation (Dorward 1987). Nor is it necessarily of real assistance in maximising long-run profits because the target rate of return that is aimed for and used in the pricing calculation is usually an accounting rate of return, not a true economic rate which would reflect the time-value of money.

Another approach to pricing, which has also been referred to briefly above in the section on pricing objectives, is *going rate* or *market-determined or competition-oriented* pricing. In its simplest form this is the type of pricing policy that is imposed by market forces on firms operating in a perfectly competitive industry. Each firm is obliged to charge the same price as the others, or lose all of its customers. In more complex situations a firm may not simply set exactly the same price as its competitors, but may use their prices as a 'benchmark' against which it adjusts its own price to take account of differences between them. For instance, a firm that is producing a high cost/high quality variant of the product will set its price above that of the competition, while a firm aiming for cost leadership may set it lower. A firm attempting to enter a new market may set its price lower than that of rivals in order to overcome existing brand loyalties and build a large enough volume of sales to allow economies of scale and capacity utilisation to be achieved.

In so far as competition-oriented pricing takes proper account of rivals' prices and their impact on the demand conditions facing the individual firm, then it potentially offers a means of securing maximum profit. Whether it actually does so depends upon the firm's ability to judge the appropriate differences between its own price and that of the competition. In the case of perfect competition this judgement is simple as the difference must equal zero. In other market conditions it may be more difficult, especially in oligopoly where a firm's rivals will react to its price-setting. One situation where this problem may be resolved is that of price leadership, discussed in Chapter 10. If one firm in an oligopolistic industry acts as a price leader, followers may respond by setting the same price, or one that has been adjusted in a way that is mutually understood by all, so that the rivals know how each other will react, thereby creating an 'orderly' form of competition.

A final approach to pricing which merits attention is the process of *competitive tendering* or *sealed bid pricing*. In this situation, which is commonly associated with government purchases of large quantities of goods or services, or with major construction projects, the purchaser advertises the specification that it wishes to meet and invites potential suppliers to submit the prices at which they are prepared to supply to that specification. Bids are made in confidence (hence 'sealed bids') in order to avoid collusion and the firm that offers to meet the specification at the lowest price is awarded the contract, provided that the purchaser is satisfied that the supplier will be able to deliver on time and to a satisfactory quality.

Firms attempting to set a price at which to bid for a competitive tender face a number of difficult problems. In the first place, if their own costs depend upon the degree of capacity utilisation, they will have to make some assumption about the level of orders they will be meeting at the time when they will be fulfilling the tender contract, in order to estimate the cost of fulfilling the contract. If they fear that they will have idle capacity they will be willing to tender at a relatively low price, because the marginal cost of meeting the order will be low and it would be profitable to accept business at a relatively low price. However, if this expectation turns out to be false, and the firm finds that it has no spare capacity with which to fulfil the order, meeting the contract may involve incurring higher costs than revenues. On the other hand, the firm could have the opposite problem. It could fear that meeting the order will be expensive, as it expects its capacity to be fully utilised, in which case it would offer to fulfil the contract at a relatively high price and then find that it fails to secure the order and has under-used capacity. Clearly this is only a problem if costs are sensitive to the degree of capacity utilisation, but that is almost always going to be the case. For very large and long-term orders the problem may be resolved by including the cost of the production capacity in the price that is bid, but that will not be possible for smaller contracts.

The other major problem concerns the behaviour of competing companies and the prices at which they are likely to bid. If rivals have very similar cost structures then each firm will be well informed about the minimum price at which others will be prepared to bid, but does not know where the actual bid is likely to be placed. In order to secure a high probability of winning a contract, firms may offer to meet the specification at a price that is very close to the incremental cost of production. As this incentive applies to them all, the prices that are offered and accepted will tend to be very low (which is, after all, the purchaser's objective). This effect may be tempered by the purchaser's fear that suppliers may go bankrupt if they offer prices that are too low, but there is clearly an incentive for suppliers in this situation to collude with each other in order to ensure that prices are fixed at higher levels than would otherwise be the case.

If collusion is ruled out, the major problem facing a firm that is bidding for a competitive tender lies in taking account of the likely behaviour of its competitors. If their identity is unknown, or there is little information about their bidding behaviour, there is very little that can be done. However, if there is an established record of competitors' bids for a large number of previous contracts it is possible to use this information to adopt a rational strategy towards bidding. The starting point is to assume that a competitor faces roughly the same costs in meeting a contract as the firm that is developing a strategy. In that case the competitor's previous bids can be expressed as a percentage of costs, and a frequency distribution can be set out, showing how the competitor has bid on those previous occasions. Table 15.1 gives an example.

The firm attempting to construct a bid can then identify a number of possible prices at which it may bid and construct a pay-off matrix showing the pay-offs for each bid, given the price at which its competitor has bid. Table 15.2 shows such a matrix for an example where the bidding firm considers five possible prices, ranging from 70 per cent of cost to 150 per cent of cost.

As the table shows, it is assumed that the firm that tenders the lowest bid will secure the contract. For each different price that might be bid an expected monetary value can be calculated, as explained in Chapter 12, and the bid price

Table 15.1 Frequency distribution of rival bids

Competitor's price as a % of cost (C)	Relative frequency
0.75C	0.20
1.00C	0.20
1.25C	0.50
1.50C	0.10

Table 15.2 Pay-off matrix

Firm's bid	Competitor's bid			
	0.75C (Pr = 0.2)	1.00C (Pr = 0.2)	1.25C (Pr = 0.5)	1.50C (Pr = 0.10)
0.70C	−0.3C	−0.3C	−0.3C	−0.3C
0.90C	0	−0.1C	−0.1C	−0.1C
1.10C	0	0	+0.1C	+0.1C
1.30C	0	0	0	+0.3C
1.50C	0	0	0	+0.5C

Source: Wilson and Darr (1979, p. 322).

that yields the highest expected value can be chosen. In the example given, this yields a bid price equal to 110 per cent of cost, which leads to an expected profit of 0.06C.

This technique can be adjusted in a number of ways, to take account of additional information. For instance, if the competitor is known to be operating at full capacity then they are less likely to submit a low bid, and the probabilities can be adjusted accordingly. If the competitor is known to have a large amount of spare capacity the probabilities can be adjusted in the opposite direction as they are more likely to be prepared to submit a low bid.

The example given here is a very simple one, with a single competitor, who is not aware of the technique being used to construct a bid. If there are multiple competitors the situation becomes more difficult and it becomes even more complex if the competitor comes to realise that there is a pattern in the bids being made. In that case the competitor may use their knowledge of the bidding pattern to amend their own bids in which case the situation becomes a game between interdependent players which may be best modelled through the techniques of game theory.

Transfer pricing

The prices discussed thus far have been those that the firm sets for transactions between itself and its customers. However, in an era of large multi-divisional firms, prices may also need to be set for transactions that take place between one part of the firm and another. These are known as *transfer prices*.

If a firm wishes each of its divisions to behave autonomously, choosing its own level of output and maximising its own profits, and yet still achieve maximum profits for the firm as a whole, the question of transfer prices becomes an important one. There are a number of different cases that need to be considered.

Transfer pricing in the absence of an external market

The first case that can be considered concerns the situation where a firm has two divisions, manufacturing and distribution. The manufacturing division produces an intermediate product which is sold to the distribution division, and for which there is no external market. In this case the amount that the manufacturing division chooses to produce and sell internally must equal the amount sold externally by the distribution division, and that amount must equal the profit-maximising level of output for the firm as a whole. The analysis can be seen graphically in Figure 15.1.

In Figure 15.1, the curves marked MC_{firm} and MR_{firm} show the marginal revenue and marginal cost for the firm as a whole. The profit-maximising level of output is given by $Q_{profit-max}$ and the price to be set for external sales is $P_{profit-max}$.

If the firm is composed of two different divisions, manufacturing and distribution, it is necessary to identify the cost and revenue conditions facing each of those divisions. For the distribution division, revenue conditions are given by the revenue conditions for the firm as a whole. Its costs are given by the costs of distribution plus the cost of purchasing the intermediate product from the manufacturing division. For the manufacturing division, costs are equal to the costs of manufacturing and revenues are given by the transfer price at which it

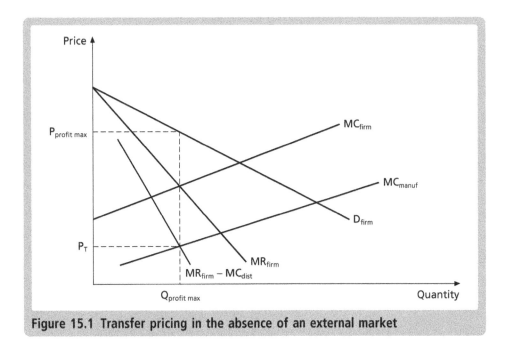

Figure 15.1 Transfer pricing in the absence of an external market

sells to the distribution division, multiplied by the number of units that yield it maximum profit.

The appropriate transfer price can be found by first considering the *net marginal revenue* curve for the distribution division, shown on the diagram as $(MR_{firm} - MC_{dist})$. This is found by taking the marginal revenue to the firm as a whole and subtracting the marginal cost of distribution. For each marginal unit this gives the net marginal contribution to the distribution division, before taking account of the cost of purchasing units from the manufacturing division.

The next step is to identify the marginal cost of manufacturing, which is equal to the difference between the marginal cost to the firm as a whole and the marginal cost of distribution, given in the diagram as MC_{manuf}. As the diagram shows, this must intersect the net marginal revenue for distribution curve at the profit-maximising level of output. This must be so because at that level of output:

$$MC_{firm} = MR_{firm}$$

and subtracting MC_{dist} from both sides gives:

$$MC_{firm} - MC_{dist} = MC_{manuf} = MR_{firm} - MC_{dist}$$

It can now be seen that if the manufacturing division is to choose to supply level of output $Q_{profit-max}$, the transfer price will have to be set at P_T. That price represents the marginal revenue for the manufacturing division, which will maximise its own profit by equating that to its own marginal cost, at level of output $Q_{profit-max}$.

In a similar way the distribution division will choose to purchase quantity $Q_{profit-max}$ from the manufacturing division because, in order to make maximum profit, it will wish to distribute every unit of output for which the net marginal contribution, given by $(MR_{firm} - MC_{dist})$ exceeds the cost of purchasing the unit from manufacturing. In other words, the curve $(MR_{firm} - MC_{dist})$ is essentially the distribution division's demand curve.

To summarise the analysis in this case, if there is no external market for the intermediate product, the optimal transfer price is equal to the marginal cost of manufacturing the intermediate product, at the level of output that maximises the firm's overall profit. If central management sets the transfer price at this level it can then simply order each division to maximise its own profit and the result will be consistent with profit maximisation for the firm as a whole. Alternatively, instead of actually setting that price, central management could provide the divisions with information about each other's situation which would lead to that price being arrived at without central intervention. If the distribution division is informed of the manufacturing division's marginal cost curve and told that this represents the supply function which determines the amount that manufacturing will supply to distribution at each price, distribution will choose to offer the transfer price P_T, which will induce manufacturing to produce just the correct amount. In a similar way, central management could provide the manufacturing division with information on the distribution division's net marginal contribution curve and order it to treat that as its own marginal revenue curve when deciding how much to supply.

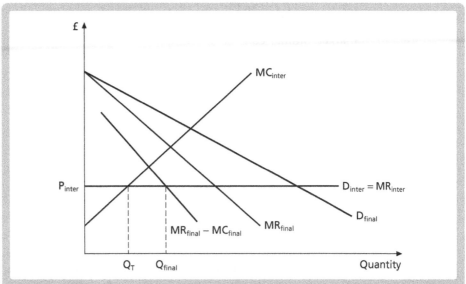

Figure 15.2 Transfer pricing with a perfectly competitive external market for the intermediate

Transfer pricing in the presence of a perfect market for the intermediate product

The second case to be covered in the analysis of transfer pricing is where the intermediate product may be bought or sold in a perfect market. In this case, examined by Hirschleifer (1956), the quantities supplied by the manufacturing division need not equal those required by the distribution division and the analysis can be explained with the help of Figure 15.2.

The starting point lies in the demand and marginal revenue curves for the final product, shown by the sloping curves marked D_{final} and MR_{final}, and the horizontal demand curve for the intermediate product, shown by D_{inter}, which also represents the marginal revenue for the intermediate, indicated by MR_{inter}. The analysis also requires information on the marginal cost of producing the intermediate product, labelled MC_{inter}, and the marginal contribution made by units of the final product, before making payment for the transferred intermediate product. This curve is labelled $MR_{final} - MC_{final}$.

For the department producing the intermediate product, profits will be maximised at level of output Q_T, where the marginal cost of producing the intermediate product is equal to its marginal revenue. However, for the department selling the final good, profits are maximised at level of output Q_{final} where the marginal cost of purchasing the intermediate product is just equal to the marginal contribution earned by units of the final product.

As Figure 15.2 shows, the division selling the final product requires more of the intermediate product than will be produced within the firm. However, that poses no difficulty as the difference can be made up by purchases on the open market. If the firm itself were to supply all of the intermediate product needed, profits would fall as the cost of supplying the additional units of the intermediate product beyond Q_T is higher than the cost of purchasing them on the open market. Similar considerations apply if the division producing the intermediate product should wish to produce more than is required by the final product division. In that case the excess internal supply would simply be sold on the open market.

More complex issues in transfer pricing

The analyses set out above have considered two simple transfer pricing situations and identified two simple rules. If there is a perfect market for the intermediate product, the transfer price should equal the market price. If there is no such external market, the transfer price should be equal to the marginal cost of producing the intermediate product, at the profit-maximising level of output.

Unfortunately these cases are much too simple to be of very general application, and a full treatment of the complex cases lies beyond the scope of this text. A number of complications are worth noting. First, there may be an external market for the intermediate, but it may be imperfect, a situation examined by Hirschleifer (1956). Second, there may be differences in the cost and the degree of risk associated with transactions carried out internally and those carried out between independent firms as examined in Chapter 3. Third, there may be different divisions competing for the use of the intermediate product, and finally there may be interdependencies between the costs and the demand for the intermediate and the final product. If all of these complicating factors occur together it becomes extremely difficult even in theory to identify the appropriate transfer price. As firms rarely have the kind of cost and demand information that would be required to calculate optimal transfer prices in such situations, it is hardly surprising that the evidence on transfer pricing in practice suggests that external market prices are used wherever possible (Emmanuel 1976, Vancil 1979). Where there is no external market for an intermediate most firms use some form of simple cost-plus formula for the setting of such prices (Hague 1971). This latter practice can lead to inefficiencies in the supplying division, which is able to pass excessive costs on to 'downstream' users unless some form of standard cost is used in the calculation, rather than costs actually incurred.

Pricing in public enterprises

The marginal cost pricing rule

The basic assumption that has been maintained throughout this chapter is that the aim of price-setting is to maximise profits. However, in the case of publicly owned firms, that is not always appropriate as public enterprises often have a different set of objectives. In so far as these have sometimes been complex and confused (Rees 1976), it can be difficult to analyse appropriate pricing policies for such firms. Nevertheless, it is possible to proceed with the economic analysis of public sector pricing by assuming that the basic objective of such organisations is to be economically efficient or to maximise social welfare.

It has been shown in Chapter 10, in the analysis of perfect competition, that a perfectly competitive industry will automatically be economically efficient because market forces ensure that price is equal to marginal cost, which is the basic requirement for welfare maximisation. That provides the starting point for the economic analysis of public sector pricing which simply states that price should be set equal to marginal cost (Webb 1976). That proposition in turn raises a number of other issues that merit consideration.

Pricing at short- or long-run marginal cost?

One of the questions that is raised with respect to public sector pricing concerns the choice between short-run and long-run marginal cost as the basis for setting the optimal price. In fact, this problem disappears if the firm is utilising the correct set of plant and equipment for the level of output that it is producing, for in that case short-run and long-run marginal cost will be the same. This can be seen with reference to Figure 15.3.

As Figure 15.3 shows, at each level of output where the short-run average cost curve just touches the long-run cost curve (Q_1, Q_2, and Q_3) both short-run and long-run average costs and short-run and long-run marginal costs are equal to each other. It is easy to see that the average costs are equal but some brief mathematical analysis may be needed to understand why the marginals are also equal. Short-run marginal cost at output Q_1 is given by the equation:

$$SMC = \frac{dTC}{dQ} = \frac{d(SAC_1 \cdot Q_1)}{dQ}$$

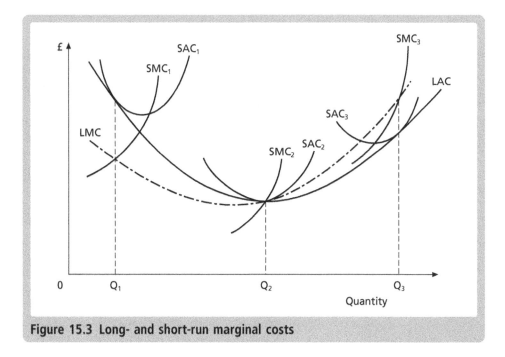

Figure 15.3 Long- and short-run marginal costs

Long-run marginal cost is given by:

$$LMC = \frac{dTC}{dQ} = \frac{d(LAC_1 \cdot Q_1)}{dQ}$$

As SAC_1 is equal to LAC at output Q_1 and Q_1 is common to both equations, it follows that LMC = SMC at that level of output. To explain it without the mathematics, at level of output Q_1, Q_2, or Q_3, total cost is the same in the short run and the long run, average costs are the same and the slope of the average cost curve is the same. As a result short- and long-run marginal costs must be equal. Provided the firm is utilising the lowest cost set of plant and equipment for the level of output, there is no need to decide between short- and long-run marginal cost in order to set the price.

Marginal cost pricing and financial surpluses or deficits

The adoption of the marginal cost pricing rule has implications for the financial position of the enterprise. If average costs are falling, as at level of output Q_1 in Figure 15.3, then marginal costs must be below average costs and setting marginal cost prices will necessarily involve incurring a financial deficit. On the other hand, if average costs are rising, as at Q_3, setting a price equal to marginal cost will imply making a surplus. Only if average cost is equal to marginal cost (at Q_2 where the average cost curve has a slope of zero) will the firm break-even exactly. In practice it is highly likely that public enterprises will have downward-sloping long-run cost curves, if only because one of the most common reasons for locating firms in the public sector is the danger of monopoly power where there are substantial scale economies. As a result, it is to be expected that the adoption of the marginal cost pricing rule would lead to substantial financial deficits (Webb 1976, Rees 1976).

Various solutions may be offered to this problem. The classic theoretical prescription is for government to cover the deficit by imposing lump-sum taxes (Hotelling 1938). As these do not affect the marginal conditions for consumers or firms, they will leave economic behaviour unchanged and will therefore not introduce any distortions into the economy's price mechanism. If lump-sum taxes (like a poll tax, for instance) are not feasible then some other solution to the deficit must be found. One of the most useful is the device of the two-part tariff. In this case the price that a buyer is charged is made up of two components. The first is a price that is set equal to marginal cost, so that consumers taking decisions at the margin are comparing the benefit they receive from an additional unit of the commodity with the additional cost of that unit. The second part of the tariff is a lump-sum per period, paid by all consumers of the good, which corresponds quite closely to the lump-sum tax.

Whichever method is adopted to cover public enterprise deficits attributable to marginal cost pricing there are associated difficulties, either with maintaining undistorted marginal conditions, or with non-economic considerations such as equity or fairness. There is also the managerial difficulty that if a public enterprise is implicitly ordered to make losses it may do so not because of the marginal cost pricing but because of general X-inefficiency and the two different causes of the losses may be difficult to disentangle in practice.

Second-best considerations

A third, and potentially very complex, issue which is raised in respect of marginal cost pricing concerns the question of *second-best*. It has been shown above that economic efficiency requires that prices be set equal to marginal cost. An economy is said to be at a 'first-best' optimum when all prices in all industries are equal to marginal cost. This would be the case if every industry were either perfectly competitive or a public enterprise following a policy of marginal cost pricing. However, it may be the case that in some industries there is a degree of monopoly power so that prices exceed marginal cost and it may be impossible to force them down to the marginal cost level. In this case, the 'first-best' will be unattainable and the important question becomes 'what is the second-best optimum?', i.e. the best position actually achievable. This is a question to which the theoretical answer is rather depressing, because it is simply not possible to identify the precise nature of the second-best solution. What is even more depressing is that theoretical analysis does show that if one of the conditions needed for the first-best optimum is not achieved, then the others may no longer be desirable and might even be counter-productive. In other words, if marginal cost pricing cannot be achieved in every industry, there may be no benefit in achieving it in any.

This last point can be made clear with an example. If every industry in the economy practised marginal cost pricing except the coal industry, which charged higher prices, the result would be an allocation of resources in which too little coal was produced, relative to the optimum. That would divert demand towards substitutes for coal, like gas, and as a result too much gas would be produced relative to the optimum. In this case the appropriate action could be for the gas industry to 'lean against the distortion' by also charging prices above marginal cost, thereby invalidating the rule that prices should equal marginal costs.

There are two potential solutions to the second-best problem. The first would be to build a complete and detailed general equilibrium model of the economy, which would identify all inter-connections between all activities in the economy, thereby allowing the model to be 'solved' in a way that would identify the necessary prices for everything. Clearly, that is impossible to achieve. The alternative is to adopt a piecemeal approach, applying the marginal cost pricing rule as a starting point and then making adjustments to compensate for the most obvious and significant distortions. That approach is at least operational, although serious doubts must remain concerning the soundness of its rationale. The final conclusion with respect to public sector pricing, then, has to be that there are no entirely satisfactory solutions. This difficulty provides one aspect of the rationale for the 'privatisation' of public utilities, examined in more detail in Chapter 21.

| Illustration | **Accountants misunderstand economists – interpreting evidence on the use of cost data in price decisions** |

Economists and management accountants both deal with the links between costs and price, but they approach the issue from different perspectives and often fail to understand each other's position adequately. A good example of this misunderstanding, accompanied by some useful data on costs and prices, is to be found in a paper by Govindarajan and Anthony (1983), referred to below as G–A.

G–A begin by declaring that economists and their courses disseminate two 'myths'. The first is that allocated costs are irrelevant to pricing decisions, and the second is that historical costs are irrelevant. According to G–A, economists advocate variable cost pricing, which ignores fixed costs, allocated costs and full costs. In order to 'prove' that the economists are wrong, G–A carried out a survey of the 'Fortune 1000' companies, designed to identify whether these firms used variable cost pricing, as advocated by the economists, or full cost pricing. Out of 505 respondents only 84 (17 per cent) used variable costs as the basis for pricing, while the other 83 per cent used some version of full costs. G–A explain that managers use full-cost pricing because 'the profit-maximising model cannot be applied in most real-world situations'. This, they claim, is because managers do not have perfect information, particularly with respect to the demand curve. Price is but one element in the marketing mix, and in any event some decisions that would increase profit are considered unethical by managers. In order to further support their claim that economists adhere to a set of myths, G–A go on to examine the use of historical cost versus replacement cost, finding that the vast majority of managers use historical cost depreciation instead of the replacement cost recommended by economists.

Taking these two pieces of survey evidence together G–A suggest that their results 'will make many economists uncomfortable' and claim that at least one of their economist colleagues was 'somewhat shaken by the results of the survey'. They even go so far as to claim that 'the results of our survey unequivocally destroy the two myths'.

Such a claim is entirely unfounded, revealing substantial ignorance of the nature and purpose of economic theory, and of the links between theory and evidence. Ever since the findings of the Oxford group in 1938, it has been well known among economists that managers do not set prices in the way that is described by the simple profit-maximising model. The G–A survey results are not in the least bit surprising to economists. Indeed, they simply (but usefully) replicate results that are well known. The fact that managers do not describe their price-setting behaviour in terms that directly mirror the profit-maximising model does not mean that the profit-maximising model is a 'bad model' or that the concepts associated with it have no value. The purpose of the model is not to describe how managers behave, but to identify the characteristics of the optimal price when profit is the objective, and to make predictions about the level of price and how it will respond to changes in the environment. For instance, the profit-maximising model, which G–A claim to have destroyed, predicts that when demand for a product rises, its price will rise. That prediction is constantly being validated by the behaviour of prices in practice, and yet it is absolutely inconsistent with G–A's finding that prices are set on a full-cost-plus basis. If the G–A survey really showed how prices are set in American industry it would imply that US companies completely ignore the market environment in which they operate, using costs as the sole basis for pricing. In fact we know from other evidence that firms are not usually so short-sighted as to set prices with sole reference to costs. Although they use a figure for full cost or standard cost as a rough benchmark, their calculation of that cost, and the margin that is added in order to arrive at a price, is sensitive to market conditions in a way that allows them to at least approximate the profit-maximising model. If competition is intense, and customers are thin on the ground, firms often reduce their prices. If the firm has a strong market position and customers who are able and willing to pay, prices will be higher, independent of cost. The economists' model is a much better 'real-world' predictor of prices and their changes than a naïve accountants' model which imagines that prices are set through the use of mechanical cost-plus pricing rules which completely ignore the existence of both customers and competition. G–A need to think again about the real implications of their evidence.

References and further reading

P.W.S. Andrews, *Manufacturing Business*, London, Macmillan, 1949.

B. Atkin and R. Skinner, *How British Industry Prices*, London, Industrial Market Research Ltd, 1975.

R.H. Barback, *The Pricing of Manufactures*, London, Macmillan, 1964.

N.M. Dorward, *The Pricing Decision: Economic Theory and Business Practice*, London, Harper and Row, 1987.

R.S. Edwards, 'The Pricing of Manufactured Products', *Economica*, 1952.

C.R. Emmanuel, 'Transfer Pricing in the Corporate Environment', PhD thesis, University of Lancaster, 1976.

B. Fog, *Industrial Pricing Policies*, Amsterdam, North-Holland, 1960.

W. Fruhan, 'Pyrrhic Victories in Fights for Market Shares', *Harvard Business Review*, vol. 50, 1972, pp. 100–7.

J.R. Gould, 'Internal Pricing in Firms When There Are Costs of Using an Outside Market', *Journal of Business*, 1964.

V. Govindarajan and R.N. Anthony, 'How Firms Use Cost Data in Price Decisions', *Management Accounting USA*, 1983.

D.C. Hague, *Pricing in Business*, London, George Allen and Unwin, 1971.

R.L. Hall and C.J. Hitch, 'Price Theory and Business Behaviour', *Oxford Economic Papers*, 1939.

R. Harrison and F.M. Wilkes, 'A Note on Jaguar's Pricing Policy', *European Journal of Marketing*, vol. 7, no. 3, 1973, pp. 241–6.

J. Hirschleifer, 'On the Economics of Transfer Pricing', *Journal of Business*, vol. 29, 1956, pp. 172–84.

H. Hotelling, 'The General Welfare in Relation to Problems of Taxation and of Railway and Utility Rates', *Econometrica*, 1938.

R.F. Lanzillotti, 'Pricing Objectives in Large Companies', *American Economic Review*, vol. 48, December 1958, pp. 923–9.

T. Nagle and R. Holden, *The Strategy and Tactics of Pricing*, 2nd edn, Englewood Cliffs, NJ, Prentice Hall, 1995.

R. Rees, *Public Enterprise Economics*, London, Weidenfeld and Nicolson, 1976.

A. Roy, D. Hanssens and J. Raju, 'Competitive Pricing by a Price Leader', *Management Science*, vol. 40, no. 7, July 1994, pp. 809–23.

E. Sim and E. Sudit, 'How Manufacturers Price Products', *Management Accounting*, vol. 76, no. 8, February 1995, pp. 37–9.

R.C. Skinner, 'The Determination of Selling Prices', *Journal of Industrial Economics*, vol. 18, July 1970, pp. 201–17.

R. Smyth, 'A Price-Minus Theory of Cost', *Scottish Journal of Political Economy*, vol. 14, 1967, pp. 110–67.

J. Urbany and P. Dickson, 'Evidence on the Risk Taking of Price Setters', *Journal of Economic Psychology*, vol. 15, no. 1, 1994, pp. 127–48.

R.F. Vancil, *Decentralisation: Ambiguity by Design*, New York, Irwin, 1979.

M.G. Webb, *Pricing Policies for Public Enterprises*, London, Macmillan, 1976.

F. Webster, 'Top Management's Concerns About Marketing: Issues for the 1980s', *Journal of Marketing*, vol. 45, 1981, pp. 9–16.

J.F. Weston, 'Pricing Behaviour of Large Firms', *Western Economic Journal*, 1972.

J.H. Wilson and S.G. Darr, *Managerial Economics*, New York, Harper and Row, 1979.

Self-test questions

1. Which of the following statements is true and which is false in the light of the evidence on cost-plus pricing?

   (a) prices are set with sole reference to costs

   (b) the figure for cost is the actual cost incurred

   (c) margins are calculated with reference to industry norms

   (d) demand-side factors influence the calculation of cost

2. Hall and Hitch argued that their evidence on pricing showed that the standard model of the firm was inappropriate. Was this because:

   (a) firms made no reference to marginal cost and revenue?

   (b) firms did not see profit as their objective?

   (c) firms did not have perfect information as assumed in the standard model?

3. Draw a diagram showing the optimal transfer price between a manufacturing division and a distribution division where there is no market for the intermediate product.

4. In which of the following situations will marginal cost pricing not lead to a financial deficit?

   (a) economies of scale

   (b) constant returns to scale

   (c) diseconomies of scale

5. Write one sentence explaining why the theory of second-best is potentially so destructive of the case for marginal cost pricing.

Essay question

Explain why the evidence on cost-plus pricing was first felt to cast doubt on the value of the economic model of the firm and then to support it.

16 Non-price competition and the marketing mix

This chapter is concerned with the analysis of non-price decisions. It begins by outlining the components of the 'marketing mix', and goes on to examine each in turn. Attention is paid to the level of advertising and promotional expenditures, to decisions concerning products, and to the choice of marketing channels. The chapter also considers the location of production and the role of R&D spending.

The marketing mix

Economic analysis and the marketing mix

The 'marketing mix' was defined by McCarthy (1960) as the 'four Ps':

- *Price* – including policy and practice with respect to discounts, allowances, payment periods and credit terms.
- *Product* – the attributes of the goods or services offered to buyers, including the range of products and their quality, brand names, packaging, service agreements and warranties.
- *Promotion* – advertising, publicity, sales promotion and personal selling.
- *Place* – the location in which the firm's products are offered to potential buyers and the marketing channels through which they reach that location.

The economic analysis of the firm pays attention to each of these issues, though not at the level of detail that would be required to offer managerial prescriptions. As in the case of pricing decisions it should be remembered that the central concern of economic model-building is to strip away the complications of the real world in order to identify the major factors that determine the optimal solutions to business problems. Detailed formulae for the day-to-day determination of operational decisions like branding or packaging are therefore not likely to be available.

The need to balance the four components of the marketing mix

Despite this reservation, even a simple approach to the economic modelling of the marketing mix illustrates the importance of achieving the correct balance between the different components of the mix.

If the firm is assumed to be a profit-maximiser, then:

Profit ($) = Total revenue (q) − Total cost (q)

or

($) = R(q) − C(q)

In the simple model of the firm, both revenue and cost depend upon a single variable, which is the level of output produced and sold (q). As each component of the marketing mix affects both the demand for the firm's output and the cost of producing and selling it, the extension of the model to include these four factors gives the more complex version:

$$\$ = \frac{R \text{ (price, product,}}{\text{promotion, place)}} - \frac{C \text{ (price, product,}}{\text{promotion, place)}}$$

If each of the marketing mix variables were measured quantitatively then this model could be solved for the profit-maximising level of every variable. In principle, this is simple enough, the first-order conditions for profit-maximisation being:

$$\frac{d\$}{\text{(d) price}} = \frac{d\$}{\text{(d) product}} = \frac{d\$}{\text{(d) promotion}} = \frac{d\$}{\text{(d) place}} = 0$$

In order for profits to be maximised, the marginal contribution of each element in the marketing mix should be equal to each other and equal to zero. If this were not the case then it would be possible to increase the level of contribution and profit by spending more on some marketing activities and by shifting the emphasis from one component of the mix to another. While this simple exposition provides little assistance to a company attempting to establish the details of its own marketing mix, it does provide a clear justification for the marketing maxim that the four Ps should be in an appropriate balance.

Advertising, promotion and selling

A formal model of advertising and promotion expenditures

Economic models of advertising and promotion are generally concerned with identifying the optimal level of advertising and promotional budgets, rather than with the specific activities that should be carried out. Spending upon advertising and promotion affects the firm's demand curve and also increases costs, so that the model of the firm can be written as follows:

$\$ = R − C − A$ where:

R = Total revenue = $P \cdot q(P, A)$
C = Total cost of production = $C(q)$
A = Spending on advertising and promotion
P = Price
q = Quantity produced and sold = $q(P, A)$

So that:

$$\$ = P \cdot q(P, A) - C[q(P, A)] - A$$

The decision variables in this version of the model are price (P) and advertising expenditure (A). If the firm maximises profit the first-order conditions are:

$$\frac{d\$}{dA} = \frac{P \cdot dq}{dA} - \frac{dC}{dQ} \cdot \frac{dq}{dA} - 1 = 0$$

$$\frac{\$d}{dP} = \frac{P \cdot dq}{dP} + Q - \frac{dC}{dQ} \cdot \frac{dq}{dP} = 0$$

The first of these conditions can be simply rearranged to give:

$$\frac{dq}{dA}(P - MC) = 1$$

and multiplying both sides by $\frac{A}{Pq}$ gives:

$$\frac{dq}{dA} \cdot \frac{A}{q} \frac{(P - MC)}{P} = \frac{A}{Pq}$$

Closer examination of this equation reveals that the term $\frac{dq}{A} \cdot \frac{A}{q}$ is simply advertising elasticity of demand (Ea).

The second first-order condition can also be rearranged, to give the familiar profit-maximising condition that:

$$\frac{P - MC}{P} = \frac{1}{-E_d}$$

Combining the left-hand side of these last two equations gives a result that is often referred to as the *Dorfman–Steiner condition*, which states that:

$$\frac{A}{Pq} = \frac{E_a}{-E_d}$$

This shows that, for profit maximisation, the ratio of advertising expenditure to sales revenue should be equal to the ratio of advertising elasticity of demand to price elasticity of demand.

Instead of presenting the model in terms of the ratio of elasticities, it can also be reworked in terms of the familiar marginal conditions. In this framework it can be seen that the firm should be willing to spend an extra £1 on advertising, provided that the extra revenue raised is sufficient to cover both that £1 spent on advertising and the extra production costs incurred in producing the extra output for sale. The maximising condition thus becomes:

$$\frac{dR}{dA} = \frac{dC}{dA} + 1$$

The determinants of advertising elasticity of demand

The Dorfman–Steiner model illustrates the importance of advertising elasticity as a determinant of the profit-maximising advertising budget. Such a result is intuitively plausible because E_a is essentially a measure of the effectiveness of advertising, and the model provides a formal demonstration of the proposition that if advertising is highly effective it will pay to do more of it, which is hardly surprising. Rasmussen (1952) first identified the factors that will determine the advertising elasticity of demand.

The first is the *absolute level of advertising expenditure*. The links between advertising effectiveness and the level of spending may take a number of forms, the most plausible of which is shown in Figure 16.1.

As the figure shows, low levels of advertising expenditure have no effect upon the level of sales until a 'threshold' level is reached, at which point sales begin to be affected by the spending. As spending increases, effectiveness increases until eventually the point of saturation is reached and diminishing returns to advertising set in.

The second factor that determines the effectiveness of advertising is the *type of commodity* involved. Advertising elasticity will tend to be higher for new products than for old ones, and higher for luxuries than for necessities. There will also be differences between durable and non-durable goods, and those that are purchased frequently as opposed to those that are only bought occasionally. As theoretical analysis offers little guidance on the size of these effects, rational decisions on the advertising budget will depend to a great extent upon the marketing department's skill in estimating them.

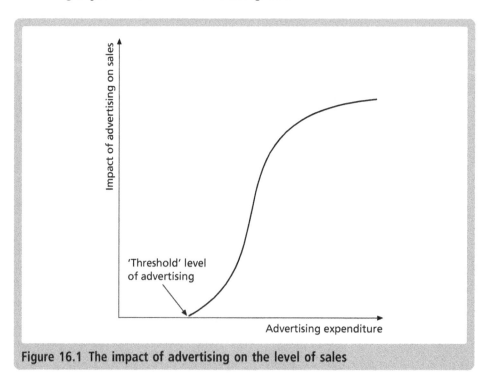

Figure 16.1 The impact of advertising on the level of sales

The third set of factors that will determine the advertising elasticity of demand concerns the *competitive structure and behaviour of the industry* and in particular the firm's market share and its rivals' reactions. The larger the firm's market share, the lower advertising elasticity of demand is likely to be. If rivals react to increases in the firm's advertising by increasing their own promotional spending, then these expenditures will tend to cancel each other out, reducing the advertising elasticity of demand.

Finally, the effectiveness of advertising will depend *upon the state of the economy in general.* If economic conditions are generally good and households have a high level of discretionary income they are more likely to respond to advertising than when incomes and expenditures are more tightly constrained.

Advertising with lagged effects

The analysis that leads to the Dorfman–Steiner condition is a single-period model in which this period's sales volume is affected by this period's advertising, but there are no spill-over effects from one period to another. While this may be appropriate for some goods, in many cases advertising will have an effect beyond the period in which it takes place and these lagged effects should be taken into account.

One model that tackles this problem is that of Nerlove and Arrow (1962), who approached it through the concept of the optimal stock of goodwill. Advertising expenditures (A) are treated as gross investment in goodwill (G), which depreciates at rate 'a'. The rate of change of goodwill over time is then given by the equation:

$$\frac{dG}{dt} = A - aG$$

As the stock of goodwill affects sales volume it is possible to examine the conditions required to maximise the present value of the firm, which yields the following condition:

$$\frac{G}{R} = \frac{E_a}{E_d(r + a)} \qquad \text{where:}$$

$$r = \text{discount rate (see Chapter 17)}$$

As the equation shows, the result is essentially a multi-period version of the Dorfman–Steiner condition.

While the Nerlove–Arrow model embodies the important insight that advertising has lagged effects, it ignores the impact of past prices, and consumers' past purchases, both of which are also likely to affect the stock of goodwill. Schmalensee (1972) constructed an alternative which takes these into account and provides another long-run version of the Dorfman–Steiner condition. Such dynamic models can easily become too complex to be of any practical interest, although Dorward (1987) notes that if the lags that determine the impact of price and advertising on sales over time have the same structure, the optimal advertising to sales ratios will be the same in the short run as in the long run and the simple Dorfman–Steiner conditions holds for both. In that case, management can ignore the complexities introduced by the dynamic effects. In other cases, the results of the models are largely of academic interest, being too complex to have any practical value.

Advertising and market structure

The models described above have focused on the individual firm's advertising decision, without explicit reference to the market structure in which it operates. That is a shortcoming because market structure will affect the profitability of advertising, while advertising is itself a determinant of market structure (see Chapter 11, for example). Two issues in particular merit consideration. The first concerns the relationship between advertising and the level of concentration in the industry, and the second concerns the use of advertising as a means of raising entry barriers.

The link between advertising and concentration can be explored by considering the impact of concentration on the advertising to sales ratio indicated by the Dorfman–Steiner condition (see Waterson 1984 for a more extensive treatment). This can be written in expanded form as:

$$\frac{A}{R} = \frac{E_a}{E_d} = \frac{(E_A + E_{conj}E_{Ar})}{\dfrac{(E_m + E_s S_r)}{S_f}} \qquad \text{where:}$$

E_A = the firm's advertising elasticity of demand, given that other firm's advertising remains constant

E_{conj} = responsiveness of rivals' advertising to changes in this firm's advertising

E_{Ar} = elasticity of this firm's demand with respect to rivals' advertising

E_m = market price elasticity of demand

E_s = elasticity of rivals' supply with respect to changes in the firm's price

S_r = rivals' market share

S_f = the firm's market share

As concentration increases, most of the terms in the equation will be affected so that the link between concentration and advertising is the result of complex interactions. Some observers have suggested that the most important effect derives from economies of scale in advertising (Kaldor 1950). If such economies are the dominant factor, E_a will tend to increase with concentration and the advertising/concentration relationship will be positive. On the other hand, the evidence for such economies is less than convincing (Simon 1965) and it might be argued that at very high levels of concentration, approaching monopoly, the returns to advertising are low because the firm has already attracted most of the buyers in the market. A number of authors (Cable 1972, Sutton 1974, Greer 1971) have suggested that the most likely relationship between advertising and concentration is as shown in Figure 16.2.

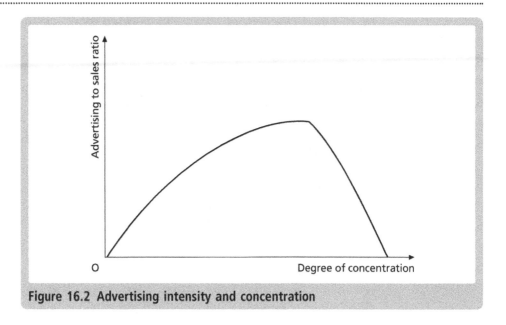

Figure 16.2 Advertising intensity and concentration

At low levels of concentration (with perfect competition setting the limit) advertising intensity is low because price elasticity of demand is very high. As concentration increases and the industry becomes oligopolistic, A/R rises because price elasticity becomes smaller and rivals' reactions become more important. Once the highest levels of concentration are reached, A/R falls as the dominance of the leading firms reduces the returns to advertising.

Traditional treatments of the concentration/advertising relationship treat the level of concentration as exogenous and then consider its implications for advertising. A more recent approach, built around advanced game theory techniques, focuses on the relationship between *endogenous sunk costs* (of which advertising is just one example) and concentration. Sutton (1996, 1999) identifies 'high-alpha industries' as those in which spending on sunk costs like advertising (or R&D) has a powerful effect on the demand for a firm's product. If such an industry is modelled as a two-stage game where firms first spend on sunk costs and then decide on price and output levels, there tends to be a competitive escalation of spending in sunk costs in the first stage, and a lower limit is set to the level of concentration in the second stage. In other words, the more responsive customers are to advertising, the more concentrated the industry tends to become. In that case it is advertising elasticity of demand that determines both industry structure and the amount that is spent on advertising. While these new models represent a much higher level of modelling sophistication, they retain the key feature of the Dorfman–Steiner approach in that higher advertising elasticites lead to higher advertising spending. However, they also go much further in explaining the evolution of industry structure over time.

The second aspect of market structure that is related to advertising concerns the condition of entry. If advertising creates entry barriers it will affect profitability in the long term by deterring entry into the industry where incumbents are earning high levels of profit, and allowing those supernormal profits to be maintained.

Advertising may contribute to entry barriers in three ways. First, it may give the incumbent firms an absolute cost advantage by creating buyer loyalty, which is expensive for new entrants to overcome. Second, if there are scale economies in advertising, newer and smaller firms will be placed at a disadvantage. Third, the cost of advertising required to establish an initial market position will increase the initial capital requirement needed to enter the industry, and render the investment more risky, which may also act to deter entry.

The effectiveness of advertising as an entry barrier is a matter of debate. Some authors, notably Comanor and Wilson (1967), have argued that both theory and evidence support the view that advertising creates entry barriers and increases profits for firms in industries having high advertising intensities. Others are more sceptical (Schmalensee 1974), noting that advertising may be just as effective a competitive weapon for entrants as for incumbents. Most of the arguments suggesting that advertising creates entry barriers rely for their validity on a hidden assumption that there is some asymmetry between entrants and incumbents with respect to basic cost and demand conditions, which allows incumbents to secure a greater benefit from advertising than entrants. Whatever the general outcome of this unresolved debate, individual companies spending on advertising need to consider whether they are able to use that spending to deter other firms from entering their industry, perhaps by establishing 'first-mover advantages'.

Setting advertising budgets in practice

The advertising decision process in companies can be divided into three stages (Mitchell 1993). First, a decision is taken on whether to advertise. Second, the advertising budget is decided, and third, the allocation of that budget across the competing media is decided. Just as many firms adopt cost-plus methods when setting prices, so the evidence suggests that firms adopt various 'rules-of-thumb' when setting advertising budgets. Each of these may be considered in the light of the profit-maximising conditions identified in the Dorfman–Steiner model.

One of the most common approaches is the *percentage-of-sales* method. Many firms determine their advertising and promotion budgets as some predetermined percentage of their current or expected sales revenue. This is seen by many as a 'safe' way to budget for advertising, as it restricts spending according to the amount of revenue available. It also provides for increasing advertising as sales grow, and the adoption of a common percentage by all firms in the industry could provide a means of securing competitive stability. However, there are serious disadvantages to the approach. In common with mechanical cost-plus pricing (see Chapter 15) it involves a problem of 'circularity' in that the level of sales determines the amount spent on advertising, which in turn determines the level of sales.

While the percentage-of-sales method is consistent in form with the profit-maximising model, which specifies a ratio of advertising to sales revenues, it will only yield the profit-maximising solution if the percentage is calculated with reference to estimates of elasticity, or if the appropriate ratio is approximated in some other way. Furthermore, most of the evidence suggests that the percentage of sales that is spent on advertising is kept relatively constant, so that opportunities for a profitable increase in advertising spending, which will arise if general economic conditions improve or if competitors alter their behaviour, will be ignored. The percentage-of-sales approach also involves the danger that a temporary dip in sales may set up a self-reinforcing cycle whereby a reduction in sales leads to a reduction in the advertising budget, which leads to a further reduction in sales until a potentially profitable firm or product line is driven from the market altogether.

A second approach to the determination of advertising budgets is known as the *all-you-can-afford* approach. This involves the firm spending as much as it can without breaking the profit constraint. Clearly, there is no obvious mechanism through which this decision process could lead to the profit-maximising result. It is perfectly feasible that where there are very high returns to advertising it would pay the firm to borrow in order to spend more on advertising than it can 'afford'. At the other extreme it would clearly be inconsistent with profit maximisation to incur advertising expenditures up to a firm's profit constraint in a situation where the effectiveness of advertising is very limited. There is, however, one situation where the all-you-can-afford approach would lead the firm to achieve its maximising objective. That is where the firm's objective is sales-revenue maximisation, as in Baumol's model (see Chapter 2).

The third method that is commonly employed in determining advertising budgets is the *competitive parity* method, where firms set their budgets by matching the percentage of sales devoted to advertising by their rivals. If all firms had the same advertising and price elasticities and the percentage of sales set by all firms happened to coincide with the ratio of these elasticities at the optimal level of output, then the competitive parity approach would lead to profit maximisation. However, as Kotler and Armstrong (1998) point out, companies within an industry often face such different opportunities that simply mimicking rivals' behaviour is unlikely to lead to the setting of optimal advertising budgets.

Each of the methods described above is concerned with setting a total advertising budget, after which individual activities can be planned within the total. The *objective-and-task* approach tackles the problem from the other direction. The starting point is to set a number of objectives that are to be met through advertising. For instance, the firm may wish to achieve a specified market share in a particular geographical area. Having set the objectives the firm then identifies the tasks that need to be carried out in order to meet those objectives. In the example given it may be estimated that, in order to meet the objective, potential consumers need to be exposed to two television advertisements per day for two months. The costs of achieving the various objectives set are added together to determine the total advertising budget.

The objective-and-task approach to the advertising budget is not in itself likely to lead to profit maximisation, because it does not directly take account of costs and revenues. However, if a firm identified a wide range of objectives and associated tasks and estimated the incremental revenues and incremental costs arising from meeting each objective, that could provide the basis for reaching an optimal budget. If the firm simply agreed to meet every objective for which the incremental revenue exceeded the incremental cost, then it would have a mechanism for at least approximating the profit-maximising advertising budget.

The evidence on company practice in respect of setting advertising budgets suggests that managers have become increasingly sophisticated in their approach (Lynch and Hooley 1990). More resources have been devoted to collecting data on which to base the decision, and approaches that are at least potentially economically rational have become more common. Synodinos *et al.* (1989), for instance, examined practice in 484 firms in fifteen countries and found that the objective-and-task approach was most commonly used (by 64 per cent of respondents), followed by per cent of sales (48 per cent) and 'executive judgement' (33 per cent). Corfman and Lehmann (1994) found evidence that those setting advertising budgets behave consistently with an understanding of the prisoner's dilemma. They based decisions on their expectations of opponents' behaviour and the history of those behaviours, as well as the short- or long-run nature of their own profit objectives. At the same time, other studies warn against forgetting the analysis of previous chapters that have emphasised managers' ability to pursue their own interests, the limits to information and the impact of attitudes to risk. Piercy (1987) found that the amount spent on advertising may be regarded as the outcome of a political process within the firm, with the power of the marketing department being a key influence. Lee (1994) found that if a firm had experienced recent poor performance, it became less risk averse and therefore spent more on advertising.

The promotional mix

It has been emphasised that the marketing mix consists of a number of different components that have to be in balance if the firm is to meet its objective. Price, promotion, product and place all have to be considered together. Similarly, within advertising and promotion, there are various different activities across which the budget has to be spread. If the aim is to make maximum profit, then the general principle of marginal equivalency can be used to identify the optimal mix of activities.

For instance, if the total advertising budget has been set, providing the constraint within which the marketing department has to operate, and there are three different advertising media on which the budget might be spent (television, radio and newspapers), then as Reekie (1981) pointed out, the optimal allocation of the budget requires that the following condition be fulfilled:

$$\frac{\text{MSR}_{\text{TV}}}{P_{\text{TV}}} = \frac{\text{MSR}_{\text{radio}}}{P_{\text{radio}}} = \frac{\text{MSR}_{\text{newspapers}}}{P_{\text{newspapers}}} \qquad \text{where:}$$

$\text{MSR}_{\text{TV,radio,newspapers}}$ = marginal sales response to a unit of advertising in each medium

$P_{\text{TV,radio,newspapers}}$ = the price of a unit of advertising in each medium

If the condition were not fulfilled then it would be possible to shift spending from one medium to another and increase sales volume with the same budget.

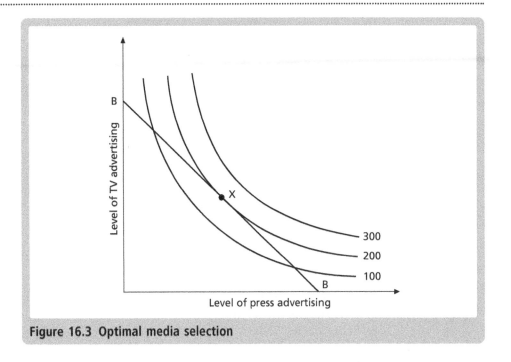

Figure 16.3 Optimal media selection

This analysis can also be presented graphically, which makes it clear that the problem is fundamentally the same as that facing a consumer deciding which combination of goods to buy, given a limited income, or a firm involved in identifying the cost-minimising combination of capital and labour required to produce a given level of output. Figure 16.3 sets out the position.

The curves marked 100, 200 and 300 in the diagram, which closely resemble indifference curves or isoquants, are *iso-sales lines*, showing the different combinations of TV advertising and press advertisements that will lead to sales volumes of 100, 200 and 300 units of output. The line BB is the budget line, showing the different combinations of the two advertising media that can be purchased within the marketing department's budget. The optimal combination of TV and press advertising is given by the point of tangency, X.

This analysis illustrates the fundamental principles of promotional mix selection, but makes light of many of the practical problems. In order to apply the analysis, quantitative estimates are required of the responsiveness of sales to advertising through different media. These might be estimated through econometric techniques, but Chapter 8 has shown that such methods are not powerful enough to be relied upon with any confidence. A more practical approach would be to collect data on the number of potential buyers who are exposed to an advertisement, and to measure the extent of their awareness of the product as a result of that exposure. Media planning could then take place on the basis of maximising customer awareness, rather than maximising the sales response. If awareness is a good proxy for sales, this will be a perfectly adequate substitute and the method has the advantage of taking into account the 'creative' aspects of the advertising message. However, awareness and sales response are by no means the same thing and decision-making based entirely around buyer awareness could pose considerable risks.

Product policies

The scope of product policy

The term 'product' refers to anything that a firm may offer to buyers in order to satisfy their needs and wants. It includes goods in the sense of physical objects, but also extends to cover services, facilities, organisations, people and even ideas. Kotler and Armstrong (1998) distinguish between three different levels at which the concept of the product may be considered. First, there is the *core product*, which is the fundamental benefit that the buyer is seeking. Second, there is the *tangible product*. This is the actual item purchased by the customer which may vary in five major respects:

1. Features offered.
2. Quality level.
3. Brand name.
4. Styling.
5. Packaging.

Finally, there is the *augmented product*, which includes additional services and benefits that accompany the tangible product. In the case of a motor-car, for instance, the core product is mobility, the tangible product is the vehicle itself and the augmented product includes credit terms, delivery dates, guarantees and after-sales service.

Firms have two major types of product decision to take. The first are product-mix decisions, concerning the range of products that the firm should produce and the circumstances under which the product range should be expanded or reduced.

The second are product attribute decisions, concerning the characteristics of the individual products, including their branding, packaging and labelling and service components. Each of these may be considered in turn.

Product-mix decisions

In simple models of the firm and the industry each firm produces only one product and the choice of product or industry is determined by the returns on capital that are available. Firms choose to produce the single product that they believe will bring the highest return on capital. In practice, most firms produce multiple products and it is necessary to consider the factors that will determine the range and variety of products that a firm will choose to produce.

A formal, and very limited, analysis of the product-mix decision can be carried out with the aid of a production possibility frontier. In Figure 16.4 the line XY shows all the combinations of two different goods that a firm is capable of producing, given that there is a fixed level of resources available to it. The curve is

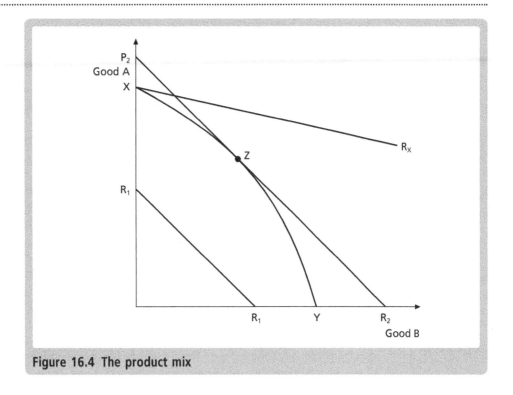

Figure 16.4 The product mix

concave, viewed from the origin, indicating that resources are not perfect substitutes for each other in the production of the two goods.

As the level of resources in use is fixed, total cost is constant for every combination of the two goods, and profits will be maximised when revenue is maximised. If it is assumed that there is a perfect market for both goods then any amount of either product can be sold for its market price. In that case, it is possible to draw *iso-revenue lines*, like R_1R_1 and R_2R_2 showing the different combinations of the two goods that yield the same level of revenue. These lines are straight as they represent a linear equation of the form:

$$TR = XP_X + YP_Y \qquad \text{where:}$$

$$TR = \text{a constant level of revenue}$$
$$X, Y = \text{amounts of product X and Y}$$
$$P_X, P_Y = \text{prices of X and Y}$$

The optimal product mix is that which allows the highest level of revenue to be earned, as indicated by point Z in the diagram. In that example, the firm chooses to produce both products. However, the combination chosen depends upon the shape of the production possibility frontier and the relative prices of the products. If the prices of the products should change so that iso-revenue curves have the slope given by the line XR_X then the firm would choose to operate at point X, producing a single product.

This analysis provides a formal statement of the rather obvious finding that the optimal product mix depends upon the prices that can be secured for different products (which determine the slope of the iso-revenue lines) and the opportunity costs of producing the two products (given by the shape of the production frontier). It also confirms that it will pay the firm to produce more of a product as its relative price is higher.

The question of product mix may be approached less formally from a number of other directions. The decision to produce a number of different products is essentially concerned with the firm's degree of diversification and its scope, both of which have been considered elsewhere in this book. Chapter 4 has examined diversification while Chapters 3 and 9 have considered the question of 'scope'. For the current purpose it suffices to note that a firm will choose to produce multiple products if it is able to do so profitably in the competitive circumstances in which it finds itself. Given that market opportunities are open to all firms, an extended product line will only provide competitive advantage if it allows the exploitation of links and interdependencies with the firm's existing activities. There are three such interdependencies that will encourage profit-seeking firms to produce a range of products. The first is *cost interdependency*, where the costs of producing one product are affected by the production of another. If there are economies of scope, so that a range of products can be produced more cheaply than a single line, there will be synergy between different product lines and an incentive for multi-product firms to develop. One of the most important sources of economies of scope arises where there is complementarity of supply so that production and marketing of two or more products share the same resources or key skills.

In a similar way, there will be incentives to produce a full range of products if there are *demand interdependencies* so that the demand for one product is enhanced by the fact that the firm is producing other, related, items.

Third, there is the *reduction of risk*. If the returns associated with different products are negatively correlated with each other, so that poor performance in one product line is usually accompanied by good performance in another, then the firm will be able to reduce the variability of its profits by producing and selling both lines.

The optimal product mix is therefore determined by a combination of cost drivers and demand conditions. As both sets of factors are subject to change over time, a profit-seeking firm will keep its mix under continual review, pruning or expanding the product line when appropriate. Pruning the line will become necessary if a product ceases to make a contribution to profits, which will tend to happen as it reaches the later stage of its product life cycle and demand both falls and becomes more price elastic. Pruning will also be necessary if the firm has limited capacity and is unable to produce every product for which incremental revenues exceed incremental costs. In that case profit maximisation requires that it concentrate its production and marketing effort on the most profitable lines. Conversely it will be appropriate to expand the product line if additional products will add more to revenues than they do to costs and the firm has the capacity to increase output.

The relationship between capacity utilisation and the optimal product mix implies that at times when demand is high, the number of products produced should be cut back in order to concentrate on the most profitable, while at times of low demand the firm should enhance its product range in order to produce all product variants that can make a contribution.

Product attributes

It has been noted in the section on the scope of product policy that the attributes of a product have at least five dimensions. These are:

1. Product features and performance characteristics.
2. The level of product quality.
3. Styling and aesthetic considerations.
4. Brand names.
5. Packaging.

Economic analysis tends to bundle these different dimensions together with advertising and promotion under the general heading of product differentiation. A profit-maximising firm will attempt to differentiate its product from that of its rivals in order to achieve two objectives. First, it seeks to raise the level of demand for its product, and second, it seeks to reduce the price elasticity of demand. A firm may seek successful product differentiation in a number of ways. It may spend on advertising and promotion, rather than on the tangible attributes of its product. Alternatively it may attempt to configure the features and performance of the product and its packaging in such a way that it has enhanced appeal to buyers. In terms of Lancaster's 'characteristics' model of demand, outlined in Chapter 7, the firm may attempt to construct a product variant that has characteristics that consumers value highly in proportions that match their preferences. As part of the product differentiation process the firm may choose to opt for branding by attaching a brand name or a brand mark to its product, allowing for easier identification by consumers and creating an element of distinctiveness. While branding involves the firm in additional costs it offers a number of advantages over simply offering a generic product.

First, branding can provide legal protection for any special features of the product, preventing rivals from selling copies. Second, it allows the development of brand loyalty among consumers, reducing the price elasticity of demand and weakening the power of wholesalers and distributors. Third, branding can assist with market segmentation and price discrimination, by allowing different brands within the product line to be targeted on the needs of different groups of users. Finally, branding may be linked to the firm's overall corporate identity, reinforcing consumers' positive views of the firm and its products.

The appropriateness of product differentiation, and its form, can be linked to the corporate strategy that the firm is attempting to pursue. If the strategy is one of *differentiation* then the firm needs to seek out those product attributes that buyers in general value highly, which the firm can provide cost-effectively, and which rivals are ill-equipped to provide. If the strategy is one of *focus*, the product's attributes should reflect the needs of the target group of consumers. On the other hand, if the strategy is one of *cost leadership*, the major need will be to produce a product whose characteristics allow it to be produced at lower cost than that of rival firms, subject to its performance characteristics maintaining proximity to those of its rivals.

However the firm specifies the characteristics of its product and packaging, success will depend to a substantial extent upon whether or not the result can be considered 'good design', for which there are three criteria (Davies 1989). The first is *functionality* or *fitness for purpose* – the design should carry out the required functions effectively. The second is *makeability* – it should be possible to produce the design at an acceptable cost. Third, the design should have *appropriate stylistic and aesthetic qualities*. Successful achievement of all three objectives demands an effectively coordinated performance on the part of the marketing and production departments in setting the design brief, and good creative skills on the part of the design team.

Marketing channels

'Place' as a component of the marketing mix

The fourth 'P' in the marketing mix is place, which refers to the locations in which the firm's product is offered to buyers and the distribution channels through which the product passes in order to reach those locations. In the textbook economic model of the firm no reference is made to these channels, the implicit assumption being that the product is sold directly to consumers. However, such direct marketing is comparatively rare and attention needs to be paid to the nature and function of other marketing channels or intermediaries.

The functions of marketing channels

Kotler and Armstrong (1998) define the functions of marketing channels as follows:

- *research* – gathering the information needed to make exchanges between buyers and suppliers
- *promotion* – disseminating persuasive communications about the product on offer
- *contact* – finding and communicating with buyers
- *matching* – adjusting the product to buyers' needs through activities such as grading, assembling and packaging
- *negotiation* – setting final prices and other aspects of the offer so that transfer of ownership can be effected
- *physical distribution* – transport and storage
- *financing* – bearing the costs of channel work
- *risk-taking* – bearing some of the risk associated with channel activities.

Each of these functions has to be undertaken by some organisation, but their allocation between the manufacturer of the product and other firms is variable, depending upon the relative efficiency of alternative channel configurations.

Alternative channel configurations

The marketing channel from manufacturer to consumer may have a number of levels. In the case of direct marketing, none of the channel activities are carried out by independent firms, and the configuration is known as a *zero-level channel*. At the other extreme, there may be a large number of intermediaries. In Japan, for instance, where the distribution system is notoriously complex and inefficient, it is estimated that the average consumer product passes through approximately a dozen different firms between the manufacturer and the consumer, in what marketing analysts would call a *twelve-level channel*. In Europe and the United States, channels more commonly have between one and three levels. A one-level channel consists of retailing organisations that either purchase from the manufacturer and sell to the consumer from a retail location or act as sales agents. A two-level channel includes wholesalers and a three-level channel also contains jobbers who purchase from wholesalers and then distribute to retailers.

Whatever the configuration of the marketing channel, it coordinates the flow of goods and services (and the legal title to them), payments, information and promotional messages from the manufacturer to the final buyer.

Channel design and selection

In designing and selecting a marketing channel a firm has to take a number of major decisions. The first concerns the number of levels in the channel. The second is the number of intermediaries to be dealt with at each level, and the third concerns the selection of the individual organisations to be dealt with. It is also important to establish mechanisms for the monitoring, control and motivation of each component in the chain. This represents a complex set of decisions that lie beyond the scope of this text. Nevertheless, it is possible to outline briefly some of the factors that will influence the design of optimal channels.

Customer's characteristics will be a major influence. If buyers are very widely dispersed and buy small amounts very frequently, as in the case of convenience goods, then relatively long channels will be needed because the creation of direct links between the manufacturer and thousands of customers would be prohibitively expensive. On the other hand, if there are few buyers who purchase infrequently, more direct marketing will be appropriate.

Product and company characteristics will be important. If the product is highly complex and customised to individual buyers' requirements (asset specificity), it will require close links between manufacturer and buyer which will be difficult to maintain down multi-level channels. Products that involve high transport costs will require a channel configuration that minimises those costs through bulk transport. Perishable products require speed and the minimisation of handling. All of these factors may be important in channel design. Similarly, the company's size, financial resources and the range of its product mix will determine the balance between in-house channel activities and those that are handled by independent organisations.

Intermediary characteristics will also have an influence. A firm's own sales employees will provide a substantial selling effort to each client contacted, as they are solely concerned with selling their own company's products. Sales representatives, in contrast, will provide a less intensive sales effort as they will be selling the products of a number of companies. On the other hand, an independent sales agent may cost less per sales contact as their costs are spread across a number of clients. Anderson (1985) used transaction costs analysis to examine this decision, noting that if there is a high degree of asset specificity involved in selling, firms will prefer to use their own employees.

Individual intermediaries will each have strengths and weaknesses with respect to the effectiveness and cost with which they can carry out the various different channel functions, which will affect optimal channel design. It should also be remembered from Chapter 11 that 'buyer power' is an important determinant of the nature of competition in an industry, to be taken into account when considering how best to build competitive advantage.

This last point makes it clear that competitive conditions and corporate strategy will also be determinants of optimal channel selection. Channel activities are an aspect of competition between firms, just like pricing and promotion. The extent of the firm's direct involvement in the marketing channel is an aspect of its scope, which is one of the key features of corporate strategy. The form of the marketing channel will also be influenced by the firm's choice of 'generic strategy' (see Chapter 18). If the business is aiming to compete through cost leadership, a very different channel configuration will be required to that which will be suitable if the aim is to focus or differentiate.

Finally, it is clear that the *economic and legal environment* will affect channel choice. If economic conditions are generally depressed, there will be advantage in using 'stripped-down' marketing channels that deliver the product to the final buyer at least cost with the minimum of inessential services added. In more prosperous times and places, the buyer may seek additional services that can be used to add value to the product. The law, especially that on competition (see Chapter 20), may place restrictions on channel designs which are seen to restrict competition or to create monopoly power.

To summarise, it can be seen that the design and implementation of appropriate marketing channels is an important and potentially complex component in the establishment of competitive advantage. As many of the determinants of the optimal configuration are subject to change, a successful firm needs to keep them under constant review and to modify the configuration with respect to levels, participants and management control whenever necessary.

The location decision

While 'place' in the marketing mix is usually interpreted to mean the route by which the product reaches the final buyer, firms also have to consider the physical and geographical location of their production, distribution and administrative facilities. Selection of an optimal location is influenced by three major factors, namely:

1. The impact of location on costs.
2. Proximity to the market.
3. Government policy.

The impact of location on costs

If the cost and quality of inputs, or their availability, varies from place to place, that will give firms an incentive to locate in the lowest cost location, other things being equal. For some inputs, like capital, there is very little variation in cost from place to place, even at the global level, and they have little influence on firms' location decisions. For some other resources, like power, there are important differences from one country to another but relatively small differences within the same national economy, in which case only global location decisions will be affected. For most industries, the inputs whose costs may vary with location are labour and raw materials. As these are naturally less mobile from place to place (and almost completely immobile from one country to another), market forces do not completely eliminate locational differentials, providing incentives for firms to move towards lower cost sites.

Differences in relative labour costs are therefore one determinant of the location decision. As wages are considerably lower in mainland China than in Hong Kong, for instance, many Hong Kong companies have moved their labour-intensive activities into China, in order to maintain cost leadership in a way that would be impossible if the activities were kept in Hong Kong. Computer companies, having produced the early versions of their machines in relatively high wage economies, have shifted the manufacture of mass-produced, technologically mature machines to the Far East, where labour costs are low. At the global level, differences in labour costs remain a major determinant of the optimal location. Within an individual national economy differences in labour costs from region to region tend to be smaller, but they may still be sufficient to have an appreciable impact on costs.

The importance of raw materials as a factor determining location is more problematical. While there are a number of obvious examples where the availability of raw materials virtually dictates the location of an activity, like coal-mining or steel production, the improvement of transportation systems and the fact that in many industries raw materials account for smaller proportions of total cost, mean that industrial activity has become less tied to the sources of such materials. As a result firms have become more free to choose locations on other criteria.

Another factor that may influence the cost of operating in different locations is the presence or absence of *agglomeration economies*, which are a form of external economies of scale. If a group of firms in the same industry, or involved in similar types of activity, are located in close proximity to each other, they may be able to secure cost savings which are available to them all, but could not be exploited by a single firm. Such savings could arise from a number of sources. Local educational institutions could specialise in the types of course needed by the industry. Local management consultants could develop specialist expertise. The transport infrastructure could be developed to suit the special needs of the industry, and the agglomeration of firms with similar requirements could produce a pool of workers and managers with the skills needed, thereby smooth-ing the workings of the local labour market. Such agglomeration economies are difficult to quantify, and have to be set against the costs of congestion which can arise if a large number of firms attempt to locate themselves close together. Nevertheless, it may be a significant phenomenon. In the case of 'Silicon Valley' in the United States, for instance, it has been shown that a large number of high technology firms chose to be located together in California, not only because the climate is very pleasant, but also because the area already had a high con-centration of similar firms and related academic institutions which provided a source of highly skilled staff, and the new entrepreneurs, which the industry needed in order to develop.

While cost minimisation may drive some activities to particular locations it is important to recall that managers may have their own preferences which will form an important input into the location decision. If a location is regarded as particularly desirable, like California in the United States, or the South-east in the United Kingdom, that location may be chosen in preference to one invol-ving lower costs.

The pull of the market

While the relative cost of resources is one factor determining location, another is proximity to the market. In part this is a question of the relative costs of transporting raw materials in comparison with the cost of transporting the final product. If the raw material can be transported more cheaply than the final product then profit-seeking behaviour will drive activities closer to the market and further away from the raw material. However, closeness to the market may also provide other advantages through better market intelligence, less extended marketing channels and closer liaison with buyers, allowing for a more rapid and flexible response to changing market needs. There may also be economies to be had through locating after-sales service and maintenance activities along-side production facilities.

Government policy

Government policy may affect the location of industry in two major ways. In the first place, at national level, governments may impose tariffs on imports or other restrictions on trade. In that case, a firm that seeks to exploit a particular market will be forced to locate production within it. Japanese motor companies, for instance, seeking to circumvent restrictions on their sales into the European market, established production and assembly facilities in Europe in order to allow them to exploit the single European market of 320 million consumers which came into force at the end of 1992. When Britain first entered the European Economic Community there was an influx of American foreign direct investment, seeking to use a country with a common language as a base from which to develop the wider European market.

Within national economies governments may attempt to alter the location of industry in order to secure a more equitable distribution of income and employment, and in order to reduce the costs of congestion. This is attempted in a number of ways. Foremost among them is the provision of financial incentives which can reduce the costs of operating in some locations, thereby making them more attractive than they would be if market forces operated without any government intervention.

Technology development

Invention, innovation and science

In the elementary model of the firm, the starting point on the supply side is the existence of a production function, which represents a given state of technology that is exogenously determined. While this is useful for the analysis of the short-run problems facing the firm, it abstracts away from innovation and technological development which lie at the heart of the process of competition (see Chapter 20 for further discussion). It is important, therefore, to devote some attention to the process of technological change.

Schumpeter (1954) drew a useful distinction between *invention* and *innovation*. An invention is an idea, a sketch or a model for some new or improved device, product, process or system. Inventions do not necessarily, or usually, lead to an innovation, which is accomplished only when the first commercial transaction takes place involving the application of the invention. Innovation therefore involves making the connection between a new technical achievement and a potential market.

Innovations may be divided into *product innovations*, which introduce new or improved products, and *process innovations*, which change the way in which existing products are produced. Such new developments may arise from a number of sources. One of the earliest observers, Adam Smith (1776), identified three major sources of innovation:

1. *Worker innovation* – where those intimately involved in the production process identify improvements that may be made.
2. *The capital goods sector* – where product innovations in the sector become process innovations for other sectors.
3. *Science* – where specialist workers trained in scientific principles identify the inventions on which innovations may be based.

Freeman (1974) argued that 'science' has been increasingly important as the major source of invention and innovation in the twentieth century. The scientists who are responsible for innovations may be located in a number of different organisational situations. At one extreme there is the 'lone inventor', working on their own projects without direction from any firm or corporate body. At the other extreme there are workers in the research, development and design departments of large corporations, working on projects with commercial objectives set by the company. In between these extremes there are research workers in educational institutions and specialised research establishments whose work may be placed anywhere on a broad spectrum from the highly applied, for which there are known and immediate applications, to the most fundamental, for which there are currently no known commercial applications.

Innovation, firm size and competitive structure

One of the most important debates in the field of innovation concerns the extent to which technological progress has become the province of the largest firms and their R&D departments. Some observers, following Schumpeter (1954), have suggested that the very largest firms, and those having substantial market power, tend to dominate the introduction of innovations. They have the financial resources needed to fund risky projects and their market share allows them to reap the returns on any new products or processes that they may introduce. However, the evidence on the issue is mixed. A number of studies have found that employment in R&D tends to increase with firm size but the relationship is weak and highly variable across industries and there is little evidence to suggest that R&D intensity, measured by the ratio of research workers to total employment, has a strong positive relationship with firm size. Similar findings have resulted from the examination of research outputs, in the form of patents, instead of research inputs.

If market power is measured by the level of concentration it might be expected, on the 'Schumpeterian hypothesis', that more concentrated industries would be more research intensive. Again, however, the evidence suggests that there is no such simple relationship. If the evidence does reveal any pattern it would appear that, for both firm size and the level of concentration, research intensity at first increases from small size and low levels of concentration but then peaks and goes on to decline as very high levels of firm size and of concentration are reached. The pattern varies very widely across industries which has led many observers to attribute the variation in technological effort to the intrinsic differences in the *technological opportunities* facing industries. In the 'science-based' industries like aerospace, electronics and chemicals there is a higher level of innovative activity, regardless of firm size and market structure, than in other sectors with more established technologies like textiles, clothing, furniture and food.

The sources of invention

Just as there has been debate over the impact of firm size and industry concentration on the rate of innovation, so there has been argument over the relative importance of the 'lone inventor' or the small entrepreneurial firm in comparison with the R&D departments of large corporations. While it is certainly true that a large proportion of the inputs to the innovation process are concentrated in large firms, and that the same applies to research outputs if measured by indicators like patents filed, that does not mean to say that the most important innovations have stemmed from inventions within large firms. A classic study by Jewkes *et al.* (1969) found that a majority of major innovations in the first half of the twentieth century stemmed from inventions by outside inventors. Studies of the steel industry, petroleum refining and the chemical giant Du Pont all showed that important innovations tended to stem from developments outside the dominant firms in the industry. On the other hand, if the distinction between invention and innovation is remembered, it is equally clear that the vast bulk of the development work required to turn an invention into an innovation is carried out within large or medium-sized firms, and not by lone inventors or technology-based small firms. The overall judgement on the issue would seem to be that 'corporate laboratories are responsible for a minority of major and a majority of minor or derivative inventions' (Devine *et al.* 1979, p. 221).

Given that the level of uncertainty is higher as the invention in question is more basic or fundamental, it seems hardly surprising that profit-seeking firms concentrate their technological efforts on those parts of the process that are closest to the point of commercial application.

Technology development and corporate strategy

Porter (1985) defines technology strategy as 'a firm's approach to the development and use of technology'. Such a strategy has to address three major issues. The first concerns the nature of the technologies that should be developed, which in turn is related to the firm's overall corporate strategy (see Chapter 18). If the firm's generic strategy is one of cost leadership then both product and process-related R&D should be directed towards that end. Product improvement can be geared towards cost reduction and process development can attempt to take maximum advantage of the various cost drivers in order to lower the cost at which buyers' needs can be met. The introduction of flexible manufacturing systems (FMSs), for instance, often reduces the minimum efficient scale of production, allowing the firm to produce smaller batches at low cost, and to compete on cost in much smaller market segments than was previously the case.

If the firm is attempting to compete through differentiation, its technological effort will be aimed at a different set of objectives. Both product and process development need to be geared towards enhancing the quality and features of the product, including the response time to orders and product 'deliverability'.

In a similar way a firm that is competing through a strategy of focus needs to direct its technological effort towards the specific requirements of the target sector it is aiming at, either by reducing costs for the targeted buyers or by differentiating in ways that are specific to that segment and less well met by more broadly targeted competitors.

Once a firm has established the objectives of its technology development programme it then has to consider whether it wishes to be a technological leader, being the first to introduce new technologies, or whether it would prefer to be a follower. The balance of advantage between the two approaches depends to a great extent upon the advantages and disadvantages associated with being a first-mover. If, for instance, there are pronounced learning effects in an industry, or if buyers can be 'locked in' to the first supplier of a commodity through the effect of switching costs, or if the first-mover secures access to the most favourable market niches and distribution channels, then it will pay to be a first-mover and technological leader. On the other hand, the first-mover often has to bear costs that can be avoided by followers, there is no certainty that its effort will be successful in either technological or commercial terms, and the lead gained may be very short-lived if the new technology can be cheaply and easily imitated by rivals. The choice between leadership and followership depends upon the competitive circumstances in which the firm finds itself, and the behaviour of its rivals.

If a firm decides to be a technological follower, then it has to consider how it will gain access to new technologies developed by leaders. In some cases, publicly available information concerning the new technology will be sufficient for the firm to develop its own variant of an innovation, while avoiding the full costs of reproducing the leader's own R&D effort. If this is not possible, followers may have to consider licensing-in new technologies from leaders. While this will be a viable route in some circumstances, it has to be remembered that licensed-in technology may still require development work and technological leaders will be anxious not to damage their own lead by licensing-out major components of their technological advantage. It may, therefore, only be possible to license-in relatively outdated technology, or technology owned by firms that have no major interest in the market in question.

Illustration   Marketing expenditures – an analysis of their determinants

One of the most important questions that marketing managers have to resolve concerns the amount they should spend on marketing and the distribution of that spending across different activities. Buzzell and Farris (1976) attempted to provide insights into this issue, in the particular context of industrial marketing, by carrying out a statistical analysis of the relationship between measures of marketing spend and a range of other variables.

The objective of the study was 'to identify those factors which best explain variations in marketing cost among industrial manufacturing businesses'. The dependent variables chosen were as follows:

- total marketing expense as a percentage of sales
- advertising and sales promotion as a percentage of sales
- advertising as a percentage of sales
- sales force expenditure as a percentage of sales.

For each of these variables a series of multiple regressions were carried out, using a set of independent variables which could be divided into five general categories. These were:

1. *Product variables* – purchase frequency, high amount of purchase, low importance of purchase to user, produced to order, importance of service to the product, R&D intensity.
2. *Market factors* – market growth, recent entry of competitors, stage of the product life cycle.
3. *Customer factors* – concentration of users, high number of users, low number of customers, percentage of individual users, percentage of institutional users.
4. *Strategy factors* – percentage of sales through wholesalers, percentage of sales direct to end users, common distribution channels, regional sales only.
5. *Cost structure and market share factors* – trading margin, relative price, percentage of sales within the company, market share.

The regressions were run for three separate industrial groupings – capital goods, raw materials and components, and supply businesses – using data drawn from the PIMS (profit impact of marketing strategies) database. The results showed that variations in the independent variables accounted for between 30 per cent and 45 per cent of the variation in the marketing effort variables, which is statistically significant though a weaker relationship than that found in consumer goods industries.

The detailed findings with respect to the signs and significance of the coefficients on the individual independent variables are summarised in Table 16.1.

Table 16.1 Summary of regression results (signs and significance of coefficients)

	Materials		Components		Supplies				Capital goods			
	(A+P)/S	A/S	SF/S	Mktg/S	(A+P)/S	A/S	SF/S	Mktg/S	(A+P)/S	A/S	SF/S	Mktg/S
Product variables												
High purchase frequency	n.s	*	***	***								
Low purchase frequency										*		
High amount of purchase	–*	–*	n.s	–***					**	n.s	–***	–***
Low importance to user						+**	+***	+**				
Produced to order	n.s	n.s	+***	+*					–***	–*		–**
Service importance	n.s	n.s	+***	+*					+***	+*	+*	+**
R&D intensity	+***	+**	+*	+***	n.s	+**	n.s	n.s	+***	n.s	+**	+***
Market factors												
Market growth	n.s	+**	n.s	+*								
Entry of competitors					+***	+*				+**	–**	–**
Decline stage									–*	–*		
Customer factors												
User concentration	+**	+*	n.s	+*								
High number of users	+**	+**	+***	+***								
Low number of users	n.s	n.s	–***	–***								
% Individual users					+***	+***	–*	n.s				
% Institutional users					+***	n.s	n.s	n.s				
Strategy users												
% Through wholesale	+***	+***	n.s	+**								
% Direct to users									–***	–***	+*	n.s
Common channels	n.s	+*	–**	–**					n.s	n.s	+***	–**
Regional only					–**	n.s	+***	+**	n.s	n.s	+**	n.s
Shared programs	–*	n.s	n.s	n.s	n.s	n.s	n.s	n.s	–***	n.s	–*	–***
Cost structure/market share												
Trading margin	+***	+***	+***	+***	+**	n.s	+***	+***	+***	+**	+***	+***
Relative price					+*	+*	n.s	+*				
% Internal sales					n.s	–*	–*	n.s				
Market share	+**	n.s	–***	–***	n.s	n.s	–***	–***	n.s	n.s	–*	–*

Key:
n.s not significant
*   significant at 10 per cent level
**   significant at 5 per cent level
*** significant at 1 per cent level
Blank cells indicate variables that were considered inappropriate for the industry in question

Adapted from: Buzzell and Farris (1976).

▶

Examination of the table suggests a number of features. In the first place, the signs show a remarkable consistency across the different dependent variables, suggesting that the different measures of marketing effort are related to the same independent variables in the same way. Scanning the results for common patterns suggests that marketing intensity for industrial products is positively related to the following:

- the importance of service
- R&D intensity
- high number of users
- percentage of sales through wholesalers
- trading margins

and negatively related to:

- high frequency of purchase
- high amount of purchase
- percentage direct to users
- market share.

The authors note that regressions never prove causality, merely association, so that the direction of causality could often be in either direction. However, they also note that many of the factors that are significantly related to the marketing effort lie outside the control of marketing managers, being inherent in the nature of the industry. The results suggest, then, that the degree of latitude that management has over its marketing costs may be more limited than is often supposed. They also suggest that the equations fitted might be used by the managers of new businesses to set the general level of their marketing budgets.

References and further reading

E. Anderson, 'The Salesperson as Outside Agent or Employee: A Transaction Cost Analysis', *Marketing Science*, vol. 4, Summer 1985, pp. 234–54.

R.D. Buzzell and P.W. Farris, *Industrial Marketing Costs: An Analysis of Variations in Manufacturers' Marketing Expenditures*, Marketing Science Institute Report No. 76–118, Cambridge, MA, 1976.

J. Cable, 'Market Structure, Advertising Policy and Inter-Market Differences in Advertising Intensity', in K. Cowling (ed.) *Market Structure and Corporate Behaviour*, London, Gray Mills, 1972.

W.S. Comanor and T.A. Wilson, 'Advertising, Market Structure and Performance', *Review of Economics and Statistics*, vol. 49, 1967, pp. 423–40.

K. Corfman and D. Lehmann, 'The Prisoners' Dilemma and the Role of Information in Setting Advertising Budgets', *Journal of Advertising*, Vol. 23, no. 2, June 1994, pp. 35–48.

H. Davies, 'The Designers' Perspective: Managing Design in the UK', *Journal of General Management*, Vol. 14, No. 4, Summer 1989, pp. 77–87.

P.J. Devine, N. Lee, R.M. Jones and W.J. Tyson, *An Introduction to Industrial Economics*, London, George Allen and Unwin, 1979.

N. Dorward, *The Pricing Decision*, London, Harper and Row, 1987.

C. Freeman, *The Economics of Industrial Innovation*, Harmondsworth, Penguin, 1974.

D.F. Greer, 'Advertising and Market Concentration', *Southern Economic Journal*, 1971.

J. Jewkes, D. Sawers and R. Stillerman, *The Sources of Innovation*, London, Macmillan, 1969.

P. Kotler and G. Armstrong, *Principles of Marketing*, London, Prentice Hall, 1998.

D. Lee, 'The Impact of Firms' Risk-taking Attitudes on Advertising Budgets', *Journal of Business Research*, vol. 31, October/November 1994, pp. 227–46.

J. Lynch and G. Hooley, 'Increasing Sophistication in Advertising Budget Setting', *Journal of Advertising Research*, vol. 30, no. 1, February/March 1990, pp. 67–75.

E.J. McCarthy, *Basic Marketing: A Managerial Approach*, Homewood, IL, Richard D. Irwin, 1960.

L. Mitchell, 'An Examination of Methods of Setting Advertising Budgets: Practice and the Literature', *European Journal of Marketing*, vol. 27, no. 5, 1993, pp. 5–21.

D. Needham, *The Economics of Industrial Structure, Conduct and Performance*, London, Holt, Rinehart and Winston, 1978.

M. Nerlove and K.J. Arrow, 'Optimal Advertising Policy Under Dynamic Conditions', *Economica*, N.S. 29, 1962, pp. 129–42.

N. Piercy, 'Advertising Budgeting: Process and Structure as Explanatory Variables', *Journal of Advertising*, vol. 16, no. 2, 1987, pp. 34–40.

M. Porter, *Competitive Advantage*, New York, Free Press, 1985.

A. Rasmussen, 'The Determination of Marketing Expenditure', *Journal of Marketing*, 1952.

W.D. Reekie, *The Economics of Advertising*, London, Macmillan, 1981.

R. Schmalensee, *The Economics of Advertising*, Amsterdam, North-Holland, 1972.

R. Schmalensee, 'Brand Loyalty and Barriers to Entry', *Southern Economic Journal*, vol. 40, 1974, pp. 579–88.

J.A. Schumpeter, *Capitalism, Socialism and Democracy*, London, Allen and Unwin, 1954.

J.L. Simon, 'Are There Economies of Scale in Advertising?', *Journal of Advertising Research*, 1965.

A. Smith, *The Wealth of Nations*, 1776.

C.J. Sutton, 'Advertising, Concentration and Competition', *Economic Journal*, vol. 84, 1974, pp. 56–69.

J. Sutton, *Sunk Costs and Market Structure: Price Competition, Advertising and the Evolution of Concentration*, Cambridge, MA, MIT Press, 1996.

J. Sutton, *Technology and Market Structure: Theory and History*, Cambridge, MA, MIT Press, 1999.

N. Synodinos, C. Keown and L. Jacobs, 'Transnational Advertising Practices: A Survey of Leading Brand Advertisers in Fifteen Countries', *Journal of Advertising Research*, vol. 29, no. 2, April/May 1989, pp. 43–50.

M. Waterson, *Economic Theory of the Industry*, Cambridge, Cambridge University Press, 1984.

Self-test questions

1. List the four 'Ps' that make up the marketing mix and identify the components of each one.

2. Consider how price and advertising elasticities are likely to vary over the different stages of the product life cycle and consider the implications for the level of advertising in each stage.

3. How would you describe the following in the case of a micro-computer?

   (a) the core product
   (b) the tangible product
   (c) the augmented product

4. List the advantages of branding.

5. How would you expect the marketing channels to vary between:
   (a) machine tools?
   (b) breakfast cereals?

Essay question

Identify two different rules-of-thumb that are commonly used to set advertising and promotion budgets and consider how they may help or hinder a firm in maximising its profits.

17 Investment decisions and the cost of capital

This chapter examines the issues raised by long-term decisions concerning the firm's investment in capital goods and equipment. The first part examines the techniques that are available for the appraisal of investment projects and the second part addresses the problem of estimating the cost of capital for a firm taking such investment decisions.

Investment appraisal

The purposes and types of investment decision

The fundamental purpose of investment spending is to meet the firm's objectives, which were discussed in Chapters 2 and 4. As the central objective is taken to be profit, expressed in the long run as the maximisation of shareholders' wealth, then the usual starting point for any discussion of investment appraisal is the assumption that the ultimate objective of investment spending is to maximise the value of the firm.

Firms aiming for profit may invest in new capital goods and equipment for a number of reasons. First, they may invest in order to *replace existing equipment*, either because it is worn out and cannot be used any longer, or because new equipment will allow cost savings to be secured. Second, investment may be needed *in support of expansion*, either of existing products and markets or into new products and markets. Third, investment may be required for reasons of *compliance with government regulations*. Whatever the immediate objective of an investment project, its fundamental purpose is to enhance the value of the firm and the techniques used to appraise them are essentially the same.

Investment decisions may also be divided into three categories according to the nature of the decision that has to be taken. The first type of decision is simply to *accept or reject* an individual project. The second involves *ranking projects* and the third involves *choosing between mutually exclusive alternatives*. Each of these will be considered below.

Simple techniques for the appraisal of investments

The simplest criterion for the appraisal of investments is the *pay-back method*. That involves estimating the net profit generated by an investment project and calculating the number of years required to repay the initial investment. The results can be used in a number of ways. If the aim is simply to accept or reject projects then the firm's management may choose a cut-off period of (say) three or five years and accept any project that pays back its investment over that period. If the aim is to rank projects, those with the shortest pay-back period are ranked highest, while the choice between mutually exclusive projects is made by selecting that with the shortest pay-back period.

The pay-back method is widely used in practice because it is seen as a means of avoiding risk and ensuring that firms maintain adequate liquidity. However, it has a number of shortcomings. The first is that it ignores any returns that accrue after the pay-back period, which is itself chosen arbitrarily. For example, if two projects have identical pay-back periods of three years, but one of them yields very substantial profits in year four and the other yields nothing, the technique will not discriminate between them. The second shortcoming is that the pattern of returns within the pay-back period is ignored. Hence, a project that yields very rapid returns within the first two years of a five-year pay-back period will be rated in exactly the same way as a project that pays back nothing until a full repayment in the fifth year. The third, and most fundamental, weakness of the pay-back method is that it ignores the time-value of money. The returns to an investment are simply added together year on year until they equal the original outlay, at which point the pay-back period is established. As a result an amount of money that accrues in year one of a project carries exactly the same weight as the same amount of money accruing in year three, provided that the cut-off point for acceptance of a project is three years or more. However, this ignores the fact that money accruing in year one could be invested with interest for two years and be worth more than the original amount by year three.

The second simple technique for the appraisal of investment projects is the *accounting rate of return* method. This can take a number of different forms but consists essentially of estimating the net profits accruing to a project over its life, calculating an average profit per year, and then expressing that profit as a percentage of the initial outlay, to give an estimated rate of return. Projects are then accepted if the rate of return calculated exceeds the firm's minimum requirement and projects are ranked by their rate of return.

The accounting rate of return method suffers from the same fundamental flaw as the pay-back criterion in that it ignores the time-value of money. If this is to be properly taken into account, more sophisticated methods have to be employed.

The principle of discounting

If the time-value of money is to be taken into account, some method has to be found of assigning appropriate and comparable values to amounts of money accruing at different times. This is done through a method known as discounting, which is closely associated with the arithmetic of compound interest.

If £1,000 is invested at an interest rate of 'r' per year, payable in a single instalment at the end of each year, then the value of the sum invested at different times is as shown in Table 17.1.

Table 17.1 The value of £1,000 invested at interest rate 'r'

Time	0	After 1 year	After 2 years	After n years
Value	1,000	$1000(1 + r)$	$1000(1 + r)^2$	$1000(1 + r)^n$

The value of £1,000 invested at interest rate 10%

Time	0	After 1 year	After 2 years	After n years
Value	1,000	1,100	1,210	$1000(1.1)^n$

In a fundamental sense, each of the figures in the rows above are the equivalent of each other. At an interest rate of 10 per cent, £1,000 today is the equivalent of £1,100 in one year's time, or £1,210 in two years' time.

When calculating compound interest, the value of a sum of money available today is being projected forwards in order to measure its value in future periods. However, exactly the same arithmetic may be used in reverse, in order to estimate the present value of a sum of money that does not accrue until some future period. If £1,210 is expected to accrue after two years, and the interest rate is 10 per cent, the present value of that £1,210 may be said to equal £1,000. The figure of £1,210 has been discounted by dividing it by 1.21, which is $(1 + r)^2$ where $r = 0.1$.

In general, the present value of a sum of money X which does not accrue until 'n' periods into the future is given by the formula:

$$\text{Present value} = \frac{X}{(1 + r)^n}$$

The amount X is said to have been discounted 'n' times at interest rate 'r'.

Net present values

As the essence of investment appraisal lies in comparing the values of outlays and returns that accrue at different times, the principle of discounting provides a solution to the basic problem involved. The stream of returns accruing over the lifetime of a project may be reduced to a single figure, representing the present value of that stream of returns. This can be compared with the cost of the project, and the project can be accepted if the present value of the returns exceeds the present value of the costs. To put it more formally, an investment project should be accepted if it has a *net present value (NPV)* which is greater than zero, where NPV is given by the formula:

$$NPV = -K + \frac{NCF_1}{(1 + r)} + \frac{NCF_2}{(1 + r)^2} + \ldots + \frac{NCF_n}{(1 + r)^n}$$

where:

K = capital cost, accruing in full at the beginning of the project
$NCF_{1,2,\ldots n}$ = net cash flows arising from the project in years 1 to n
r = the opportunity cost of capital

If the analysis is to be carried out correctly both the net cash flows (NCFs) and the opportunity cost of capital must be properly calculated. The figures for NCF in each year should include *all and only incremental cash flows after taxes*. Costs that the firm would incur even if it did not carry out the project should not be included, because they are not incremental and are therefore irrelevant. Depreciation should not be included directly as a cost because it is not an outflow of cash, although the impact of depreciation on the firm's tax position should be taken into account as that will affect outflows of cash arising from the project. If the equipment is to be sold for scrap at the end of the project's life, the revenue from that sale should be included in the NCF for the last period.

The calculation of an appropriate figure for the opportunity cost of capital is a complex issue which takes up the second part of this chapter. At this stage it suffices to note that when a firm puts resources into an investment project it is foregoing the opportunity to put those resources to an alternative use, and the figure for the cost of capital used in the NPV calculation should reflect the return that could be earned in that alternative use. This in turn depends upon rates of return in financial markets in general, and upon the riskiness of the projects involved.

Internal rate of return

A closely related technique for investment appraisal, which has its roots in the same discounting technique, involves calculating the *internal rate of return (IRR)* on a project. Instead of setting a value for 'r' in the NPV equation set out above, 'r' is treated as an unknown and NPV is set equal to zero. The IRR is then the value for 'r' that satisfies the equation. In other words, the IRR is the discount rate that renders the NPV of the project equal to zero. If this method is used to appraise investments, the criterion for acceptance is that the IRR on a project should exceed the opportunity cost of capital to the firm.

Precise direct calculation of the IRR may be mathematically difficult, as the NPV equation is a complex polynomial. However, the result may be arrived at through *linear interpolation*, which involves a series of steps. First, a guess is made with respect to the value of the IRR, and the NPV associated with that guess calculated. If the resulting NPV is positive, the guess is known to have been too low, and if the NPV is negative the guess is known to have been too high. A second guess is then made, with the intention of 'overshooting' the target. If the first guess yielded a positive NPV, the second guess should be higher by an amount that is expected to yield a negative NPV. The correct result is then known to lie between the two guesses and can be approximated by graphing the two results on NPV and IRR, connecting them with a straight line and reading off the rate of return at which NPV equals zero. Figure 17.1 illustrates this procedure for a simple example.

In most situations the IRR method will yield the same results as the NPV method, as might be expected. However, there are a number of problems that can arise. The NPV formula is a polynomial and the mathematics of polynomials implies that there may be more than one value for the IRR that satisfies the equation. This will not happen in the most common type of investment project, where

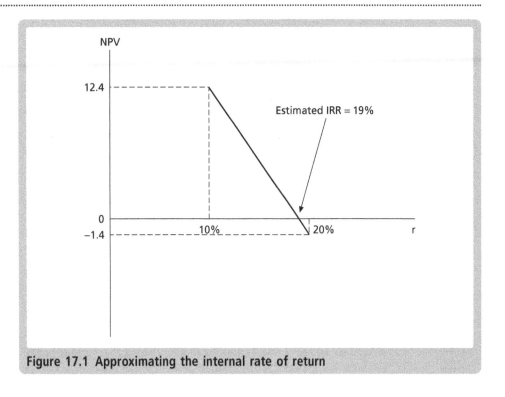

Figure 17.1 Approximating the internal rate of return

an outflow of cash at the beginning of the project is followed by inflows until the end of the project, because in that situation the sign of the cash flows changes only once, from negative to positive, which dictates that there can be only one positive value for 'r' (see Lorie and Savage 1955 and Pratt and Hammond 1979 for more detailed expositions). However, if the sign of the cash flows changes more than once in the life of the project, there may be multiple solutions to the equation and hence multiple IRRs, which lead to a number of difficulties. In the first place, having found one solution to the equation, the decision-maker may not be aware that others exist and may take a decision on the basis of incomplete information. Second, if there are multiple solutions, neither of them may be an appropriate figure for the appraisal of the investment project. Further exploration of these problems may be found in most financial management textbooks (van Horne 1980, Franks *et al.* 1985, Copeland and Weston 1983), which show that it is possible to adapt the IRR rule in order to cope with these difficulties. However, as Brealey and Myers (1984, p. 75) note of such adaptations: 'Not only are they inadequate, they are unnecessary, for the simple solution is to use net present value.'

Choosing between mutually exclusive investment projects

The problem of multiple solutions is not the only difficulty that arises with the IRR approach. It can also be misleading in situations where a firm is attempting to choose between mutually exclusive investment opportunities. Table 17.2 sets out the basic data for two alternative projects, A and B.

Table 17.2 Cash flows, NPV and IRR for two mutually exclusive projects

	Year				NPV at 15%	IRR
	0	1	2	3		
Project A cash flow	−100,000	45,000	55,000	50,000	13,630	22.8%
Project B cash flow	−60,000	30,000	37,000	28,000	12,496	27.2%

As the table shows, the two criteria give different results. If NPV is adopted, using a discount rate of 15 per cent, which is assumed to correspond to the actual opportunity cost of capital for the firm, then Project A is selected. On the other hand, Project B has a higher IRR and would be selected on that criterion.

The reason for this conflict can be better understood if the relationship between NPV and the discount rate is explored for each of the alternative projects. Figure 17.2 shows the NPV of each project for every discount rate between zero and 30 per cent.

As the cash flows associated with both projects are 'well behaved', with no sign changes, the relationships between NPV and the discount rate are relatively simple. In both cases, the NPV declines as the discount rate rises, and in both cases there is only one IRR, where the discount rate equates the NPV to zero. However, the curves for the two projects have different slopes and intersect the axes at different points, while they intersect each other at a discount rate of approximately 18 per cent. For discount rates below 18 per cent, Project A has the higher NPV, while for discount rates above 18 per cent, the ranking is reversed and Project B has the higher value.

The conflict between the two different criteria can now be explained in a number of ways. The simplest is to note that when evaluating an investment

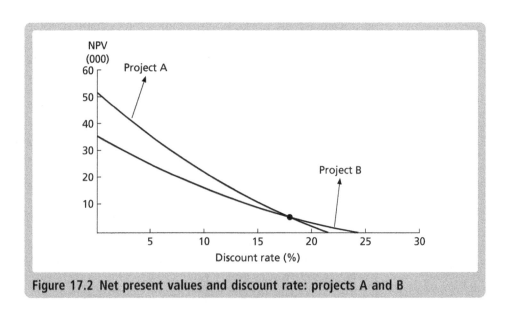

Figure 17.2 Net present values and discount rate: projects A and B

the key issue is that the firm should take account of the opportunity cost of using its funds for the project. In the example used in Table 17.2 the opportunity cost of capital is 15 per cent, and that figure is of central importance. If the two projects are compared using present values at this discount rate, Project A is seen to be superior to Project B and that is the correct evaluation. The figures for IRR show the cost of capital at which NPV would equal zero and they would be appropriate if the cost of capital were actually at that level. However, as the cost of capital is actually 15 per cent and not 22.8 per cent or 27.2 per cent, the IRR is essentially providing information with respect to a hypothetical situation in comparison with NPV, which is evaluating the actual situation.

Another way to explain essentially the same point is to note that the difference between the two criteria may be seen as involving two different assumptions with respect to the rate of return at which returns from the project may be reinvested. The NPV rule compares projects by using the actual opportunity cost of capital as the discount rate and is thereby implicitly assuming that shareholders can reinvest their money at that rate, which is correct. The IRR rule, in contrast, assumes that shareholders can reinvest at the IRR, which is in contradiction to the known fact that the opportunity cost of capital takes a different value.

The IRR method is inferior to NPV for a third reason: it is expressed in terms of a percentage rate of return, rather than in terms of a project's absolute effect on the wealth of shareholders. If a firm has a mutually exclusive choice between an investment costing £1, with an IRR of 100 per cent and an investment of £1,000,000, with an IRR of 15 per cent, the IRR criterion will dictate that the firm choose the investment of £1, whereas the investment of £1,000,000 will have a much more beneficial effect upon the wealth of the shareholders, which is the basic objective being pursued.

The conclusion with respect to the IRR rule, then, is that it has serious deficiencies in comparison with NPV and should only be used if careful thought is given to its shortcomings. Given that the IRR method is also more laborious than NPV it may be legitimate to wonder why financial management textbooks devote so much space to considering it. The usual argument put forward is that companies often use IRR, being intuitively more comfortable with the concept of a percentage rate of return, than with an absolute net present value, and that its disadvantages therefore need to be spelt out in detail.

Investment appraisal with capital rationing

If the aim of the firm is to maximise the wealth of its shareholders it should accept every investment project that has a positive net present value. However, there may be situations where this is not appropriate. If projects are mutually exclusive, the choice of one precludes investment in the others. A more general problem arises where a firm faces a number of projects that are not mutually exclusive but which cannot all be accepted because the amount of capital available is limited. Clearly, this situation could not arise in a world of absolutely perfect capital markets because it would be possible to borrow funds at the opportunity cost of capital to finance any project with a positive NPV at that cost of

Table 17.3 Project selection under capital rationing

Project	Initial outlay	NPV	PI
A	2,000	1,000	1.5
B	1,000	400	1.4
C	2,000	700	1.35
D	1,000	250	1.25
E	1,000	200	1.2

capital. Nevertheless, capital markets are not perfect and in practice firms may have to decide how to distribute the limited investment funds available among the opportunities that face them. They have to solve the problem of *capital rationing*.

Firms faced with this problem may a use variety of techniques in the attempt to find a solution. The simplest, which is referred to in most textbooks, involves the use of the *profitability index*, defined as follows:

$$PI = \frac{(NPV + I)}{I} \qquad \text{where:}$$

$$PI = \text{Profitability index}$$
$$NPV = \text{Net present value of the project}$$
$$I = \text{Initial investment outlay}$$

The PI provides a measure of the present value per pound of initial investment outlay and may be used to rank projects by giving the highest priority to those having the highest PI. A solution to the capital rationing problem may then be found by sequentially accepting projects, beginning with those having the highest PI, until the capital constraint is reached. However, while this procedure 'can lead to a reasonable approximation for allocating funds that are limited in a single period' (Franks *et al.* 1985, p. 105) it is easily shown that the method may fail to identify the optimal grouping of projects, even in a relatively simple example. Table 17.3, for instance, shows an example adapted from Reekie and Crook (1982), showing five possible projects being considered by a firm facing an investment constraint of £4,000.

If the PI criterion is applied as suggested, projects A and B will be selected first, yielding a present value of £1,400, and unused capital of £1,000. As that £1,000 is insufficient to fund project C, the firm then selects project D, using up all of the capital available and securing a total NPV of £1,650. However, simple inspection of the table shows that the firm could have secured an NPV of £1,700 by choosing projects A and C.

If the situation is more complex, with a large number of possible projects, capital spending constraints in every year and the possibility of using cash flows generated from earlier projects to fund later ones, some more formal method of solving the problem is needed.

One possibility is to use *linear programming*. If we assume that each of the available projects is perfectly divisible, so that it is possible to carry out a proportion of each project, then the NPV for the total package of projects is given by the sum of the NPVs for the individual projects, each weighted by the proportion of the project that is undertaken. For the projects listed in Table 17.3 above, the total NPV for the package of projects, or part-projects, is given by the following equation:

$$NPV = 1,000X_A + 400X_B + 700X_C + 250X_D + 200X_E$$

where:

$X_{A,B,C,D,E}$ = proportion of each project undertaken

The problem is to maximise NPV, subject to the constraint that the total outlay in the first year does not exceed £4,000, and that the proportion of each project accepted must be between 0 and 1. If there are other constraints, perhaps on capital outflows in years other than the first, these can also be added in. The result is a linear programming problem which can be solved using standard techniques.

The obvious weakness of the linear programming approach to the capital rationing problem is that it assumes that every project is infinitely divisible. While this may be true in some cases and it may be possible to invest in 45 per cent of a project to install 1,000 square feet of floor space, for instance, most projects are either completely indivisible or only divisible into discrete 'chunks'. In this case, the solution to the linear programming problem may be impossible to implement and the technique has little value.

If fractions of projects are not feasible, decision-makers may have recourse to an alternative mathematical technique known as *integer programming*, in which the solutions are constrained to take the values of 0 or 1. This technique offers some assistance with the capital rationing problem, but a detailed examination of it lies outside the scope of this text. (See Franks *et al.* 1985, pp. 112–14 for a more extended treatment and further references on this issue.)

The cost of capital

The first part of this chapter has shown that the NPV technique is the most appropriate way to evaluate investment projects and that use of the method requires the identification of a discount rate that is to be used in the calculations. However, little has been said about that discount rate, apart from noting that it should represent the opportunity cost of capital to the firm taking the investment decision.

The second part of this chapter considers how to measure the cost of capital, a topic that raises a number of fundamental issues and has led to a number of hotly contested academic debates.

The weighted average cost of capital

A firm may raise the funds for investment projects in a number of ways, including loans, debentures, retained earnings and equity issues. Each of these may take a variety of forms in detail and each is subject to different accounting, legal and tax procedures, which render a detailed and comprehensive discussion impossibly complex. For simplicity, just two different types of capital will be considered. The first is *debt* and the second is *equity*.

The key characteristics of debt are that those who hold it have first call on any operating profits earned by the firm and they bear the risk of default. The key characteristics of equity are that its holders are the owners of the firm, they are the beneficiaries of any increase in the firm's value, they have the right to any profits made after interest payments have been made and they bear the equity risks associated with the variability of the firm's profits.

The cost of debt and the cost of equity need to be defined. The cost of debt consists of the interest rate that must be paid on new debt issues, adjusted for taxation. As the interest on debt is deductible for the purpose of corporate taxation, its cost to the firm is reduced so that the actual cost is given by the formula:

After-tax cost of debt = (Interest rate) × (1 − Tax rate)

The *cost of equity* may be defined as the rate of return that shareholders require on the ordinary shares of the firm in order to persuade them to continue holding those shares, or more formally, 'the minimum rate of return that the company must earn on the equity-financed portion of its investments in order to leave unchanged the market price of its stock' (van Horne 1980, p. 221). The calculation of this rate of return is a complex issue, which is examined in detail below. For the current purpose it is enough to note that it depends upon conditions in the capital market and the degree of risk attached to the operations of the individual firm.

If a firm is entirely financed through equity, it is clear that the cost of capital is the same as the cost of equity. At the other extreme, it is clear that for a firm that is financed entirely by debt, the cost of capital is the cost of debt. What is much more difficult, and contentious, is the calculation of the cost of capital for the vast majority of firms which are financed through a mixture of debt and equity, and the impact of *leverage* or the *gearing ratio* on that cost.

The traditional view of the weighted average cost of capital

The starting point for the debate is to be found in the 'traditional' view of the issue which states that the cost of capital is given by a weighted average of the cost of equity and the cost of debt, as given by the formula for the weighted average cost of capital (WACC):

WACC = (After-tax cost of debt × Proportion of debt financing)

+ (Cost of equity × Proportion of equity financing)

Both the cost of debt and the cost of equity are held to vary with the gearing ratio, as shown in Figure 17.3 below, which also shows the WACC.

As the figure shows, the cost of debt is held to be lower than the cost of equity, whatever the gearing ratio, because the holders of debt have the first call on the firm's profits. They are therefore exposed to less risk and will accept a lower level of return. As the gearing ratio increases, the cost of debt increases because the higher the level of debt, the higher the probability that the firm's profits are

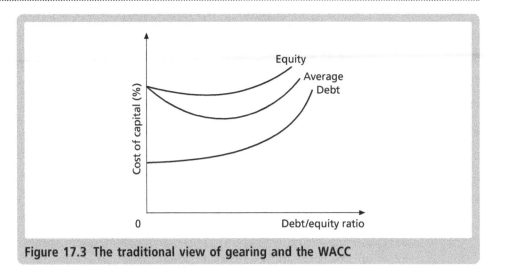

Figure 17.3 The traditional view of gearing and the WACC

insufficient to service the debt and make repayments when due. At higher levels of gearing, the holders of debt are exposed to greater risk and therefore require a higher rate of return.

Similar considerations apply to the cost of equity. It begins at a higher level than the cost of debt because equity-holders bear a greater degree of risk, and it rises with the gearing ratio because a higher level of debt increases the risk to equity holders as well as to debt holders. The cost of debt and the cost of equity curves are therefore as shown in Figure 17.3. The WACC that corresponds to these curves is U-shaped, as shown, because as the gearing ratio rises from a low level, the increasing proportion of cheaper debt lowers the average until it reaches the minimum point, after which the increasing risk attached to greater proportions of debt raise the WACC.

The Modigliani–Miller proposition

The traditional view of the relationship between the gearing ratio and the cost of capital has been challenged by Modigliani and Miller (M–M) in perhaps the most famous article ever written on the theory of finance (Modigliani and Miller 1958). According to M–M, the cost of capital is not affected by the gearing ratio, as it is constant and equal to the cost of equity in a firm that has no debt. That result appears so unlikely at first sight that it requires closer attention.

The starting point for the M–M proposition lies in a very rigorous set of assumptions. These are:

- there are no taxes
- the capital market is efficient and competitive
- there are no transactions costs
- there are no costs associated with bankruptcy
- shareholders can borrow on the same terms as corporations
- the cost of debt is constant, whatever the level of gearing.

If these assumptions hold, the total market value of two firms that are identical except for their levels of gearing must be the same, and their WACCs must be the same. If they were not, investors could improve their position by 'arbitrage', selling the shares of one and buying shares in the other, which would alter the relative prices of shares until the WACCs become equal. The level of gearing is therefore irrelevant to the WACC and the value of the firm.

This very striking proposition requires further explanation if it is to be fully understood. The total market value of a firm is given by the following equation:

$V = D + E$ where:

> V = total market value
> E = market value of equity
> D = market value of debt

The market value of equity (E) is equal to the present value of the future stream of dividends, and the market value of debt (D) is equal to the present value of future interest and redemption payments. If we assume for simplicity that annual dividends are constant in perpetuity and debt consists of irredeemable debentures, and we also assume that all of the firm's net cash flow is paid out as interest or dividends, then the firm's net cash flow (Y) is a constant and is given by the equation:

$Y = d + I = [E \cdot K_e + D \cdot K_d]$ where:

> Y = net cash flow
> d = dividends paid
> I = interest paid
> K_e = cost of equity capital
> K_d = cost of debt capital

The total value of the firm (V) is linked to the net cash flow (Y) and the WACC (K_o) in the following way:

$$V = \frac{Y}{K_o} \quad \text{or} \quad K_o = \frac{Y}{V}$$

If we now take two firms that have the same net cash flows and the same level of business risk, it is possible to show that they must have the same WACC and the same market value, even if they have different levels of gearing.

Consider an example of two firms, adapted from Lumby (1982). Firm A is financed entirely through equity in the form of 20,000 ordinary shares. Firm B is financed through £4,000 of debt at a cost of 4 per cent, plus equity in the form of 6,000 ordinary shares. Both firms have an annual net cash flow of £1,000, all of which is distributed in either dividends or interest payments. Table 17.4 shows how the WACC and share prices will be determined for firm A, which the stock market values at £10,000.

As the table shows, the WACC is equal to the cost of equity, at 10 per cent, the value of the firm is £10,000 and the share price is 50 pence.

A similar exercise can be carried out for firm B. This has the same risk attached as firm A and the same net cash flow, but is partly funded through debt. In

Table 17.4 WACC for firm A: an all-equity firm

Annual net cash flow (Y)	1000
Market value of debt (D)	0
Cost of debt capital (K_d)	0
Annual interest flow ($D \cdot K_d$)	0
Dividends paid ($d = Y - D \cdot K_d$)	1000
Market value of equity (E)	10,000
Cost of equity ($K_e = d/E$)	0.10
Total market value (V)	10,000
WACC ($K_o = Y/V$)	0.10
No. of shares (N)	20,000
Price of shares (E/N)	0.50

Table 17.5 WACC for firm B: partly debt funded

Annual net cash flow (Y)	1000
Market value of debt (D)	4000
Cost of debt capital (K_d)	0.04
Annual interest flow ($D \cdot K_d$)	160
Dividends paid ($d = Y - D \cdot K_d$)	840
Market value of equity (E)	7,000
Cost of equity ($K_e = d/E$)	0.12
Total market value (V)	11,000
WACC ($K_o = Y/V$)	0.091
No. of shares (N)	6,000
Price of shares (E/N)	1.167

contradiction to the M–M proposition, the stock market values the equity of firm B at £7,000, giving a total value for the firm of £11,000, compared with the £10,000 for firm A. The figures for B are shown in Table 17.5.

Because the market values firm B more highly, the WACC differs between A and B and the M–M proposition does not hold. However, the central argument in the M–M debate is that if such differences do arise they represent a short-term disequilibrium in which firm B's shares are overvalued. Shareholders can improve their financial position by selling shares in B and buying shares in A. But if B's shares are being sold and A's shares being bought, the price of B's shares must fall while the price of A's rise. This process must continue until the value of both firms is the same, and their WACC is the same, despite the difference in their gearing.

Continuing with the example, the figures set out in Tables 17.4 and 17.5 above can be used to show how this process of arbitrage takes place. If we take an individual who owns 60 shares in company B, that investor's holding is worth £70(60 × £1.167), it yields £8.40 per year, and it bears the level of financial risk associated with holding equity in a firm with a 4:7 gearing ratio. If the investor sells their holding for £70 and uses that money to buy shares in A, they can buy 140 shares yielding £7. However, they will also have altered the level of risk borne as their holdings are now in an ungeared firm. As the individual's

Table 17.6 Post-arbitrage WACCs and values: ungeared firm A, geared firm B

	A	B
Annual net cash flow (Y)	1,000	1,000
Market value of debt (D)	0	4,000
Cost of debt capital (K_d)	0	0.04
Annual interest flow ($D \cdot K_d$)	0	160
Dividends paid ($d = Y - D \cdot K_d$)	1,000	840
Market value of equity (E)	10,500	6,500
Cost of equity ($K_e = d/E$)	0.0952	0.1292
Total market value (V)	10,500	10,500
WACC ($K_o = Y/V$)	0.0952	0.0952
No. of shares (N)	10,000	6,000
Price of shares (E/N)	1.05	1.083

original position involved the risk associated with a 4:7 gearing, and as we need to compare like with like, the investor can re-establish that level of gearing and risk by borrowing £40, at the cost of debt, and spending that £40 on a further purchase of shares in A. The individual investor then has a 'home-grown' gearing ratio of 4:7, a holding of £110 worth of shares in A, which yields £11, and a liability for interest payments of £1.60, giving a net return of £9.40, compared with only £8.40 on the original investment in B.

Clearly, there is an incentive to all investors in company B to sell their holdings and purchase shares in company A, which will tend to reduce the price of B's shares and raise the value of A's. These incentives will continue to be in place until the total values of the two firms, and their WACCs, are the same. In Lumby's example used above, this will produce an eventual share price of £1.05 for firm A and £1.083 for firm B, at which point the data for each firm are as given in Table 17.6.

If the assumptions made by M–M are valid, the WACC is independent of the gearing ratio and is equal to the cost of equity in an ungeared firm. The relationship between the cost of debt, the cost of equity and the WACC is as given in Figure 17.4. The WACC is constant, the cost of debt is constant and the cost of equity increases in a linear fashion with the gearing ratio (see Lumby 1982, p. 135 for further details).

While the M–M proposition provides a rigorous approach to the cost of capital, and illustrates the weaknesses of the traditional approach, its assumptions are extremely restrictive and the conclusions change if they are relaxed. The existence of transactions costs will affect the process of reaching equilibrium, although exactly how is not clear. If individuals and corporations cannot borrow at the same cost and risk, then 'home-made' gearing cannot provide a perfect substitute for corporate gearing, and the arbitrage process will be impeded. If there are costs associated with bankruptcy then the higher probability of bankruptcy that is associated with a higher gearing ratio will mean that investors require a higher rate of return from more highly geared firms.

Perhaps the most important issue of all in practice concerns the M–M assumption that there are no corporate taxes, which is clearly unrealistic. If the existence

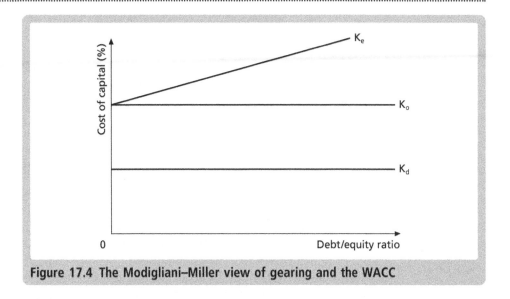

Figure 17.4 The Modigliani–Miller view of gearing and the WACC

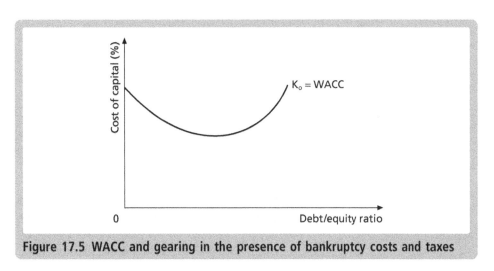

Figure 17.5 WACC and gearing in the presence of bankruptcy costs and taxes

of taxation is recognised, and the interest on debt is tax deductible, then a higher level of gearing allows the firm to increase its net cash flows. The market value of the firm increases as gearing increases, and the WACC declines. As a result, a firm seeking to maximise its total market value would have a capital structure consisting of 99.99 per cent debt and the minimum possible amount of equity. This is an uncomfortable result in many ways because while it is clearly more realistic to assume that taxes are present, the conclusion drawn as a result is not one that matches firms' real-world behaviour where very high gearing ratios are rarely observed. As a result, the debate remains unresolved. Perhaps the most satisfactory, though tentative, conclusion (van Horne 1980, p. 283; Lumby 1982, p. 152) is that the combined effects of bankruptcy costs and taxation lead to a WACC curve as shown in Figure 17.5.

As the figure shows, at low levels of gearing, WACC declines with higher gearing, due to the advantages of tax relief on debt interest. However, beyond some point, these advantages begin to be offset by the bankruptcy costs associated with higher gearing. At very high levels of gearing, the bankruptcy effect is more powerful than the tax effect and the WACC begins to rise. If this conclusion is valid, capital structure does have an effect upon the WACC and the M-M proposition no longer holds.

The cost of equity capital I: the dividend valuation approach

It has been noted above that the cost of equity capital (K_e) is the rate of return that the firm must earn on its equity in order to leave the market price of its stock unchanged. The estimation of that rate may be approached in two different ways, based upon the *dividend valuation model* or the *capital asset pricing model*, each of which merits brief consideration.

The dividend valuation approach to the cost of equity capital is based upon the relationship between dividends, market price and the expected return on an investment. As the market price of a firm's equity (E) is equal to the present value of the dividends it earns (d), discounted by the required rate of return (K_e), the value of a firm that produces an annual flow of dividends that is constant (i.e. 'd' is the value of a perpetuity) is given by the equation:

$$E = \frac{d}{K_e} \quad \text{which rearranges to give } K_e = \frac{d}{E}$$

This is a very simple method to use for the estimation of the cost of equity and is restricted to the case where dividends are constant over time. A more sophisticated version may be developed for the case where dividend growth is constant over time, rather than the dividend level.

If d_1 is the dividend payable at the end of the first year, and 'g' is the growth rate of dividends, the market value of equity is given by the DCF calculation:

$$E = \frac{d_1}{(1 - K_e)} + \frac{d_1(1 + g)}{(1 + K_e)^2} + \frac{d_1(1 + g)^2}{(1 + K_e)^3} \dots + \frac{d_1(1 + g)^{n-1}}{(1 + K_e)^n}$$

Simple algebraic manipulation of this equation (see Lumby 1982, p. 78) allows it to be rearranged as follows:

$$E = \frac{d_1}{K_e - g} \quad \text{or} \quad K_e = \frac{d_1}{E} + g$$

In order to make use of this formula, some estimate has to be made of the dividend growth rate 'g'. The simplest approach is to extrapolate the past rate of growth, adjusted in the light of any additional information which is available, or more sophisticated forecasting techniques might be preferred. Whichever method of estimation is chosen, the basic approach remains the same, using the present value of the expected future stream of dividends to establish the relationship between dividends, market price and the expected rate of return.

The cost of equity II: the capital asset pricing model

The dividend valuation approach makes no explicit reference to the degree of risk attached to the ownership of equity, being based entirely upon the future flow of benefits that it is expected to generate. An alternative approach, which places the valuation of risk at the heart of the analysis, is known as the *capital asset pricing model (CAPM)*. This has its basis in a relatively complex body of financial analysis, known as portfolio theory, which lies outside the scope of this text. Nevertheless, it is possible to outline the basic principles involved, leaving a fuller treatment to the financial management textbooks.

The starting point for a brief overview of the CAPM is to note that the required return on a risky security may be divided into two components. The first is the return that could be earned on a riskless security and the second is a premium in compensation for the risk involved. (It is generally assumed that investors are risk averse to some degree, and not risk lovers.)

The risk-free return depends upon general conditions in financial markets and may be reasonably approximated by the return on government bonds. The premium for risk which is to be applied for an individual firm is calculated by measuring the variability of the return on the firm's stock, and comparing it with the variability of the *market portfolio* of stocks, which reflects the variability of the stock market as a whole. This is encapsulated in a measure known as the *beta coefficient* for the individual stock. If the shares of a firm have a 'beta' that is greater than 1, investing in those shares is more risky than investing in the stock market as a whole. If the beta is less than 1, the shares are less risky than the market as a whole, and if beta equals 1, investing in the shares bears exactly the same risk as investing in the market as a whole. The expected return on a security is then given by the following equation:

$$K_e = R_F + b[K_M - R_F] \qquad \text{where:}$$

R_F = the return on a risk-free security
b = the 'beta' for the individual security
K_M = the return on the market portfolio of shares, representing the market as a whole

As the equation shows, if the security has a beta of 1, the expected return will be the same as that for the market as a whole. If beta is larger than 1, the return will be higher; if beta is less than 1 it will be lower, reflecting the lower level of risk associated with the individual security being assessed.

Clearly, the calculation of beta is of central importance to the application of the CAPM. It may be defined as the co-variance between the returns on a security and the returns to the market as a whole, divided by the variance of the returns to the market. Investment advisory services publish estimates of 'beta' for most stocks, which allow the CAPM to be used to calculate the cost of equity capital for the stock of most major companies.

Whether the CAPM is an entirely effective means of estimating the cost of equity capital remains a matter for debate and for empirical testing, which is extremely difficult. All of the returns referred to in the model are expected returns, which are not directly observable and may not be well approximated by historical returns. The market portfolio, whose returns and variability are central to the analysis, is very difficult to construct but should in principle contain every asset available to investors, including human capital, personal money and jewellery, and a whole range of assets that are non-marketable and whose returns cannot be directly observed. The empirical tests that have been carried out (see Copeland and Weston 1983, p. 207) suggest that the CAPM has some predictive value, but have also tended to find that low beta stocks earn more than the CAPM would predict, while high beta stocks earn less. Factors other than beta, like price/earnings ratios and firm size, also seem to have an influence on the rate of return, which reduces the usefulness of the CAPM equation which relies entirely upon beta as the determining variable.

Illustration   ## Investment appraisal – a worked example of NPV and IRR

The Wizzo Lollipop Company is considering the installation of a new production line, which will allow it to produce chocolate ice cream.

The initial investment required is estimated to be £1,000,000. The life of the new line is estimated to be five years and the marketing department estimates that initial sales revenue will be £1,000,000, rising at the rate of 10 per cent per year. The production department estimates that production of chocolate ice cream will incur fixed costs of £150,000 per year plus incremental variable costs of 50 pence for each £1 of sales revenue. Tax is chargeable at 40 per cent of profits, calculated as revenue minus costs, including depreciation. Wizzo uses the straight-line method to calculate depreciation over the five-year life of the equipment.

At the end of the project it is estimated that the equipment will be sold as scrap for £350,000. The cash flows from the project are shown in Table 17.7.

Table 17.7 Estimated cash flows

Year	1	2	3	4	5
Revenue	1,000,000	1,100,000	1,210,000	1,331,000	1,464,100
Variable costs	500,000	550,000	605,000	665,500	735,050
Fixed costs	150,000	150,000	150,000	150,000	150,000
Depreciation	200,000	200,000	200,000	200,000	200,000
Profit before tax	150,000	200,000	255,000	315,500	382,050
Income tax	60,000	80,000	102,000	126,200	152,820
Profit after tax	90,000	120,000	153,000	189,300	229,230
Plus depreciation	200,000	200,000	200,000	200,000	200,000
Revenue from sale of scrap					350,000
Net cash inflow	290,000	320,000	353,000	389,300	779,230

As Table 17.7 shows, depreciation is first deducted, in order to arrive at profits before tax, and then added back in, in order to calculate net cash inflow. This is because depreciation is not in itself a cash flow, but it affects cash flows because of its impact on the tax deducted.

If the cost of capital to Wizzo is 12 per cent, the net present value (NPV) of the chocolate ice cream project is given by the equation:

$$NPV = \frac{290{,}000}{(1 + 0.12)^1} + \frac{320{,}000}{(1 + 0.12)^2} + \frac{353{,}000}{(1 + 0.12)^3} + \frac{389{,}300}{(1 + 0.12)^4} + \frac{779{,}230}{(1 + 0.12)^5}$$
$$-1{,}000{,}000 = 466{,}193$$

At the given discount rate of 12 per cent, the project adds to the value of the firm, and should therefore be undertaken. If the discount rate had not been known, the firm may have preferred to use the internal rate of return (IRR) method, to evaluate the project. Most financial calculators allow this to be done directly, and there is a wide range of computer software that would carry out the task with ease. In the absence of such aids, or in order to have a better 'feel' for the project, the IRR could be estimated by making successive guesses and adjusting the estimate each time, in the light of the result.

Beginning with an estimate of 10 per cent gives an NPV in excess of £500,000, indicating clearly that the IRR is higher than 10 per cent. Recalculation for 20 per cent still gives a positive figure, of approximately £170,000, showing that the IRR is above 20 per cent. At 28 per cent the NPV calculation yields a negative result and at 24 per cent a positive one, indicating that this pair of estimates 'bracket' the true result. Confirmation with a calculator shows that the IRR is in fact 26.3 per cent.

In this example, calculation of the IRR raises no difficult mathematical problems because the sign of the cash flows changes only once and the solution is unique. When adopting the iterative approach to solving for IRR it should always be remembered that in complex cases there may be multiple solutions, which could be missed by this simple technique.

References and further reading

R. Brealey and S. Myers, *Principles of Corporate Finance*, London, McGraw-Hill, 1984.

T.E. Copeland and J.F. Weston, *Financial Theory and Corporate Policy*, Reading, MA, Addison-Wesley, 1983.

E.J. Douglas, *Managerial Economics*, Englewood Cliffs, NJ, Prentice Hall, 1979.

J.R. Franks, J.E. Broyles and W.T. Carleton, *Corporate Finance: Concepts and Applications*, Boston, Kent, 1985.

J.H. Lorie and L.J. Savage, 'Three Problems in Rationing Capital', *Journal of Business*, vol. 28, October 1955.

S. Lumby, *Investment Appraisal and Related Decisions*, Walton-on-Thames, Nelson, 1982.

F. Modigliani and M. Miller, 'The Cost of Capital, Corporation Finance and the Theory of Investment', *American Economic Review*, vol. 48, 1958, pp. 261–97.

J.W. Pratt and J.S. Hammond, 'Evaluating and Comparing Projects: Simple Detection of False Alarms', *Journal of Finance*, vol. 34, December 1979.

W.D. Reekie and J.N. Crook, *Managerial Economics*, Oxford, Philip Allan, 1982.

J. van Horne, *Financial Management and Policy*, Englewood Cliffs, NJ, Prentice Hall, 1980.

Self-test questions

1. Which of the following statements is true?

   (a) if there were no inflation it would not be necessary to discount the value of future cash flows in order to reach present values

   (b) discounting is necessary in order to recognise the time-value of money

   (c) depreciation, using the straight-line method, should be included when calculating cash flows for NPV analysis

2. Calculate the internal rate of return for the following stream of cash flows:

Year	0	1	2
Cash flow	−100	+100	+20

3. List three reasons for preferring net present value to the internal rate of return as a criterion for evaluating investment projects.

4. Name the mathematical technique that may be used to solve the problem of capital rationing:

   (a) when projects are perfectly divisible

   (b) when projects cannot be sub-divided

5. Write down the equations that determine the cost of equity capital according to:

   (a) the dividend valuation model

   (b) the capital asset pricing model

Exercise

'The Modigliani–Miller proposition undermines the traditional view that there is an optimal degree of gearing, but is itself undermined by the recognition of the impact of bankruptcy costs and taxation.' Explain this statement.

18 Economics and business strategy

As Rumelt *et al.* (1991, p. 26) confirm, 'economics and strategic management are not the same, in research or in practice'. Nevertheless, the two subjects bear an important relationship to each other and economics has made a significant contribution to the study of business strategy over the years. This chapter sets out some of the basic ideas that inform the analysis of strategy and examines the way in which economics has made a contribution to the development of the field.

Definitions of strategy

The term 'business strategy', sometimes rendered as 'strategic management' or 'business policy', is open to a wide range of interpretations. McMillan (1992, p. 3) traces the term back to its roots in the Greek word *strategos* which meant the leader of an army, and he defines strategy as 'a game plan; a specification of actions covering all possible eventualities'. That definition is helpful in the context of game theory but the implication that there is no strategy to study unless firms have specified all of their possible future actions is much too restrictive to characterise most of the work that has been done in the strategy field. Broader alternative interpretations of business strategy include:

- strategy as purposive action – the resource allocations that firms plan and implement in order to position themselves in markets and to compete with others
- strategy as the 'fit' between a firm's use of resources and its environment
- strategy as an ongoing, unplanned and 'unintended' process of interaction between the firm's internal structures and its environment.

While strategy itself is the focal concept, the literature is largely concerned with the interrelationships among four key sets of constructs:

1. *Strategy* – in its various interpretations.
2. *Structure* – the internal organisation of the firm.
3. *Environment* – the external circumstances in which the firm operates.
4. *Performance* – the outcomes achieved.

The sheer breadth of this research agenda allows many different academic disciplines to contribute, including organisation theory, sociology, psychology and political science, as well as economics. As a result the subject area is enormously rich and interesting but also somewhat inchoate. In order to render it manageable this chapter begins by examining the ways in which 'business performance' is interpreted in economics and in the strategy literature. It then goes on to consider how different schools of thought in economic analysis have contributed to the explanation of that performance.

The conceptualisation of business performance

Both economics and the analysis of business strategy are centrally concerned with the performance of firms and industries. In economics, however, there are two distinctly different levels at which performance may be measured. First, from a public policy perspective and for the economy as a whole, performance is interpreted in terms of economic efficiency, meaning both static efficiency (is price equal to marginal cost?) and dynamic efficiency (does innovation take place?). These are the central concerns of economic analysis, which focuses on whether society is functioning effectively in the production of social welfare. At the level of the individual firm it is generally assumed in economics that the objective is to maximise shareholder wealth. Hence performance is interpreted as financial performance and there is relatively little discussion of alternatives.

The strategy literature is not concerned with social welfare or the overall performance of the economic system, and attention is restricted to the performance of individual firms or sub-units within firms. However, the conceptualisation and operationalisation of performance is broader and can be more complex. Venkatraman and Ramanujam (1986) use Figure 18.1 to illustrate the different but overlapping domains of the performance construct.

As the figure shows, the narrowest conception of business performance is financial performance. From that perspective, the success of a business may be measured by its: market value; return on assets, equity, investment or sales; earnings per share; or *Tobin's* Q, which is the ratio of the market value of the firm to the replacement value of its assets (Lindberg and Ross 1981).

In economics the assumption that profit maximisation is the objective ensures that financial performance is the usual measure of success and that approach has also tended to be the most common in business strategy (Capon *et al.* 1996). However, the performance construct may be widened, first by extending it to include indicators of operational performance, such as market share, new product introduction, product quality, marketing effectiveness, value-added, efficiency/productivity and productivity growth. These additional indicators may either be interpreted as performance indicators in their own right, or as lower-level, intermediate 'success factors' which may lead to higher levels of financial performance.

The notion that there may be a hierarchy of performance variables has been taken further by Seashore and Yuchtman (1967). They propose that at the apex of the hierarchy there is the 'ultimate criterion' – 'some conception of the net output performance of the organisation over a long span of time in achieving its formal objectives, with optimum use of environmental resources and opportunities' (p. 378). They suggest that the ultimate criterion can probably never be measured, except possibly by historians, but that lesser performance criteria

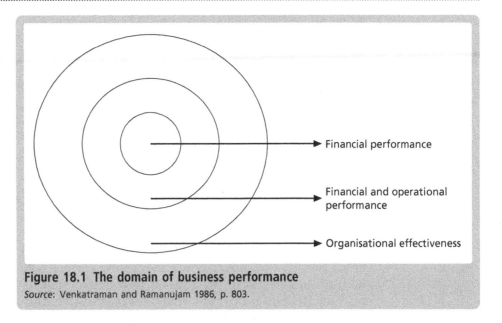

Figure 18.1 The domain of business performance
Source: Venkatraman and Ramanujam 1986, p. 803.

might be judged according to whether they contribute to its achievement. That suggests the idea of 'organisational effectiveness' as a broader and multi-dimensional set of measures that together constitute the broadest interpretation of performance. Seashore and Yuchtman (1967, p. 393) define the effectiveness of an organisation as 'its ability to exploit its environments in the acquisition of scarce and valued resources to sustain its functioning'. That also reflects the 'resource dependence' approach in organisational theory (Aldrich 1976, Pfeffer and Salancik 1978) which sees organisations as being dependent upon their environment for resources and engaged in a constant struggle to reduce that dependence.

If organisational effectiveness is adopted as the interpretation of performance, the firm is seen as a 'system' whose long-term viability is the object of concern. In that case 'system performance' can be measured using a wide variety of lower level concepts, including *long-term* profitability, productivity, the ability to generate innovation, the ability to attract and develop human resources and the ability to secure customer loyalty. 'System performance' may be contrasted with 'goal performance' where success or failure is interpreted not in terms of the ongoing viability of the organisation, but in terms of the achievement of more specific and limited goals. That distinction may be important when drawing the most appropriate conclusions in respect of performance. For example, there has been a great deal of interest in the performance of joint ventures in the last two decades and many studies have concluded that the 'failure rate' of joint ventures is very high because they are frequently terminated by their parents. From a 'system performance' perspective those joint ventures can properly be classified as failures because they were not viable in the longer term. However, from the parent company point of view, they may have been very successful in that they achieved the specific goals set for them and were therefore no longer needed. For instance, many joint ventures have been characterised as 'races to learn' where the host-country partner seeks to acquire technology from the foreign firm, while the foreign firm seeks to learn about the local market through its partner. If either partner succeeds in their goal, the purpose of the venture has been achieved, a high level of 'goal performance' is secured but the venture may then be terminated, having served its purpose.

Clearly, the analysis of business strategy allows a much broader and richer characterisation of business performance than that which is to be found in economic analysis. At the same time, the dominant emphasis has been on financial performance and in that respect the two disciplines retain a great deal in common with each other.

The determinants of business performance: SWOT analysis as an overall framework

One of the simplest and yet most useful approaches to strategy is known as SWOT analysis, which was originally put forward by Learned, Christiansen, Andrews and Guth in 1969. Their purpose was to help managers to develop their business strategies and hence their analysis was normative and prescriptive, unlike the economists' approach, which is positive and predictive. They interpreted strategy as purposive action and they advised managers to begin planning their strategy by carrying out a SWOT analysis. That involves two types of appraisal. The first is an internal appraisal of the firm's strengths (S) and weaknesses (W) and the second is an external appraisal of the opportunities (O) and threats (T) offered by the environment. That simple framework, emphasising the distinction between internal and external factors as determinants of performance, has remained unchanged as a basic organising principle for the field of strategic management (Barney 1995). However, as the analysis of business strategy has developed over the years, attention focused first on the external factors and then shifted to the internal factors, perhaps losing sight of the original SWOT insight, which was that both sets of factors need to be considered. Throughout the debate, inputs from economic analysis were important and they may be examined in turn.

Business strategy and the structure–conduct–performance approach to industrial organisation

The economic analysis of industrial organisation (IO) has been one of the most important influences on the analysis of business strategy in its attempts to explain business performance (Capon *et al.* 1996). For many years, the dominant form of IO was the 'structure–conduct–performance' (S–C–P) paradigm (Bain 1968, Scherer 1980). In that approach attention focused on explaining the average profitability of different industries. As conduct was left largely implicit, the S–C–P approach hypothesised that industry-level profitability was determined by industry structure. In particular it was suggested that market concentration, entry barriers and product differentiation would limit the degree or intensity of competition and hence have a positive effect on profitability. Given the public policy orientation of most economic analysis, the existence of supernormal profits was interpreted as poor performance in terms of allocative efficiency, rather than superior business performance.

As long as the S–C–P approach lay within the bounds of economics, it remained relatively formal and retained its public policy focus. The purpose of the analysis was to help governments identify the circumstances in which government intervention is needed in order to prevent the abuse of market power. However, that perspective changed dramatically when Porter (1980, 1981) brought S–C–P into the strategy domain in the form of the 'five forces' model of competitive structure, examined in Chapter 11. In that analysis the 'attractiveness' of a sector (most obviously interpreted as its potential profitability) is determined by: the intensity of competition among incumbents; the threat of entry; the threat of substitutes for the sector's output; the power of buyers; and the power of suppliers.

At first sight, the S–C–P approach seems to be in opposition to the whole purpose of the strategic management discipline. In strategic management a high level of profit is a desired outcome, representing good financial performance, whereas in S–C–P a high level of profit is an indication of undesirable market power. Furthermore, as the entire rationale for the study of strategic management rests on the idea that managers have the ability to determine performance through their actions, an analysis that attributes performance to the external environment seems to sit uncomfortably with the rest of the discipline.

In fact, however, the conflict between the industrial organisation and strategic management approaches was resolved by the ingenious way in which Porter (1980, 1981) used the ideas drawn from S–C–P. First, he simply switched the perspective from which the same basic ideas were viewed. Instead of seeing supernormal profits as the illicit earnings accruing to market power, he interpreted them as the legitimate reward earned by firms that position themselves as incumbents in attractive sectors. Second, he did not present the 'five forces' analysis simply as a means by which a fixed environment could be described and its consequences predicted, which is how the economists had approached it. Instead he presented it as an analytical tool through which managers could assess alternative environments and evaluate the tractability of their components. They could then use that knowledge either to choose more attractive environments in which to operate or to take action to improve the attractiveness of any given environment (by raising entry barriers or reducing rivalry among incumbents, for instance). Hence, the 'five forces' became a management tool, whereas the S–C–P approach was essentially a predictive device.

The introduction of the S–C–P paradigm into strategic management marked a major development in the analysis of strategy. The task of the senior executive was increasingly seen in terms of understanding the technologies and market conditions that shape the 'five forces' and then devising product and market positioning strategies and resource allocations that would best meet the opportunities and threats posed by the competitive structure of the environment. In order to assist in the latter task Porter (1985) later went beyond the S–C–P-derived techniques for analysing industries and competitors to suggest a taxonomy of 'generic strategies' – cost leadership, differentiation and focus – from which firms could choose in order to secure maximum profit from the environment in which they find themselves.

The assimilation of the S–C–P paradigm into strategic management led to a number of associated developments. As the unit of analysis was the industry, rather than the individual firm, one question that arose naturally was 'at what level of aggregation should the industry be defined?' From a theoretical point of view, an industry is a group of firms that compete with each other, so that the same question could be expressed as 'with whom do firms compete?' Traditional S–C–P analysis paid little attention to that question, perhaps because its empirical work drew heavily on secondary data from government sources, organised according to standard industrial classifications. However, strategy researchers noted that within an industry as defined by the standard classifications there are often sub-groups of firms whose members compete with and resemble each other more than they do members of other sub-groups. Hence, it was argued that the appropriate unit of analysis lay somewhere between the industry as defined in the classifications and the individual firms, in an aggregation of firms described as a 'strategic group' (McGee and Thomas 1986).

While the concept of the strategic group seems at first sight to be of relatively little consequence, simply dividing industries as conventionally defined into smaller units, Thomas and Pollock (1999, p. 130) point out that it 'turned the S–C–P paradigm on its head'. That was because each strategic group contained firms whose strategies were closer to each other than to members of other groups. But in that case the structure of an 'industry' – now interpreted as a set of strategic groups – depends upon the voluntaristic behaviour of the firms within it. Industry structure is not the exogenous, independent variable that determines conduct and performance. Instead it becomes an endogenous variable, dependent upon the ways in which firms choose similar or dissimilar strategies.

While the strategic group approach marked a significant move away from the S–C–P perspective, some of the most important ideas from that paradigm were carried over into the more disaggregated setting. Most important, Caves and Porter (1977) developed the idea of 'mobility barriers' which echoes that of entry barriers. Just as entry barriers exist to reduce the threat of entry into an industry, protecting the profits of incumbents, so do 'mobility barriers' make it more difficult for firms within an industry to move from one strategic group to another. If a high-performing strategic group can erect mobility barriers to prevent other firms from implementing the same strategy, they will similarly be able to protect and maintain their high level of performance.

The strategic group approach cast doubt upon the S–C–P paradigm by suggesting that the unit of analysis should be more disaggregated than the industry and that the appropriate grouping should consist of firms that have chosen to adopt similar strategies. However, other analysts of business strategy have gone further, arguing that the sources of supernormal profit do not lie in the 'common property of collections of firms, but arise instead from the unique endowments and actions of individual corporations or business units' (Rumelt 1991, p. 167). One way to explore that issue empirically is to examine and compare the dispersion of returns across industries and across firms within industries. If the S–C–P paradigm is correct then most of the variation in profitability will be found across industries, with relatively little dispersion within them. On the other hand, if the business strategy view is correct, variation among firms in the same industry will be greater than variation across industries. The first study to examine this issue was carried out by Schmalensee (1985) who estimated the variance components of profit rates in the United States, using the Federal Trade Commission's Line of Business (LB) data. The total variance in the rate of return on assets in the 1975 LB data was decomposed into three components – that due to industry effects, that due to corporate effects and that due to market share effects. The results were highly supportive of the S–C–P approach and industry-level analysis, in that they found no corporate effects while industry effects accounted for 20 per cent of the variance in business unit returns and 75 per cent of the variance in industry returns. However, Rumelt (1991) pointed out that Schmalensee's results arose from the analysis of a single year's data. As the theory is couched in terms of the variation in long-run returns it would be more appropriate to use data for a longer period and to distinguish between 'stable' effects and 'transient' effects. By reworking the data for the same sample for a longer period, 1974–77, Rumelt found that there were significant business unit effects (though not corporate effects) and that the variance among business effects was at least six times larger than the variance among industry effects. The Schmalensee results were in effect reversed and Rumelt concluded that 'work seeking to explain an important portion of the observed dispersion in business-unit profit rates must use the business unit . . . as the unit of analysis'.

Overall, those who take the business strategy view believe that 'industry does not matter much' and they seek explanations of performance at the business unit level. Hence a move in the strategy literature away from the S–C–P paradigm as the central explanation for performance and towards explanations based on differences between business units in the same industry. Nevertheless, a more recent empirical analysis by McGahan (1999), covering the financial performance of US corporations for 1981–94, suggests a more nuanced view. According to that analysis, firm effects were indeed more important for performance than industry effects, supporting the business strategy view. However, industry effects did exist and they were more predictable and sustainable than the firm-level effects. According to that analysis, there is still a place in the explanation of performance for the industry.

Resources, capabilities and competences

As the analysis of business strategy has turned away from the S–C–P industry-based approach, so it has turned towards an alternative approach that also has its roots in earlier work by economists. In 1959 Edith Penrose developed a view of the firm as 'both an administrative organisation and a collection of resources'. That basic insight led to what has become known as the 'resource-based perspective' (RBP) on the firm. The starting point for the RBP begins with two empirical generalisations (Foss 1997). The first of these is that there are systematic differences between firms, even in the same industry, in the extent to which they control resources that allow them to implement strategies. The second is that those differences are relatively stable over time. It is assumed, as in economics, that firms aim to earn supernormal profits and the fundamental assumption underlying the whole approach is that the differences in profitability across firms are caused by differences in their resource endowments, as opposed to differences in the environments they occupy. In terms of the simple SWOT analysis, the RBP switches attention away from the external opportunities and threats and towards the strengths and weaknesses.

The idea that performance is determined by a company's resources opens up a number of key questions, most notably 'what kind of resources lead to enhanced profitability?' Peteraf (1993) drew very directly upon economic thinking in order to identify four characteristics that a resource needs to possess if it is to allow the firm to earn 'rents'. The first characteristic is *heterogeneity* – a rent-yielding resource must be different from the resources owned by other firms because if all firms had access to the same resources (as in perfect competition) there could be no supernormal profits. The required heterogeneity could arise in a number of ways. It might stem from the kind of 'mobility barriers' identified by Caves and Porter (1977), which prevent firms from joining more successful strategic groups. Those in turn might arise from size advantages, irreversible commitments (Ghemawat 1991) or 'first-mover advantages' (Lieberman and Montgomery 1988).

The second characteristic that must be in place for a resource to provide a sustainable competitive advantage is that there must be *ex post limits to competition*. That is to say that after a firm has acquired a rent-yielding heterogeneous resource there must be some reason that more of that resource, or a close substitute for it, cannot be produced. RBP theorists have suggested two basic mechanisms that limit competitors' ability to reproduce an important resource, namely *imperfect imitability* and *imperfect substitutability*. There must be some *isolating mechanism* (Rumelt 1984) in place that preserves the resource owner from imitation, and hence the erosion of the rents earned. Various suggestions have been made with respect to those mechanisms. Rumelt (1987) identifies a considerable list, including:

- property rights like patents and copyrighted brand names
- time lags and learning effects
- information asymmetries
- buyer search and switching costs
- reputation
- channel crowding
- economies of scale in specialised assets.

Lippman and Rumelt (1982) point to *causal ambiguity*. If no one, including the resource owner themselves, knows exactly what the key resource is, it will be impossible for others to imitate. Clearly, Rumelt's 'isolating mechanisms', which prevent firms from imitating others' rent-yielding resources, are very similar to Caves and Porter's 'mobility barriers' which prevent firms from joining successful strategic groups, which in turn are similar to the S–C–P framework's 'entry barriers' which prevent firms from entering attractive industries. The debt to economic analysis is clear.

The third characteristic required of a resource if it is to provide long-term sustainable competitive advantage is that it should be *imperfectly mobile*. Dierickx and Cool (1989) point out that the resources that generate rents must be *non-tradeable*, at least for their full value. If they were tradeable and their full value could be realised through that trade it would be more sensible for a resource owner to sell the resource, and avoid the costs and risks of using it in product markets. Non-tradeability may arise in a number of ways. Most obviously, a resource may be specialised to a particular firm's needs, having no other use outside that firm. In that case the resource is perfectly immobile. Assets may be *co-specialised* (Teece 1986) in the sense that they need to be used in combination with some other asset, so that there is asset specificity as examined in Chapter 3. A resource may also be tradeable but less valuable to other firms because of switching costs (Montgomery and Wernerfelt 1988) or because the transactions costs associated with their transfer to a new owner are very high (Williamson 1975). Imperfectly mobile assets will remain available to the firm and will be the source of any monopoly rents earned.

The fourth condition required for a resource to provide a long-term competitive advantage is that there must be *limited ex ante competition*. That simply means that before the firm acquires the resource in question, there must have been limited competition to acquire it. If that were not the case then bidding for the resource would take its price to the level where no additional profit could be made from its acquisition. Indeed, the phenomenon of the 'winner's curse' (see Chapter 13) could mean that the firm that succeeds in purchasing the resource earns lower profits as a consequence of paying too high a price for it. As Barney (1986) emphasised, the return on a strategic resource depends upon the cost of acquiring and using it, as well as the revenues it generates.

Peteraf (1993) suggests that this analysis of the four characteristics required for resource-based competitive advantage can be used to carry out a more sophisticated version of the strengths and weaknesses component of SWOT analysis. By making an inventory of a firm's assets and then considering the extent to which each one has the required characteristics (or could be re-configured to have them) managers can identify ways in which a competitive advantage might be established or maintained.

While the resource-based approach appears to be entirely focused on the internal characteristics of the firm, and Porter (1994) has accused its proponents of being too 'introspective', that may be unfair. Foss (1997) points out that the heterogeneity requirement, limits to *ex ante* and *ex post* competition, and imperfect mobility all require consideration of specific other players in the firm's environment. Hence, the RBP does not forget the environment totally.

As it has become the dominant paradigm in the analysis of business strategy, so the RBP has generated a number of central themes. One such has been the tendency to interpret the most important resources as residing in the firm's stock of knowledge, especially the tacit (hence inimitable) knowledge that is built up over a long period of time and is often embodied in the firm's routines, structures and culture. Such resources are often referred to as 'competences' or 'capabilities', perhaps to distinguish them from more tangible assets. Hence Prahalad and Hamel (1990) define the 'core competence' of the corporation as 'the

collective learning of the organisation, especially how to co-ordinate diverse production skills and integrate multiple streams of technology'. Langlois (1991) refers
to 'capabilities' while Kogut and Zander (1992) examine the 'combinative capabilities' that allow a firm to synthesise current knowledge with newly acquired
knowledge and apply them together. While knowledge is clearly a key asset, and
one that exhibits all four key characteristics, it may be unnecessarily restrictive
to see it as the whole picture. As Collis and Montgomery (1995) point out,
in some circumstances physical assets like a good location or possession of a
transmission network may also be a key resource.

A second theme that has arisen in the RBP research programme is that of
diversification. That is very much a reflection of the literature's origins because
the central focus of Edith Penrose's seminal contribution in 1959 was to outline
a theory of the growth of the firm. The central idea outlined there was that a
firm grows and diversifies by making use of its basic competence in new areas.
A firm that has experience in making cookers may extend into refrigerators because
the competence acquired in making one can be used to make the other. Teece
(1980) extended that idea in order to examine the relationship between economies
of scope, transaction costs and the multi-product firm, concluding that economies
of scope alone cannot explain diversification. Only when the production of two
products requires the same non-transactable know-how or when two products
require a specialised and indivisible resource will diversification become necessary. Montgomery and Wernerfelt (1988) take up a similar idea, testing the hypothesis that firms diversify in order to use rent-yielding assets that they have in
excess supply and which cannot be sold or rented out in the marketplace.

The RBP draws very heavily on economic analysis. The basic idea that resources
are only valuable if they are different and not subject to *ex post* or *ex ante* competition is drawn by contrast with the perfectly competitive model where such
characteristics are not found. The terminology of 'rents' is drawn from economics
and the RBP makes explicit use of concepts like economies of scope, transactions
costs and specificity. Conner (1991) provides a detailed comparison of RBP with
five different schools of thought within industrial organisation economics,
ranging from the perfect competition model, through the S–C–P paradigm,
Schumpeter and the Chicago School to transaction cost economics. Her conclusion
is that RBP both incorporates and rejects at least one major element from each
of them, thereby reflecting a strong economics heritage while retaining fundamental differences.

Before moving on to consider two other aspects of the relationship between
economics and strategy it is worth commenting on the 'contest' between the
S–C–P approach to performance, which emphasises the impact of external factors
on performance, and the RBP approach, which emphasises internal factors.
Viewed from the original SWOT perspective, both of these approaches are
under-specified in the sense that they omit factors that have an important
bearing on the dependent variable. After an extensive 'meta-analysis' of the
factors determining financial performance, Capon *et al.* (1996) conclude that the
field has suffered from excessive fragmentation and partial explanation, and that
may be the main reason that it has proved difficult to identify and develop a
consistent picture of what is important in shaping business performance. They

argue strongly for the need to achieve greater inclusivity among explanations for performance and integration between them. Despite its simplicity, the SWOT framework encapsulates an important point, which is that the different forms of explanation for performance are not mutually exclusive and are best taken together as reinforcing rather than conflicting components of an explanation.

Business strategy and the 'new' industrial economics

It has been explained in Chapter 13 that the S–C–P approach to industrial economics has been supplanted by an approach based on game theory. Given the close relationship between industrial economics and the analysis of business strategy it might be expected that the game theory revolution would 'spill over' from one field into the other. Furthermore, the shift in emphasis in the strategy literature towards the importance of making commitments to firm-specific resources might be expected to reinforce that tendency. However, as Ghemawat (1997, p. 1) points out, that has not taken place to any great extent. There has been interest in two sets of game theory results. The first, as expected, are those concerning commitment, where game theory has shown that investing in specific assets and excess capacity may have an influence on the behaviour of rivals. The second concerns the importance of reputation effects, where customers may develop beliefs about a supplier that have value and are based upon the way in which the supplier has behaved in the past. Apart from these two narrow sets of propositions, game theory has not overwhelmed the strategy literature as it has done in industrial economics. Ghemawat (1997) found only fourteen game-theory-based articles in the five most cited management journals over the period 1975–94. Of those, four were published in the 'peak year' of 1991 and three of those were found in a special issue of the *Strategic Management Journal* which was focused on the relationship between economics and strategy. Rumelt *et al.* (1991), in one of those articles, suggest five reasons for this lack of interest. First, the phenomena that are of interest to strategists tend to lie outside the scope of game theory. Most notably, game theory says little about the causes of performance, except incidentally, being focused on the characteristics of Nash equilibria. Second, game theory focuses on whether interactive effects exist without paying much attention to their practical significance. Third, game theory models strategic phenomena in a very piecemeal and detailed way, taking a very small number of variables into account. Fourth, it may be unreasonable to expect that game-theoretic equilibria are actually reached because they assume such a high degree of rationality in the face of complex situations. Finally, in contradiction to the RBP, game theory places interaction between firms as the most important phenomenon, just at a time when the emphasis has shifted towards the examination of internal factors as the key determinants of performance.

In addition to these five objections to the use of game theory in the analysis of strategy Ghemawat (1997) suggests that a further key weakness lies in its limited ability to engage with the empirical evidence. The 'old' S–C–P approach to industrial organisation led to hundreds of empirical studies in both economics and strategy, many of them involving dozens of sectors and hundreds of firms.

Game theory, by contrast, has found it difficult to develop testable propositions that can be confronted by evidence from large samples. Ghemawat's proposed solution to this difficulty is to replace the large sample regression analyses that typify the S–C–P approach with detailed analyses of individual cases. However, as noted in Chapter 13, the result of that approach has tended to be that the usual process of research is reversed. Instead of using a theory to make predictions and then testing those predictions against the evidence, the evidence is considered first and an attempt is then made to find a convincing game-theoretical explanation. Unfortunately, there often turn out to be many such explanations and there are no obvious means by which they may be compared.

Illustration ## Resource-based competition in the bearings industry

The resource-based perspective (RBP) is often described and explained in rather abstract terms, which can make it difficult to understand. Collis (1991) provides a useful study of three firms in a specific industry, which helps to make the analysis more concrete.

The anti-friction bearings industry produces two generic types of bearing – ball and roller – and more than 200,000 different product variants. The auto industry is the largest single customer, purchasing around 30–40 per cent of the total and bearings are either produced to stock in standard designs, or customised to meet the specialised needs of individual customers. With so many different applications and so many different users, the industry offers ample room for the exercise of strategic choice. Collis examined the strategies adopted by three firms: Minebea of Japan, SKF of Sweden, and RHP of the United Kingdom.

Minebea was founded in 1951 by the charismatic and unorthodox Mr Takahashi. Its basic approach to competition has been to pursue a 'low-cost focus' strategy, producing a limited range of products at high volume and low cost. That strategy is made viable by the importance of learning effects and scale economies at the product-line level, so that by having product-line volumes at least 100 per cent larger than its rivals, much lower costs can be secured. In order to maintain that competitive advantage Minebea built dedicated and highly automated product lines which were vertically integrated from the input of bar steel to the output of complete bearings. Labour cost is still important in bearing production, so that the highest volume product lines were transferred to Thailand in order to take advantage of lower cost labour. In terms of core competences, Minebea sees its strength as lying in the process technology and production management needed for high quality, volume production of precision products. By focusing on the automation and coordination of high volume production, which requires careful attention to facilities layout and training, by employing large numbers of quality control workers and by implementing total quality management (TQM), the company is able to make more than 500 million bearings every year, to the highest standards of quality.

This core competence allowed Minebea to be successful in a market segment that would have been deemed highly 'unattractive' according to a 'five forces' type of economic analysis. When the company entered the bearings industry, it was dominated by US firms which had built up their experience during the Second World War. The Japanese market was highly undeveloped and Japanese quality levels were too low to compete in international competition. However, Chairman Takahashi's vision of Minebea's potential core competence led him to choose 'head-on' competition. That decision was essentially repeated and again vindicated when Minebea later entered the dynamic random access memory (DRAM) industry. In that sector, there were huge barriers to entry in the form of high capital costs, learning effects that yield 68 per cent cost savings, and an entrenched group of just four Japanese competitors. Intel and Motorola were exiting the industry and prices had fallen by 30 per cent in the year before Minebea's entry. Nevertheless, Mr Takahashi's company became the world leader in DRAM production within a few years, by using the same core competence in high quality, high volume precision production.

While the core competence was central to the firm's success, the resource-based perspective suggests that it can only lead to a long-term sustained advantage if the firm also has the 'organisational capability' to upgrade that competence continually. In the case of Minebea, Mr Takahashi emphasised that senior management should be completely familiar with the details of the technology in use. Manufacturing personnel were accorded high status and huge expenses were incurred in technological training, to the point where nearly 3,000 operatives from the Thai plants were flown to Japan for training, despite the fact that many were not expected to stay with the firm for more than a short time. The transfer of production to Thailand was widely viewed as a high-risk move by industry observers but the shift to less developed country production was handled so well that within four years labour productivity in Thailand was higher than in Japan.

The third element in the Collis (1991) analysis of Minebea's success concerns its 'administrative heritage' – the organisational culture and physical facilities that constrain the company's ability to implement actions. Mr Takahashi was widely known, and widely criticised within Japan, as a 'maverick'. He exerted personal control over the company, he ignored the Japanese tradition of working through consensus and he rewarded performance instead of seniority. By imprinting the organisation with his own personality he was able to overcome the (quite reasonable) objections to the move to Thailand and the entry into the DRAM industry, allowing the core competence to be used effectively.

The three elements of core competence, organisational capability and administrative heritage can be examined for two other, very different competitors in the same industry. SKF of Sweden, which was the overall world market leader, followed a strategy of broad differentiation, almost the opposite of the Minebea approach. By developing new products first, across a wide range of applications and over a long period of time, SKF developed a durable product market advantage. Because it has a broad scope it is able to share learning across product lines and spread the results of extensive R&D spending. Instead of producing more than 300,000 units of a single product per month, as does Minebea, SKF will custom-design a bearing for a particular need, deliver it on time and support it in use. In order to do that they need to be close to the market and they have production and marketing facilities in all major regions of the 'triad' economies – North America, Europe and Japan.

The core competence developed by SKF is reflected in its philosophy of 'the right bearing in the right place'. They have extensive technology development capability linked to sales and marketing expertise which effectively leverages well-developed customer relationships. The organisational capability to update that competence continually is linked to three different market segments. For sales to distributors the company has a state-of-the-art logistics and service network which gave customers direct access to its order and delivery system long before the Internet existed. For specialty customers SKF designers become a part of the product development team. For original equipment manufacturers (OEM), producing for other companies, CAD/CAM and just-in-time delivery provide the added value that they are willing to pay for.

A particularly interesting aspect of the SKF case is that the company's 'administrative heritage' was not a very positive contributor to its success. A decree in the US courts in 1953 forced the company to compete with its own subsidiary in that market and led to a culture of independence for plants in different locations. The allocation of products to facilities was driven by 'which plant volunteers to make which product', which prevented the optimisation of costs. When the five largest subsidiaries set up a joint R&D facility it was placed in Holland, because that country was 'neutral' in terms of company politics, having no SKF production facility. If it had been placed in the same country as a production facility, it would have been perceived as having been 'captured' by that division of SKF, leaving the others at a disadvantage.

The third company examined in the Collis (1991) study was RHP of the United Kingdom, which illustrates the problems that arise if inappropriate strategies, unsupported by core competences, organisational capabilities and an appropriate administrative heritage are attempted. RHP was created in 1969 by the UK government's Industrial Reorganisation Corporation, which merged the nation's three largest bearings firms. It first tried to become a broad-line low cost producer servicing the auto industry, but failed because its market share was too small. It then tried to diversify into electrical equipment and failed, again because its share was too small to support low cost competition. Only after 1987, when a management buy-in took place, did it begin to be successful as a focused differentiator in markets that were less price sensitive than the auto sector and more dependent upon technical expertise. RHP's core competence was engineering expertise which allowed it to respond quickly to customer demands for customised bearings. However, that was not helpful to it in the context of the auto industry because other firms had developed similar expertise. Core competences only have value in so far as they are unique in some respect. Only by moving into market segments where others did not have the same competence could RHP be successful.

As RHP was producing small batches of 5,000 units, and more than 200 different products per month (the Japanese market leader NSK was producing only six varieties per year), the key element in determining cost was set-up time rather than cycle time. The company therefore configured production facilities to allow flexible manufacturing and integrated its information systems to support that thrust. The introduction of activity-based costing systems allowed costs to be better tracked and allocated to products, and sales people were encouraged to narrow the customer base down to those purchasing the more profitable products. A system of highly intense incentives was put in place so that workers could increase their pay by up to 100 per cent with good performance, and the message was passed throughout the company that RHP would be the company that 'will make it'.

The administrative heritage of RHP reflected the influence of the capital market. Initial funding for the merger came from the government but there was pressure to replace that with private funding as soon as possible. That was achieved and satisfying the shareholders became the major concern of senior management. However, as the bearings industry is highly cyclical, senior management interpreted serving the shareholders to imply diversifying away from the bearings sector (the analysis of Chapters 3 and 4 suggests that might have been a self-serving rationalisation on the part of the managers, but they did behave in that way). The bearings division was used as a 'cash cow' to support unsuccessful acquisitions in the electrical industry and overseas production facilities were not acquired at a time when they were a necessity if overseas sales were to be made. Only when the management buy-in gave a new group of senior managers a direct equity stake in success was the perception that the owners required diversification away from the firm's core competence abandoned.

Overall Collis (1991) draws a number of conclusions from the bearings industry case. The first is that the economic analysis of strategy, based on the firm's product and market position, is complementary to the resource-based approach, which focuses on core competences and organisational capabilities. The initial insight embedded in the SWOT framework is supported. However, both approaches do need to be taken together. A strategy formulated entirely in terms of the optimal product and market configuration may be impossible to implement if the firm does not have appropriate competences. On the other hand, a strong set of competences may allow a firm to be successful in a competitive environment that economic analysis would reject as being highly unattractive for other firms. Minebea knowingly entered a highly unattractive market with high entry barriers and intense competition among incumbents because its founder correctly perceived that its core competence would allow it to be profitable in that sector. To secure superior performance, firms need to examine both the opportunities and threats in their external environment and their own internal strengths and weaknesses. Thirty years of analysing business strategy leads back to the starting point, albeit with a much enriched understanding of the details involved.

References and further reading

H. Aldrich, 'Resource Dependence and Inter-organizational Relations', *Administration and Society*, vol. 7, 1976, pp. 419–54.

J. Bain, *Industrial Organization*, New York, John Wiley, 1968.

J. Barney, 'Strategic Factor Markets: Expectations, Luck and Business Strategy', *Management Science*, vol. 32, no. 10, 1986, pp. 1231–41.

J. Barney, 'Looking Inside for Competitive Advantage', *Academy of Management Executive*, vol. 9, no. 4, November 1995, pp. 49–61.

N. Capon, J. Farley and S. Hoenig, *Towards an Integrative Explanation of Corporate Financial Performance*, London, Kluwer Press, 1996.

R. Caves and M. Porter, 'From Entry Barriers to Mobility Barriers', *Quarterly Journal of Economics*, vol. 91, 1977, pp. 241–6.

D. Collis, 'A Resource-based Analysis of Global Competition: The Case of the Bearings Industry', *Strategic Management Journal*, vol. 12, 1991, pp. 49–68.

D. Collis and C. Montgomery, 'Competing on Resources: Strategies in the 1990s', *Harvard Business Review*, vol. 73, July/August 1995, pp. 118–28.

K. Conner, 'A Historical Comparison of Resource-based Theory and Five Schools of Thought Within Industrial Organization Economics: Do We Have a New Theory of the Firm?' *Journal of Management*, vol. 17, no. 1, 1991, pp. 121–54.

I. Dierickx and K. Cool, 'Asset Stock Accumulation and the Sustainability of Competitive Advantage', *Management Science*, vol. 35, no. 12, 1989, pp. 1504–11.

N. Foss, *Resources, Firms and Strategies*, Oxford, Oxford University Press, 1997.

P. Ghemawat, *Commitment: The Dynamic of Strategy*, New York, Free Press, 1991.

P. Ghemawat, *Games Businesses Play: Cases and Models*, Cambridge, MA, MIT Press, 1997.

B. Kogut and U. Zander, 'Knowledge of the Firm, Combinative Capabilities and the Replication of Technology', *Organization Science*, vol. 3, 1992, pp. 383–97.

R. Langlois, 'Transaction-cost Economics in Real Time', *Industrial and Corporate Change*, vol. 1, no. 1, 1991, pp. 99–127.

E. Learned, C. Christiansen, K. Andrews and W. Guth, *Business Policy*, Homewood, IL, Irwin, 1969.

M. Lieberman and D. Montgomery, 'First-Mover Advantages', *Strategic Management Journal*, vol. 9, 1988, pp. 41–58.

E. Lindberg and S. Ross, 'Tobin's q Ratio and Industrial Organization', *Journal of Business*, January 1981, pp. 1–32.

S. Lippman and R. Rumelt, 'Uncertain Imitability: An Analysis of Interfirm Differences Under Competition', *Bell Journal of Economics*, vol. 13, 1982, pp. 418–38.

A. McGahan, 'The Performance of US Corporations: 1981–94', *Journal of Industrial Economics*, vol. XLVII, no. 4, 1999, pp. 373–98.

J. McGee and H. Thomas, 'Strategic Groups Theory, Research and Taxonomy', *Strategic Management Journal*, vol. 7, 1986, pp. 141–60.

J. McMillan, *Games, Strategies and Managers*, Oxford, Oxford University Press, 1992.

C. Montgomery and B. Wernerfelt, 'Diversification, Ricardian Rents and Tobin's q', *RAND Journal of Economics*, vol. 19, no. 4, 1988, pp. 623–32.

E. Penrose, *The Theory of the Growth of the Firm*, London, Oxford University Press, 1959.

M. Peteraf, 'The Cornerstone of Competitive Advantage: A Resource-Based View', *Strategic Management Journal*, vol. 14, 1993, pp. 179–219.

J. Pfeffer and G. Salancik, *The External Control of Organizations: A Resource Dependence Perspective*, New York, Harper and Row, 1978.

M. Porter, *Competitive Strategy*, New York, Free Press, 1980.

M. Porter, 'The Contributions of Industrial Organization to Strategic Management', *Academy of Management Review*, vol. 6, 1981, pp. 609–20.

M. Porter, *Competitive Advantage: Creating and Sustaining Superior Performance*, New York, Free Press, 1985.

M. Porter, 'Toward a Dynamic Theory of Strategy', in R. Rumelt, D. Schendel and D. Teece (eds) *Fundamental Issues in Strategy*, Boston, Harvard Business School Press, 1994.

C. Prahalad and G. Hamel, 'The Core Competence of the Corporation', *Harvard Business Review*, May/June 1990, pp. 79–91.

R. Rumelt, 'Towards A Strategic Theory of the Firm', in B. Lamb (ed.) *Competitive Strategic Management*, Englewood Cliffs, NJ, Prentice Hall, 1984.

R. Rumelt, 'Theory, Strategy and Entrepreneurship', in D. Teece (ed.) *The Competitive Challenge: Strategies for Industrial Innovation and Renewal*, Cambridge, MA, Ballinger, 1987.

R. Rumelt, 'How Much Does Industry Matter?', *Strategic Management Journal*, vol. 12, 1991, pp. 167–85.

R. Rumelt, D. Schendel and D. Teece, 'Strategic Management and Economics', *Strategic Management Journal*, vol. 12, 1991, pp. 5–29.

F. Scherer, *Industrial Market Structure and Economic Performance*, 2nd edn, Boston, Rand McNally, 1980.

R. Schmalensee, 'Do Markets Differ Much?', *American Economic Review*, vol. 75, no. 3, June 1985, pp. 341–51.

S.E. Seashore and E. Yuchtman, 'Factorial Analysis of Organizational Performance', *Administrative Science Quarterly*, vol. 12, no. 3, 1967, pp. 377–95.

D. Teece, 'Economies of Scope and the Scope of the Enterprise', *Journal of Economic Behaviour and Organization*, vol. 1, 1980, pp. 223–33.

D. Teece, 'Profiting from Technological Innovation', *Research Policy*, vol. 15, no. 6, December 1986, pp. 285–305.

H. Thomas and T. Pollock, 'From IO Economics' S–C–P Paradigm Through Strategic Groups to Competence-based Competition: Reflections on the Puzzle of Competitive Strategy', *British Journal of Management*, vol. 10, 1999, pp. 127–40.

N. Venkatraman and V. Ramanujam, 'Measurement of Business Performance in Strategy Research: A Comparison of Approaches', *Academy of Management Review*, vol. 11, no. 4, 1986, pp. 801–14.

O. Williamson, *Markets and Hierarchies: Analysis and Anti-trust Implications*, New York, Free Press, 1975.

Self-test questions

1. Distinguish between core competence, organisational capability and administrative heritage.

2. Explain the difference between 'system performance' and 'goal performance'.

3. Define entry barriers, mobility barriers and isolating mechanisms.

4. List the characteristics that a resource must have if it is to earn rents in the long term.

5. List *three* reasons for the limited application of game-theory-based economics to issues of business strategy.

Essay question

Evaluate the view that the analysis of business strategy lost sight of the key insights offered by SWOT analysis, only to rediscover them.

19 Network economics and the information sector

This chapter examines the 'network industries'. It outlines the idiosyncratic features of their cost and revenue conditions, the implications of these conditions and the debate over the 'lock-in' and increasing returns.

The explosive development of the software industry, the 'information economy' and the Internet have led to suggestions that the 'old' rules of economic life have been suspended, at both macro- and microeconomic level. At the macro level it has been argued that the productivity gains arising from the new technology have changed the relationship between inflation, employment and output growth. In that case the economy (especially the American economy) may be able to sustain high growth and high employment without triggering the inflation that was previously regarded as their inevitable accompaniment.

At the micro level, conventional wisdom on the importance of revenues, costs and profits seemed to have been left behind in 1999 as Internet firms which had never made a profit were given billion dollar valuations by stock markets all over the world.

Neither of these developments justifies the assertion that the established rules of economic life have been suspended. At the macro level it might be true that the 'natural rate of unemployment' has fallen somewhat. However, that is in line with simple conventional macroeconomic theory and requires no radical rethinking. At the micro level, the year 2000 saw a return to rational behaviour in stock markets as 'dot.coms' with no perceptible profit streams ran out of funds and their valuations crashed. The characteristics that make the 'information economy' and the Internet so different from other aspects of business life are not new and they are reasonably well understood. They are shared by other businesses, they have been experienced before and they can be examined with the tools of economic analysis. As Shapiro and Varian (1999, pp. 1–2) put it: 'Technology changes, economic laws do not'. Goods and services whose value derives from their information content, and the Internet phenomenon as a whole, are no less (and no more) susceptible to economic analysis than any other form of business activity. However, while their special characteristics are shared with activities in other industries, they are not clearly identified in magazine and newspaper coverage, they have been given relatively little attention in the non-specialist professional literature and they are not usually examined in undergraduate-level textbooks. Hence it is useful to set out a non-technical introduction to the issues, in order to make them more accessible. This chapter provides that introduction.

The structure of costs and revenues in the information economy

The standard model of the firm, set out in Chapter 2, describes a firm whose aim is to maximise profits. That assumption will be maintained here, although the intervening chapters have shown that more sophisticated interpretations are possible and the firm does not necessarily need to be modelled as a single, purposive, entity. The profit-maximisation assumption is a useful fiction that allows attention to be focused on the firm's relationships with the outside world, as opposed to its internal mechanics.

Profit is simply the difference between revenue, which depends on demand conditions, and cost, which depends on the technological conditions of production. That suggests that the information economy and the impact of the Internet can be explored systematically by considering how they affect those determinants of the firm's performance. There are two major phenomena that need to be considered in that respect. The first of these is *network effects*, which have an important impact on the demand for a firm's output. The second is *sunk costs*, which affect the way in which cost per unit is related to the firm's level of output. Both of these are related to the broader issue of *increasing returns*, which has been touched on in brief in Chapter 9 where cost/output relationships were examined.

Networks and their effects

A 'network' may be defined most generally as a set of 'nodes' connected by 'links'. (Economides 1996). 'Networks' have attracted a good deal of attention across a wide range of disciplines, from computer science and economics to marketing and sociology. In each discipline the units of analysis – the 'nodes' and the nature of the links between them – are defined in different ways. Computer science is concerned with the electronic links between computers, marketing is concerned with the commercial exchanges between the buying and selling functions of firms, and sociology is concerned with the social exchanges between people as social animals. In economics the nodes are economic actors (firms or individuals) and the links may be roads, railway lines, electricity cables, water and gas mains, copper cable or optical fibres.

Networks have a number of important economic characteristics. First, there is a high degree of *complementarity* among the different components. A service cannot be provided unless all of the necessary components are in place. Water cannot flow from the reservoir to the kitchen sink unless the pumping station, the treatment works, the water storage tank and the pipes are all in place. An e-mail message cannot be read or an on-line transaction made unless the personal computers, servers, software and connecting cables and fibres are all in place. Networks may be either two-way, where services can travel in either direction like roads, railways and e-mail systems, or they may be one-way, like paging services or radio and TV broadcasting. For both types of network the nodes and the links between them must be *compatible* with each other and it is that compatibility that makes the complementarity operational. If all of the nodes in a network belong to a single firm, compatibility can be assured by the firm's internal coordination mechanisms. The management will use its authority to ensure that the different components all work together. However, if different nodes belong to different organisations some other coordinating device will be needed, like the development of industry standards, and the various players in the industry will face a number of key decisions with respect to the standards they adopt and the technologies they develop.

Before considering the economic analysis of those decisions, it is necessary to examine the most fundamental property of networks. That is the existence of *network effects*. On the demand side, the value of a network to potential customers increases more than proportionally as the number of people or firms connected to it increases. A two-way network that connects just two people, A and B, provides two potentially valuable services, A to B and B to A. A network that connects three people is 50 per cent larger in terms of membership but it allows six different connections to be made, an increase of 200 per cent. Adding one more node (an increase of 33 per cent) creates a network that allows twelve bilateral connections (a 100 per cent increase). In general a network having 'n' nodes allows $(n^2 - n)$ bilateral connections and the increase in connections arising from the addition of one node is equal to $2n$. Hence if one node is added to a network that has already has one million nodes, a total of 2,000,000 additional connections are put in place. Clearly, if the value of the network to its members is determined by the number of connections that it allows, then that value increases dramatically as the size of the network increases. That feature of networks means that the demand for the services it provides is unusual in that the unit value of a network service – the amount that someone is willing to pay for it – increases as more people consume it. For most goods, as noted in Chapter 7, the unit value declines as more units are sold. However, this does not mean that the demand curve for network services slopes upwards, but rather that a downward-sloping demand curve shifts upwards as more consumers are connected (Economides 1996).

This network effect arises because of the complementarity of the different components required – servers and personal computers for instance. If more network-enabled computers are purchased then the value of servers is increased and the demand for them will increase. But as there are more servers, so does the value of computers increase. Hence the demand for the components of a network will tend to grow explosively.

A key question in respect of network effects concerns the way in which they relate to *network externalities*. A network externality arises if a decision-maker does not bear the full cost (or receive the full benefit) of the actions they take in respect of a network. In that case markets will tend to provide sub-optimal results. In some treatments of network issues, network effects are referred to universally as network externalities. However, as Liebowitz and Margolis (1999) point out, mechanisms exist that may eliminate the inefficiencies that might arise in this way. Figure 19.1 illustrates their analysis.

In Figure 19.1 the line AB shows the average benefit that each participant in the network enjoys. For rational participants that benefit also represents the maximum amount that each participant would be willing to pay to participate

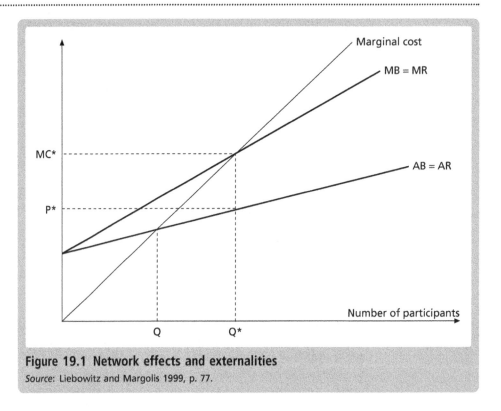

Figure 19.1 Network effects and externalities
Source: Liebowitz and Margolis 1999, p. 77.

with one connection to the network. The line MB represents the marginal benefit, showing the increase in total benefit that takes place when one more participant is added to the network. Because network effects are present, both of these curves slope upwards. The MB is above the AB because AB is rising. It should also be appreciated that when a new member joins they receive the average benefit, which is below the marginal benefit because the marginal benefit includes the gains to other network members arising from the increasing network size.

The line MC shows the marginal cost of supplying another connection to the network. It is shown sloping upwards here for simplicity, and that assumption can be justified on the grounds that networks are usually first connected to the closest nodes, gradually extending further outwards at higher cost, and that greater demand for the network's hardware tends to increase its price. (However, it should also be noted that the analysis does not provide a stable equilibrium unless the slope of the marginal cost curve exceeds the slope of the marginal benefit curve and this needs to be kept in mind.)

If the network is not owned by anyone, as in the case of the Internet, independent participants pay the marginal cost of joining. In that case participants will join up to the point Q where their marginal cost equals their AB (Liebowitz and Margolis 1999, p. 79). However, if the network has an owner, who bears the costs and charges a price to participants, the owner will set output at the level where their marginal cost and marginal revenue are equal, which is Q*, and set the corresponding price P*. This equilibrium has the odd characteristic that price is less than marginal cost. However, that does not mean that the owner is making losses; it arises instead from the positive slope of the AR and MR curves. Total revenue is equal to the area under the MR curve at Q* and clearly exceeds total variable cost, which is the area under the marginal cost curve at Q*.

A key point to be noted from this analysis is that the socially optimal or economically efficient level of network participation is where MB = MC which is the level of output provided in an owned network. In that case, the network effect is not an externality because the decision-maker – the owner – does take all of the costs and benefits into account. However, in a network that is not owned, the Internet being the major example, the network effect is an externality. That is because each independent person deciding to join only takes into account the benefit to themselves from joining, ignoring the benefit that other network members receive from the consequent expansion of the network. The network owner takes these interactions into account, and profits from them. As Liebowitz and Margolis (1999) point out, this is essentially an example of the 'tragedy of the commons'. If a resource, like a fishing ground, is held in common ownership it will tend to be over-used. That is because the average benefit from fishing exceeds the marginal benefit and hence too many fishermen seek to use it. In the case of a network that is not owned, the problem lies in the opposite direction. Because the average benefit is less than the marginal benefit, too few participants join the network. In both cases, the externality can be internalised by placing the common resource under single ownership.

Other economists, including Katz and Shapiro (1985), Economides (1996) and Economides and Himmelberg (1995), have approached the analysis in a rather different way in order to examine the implications of network effects for the market outcome under perfect competition, monopoly, monopolistic competition and oligopoly. They do not assume rising marginal costs and they model the demand side by beginning with the idea of a *fulfilled expectations demand curve* as shown in Figure 19.2.

In Figure 19.2 each demand curve, D_1 to D_8, shows the demand for the network good at different prices, given that buyers expect n_1 to n_8 sales to be made. As the expected number of sales increases, so the buyers' willingness to pay and demand curve are higher. As the level of sales approaches infinity it is assumed that willingness to pay approaches zero, so that demand curves form the pattern shown in the figure. (At a price of zero there must be a limit to the number of participants, although that number may be very large.) The actual willingness to pay for each level of output n_1 to n_8 is given by the point on the demand curve corresponding to that level of output being expected. For instance, if buyers expect the level of output to be n_1 they will have demand curve D_1. If their expectations are fulfilled, the amount they are willing to pay is given by the point on D_1 corresponding to the left-hand end of the thick line in Figure 19.2. As the figure shows, the fulfilled expectations demand curve rises at low levels of network participation and then falls for large 'n'. In this situation, the network is said to exhibit *positive critical mass under perfect competition*. At any marginal cost above C_0 the network will not be provided. However, at any marginal cost below C_0 the equilibrium will be given by the intersection of the marginal cost curve and the downward-sloping portion of the demand curve. (An equilibrium on the upward-sloping portion would be unstable.)

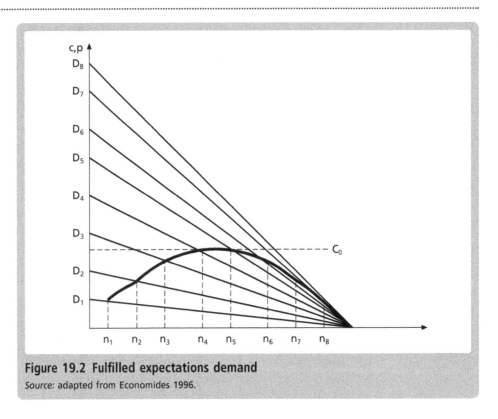

Figure 19.2 Fulfilled expectations demand
Source: adapted from Economides 1996.

Having developed the idea of the fulfilled expectations demand curve Economides and Himmelberg (1995) reaffirm that under perfect competition the most efficient level of output will not be produced, on grounds that correspond to those invoked by the Liebowitz and Margolis (1999) analysis. The marginal social benefit of network expansion is larger than the benefit accruing to a particular participant. Under monopoly they find that the network formed will be even smaller and the price higher, so that the standard comparison of economic welfare between competition and monopoly is not reversed and network externalities do not provide a justification for monopoly. In a Cournot oligopoly (refer to Chapter 13) where the firms all produce compatible products, the size of the network varies directly with the number of incumbents. If that number is very large the network is the same size as that which would be provided by a perfectly competitive industry. As the number of firms decreases, so does the network size, approaching the monopoly solution.

The choice of standards

The analysis becomes more complex if at least some firms produce incompatible products. In that case it becomes possible to determine the incentives that consumers and firms have to choose technologies that are compatible or incompatible. This is one aspect of the issue of 'standards', which are central to the working of network industries and an important determinant of both private profitability and social welfare. Liebowitz and Margolis (1996) provide an accessible model of standards choice.

The starting point for this model is to note that standards allow *synchronisation* among individuals. By using the same operating system and software, individuals can exchange files. Using the same video format allows tapes or disks to be played on different machines and using the same keyboard layout allows an individual to use different computers. The value of such commodities therefore depends upon the number of other users who have adopted the same format, just as the value of a network depends on the number of other users connected to it. For an individual consumer the value of a good may be seen as made up of two components. The first is its *autarky value*, which is the value it has to a customer if no one else uses it. The second is its *synchronisation value*, which is the additional value arising from the product format being adopted by others, and which increases as the market share of the format increases. For any potential customer, the *net value* of a product having a particular format is equal to the difference between the supply price of the product (the amount that the customer pays for it) and the total value, made up of autarky plus synchronisation value. Figure 19.3 brings these concepts together.

In the example shown, net value increases as the market share of format A increases because the slope of the total value curve is greater than the slope of the supply price function. If that were not the case the net value curve would fall from left to right and the key feature of the standards issue would not be present. A unit of the product would not be worth more to buyers as its market share increased and the phenomenon being examined would disappear.

If there are just two competing formats, A and B, the net value curves are the opposite of each other, as shown in Figure 19.4.

In this figure, point X is the market share at which the consumer is indifferent between the two formats. If the seller of format A wishes to lower the market

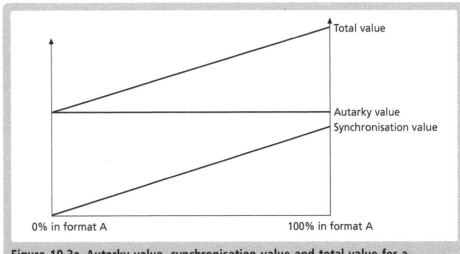

Figure 19.3a Autarky value, synchronisation value and total value for a production in format A

Source: Liebowitz and Margolis 1999

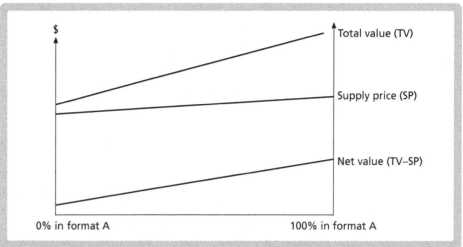

Figure 19.3b Total value, supply price and net value for product in format A
Source: Liebowitz and Margolis 1999

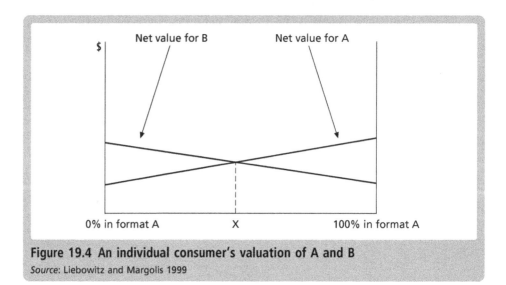

Figure 19.4 An individual consumer's valuation of A and B
Source: Liebowitz and Margolis 1999

share at which a consumer will prefer their version, they may do so by selling the product at a lower price, which shifts the net value curve for that format upwards and the indifference point to the left.

The point X applies to a single consumer, but if all consumers have the same valuations it will be the 'tipping point' at which the market share of each format switches between 0 per cent and 100 per cent. If format A currently has less than X then in the next period 100 per cent of sales will be in format B. Conversely, if format A has more than X then A will take 100 per cent of the market in the next period.

This feature of network products, whereby a larger market share leads to a standard becoming completely dominant and driving the other one out, is an important result and one that is often seen as raising major issues for public

policy. However, as Liebowitz and Margolis (1999) emphasise, it is also important to note that it depends upon the net value curve for A being upward sloping.
If it is downward sloping, which would be the case if the supply price function
has a greater slope than the synchronisation value curve, point X would not be
a 'tipping point' but an equilibrium market share for both formats. At market
shares below X customers would prefer A, all new customers would buy it and
its market share would rise. However, as its market share rose, the increasing
supply price would reduce the net value until point X is reached. At that point
new customers would be indifferent between A and B. If for any reason market
share of A should increase beyond X, new customers would then prefer B and
A's share would fall. Even if there are network effects in the form of synchronisation value, multiple formats may coexist if there are diseconomies of production
that offset the synchronisation advantages.

The model developed thus far may be extended by changing the assumptions
on which it is built in order to investigate two key issues. The first concerns the
impact of different customer preferences. If point X varies from customer to
customer, determined by their different assessment of the two formats or different valuations of the synchronisation effects, multiple formats may exist in
equilibrium even if the net value curves slope upwards (see Liebowitz and
Margolis 1999, pp. 104–6). The second concerns whether superior products will
necessarily dominate the market or whether there are circumstances in which
an inferior product could prevail. If one product is so far superior to another
that it has higher net values for all customers at all market shares, it is obvious
that it will take 100 per cent market share. However, even if one format (A) is
only superior in the weaker sense that A with z per cent share is preferred to B
with z per cent share, then it will also dominate the market. There is, however,
a circumstance in which a market can become locked in to an inferior product,
as illustrated in Figure 19.5.

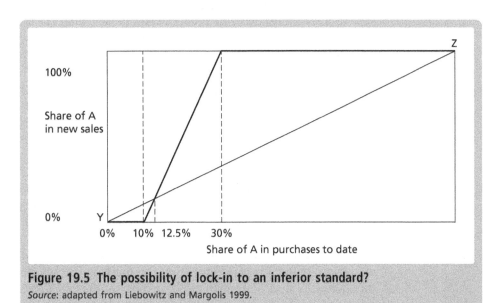

Figure 19.5 The possibility of lock-in to an inferior standard?
Source: adapted from Liebowitz and Margolis 1999.

In the situation shown, format A is superior to the alternative for all customers, and point X in Figure 19.4 varies across customers, from 10 per cent to 30 per cent. In other words, some customers will choose A if its recent share has been as low as 10 per cent, while others will not choose it unless its recent share has been as high as 30 per cent. The superiority of A is demonstrated by the fact that all of the point Xs are less than 50 per cent. Every customer will prefer A if both formats have equal shares. Indeed, every customer will prefer A as long as the rival format has less than 70 per cent of the market and some will prefer A even if the rival has 89 per cent of the market. If A's recent market share has been above 30 per cent, all customers will choose it, as shown by the thick line in Figure 19.5. If A's market share has been between 10 per cent and 30 per cent a rising proportion of customers will choose it (in a straight-line relationship if the different point Xs are evenly distributed across the population of customers). However, as no customer has a point X below 10 per cent, if A's recent market share has been below that level (so that the rival's share has been above 90 per cent) every customer will prefer the rival format.

The thick line in Figure 19.5 illustrates how format A's share of new sales will be related to its recent market share. The thin line joining points Y and Z shows all points where current share equals recent share. If these are not equal to each other then the situation cannot be 'at rest' because one or other must be changing. Hence the line YZ indicates all possible equilibrium points. In the situation shown there are three apparent equilibria, at point Y, point Z and at a 12.5 per cent market share for format A. The last of these three 'equilibria' is in fact unstable because any slight move away from it would lead to a cumulative and continuing move in the same direction. For instance, if there was a slight move along the thick line towards Z, A's share in new sales would exceed its recent market share and its recent market share would rise. That would trigger an increase in current sales, raising recent market share, raising current sales until point Z is reached. Similarly, if sales were at the 12.5 per cent 'equilibrium' but then fell very slightly the share in new sales would be less than the share in recent sales, the latter would fall, the former would fall and point Y would eventually be reached. In Figure 19.5 the only stable equilibria are at Y and Z.

It is now possible to consider the possible outcomes in the contest between format A and its rival. If superior format A is established first, having a 100 per cent market share in the first period, the equilibrium will be at Z. The rival will only be able to dislodge it if it can achieve 87.5 per cent market share or better in its first period of entry. That could be possible if the owners of the rival format offer customers inducements to purchase their product, but it will be expensive given the large market share needed. Hence A is likely to dominate, with 100 per cent market share. If the inferior rival format arrives first, the equilibrium will be at Y. The industry will be dominated by an inferior format. However, as before, the other format could shift this equilibrium by offering inducements to customers. As format A is superior its owners only need to persuade 12.6 per cent of customers to adopt it and the equilibrium will shift to point Z, with the superior format dominating the market. The key point highlighted by the Liebowitz and Margolis (1999) analysis is that an inferior standard might come to dominate an industry but there are means by which the superior standard can prevail, and it will be easier for a superior standard to dislodge an inferior one than vice versa. This point will be returned to below in the discussion on 'lock-in' and the debate over 'increasing returns'.

The analysis of standards thus far has centred on customers' choice between two rival standards. Economides (1996) approaches the issues from a different direction by examining the interaction of oligopolists producing incompatible goods. From that perspective an industry can be divided into 'coalitions' where each coalition is a group of firms adopting the same technical standard. If every firm adopts the same standard the industry is made up of a single coalition. At the other extreme, if every firm adopts its own idiosyncratic standard the number of coalitions is equal to the number of firms. The nature of the equilibrium coalition structure (the number of coalitions and the size of their membership) depends partly on the type of cooperation that takes place between the individual firms. In the simplest situation firms make no side payments to each other. In that case, a firm will only join a coalition if the profits arising from its own sales increases as a result. Alternatively the members of a coalition may divide up the total profits made, in order to induce firms to enter. Katz and Shapiro (1985) provide a starting point for the analysis by showing that industry output is always larger when there is complete compatibility. However, as Economides (1996) points out, that does not in itself tell us very much about the incentives that firms face when deciding on the standard to adopt.

For an individual firm that is considering whether to join a coalition the decision depends upon three factors: first, the size of the extra benefit to potential customers that is created by the firm joining the coalition (as that benefit increases, so does the incentive to join the coalition become more intense); second, the size of the coalition that is being joined (as that becomes larger, so does the incentive to join become more powerful); third, the extent to which joining the coalition increases competition within it. If joining increases competition very substantially that effect may offset the benefits of joining. Similarly, for the incumbent members of the coalition, they will benefit from the addition of a new member if the marginal externality is large, if the new member firm is large and if its entry does not significantly increase competition.

The first of these three factors works in the same direction for both the potential new member of the coalition and the incumbents. Hence, the impact of a large marginal benefit will be straightforward. It will increase the number of firms that choose to adopt the same standard. However, for both the new member and the incumbents the second and third factors may come into conflict and that helps to identify an equilibrium coalition structure. Katz and Shapiro (1985) show that the outcome also depends upon the costs of achieving compatibility relative to the increase in profits for individual firms and relative to the social benefits to be gained. If the cost of achieving compatibility is less than the extra profits for every firm then the industry will achieve complete compatibility and that will be socially beneficial. However, there may be a situation where for some firms the cost of achieving compatibility is more than the extra profit to be earned. In that case the outcome represents the classic problem of externalities. A socially beneficial result is lost because when an individual firm takes decisions it ignores the impact on other firms' profits and on consumer surplus.

The question of compatibility may also be approached through *mix and match* models (Matutes and Regibeau 1988) which do not depend upon the assumption of network externalities, but in which such effects do arise. We can first consider two components of a network, like a personal computer (PC) and its operating system (OS), and assume that there are two brands of each, produced by two different firms. Each firm is vertically integrated, producing both components, and the question is whether they will want to make their components compatible with each other. If the components are made compatible in both directions then *hybrid products* are available consisting of the PC from one firm and the OS from another. The incentive to produce compatible products arises from the fact that compatibility increases demand by allowing those hybrid products, but at the same time it increases competition for the individual components. The optimal choice for each firm therefore depends upon the size of the demand for hybrids, relative to the demand for its own product. If it is large a firm will opt for compatibility. If it is small it will not. Two firms may find themselves in different positions. If one has relatively small demand for its own product, but there is significant demand for hybrids, that firm will prefer compatibility. However, if the other is in the opposite situation it will prefer incompatibility, which will prevail unless the firm that prefers compatibility can always counteract any incompatibility introduced by engineering around it, legally and at acceptable cost.

The question of compatibility becomes increasingly complex as different possibilities are examined. In the situation just described it was assumed that both firms are vertically integrated and the decision on compatibility was examined in that setting. However, as Economides (1996) points out, a firm's decision on compatibility is actually less reversible than its decision on vertical integration. Hence it makes more sense to think in terms of a series of decisions which begins with the decision on which technology to adopt (and hence compatibility) and then proceeds first to the decision on vertical integration and then to decisions on price and quantity. Such models become too complex to consider here.

Another issue that arises in networks concerns the quality of the final product and the necessity for coordination. In many network situations the quality of the service received – the quality of voice in a telephone conversation, the speed of the Internet connection – is determined by the weakest component in the system. A firm may therefore offer a fast quality server, for instance, but find that its quality is negated by the lower quality of the components to which it is connected. Economides and Lehr (1995) show that for a network service involving two components a vertically integrated monopolist will choose to produce a higher quality composite product (one that has higher quality components at both stages) than two monopolists, one for each component.

Earlier chapters in this book have examined the question of entry barriers, where the key issue lay in the extent to which incumbent firms could protect their profits by erecting entry barriers and deterring entry to their industry. This is an issue where network industries exhibit important counter-intuitive tendencies because in certain circumstances network effects make it profitable for firms to invite entrants into the industry and even to subsidise them. The existence of network externalities means that demand for a product increases as the *expected* number of users increases. If the industry is a monopoly, potential customers know that there is an incentive for the monopolist to restrict output and increase price. Hence they will expect a relatively small number of users and demand will be lower than it would be if there were more firms in the industry. The monopolist could promise to produce a high level of output but that promise would lack credibility. Therefore the monopolist may invite other firms to join the industry, and license the technology to them, in order to convince customers that there will be a large number of users. The monopolist loses because of the increased competition but gains because of the increased demand. Provided that the increased demand compensates for the increased competition, it will be rational for the monopolist to give away the monopoly position. Hence Intel licensed its chip technology to AMD in order to convince buyers that the market would not be restricted.

Before moving to other aspects of the information economy it should be noted that the existence of network effects means that timing and history are important determinants of the outcomes faced by individual firms. Consumers and producers are both influenced by their expectation of the future size of the network, which in turn is related to the current 'installed base' – the number of current users – and future expectations of its growth. The same technology and the same pattern of customer preference can lead to very different outcomes depending on the moves made by firms in the early stages of a network industry's development. Hence, being the 'first mover' and making the correct first moves may create long-term advantages for an industry's pioneers.

The cost structure of information industries

The second key feature of information industries lies in the structure of their costs. As explained in Chapter 9, costs can be divided into fixed costs and variable costs. Fixed costs are those that are invariant with the level of output and which must be incurred even if the firm produces nothing. Variable costs are those that depend upon the level of output produced, increasing as output per time-period increases. Marginal costs are the additional costs incurred in the production of one additional unit of output.

For many of the products associated with the software sector and the information industries the structure of costs is unusual. Almost all of those costs are fixed. Furthermore, the fixed costs have the special characteristic of also being *sunk costs*. That means that they cannot be recovered if the firm should decide to close and exit the industry. In many industries, fixed costs are not sunk. For instance, if a company rents a factory or uses its own premises for production, the cost of that facility is a fixed cost in that it does not depend upon the level of output produced. However, it is not a sunk cost because if the firm decides to exit the industry it can stop renting the factory or it can sell or rent the premises to some other user. If a software company spends billions of dollars in developing and advertising a new word-processing package and then fails to make profits, the cost of developing the package cannot be recovered. The costs are sunk costs. In the information sectors, there are usually two kinds of sunk costs involved. First, there are the 'first-copy' costs involved in developing and testing the product.

Then there are the marketing costs of advertising and promoting the product so that potential customers are made aware of it and drawn towards its purchase. Taken together these can be enormous, making the stakes at risk very high indeed.

The other key characteristic of most information goods and services is that the marginal cost of production is almost zero. Producing a movie, a music CD, a book, a suite of software or a website requires a heavy investment in sunk costs in the initial stage of operation. However, when the product has been made once, the cost of reproduction is very small, it does not increase as output increases and there are effectively no natural limits to the volume of output that can be produced.

The implications of near-zero marginal costs

The impact of this unusual cost structure can be seen by using standard economic models. In a perfectly competitive market, where there is a high level of competition, where firms have the same costs and products are identical, price is forced down until it equals marginal cost, which in this case is close to zero. Similarly in a duopoly or oligopoly with Bertrand competition (on price, which is the appropriate model in this case, refer to Chapter 13) price is also forced down to the level of marginal cost. The key lesson here, of course, is that if firms all face the same cost conditions, there is no long-term profit to be had in the information industries by producing a product that is the same as that produced by others. For such a product the price will be close to zero and the sunk costs will be lost.

If a firm is to escape from the difficulties imposed by high fixed and low marginal costs it can follow two routes. The first is that it may seek to achieve lower costs than others by exploiting economies of scale or scope. In that case, price will be forced down to the marginal cost of the less efficient firms and the cost leader will be able to make a profit, even in a commodity market. If marginal cost really is zero (and hence the same for everyone), or cost leadership is not a viable strategy, then the alternative route is that the firm offers a product that is different from that offered by others, in a way that is valued by customers. If neither cost leadership nor valued product differentiation can be achieved, and just one other firm produces a perfect substitute at the same cost, the economics of oligopoly markets shows that the information good in question will become a 'commodity' whose price is forced down to its marginal cost. The 'business model' will not be viable and the shareholders will never see a significant return on their investment. However, as explained below, one firm's product may be differentiated from others by the switching costs required to change to those others, and this is an important feature of information industries.

Price discrimination and profitability

The analysis above makes it clear that long-term profitability in an industry where marginal costs are close to zero requires that at least one of two conditions be met. The firm must either have significantly lower marginal costs than others (which is difficult at such low costs) or it must have an element of market power in the form of product differentiation which is valued by customers. Those conditions are fundamental. If they are not met, a firm that has made a significant investment in sunk costs must eventually go bankrupt and there is no point in further analysis.

If a firm is able to differentiate its product from those offered by its rivals, it will be able to survive and it then has a number of options through which additional profits can be raised. These are:

● *price discrimination* – charging different customers different prices for the same product, according to their 'willingness to pay'
● *product differentiation or proliferation* within the firm's product line – referred to by Shapiro and Varian (1999) as *'versioning'*.

Each of these can be considered in turn.

Chapter 14 has examined a number of different forms of price discrimination. 'First-degree' price discrimination is where each individual customer is charged a different price for the same product. Practical examples have been relatively difficult to find in the past because this degree of discrimination is only possible if the seller is a monopoly, if it can discover each individual buyer's willingness to pay, and if each individual customer cannot sell its purchase on to others. However, as retailing on the Internet, and 'smart' use of customer information databases, provide 'one-to-one' communication channels between buyer and seller, they make 'personalised pricing' a possibility. A seller may be able to discover a buyer's willingness to pay either directly through on-line auctions like those provided by Amazon or e-Bay, or by using information about the buyer's previous purchasing behaviour. For example, Lexis-Nexis sells access to databases at prices that vary for almost every user (Shapiro and Varian 1999, p. 41). If you are an impecunious student who uses the facility only occasionally and who provides a credible signal of poverty by being prepared to dial up at night and to view the data on screen without printing it out, the price will be very low. On the other hand, a major corporate user printing frequent reports during the day will pay a much higher price. The same product is being sold at different prices (although it could be argued that this is really an example of 'versioning', the same data being a different product at different times – the quibble is semantic).

Another type of price discrimination which has been explained in Chapter 14 is 'third-degree price discrimination' which is where different prices are charged to identifiably different groups of customers, while the same price is charged within the same group. In practice the boundaries between first-degree and third-degree price discrimination are somewhat blurred. If any two customers have the same willingness to pay then first-degree price discrimination involves charging them the same price and hence is the same as third degree for that group. Strictly speaking, most practical examples of first-degree discrimination come into this category because it is rarely possible to extract all of the consumer surplus from every single customer.

It will be possible and profitable to charge different prices to different groups of customers if the standard conditions for price discrimination apply. The firm must have a monopoly for the product in question (meaning that there are no very close substitutes), different groups must have different price elasticities of demand (which are known to the seller) and the different groups must be unable to buy at the prices set for other groups or to trade the product with each other. This latter point indicates a potential problem that the Internet poses for third-degree price discrimination. If the same product is offered for sale on the Internet at different prices to different customers – a low price for customers in developing countries and a high price in rich countries, for instance – it may be difficult for the seller to enforce the separation of markets. A customer in the United States may try to purchase the product at the poor country price. The seller could refuse to deliver the product to the United States at that price. If the product must be physically delivered to the buyer, that might solve the seller's problem but the purchaser could then simply purchase the product 'by proxy', having a friend in a poor country buy it at the low price and then ship it to the United States. Indeed, if the difference between poor country and rich country prices is substantial, a sharp-eyed entrepreneur will soon realise that there is a profit opportunity here. They will provide an arbitraging intermediary service which effectively prevents price discrimination taking place and forces all sales to be made at the lower price. Of course, if the extra costs of shipping the product from the seller to the intermediary to the buyer are significant, a price differential can be maintained. However, if the product is an item of software which is delivered by downloading, a basic requirement for price discrimination is not met as buyers in different locations can purchase at the lowest price offered.

One final point to make in respect of price discrimination is that the analysis impacts on the development of information products and services in two different ways. First, information products themselves may be sold at different prices to different customers. Second, information services like on-line retailing and customer databases may allow more effective price discrimination to be carried out for other products. Books, airline tickets and hotel rooms provide the most obvious examples, all of them being available for on-line purchase (or on-line assisted purchase).

'Versioning' and pricing information products

Shapiro and Varian (1999, p. 39) use the term 'versioning' to describe the situation where the firm offers a range of different product variants – 'versions' – and allows customers to choose the variant that suits them best. Some of the examples of third-degree discrimination outlined above may be re-packaged conceptually as 'versioning' (like the same data accessed at different times of the day) and the practice is central to profitability in the information sectors.

'Versioning' provides a number of benefits to the firm. In the first place, it provides useful market intelligence that helps to identify those aspects of a product that are most highly valued by customers. Second, it provides a way in which different customers can be charged different prices for 'almost the same thing' which can itself be produced at almost zero marginal cost. Microsoft Office, for instance, is available in various different versions, suitable for home or small business (the database and presentation components are missing), suitable for professional users (all components are included) or suitable for networked use in larger organisations (all components are included in a server version). Shapiro and Varian (1999, p. 62) provide a list of dimensions along which a product may be 'versioned' in order to meet different customer needs. These are:

- *Delay* – stock prices or other time-sensitive information may be delivered in 'real time', which will significantly enhance its value for one group of users, or with different degrees of delay, longer delays being associated with lower prices.
- *Complexity and power of the user interface* – databases may offer more or less complex search facilities, suitable for users with different needs.
- *Convenience* – access to an information product can be made more convenient by extending the times and locations at which it can be accessed, and less convenient by restricting them.
- *Image resolution* – images are the most accessed type of information on the Internet and they may be versioned by offering different resolutions. Lower resolutions will meet the needs of one set of customers while others may be prepared to pay more to receive enhanced detail. Professionals using downloaded pictures for use in commercial brochures (or pornography addicts) will value the enhanced detail and be prepared to pay for it.
- *Speed* – some users may need and value high speeds, others will not.
- *Flexibility of use* – some versions may be copy-protected, and non-transferable to other media (through printing, for instance), while others are open to a wider range of uses.
- *Capability, features and functions* – software can vary in respect of the range of tasks that it can carry out, and the number of those tasks with which it can cope. Statistical software like the Statistical Package for the Social Sciences (SPSS) is sold in modules so that users can choose which applications they need. If they require comprehensiveness they can purchase every module. Student versions of some statistical packages, like AMOS, for instance, are often made available at low or even zero prices but they are only able to deal with a limited number of variables. Fully specified versions are very much more expensive.
- *Annoyance* – an inexpensive version of an information service, a radio station, a TV service or a home movie channel may irritate the user with advertisements. Or it may keep breaking into the service offered with announcements or requests to register for a more expensive version of the same product that does not include such irritants.
- *Technical support* – some users will value a high level of technical support, others will not, creating another opportunity for versioning.

In terms of the analysis presented in Chapter 7, these dimensions all represent product 'characteristics' and each version is made up of a different bundle of these characteristics, as in Lancaster's 1966 model. That naturally raises questions concerning the profit-maximising number of product variants and optimal pricing for multi-product companies. With respect to the optimal number of product variants there is a substantial economic literature on product diversity under

413

different market conditions. However, it offers relatively little direct guidance. For a firm that is a multi-product monopolist it can be shown (Tirole 1988, p. 105) that such a firm may produce too many product variants, relative to the social optimum. That is because the monopolist's ability to charge a price above marginal cost for one product variant increases demand for the other, relative to the level it would have if the first product were priced at the socially optimal level. That increase in demand might make the second variant profitable even if it would not be so in the presence of socially optimal prices. Furthermore, a monopolist may try to use brand proliferation as a way to deter entry into the industry by 'crowding the product space' (Tirole 1988, p. 285) and an incumbent monopolist may have more incentive to introduce additional brands than an oligopolist. In the case of monopolistic competition or oligopoly, firms will not want to occupy the same product space (i.e. produce perfect substitutes for each other's product) because that will trigger a price reduction down to marginal cost. Hence they will seek different market niches and the optimal number of products to produce, for the firms as a whole, depends on the number of such niches.

This analysis is not very useful in terms of practical guidelines. Shapiro and Varian (1999) suggest more helpfully that firms should search their markets for groups of customers who are identifiably different from each other and then examine their product for versioning opportunities that might match the needs of different segments. If that approach does not produce a clearly specified set of versions they propose that a 'Goldilocks' approach be taken where three versions are offered. The logic of choosing three versions is drawn from Simonson and Tversky's study in the *Journal of Marketing Research* (1992), which found that customers are averse to choosing products priced at the extreme points of the scale. Faced with a cheap version and a mid-range version, buyers tended towards the cheaper offering. However, faced with the same cheap and mid-range products, plus a more highly priced 'top-end' version, a much larger proportion of buyers chose the mid-range version. Few of them bought the most expensive version but its availability encouraged a move away from the lower end of the range.

When the number of versions has been decided upon, they need to be priced. The key issue here concerns whether the different versions of the product are substitutes or complements for each other. For instance, a low specification student version of a statistical software package is probably a complement rather than a substitute for the fully specified version aimed at professors and corporate market researchers. In that case, giving it away free can be a perfectly rational approach because that will increase demand for the more expensive version. In a similar way, on-line versions of some products, most obviously books and magazines, are much less convenient to use than the printed version. Hence, the two different formats are complements rather than substitutes for each other and the on-line version can safely be given away. *The Economist* magazine takes this one step further in that it offers a printed edition, an Internet edition and a further mobile edition that can be downloaded weekly onto palm personal digital assistants. The cost of the full package is slightly more than a subscription to the printed version alone, and represents about half the price of buying the magazine from a newsagent every week.

If two versions of an information product are complements for each other, a lower price for one will increase the demand for the other. On the other hand, different versions of information products are more often relatively close substitutes for each other. In that case pricing one version at zero would be disastrous because no one would buy the other, and revenues would be equal to zero.

The unusual structure of costs for information products affects the costs of producing different versions, in ways that may be perverse. In particular, the costs of producing lower quality versions may be higher than the costs of higher quality versions. This will be true whenever a lower quality/higher quality pair of versions is most cheaply produced by first making the high quality version and then degrading it at additional cost. A high quality/low quality pair of images is most cheaply made by producing the top quality version at high resolution and then deliberately 'fuzzing it up' for cheaper versions. If stock market information is collected and disseminated in real time for a high quality product it may then need to be held in storage at extra cost before being sold as a lower quality product. Hence firms may rationally incur additional costs in order to produce a lower quality product to be sold at a lower price. (Of course, this arises from the joint nature of production for the two commodities. It would not be profitable to produce a single low quality product by first producing a high quality product and then degrading it.)

A final set of issues that arises in respect of versioning concerns the 'bundling' of products into multi-product versions which are sold at a single price. Microsoft Office is the most obvious example, combining Word, Excel and PowerPoint into a single product. The basic principles associated with bundling have been examined by Shy (1995), Lewbel (1985) and McAfee *et al.* (1989). In the software industry tying offers the customer a guarantee that the products are compatible with each other, which will increase demand for the package. However, the benefit to the seller arises independently of that gain. If two customers place different valuations on the components that are tied together (and their valuations are negatively correlated) a monopoly seller can increase revenue by tying. Furthermore, as Adams and Yellen (1976) showed, revenue can be increased further by 'mixed tying' which involves selling a tied package of both components, plus the components individually.

Switching costs and lock-in

Network effects on the demand side, and a high sunk fixed/low marginal cost structure, are two of the key characteristics of the information sector. The third is *lock-in*, which may be defined as the tendency of customers to persist with the use of a particular product as a result of *switching costs*.

If the use of a particular product involves investment *in complementary assets that are specific to that product*, then switching costs are created. Examples of these complementary assets include:

- collections of long-playing records or CDs, which make it expensive to switch to Mini-Discs or MP3 players

- printers that only work with one brand of computer, creating additional expense if the user switches to a different brand
- the investment in human capital built up through experience with a particular software package, requiring retraining if a new package is adopted
- corporate databases that can only be processed using a particular set of hardware and software, requiring substantial expense on rebuilding the datasets if the hardware is changed
- telephone networks that will only function with a specific set of switches provided by one supplier
- the time and effort involved in giving your mobile phone number to friends and acquaintances if that number can only be used with one telephone company's network.

Lock-in means that 'history matters' because a decision made at one point in time can restrict the options available in future, hence the term *path dependence* which is sometimes used to describe the resulting phenomenon. Lock-in through the creation and maintenance of switching costs can enhance profitability for an incumbent firm, as indicated in Porter's 'five forces' model of Chapter 11. By the same token, it is expensive for customers who are locked in and it creates an entry barrier against firms seeking to compete against those profiting from the lock-in. Both sides of the relationship need to be examined.

Lock-in creates profit through a number of mechanisms. Most directly, it allows the price charged for the product to rise above the (quality-adjusted) cost of competing suppliers by the amount of the switching cost. If quality and marginal cost are the same for two products, and there is a switching cost of s_c for existing customers, the supplier will be able to charge a price equal to (marginal cost + s_c) without losing the customer to the other supplier. When it is remembered that marginal cost is often close to zero for information products, it is clear that s_c is a crucial determinant of profitability. In the case of telephone companies, where lock-in to equipment suppliers is created through the purchase of electronic switches, the number of customers is small and the switching cost per customer is very large. On the other hand, for information products like telephone calls, e-mail services and websites the switching costs per customer are very small, but they apply potentially to millions of customers and hence have significant total value.

If the cost of supplying a customer is the same for an existing supplier and a challenger then the analysis above is sufficient. However, if a customer shifts to a new supplier that firm will usually face some additional cost that does not need to be incurred by the current supplier, for whom it is a sunk cost incurred in the past. For instance, if a subscriber shifts from one telephone company or Internet Service Provider (ISP) to another, the new company will have to set up an account and enter the subscriber into the accounting and operations databases. This adds to the marginal cost of the challenger firm in the form of an additional switching cost s_s. The price that the existing supplier can now charge is equal to (marginal cost + s_c + s_s). Note that it is the total switching cost that creates the profit margin for the incumbent, not its distribution between the customer and the new supplier. If the new supplier tried to reduce switching costs for customers by paying them a 'new customer bonus', that would simply increase the new supplier's switching cost by the same amount, leaving the situation unchanged. However, if the new supplier can offer the customer something that the customer values more highly than the supplier, total switching costs can be reduced. That is because the supplier's costs rise by less than the reduction in the customer's costs. If the customer values a ten-minute phone call at ten pence and it costs the new supplier five pence to provide it, offering such a call free to a new customer will reduce total switching costs by five pence.

The final amendment that needs to be made to the analysis is to recognise that quality-adjusted marginal cost may not be the same for the existing supplier and the challenger. If the incumbent's marginal cost is lower than that of the challenger, or its quality is higher for the same cost, there will be a further margin to be earned (and vice versa if the challenger has lower quality-adjusted costs).

While the margin to be earned on information products is largely determined by switching costs, total profit depends upon the size of the *installed base* – the total number of users who are locked in. That in turn decides the valuation of such a base and consequently the level of investment that should rationally be made in order to achieve it.

The analysis thus far has focused on the case where revenues are earned through the sale of an information product at positive prices. However, an alternative model is where the apparent 'product' is given away to customers and the revenue is raised through advertising. The classic example is the Hotmail e-mail service provided free by Microsoft (after it purchased the original supplying company). Users receive e-mail services at zero cost and are then locked in by the switching costs associated with changing their e-mail address. Instead of exploiting this profit opportunity by charging for the service (perhaps after a free initial period) the supplier earns revenue through selling advertising to the very large installed base of customers.

Shapiro and Varian (1999, p. 117) identify seven common sources of lock-in, which are as follows:

1. *Contractual commitment to buy from a particular supplier* – which imposes the switching cost of compensating that supplier if an alternative is to be used.
2. *Durability of purchases* – which imposes the cost of premature replacement, which declines as the purchases become obsolete.
3. *Brand-specific training or learning* – which imposes the cost of learning to work with a new system.
4. *Formatted information* – imposing conversion costs.
5. *Sole supplier having the appropriate capability* – requiring the redevelopment of capability.
6. *Search costs* – requiring an investment in time and resources to identify and evaluate alternative sources of supply.
7. *Loyalty programmes* – imposing the loss of accrued benefits.

For incumbent firms the aim is to secure and maintain the lock-in of existing customers and to attract and lock in new ones. For challengers the aim is to overcome that lock-in, replacing it with lock-in to their own products, while for customers the aim is to free themselves from lock-in. While the actions that the various protagonists can take follow straightforwardly from the analysis above (Shapiro and Varian 1999, pp. 135–71) the likely outcome of this competitive process is a matter of intense debate. It determines how well a market economy works, the impact of the information industries on welfare and the appropriate actions that the anti-trust authorities should take. This chapter therefore closes with a review of the arguments, paying particular attention to the way in which managerial decisions can affect the outcomes.

The debate over 'increasing returns'

Perhaps the most important economic issue of all concerns whether a decentralised market economy works effectively. As the second millenium drew to a close the collapse of planned economies around the world and the overwhelming practical and intellectual dominance of the market model led Francis Fukuyama (1992) to declare the 'end of history'. That was not intended to mean that time had stopped but that the ongoing battle between alternative social and economic systems had effectively been won. Civil society, governed by democracy and the rule of law, and driven by a competitive market economy, was accepted as the best available solution to the problem of human organisation. The world's wealthiest societies practised an approximation to that model, and sought to adopt it more closely, while the world's largest and poorest (China, India, Indonesia and Russia) accepted that their proposed alternatives had failed. And yet, ironically, history may have taken its revenge because at exactly the same time the increasing importance of the information industries drew attention to a phenomenon that might prevent the market economy from working.

Such a grandiose concern might seem out of place in a textbook on managerial economics. However, it relates directly to the economics of the information business, it depends heavily on the actions that managers may take, and it provides a useful background to Part IV of this book, which is concerned with public policy. An overview is therefore relevant to this book's central concerns.

The key issue is that of 'increasing returns' which simply means that returns to an activity increase as the size of that activity increases. The simplest example concerns increasing returns to scale in production, as discussed in Chapter 9. If the technology of production for a good or a service exhibits increasing returns to scale, then unit costs decline as the level of output increases. In that case, larger firms have lower costs and in a competitive situation the largest firm will become dominant. But in that case the industry in question will become a monopoly and it is well known that a market economy 'fails' in the presence of monopoly. If economies of scale were highly significant in many industries, the 'competitive market economy' which provides the basis for the society at the end of history would be a contradiction. Market forces would effectively end competition and hence government intervention and some form of planning would be required.

Economies of scale in production are just one aspect of the 'increasing returns' phenomenon. An influential group of economists led by Paul David and Brian Arthur have pointed out that network effects and lock-in have similar effects,

Table 19.1 Pay-offs to alternative technologies

Number of adoptions	0	10	20	30	40	50	60	70	80	90	100
Technology A	10	11	12	13	14	15	16	17	18	19	20
Technology B	4	7	10	13	16	19	22	25	28	31	34

Source: Liebowitz and Margolis (1999), p. 57.

whereby larger firms tend to take increasing shares of the market. Furthermore, they have argued that the costs associated with the presence of increasing returns go beyond the static inefficiencies associated with monopoly, and the lack of innovation that may follow from an absence of competitive pressure. They suggest that the existence of path dependence and lock-in means that a market economy may actually select inferior technologies. The dominant firm does not attain its position because it has lower costs and is more efficient, as in the straightforward case of scale economies. Instead the dominant firm overwhelms its competitors because earlier events give it 'first-mover advantages', even if it is selling a product that is inferior.

This argument has often been set out as the received truth, despite the fact that it has been vigorously contested. Both sides merit consideration.

Some of the key arguments in favour of the 'increasing returns' position are to be found in Arthur (1989, 1994) and David (1985, 1986). Arthur (1989) uses figures like those set out in Table 19.1 to illustrate the basic point.

In the situation shown, technology B is more efficient once the number of adoptions exceeds thirty. However, the first adopter will choose A and B will therefore never be chosen. The best-known example of this phenomenon concerns the ubiquitous QWERTY keyboard, so-called because of the layout of the top row of alphabetic characters. According to David (1985, 1986), the QWERTY layout originated in a problem with the early mechanical typewriters, whereby they would jam if the typist operated the machine too quickly. The QWERTY arrangement slowed down the keyboard action and prevented jamming. However, as typewriters improved and were replaced by computers the original rationale for the design became irrelevant and indeed a keyboard that allowed more rapid typing became more desirable. Nevertheless, despite the availability of more efficient keyboard designs, like the Dvorak Simplified Keyboard, QWERTY remains the dominant design.

This example provides a vivid illustration of a number of issues raised above. It has taken a place within the received wisdom and has been quoted with approval by a number of authors including Farrell and Saloner (1985) in a key paper on standards, and by Tirole (1988) in a standard advanced textbook on industrial organisation. QWERTY has a very large installed base and the switching costs involved in retraining typists and replacing keyboards create the lock-in that is such an important feature of information industries. Hence it has persisted as the standard, despite its inferiority. Increasing returns cause market failure.

While this analysis of the QWERTY phenomenon seems convincing at first, Liebowitz and Margolis (1990, 1999) have examined it in more detail and shown that it is crucially flawed, both in theory and as a piece of history. The evidence in support of the superiority of the Dvorak keyboard is totally unconvincing, not least because some of the evaluations were carried out by Dvorak himself. Other tests, carried out by independent researchers, failed to find that the QWERTY layout led to inferior typing speeds. It is not true that a superior design was locked out by the early choice of an inferior alternative.

The theoretical flaw can be seen by re-examining Table 19.1. According to the logic of that argument, the superior technology B is never adopted because at each stage adopters making the choice between two alternatives prefer technology A. As no one adopts B, the returns to its adoption by the next firm making the decision remain low, although they would be high if everyone opted for it. The problem with that analysis is the implicit assumption that decision-makers cannot, or do not, look ahead. If adopters looked beyond the immediate situation to one where more than thirty adoptions have taken place, they would realise that B is superior. They would also realise that others would make the same judgement. Hence decisions would be made on the expectations associated with the superior technology being adopted. Purchasers have an interest in seeing the superior technology adopted and they may therefore organise themselves in order to achieve that objective. The formation of user groups is common among computer users, and may be seen as a means to this end.

It might be argued that purchasers themselves are uncertain about the relative merits of the alternative technologies, except in the immediate circumstances, and hence the QWERTY story can be revived. However, if the superior technology B is owned by someone, the owner has an incentive to bring it into use because its superiority will create a profit opportunity. It will therefore pay the owner to invest in a variety of stratagems designed to ensure that the first thirty adoptions do take place, after which adopters will choose B. Such stratagems are what Shapiro and Varian (1999) describe as 'ways to manage lock-in', and they include:

- *leasing the technology with a cancellation option* – that allows adopters to sample the technology at low cost, with the option to shift to another if they prefer
- *publicise adoptions, especially those by large or influential customers* – that helps to reassure other adopters that the required level of adoptions will be reached
- *bribe early adopters with low prices or other benefits* – in order to ensure that the early adoptions take place
- *advertise heavily, stressing the product's advantages* – in order to encourage early sales
- *give distributors and retailers incentives* – to encourage them to attract the required early adopters.

All of these tactics involve costs and a technology owner who spends too much on them, or who spends to poor effect, will necessarily fail. However, the central argument is that the owner of the superior technology will be able, and will have the incentive, to spend more than the owner of an inferior technology. At the same time potential customers also have an incentive to see the superior technology put in place, simply because it is superior. In the face of these incentives, and subject to the usual margins attributable to bounded rationality and information asymmetries, entrepreneurial activity in the market should ensure that inferior technologies are replaced. This does not only apply to the initial choice between two technologies. It also applies when a new technology emerges that is superior to the old (initially superior) version. In that case a number of other stratagems may be used. *Backward compatibility* means that the new product can be used with components from the older version. That reduces switching costs and helped Microsoft Word replace Wordperfect as the standard word-processing package. Failure to provide backward compatibility also seriously damaged the reputation of the Macintosh computer and helped the (supposedly inferior) IBM PC to win that particular 'standards' war.

Before concluding this review of the 'increasing returns' debate in the context of the network economy, it is worth revisiting the two central phenomena that distinguish networks and network products. These are the increasing value of a network to its participants as the number of participants increases, and the very low average variable and marginal cost of production for network products. With respect to the first of these, it must be true as a matter of arithmetic that as a network is larger each additional participant generates an increasingly large number of new connections. That forms the basis of the argument that users will be willing to pay more to join a network as it get bigger. However, simple economic logic suggests that links between nodes have different values and that the more valuable links are likely to be put in place first. In that case, the links that are added later will be less valuable than those added earlier and the phenomenon of increasing returns on the demand side is rather less certain. For the academic community, rapid communication links are very valuable and academics were among the first to participate in the Internet. However, once most academics became linked it is not clear whether the addition of further nodes necessarily raised the value of the network for the academics, or whether the value of the network for the new participants was really larger than its value to the earlier comers. Similarly with respect to standards. A grandfather will gain from having a video player in the same format as his son, because they can then share family videos. There will also be a gain if their immediate acquaintances use the same standard. However, at some point a limit is reached. It makes little difference to a family in Japan that a family in the United Kingdom uses the same video standard.

There are also reservations to be raised in respect of the idea that in the network economy marginal costs are near to zero and output can be scaled up almost infinitely at the same near-zero cost. That may be true for music CDs, but the purchasers of more complex products may need complementary goods or services in order to receive the full benefit. For software products, for instance, it is true that a very large number of copies can be made for almost zero cost. However, many users will also need software support whose supply is not infinitely scalable at zero cost. Furthermore, in order to sell more of a network product, sellers may need to advertise and the cost of attracting an additional purchaser may become increasingly high as the volume of sales increases. In other words, network products that are not subject to decreasing returns may be closely tied to 'old economy' products that are. As a result, the idea that larger volumes of network products can be sold under conditions of non-increasing cost per unit may have serious limits.

In conclusion, then, there remains considerable room for debate with respect to the threat that is posed by increasing returns to the efficient working of a market economy. It is clear from the analysis above that path dependence, leading to 'lock-in' and the possible dominance of inferior products, has been of major concern to analysts, policy-makers and those who fear that they may suffer from its effects. The judgment against Microsoft in the year 2000 was partly a reflection of that concern. At the same time it may be argued that in a market economy populated by alert profit-seekers the inherent profitability of a superior solution will lead to its adoption, as wily entrepreneurs find ways to overcome lock-in effects that are more real than apparent. It may also be argued that the network economy is not quite as different from its predecessor as appears at first sight.

Illustration **Microsoft in operating systems, spreadsheets, word processing and financial software**

The performance of Microsoft in different product segments provides a valuable illustration of many of the issues that have been covered in this chapter. A logical starting point lies in the history of its Windows operating system, which forms the platform for its other software products. Liebowitz and Margolis (1999) provide a detailed history and analysis.

In the mid-1980s a number of personal computers (PCs), most notably the Apple Macintosh, already had graphical user interfaces (GUIs). However, most PCs were still using the text-based DOS operating system. Digital Research produced a GUI known as GEM, Quarterdeck introduced Deskview, IBM developed Topview and Microsoft introduced Windows 1.0 in 1985. None of these products was successful. That was partly because they were slow and inclined not to work, partly because users had not yet decided in sufficient numbers that the mouse was the best approach to controlling a PC, and partly because it was known that Microsoft and IBM were working on a new operating system – O/S2 – which might well become dominant.

Only in 1990 did Microsoft introduce Windows 3.0, which marked the beginning of its dominance. That was based upon two key insights into the market. The first was that for a GUI to succeed there must be a large number of applications written for it. The second was that there must be backward compatibility so that older DOS applications could be run on the same PC. In 1992 both DOS and Windows were being used for spreadsheeting on around four million machines. By 1995 DOS spreadsheets had almost disappeared and Windows spreadsheets were operating on sixteen million machines. Leading competitors, notably Lotus and Novell, failed because they focused their development efforts on applications for OS/2, having been 'blindsided' by Bill Gates's assertion that it would become the next operating system of choice and that Windows was simply an intermediate step.

At this point, Microsoft began to move from selling operating systems and stand-alone applications to selling Office suites. As Windows 1.0 and 2.0 had sold relatively poorly, the company recognised that it needed to encourage users to adopt 3.0 and the combination of the new operating system with the suites allowed users to run the three major applications – word processor, spreadsheet and database

– simultaneously. The major competitors were Lotus in spreadsheets, Wordperfect in word processing and Borland in databases. In an attempt to assemble a competing suite Borland and Wordperfect constructed Borland Office. However, that consisted of two independently developed products that had little in common. Novell purchased Wordperfect and Borland's QuattroPro in order to integrate the components more effectively but it paid too much, failed to create a consistent strategy or identify a market niche for itself and badly damaged Wordperfect's valuable support organisation. Eventually the suite was sold to Corel and there was effectively no challenge to Microsoft Office.

Two different types of explanation are available for Microsoft's dominance. The first is based on the lock-in, path dependence, increasing returns interpretation of the situation. From that perspective, Microsoft came early to the market and as it gained market share the advantages of having software compatible with the largest possible number of users drew customers away from other products and created a lock-in to a (possibly inferior) product. As a result Microsoft gained significant market power which led to the anti-trust judgment against it in 2000. The alternative perspective is simply that Microsoft had the better products and secured market dominance, but not market power, because customers preferred those products.

Liebowitz and Margolis (1999) compare these alternatives by examining the evolution of some of the most important product segments, notably spreadsheets, word processors and financial software. In spreadsheets, the early market leader was Lotus 1-2-3, introduced in 1983. Microsoft Excel was originally launched for the Macintosh in 1985 and only entered the PC market in 1987. Hence it was not a first-mover that gained market share simply by virtue of having market share. However, its experience with the Macintosh did mean that it knew how to link spreadsheets with a GUI. When Excel entered, the market was divided among Lotus, Excel and QuattroPro. As Excel was linked to Windows, reviewers clearly saw it as the leader in terms of capabilities. Its only serious weakness in comparison with the competition was that it required relatively powerful hardware to function at its best. As hardware grew both more powerful and cheaper, so Excel's advantage over the competition grew. Nevertheless, there was little sign of the 'tipping' effect whereby almost all customers switch to a single supplier as soon as it secures a critical market share. Instead there was a steady decline in the share held by Lotus, and a steady increase in that held by Excel, so that it took six years for the market to shift from 70 per cent of revenues going to Lotus to 70 per cent of revenues going to Excel.

A similar pattern is revealed in the market for word processors. The early leaders were Wordperfect and Wordstar, running under DOS. Wordstar lost market share because its quality failed to keep up with its rivals. Wordperfect, on the other hand, was an excellent product in the DOS version and deserved its market dominance. However, it fell behind in developing a Windows-based version and in linking its product to an Office-type suite. Early releases of Wordperfect for Windows suffered from bugs so that when purchasers began to shift to Windows the best product on offer was Word which could be bundled with Excel.

The key conclusion drawn by Liebowitz and Margolis in respect of the spreadsheet and word-processor markets is that they did not display the features expected if lock-in and path dependence were a major determinant of the industry's development.

In both cases, the product that held an early lead lost it, which would not happen if network effects on the demand side were very powerful. While both markets eventually came to be dominated by a single product – Excel and Word – those products were not inferior. Judged by independent reviewers in the IT industry they were both judged superior to their rivals.

This view is reinforced if the market for personal software is examined. In that sector sales are divided among Microsoft Money, Managing your Money by Meca and Quicken Intuit. Managing your Money in the DOS version was originally most highly rated by reviewers and it had the highest market share. However, Meca was slow to introduce a Windows version whereas Intuit had experience with GUIs in the Macintosh market. Hence when users shifted to Windows, reviewers began consistently to rate Quicken as the best product and Quicken took the largest market share. As in the case of spreadsheets and word processors, the shift to Windows was crucial but in this case it was not Microsoft who gained, but a rival. Again, one product dominated the market in an early stage but it was replaced by a superior version.

Overall, these examples seem to suggest that market forces do function effectively, even in the sector where network effects might be expected to be most marked. Liebowitz and Margolis (1999) conclude that the benefit to buyers of using common software packages does not tend to lock them into inferior products, come what may, and that ownership of Windows does not give Microsoft the ability to impose its other products on users. As Linux and other contenders for the operating system market begin to take sales away from Microsoft it will be interesting to see if the software behemoth itself might eventually follow Lotus and Wordperfect to become a thing of the past, or whether it can remain nimble enough to keep its products in their leading positions.

References and further reading

W. Adams and J. Yellen. 'Commodity Bundling and the Burden of Monopoly', *Quarterly Journal of Economics*, vol. 90, 1976, pp. 475–98.

B.W. Arthur, 'Competing Technologies, Increasing Returns and Lock-In by Historical Events', *Economic Journal*, vol. 99, no. 397, 1989, pp. 116–31.

B.W. Arthur, *Increasing Returns and Path Dependence in the Economy*, Ann Arbor, University of Michigan Press, 1994.

P. David, 'Clio and the Economics of QWERTY', *American Economic Review*, vol. 75, no. 2, 1985, pp. 332–37.

P. David, 'Understanding the Economics of QWERTY: The Necessity of History', in W. Parker (ed.) *Economic History and the Modern Economist*, Oxford, Basil Blackwell, 1986.

N. Economides, 'The Economics of Networks', *International Journal of Industrial Organization*, October 1996, pp. 000.

N. Economides and C. Himmelberg, 'Critical Mass and Network Size with Application to the US Fax Market', Discussion Paper EC-95-11, Stern School of Business, New York University, 1995.

N. Economides and W. Lehr, 'The Quality of Complex Systems and Industry Structure', in W. Lehr (ed.) *Quality and Reliability of Telecommunications Infrastructure*, Hillsdale, Lawrence Erlbaum, 1995.

J. Farrell and G. Saloner, 'Standardization, Compatibility and Innovation', *RAND Journal of Economics*, vol. 16, 1985, pp. 70–83.

F. Fukuyama, *The End of History and the Last Man*, New York, Free Press, 1992.

M. Katz and C. Shapiro, 'Network Externalities, Competition and Compatibility', *American Economic Review*, vol. 75, no. 3, 1985, pp. 424–40.

K. Lancaster, 'A New Approach to Demand Theory', *Journal of Political Economy*, vol. 74, 1966, pp. 132–57.

A. Lewbel, 'Bundling of Substitutes or Complements', *International Journal of Industrial Organization*, vol. 3, 1985, pp. 101–7.

S. Liebowitz and S. Margolis, 'The Fable of the Keys', *Journal of Law and Economics*, vol. 33, 1990, pp. 1–26.

S. Liebowitz and S. Margolis, *Winners, Losers and Microsoft*, Oakland, The Independent Institute, 1999.

C. Matutes and P. Regibeau, 'Mix and Match: Product Compatibility Without Network Externalities', *RAND Journal of Economics*, vol. 19, 1988, pp. 221–34.

P. McAfee, J. McMillan and M. Whinston, 'Multiproduct Monopoly, Commodity Bundling and Correlation of Values', *Quarterly Journal of Economics*, vol. 19, 1989, pp. 221–34.

C. Shapiro and H.R. Varian, *Information Rules: A Strategic Guide to the Network Economy*, Boston, Harvard Business School Press, 1999.

O. Shy, *Industrial Organization: Theory and Applications*, Cambridge, MA, MIT Press, 1995.

I. Simonson and A. Tversky, 'Choice in Context: Tradeoff Contrast and Extremeness Aversion', *Journal of Marketing Research*, vol. 29, 1992, pp. 281–95.

J. Tirole, *The Theory of Industrial Organization*, Cambridge, MA, MIT Press, 1988.

Self-test questions

1. Which of the following applies to network products?

   (a) the demand curve slopes upwards

   (b) the value of the good to a user increases as the number of users increases

   (c) all users will prefer the same product if there is a choice

2. Explain why a network that has no owner will have too few participants and why a perfectly competitive industry producing network products will produce too few.

3. Which of the following is true for the case of the QWERTY keyboard?

   (a) the QWERTY keyboard is less efficient than the available alternatives

   (b) there are switching costs involved in shifting to another keyboard

   (c) keyboard users are locked in to the inefficient QWERTY keyboard

4. If a network industry produces undifferentiated products and competes on price (Bertrand competition), what will price be equal to?

5. You have a technology that is superior to the current standard, which dominates your industry. List *three* actions you can take to secure the adoption of your new standard.

Essay question

What does the history of Lotus 1-2-3, Wordperfect and Microsoft Office suggest about the efficiency problems of the network industry?

PART IV

Public policy

20 Competition and competition policy

In every economy, government has a significant influence on industry and commerce. Hence managers need to understand the regulatory environment in which they are working. This chapter examines policy towards competition, while Chapter 21 covers government regulation and privatisation.

Competition policy is a means by which governments hope to improve the competitive environment in which firms operate, in order to enhance the overall performance of the economy. However, in common with most important issues in economics, theory offers a variety of approaches and practice differs from place to place and from time to time. The analysis here examines the rationale for competition policy and outlines the major features of competition policies in the United Kingdom, the European Union and the United States. Alternative concepts of competition, including perfect competition, 'workable competition' and the 'Austrian view' are outlined and their implications for the social cost of monopoly power examined. The chapter then goes on to consider the legal control of 'dominant position', mergers and restrictive trade practices.

Alternative concepts of competition and monopoly power

Resource allocation under competition

In economics textbooks, and in large parts of the professional economics literature, the term 'competition' is synonymous with *perfect competition*, explained in Chapter 10. In that type of market structure an industry consists of a large number of small firms, producing identical products. New entry to the industry is completely free and this combination of circumstances guarantees that firms have absolutely no market power at all. The outcome of such a situation is that prices will be set equal to marginal cost, and the resulting allocation of resources is optimal, in the sense that social welfare is maximised, that being defined as the difference between benefits to consumers and costs to the economy.

The textbook analysis of monopoly refers to the very restricted circumstance of *pure monopoly* where there is only one firm in the industry and no possibility of entry. In that situation it can be shown that price will exceed marginal cost so that social welfare is not maximised, and firms will be able to exert considerable market power, allowing them to earn supernormal profits in the long run. The case in favour of competition and against monopoly can be understood in terms of this analysis. Monopoly leads to a misallocation of resources or allocative inefficiency, because price is not set equal to marginal cost.

The limitations of the textbook models

The textbook analysis of competition and monopoly provides a basic rationale for anti-monopoly or anti-trust policy. However, that approach is subject to criticism on the grounds that the two cases examined are highly unrealistic and markets that conform to their very tight specifications are rare and perhaps even non-existent. It has been pointed out in Chapter 1 that for some of the purposes of economic analysis this lack of realism is not necessarily a weakness. If the models are to be used for purely positive and predictive purposes then unrealistic assumptions are quite acceptable, even necessary.

On the other hand, if the analysis is to be used for 'normative' purposes, that is to make statements about how the economy *should* behave and what sort of policy *should* be introduced, the problems are real. If economic analysis is to be used to decide whether one real-world situation is superior to another, and neither conforms closely to either 'pure' model, then it is difficult to see how the models can be used convincingly.

It might be argued that most industries are a fair approximation to either perfect competition or monopoly and those that are roughly competitive could be left alone while those that are roughly monopolistic could be made subject to control. Unfortunately this argument is badly flawed. In the first place the dividing line between 'approximately competitive' and 'approximately monopolistic' is impossible to draw. In the second place, and more fundamentally, there is the *second-best problem*. Although perfect competition in all industries can be shown to give a first-best optimal allocation of resources, it is not at all clear what is the second-best optimum if perfect competition is not achievable everywhere. It could well be the case that the lack of perfect competition in some industries means that the best available allocation of resources requires monopoly behaviour in some other industries. These difficulties have led economists to search for a variety of solutions to the problem.

The search for 'workable competition'

If the requirement that all industries be perfectly competitive is an unattainable counsel of perfection, then an obvious response is to try to identify 'workable competition', defined by Clark (1940) as 'the most desirable forms of competition, selected from those that are practically possible'.

The difficulty is that we have very little to guide us on the characteristics of such a market structure, and the theory of second-best makes it clear that simply approximating to perfect competition is not the answer. Clark recognised this and his work on the issue provides an early intuitive statement of the second-best problem. Unfortunately, its implications have often not been taken up by other writers on the subject. Attempts to identify 'workable competition' have often consisted of long lists of structural and behavioural 'norms' to which an industry has to conform before being deemed workably competitive.

However, many of the norms consist of nothing more than approximations to perfect competition, for which there is no sound rationale. As a result one observer (Stigler 1956) suggested, rather cynically, that it is a simple matter to decide whether an industry is workably competitive or not. All that is required is to have a graduate student write a thesis on it. There is, however, a further condition, which is that no other student should ever be allowed to decide whether the industry is workably competitive or not, because he would be certain to reach the opposite conclusion.

The search for 'workable competition' has not, therefore, proved very fruitful although it is worth noting (and somewhat worrying) that the law on competition often seems to assume that some undefined version does exist and is understood. Indeed, if the law on competition outlaws certain market structures, or certain actions on the part of firms, that does imply that such structures and actions are known to be incompatible with workable competition, which in turn implies that the concept is understood by someone.

Structure–conduct–performance paradigm

In view of the failure to identify clearly the characteristics of workable competition an alternative approach is to turn away from theory and examine the facts about industries' activities, in order to identify those factors that lead firms to behave in unacceptable ways, and those that lead to satisfactory performance. This approach was suggested by Mason (1937) who noted: 'It is not sufficient to conduct purely analytical . . . studies . . . A further study of different types of industrial markets and business practices . . . is the only way in which economics can contribute directly to the shaping of public policy.'

This call was taken up by economists using increasingly sophisticated statistical methods in the attempt to identify the empirical links between industries' performance, their structure and the conduct of the companies within them. Many different relationships were examined but the most common hypothesis to be tested was that profitability in an industry may be positively linked to the level of concentration, the height of entry barriers, the extent of product differentiation and the rate of growth of demand.

As with so many issues, opinions vary widely on the value of this approach, which is known as the structure–conduct–performance paradigm. Many of the studies (though by no means all) confirmed the existence of a positive relationship between the level of concentration in an industry and its profitability. That in turn confirmed the view of many writers that concentration confers monopoly power and that government regulation of highly concentrated industries is therefore justified. Unfortunately, there are a number of reasons that such a conclusion cannot be held to with great confidence.

The first problem concerns the difficulties associated with the statistical methods used to identify the links between the various different variables. Many of the central concepts, like concentration, entry barriers and product differentiation, are difficult to measure and researchers are forced to approximate them using 'proxy' variables. As a result the findings of the different studies tend to vary widely with the sources of data used and the samples chosen. Very similar studies have often produced radically different, even diametrically opposite, conclusions.

There are also difficulties with the mis-specification of the relationships between the variables. In most structure–conduct–performance investigations it is assumed that the direction of causation runs from industry structure to industry performance. However, even a simple model like that of perfect competition makes it clear that performance (in the shape of a high level of profits) can affect structure (by inducing entry). If the relationships between structure and performance run in both directions, then the results of simple statistical techniques using just one equation provide very little meaningful information about how industry works.

The second problem is more fundamental, because it concerns the interpretation of the results and the use to which they are put. If it is accepted, for the sake of argument, that the evidence does show a positive link between concentration and profitability, the most common interpretation of that finding is that concentration bestows monopoly power and that there are gains to be had from an active policy against concentration and mergers. However, as Demsetz (1973, 1974) and others have noted, the same factual relationship between concentration and profitability could arise from a wholly different mechanism. Higher profits could simply be the result of greater efficiency, and high levels of concentration could simply be the incidental result of market share becoming concentrated in the hands of firms that have 'got it right'. If the cost structure of an industry exhibits substantial scale economies, or if a few firms have strong management teams while others do not, then the industry will become concentrated in the hands of a few highly profitable firms. That concentration will have little to do with the pure monopolist's raising of price through the restriction of output.

There are therefore two completely different interpretations of the concentration –profitability relationship. The 'market power' interpretation sees it as evidence of powerful firms' ability to acquire and use monopoly power, to the detriment of the public. The 'competitive' view argues that concentration may be the result of a desirable competitive process. It is unfortunate, then, that Mason's challenge to economists to improve their understanding of the issues by examining the evidence has not fulfilled the aspirations of those who hoped that an appeal to the facts, over the head of theory, would help in the construction of policy.

Competition as a process, rather than a state

The 'competitive' interpretation of the concentration–profitability relationship clearly implies a completely different conception of competition from that embodied in the model of perfect competition, or approximations to it. The perfectly competitive world is completely static and there is no reference to behaviour over time. The basic picture of the economy that it represents is one of a group of households who have fixed tastes for a set of known products, facing a group of firms having a fixed set of technologies available to them. Everybody is perfectly informed about everything and the abstract forces of supply and demand ensure that consumer satisfaction is maximised. In that concept of competition there is no rivalry among firms, which simply face 'the market'. Emphasis is placed upon how an industry will behave in equilibrium and profits are simply a temporary aberration, which are eliminated in the long run by entry. Such a model has no room for the entrepreneur. There are no innovations and no rivalries between individual firms.

A very different view of competition, which links back to much earlier conceptions, and is much closer to the layman's interpretation of the term, is that which is sometimes referred to as the Austrian view (Reekie 1979). In this view competition is not a state, but a process taking place through time in a world that is never in equilibrium. All of the possibilities are not known to everyone, firms have differing abilities and the entrepreneur who exercises creativity and foresight is able to alter the world they inhabit in ways that allow them to create profit opportunities. In this situation a company may develop a monopoly position.

However, unless the monopoly arises from some government-imposed restriction, or the sole ownership of a resource that has no substitute, it will tend to be a temporary one. Other firms will recognise the opportunities and enter the industry, or devise substitute products for the one that is earning high prices and profits. In the Austrian view (which seems consistent with much of the literature on corporate strategy) entrepreneurs are constantly trying to become temporary monopolists by being the first to invent a new product or identify a new market. At the same time, others are constantly trying to break down existing monopolies by entering markets that are seen to offer the prospect of profits.

From this perspective, profits may arise in three different ways. First, there are *true monopoly profits*, arising from the firm being protected from competition in some way. These are undesirable and policy should prevent firms from having such advantages. Second, there are *'windfall' profits* which arise as a matter of chance because cost and demand conditions turn out to be more favourable than anyone expected. Third, there will be an element of *'entrepreneurial' profit*, arising because some firms have a greater ability to identify profit opportunities or to go further and create opportunities that did not exist before. This last form of profit owes nothing to monopoly power, because the new opportunities are open to all, and it should not be seen as an indicator of misallocated resources.

Clearly, this interpretation has radical implications for the interpretation of profits, and for policy towards competition. If the notion of competition as a process is superior to the static conception set out in the economics textbooks then the existence of profits is at least partly the result of socially beneficial creative behaviour. Profits do not signal the existence of damaging monopoly power and it would be a mistake to introduce policies designed to eliminate the situations that lead to those excess profits.

The difficulty with this approach is that once the benchmark of perfect competition is abandoned there are no clear guidelines for deciding what kind of situations should be made subject to control through monopoly policy. Littlechild (1981) suggested that case studies of individual firms might allow some separation of the different sources of profits ('good' entrepreneurial activity, random variations in the environment and 'bad' monopoly power). Demsetz (1969) suggested a 'comparative institutions' approach, comparing the likely development of the market process under different types of policy regime. However, it is difficult to see how this could be achieved in practice. Perhaps the only clear prescription that emerges, in common with the more orthodox approach, is that the removal of entry barriers should be a major focus for competition policy.

The contestable markets approach

What is a contestable market?

The importance of entry conditions is also a key feature of an alternative approach to the analysis of competition, known as the *contestable markets* approach (Baumol *et al.* 1982). In some respects this development has elements in common with the Austrian view because its general conclusions are that an industry may perform in a socially acceptable way even if it contains a very small number of firms and does not correspond even remotely to the specification of perfect competition. However, the origins of the approach lie much closer to the mainstream of industrial economic theory, and it has the advantage of resting upon more conventional analytical foundations than the Austrian view. A full exposition of 'contestable markets' lies beyond the scope of this text but it is possible to provide an outline.

The most important concept is that of 'contestability'. A perfectly contestable market is one in which entry is free, exit is costless, and entry is a comparatively fast process. A crucial feature of a contestable market is its vulnerability to 'hit-and-run' entry. Potential entrants will not neglect any transient opportunity of earning economic profit. Should such opportunity come about, they will enter the market, collect the gains and exit the market costlessly before prices change. As the speed of entry is very fast, both the incumbents and entrants compete on equal terms, and potential entrants are not deterred by the threat of retaliatory price-cutting by incumbents.

If an industry has the features of a contestable market, then the threat of entry alone would be enough to discipline an incumbent monopolist to earn zero profit with efficient production. In such a market it can be shown that the benefits associated with perfect competition will accrue, even if there is a single firm, or if there are very few firms in the industry. As the contestability theorists themselves put it:

> Monopolists and oligopolists who populate such markets are sheep in wolves' clothing, for under this arrangement potential rivals can be as effective as actual competitors in forcing pro-social behaviour upon incumbents, whether or not such behaviour is attractive to them. As we have seen . . . this may be true where observed market phenomena are far from the competitive norm, and even where they superficially assume some pattern previously thought to be pernicious *per se*. (Baumol *et al.* 1982, p. 350)

Clearly, the concept of a contestable market is related to the idea of entry barriers and such a market might simply be thought of as one in which entry barriers are limited. However, the theory also suggests that in many instances barriers to entry are less formidable than has previously been supposed. In particular, the analysis points to the importance of sunk costs as the major real deterrent to entry. (Sunk costs are those that cannot be eliminated, even by cessation of production.) If sunk costs are small, entrants will have little difficulty in competing with existing firms on equal terms and the threat of this competition will force incumbents to behave like perfect competitors. Baumol *et al.* (1982) provide a good example in a small airline market.

If we consider the market for air travel between two towns where the number of people travelling is only enough to fill one aeroplane, we have an example of a 'natural monopoly'. It is always cheaper for the route to be served by a single airline than for two or more to fly in competition. As a result the market will be monopolised, in the sense that there is only one supplier. However, that supplier will not be able to operate like a textbook monopolist. If aircraft can be rented, or if there is an active market for second-hand planes, then sunk costs are very limited. Sunk costs are those costs that cannot be recovered even if the firm decides to leave the industry. If the incumbent airline is creating a profitable opportunity by charging high fares, what an entrant needs to do is to fly their aircraft onto the tarmac, undercut the incumbent and make a profit. If the incumbent then cuts their price, the entrant can literally fly away and either use the plane on another route or sell it (or cease renting it). The absence of sunk costs makes entry cheaply reversible and the threat or the reality of easy entry will discipline the incumbent 'monopolist'.

The contestable markets approach has a number of implications for competition policy. First, it shows that it is not appropriate to decide on whether to intervene in an industry by making reference to the degree of departure from the conditions of perfect competition. Second, it provides an alternative benchmark to the unattainable criterion of perfect competition, that of 'contestability'. When considering the structure and behaviour of an industry, the first step is to decide whether or not it constitutes a contestable market. If it does, government interference is not needed, even if the industry exhibits symptoms that have in the past been accepted as indicators of poor market performance, such as high concentration, price discrimination, mergers and vertical integration.

On the other hand, if the industry is not contestable then intervention to make it so needs to be considered. First and foremost governments need to consider means by which entry to and exit from an industry can be made easier. In particular, policy needs to reduce the level of sunk costs, which form the major barrier to exit and the main impediment to contestability. Measures could include having sunk costs borne by government, which would then lease facilities to firms, or by mandating that sunk costs should be shared by a consortium. Alternatively, sunk costs might be reduced by tax advantages for rapid depreciation, for retooling, or for the reuse of old plant in new activities. Anything that improves the efficiency of second-hand equipment markets would also be useful.

Contestable market, natural monopoly and government intervention

If an industry is contestable, the forces of potential competition will constrain the incumbents to earn zero economic profit. Even if there exists only one firm in the market, or the industry is a natural monopoly, the government need not regulate the firm if the market is contestable with free entry. However, not all types of entry are efficient. Under some situations, government's entry restrictions are needed to protect a natural monopoly from inefficient entry.

By definition, an industry is a natural monopoly if the cost of supplying the products by a single firm is lower than by any combination of several firms due to scale economies or scope economies. In other words, the cost of supplying the products via a single system is less than the cost of supplying via multiple systems. The cost function is said to be *sub-additive*. Consider an example. Suppose that the total cost of supplying one product by a single firm is $6, while the total cost of supplying two products is $8. In this example, it is less costly for a single firm to produce the two products. If there are two firms in the industry, each supplying one product, then the total cost will be $6 × 2 = $12. Hence, the industry is a natural monopoly.

Suppose now we extend the example to three products. The cost of supplying three products by a single firm is $13. In this three-product case, the cost function is still sub-additive: the total cost of supply by a single firm is lower than by any combination of several firms. If we have three firms in the industry, each supplying one product, then the total cost will be $6 × 3 = $18. If there are two firms, with one supplying two products and the other supplying one product, the total cost will be $8 + $6 = $14, which is still higher than the single-firm situation. Hence, the industry is a natural monopoly.

However, in the three-product case, the natural monopoly is not *sustainable*. A natural monopoly is sustainable if there exist prices that will not attract entry. Conversely, a natural monopoly is non-sustainable if there exist no prices that will not attract entry, even though single firm supply is efficient. In the two-product case, the average cost of supplying by one firm is $8/2 = $4. If the incumbent charges a uniform price of $4 for each product, it will not be profitable for any entrant who is equally efficient to enter the market to supply one (at a cost of $6) or two products (at a cost of $4). Entry is not attracted at this price and the natural monopoly is sustainable.

In the three-product case, the average cost of supplying by one firm has increased from $4 to $13/3 = $4.33. If the incumbent charges a uniform price of $4.33, then a two-product entrant, with an average cost of $4, can profitably enter the market and take away two-thirds of the incumbent's business. This will leave the incumbent with a loss on its remaining activity, as the cost of supplying one product ($6) is higher than the price ($4.33). This is referred to as *cream-skimming* or *destructive* competition, in the sense that a rival takes a profitable component of the incumbent's business, leaving the incumbent with a loss on the rest. The example has shown that if the average cost of the natural monopoly does not decrease continuously, then there is an opportunity for inefficient entry or cream-skimming. In such a situation, government entry restrictions may be needed to prevent inefficient entry which will increase the total costs of supplying the products.

The above example provides a good case for government's protection of natural monopolies. In the long run, however, a natural monopolist may use its protected position to become X-inefficient. Furthermore, although it is theoretically possible that natural monopolies are not sustainable, there is little evidence to show that actual cost conditions in regulated industries meet the conditions for non-sustainability. Experiences in deregulation have shown that even for some utility industries like telecommunications and electricity supply, which are traditionally regarded as natural monopolists, introduction of competition and promotion of free entry can be both feasible and efficient. Unless there is a strong case to prevent inefficient entry and destructive competition, government policies should be aimed at promoting competition rather than restricting entries.

The rationale for competition law

Measuring the cost of monopoly: Allocative inefficiency, X-inefficiency and rent dissipation

If an anti-monopoly policy is to be introduced to encourage market competition, it will use resources and impose costs on the economy. It is important, therefore, to consider whether the allocative inefficiency caused by monopoly is sufficiently large to justify the expenditure incurred in correcting it. This in turn requires some estimate of the 'cost of monopoly power'. It is hardly surprising, in the light of the preceding discussion, to discover that estimates of the cost of monopoly power vary widely with the method of calculation used and with the analyst's interpretation of the nature of competition and the source of profits. The mechanics of the measurement process are too complex to detail here, beyond noting that they begin from the proposition that monopoly power will reduce consumer satisfaction and increase profits. Published figures for profits are then used as the basis for measuring the size of the loss involved.

The earliest attempt to make an estimate in this way was carried out by Harberger (1954) who concluded that the loss was very slight, at approximately 0.1 per cent of national income (for the United States), a figure that has been refined but not radically altered by others using similar methods who also found the losses due to monopoly to be small.

If such estimates are correct, there are empirical grounds for questioning whether monopoly policy is justified at all. However, as might be expected, other commentators have criticised the basic method and produced much larger estimates. Apart from causing allocative inefficiency by setting a price higher than marginal cost, a monopolist is under little pressure to keep its costs down and it will tend to be 'X-inefficient'. That means that the firm incurs higher costs than are strictly necessary through organisational slack, laziness and general lack of tight control. Leibenstein (1966) emphasises the importance of X-inefficiency and considers it another major source of inefficiency due to monopoly.

In the standard neo-classical, profit-maximising model it is assumed that the firm incurs the minimum cost achievable for the level of output being produced, given the set of plant and equipment that has been installed. Such a firm may be described as being X-efficient or 'operationally efficient'. However, this may not be the case under monopoly. A firm possessing monopoly power may aim at maximising managerial utility, rather than maximising profits of the shareholders.

This is particularly true for a monopoly under government profit control (see Chapter 21). Because of the lack of competitive pressure to minimise costs and because profits cannot be above the permitted levels set by the regulator, a regulated monopolist will tend to spend more on staff and on 'perks' for the management than is necessary, in which case it is X-inefficient.

In non-regulated markets the degree of X-inefficiency will tend to be higher if the market structure in which the firm operates is less competitive. If there are a small number of rivals who are able to avoid direct competition with each other, and they are protected by barriers to entry into the industry, there will be few penalties for slackness and X-inefficiency is correspondingly more likely to result.

Some other economists have suggested that monopoly not only results in losses arising from allocative and X-inefficiencies, but that would-be monopolists use up scarce resources in the attempt to secure their monopoly positions, and the cost of those resources should be added in to the social losses caused. Posner (1975), Buchanan and Tullock (1967), for instance, argued that if acquiring (and protecting) a monopoly position is itself a competitive activity, then the costs of becoming a monopolist will just equal the monopoly profits to be made. Tariffs, quotas, monopolies and any other artificial barriers to entry created by the government will have redistributive effects on wealth. Firms and individuals will spend resources to obtain political favours. They engage themselves in profit-seeking (or rent-seeking) activities to make or prevent wealth transfers. The monopoly profit (or rent) is dissipated in the competitive process for monopoly rights or government protections. In that case, the cost of monopoly is much higher than that estimated by Harberger and others using similar methods.

Cowling and Mueller (1978) extended these arguments to calculate a number of different estimates of the cost of monopoly in the United States and the United Kingdom, using information on individual companies rather than whole industries. Their conclusion was that for the United States the losses attributable to General Motors alone amounted to US$1.75 billion, which exceeded Harberger's estimate for the whole economy. For the 734 largest firms in the economy the loss attributable to monopoly power was equal to 13 per cent of the gross output of those firms. In the UK case it was concluded that monopoly losses could be as high as 7 per cent of output, with three firms alone (Shell, BP and BAT) accounting for losses of £186 million.

If these latter estimates are correct, the case for anti-monopoly policy is strengthened and the estimates of losses attributable to individual firms could provide the starting point for enforcement. However, that takes the debate back to the differences between the 'market power' and the 'competitive' approach to concentration and profits. Littlechild (1981) has argued that the whole conceptual framework used by Cowling and Mueller introduces an upward bias into the calculations, which therefore give highly exaggerated results. The basic problem is that all the attempts to measure the cost of monopoly power take place within a framework of long-run equilibrium. The investigators assume that the profits observed will be maintained in the long run and are entirely due to the monopoly position held by the firms. Under that assumption, all profits represent welfare losses.

However, that is a very strong assumption and if the industries were not in long-run equilibrium at the moment of observation then the profits and price/cost margins observed cannot be attributed to monopoly power. Even in a perfectly competitive industry, where there is no monopoly power at all, large profits can be made in the short run if demand increases. It has also been noted above that there are three components to supernormal profit – true monopoly profit, windfall gains and 'entrepreneurial' profit. Only the first arises from socially harmful behaviour and to assume that all profit is of this type seems certain to lead to overestimates of the cost of monopoly.

Economics and competition law

As in so many other areas of economic analysis, there is no consensus on the importance of the need for competition law. Some economists argue that monopoly power is a major impediment to the efficient use of the economy's resources, imposing substantial costs on the economy. Others take the view that the dangers have been exaggerated and that the need for intervention is much less marked. As a result, economic analysis has not provided the law-maker with a clear set of guidelines concerning the types of industrial structure and market behaviour that lead to acceptable levels of performance.

Although the rationale for competition law is fundamentally economic, the connections between the law on competition and the economic analysis of competition are much more limited than might be expected or hoped for. The best that can be said is that economic analysis illustrates that there are three dimensions to the concept of competition. The first concerns the structure of an industry, where the number of firms, their market shares and the condition of entry are of central importance. Second, there is the dimension of company behaviour, encompassing firms' objectives and the methods they adopt in order to achieve those objectives. Third, there is the industry's performance with respect to prices, costs, profits, productivity, efficiency and equity. The law on competition is concerned with both structure and behaviour because of their perceived impact on performance, as is shown below.

Different approaches to monopoly policy and competition law

Sector-specific versus comprehensive competition laws

A government may take either a sector-specific or a general competition authority approach to introducing competition policy. In many countries, including the United Kingdom and the United States, comprehensive competition laws covering all sectors coexist with sector-specific regulations.

Some countries opt for a sector-specific approach to competition policy without setting up any competition authorities. In Singapore and Hong Kong there are neither general competition laws applying across all industries nor independent agencies to enforce the law. The governments in these two economies adopt a sector-specific approach. Under that approach, if a government finds that effective competition does not prevail in certain industries, or dominant firms abuse their market powers, it will take *ad hoc* action to promote competition. Such actions include the establishment of sector-specific regulatory authorities and the enactment of sector-specific competition laws. Other countries, like New Zealand, take the opposite approach, adopting a general competition authority approach without sector-specific regulators in industries like telecommunications and electricity supply.

The debate on 'rules versus discretion'

There are two fundamentally different approaches to the law on competition. The first, which forms the basis for much of the American system of anti-trust legislation, is known as the 'rules' approach. In a system based upon rules certain types of market structure or behaviour are illegal *per se*. It is not necessary to show that the structure or the behaviour in question has been harmful because the illegality arises from the structure or the behaviour itself, not from any result that follows.

The alternative system is known as the 'discretionary' approach around which the UK system is largely based. In that type of system there is no automatic presumption that certain types of market structure or certain types of behaviour are necessarily harmful. Instead it is noted that some structures or behaviours may allow firms to damage the public interest, and it is that damage that the law aims to prevent. In other words, in the American system it is monopoly power that is illegal. In the UK system it is the abuse of monopoly power that is illegal.

The advantages and disadvantages of these alternative approaches to competition policy are themselves the subject of debate. The 'rules' approach has a number of advantages:

● firms have a clear understanding of what is permitted and what is not
● the criteria on which policy is based are objective
● the system is relatively inexpensive to administer
● the costs of legal procedures are lower than in a situation where the law has to be decided case by case (although the American example shows that the cost of lawyers does not become negligible)
● firms have less encouragement to waste resources by lobbying those they believe will have influence in deciding their case, or potential cases.

The first major disadvantage of the 'rules' approach is that the system is potentially inflexible and unable to deal effectively with the special circumstances of individual cases. This could be overcome by having an increasingly complex set of rules, setting out how different circumstances are to be treated (Hay 1988), but as the rules become more complicated their application becomes more open to interpretation and the basic advantages of the 'rules' approach are lost. The second major problem, which follows from the discussion above, is that analysis has provided no clear indication of what exactly the rules should be. The 'rules' approach therefore involves the simple and efficient application of rules that may be incorrect.

The advantages and disadvantages of the 'discretion' approach are essentially the converse of the 'rules' approach. As there is no presumption that certain types of structure or behaviour are necessarily harmful, each case has to be decided upon its individual merits. That allows a degree of flexibility that is not available under the rules approach. On the other hand, each case has to be investigated in depth, which is expensive, and companies are uncertain with regard to the permissibility of some actions. As a result they may be deterred from carrying out legitimate activities for fear of government intervention, and there is the danger that cases are decided on political rather than economic grounds. Given the uncertain application of the law under this approach, companies may also waste scarce resources in lobbying to attempt to influence the outcome of cases in which they are involved, or to prevent their actions from being subject to legal proceedings at all.

Alternative institutional and legal frameworks

Apart from the differences between the 'rules' and 'discretion' approaches, competition policies may differ in the way in which they relate to the legal system, which may be through administrative controls, the criminal law or the civil law.

In the American system, anti-trust policy is associated most closely with the criminal law, and it is a criminal offence to monopolise a market or to collude with others to restrict competition. Under European Union legislation, fines can be imposed upon offenders but civil sanctions involving injunctions and damages are also used to restrain anti-competitive activity. In the United Kingdom the system is based almost entirely around administrative controls and limited civil sanctions, with very little use being made of criminal sanctions.

Policy towards monopoly or 'dominant position'

The concept of market dominance

Competition policies are often targeted at firms having a *dominant position* in the market. The debate on whether a firm is dominant revolves around the definition of the market. According to the Federal Communications Commission (FCC) in the United States, a carrier is declared dominant only if it possesses market power in the relevant product and geographic market (FCC 1995). The definition of the 'relevant market' is therefore crucial. The Merger Guidelines of the US Department of Justice and the Federal Trade Commission define the relevant market as 'the narrowest product and geographic area in which a hypothetical monopolist could profitably raise and maintain prices above the competitive level significantly (of the order of 5%) for a substantial period of time'. This is also called the 'hypothetical monopolist' test.

The 'hypothetical monopolist' test involves asking whether, if all suppliers of the products raised their prices by 5%, their collective profits would rise. If the answer to this question is 'yes', then the 'relevant market' is defined as that which covers the products under consideration. If the answer is 'no', because quite a large number of customers would shift to other substitutes, then the boundary of the 'relevant market' has to be extended by adding other substitutes. After adding the closest substitute into the potential market, we apply the test again. This process is repeated until the answer is 'yes', which implies that suppliers could profitably raise and maintain prices above the competitive level. Of course, when more products are added into the 'relevant market', the market share of a single firm will become smaller.

Apart from applying the 'hypothetical monopolist' test, other indicators used in assessing market power in the relevant market include market concentration, market share, the degree of price correlation in the market, supply elasticity of the market, demand elasticity for the product and the degree of substitutability between products.

The measurement of market concentration

The term 'concentration' refers to the extent to which industrial activity is concentrated in the hands of a small number of firms. While concentration is only one aspect of industrial structure it is probably the single most important determinant of competitive behaviour and performance and therefore merits close attention. If an industry is highly concentrated, the firms within it may be able to exert some degree of market power, resulting in a misallocation of resources to the detriment of consumers and a less efficient price system. On the other hand, a high level of concentration may be needed if firms are to operate at minimum cost by exploiting all of the available economies of scale and economies of scope.

The degree of concentration may be examined at two different levels. First, there is the overall level of concentration, which refers to the extent to which the largest firms in an economy dominate total employment and output. Second, there is the level of market concentration, which refers to the level of concentration in an individual industry or market.

Overall concentration is a highly aggregated phenomenon which may mask wide variations across individual industrial sectors. For the purposes of managerial economics, it is market concentration that is of the greatest interest, as it is concentration at that level that forms a major determinant of the environment in which individual firms operate.

Market concentration may be measured in a number of different ways. A useful starting point is with the concentration curve, which traces out the cumulative percentage of market output (or sales or employment or assets) against the cumulative number of firms, ranked from largest to smallest. Figure 20.1 shows a number of such curves.

The advantage of the concentration curve is that it provides a graphical summary of the information relating to every firm in the industry. However, such a complete set of information is very expensive to collect and if empirical work is to be carried out some form of quantitative empirical measure needs to be derived from it.

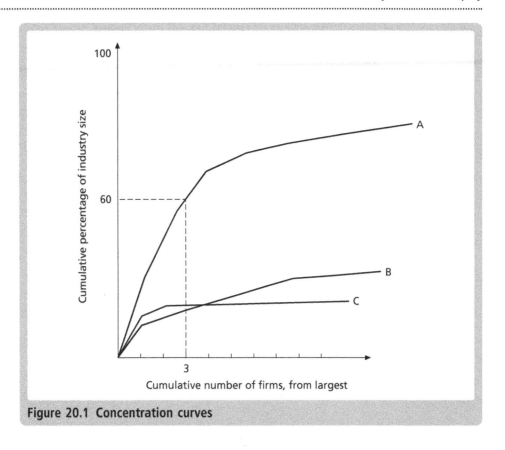

Figure 20.1 Concentration curves

The most commonly used measure of concentration is the concentration ratio, which is the proportion of an industry's size accounted for by a group of the very largest firms. The three-firm concentration ratio, for instance, often denoted CR_3, shows the proportion of industry size accounted for by the three largest firms, shown for industry A in Figure 20.1 as 60 per cent.

As the concentration ratio is simple to understand and relatively cheap to construct it is available for most industries in many industrialised economies. Unfortunately it suffers from a number of disadvantages. In the first place, the ranking of industries by their level of concentration may vary with the number of firms included in the calculation of the ratio. If, for a pair of industries, the concentration curve for one lies above that of the other for the whole of its range there is no difficulty. Whichever number of firms are included in the concentration ratio, one industry will always record a higher level of concentration than the other, as with industries A and B in Figure 20.1. However, if the concentration curves cross each other, as for industries B and C, the ranking of the two industries will vary with the number of firms chosen, providing inconsistent measures of the degree of concentration.

The concentration ratio also suffers in that it provides no information at all about the relative sizes of either the firms not included in the index or the firms that have been counted. An industry could have a three-firm concentration ratio of 60 per cent and the remaining 40 per cent of the industry's size could be distributed across just two additional firms having 20 per cent each, thereby being a five-firm oligopoly. On the other hand, the remaining 40 per cent could be quite evenly distributed across hundreds of other firms. Within the 60 per cent accounted for by the largest three firms there could be either an even distribution of around 20 per cent each, or a single firm could have 50 per cent with the two second largest having only 10 per cent between them. Such differences in market structure are likely to have important implications for the behaviour and performance of the firms but they will be hidden within the summary index. A further difficulty with concentration ratios is that there is no theoretical reason for preferring a three-firm ratio to a five-firm or an n-firm ratio. The choice of the number of firms to include is entirely arbitrary.

An alternative measure of concentration, which does take into account the role played by all firms in the market and yet still provides a single summary measure, is the *Herfindahl index*. This is defined as the sum of the squares of the market shares of all firms, so that:

$$\text{Herfindahl index} = \sum S_i^2, \qquad \text{where } S_i = \text{share of the i'th firm}$$

This index reflects both the number of firms in the industry and their relative size. It also has the intuitively useful property of providing a *numbers equivalent*. If an industry contained two firms of equal size, the Herfindahl index would have a value of 0.5. If an industry had four firms, the index would be equal to 0.25. If an industry has a Herfindahl index calculated as 'n' then it has the same index value as an industry containing 1/n firms of equal size, which helps to provide an intuitive 'feel' for the meaning of the measure. On the other hand, this could be misleading because there is no reason to suppose that an industry having index 'n' actually contains 1/n firms of the same size.

The level of concentration in an individual industry, and changes in that level, may be determined by a number of factors. The most obvious are economies of scale. It is also important to remember that scale economies are not limited to production alone. In consumer goods in particular, firms that can afford high levels of advertising may be able to secure discounts from the advertising media and the impact of advertising and promotion may be cumulative so that heavy spending on advertising secures consumer loyalty to a much greater extent than lower levels. Recent work by Sutton (1996, 1999) suggests that in some sectors, described as 'high alpha' industries, customers react strongly to firms' spending on sunk costs like advertising and R&D so that firms who escalate such spending can take rapidly increasing market shares.

If concentration were solely determined by economies of scale, firms would not expand beyond the size needed to reap all of the known scale economies. However, there is evidence that in some industries concentration is greater than is needed to secure the scale economies available. In that case the most important determinant of concentration lies in firms' attempts to secure the profits arising from having market power, by erecting entry barriers to limit new firms' access to the market or by merging with other firms in order to secure larger market shares. It is certainly the case that mergers have played a very important role in the process of concentration in both the United Kingdom and the United States. One study of increasing concentration in UK manufacturing (Hannah and

Kay 1977) found that in the postwar period mergers actually accounted for more than 100 per cent of the increase in concentration, a result that implies that in the absence of mergers, concentration would have actually declined.

The links between concentration and the possibility of harmful abuse of market power are complex and causality may run in both directions. Concentration may provide firms with the monopoly power to exploit consumers, or it may be the drive to secure monopoly power that causes higher levels of concentration. Whichever way the relationship operates, there is clearly a risk that in concentrated industries the beneficial forces of competition may be weakened. For that reason many countries, including the United Kingdom and the United States, have policies that are designed to guard against that possibility, either by preventing firms from gaining a dominant position or by making illegal the abuse of a dominant position.

Policies towards market dominance

A dominant position acquired by a firm in the market can either be the result of anti-competitive behaviour by the firm, or the result of its superior competitive performance. In most market economies, governments have designed competition or anti-trust policies to avoid the emergence of market dominance and to prevent the abuse of a dominant position. The focus of the European Union's competition policy is on the abuse of dominance, not market dominance *per se*. The competitive authorities in the United Kingdom follow the Union's policy on preventing the abuse of dominance.

The policy in the United States regarding market dominance is based upon a much more hostile view. Anti-trust policy is aimed at the prevention of market dominance and monopolisation, firms are prohibited from monopolising or *attempting* to monopolise a market, and the growth of a dominant position is restrained at an early stage. In other words, the policy is aimed at preventing dominance, rather than preventing the abuse of dominance. The provisions in the anti-trust laws are directed against anti-competitive behaviour, rather than the possession of a dominant position. A similar approach seems to have been adopted in the United States with the Department of Justice's anti-trust suit against Microsoft (Lam 2000).

The UK approach to market dominance

The UK approach to monopoly or 'dominant position' is based on a series of legislative developments, from the Monopolies and Restrictive Practices Act of 1948 to the Competition Act 1998 (Parker 2000) and currently involves three main legal channels:

1. A monopoly reference under the Fair Trading Act 1973.
2. A competition reference under the Competition Act 1980 (as amended in 1998).
3. A prohibition of the abuse of a dominant position within the Common Market, under Article 86 of the Treaty of Rome (which under the Amsterdam Treaty became Article 82 from May 1 1999).

Under the Fair Trading Act 1973 the Director General of Fair Trading (DGFT) had the power to refer a monopoly situation to the Monopolies and Mergers Commission (MMC). Under that Act a 'legislative monopoly' could be deemed to exist if at least 25 per cent of goods or services of a particular description were supplied in the United Kingdom by one firm (a 'scale monopoly') or two or more firms acting in such a way as to restrict competition between them (a 'complex monopoly'). However, the 1973 Act did not prohibit any specific business conduct or presume that any particular conduct was unlawful *per se*. Instead, it invoked the 'public interest test' and required the MMC to take account of 'all matters which appear to them . . . to be relevant' when deciding whether a legislative monopoly was in the public interest. The Competition Act 1998 extended the legislation in a number of ways. First, it replaced the MMC with a Competition Commission (largely staffed by the personnel of the MMC). More significantly, it provided an alternative approach to dominance by introducing a prohibition on 'any conduct . . . which amounts to the abuse of a dominant position of a market . . . if it may affect trade within the United Kingdom'. The Act borrows directly from Article 82 (previously Article 86) of the European Community Treaty in providing examples of conduct that could constitute such abuse. Further guidelines divide abuses into two categories. The first of these is 'exploitive' abuse, which is where the monopoly charges excessive prices or discriminatory prices. The second is 'exclusionary' abuse, which covers predatory attempts to exclude competition or to prevent customers from dealing with potential competitors.

The DGFT has also revised the 25 per cent market share criterion by suggesting that an undertaking with less than a 25 per cent share would not normally be considered dominant, while one having a share of more than 40 per cent 'may well be dominant'. UK competition policy therefore has a number of different market share criteria. The 25 per cent threshold applies to investigations and inquiries under the 1973 Act but a 40 per cent share is the presumed threshold for dominance under the 1998 Act.

Clearly, the definition of the market to which the 25 per cent or 40 per cent criteria apply is important, as any firm would be a monopolist if the definition were drawn narrowly enough. In principle the market that is defined should take into account a group of products or services that are very close substitutes for each other, having high cross-elasticities of demand, and the geographical area served by the firms under investigation. In practice it can be extremely difficult to decide on an appropriate definition of the market covered and companies coming under investigation could spend considerable time and effort attempting to redefine the boundaries of the market in such a way as to render them immune from investigation. In order to avoid this problem the Fair Trading Act 1973 simply states that in making the reference the Director General or Secretary of State should state the criteria on which goods and services are to be included. When a reference is made to the Competition Commission, it has to consider a number of questions, namely:

- Does a monopoly situation exist?
- In whose favour does it exist?
- Are any steps being taken to exploit or maintain the monopoly position?
- Are these steps contrary to the public interest and what are the adverse effects?

If the Competition Commission should find against a firm, or group of firms, the DGFT then usually seeks undertakings from them, designed to remedy the abuse that has been found. If such undertakings are not forthcoming, or not kept, the minister responsible has wide powers to make an order prohibiting the anti-competitive behaviour, or even ordering disinvestment (or divestiture). Should such orders be breached, enforcement is by civil procedures.

A monopoly reference has a number of limitations, as it can only be used when there is a monopoly situation as defined. The whole of the market has to be investigated, which is expensive and time consuming (some investigations take years to complete) and the sanctions are limited. As a result, the Competition Acts (1980, 1998) gave powers to the DGFT to investigate the practices of a single firm if he believed it to be engaged in anti-competitive practices likely to restrict, distort or prevent competition in the United Kingdom. The Act makes no direct reference to monopoly or dominance in this respect, but it is unlikely that the terms could be applied to a firm that did not have substantial market power. The DGFT himself can make an investigation, rather than referring it to the Competition Commission, and can try to obtain any undertakings deemed necessary from the firm in question. If these cannot be obtained satisfactorily then a 'competition reference' may be made to the Competition Commission, which must report back within six months.

Satisfactory evaluation of the UK policy on dominance or monopoly is difficult, given the failure of economic analysis to provide an adequate definition of workable competition, and given that the essence of a discretionary policy is to treat each case on its merits in the light of the public interest. It is certainly the case that 'contestability theory' casts very serious doubt on the market share criterion as a means of identifying situations in which market power is being abused (Hay 1988). Various other commentators have suggested that the lack of clear rules has led to inconsistent judgments where different conclusions have been reached in situations where the facts of the case appear to be substantially similar. At a more practical level it is also the case that practices such as high prices, refusing to supply, or keeping other firms out of the market are not illegal under the UK system unless there has been a monopoly report. As only a limited number of such reports can be produced, and as the process of investigation is often drawn out over a long period of time, the policy is unlikely to have a major effect on industrial structure, conduct or performance.

The impact of the European Union in respect of dominance

Since the United Kingdom joined the European Union, EU rules on competition form part of the law of the United Kingdom. These provide for a different approach to the control of economic power. Article 86 of the Treaty of Rome (Article 82 following the Amsterdam Treaty) states that any abuse of a dominant position within the EU market, or a substantial part of it, shall be prohibited in so far as it affects trade between member states. Dominant position is not defined, either in terms of market share or any other criterion, being left to judicial interpretation, which has defined it in one case (*Sirena* vs *Eda*, 1971) as 'the power to prevent effective competition in an important part of the market' and in another

(*EC Commission* vs *Continental Can*, 1972) as 'the power to behave independently without having to take into account competitors, purchasers or suppliers'.

Under the EU rules, evidence that a firm has a dominant position does not in itself lead to action being taken against the firm. The principle adhered to, as in the United Kingdom, is that it is abuse of a dominant position that is prohibited, not the position itself. Various such abuses have been condemned by the EU and the European Court of Justice, including unfair prices, discriminatory pricing, predatory pricing designed to drive rivals from the market, refusal to supply and unfair trading practices.

Under the Treaty of Rome such practices are not subject to Article 86 (now 82) unless they affect trade between member states and in early judgments this was often taken to imply that imports and exports between member states had to be directly involved before the abuse of a dominant position could come within the remit of the EU's rules. However, as Agnew (1985) pointed out, later judgments broadened that interpretation considerably, to the point where abuse of a dominant position affecting competition anywhere within the EU is interpreted as potentially having effects upon intra-EU trade. As a result, EU law on competition has begun to enter into areas previously reserved for national legislation.

Enforcement of Article 86 can take place in three different ways. The first is where the European Commission itself makes an order to end an infringement or imposes fines. The second is where national authorities themselves enforce the Article, although they can only do so if the Commission has not commenced proceedings, and the Office of Fair Trading has never taken such a step. Third, an individual or company who has suffered harm as a result of an infringement of the Article could themselves bring an action for damages.

Evaluation of the impact of the EU's rules on dominance has been very limited. In so far as they embody similar principles to those underlying the UK approach, they are probably subject to the same shortcomings. Korah (1975) suggested that Article 86 is used to protect small and medium-sized firms from competition from larger rivals, which may be counter-productive if those rivals are more efficient. Agnew (1985) suggests that in at least one case a firm's attempt to rationalise its distribution system was put at risk because a former distributor who was excluded from the new, supposedly more efficient, system brought in an action for damages on the grounds of refusal to supply.

The US approach to dominance

The US policy on anti-trust pre-dates the UK and European policy by a considerable margin, being traceable back to the Sherman Act. In 1890, the US Congress passed that Act in response to the alleged monopolistic behaviour of the railroad, tobacco, steel and oil trusts of the time. As explained above, US anti-trust policy rests upon different principles, being closer to the 'rules' approach where certain aspects of market structure are made illegal *per se*, as opposed to the discretionary approach where each case is considered on its merits. The Sherman Act aims at prohibiting firms from restraining trade to lessen competition. Section 1 of the Act prohibits collusive combinations and conspiracies among firms that lessen competition in the market, while Section 2 prohibits firms from monopolising or attempting to monopolise a market. As Section 2 of the Act puts it: 'Every person who shall monopolise, or attempt to monopolise . . . any part of the trade or commerce . . . shall be deemed guilty of a felony.' The body of anti-trust law in the United States empowers the Department of Justice and the Federal Trade Commission to prosecute violators.

In the original formulation of the Sherman Act, emphasis was placed upon the word 'monopolise', in order to mean an active process of securing monopoly power, rather than simply possessing it, perhaps as a result of superior efficiency. As a result, the possession of large market shares was not itself seen as illegal, most notably in the early case of US Steel, which had a 65 per cent share of total output in 1901. In that case it was argued that a dominant position was only illegal if the firm actively attempted to use it or maintain it. However, that view was developed in the Alcoa case of 1954 in such a way as to effectively overturn earlier judgments. In the Alcoa case it was found that illegal monopolisation could be inferred without any evidence of unreasonable practices on the part of the firm in question. It therefore came very close to outlawing monopoly position *per se*, a position that was reinforced by other judgments. Some of the world's best-known firms, including Standard Oil, Eastman Kodak, General Motors, Xerox, American Telephone & Telegraph (AT&T) and Microsoft have been effectively forced, often through out-of-court agreements, to facilitate new entry by other firms into their industry, following the attentions of the Department of Justice.

In 1914, the US Congress decided that the focus of anti-trust law should be on preventing the growth of monopoly at an early stage and passed the Clayton Act. That Act addressed potentially anti-competitive behaviours like price discrimination, tying arrangements, exclusive arrangements and mergers. The Act also declared that the specified business practices would be illegal only where the 'effect may be to substantially lessen competition or tend to create monopoly'. The perceived balance between the costs and the benefits arising from these actions depends upon the concept of competition that is adopted. If firms have acquired a monopoly position through superior performance, to force them to assist less efficient firms to enter and to allow those less efficient firms to survive is unlikely to be in the public interest. On the other hand, if dominant position secures monopoly power and misallocates resources, such policies can be justified.

Policy towards mergers

Mergers may be of three main types, as outlined in Chapter 4. The first is the horizontal merger, where two or more firms in the same industry, and at the same stage of the distribution process, join together. The second is the vertical merger, where a firm becomes more vertically integrated by linking with another that is either closer to the final buyer ('forward' integration), or closer to sources of supply ('backward' integration). The third is the conglomerate, or diversified merger, where firms carrying on business in unrelated sectors come together. All three types of merger may have implications for competition but it is horizontal mergers that raise the salient issues.

Cost–benefit analysis of horizontal mergers

If a government has a policy towards dominant position and monopoly, it must also have a policy towards horizontal mergers, as they are one of the most common mechanisms through which a dominant position can be established. As in the case of monopoly, there are two basic approaches that policy can take. The first is to have rules, which would prevent firms from growing beyond a certain size, or having more than a certain specified market share. The alternative is to treat each case on its individual merits, measuring the costs and benefits that arise in each case and ruling accordingly.

Williamson (1968) put forward a simple analysis that might be used to measure the costs and benefits associated with an individual merger, as shown in Figure 20.2.

The starting point for the analysis is the assumption that if the merger takes place, costs of production will fall, as a result of scale economies or synergy, but price will rise as a result of the monopoly power secured. In the simplest case it is assumed that before the merger takes place, price is set at a level that equals average cost. In Figure 20.2 the pre-merger position is given by the cost curve AC_1 and the price P_1. If social welfare is defined as the difference between the benefit to consumers and the cost to the economy, it can be seen that the gross benefit to consumers is found by adding together the areas marked S, A, B, C, D, E and F. The cost to the economy is given by adding together the areas C, D, E and F. As net benefit is given by the difference between the two, it is equal to the areas S, A and B. If the merger leads cost to fall to AC_2 and price to rise to P_2 it can be seen that after the merger gross benefit to consumers is equal to the sum of areas S, A, C and E, while cost to the economy is equal to area E, giving a net benefit that is equal to areas S, A and C. Comparing the pre-merger and post-merger position it can be seen that on balance the merger leads to a

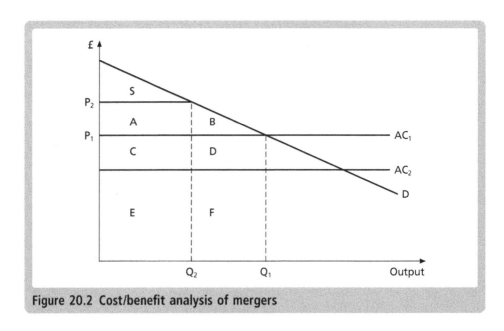

Figure 20.2 Cost/benefit analysis of mergers

gain given by area C and a loss equal to area B. The relative size of these effects determines the balance of advantage.

Clearly, the net advantage of a merger depends upon the particular circumstances, which are determined by the extent of the price rises, the size of the cost savings and the slope of the demand curve. Williamson sets out a table showing the relative size of cost and benefit for a range of different values for these variables, an exercise suggesting that a relatively small reduction in cost will compensate for quite a large increase in price. For instance, if elasticity of demand is equal to –0.5, and the merger leads to a price increase of 20 per cent, a unit cost reduction of only 1 per cent would be sufficient for the benefits to outweigh the costs.

This simple analysis suggests that in general mergers may be justified on cost–benefit grounds. However, as always, there are further complications that need to be taken into account. The model set out in Figure 20.2 assumes that firms possessed no market power before the merger took place. If there was pre-existing market power, the analysis needs amendment in ways that suggest that larger cost reductions may be needed to compensate for similar price increases. The analysis is restricted to a partial equilibrium, examining the firms in question without any reference to their links to other sectors. That leads back to the second-best problem discussed above. If the characteristics of the overall second-best optimum are not known, it is not possible to know whether an apparent improvement in one part of the economy really involves an overall improvement.

There are also questions of timing. If the costs arising from a merger are felt immediately, while the benefits do not accrue until some time in the future, a calculation that takes into account the value of time may show that the costs outweigh the benefits, even if the balance for a single period is in the opposite direction. Furthermore, the merger may slow the rate of technical progress, or trigger other mergers that are not in the public interest. Crew and Rowley (1970) draw attention to the further point that the analysis ignores the implications of the merger for X-inefficiency. If one result of the merger is to give the firm greater market power, this may give managers greater discretion to indulge themselves in organisational slack so that the potential cost savings are not actually achieved. In that case, the balance of the argument clearly shifts away from a general presumption that mergers will be in the public interest.

UK policy towards horizontal mergers

In the UK system, merger control is effected through the Fair Trading Act of 1973, which defines a merger to have taken place when two or more enterprises have ceased to be distinct from one another. This may happen either because they have been brought under common control or because one has ceased to carry on activities as a means of preventing competition with the others.

For a merger to be referred to the Competition Commission, either the value of the assets taken over must exceed a certain amount, or a monopoly position must be created or intensified. The criterion on which the latter is judged is the same as for a monopoly reference, namely that 25 per cent or more of the market referred to has come into the hands of a single enterprise or group of enterprises acting together. If either of the criteria are fulfilled, the Secretary of State may decide to refer the merger to the Competition Commission, a decision that is taken in the light of advice from the Mergers Panel, chaired by the Director General of Fair Trading. If such a reference is made, the Competition Commission is required to investigate first whether a merger situation that qualifies for reference has been created, and second, whether that situation is expected to operate against the public interest. The term 'public interest' is not defined and it is the Authority's responsibility to identify the balance between costs and benefits for the individual case in hand.

In practice, policy appears to embody the view that mergers are, by and large, expected to be in the public interest. Whether this is appropriate clearly depends upon the view taken of competition. In the 'competitive' view of the economy, mergers are part of the process whereby more efficient firms take over the less well run, leading to an improvement in the allocation of resources. Scale economies, 'synergy' and improved management are likely to be the result. In that case a lenient view of mergers is appropriate. In the 'market power' view of competition, horizontal mergers will lead to monopoly power, raised prices and X-inefficiency in which case the UK policy towards mergers offers considerable scope for more rigorous enforcement.

EU policy on mergers

The Treaty of Rome provides no direct mechanisms for the control of mergers. Nevertheless, it can have an influence on them, through the Commission's interpretation of Article 86 (now 82). In the case of Continental Can, for instance, the European Court of Justice found that 'Article 86 is . . . aimed at . . . an effective competition structure . . . Abuse may therefore occur if an undertaking in a dominant position strengthens such a position in such a way that the degree of dominance reached substantially fetters competition.' While this confirms the applicability of Article 86 to mergers, it provides a very limited instrument of control. Action is only possible if a dominant position already exists, so that a merger involving the creation of a dominant position by two firms, neither of whom previously has a dominant position, could only be tackled after it had taken place. There have been proposals to strengthen European anti-trust law in this respect but they remain the object of controversy.

US policy on mergers

While UK policy towards mergers embodies a presumption that in general they are 'a good thing', American policy is based upon a much more hostile view. Under the Sherman Act any merger is forbidden if its effect would be to eliminate competition. In contrast to the discretionary cost–benefit approach adopted in the United Kingdom, there are no exemptions to this prohibition and it cannot be argued that a merger be allowed because there are offsetting advantages in the form of scale economies, lower prices, improved management or the avoidance of unemployment. A horizontal merger is presumed to be illegal if it leads the merged firm to have a substantial market share or results in a significant increase in concentration.

While the Sherman Act adopts a comparatively tough stance towards mergers it only has effect if the merging firms are about to attain substantial monopoly power, which may mean that it can only be applied too late to save competitive market structures. For that reason the American Congress passed the Clayton Act in 1914 whose purpose was to 'arrest the creation of . . . monopolies in their incipiency and before consummation'. Under this Act no firm engaged in commerce shall acquire any of the stock of any other firm if the effect will be substantially to reduce competition or to create a monopoly. The wording of this Act proved to have a loop-hole in that firms could merge through asset acquisition rather than stock acquisition until the loop-hole was plugged by the Celler-Kefauver Anti-merger Act of 1950, which also reinforced the determination of Congress to pursue a vigorous anti-merger programme.

Clearly, the US policy towards mergers is already much more aggressive than its UK counterpart. Nevertheless, the presumption against mergers is so strong in the United States that there is continuing pressure to strengthen anti-merger controls, perhaps to the point where firms wishing to merge must demonstrate that there are positive benefits to be had from the merger, rather than the weaker requirement that the level of competition is not reduced.

Policy towards restrictive practices

UK policy on restrictive trades practices

While the UK policy towards monopoly and mergers is relatively permissive, the approach towards restrictive trade practices has been more firm. Controls first came into effect with the Monopoly and Restrictive Practices Act 1948 which was followed by a substantial amount of legislation. The Restrictive Trade Practices Act 1956 established a Restrictive Practices Court, the Resale Prices Acts 1964 and 1976 abolished resale price maintenance, and the Restrictive Trades Practices Act 1968 extended the scope of the legislation which was then drawn together with that concerning monopoly and mergers under the Fair Trading Act 1973 which established the Office and Director General of Fair Trading. Finally there has been a degree of consolidation through the Restrictive Practices Act 1976, the Competition Act 1980 and the Competition Act 1998.

The starting point for policy has been the presumption that restrictive agreements between firms are against the public interest unless they can be proved otherwise. Hence agreements should be registered with the Office of Fair Trading (OFT). Under the Restrictive Trades Practices Act 1956 only restrictive agreements concerning goods were to be registered. However, the scope of the legislation was gradually expanded. It was realised that by exchanging information about prices, firms could achieve much the same result as if they had a price-fixing agreement, a loop-hole that was covered in the 1968 Act which required that information agreements concerning goods should also be registrable. The Fair Trading Act 1973 and the 1976 Act extended the requirement to register to the service sector, covering both restrictive and information agreements so that both types of agreements for both goods and services come within the remit of the legislation. The legislation covers both 'agreements' in the sense of formal undertakings between firms and 'arrangements' in the sense of informal under-standings. The legislation is therefore not restricted to legally enforceable rela-tionships between firms but extends to much looser arrangements, the limits being set by decisions of the court rather than by definition.

All arrangements covered by the legislation were to be registered with the Office of Fair Trading and it was then the duty of the DGFT to refer each agreement to the Restrictive Practices Court. In practice the DGFT attempted to persuade the parties involved to withdraw any restrictions, or end the agreement, in order to avoid the expense of involving the court. When the legislation was first introduced, more than 2,000 agreements were registered in the first few years, covering almost every sector in the Standard Industrial Classification. However, the vast majority were voluntarily abandoned by firms. By 1972 the Court had heard 37 cases, finding against the firms in 26 of them, and more than 300 cases referred to it had been abandoned by firms, because their agreements were similar to others that had been disallowed.

If the parties to an agreement did not abandon it, and wished to defend it in the court, they were obliged to show that the agreement was capable of passing through at least one of eight 'gateways'. These were defined as follows:

1. The restriction is necessary to protect the public from injury.
2. The removal of the restriction would deny the public substantial benefits.
3. The restriction is necessary to counteract measures taken by someone who is not a party to the agreement.
4. The restriction is necessary to enable those who are party to it to negotiate fair terms for the supply of goods or services from a person who is in a dominant position.
5. The removal of the restriction would have a serious effect on the level of unemployment.
6. The removal of the restriction would cause a reduction in the level of exports.
7. The restriction is necessary to support another restriction that is not against the public interest.
8. The restriction does not directly or indirectly restrict competition to any material degree.

In addition to being eligible to pass through one of these 'gateways', the court had to be satisfied that the restriction was 'not unreasonable', having regard to the balance between the benefits of the agreement and any detriment that might be caused to others.

UK policy towards restrictive practices has clearly been much more vigorous than that towards dominance and mergers and a very substantial number of restrictive agreements have been eliminated by the legislation. However, there continued to be reservations on at least four counts. The first concerned the rationale for the 'gateways', where Stevens and Yamey (1965) argued that the first gateway is redundant in the light of other legislation and others have suggested that a concern for unemployment and exports is inappropriate for legislation concerned primarily with competition.

The second reservation concerned the validity and consistency of the court's judgments. In the case of the *Black Bolt and Nut Association*, for instance, a price-fixing agreement was upheld on the grounds that if firms charged a common price, buyers were saved the effort of shopping around, which seems a little dubious and was not accepted as a valid defence in other cases of price-fixing. (On the other hand, the Black Bolt case involved forty-four firms producing over 3,000 standard items of very low unit value, and it could be argued in these circumstances that the transactions costs incurred by buyers attempting to identify the lowest prices would be very high in relation to the value of the product, and could be avoided by the price-fixing agreement.)

The third reservation concerned the very limited resources and sanctions available in support of the legislation. The Office of Fair Trading was only able to mount a small number of investigations at any one time, and if anti-competitive practices were taking place there was no power to impose fines under the national legislation, unlike the EC rules or those of other countries, including Germany.

The fourth reservation concerned the existence of important loop-holes (Parker 2000). Agreements could be designed to avoid registration by having only one party accept a restriction on its conduct, attention focused on registration rather than the prevention of important agreements and there were no provisions for retrospective penalties. Hence when unregistered practices were discovered, like secret price-fixing in ready-made concrete in 1991, penalties could not be imposed or damages recovered.

As a result of these weaknesses the 1998 Competition Act replaced the need for registration with a general prohibition. Chapter I of the Act prohibits agreements that 'have as their object or effect, the prevention, restriction or distortion of competition within the United Kingdom'. It covers 'concerted practices' involving collusion that fall short of a formal agreement and provides an illustrative, non-exhaustive list of prohibited practices, using wording identical to that in Article 81 of the EC Treaty (previously Article 85 of the Treaty of Rome).

As a result of the 1998 Act all agreements falling within the prohibition are void when they have a significant impact on competition. The DGFT issued guidelines stating that agreements involving less than 25 per cent market share would be known as 'small agreements' and these would not be regarded as having a significant effect unless they involved price-fixing. Hence all price-fixing agreements are void.

Restrictive practices in the European Union

The creation of a single European market would be of little significance if restrictive practices among firms prevented competition from taking place within that market. Article 85 of the Treaty of Rome (now Article 81) therefore provided that all agreements and concerted practices between undertakings, which have as their object or effect the prevention, distortion or restriction of competition within the European Union (EU) (formerly called the Common Market), and which affect trade between member states, shall be prohibited. The Article also provides an illustrative, but not exhaustive, list of the types of practice that are forbidden, which includes price-fixing, limiting production, sharing markets, discriminating between different partners to transactions and attaching supplementary obligations to contracts that have no connection with the subject of those contracts.

If firms are found to have infringed Article 81 then the agreement concerned is void in law, and cannot be enforced by any party that seeks to do so, which is the only sanction contained in the Article itself. However, further regulations give the European Commission considerable powers to enforce the rules on competition, including the ability to order the termination of an agreement or practice and the ability to impose fines.

Not all restrictive agreements between firms that affect trade in the EU are subject to proscription under Article 81, which provides for the exemption of some agreements and negative clearance for others. If an agreement contributes to improving the production or distribution of goods or to promoting technical or economic progress, while allowing consumers a fair share of the resulting benefits, and if the agreement does not contain unnecessary restrictions or eliminate competition, then it may be declared exempt from the rules. In addition to exemption for individual agreements the rules also allow for the 'bloc' exemption of certain classes of agreement including exclusive distributorships, selective distribution of automobiles, patent licensing agreements and R&D agreements. Such exemptions are necessary in part because the European Commission has been concerned to foster collaboration between small and medium-sized companies and offers financial incentives to firms to enter into arrangements that might otherwise fall foul of the Commission's own competition policy.

Negative clearance is essentially a weaker form of exemption. The Commission may declare its opinion that an agreement or a class of agreements does not come within the scope of the competition rules. Such a declaration is not binding on the Commission or on national courts, but it is unlikely that significant action would ever be taken against agreements that have been given negative clearance which include agreements of minor economic importance, certain exclusive agency contracts, cooperation agreements, sub-contracting and a number of clauses common to patent licensing agreements.

Unlike the UK system for dealing with restrictive practices there is no duty to notify restrictive agreements to the European Commission. However, exemption and negative clearance can only be given to agreements that have been formally notified, which provides a powerful incentive to notify.

Restrictive practices in the United States

Like other aspects of anti-trust legislation, American policy towards restrictive practices has its origins in the Sherman Act of 1890, Section 1 of which provides that 'every contract, combination . . . or conspiracy in restraint of trade or commerce . . . is hereby declared to be illegal'. As the Act itself makes no attempt to define those types of restrictive agreements that are illegal, any arrangement, formal or informal, that can be construed to be in restraint of trade could be illegal in principle. However, this extreme position has been moderated through the application by the courts of what is known as 'the rule of reason' whereby contracts in restraint of trade were held to be illegal in some cases only if they were unreasonable. This has led to two different categories of violation. The first is those that are illegal *per se*, and the second is those that are only illegal if unreasonable. Any agreement whose main object is to restrict competition is illegal *per se* which has led to the automatic prohibition of price-fixing agreements, market sharing, collective boycotts and limitations on supply. Other agreements may be anti-competitive, but that may not be their main object, in which case they are not illegal *per se*, but only if they are found to be unreasonable.

Illustration **Different approaches to the cost of monopoly**

Different approaches to the nature of competition and the cost of monopoly are well exemplified by the debate between Cowling and Mueller (1978) (henceforth C–M) and Littlechild (1981) over the empirical estimation of the cost of monopoly in the United Kingdom and the United States.

C–M's starting point is with Harberger's analysis of 1954, which can be explained using a simple diagram (see Figure 20.3).

In Figure 20.3 the price and output for a perfectly competitive industry are shown as P_1Q_1. If the industry becomes monopolised, price rises and output falls to the new combination P_2Q_2. The welfare loss is given by the shaded triangular area ABC. Harberger attempted to estimate the sizes of these triangles for US industry by deriving a relationship between the welfare loss and profits earned and then using the figures for profitability to give estimates of the welfare losses. This produced an estimate of the losses associated with monopoly power in the United States which was around 0.1 per cent of GNP. Such a figure was regarded as very small, implying that there need be little concern over the cost of monopoly.

C–M took issue with the Harberger approach on a number of essentially technical points. First, they noted that Harberger assumed an elasticity of demand equal to –1 in every industry. When he then observed relatively small increases in price (ΔP) due to monopoly, this assumption about elasticity led to relatively small

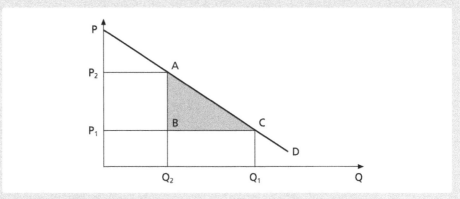

Figure 20.3 Harberger's analysis

estimates of the change in quantity (ΔQ) and to small estimates of welfare loss. Secondly, C–M noted that, when calculating monopoly profits, Harberger identified the competitive profit rate with the average rate, which could itself involve an element of monopoly profit. Monopoly profits were therefore underestimated, again leading to small estimates of welfare loss. This problem was further compounded by the fact that industry profit rates were used, so that if some firms made losses these were subtracted from the profits of the monopolists, again underestimating their importance.

Third, C–M argued that Harberger's estimates of the cost of monopoly were based solely upon the losses arising from the reduction in output and increase in price attendant upon monopoly behaviour, as shown in Figure 20.3. However, if resources are also used up in the attempt to secure monopoly power, those resources represent an additional social cost that should be taken into account.

Having made these essentially technical criticisms of the Harberger approach, C–M produced a series of estimates of their own, based upon four alternative measures. Their conclusion was that in the United States, the cost of monopoly could be as high as 13 per cent of the Gross Corporate Product of the major companies, while in the United Kingdom the figure could be as high as 7.2 per cent. Such estimates are very much larger than those found by Harberger and others, strengthening the justification for anti-monopoly policy.

The C–M estimates have been attacked by Littlechild (1981) in two different ways. First, he examined their calculations within the confines of their own model, making various technical comments suggesting that they overestimated the cost of monopoly, even if that framework is accepted. Second, and more importantly, he criticised the whole conceptual framework that C–M shares with the Harberger study and others like it. The central assumption in all of these studies is that when firms are observed they are in long-run equilibrium. If that assumption is valid then the profits that are observed can be maintained in the long run and can be attributed to the abuse of monopoly power. However, the data used by C–M also include examples of loss-making firms that cannot be in long-run equilibrium. If some firms are making losses through short-term bad luck or poor judgement, then it also has to be accepted that some of the profits observed may be due to short-term good luck or superior judgement, rather than the possession of monopoly power. In other words, not all profits are an indication of social losses.

Littlechild further pointed out that above-average profits could arise from two sources, other than the possession of monopoly power. The first, which has already been referred to, is the occurrence of unexpected events, which lead to 'windfall' profits (and losses). The second is differences between firms in their ability to create or identify profitable opportunities which are open to everyone but not noticed by all. To interpret all profits as arising from monopoly would be to ignore these other sources of profit.

Behind Littlechild's critique lies a conception of competition that is very different from that which underlies the textbook models. If competition is viewed as a process, rather than an equilibrium state, then it can be seen as a constant battle among firms to become temporary monopolists by being 'first in the field'. If a firm succeeds in spotting an opportunity that has gone unnoticed by its rivals, it will be able to make superprofits for a while, but they will soon be eroded as others imitate or improve on the original idea. In the meantime a truly entre-preneurial company will have spotted a new idea and will be making another round of superprofits from that new temporary monopoly. None of the profits that are observed can be interpreted as measures of social loss.

Indeed, the diagram set out above can be reinterpreted in a completely different way. Instead of making a comparison between the situation under competition and that under monopoly, and suggesting that monopoly causes social loss, the diagram may be interpreted as showing the position adopted by an entrepreneur who has a monopoly because they are the only person to have spotted the oppor-tunity. In that case, the appropriate comparison is not between the monopoly situation and that which would arise if everyone else had shared the monopolist's insight, because they did not. The appropriate comparison is between having the product as produced by the monopolist and not having the product at all. In that case the monopolist can be seen to have generated a social gain equal to their own entrepreneurial profit, plus the consumer surplus.

References and further reading

J.H. Agnew, *Competition Law*, London, Allen and Unwin, 1985.

W. Baumol, J.C. Panzar and R.D. Willig, *Contestable Markets and the Theory of Industry Structure*, New York, Harcourt Brace Jovanovich, 1982.

J.M. Clark, 'Toward a Concept of Workable Competition', *American Economic Review*, vol. 30, June 1940, pp. 241–56.

K. Cowling and D.C. Mueller, 'The Social Costs of Monopoly', *Economic Journal*, vol. 88, 1978, pp. 727–42.

M.A. Crew and C.K. Rowley, 'Anti-Trust Policy: Economics versus Management Science', *Moorgate and Wall Street*, 1970, pp. 19–34.

H. Davies, 'Economic Concepts of Competition', in J. Agnew, *Competition Law*, London, Allen and Unwin, 1985.

H. Demsetz, 'Information and Efficiency: Another Viewpoint', *Journal of Law and Economics*, vol. 11, 1969, pp. 1–22.

H. Demsetz, 'Industry Structure, Market Rivalry and Public Policy', *Journal of Law and Economics*, vol. 16, 1973, pp. 1–10.

H. Demsetz, 'Two Systems of Belief About Monopoly', in H.J. Golschmid (ed.) *Industrial Concentration: The New Learning*, Boston, Little, Brown, 1974.

FFC, *Order for AT&T Corporation to be Reclassified as a Non-Dominant Carrier*, FCC 95-427, paragraphs 138 and 139, October 1995.

L. Hannah and J. Kay *Concentration in Modern Industry*, London, Macmillon, 1977.

A.C. Harberger, 'Monopoly and Resource Allocation', *American Economic Review, Proceedings*, May 1954, pp. 77–87.

D.A. Hay, 'Competition and Industrial Policies', *Oxford Review of Economic Policy*, 1988.

V. Korah, *An Introductory Guide to EEC Competition Law and Practice*, Oxford, ESC, 1975.

P-L. Lam, 'Dominance in Hong Kong's Gas Industry', *Review of Industrial Organization*, vol. 16, 2000, pp. 303–12.

H. Leibenstein, 'Allocative Efficiency vs X-Efficiency', *American Economic Review*, vol. 56, 1966, pp. 392–415.

S. Littlechild, 'Misleading Calculations of the Social Costs of Monopoly Power', *Economic Journal*, vol. 91, 1981, pp. 348–63.

E.S. Mason, 'Monopoly in Law and Economics', *Yale Law Journal*, 1937.

D. Parker, 'The Competition Act 1998: Change and Continuity in UK Competition Policy', *Journal of Business Law*, July 2000, pp. 283–302.

R.A. Posner, 'The Social Costs of Monopoly and Regulation', *Journal of Political Economy*, vol. 83, no. 4, 1975, pp. 807–27.

W.D. Reekie, *Industry, Prices and Markets*, Oxford, Philip Allan, 1979.

R. Stevens and B. Yamey, *The Restrictive Practices Court*, London, Weidenfeld and Nicolson, 1965.

G. Stigler, 'Report on Anti-Trust Policy Discussion', *American Economic Review*, vol. 46, May 1956, p. 505.

J. Sutton, *Sunk Costs and Market Structure: Price Competition, Advertising and the Evolution of Concentration*, Cambridge, MA, MIT Press, 1996.

J. Sutton, *Technology and Market Structure: Theory and History*, Cambridge, MA, MIT Press, 1999.

O. Williamson, 'Economies as an Anti-Trust Defence: The Welfare Trade-Offs', *American Economic Review*, vol. LVIII, 1968, pp. 18–36.

Self-test questions

1. Which of the following is an implication of the second-best problem?
   (a) failure to achieve perfect competition in one industry means that it is not necessarily desirable in others
   (b) workable competition is not achievable by approximating perfect competition
   (c) monopoly power need not be controlled

2. Which of the following variables represent market structure, which relate to conduct and which are indicators of performance?

   concentration, growth of demand, advertising intensity, collusive agreements, productivity growth, entry barriers, profitability, degree of diversification, company objectives

3. List the three different sources from which profits may arise in the Austrian view of competition.

4. Which of the following conclusions drawn from the orthodox analysis of the industry is rejected by contestability theorists?
   (a) barriers to entry are important features of structure
   (b) firms in an industry with a high level of concentration will be able to exert significant market power
   (c) monopolies charge prices that exceed average cost

5. List the advantages and disadvantages of the 'rules' approach to competition policy.

Essay question

Consider the view that policies designed to prevent the abuse of monopoly power are unnecessary and misguided.

21 The economics of regulated industries

Governments adopt a variety of approaches to improving the efficiency and effectiveness of the economy. Some place most emphasis on competition policy (examined in Chapter 20), while others tend to address perceived market imperfections by imposing government controls. This chapter considers the economic analysis of government intervention at industry level, focusing on the various regulatory policies that the government may use to improve industrial performance.

Theories of regulation

If managers are to deal effectively with officialdom (and vice versa) it is important that they understand why and how government bodies become involved in regulating commercial and industrial activity. A number of perspectives are helpful in this respect, namely:

- public interest theory
- private interest or 'capture' theory
- regulation as taxation
- a general theory of regulation.

Public interest theory

The simplest (and perhaps rather naïve) approach to government regulation assumes that it is entirely driven by the need to protect the consumer or the public interest. From that perspective, regulation is required in the following situations:

- *Monopoly*: if an industry is not contestable and is monopolised by a firm (or a few firms), or if it is a non-sustainable natural monopoly, it will fail to achieve an efficient outcome. Hence regulation is needed to prevent monopolistic behaviour.
- *Externalities*: in the presence of externalities in the market, private benefits and private costs are not the same as social benefits and social costs. These divergences lead to under-production and over-production of goods and services. Taxes, subsidies or controls are needed to correct the market imperfections.
- *Provision of public goods*: a public good is a commodity which it is difficult to exclude non-payers from consuming and where more consumption by one

user does not lead to less being available for others: lighthouses, public roads, national defence, law and order, flood defence and fire protection are all examples. The market tends to under-provide public goods because potential users attempt to 'free ride' on provision paid for by others and it is difficult for a private firm to collect payments. The government may provide public goods in order to overcome the weaknesses of the market in this respect.

● *Imperfect information*: the government may impose regulations to protect consumers, who lack information on the price, quality and safety of a product or service.

Private interest or 'capture' theory

In 1962 Stigler and Friedland published a pathbreaking paper titled 'What Can Regulators Regulate? The Case of Electricity'. They rejected the conventional wisdom, embodied in the public interest perspective, that regulations were intended to protect consumers and the public interest. That conclusion was based on the finding that the system of regulation imposed on the electric power industry in the United States had an insignificant effect on the average level of prices and was more likely to protect commercial and industrial consumers than domestic consumers. Indeed, regulation seemed to increase price discrimination against domestic consumers rather than reduce it.

Stigler (1971) suggested that the reason for this phenomenon could be found in the asymmetrical distribution of the gains and losses arising from regulations and the asymmetrical distribution of information about those gains and losses. If the gains are concentrated on a small number of recipients, each recipient will gain significantly. But if the losses are spread across a large number of losers, each one will suffer just a small loss. Regulation is decided through the political process and individual voters may lack information about the losses they will suffer, or they may not have the incentive to avoid the small loss resulting from regulation. There are also high costs of organising a large group to protect members from the damage. Regulations therefore tend to benefit industries involving a small number of firms, where the members have greater incentives to acquire information, and there are smaller costs of organising political activities. To express it in a different way, Stigler provided a model for the demand side of regulation. Regulated firms demand regulations in order to protect their interests. Economic regulation is not about the public interest at all, but a process by which interest groups seek to promote their private interests. Regulators are 'captured', or even brought into being, by the industries that they are supposed to be regulating.

Regulation as taxation

Posner (1971, 1974) argued that there are a number of deficiencies in both 'public interest' theory and 'capture' theory. The public interest theory is flawed because case studies have shown that many schemes of government regulation cannot be explained on the grounds that they increase the wealth or the justice of the society as a whole. The capture theory is also inadequate, because it cannot predict which industries will be favoured by the regulatory agencies and there is also evidence that in some cases customer interests, rather than those of regulated firms, are promoted by agencies.

Posner proposed instead that regulation be interpreted as a form of internal subsidy, whereby firms are forced to provide unremunerative services, funded by the profits from others. Like more explicit taxes, the effect of regulation is to compel members of the public to support a service that the market would provide at a reduced level, or not at all. By regulation, the government can tax some groups and subsidise others, thereby achieving the goal of income redistribution in the economy. Having contributed that insight, Posner went on to examine the advantages of using regulation as a form of taxation over other methods of taxation and subsidy.

General theory

While Posner criticised the public interest and 'capture' theories for their incompleteness, his own theory also failed to explain why some groups are subsidised and others not. Only in 1976 did Peltzman provide a powerful generalisation of previous theories, in a paper titled 'Toward a More General Theory of Regulation'. In that paper he considered how individuals organise themselves into coalitions and compete for economic rents. In his view, the key feature of regulation is that it redistributes wealth or rents from unorganised consumers to organised coalitions of consumers, or producers.

In this analysis, the regulator is assumed to be a vote-maximiser. To maximise votes, the regulator chooses the size of the group to be benefited, the amount of dollar gain to the beneficiary group, and the amount spent by that group to mitigate opposition on his behalf. (The opposition comes from those who are paying higher tax as a result of the regulations.) To secure a majority vote, the regulator has to consider both the votes gained from the beneficiary group and the votes lost from the people outside the beneficiary group. Hence, Peltzman provided a model on the supply side of regulation: how regulators supply regulations in exchange for votes.

Peltzman's 1976 paper was an extension of his earlier work 'Pricing in Public and Private Enterprise: Electric Utilities in the United States' (1971). In that paper, he argued that government-owned firms use their pricing policies to attract political support. In the electricity industry, for instance, each firm has to determine the appropriate amount of benefits through lower electricity prices to each beneficiary group.

Stigler and Peltzman's models have been criticised on the grounds that regulators are not always legislators or elected officials. Some are appointed rather than elected in which case they are simply bureaucrats, whose jobs and rewards are not linked to election results. However, it can still be argued that bureaucrats are suppliers of regulation, who rationally use their regulatory capacity to pursue their own interests. Models of regulatory behaviour based upon that proposition are more convincing than the public interest approach.

Having considered the underlying motivation for regulation, it remains to examine the impact that different forms of regulation have on the behaviour of the regulated firm. Three forms of regulation merit attention:

1. Rate-of-return regulation.
2. Price-cap regulation.
3. Franchise bidding.

Rate-of-return regulation

Public utilities in the United States have generally been subject to *rate-of-return regulation* where the regulatory body attempts to control the return on capital earned by the regulated industry. The aims of that regime are to protect the consumer by ensuring adequate service at a reasonable price while at the same time providing the company's shareholders with a 'fair' rate of return (Crew and Kleindorfer 1987).

Under this system, prices are set at a level that is estimated to earn the allowed rate of return on capital. If a public utility wishes to change the structure or level of those prices it must file a formal request to the regulator, accompanied by the submission of supporting evidence. The regulatory commission then presides over a formal proceeding where the evidence provided by the utility, along with that submitted by other parties, including commission staff and customers, is presented and examined. 'Intervenors', principally the state-appointed 'Rate Counsel' – a lawyer representing the public interest – have the opportunity to object to the utility's proposal, and then file their own testimony criticising the case. The two sides, public utility and intervenors, may either discuss their differences and agree to a 'stipulation' which has to be approved by the commission, or to litigate the case before an administrative law judge.

The litigation is similar to normal court proceedings in which cross-examination and rebuttal take place. After the hearings, the judge prepares a report that goes to the commission for a final decision. In some cases, the commission may use its own initiative to order a utility to change the level and structure of the proposed tariffs, if the tariffs are found to be inconsistent with state law.

Most state commissions operate under a vague statutory mandate which states that the commission is to set prices that are 'just, reasonable and non-discriminatory'. State statutes permit commissions to regulate the prices charged by investor-owned utilities, but not to fine or subsidise them. The basic principle of rate-of-return regulation is that utilities should be allowed to charge prices that reflect 'costs of service', if they are prudently incurred, and earn a fair rate of return on investment. The sum of all the approved costs of service is called the 'revenue requirement', and prices are then set to generate revenue to meet this revenue requirement.

Different procedures are used by different regulatory commissions to estimate the costs and levels of service. Some base their estimates on costs from previous historical 'test' years, others use forecasts of future costs. Many commissions allow automatic price adjustments for some cost items, the most common being fuel costs. Prices are set at a level to allow the utility to earn a fair rate of return. In theory, the fair rate of return on investment should be high enough to compensate the owner of the utility for the cost of capital investment, adjusted for risk. It should also provide incentives for the utility to raise capital in order to finance the investment needed to meet the demand for electric power efficiently.

The fair rate of return is an allowed, rather than a guaranteed, rate of return. That is because the usual regulatory practice precludes 'retroactive rate-making' (going back and changing past prices to reflect actual costs). Economic conditions may change during the period that the prices are in effect and, consequently, the regulated utility may earn less than the allowed rate of return. Therefore, the actual rate of return earned by the utility depends partly on the accuracy of the forecasts used to set prices, and partly on unforeseen developments. If the prices set do not yield the allowed rate of return, then the utility may file a case for a price increase.

Several financial models have been used by regulatory commissions to estimate the cost of capital or the required ('fair') rate of return for regulated utilities. These include the comparative earnings method, the dividend valuation (or dividend growth) model, and the capital asset pricing model (CAPM).

Problems with rate-of-return regulation

As the major concern of rate-of-return regulation lies with equity and fairness, it is not surprising that outcomes are inefficient. Crew and Kleindorfer (1987) identify four dimensions along which economic efficiency may be evaluated: allocative efficiency; X-efficiency; dynamic efficiency; and governance (or monitoring) cost efficiency.

Allocative efficiency is the traditional measure of static efficiency. In a competitive market, prices should be set so that total benefits minus total costs (i.e. net benefits) are maximised. In general, maximisation of net benefits requires that price equals marginal cost. However, because of scale economies, the need to cover costs and the non-existence of government subsidies, regulated prices are not likely to reflect marginal costs. Under rate-of-return regulation, prices tend to be based on average cost pricing or second-best pricing, rather than true marginal cost pricing. Unless the regulator allows an efficient two-part tariff, with a fixed fee covering fixed cost and a variable fee reflecting marginal cost, rate-of-return regulation can at best achieve only optimal second-best pricing.

X-inefficiency is a concept introduced by Leibenstein (1966). It refers to the losses or waste that occurs when firms fail to combine inputs efficiently, resulting in higher production costs than are necessary – the firm is operating above its cost curve. Rate-of-return regulation is similar to a cost-plus contract in that it provides little incentive for regulated firms to minimise costs. That is because successful cost reduction efforts would lead to returns exceeding the allowed level, after which prices would be reduced in the next review. A firm under rate-of-return regulation may intentionally spend more on staff and on 'perks' for the management than necessary, as the firm can pass the cost on to consumers. Hence, it has been argued that rate-of-return regulation fails to achieve productive efficiency.

In 1962, Averch and Johnson published a landmark paper dealing with monopolies subject to rate-of-return regulation. According to the Averch–Johnson proposition, if the allowed rate of return on capital is between the profit-maximising rate and the cost of capital, then the regulated firm will substitute capital for other factors of production and operate at an output at which cost is not minimised. Regulated firms will use too much capital and the result is a sub-optimal allocation of resources. Production costs are not minimised and productive inefficiency arises.

Dynamic efficiency refers to the ability of the regulatory system to accommodate growth and change over time. A system is dynamically efficient if it is able to encourage the regulated firms to adopt innovation and invention, and to accommodate changes in tastes and preferences. Rate-of-return regulation is also deficient in dynamic efficiency. Because profits are fixed, regulated firms have little incentive to adopt cost-saving innovations or to introduce new products.

In a competitive market, unregulated firms have to make investment decisions under conditions of uncertainty. Even when they make efficient investment decisions *ex ante*, they may end up earning more or less than a competitive return when demand and cost conditions change. Firms under rate-of-return regulation, however, are not rewarded or penalised for unforeseeable fluctuations in demand or cost conditions. Even if a firm overestimates demand and builds plants yielding excess capacity, it is still allowed to earn a rate of return on this excess capacity provided that it can defend its forecasting procedure. Thus rate-of-return regulation punishes only bad decisions, not bad luck. However, this does not eliminate risk, it simply transfers risk from the company to consumers. Consumers, whose interest is supposed to be represented by the regulator, have to bear all the risk from the investment decisions made by a regulated firm. Hence, rate-of-return regulation also fails to allocate risk efficiently.

Governance cost efficiency: in evaluating alternative governance structures for regulation, it is important to consider the transaction costs involved. If a given governance structure requires considerable expenditure on lawyers, accountants and regulators, those transaction costs should be taken into account when evaluating the net benefits. Under the rate-of-return regulation, which is common in the United States, considerable resources are spent in the process of administrative hearings and litigations, and governance costs are high. MacAvoy (1970) suggested that the governance costs of regulatory proceedings instituted by the Federal Power Commission were larger than the net benefits warranted. With the huge amount of administrative expenditure at stake, rate-of-return regulation also encourages wasteful rent-seeking activities.

Other problems: there are other problems associated with the US regulatory system. For example, there is asymmetric information, as utility managers are always better informed than regulators. Regulators are generally not able to distinguish efficient from inefficient behaviour. They simply do not have enough information to detect flawed decisions in a way that would satisfy legal standards. Utility managers have every incentive to make their decisions seem prudent by arguing that poor performance is due to bad luck, rather than bad decisions. Also, if the threat of sanctions is not credible, a regulated utility will have diminished incentive to supply electricity efficiently.

Finally, if price increases lag behind cost increases, regulatory lags may worsen the financial situations of regulated firms rather than provide incentives for them to lower costs.

Incentives under rate-of-return regulation

Despite its shortcomings, rate-of-return regulation has some features that provide incentives for regulated firms to improve efficiency. Joskow (1986) criticised many studies on rate-of-return regulation for failing to consider the actual regulatory process. In practice, regulatory commissions are not required to set prices that cover all costs incurred by regulated firms. They have the authority to 'disallow' capital costs (or any other costs) when setting rates, if they find the associated expenditures imprudent or unnecessary. That 'threat of disallowance' may limit expenditures on 'gold plating' (unnecessary capital expenditures), and provide some incentive for the utility to make efficient investment decisions.

Furthermore, in practice, regulation does not take place in a continuous fashion. Prices are set for an interval of time, during which the utility is free to choose whatever input combination it likes. The existence of regulatory lag induces utilities to reduce capital bias and allows them to keep the benefits of improved cost efficiency until they are asked by commissions to reduce prices in the next review. There also tends to be an asymmetry in the formal regulatory review process. Utilities ask for price increases when costs rise, but when costs fall they are often allowed to keep the existing prices and thus enjoy higher rates of return. Hence, as a result of regulatory lag, the actual rates of return earned by utilities may be above or below the commission-determined fair rate of return.

Price-cap regulation

The shortcomings of rate-of-return regulation prompted interest in alternatives, especially during the 1980s. In particular attention has focused on the structure of incentive contracts between regulated firms and the government. One such type of incentive contract is *price-cap regulation*, which makes use of regulatory lag to give appropriate incentives to firms. This approach was first applied to the privatised industries in the United Kingdom and is now widely adopted by regulators in the United States and other countries.

The origin of price-cap regulation

In 1982, the UK government announced its plan to privatise British Telecommunications (BT). The framework of the privatisation programme was laid down in the White Paper 'The Future of Telecommunications in Britain'. Given BT's monopoly position in the industry, the prospect of privatisation should have been accompanied by some form of regulation to contain its market power. The Department of Industry's original intention was to adopt a modified rate-of-return regulation (Beesley and Littlechild 1989). However, Professor Alan Walters, the Prime Minister's economic adviser at the time, argued fiercely against it (Vickers and Yarrow 1988). He argued that it was equivalent to 100 per cent taxation, provided poor incentives for innovation and efficiency, and that the American experience showed that the system was wasteful, bureaucratic and inefficient.

With other regulatory options under debate, a study was commissioned from Professor Stephen Littlechild of Birmingham University at the end of 1982. His report in early 1983 recommended a local tariff reduction (LTR) scheme, better known as the *RPI–X* proposal. After further discussions and investigations, this control on prices, or price cap, was finally adopted, and variants of it have been used for other privatised utilities, including electric, gas and water supply utilities. The key features of price-cap regulation are as follows:

- The regulator directly sets a ceiling for prices to be charged by the regulated firm according to a formula. The average price increase of a specified basket of services must not exceed RPI–X (rate of change in retail price index minus X), where X is an adjustment factor to share productivity gains between the company and the consumers. In other words, the prices of the regulated services must fall in real terms by X per cent per annum.
- For a specified period of time (usually several years), the regulated firm may set prices freely below the ceilings.
- Price ceilings are defined for baskets of services provided by the regulated firm. There may be different price ceilings for different baskets of services.
- The adjustment factor X is specified by the government and will be reviewed and possibly changed at the end of the specified period.
- The regulator can adjust the factor X in any review or interim review. The regulator may modify this RPI–X constraint in the regulated company's licence at any time by agreement with the licensee. If the licensee does not agree, the regulator may refer the matter to the Monopolies and Mergers Commission (MMC, now renamed the Competition Commission).

Arguments for and against price-cap regulation

Beesley and Littlechild (1989) summarised the arguments for and against price-cap regulation. First, they suggested that RPI–X is more efficient than rate-of-return regulation. It is less vulnerable to 'cost-plus' inefficiency and over-capitalisation (the Averch–Johnson effect). That is because the regulated firm can keep whatever profits it earns during the specified period, but it must also accept any losses; thus there is an incentive to produce as efficiently as possible. As efficiency increases, it is possible for both the company and the consumers to benefit. The company enjoys higher profits while the consumers buy at lower prices. Since regulated companies keep all profits, they have a greater incentive to innovate and to introduce new products, resulting in higher dynamic efficiency than under rate-of-return regulation.

Second, RPI–X allows the company greater flexibility to adjust the structure of prices, as there is no price control on services outside the basket. As a result, the regulated firm can adopt pricing arrangements to achieve optimal second-best pricing. Within the period specified under the existing price cap, the firm can learn about the structure of costs and then adjust the price.

Third, it is argued that RPI–X is easier to operate and its governance costs are lower than the US rate-of-return regulation. Both regulators and company can devote fewer resources to operating the system. It is also more transparent as the system focuses on prices, which are of greater concern to customers. Customers are guaranteed that price increases are under some form of controls. Hence, the system also helps to curb inflation and, being less discretionary, involves less danger of regulatory capture.

Like all regulatory systems, price cap has its shortcomings. Many of the arguments put forward against price cap revolve around the setting of the X factor. First, it has to be set and reset repeatedly, in order to secure a reasonable rate of return to the regulated firm. In addition to production cost and cost of capital, this process requires information on productivity gains. If the X factor is not set appropriately, allocative inefficiency will arise. In addition, there will be political pressure from the company and consumers in setting and resetting the X factor. Any shift in the X factor in favour of one group (customers) will be at the expense of the other (shareholders).

Vickers and Yarrow (1988) argued that the price-cap formulae lack any long-term provision for the decisions that will be taken when they come to be reviewed. In the absence of clear guidance on the long-term conduct of regulatory policy, private investors may be concerned that they will not be able to recover the cost of capital. Hence, because future government policy is unpredictable, there may be a real danger of under-investment in a privatised industry. The cost of capital (and prices) may be raised by the presence of this regulatory risk.

Second, companies may believe that any increase in efficiency in the short term will invite a tougher X factor in later periods, or even induce an adverse change of the X factor within the current period. If the short-term gain is more than offset by the long-term loss, they will avoid increasing productivity. This is similar to the problem of the ratchet effect in the contract made between a socialist firm and the state. If firms believe that good performance on their part will be met with a more demanding target, they will avoid performing well.

Third, some commentators have questioned whether price cap really does have greater price flexibility and transparency. Under rate-of-return regulation, the regulatory procedure, which involves public hearings and litigation, may be more transparent. Furthermore, greater price flexibility may be a disadvantage rather than an advantage since it allows price discrimination and cross-subsidisation. As costs of various services are difficult to determine precisely, price discrimination and cross-subsidisation cannot be easily detected.

Last, as price cap focuses on prices, regulated firms may shirk on quality. Therefore, the regulator must incur additional costs to monitor the quality of service provided.

Price-cap versus rate-of-return regulation

It is helpful to consider how price-cap regulation in the United Kingdom differs from rate-of-return regulation in the United States (see Waterson 1990, Weyman-Jones 1990). In the first place, under price-cap regulation, the periods between reviews are known and fixed in advance. That means that the period during which the firm is at risk from unexpected cost changes is not under the control of the regulated firms; instead it is predetermined by the regulator. Under rate-of-return regulation as practised in the United States, the regulated firm may ask for a rate review if they think they can justify it. Hence the risk period is endogenous, rather than exogenous, under the US system.

In the regulatory process, there is no requirement that regulators in the United Kingdom look at past costs in setting prices. They may make their own estimates of future costs. In that sense price-cap regulation is more forward-looking. In the US rate-of-return regulation, historical costs are often used to justify rate changes (unless the test year is based on forecasts of future costs). The lack of restriction on the information used by the regulators gives price-cap regulation in the United Kingdom a greater degree of freedom than the US rate-of-return system.

The governance costs of the two systems are also different. The UK regulators do not need to face judicial or court proceedings in determining prices. They can request a Competition Commission audit of a utility's costs over a long period if disputes arise. The threat of requesting such an investigation serves as a bargaining tool for the regulators and increases the likelihood that regulated firms will report true costs. Regulators in the United States do not possess that bargaining power. In addition, the regulatory commission framework in the United States has been found to be more costly than the regulatory office approach in the United Kingdom. Considerable resources are devoted to public hearings in the United States and it has been argued that the open hearings, which allow information to be available to potential competitors, may also affect competition in the industry (Weyman-Jones 1990).

In the UK privatised electricity supply industry, some price-cap regulations are in the form of RPI–X+Y. The Y factor represents those costs that are assumed to be outside the industry's control. RPI–X+Y regulation implies that some fraction of a utility's average price for a basket of outputs is assumed to depend on its own activities. Those costs are capped by a growth rate equal to the rate of change in the retail price index minus a constant factor X. The remainder of the price is assumed to be determined by those costs that are outside the utility's control (the Y factor) and these can be passed on to final consumers. Hence, price-cap regulation preserves automatic adjustment clauses similar to those under rate-of-return regulation. As a result, the incentive for regulated firms to minimise costs is reduced.

While the rate-of-return and price-cap approaches may appear to be quite separate, in practice the setting of the price cap is not independent of the rate of return. In the late 1990s, when the privatised utilities announced large profits, there was mounting political pressure to raise the X factor (i.e. to lower price). If regulators do not remain committed to the same X factor but change it during the current contractual period, this will affect the incentives of utilities to increase efficiency and will reduce price-cap regulation to rate-of-return regulation. Liston (1993) has reviewed the differences and similarities of the two systems and concluded that price cap in practice is not distinct from rate-of-return regulation. In fact, it can be argued that price-cap regulation is akin to rate-of-return regulation with a longer regulatory lag (of several years). The choice between price-cap and rate-of-return regulation therefore remains very much an empirical question.

Finally, under the existing licence terms, privatised electric utilities in the United Kingdom are not allowed to engage in cross-subsidisation. The generators' ability to engage in price discrimination is also limited by the requirement that they offer comparable terms to comparable purchasers. That provision extends to dealings between generation and supply businesses and also applies to regional distribution companies (Vickers and Yarrow 1991). Hence, price-cap regulation allows greater price flexibility without leading to cross-subsidisation and discriminatory pricing. However, Liston (1993) argues that discrimination and cross-subsidisation can still exist under a price-cap regime. As prices of different services are capped under a single ceiling, regulated firms may lower prices for some services and raise prices for other services, particularly those with lower demand elasticities.

Franchise bidding and regulation

Franchise bidding for monopoly rights

In 1968, Demsetz questioned the necessity of regulating industries having the characteristic of scale economies. He proposed that government regulation of utilities (using traditional rate-of-return regulation) would be rendered unnecessary if we could allow competitors to bid for the exclusive right to supply the good or service over a contract period. The franchise would be awarded to the firm offering the good or service at the lowest price – a reverse auction.

Demsetz argued that such an arrangement is feasible even when the production of the good or service involves equipment durability and uncertainty. Equipment durability need not cause wasteful duplication of facilities if they can be transferred from the original supplier to the successor supplier who offers superior terms. The problem of uncertainty can also be overcome by using long-term contracts signed between suppliers and customers. Hence, the existence of natural monopoly need not imply monopoly price and output.

Contractual problems of franchise bidding

Williamson (1976) argued that franchise bidding suffers from a number of contractual disabilities. *Once-for-all bidding schemes* are infeasible, because they would require each potential bidder to specify the terms at which they are prepared to supply service now and the conditional terms under which they will supply service in the infinite future. Such complete contingent claims contracts are impossibly complex to write, negotiate and enforce. While complete long-term contracts are an impossibility, both incomplete long-term contracts and recurrent short-term contracts also suffer from severe transactional problems at the initial award stage, the execution stage and the contract renewal stage. Winning bidders may behave opportunistically by lowering the quality of service because it is very difficult to define quality clearly in the bidding process. Penalty clauses in the contract may not be effective to eliminate this kind of behaviour.

When contracts are renegotiated, or when assets are transferred from existing franchisees to successor firms, the asset specificity of human and non-human capital would cause many problems. There would be costly bargaining and haggling over the valuation of capital assets. Employees of existing firms that have invested in training may find their services of no value to the successor firms. In order to mitigate these contractual difficulties, the government needs to introduce an extensive regulatory or arbitration apparatus. These include methods of assessing plant and equipment values, routine auditing procedures and an arbitration process in case of disputes between existing and rival firms over physical asset valuations. Williamson concluded that franchise bidding would then become similar to traditional rate-of-return regulation.

Regulation as a long-term contract

Goldberg (1976) presented a model of regulation in which the regulator is explicitly conceptualised as an agent administering a long-term contract. His analysis was principally concerned with natural monopolies or network industries, like the electricity, gas, water supply and local telephone industries, and he made the assumption throughout that the agent/regulator is a faithful representative of their principals' interests (the interests of the community at large).

In Goldberg's view regulation is akin to private or public long-term contracts designed to protect producers' right to serve and consumers' right to be served. A common feature of the natural monopolies is the huge amount of sunk investment required for developing the infrastructures, such as transmission and distribution networks. Because of the asset specificity and demand uncertainty involved, both producers and consumers prefer to enter into long-term relational contracts which may limit their future options in order to achieve optimality over time. In the regulatory process, the agent/regulator enters into a contract with the producers in order to protect both the producers' right to serve and the consumers' right to be served.

If it is to be effective, the long-term contract should permit the regulator flexibility over time in administering the contract, for example, through a flexible pricing mechanism or a flexible allowed rate of return. Contracts, or regulations, in Goldberg's view, provide procedural and flexible mechanisms for adjudicating and adjusting to future contingencies.

When administering and policing a regulatory contract the regulator will experience the usual problems encountered by all agents, such as determining and acting upon principals' preferences and interests. Increasing the producers' right to serve would make the contracts more attractive to producers while at the same time making them less attractive to consumers. The opposite is true for the consumers' right to be served. Therefore, the regulator as agent of the community at large must choose some mix of actions, which usually involves making trade-offs among different objectives.

In analysing this issue Goldberg developed the relational contracting paradigm contained in Oliver Williamson's work (see Chapter 3). He contrasted his long-term contract model with the usual discrete transaction approach used in economics. He also argued strongly that many of the problems that arise in regulated industries would be present even if the industries were not under the jurisdiction of a regulatory agency. To compare regulation with a perfectly competitive market or transaction-cost-free franchise bidding system is inappropriate and will necessarily make administrative regulation seem a poor choice because it must have imperfections. A more appropriate approach would be, first, to analyse carefully the characteristics of the services being regulated and the transactional problems associated with these characteristics. The benefits and costs of using a regulatory agent may then be compared with those for the alternative institutions that might replace it. Viewing regulation from that perspective may lead to a more favourable judgement on its merits.

Privatisation and de-regulation

The basic rationale for extending the scope of the market

There is a broad spectrum of approaches to analysing government policy towards industries. At the 'right-hand' end of that spectrum is the view that only market forces, in a competitive environment secured by the rule of law, can be relied upon to secure a dynamic and efficient economy. The arguments in favour of such a view may be put forward in a number of different ways. One approach is heavily ideological in that it sees the untrammelled operation of the market as a good thing in itself. Competition and market forces are identified with 'freedom', government intervention is seen as the thin end of a wedge that may lead to totalitarianism and 'rolling back the state' is seen as a major end in itself. Another approach is to concentrate on the improvements in economic and industrial performance that are held to flow from opening up a wider range of activities to competition and private sector management practices.

In the United Kingdom, the rationale for 'privatisation' has drawn upon both of these arguments. In the economic sphere at least, the writings of pro-market visionaries like von Hayek (1948, 1978) undoubtedly influenced thinking to the point where a general ethos of 'public sector bad, private sector good' has permeated the national environment to an extent that would have been unthinkable in the 1960s and 1970s. At the same time, the more detailed arguments around particular aspects of the privatisation programme have tended not to rely on such a general justification but to point to improvements in efficiency, reductions in cost and improvements in competitiveness and quality of service which are deemed to flow from exposing public sector activity to the pressures and disciplines of the marketplace.

Heald (1984) identifies four major components of the privatisation programme:

1. *Introduction of charges*: privatising the financing of a service that continues to be provided by the public sector – particularly the introduction of charges for services previously provided without charge. Full cost recovery can be achieved by setting up a trading fund, or by turning a public enterprise into a public corporation responsible for its profits and losses.

2. *Contracting out*: privatisation of the production of services that continue to be financed by the public sector – tendering for refuse collection by private firms, school cleaning and similar services within the National Health Service.

3. *Full privatisation*: selling off public enterprises and transferring state functions and state assets to the private sector.

4. *De-regulation and liberalisation*: the relaxation of statutory monopolies or other arrangements that prevent private sector firms from entering markets previously reserved for the public sector.

Introduction of charges

The argument in favour of charges has two elements. The first lies in the need to finance the provision of services, and the effects of alternative financing methods on the public purse and the level of taxation. If services are to be provided free of charge this imposes a burden on the government which may be met either by running a larger public sector deficit or by having a level of taxation that is higher than it would otherwise be. If public sector deficits are abhorred because of the extent to which they create problems of monetary control, and higher levels of taxation are seen as inhibiting incentives, then the introduction of charges can be supported on the grounds of financial prudence and the enhancement of the dynamic efficiency of the economy.

In economic analysis, however, prices are seen not simply as means of raising finance but as the central factor determining the efficiency of the allocation of resources. As has been seen in earlier chapters, static efficiency requires that all prices be set equal to marginal costs. If charges have not been made then it can be argued that this will have distorted the allocation of resources in that rational utility-maximising households will consume goods that are provided free up to the point where the value they place on the final unit is zero. Resources will have been 'wasted' in the production of units of output whose additional cost exceeds the additional benefit created for consumers.

This argument provides a basic rationale for charges, but requires qualification in a number of respects. In the first place, the relevant marginal cost is *marginal social cost*, which may not be well represented by the accounting costs which are usually the only cost information available. Second, there are *system effects* which need to be taken into account when setting charges for some goods and services in situations where others are not charged for. In the case of the National Health Service, for example, charging for prescriptions may lead to a reduction in the demand for medication, but a shift in demand towards other, uncharged for, services such as acute hospital provision. In the case of charges for eye tests, for instance, it has been argued that such tests provide an early aid to the diagnosis of much more serious conditions than defective sight and that to deter some users from having eye tests could lead to the worsening of undetected illness to the point where much greater and more expensive demands are made upon the hospital services. Clearly, the 'piecemeal' application of accounting-cost-based charges offers little guarantee of an improved allocation of resources.

The other issue that is raised in respect of charging for services is that charges have distributional implications, which raise questions of equity or fairness. These arguments can be raised in both directions, especially as the concept of equity has no clear definition. In favour of charges it might be argued that it is 'unfair' in a situation of scarce resources to provide free services to the well-off. On the other hand, it could also be argued that to impose charges to be paid by the poor may effectively exclude them from the benefits of some services. Such arguments have featured substantially in the arguments over charges in the National Health Service and the growing debate on charging students for courses in higher education.

Self-financing through trading fund arrangement

The trading fund arrangement originated in public sector reforms in the United Kingdom. Under the 1973 Trading Fund Act, trading funds were set up for a number of government departments in the United Kingdom for self-provision of finances. Examples include Royal Ordnance Factories, the Royal Mint and HMSO (the UK government's stationery office). These departments were given trading fund status with the aim of making them more business-oriented in operation. Under the trading fund arrangement, managers remain accountable to the minister and the employees remain civil servants. However, these government departments have their own accounts and their operations are financed by trading receipts. It is argued that this arrangement has provided a greater degree of financial autonomy and managerial independence than when services have directly been run by government departments and financed by tax revenues.

Self-financing through corporatisation

Corporatisation is the process by which a public sector organisation is separated from the general body of government and is empowered to function as a commercial company while remaining under public ownership. Strictly speaking, it is not a form of private sector participation and it may be adopted as a long-term solution to problems of public enterprises, or as a useful half-way house to private sector participation. For example, corporatisation was adopted in Scotland, when customers showed strong disapproval of the full privatisation approach adopted for the water industry in England and Wales.

In the 1980s, the governments of Australia and New Zealand attempted to improve the performance of the utility sector, and to increase the productivity of the whole economy, by adopting a policy of corporatisation. Under that policy, managers of public corporations were required to run the companies as successful business enterprises. Many industries were deregulated and competition introduced to encourage efficient production.

Contracting out

Services that continue to be financed by the public sector need not be supplied by public sector organisations. Refuse collection, for instance, has been 'contracted out' to private sector contractors instead of being provided by local authorities' own direct labour. Private contractors have provided school and hospital cleaning services. Such arrangements allow for a degree of competition in that contracts for the provision of services may be awarded on the basis of competitive tendering, which exposes the provision of the activity to the pressure and discipline of the market.

While this exposure to competition may improve efficiency and lead to savings through the introduction of better working practices and greater incentives, its opponents point out that the information required to measure the cost differences between direct production and contracting-out are bedevilled by the limitations of public sector cost accounting practices. That makes proper comparison difficult but such a comparison might show direct production to be more efficient than had been believed. It is also argued that private sector contractors may provide services for lower costs by providing inferior service or by adopting exploitative labour practices not open to public sector employers who are obliged to honour good practice in respect of employee protection, health and safety, and collective bargaining.

The position of the trade unions is an important aspect of this debate in that the employees of private contractors tend to have less bargaining power than public sector employees. That reduces the cost of private sector provision in a way that is applauded by some supporters of privatisation, but seen by its opponents as 'unfair competition'. The balance of the argument clearly depends upon the view that is taken of the trade unions and of collective bargaining. If trade unions are seen as impediments to the effective operation of markets, privatisation is to be supported on these grounds. On the other hand, if trade unions are seen as necessary defenders of the interests of employees, privatisation is simply another means of weakening their influence.

These arguments are well exemplified by the debate over the advantages and disadvantages of contracting out refuse collection. A study by Domberger *et al.* (1988) found that where this service had been tendered out by local authorities, cost savings in the order of 20 per cent had been achieved, both when outside contractors and in-house local authority organisations carried out the work. This appeared not to have reduced the quality of service offered to households, or to have been attributable to tendering companies offering 'loss leaders' to establish their position in the market. On the other hand, a rejoinder to that study (Ganley and Grahl 1988) argued that these results were heavily dependent on savings achieved by a small number of 'superstar' performers, all of whom were operating in the rather special conditions of rural areas. Working conditions for employees had deteriorated substantially, and private contractors were found to be operating very high proportions of unroadworthy vehicles and to receive a high level of complaints from users.

Full privatisation

Corporatisation and contracting out does not change the ownership of public enterprises, which remain public property. As a result, the capital market cannot be relied on to discipline the performance of the operators and to finance expansion. One alternative is full privatisation. In the United Kingdom perhaps the most visible and spectacular aspect of the privatisation programme has been the full privatisation or denationalisation of such major enterprises as British Gas, British Aerospace, British Telecom, BP and other public enterprises. Indeed, Beesley and Littlechild (1983) suggest that the term 'privatisation' is generally used to mean the transfer of nationalised activity to a Companies Act company and the sale of at least 50 per cent of the shares to private shareholders.

Full privatisation refers to the situation where the assets of the government are sold to the private sector either through a private sale or a public offer of shares – a flotation. The issues raised by full privatisation can be approached through the economic analysis of previous chapters. If a public enterprise is re-established as a private enterprise with ownership passing to the shareholders there will be a number of important changes. Instead of having objectives set (or perhaps not set clearly) by nationalisation statutes, White Papers and direct government intervention, the objectives will be those of a private company. The central objective will be profit, amended by the managers' own objectives to an extent determined by the degree of discretion that those managers are able to exert. This clarification of objectives is often seen as a major advantage of privatisation in itself, as clear objectives allow for more effective monitoring of managerial performance and give managers a much better directed set of tasks to perform.

If a firm is under pressure to maximise profits it is also under pressure to eliminate 'X-inefficiency' and to keep costs down. This will only be the case if the pressure to maximise profit is powerful, exerted through shareholder pressure, the threat of take-over and the market for corporate control. The presumption made by the supporters of privatisation is that such pressure is powerful, so that the managers of the newly privatised firms are not simply able to use the firm's resources to indulge themselves in 'organisational slack', perquisites and unnecessary costs.

The first major argument in favour of full privatisation, then, is that pressure to concentrate upon the profit objective eliminates the X-inefficiency that is said to be inherent in the public enterprise. There are examples of firms in public ownership that have achieved quite remarkable improvements in performance while still in the public sector, British Steel being the most spectacular example (Aylen 1988), but this is not typical and could be partly attributable to the knowledge that privatisation would soon take place.

The second issue raised by full privatisation concerns the structure of the market that exists after privatisation and the degree of competition that the privatised firm faces. Private ownership in itself provides a source of market discipline through the market for corporate control which may force firms to eliminate X-inefficiency. However, if the firm then becomes a private sector monopoly instead of a public sector monopoly this will lead to all the disadvantages of monopoly. Although the firm may be X-efficient, keeping its costs in check, it may charge exploitative prices and misallocate resources, thereby being economically inefficient. It may also be the case that if the market for corporate control does not achieve its full potential for exerting discipline, competition in the product market may be needed to provide a further stimulus to efficiency even in the narrow sense of X-inefficiency.

The full benefits of privatisation therefore require that vigorous competition and rivalry are established in the markets that the privatised firms are entering. This could be achieved in a number of ways. Most obviously, any statutory monopoly rights enjoyed by the firm should be abolished. Entry to the industry should be eased as far as possible, perhaps by transferring some of the assets of the existing company to new entrants. The company could be dismembered into a number of horizontally separate competing units, which could only be allowed to re-merge if they could demonstrate benefits sufficient to satisfy the competition legislation. If privatisation does not provide for the establishment of competition, it is subject to the valid criticism that little has happened apart from transforming a public monopoly into a private monopoly.

The problem of introducing competition for privatised firms varies in the level of difficulty from firm to firm. In some cases, enterprises came into public ownership for political or historical reasons which had little industrial logic and the sectors in which they operate are already relatively competitive (the National Freight Corporation is an example). On the other hand, some industries, like telecommunications, gas and water supply, were held in public hands at least partly because they exhibit many of the characteristics of 'natural monopolies'. Sunk costs are very high indeed, making entry and exit difficult and expensive, and scale economies are so substantial as to almost reserve the market for a single firm. In these circumstances it used to be argued that it is difficult to introduce effective competition. However, that argument has now been rendered obsolete by industry restructuring, rapid technological developments and innovative activities.

In the case of British Telecom, for instance, the company is now required to lease part of its network to its competitors, which reduces the sunk costs for entrants. That renders the market closer to 'contestability' but it is not likely in the short or medium term to establish a high degree of rivalry. In the long term, as technology changes and new customer needs emerge, this picture could change. Cable television networks or cellular radio could perhaps provide competition in some segments of the market. As the future is unforeseeable, and if competition is seen as a 'discovery process' (von Hayek 1978), it might be that entrepreneurial activity will lead to the breakdown of monopoly powers, provided that government ensures that obstacles to entry are not established. In the meantime some privatised firms will enjoy substantial monopoly power and methods need to be found to prevent the abuse of that power.

Two basic options offer themselves. The first is to regulate the industry, as explained in the first part of this chapter. However, as noted, the regulating agencies may simply be 'captured' by the industries they are supposed to be controlling, becoming vehicles for the companies' self-interest, or turned into 'political footballs' at the whim of trade unions and local political interests.

Another approach would be to limit prices directly, as in the case of the RPI–X formula considered above, which also has limitations.

The alternative approach, which is consistent with the general outlook on industrial policy that has led to the privatisation programme, is to place greater reliance on competition law. If the law had as its main aim the prevention of predatory practices and the protection of actual and potential competitors, and if such competitors were able to sue for very substantial damages, it might be possible to prevent the abuse of monopoly power without resort to regulation.

A mixed model: private finance initiative

In the 1990s, the private finance initiative (PFI) model was adopted in the United Kingdom. This is where the private sector funds, builds and owns an asset while the public sector simply purchases the flow of services as they occur, through a long-term commitment made at the time of construction. As the asset is financed and owned by the private sector, the investment may be provided without affecting the public sector borrowing limit (Grout 1997).

A common characteristic of PFI projects is that they are concerned with core public services that are often politically sensitive, such as health care, defence, education and the prisons. The model may also be applied to other infrastructure services, like the provision of roads, tunnels and bridges. The private provider is usually remunerated directly from the government, not the user, in the form of a fixed fee. For example, the private provider of a road is paid a fixed fee per vehicle by the government. The public sector is paying directly for the consumption of the service by the public, rather than for the provision of road services. As the fees paid depend on the number of vehicles using the road, neither the government nor the private provider accurately knows the future income stream. A substantial amount of risk is therefore transferred to the private provider of the service.

Such PFI partnerships between the government and private sector are quite similar to build–operate–transfer (BOT) contracts or the contracting-out arrangement. A major difference is that the government, rather than the user, pays for the consumption of the service. The government may use other methods, like taxation, or charges based on rental value of property, to recover part or all of the costs. Since the taxes or charges imposed are not directly related to the level of consumption, the PFI model can serve to achieve the objective of subsidising public services. In the United Kingdom, the PFI model started formally in 1992 when rules governing the use of private funds by the public sector were revised. It soon became the preferred option for capital projects.

De-regulation and liberalisation

The fourth component of the privatisation programme is the repeal of restrictions on entry into certain markets. In part this has accompanied the process of denationalisation discussed above, but there have been other examples, most notably the de-regulation of bus services, beginning with the express coaches sector which was de-regulated in 1980, and where sufficient time has elapsed for some evaluation to have taken place (Jaffer and Thompson 1986).

The basic rationale for de-regulation consists of the familiar argument that additional competition will improve efficiency and the quality of service, forcing cost savings in sectors that have hitherto been protected from competition by artificial barriers to entry constructed by government. In the case of express coaches, monopoly rights to many inter-city routes were held by National Express, part of the National Bus Company, until they were removed by the 1980 Transport Act. De-regulation was accompanied by significant entry to the industry, falling fares and the introduction of various innovations including on-board meals, videos and bus hostesses. Robbins and White (1986) showed that in some markets fares fell by half, at the same time as the new services were introduced, in a process that very closely reflects the typical claims made for de-regulation and privatisation in general. As might be expected, this experience was greeted with enthusiasm by supporters of de-regulation and used in support of the argument for the extension of the policy into other areas of bus transport.

However, many of the entrants to the industry did not remain for very long and fares began to rise again, while National Express maintained a very high market share. This development illustrates a major problem for the evaluation of de-regulation in that the increasing fares and continued dominance of a single firm do not necessarily show that de-regulation has failed to be effective. It could equally well be the case that the dominant firm is able to maintain that position because it is more efficient than others, so that de-regulation does not lead to it being ousted from its market position but does prevent it from exerting substantial market power. If the cost structure of the industry is such that efficiency requires only a small number of firms operating inter-city routes, and if entry barriers are low, an incumbent firm will not be able to exploit passengers but concentration needs to be relatively high in the interests of efficiency. On the other hand, the same observed situation might be attributable to the existence of entry barriers, in which case the judgement on de-regulation is that it removed one source of entry barrier, imposed by government policy, but left others in place which effectively prevented any gains from de-regulation.

Distinguishing between these two alternative hypotheses is difficult but Jaffer and Thompson (1988) concluded that in the case of inter-city bus travel the explanation lay not in the 'effective competition' explanation, but in the existence of entry barriers. While the initial enthusiastic judgement on de-regulation need not be completely overturned, it needs to be reassessed in the light of the evidence that entry barriers protect incumbent firms and keep prices substantially higher than they would be in their absence.

Illustration 1   Does the privatisation of refuse collection lead to efficiency gains?

The debate on the privatisation of public services in the United Kingdom is well exemplified by a series of papers on refuse collection which appeared between 1986 and 1988. In 1986, Domberger, Meadowcroft and Thompson (henceforth D–M–T) published a paper which estimated that competitive tendering by local authorities had reduced the cost of refuse collection by an average of 20 per cent. This result was arrived at by first using regression analysis to estimate costs as a function of volume and service characteristics and then using that estimated relationship to compare the costs of refuse collection for authorities that had put the service out to collection with those who had not.

Illustration 1

DMT's methods and conclusions were criticised by Ganley and Grahl (G–G) on a number of grounds. In the first place, they noted that within the group of 'privatising' local authorities there were a small number of six to eight 'superstars' whose costs were as much as 50 per cent less than expected. The overall results with respect to the magnitude of the savings to be had from privatisation were heavily dependent on this small number of atypical points. Further examination of the 'superstar' local authorities showed that all of them were in rural areas, where collection rounds may exhibit much wider qualitative differences than in urban areas. D–M–T's results might therefore reflect the geographical characteristics of the local authorities under scrutiny, rather than their adoption of privatisation policies.

While G–G's first line of criticism disputed the magnitude of the cost savings found by D–M–T it did not dispute their sign, accepting that some cost savings are apparent from the data. Their second line of attack concerned D–M–T's contention that those savings arose from increased efficiency attributable to competition.

G–G point to a number of ways in which cost savings may have been achieved without improvements in efficiency. First, they may have arisen from 'loss-leader' tactics on the part of the bidders, a suggestion that is supported by the fact that a number of successful bidders later applied for upwards revaluation of their contracts, having secured their position as suppliers. Second, bidders may have been given access to the local authorities' refuse collection facilities and equipment at prices that did not reflect their full value. Third, the cost savings may have arisen because the quality of service declined and working conditions for employees also declined. G–G quote the case of the largest contract moved to the private sector, where 84 per cent of the company's vehicles were claimed to be unroadworthy, and to other cases where employees lost access to toilets and canteens and found their working day extended by two hours. Complaints from both the public and employees have been extensive and at least one of the 'superstars' had returned refuse collection to the public sector.

These criticisms of the original D–M–T approach led to a follow-up study by Cubbin, Domberger and Meadowcroft (C–D–M), published in 1987, which attempted to identify the nature of the efficiency gains found in refuse collection. In particular, given G–G's arguments, they focused on measures of 'technical efficiency', which indicated the amounts of manual manpower and the number of vehicles used to provide the refuse collection 'outputs'. On this basis, local authorities that had tendered and contracted out had secured efficiency gains of 17 per cent over those that had not tendered, while those that had tendered but retained the services in-house had secured efficiency gains of 7 per cent. These results suggested, in response to G–G's arguments, that the cost reductions found in local authorities that had 'privatised' were attributable to improvements in the physical productivity of people and vehicles, and not to pecuniary gains arising from lower output and poorer conditions for employees.

As might be expected, G–G were not convinced by the follow-up study. A second version of their paper noted that the distribution of efficiency ratings for local authorities produced by C–D–M was completely different to that produced by D–M–T, but very similar to those produced by the Audit Commission which had not found examples of low-cost service through privatisation. They also noted that D–M–T's procedures implicitly assumed that the propensity of a local authority to privatise is independent of its costs. However, a time-series analysis of the local authorities' costs showed that those that privatised had lower than average costs already, which in turn suggests that the cost savings attributed to privatisation could at least in part be due to lower-cost operations before privatisation.

As so often happens in the analysis of the controversial policy matters, it is not possible on the basis of the evidence offered to pin down conclusively the impact of privatisation on the efficiency of refuse collection. Both sides in the debate appear to agree that costs are lower in privatising authorities, but whether those lower costs are attributed to productivity gains, losses incurred by clients and employees, or past practices independent of privatisation, remains unresolved. While the application of the policy may reduce job opportunities for refuse collection operatives, it continues to provide grist to the academic mill. As G–G note in conclusion, the results to date must be regarded as provisional until there is much more experience of contracting out. 'Further analysis will then be necessary.'

Illustration 2 Water privatisation in the United Kingdom

In the past two decades, there has been a global trend towards the full privatisation of public enterprises. This wave of privatisation is considered to have begun in the United Kingdom, and the UK experience is considered to be the most extreme form of public sector reform.

Modern change in the practice of water management in the United Kingdom can be traced back to the 1973 Water Act. Under that Act, 157 pre-existing supply undertakings, 29 river authorities and 1,393 sewage disposal authorities within England and Wales were replaced by ten Regional Water Authorities (RWAs), thus moving the control of the water supply from the local authorities to more centralised bodies. The 1989 Water Act led to the flotation of the UK water industry. Licences were issued to the privatised RWAs which are now commonly referred to as water and sewerage companies (WASCs). Today they account for the bulk of water supply and treatment in England and Wales. There are also some twenty-one smaller water-only companies (WOCs) which continue to supply water but are not involved with waste-water treatment. All of these water companies must finance their operations and construction expenses either from the revenues of water bills paid by consumers or by borrowing. Funding from local and central governments is virtually negligible.

The 1989 Water Act established the Office of Water Services (OFWAT) which is headed by the Director General. His duty is to ensure that water and sewerage operations are properly carried out, and that companies are able to earn reasonable returns on their capital so that they are able to finance the proper running of their operations (Byatt 1991). Charges by WASCs and WOCs are controlled by a price cap in the form of RPI + K. RPI is the inflation rate measured by the retail price index. The K factor is an allowable price increase above inflation to be used to finance the investment plans necessary to upgrade capacity and meet quality standards.

The privatisation of water utilities often takes place after cutbacks in the levels of government investment and service, resulting in a poor quality of water services. In the United Kingdom, new investment was required to improve infrastructure in the water industry and to meet new environmental standards. It was perceived that privatisation could free the managers of water utilities from the financial restrictions imposed on them by governments, providing them with the flexibility to raise funds to finance expansion and improve efficiency. It was also anticipated that the government could also obtain revenue from the proceeds of the sale of public enterprises.

Financial benefits aside, water utilities would gain a sense of initiative and independence after privatisation. They would also gain a greater incentive to increase productivity and diversify into new businesses in order to increase their returns. Finally, accountability would also increase because, faced with direct or indirect competition, privatised water companies would recognise the importance of meeting the needs of their consumers.

A move to private ownership necessarily means that water companies will give their shareholders priority over consumers. Hence, new regulations may be required to prevent any monopolistic behaviour on the part of the water company. Overall, the benefits of the privatisation of the UK water industry have been found to outweigh the costs (Meredith 1992, Lynk 1993). However, there has been increasing public concern over the distribution of the benefits. Water prices in the United Kingdom have been rising steadily since the end of the 1980s. Some of these increases were due to high investment costs required to meet tighter environmental standards. At the same time, huge costs were incurred in improving the poor state of many public water systems prior to the entry of private companies. Nevertheless, the perception that water companies might exploit consumers in order to serve their shareholders better remains a significant concern for public policy.

References and further reading

H. Armstrong and J. Taylor, *Regional Economics and Policy*, Oxford, Philip Allan, 1985.

H. Averch and L.L. Johnson, 'Behaviour of the Firm under Regulatory Constraint', *American Economic Review*, vol. 52, 1962, pp. 1052–69.

J. Aylen, 'Privatisation of the British Steel Corporation', *Fiscal Studies*, vol. 9, no. 3, 1988, pp. 1–26.

M. Beesley and S. Littlechild, 'Privatisation: Principles, Problems and Priorities', *Lloyd's Bank Review*, no. 149, July 1983, pp. 1–20.

M. Beesley, and S.C. Littlechild, 'The Regulation of Privatized Monopolies in the United Kingdom', *RAND Journal of Economics*, vol. 20, 1989, pp. 454–72.

D.L. Birch, *The Job Generation Process*, Cambridge, MA, MIT Press, 1979.

I. Byatt, 'UK Office of Water Services: Structure and Policy', *Utilities Policy*, January 1991, pp. 164–71.

M. Crew and P.R. Kleindorfer, 'Productivity Incentives and Rate-of-return Regulation', in M. Crew (ed.) *Regulating Utilities in an Era of Deregulation*, London, Macmillan Press, 1987, pp. 7–23.

M. Cross, 'The United Kingdom', in D. Storey (ed.) *The Small Firm: An International Survey*, 1983.

J. Cubbin, S. Domberger and S. Meadowcroft, 'Competitive Tendering and Refuse Collection: Identifying the Sources of Efficiency Gains', *Fiscal Studies*, vol. 8, no. 3, 1987, pp. 49–58.

H. Demsetz, 'Why Regulate Utilities?', *Journal of Law and Economics*, vol. 11, 1968, pp. 55–65.

A. Dilnott and C. Morris, 'What Do We Know About the Black Economy?', *Fiscal Studies*, 1981.

S. Domberger, S. Meadowcroft and D. Thompson, 'Competitive Tendering and Efficiency: The Case of Refuse Collection', *Fiscal Studies*, 1988.

J. Firn and J. Swales, 'The Formation of New Manufacturing Establishments in the Central Clydeside and West Midlands Conurbations', *Regional Studies*, vol. 12, 1978, pp. 199–213.

J. Ganley and J. Grahl, 'Competition and Refuse Collection: A Critical Comment', *Fiscal Studies*, vol. 9, no. 1, 1988, pp. 80–91.

V. Goldberg, 'Regulation and Administered Contracts', *Bell Journal of Economics*, vol. 7, 1976, pp. 426–48.

P. Grout, 'The Economics of the Private Finance Initiative', *Oxford Review of Economic Policy*, vol. 13, issue 4, winter 1997, pp. 53–67.

D. Hay, 'Competition and Industrial Policies', *Oxford Review of Economic Policy*, 1988.

D. Heald, 'Privatisation: Analysing its Appeal and Limitations', *Fiscal Studies*, 1984.

S. Holland, *The Socialist Challenge*, London, Quintet, 1975.

S. Jaffer and D. Thompson, 'Deregulating Express Coaches: A Reassessment', *Fiscal Studies*, vol. 7, issue 4, November 1986, pp. 45–69.

P. Joskow, 'Incentive Regulation for Electric Utilities', *Yale Journal on Regulation*, vol. 4, 1986, pp. 1–49.

H. Leibenstein, 'Allocative Efficiency vs. X-efficiency', *American Economic Review*, vol. 56, 1966, pp. 392–412.

C. Liston, 'Price-cap versus Rate-of-return Regulation', *Journal of Regulatory Economics*, vol. 5, 1993, pp. 25–48.

E. Lynk, 'Privatization, Joint Production and the Comparative Efficiencies of Private and Public Ownership: The UK Water Industry Case', *Fiscal Studies*, vol. 14, 1993, pp. 98–116.

P. MacAvoy, 'The Effectiveness of the Federal Power Commission', *Bell Journal of Economics and Management*, vol. 1, 1970, pp. 271–303.

C. Mason and P. Lloyd, 'New Firms in a "Prosperous" UK Sub-Region', *National Conference on Small Business Policy and Research*, 1983.

S. Meredith, 'Water Privatization: The Dangers and the Benefits', *Long Range Planning*, vol. 25, 1992, pp. 72–81.

B. Moore and J. Rhodes, 'Evaluating the Effects of British Regional Economic Policy', *Economic Journal*, vol. 83, March 1973, pp. 87–110.

A.T. O'Donnell and J.K. Swales, 'Regional Elasticities of Substitution in the United Kingdom in 1968: A Comment', *Urban Studies*, vol. 14 N.S., October 1977, pp. 371–8.

S. Peltzman, 'Pricing in Private and Public Enterprise: Electric Utilities in the United States', *Journal of Law and Economics*, vol. 14, 1971, pp. 109–47.

S. Peltzman, 'Toward a More General Theory of Regulation', *Journal of Law and Economics*, vol. 19, 1976, pp. 211–40.

R. Posner, 'Taxation by Regulation', *Bell Journal of Economics and Management Science*, vol. 2, 1971, pp. 22–50.

R. Posner, 'Theories of Economic Regulation', *Bell Journal of Economics*, vol. 5, 1974, pp. 335–58.

D. Robbins and P. White, 'The Experience of Express Coaching Deregulation in Great Britain', *Transportation*, 1986.

T. Sharpe, 'Privatisation, Regulation and Competition', *Fiscal Studies*, 1984.

G. Stigler, 'The Theory of Economic Regulation', *Bell Journal of Economics and Management Science*, vol. 2, 1971, pp. 3–21.

G. Stigler and C. Friedland, 'What Can Regulators Regulate? The Case of Electricity', *Journal of Law and Economics*, vol. 5, 1962, pp. 1–16.

D. Storey, *Entrepreneurship and the New Firm*, London, Croom Helm, 1982.

P. Townroe, 'Some Behavioural Considerations in the Industrial Location Decision', *Regional Studies*, vol. 6, 1972, pp. 261–72.

J. Twomey and J. Taylor, 'Regional Policy and the Inter-regional Movement of Manufacturing Industry in Great Britain', *Scottish Journal of Political Economy*, 1986.

J. Vickers and G. Yarrow, 'Regulation of Privatised Firms in Britain', *European Economic Review*, vol. 32, issue 2, 3, March 1988, pp. 465–73.

J. Vickers and G. Yarrow, 'Economic Perspectives on Privatisation', *Journal of Economic Perspectives*, vol. 5, 1991, pp. 111–32.

F. von Hayek, *Individualism and Economic Order*, Chicago, Chicago University Press, 1948.

F. von Hayek, *The Constitution of Liberty*, Chicago, Chicago University Press, 1960.

F. von Hayek, *New Studies in Philosophy, Ethics and Economics*, London, Routledge and Kegan Paul, 1978.

M. Waterson, 'The Major Utilities: Ownership, Regulation and Energy Usage', in K. Cowling and R. Sugden (eds) *A New Economic Policy for Britain: Essays on the Development of Industry*, Manchester and New York, Manchester University Press, 1990, pp. 174–91.

T. Weyman-Jones, 'RPI-X Price Cap Regulation: The Price Controls Used in UK Electricity', *Utilities Policy*, October 1990, pp. 65–77.

O. Williamson, 'Franchise Bidding for Natural Monopolies – in General and with Respect to CATV', *Bell Journal of Economics*, vol. 7, 1976, pp. 73–104.

Self-test questions

1. Explain the difference between the 'public interest' and 'capture' theories of industry regulation.

2. List four different approaches to 'privatisation'.

3. Identify the main problems that arise in respect of franchise bidding.

4. Why may regulation be necessary, from the 'public interest' point of view?

5. Explain what is meant by the 'demand' side and the 'supply' side of regulation.

Essay question

Compare rate-of-return regulation and price-cap regulation as means by which an industry may be controlled in the public interest.

Solutions to questions

Chapter 2

Self-test questions

1 (a) No, the firm is on its cost curve
  (b) Yes, unnecessary spending is incurred
  (c) Yes
2 (a) No
  (b) Yes
  (c) No
  (d) Yes
  (e) Yes
3 (a) Nothing
  (b) Falls
  (c) Falls
4 (a)

Model answer to essay question

The neo-classical theory of the firm is based upon the assumption that the objective of the firm is to maximise profit, and that the firm is operating in a world of certainty. Revenue conditions are determined by consumer behaviour and by the structure of the industry. Cost conditions are determined by the form of the production function which represents the technology available. Neo-classical theory assumes that firms adopt the most efficient production technique available, and use up only the level of resources that is strictly necessary for the level of output being produced. In the language of model-building, the neo-classical model is an 'optimising' model, which assumes certainty, and which takes a 'holistic' view of the firm, treating it as an entity that can have objectives and take decisions. A graphical version of the resulting model is set out in Figure Solutions 2.1, for the simple case of a firm in monopoly conditions. As the diagram shows, in the neo-classical model, the firm produces the level of output Q, at which marginal cost equals marginal revenue. Price is set at P, the level required to sell output Q, and cost per unit is AC_1 as shown by the average cost curve. The firm always operates on its cost curve, and never above it.

In the neo-classical model, the firm is always 'X-efficient' or 'operationally efficient', in the sense that it incurs no more costs than are strictly necessary for the production of the profit-maximising level of output. 'X-inefficiency' theory suggests that may not be the case. If the firm is not under powerful pressure from its shareholders, the market for corporate control, or competition, its managers may not be forced to maximise profits. In that case they will have a degree of freedom to indulge themselves in 'perks' and a 'quiet life', which will involve the firm in costs that are not strictly necessary and which

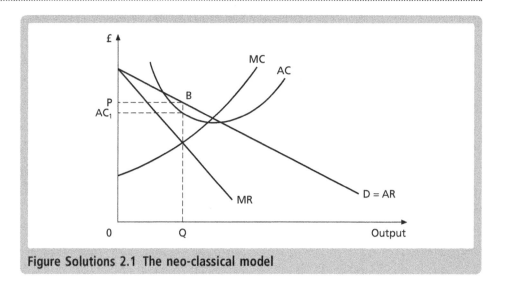

Figure Solutions 2.1 The neo-classical model

render the firm 'X-inefficient'. In terms of the diagram shown in Figure Solutions 2.1, the firm will be above its cost curve, at a point like B.

The X-inefficiency approach, therefore, does not assume that the firm is a profit-maximiser; nor does it involve a completely holistic approach. Instead of treating the firm as a 'black box', X-inefficiency theory takes account of its internal workings by suggesting that workers and managers may have motivations other than profit. The extent to which a firm actually incurs unnecessary costs depends to a great extent upon the nature of those motivations, and the framework of relationships between managers, workers and shareholders. If shareholders exert powerful pressure on managers, forming an efficient 'principal/agent' contract, and if managers are effectively able to control workers, there will be no X-inefficiency. On the other hand, if neither of these links is strong, there will be room for 'organisational slack' and X-inefficiency.

This approach also identifies links between the opportunities for X-inefficient behaviour and the structure of the market in which the firm is operating. If the market is highly competitive, profit-maximising behaviour will be needed for survival, and the opportunities for incurring unnecessary costs will be limited. On the other hand, if competition is limited, firms will have the discretion to waste a proportion of the firm's resources in order to meet their own objectives. X-inefficiency theory therefore has an important application in the debate on competition policy. If a firm has monopoly power, not only will it tend to behave in ways that are economically inefficient, it will also tend to be X-inefficient, adding to the burden on the economy created by the monopoly power.

Chapter 3

Self-test questions

1 (a) Buying a general-purpose piece of equipment
   (b) Installing the engine into the body shell on a vehicle production line
   (c) Buying a customised piece of equipment
   (d) Buying a piece of general-purpose equipment that has been modified somewhat to fit special needs

2 (a) market transaction – classical contracting
  (b) hierarchy – unified governance
  (c) neo-classical contracting
  (d) neo-classical contracting
3 (a) Site specificity: whisky distilleries are located next to the streams that provide the water giving them a special flavour
  (b) Physical or intellectual asset specificity: the moulds and dies used to make many products are specific to one particular use
  (c) Dedicated asset specificity: a firm buys a general-purpose machine tool to meet an order from a specific customer; other customers' requirements do not involve the use of that machine tool
  (d) Human capital specificity: staff are trained to carry out a set of tasks and routines that are unique to meeting the needs of a particular customer
  (e) Brand-name specificity: Actors in well-known 'soap operas' receive higher pay and other opportunities as a result of their association with that brand name.
4 (a) Yes
  (b) No
  (c) No
  (d) Yes
  (e) No

Model answer to essay question

Transactions cost analysis suggests that the choice between in-house production of a product and either the spot purchase of the product from an independent supplier or the acquisition of the product through a medium-term contract depends upon four major factors. These are:

1. *The extent to which a complete contract can be written,* which in turn depends upon the degree of complexity and the level of uncertainty associated.
2. *The threat of opportunistic behaviour* on the part of the transacting party.
3. *The extent of asset specificity* involved in the transaction.
4. *The frequency of the transaction.*

In the case of newspaper production, transactions take place very frequently in conditions of great uncertainty because papers are printed every day and there are constant changes to the copy as news comes in. Any delay in printing would lead to a huge loss in revenues so that any 'hold-up' or delay by an independent printer would be very expensive. In order to get the news into the paper very quickly, the news-gathering mechanisms, page layout systems and typesetting systems are tightly integrated into expensive facilities that could not be used for any other purpose. Therefore there is a very high level of physical asset specificity, the 'small numbers' problem is present, and unified governance is most efficient.

In the case of book publishing, a book is usually printed just once for each edition and the need for timeliness is much less urgent. If a dispute arises between printer and publisher, a book might be printed a few weeks late, but that is of relatively little importance. Hence the cost of opportunistic behaviour is much lower. Because the production of the copy and the production of the final book do not need to be so closely integrated, there is much less asset specificity and there are many jobbing printers who could produce a book, and who compete with each other, keeping costs down. Hence, publishers tend to use independent printers. This book was written in Hong Kong by the authors, copyedited in the United Kingdom by an independent editor and then proofed and printed in Hong Kong. That kind of governance mechanism is efficient for books but would be disastrous in the newspaper industry.

Chapter 4

Self-test questions

1 (a) Less likely
  (b) More likely
  (c) More likely
  (d) Less likely
  (e) More likely
2 (a) if the shareholder has a relatively small holding in the firm and purchases from the company, hence preferring lower prices
  (b) if the shareholder is a supplier to the company, preferring high prices to be paid for those supplies
3 In an 'outsider' financial system, shareholders buy shares in companies but do not take a direct role in management. Instead, they pay attention to the share price, which is determined by the market, and they exert influence by 'exit'. If they believe that a firm is being badly run, they sell its shares. That lowers the share price and puts the firm under pressure through the threat of take-over.

  In an 'insider' financial system, shareholders (often banks) take a direct role in managing the companies they hold. They exert influence over the company by 'voice', which is direct influence over company decisions.
5 (a) recent superior performance
  (b) a self-important chief executive
  (c) recent positive media publicity

Model answer to essay question

Managerial discretion is the ability of managers to use the assets of a firm in furtherance of their own ends, at the expense of profitability and shareholder interests. Alternative models of the firm, like Baumol's revenue-maximising model and Williamson's utility-maximising approach, assume that such discretion does exist.

The extent of discretion is limited by a number of factors. If shareholders place a high value on profits, if they pay close attention to managers' behaviour and if they are able to act to influence that behaviour, discretion will be limited. If the stock market – the market for corporate control – is relatively efficient, the exercise of managerial discretion will result in lower share prices (because expected profits will be lower and share prices reflect expected profits). Lower share prices will make the firm vulnerable to take-over by more efficient managers who expect to improve profits and raise share prices.

Financial liberalisation tends to reinforce these pressures in a number of ways. Most importantly, the financial institutions are exposed to competition, which forces them to pay greater attention to their own profits. However, their own profits depend to a significant extent upon the performance of the companies in which they make investments. Hence they tend to pay more attention to the ways in which the managers of those firms are performing. Evidence from the United Kingdom suggests that twenty years ago, banks and insurance companies had great potential influence on companies but did not bother to use it. In more recent times they have been forced to become more aggressive in order to compete with each other.

Financial liberalisation also tends to improve the efficiency of stock markets by opening them to a wider range of participants and by facilitating globalisation and international participation. As stock markets are followed increasingly closely by an ever growing group of well-informed investors, so are profit opportunities arising from the exercise of managerial discretion more likely to be identified and acted upon.

Chapter 5

Self-test questions

1 (a) ownership advantages
  (b) location advantages
  (c) internalisation advantages
2 Because it is almost impossible to write licensing contracts that can effectively coordinate the transfer of ownership advantages from one organisation to another without considerable risk. There are often asset specificities involved and a serious danger of opportunism.
3 (a) the development of local companies may be inhibited
  (b) there may be a net capital outflow
  (c) the government will lose some of its autonomy
4 (a) global market participation
  (b) product standardisation
  (c) uniform marketing
  (d) coordination of value-added activities
  (e) concentration of value-adding activities

Model answer to essay question

The OLI analysis has its foundation in economics. Its purpose is to identify the conditions under which multinational activity will take place. Three sets of conditions are identified. First, in order to compete in a foreign market a firm must have some kind of 'ownership advantage'. That is some kind of proprietary asset that enables it to compete with local firms. Such assets may include tangibles like patents or brand names, or more intangible factors like managerial skills and knowledge of market opportunities. Second, there must be some kind of 'location advantage' that makes it more profitable to use the ownership advantage in a new location. The most obvious such advantages are access to inexpensive immobile resources and proximity to customers. Third, there must be 'internalisation advantages'. It must be more profitable to transfer the ownership advantage to its new location inside the company, instead of transferring it to an independent company through a licensing agreement. The conditions under which internalisation advantages exist are explained by transaction cost analysis.

The OLI model is positive and descriptive, in keeping with the traditional economics approach to analysis. It allows hypotheses to be developed and tested, concerning the types of firms and activities that will tend to become multinational. The analysis of global strategy is quite different in that it aims to be normative and prescriptive. The strategy analyst hopes to identify the actions that firms can take in order to improve their performance. It is recognised that different situations require different actions, hence attention focuses on the interaction between the forces in the environment that make it profitable to adopt a 'global' approach to business and the different actions that may be taken in order to profit from the environment. Within that broad framework, there are many different approaches to global strategy. One of the most comprehensive, which draws together earlier contributions, is the Cavusgil and Zou model. In that model external 'drivers' and internal 'organisational factors' determine the extent to which global strategies like standardisation versus localisation of products and marketing tactics lead to enhanced performance. Although the fundamental purpose of strategy research is normative and prescriptive, the models generated are often used in a positive and descriptive way by testing the hypotheses they generate with respect to performance. For economists, however,

that can be problematical. If a strategy researcher identifies the key to superior performance, that key is either imitable by others or not. If it is imitable, then others will copy
it and it will cease to give good performance. If it is not imitable, the prescription has
limited value precisely because no one else can put it into practice!

Chapter 6

Self-test questions

1 (a) Correct
  (b) No
  (c) Not always
  (d) Correct
  (e) Correct
2 (a) See Figure Solutions 6.1 for apples and oranges
  (b) Straight lines at right angles to the beer axis
  (c) Straight lines at right angles to the cigarettes axis
  (d) Concave to the origin, with higher satisfaction represented by points closer to the
    origin
3 35A and 33B gives 134 juiciness and 169 sweetness
4 (a) No
  (b) Yes
  (c) No
5 (a) Yes
  (b) No
  (c) No

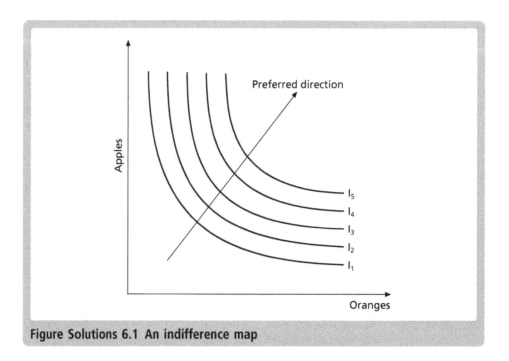

Figure Solutions 6.1 An indifference map

Model answer to essay question

Indifference analysis assumes that consumers are able to identify those combinations of goods that they prefer to other combinations and those combinations of goods between which they are indifferent. On the basis of this assumption, an indifference map can be drawn up which provides a graphical representation of a consumer's taste patterns. This map consists of a set of indifference curves, each of which shows combinations of the commodity among which the consumer is indifferent. Figure Solutions 6.1 shows such an indifference map.

Indifference curves are shown as continuous lines, with increasing slope to the left and decreasing slopes to the right. (They are convex viewed from the origin.) This general shape reflects the further assumption of a decreasing marginal rate of substitution, which implies that as a consumer has more of one commodity, they are willing to exchange more of it for a given amount of the other commodity. Higher indifference curves represent higher levels of satisfaction and the aim of the consumer will be to reach the highest possible indifference curve. The indifference map can be used to identify the optimal basket of goods for a consumer. To find this, it is first necessary to consider the household's level of income, and the different combinations of goods it can therefore afford. This is shown using a budget line, as shown in Figure Solutions 6.2.

If the budget line is placed on the same diagram as the indifference map, it is then possible to identify the optimal combination of goods, shown at point X in Figure Solutions 6.3.

It is now possible to examine the impact of a reduction in the price of one of the commodities. If the price of the commodity indicated by the horizontal axis falls, the budget line will shift, from its original position BB to the new position BB$_1$. This gives a new optimal combination of commodities at point Z. In the example shown, the consumer buys more of the good whose price has fallen. However, this could be a quirk of the particular diagram shown and it is necessary to consider whether this must be generally

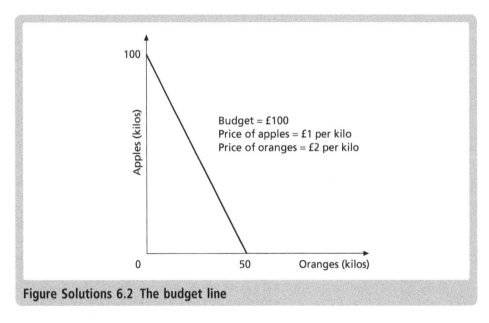

Figure Solutions 6.2 The budget line

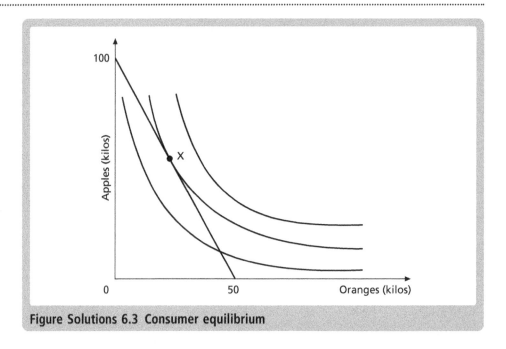

Figure Solutions 6.3 Consumer equilibrium

true. This can be examined by recognising that the fall in price leads to two separate effects. The first, known as the substitution effect, arises because the relative prices of the two goods have changed. The second, known as the income effect, arises because a fall in price means that the consumer's real income has risen, a change that will also affect the consumer's purchases.

The substitution effect can be separated out by asking the question 'how would the basket of goods purchased change if relative prices changed, but the consumer maintained the same level of real income?' As 'real income' really means the level of satisfaction attained by the consumer, this is equivalent to asking 'what would happen if the consumer stayed on the same indifference curve but relative prices changed?' This can be identified by changing the slope of the budget line so that it represents the relative prices of the goods, after the price change, but leaving the consumer on their original indifference curve. If the budget line is changed to B_2B_2 in Figure Solutions 6.4 this shows that in those circumstances the consumer would purchase the basket of goods indicated by combination Y.

This involves increasing purchases of the good whose price has fallen, and it is also clear that this must always be the case. If a good indicated on the horizontal axis becomes cheaper, the budget line becomes flatter and its point of tangency with the same indifference curve must move to the right. The substitution effect will always lead to increased purchases of the good whose price has fallen.

The income effect can now also be found. This is the change in the basket of goods that would be purchased if the consumer experienced the change in real income that follows from the reduction in price, but relative prices remained the same. That is indicated by the shift in the budget line from B_2B_2 to BB_1 and the shift in the basket of goods purchased from Y to Z. The income effect is less certain in its direction than the substitution effect. For 'normal' goods it will be in the same direction as the substitution effect, leading to more of the good whose price has fallen being bought. However, for 'inferior' goods, the effect will be perverse, leading to less being bought.

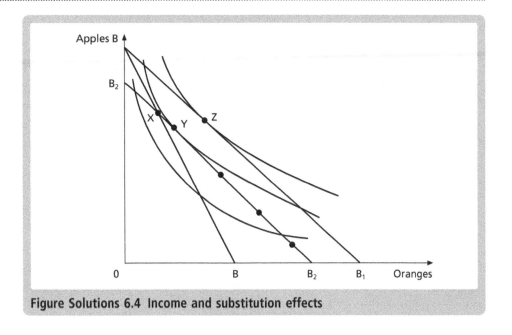

Figure Solutions 6.4 Income and substitution effects

It can now be seen that the overall impact of a change in price (the 'price effect') and the shape of the consumer's demand curve depend upon the combination of the income effect and the substitution effect. It can also be seen that there are three possible cases. For 'normal' goods, lower prices must lead to more of a good being purchased and the demand curve must slope downwards. For 'inferior' goods, the two effects work in opposite directions and the outcome depends upon which is the most powerful. For most such goods, the substitution effect will outweigh the income effect, and the demand curve will slope downwards. For a very extreme class of inferior goods, known as 'Giffen goods', the perverse income effect will outweigh the substitution effect and the demand curve will slope upwards. For instance, if a consumer is very poor indeed and spending most of their income on a staple food, whose price then falls, the consumer may actually reduce their consumption of that staple food, replacing it with something else. However, this is a very extreme case and with that exception demand curves will slope downwards.

Chapter 7

Self-test questions

1 (a) Yes
  (b) No
  (c) No
  (d) Yes
2 (a) Yes
  (b) Yes
  (c) No
  (d) No
  (e) No
  (f) No

3 (a) No
  (b) No
  (c) Yes
  (d) Yes
  (e) Yes
4 (a) Yes
  (b) No
  (c) No
  (d) No
  (e) Yes
5 (a) Falls
  (b) Falls
  (c) Rises

Model answer to essay question

Jaguar set the price of the XJ12 at a level that was well below the price of similar cars and which lost the company a large amount of revenue. At the same time, difficulties with production led to a much smaller number of cars being produced so that the low price had an even more marked effect on the company's profitability. Three different explanations are possible for Jaguar's apparently irrational decision, each involving a different level of analysis.

At the most superficial level, the price was set as the result of a cost-plus approach to pricing. The company estimated the cost of production at the expected level of output, added a margin and thereby arrived at the price to be set. Cost-plus pricing ignores the marketing side of the business, paying no attention to the behaviour of either customers or competitors. Therefore, the higher prices of similar cars were not taken into account when setting prices.

While the use of cost-plus pricing provides a partial explanation for Jaguar's decision, it is still necessary to ask 'why adopt cost-plus pricing?' The explanation may be found in the nature and background of the company's management, in their preferences and in the fact that they had significant managerial discretion. Jaguar's management was dominated by engineers who saw the company's purpose as the production and sale of beautiful cars, not the production of profits. They placed a high value on maintaining a smooth flow of production and on being able to sell every car produced. They placed little value on marketing and the revenue side of the company's operations. As neither shareholders nor the market for corporate control exerted strict discipline over the senior management, they were able to ignore shareholder value for a long period of time.

Third, it should be remembered that the political and social background to the decision was also important. The trade unions were very powerful in the UK motor industry in the 1970s and they did not hesitate to force managers to maintain overtime payments and avoid sacking lazy workers. It was not unknown for trade union activists to use physical violence against managers whose actions displeased them. In that situation managers placed a high priority on ensuring that all cars produced could be sold, and most of the managers' efforts were focused internally, on managing and placating the workforce, instead of considering customers and competitors in the external environment.

Chapter 8

Self-test questions

1 (a) Yes
  (b) No
  (c) No
  (d) No
  (e) No
2 (b), (c), (d)
3 (a) No
  (b) Yes
  (c) No
4 (a) D
  (b) A
  (c) C
  (d) B
5 (a) No
  (b) No
  (c) Yes
  (d) No

Model answer to essay question

'Estimation' involves attempting to quantify the causal links between one variable and another. In the case of the demand for a product this requires identifying the links between the quantity of the good demanded and such factors as its price, the level of advertising, consumers' income and the prices of substitute products. Estimation poses some very difficult and fundamental problems, which can only be partly resolved through sophisticated analytical methods. The most common method of estimating demand is through the application of econometric techniques to the available data on each of the variables. Estimation might also be carried out by attempting direct questioning of buyers on their response to changes in the values of the determining variables.

'Forecasting' involves attempting to quantify the future value of a variable without reference to its determinants. In a sense, forecasting involves an implicit assumption that time is the major determining variable. There are many different methods of forecasting, including:

- time-series analysis
- barometric forecasting
- surveys of buyers' intentions
- sales force opinion
- expert opinion
- market testing.

Estimation through econometric forecasting usually involves the statistical technique of multiple regression, which fits an equation to the data, showing the 'best fit' that can be found for the data set. While this is a powerful technique it also carries with it a number of problems. In the first place, the 'best fit' may not be a very good fit, in which case the estimating equation only explains a small proportion of the variation in the level of demand. In the second place, the equation will provide individual coefficients linking each of the determining variables to the variable that is being forecast. However, these will only be accurate estimates if a set of very restrictive assumptions is met.

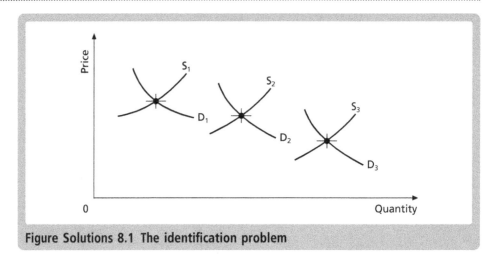

Figure Solutions 8.1 The identification problem

Third, econometric estimation has to deal with the 'identification problem'. If we focus on the link between price and demand, for instance, it is tempting to examine the set of observations on price and quantity, as shown by the set of crosses in Figure Solutions 8.1 and conclude that a line drawn through them represents the demand curve.

However, that set of points could have been generated by both the demand and supply curves shifting, as shown in the diagram. Sophisticated methods involving multiple equations can help to solve this problem but they have problems of their own which are difficult to resolve.

As estimation is difficult and often unsatisfactory, companies often restrict themselves to forecasting. If they use barometric forecasting, the technique involves identifying some other variable whose value is known to foreshadow changes in the variable to be forecast. In attempting to forecast the number of children starting school, for instance, the figures for births five years ago will provide a very useful example of a 'leading indicator'. Companies may use more general 'leading indicators' of economic activity, like orders for machine tools, or even sunspot activity, which has been found in the past to have a close correlation with fluctuations in the economy.

The success of barometric forecasting depends upon finding a leading indicator that has a reliable and robust relationship with the variable to be forecast. If there is no obvious causal link between the two variables, accurate forecasting will depend upon the continued existence of that past relationship. However, if there is a substantial change in any of the variables that determine the level of demand, the link between the leading indicator and the variable to be forecast may break down. Other types of forecasting, such as sales force opinion, expert opinion or surveys of buyers' intentions may be more reliable because these provide a means by which expected changes in the environment may have appropriate influence upon the forecast.

Chapter 9

Self-test questions

1 (a) No
  (b) Yes
  (c) Not strictly – techniques are capital or labour intensive
  (d) No
  (e) Not necessarily

2 (a) Yes
  (b) Yes
  (c) Yes
  (d) No
  (e) No
3 (a) No
  (b) Yes
  (c) Yes
  (d) No
  (e) No
4 What the lowest possible cost per unit would be for every level of output if the firm were using the most appropriate set of plant and equipment chosen from the current technology at the current set of factor prices.
5 (a) The contribution margin is £40 per delegate. Fixed costs are £500. Dividing the fixed cost by the margin gives a break-even level of 13 delegates.
  (b) Total contribution required is £1,000. Dividing that figure by the contribution margin gives 25 delegates.

Model answer to essay question

Break-even models have a number of characteristics, illustrated graphically in Figure Solutions 9.1.

As the diagram shows, total cost is made up of two components. The first is fixed costs and the second is variable costs. The curve for total variable cost is drawn as a straight line, indicating that variable cost per unit is assumed to be constant. Similarly, the curve for total revenue is drawn as a straight line, indicating that every level of output is sold at the same price. The level of output at which total revenue equals total cost, shown by Q_1, is known as the 'break-even' point.

If the cost component of the model is examined first, it is clear that the assumed structure of costs is very different from that which appears in the economic model of the firm.

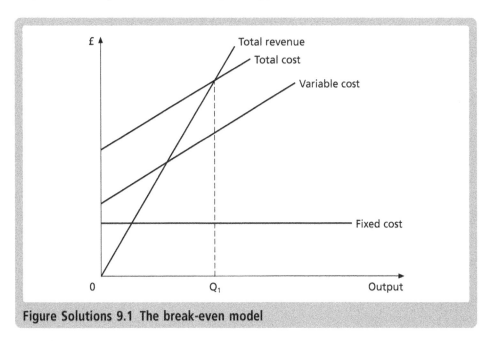

Figure Solutions 9.1 The break-even model

In the break-even model, whatever the level of output, and whatever the level of capacity utilisation, average variable cost remains the same. It is therefore assumed that the principle of diminishing returns, which leads to higher levels of variable cost per unit as more of the variable factors of production are combined with the fixed factors, does not hold. The break-even model appears to suggest that there is no limit to the output that the firm could produce, and no cost penalties for very high levels of capacity utilisation.

On the demand side, the linear form of the total revenue function reflects the assumption that every level of output can be sold at the price that is indicated. Different prices lead to different total revenue functions, with higher prices being reflected in steeper curves, and correspondingly lower break-even levels of output. The concept of elasticity of demand, and the possibility that different prices may lead to different levels of demand, has no place in the break-even model. If this model were used to answer the questions that are addressed by the economic model of the firm, it clearly produces nonsensical results. The profit-maximising level of output is infinity, as profits simply increase without limit as the level of output rises. Similarly, the profit-maximising level of price is infinitely high because the model contains no reference to the possibility that buyers may be deterred by higher prices.

If the break-even model were judged on the criteria applied to the economic model of the firm, which are that it should produce testable predictions with respect to output and price, then clearly it would be judged a failure. However, that would be to misunderstand the purposes of the model. The break-even model is not intended to predict or identify the profit-maximising level of output or the profit-maximising price. Instead it is intended to examine cost and revenue relationships within a relatively narrow range of output, in order to assist in the planning and control of business activity. In particular, it is useful for short-term profit planning, and for considering the feasibility of particular business activities. Having calculated the break-even point for some activity, that result can then be the focus for further analysis. For instance, it can be used to consider whether the volume of sales required to break even is felt to be feasible at the price indicated. Different prices may be considered in order to examine their impact on the break-even level. If the firm has an estimate of the actual level of sales, this can be compared with the break-even level to consider the 'margin of safety' available, which provides a means of examining the firm's vulnerability to unexpected changes in the volume of activity.

In summary, then, break-even analysis is directed towards a set of questions that is different from those addressed by the economic model of the firm. The fact that it ignores the principle of diminishing returns and the concept of elasticity of demand does not imply that the model has no value.

Chapter 10

Self-test questions

1 (a) Yes
  (b) Yes
  (c) No
  (d) Yes
2 (a) Yes
  (b) No
  (c) No
  (d) No
  (e) No

3 (a) Yes
  (b) No
  (c) Yes
  (d) Yes
  (e) No
4 (a) Yes
  (b) Yes
  (c) No
  (d) Yes
  (e) Yes

Model answer to essay question

Perfect competition is a market structure in which the following conditions hold:

- firms aim to maximise profits
- a large number of small buyers and sellers
- firms produce identical products
- free entry to the industry
- perfect knowledge of market opportunities
- perfect mobility of factors of production.

In this situation, firms are 'price-takers', being forced to accept the price that is deter-mined by the market forces of supply and demand. The situation for each firm, and for the industry as a whole, is shown in Figure Solutions 10.1.

The price, P, is set by the market. Each individual firm has a horizontal demand curve at the market price, indicating that it can sell as much as it chooses at that price, but nothing at higher prices. Because price is constant at different levels of output, marginal revenue and price are equal. Profit-maximising firms will choose to produce level of output q_0, which gives an aggregate output for the industry of Q_0.

This result gives an optimal allocation of resources because it ensures that price is equal to the marginal cost of production. The individual firm, maximising its profit, chooses to supply the amount indicated by its marginal cost curve, which is also the firm's supply curve. The supply curve for the industry is simply the horizontal sum of the marginal

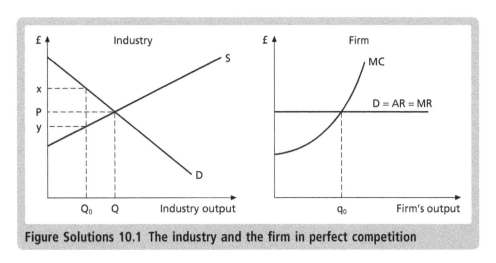

Figure Solutions 10.1 The industry and the firm in perfect competition

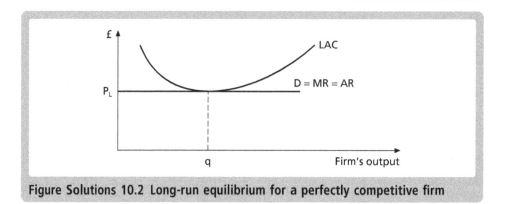

Figure Solutions 10.2 Long-run equilibrium for a perfectly competitive firm

cost curves for the individual firms, and may be thought of as the industry's marginal cost curve, as indicated on the diagram. As price is determined by the intersection of the demand curve and the supply/marginal cost curve, perfect competition guarantees that price equals marginal cost. The equality of price and marginal cost is the condition for an optimal allocation of resources because achievement of that condition implies that the economy has maximised the net benefit to consumers arising from production of the commodity in question. If the price of a good is recognised as a measure of consumers' 'willingness to pay' for it, and willingness to pay is seen as a measure of the value that the consumer places on a commodity, then maximising net benefit requires that output be set at the level where the price is equal to marginal cost.

This point can be seen more clearly with reference to the left-hand part of Figure Solutions 10.1. If the industry were to produce level of output Q_0 the allocation of resources would be sub-optimal as consumers would place a value of 'x' on the production of an additional unit which would only cost 'y' to produce. Net benefit to consumers would be foregone unless every unit for which the price exceeds marginal cost is produced. Only at Q, where price is equal to marginal cost, is this result achieved. Perfect competition therefore guarantees an optimal allocation of resources. However, a perfectly competitive market situation is only possible if there are no substantial economies of scale. This can be seen by examining the long-run equilibrium position for an individual firm in the industry, shown in Figure Solutions 10.2.

The curve LAC in the diagram indicates the long-run average cost curve for each firm in the industry. In the long run, price must settle at the level P_L because if it were any higher, new entry would take place, forcing the price down, and if it were any lower, firms would leave, pushing the price upwards. When the price reaches P_L, each firm has a horizontal demand and marginal revenue curve as shown, and chooses to produce level of output 'q' where profit is maximised. This analysis makes it clear that the size of the firm is limited by the up-turn in the LAC curve. As there is a large number of firms in the industry, the level of output at which costs begin to rise must be a very small proportion of the total industry output. If there were any substantial scale economies, so that the LAC curve sloped downwards, rather than being U-shaped, there would be no long-run equilibrium. Larger firms would have lower costs than smaller ones and the industry would tend to become more concentrated, ceasing to be perfectly competitive. If scale economies exist, then, perfect competition will be impossible.

Chapter 11

Self-test questions

1 (a) No
  (b) Yes, note that rivalry is limited because with a large number of firms the actions of one have no direct effect on the others
  (c) No
  (d) No
2 (d)
3 (a) No
  (b) Yes
  (c) Yes
  (d) Yes
  (e) Yes
4 (a) No
  (b) Yes
  (c) No
  (d) No
5 (a) Yes
  (b) Yes
  (c) No
  (d) Yes

Model answer to essay question

The economic models of perfect competition, monopoly and oligopoly are rigorously defined models of market structure, whose fundamental purpose is to provide a basis for making predictions about the behaviour and performance of firms. Each model is based upon a series of assumptions about market structure, which include:

● the number of firms in the industry
● the condition of entry
● the extent of product differentiation.

These formal models of competitive structure are not intended to be descriptively realistic or to provide decision-makers with a directly applicable tool for the analysis of individual industries. Their aim is to abstract away from the complexities of the real world in order to identify the major factors that determine the outcome of competitive situations. The method used is to set up tightly defined models for which equilibrium situations can be identified and then to examine the nature of those equilibria and the mechanisms through which they can be reached. The models show clearly how factors like the number of firms, entry barriers, economies of scale, rivals' reactions and product differentiation all affect the outcome of a competitive situation.

Porter's 'five forces' analysis differs from the economic approach in a number of ways. In the first place, the objective of the analysis is quite different. Instead of aiming to make predictions on the basis of highly simplified 'ideal types' of market structure, the 'five forces' analysis aims to provide managers with a means of systematically describing the nature of competition in the complex situations faced by real firms. This is achieved by examining a checklist of the factors that determine each of the five forces, which are as follows:

1. The intensity of rivalry among incumbents.
2. The threat of entry.
3. The threat of substitution.
4. The power of buyers.
5. The power of suppliers.

When the factors determining the five forces have been examined, they can each be summarised in a qualitative fashion in order to characterise the major features of competition in the industry in question. No attempt is made to identify the equilibrium position towards which an industry will tend and the end result of the analysis is not a detailed description of its performance but a much more general categorisation of its structure as either 'attractive' or 'unattractive' to its incumbents.

Despite these major differences in their objectives and method, there are substantial overlaps between the two approaches to competitive structure. Each of the 'five forces' identified in Porter's approach is a generalisation and extension of aspects of market structure that appear in the formal economic models. As a result, each of the formal models can be characterised in the Porter framework. Perfect competition, for instance, could be described in 'five forces' terms as an industry with a low level of rivalry, high threat of entry, limited buyer and supplier power, and a threat of substitution which varies from individual case to case. That suggests an industry that is likely to be relatively unattractive in 'five forces' terms, a conclusion that is reflected in the formal model by the fact that in the long run no supernormal profits can be earned. The 'five forces' model may therefore be seen as an attempt to develop the formal models in order to make them operational as a means of characterising the complex competitive structures that are to be found in real industries.

Chapter 12

Self-test questions

1 (a) Yes
  (b) No, uncertainty
  (c) Yes
2 (a) No
  (b) No
  (c) Yes
3 (a) No
  (b) Yes
  (c) No
4 (a) No
  (b) Yes
  (c) No
5 (a) No
  (b) Yes
  (c) No

Model answer to essay question

The terms 'certainty', 'risk' and 'uncertainty' refer to differing 'states of information'. A situation of certainty exists when decision-makers are perfectly informed about the outcomes of actions they may take. 'Risk' is a situation where decision-makers are not perfectly informed about the outcomes of actions, but they are able to enumerate all the possible outcomes and to attach probabilities to each of those outcomes. 'Uncertainty' is a state of even more limited information, where a decision-maker does not know the possible outcomes of actions, or cannot attach probabilities to them.

In a situation of certainty, decision-makers can choose between alternative actions by comparing the known value of their outcomes. In the presence of risk, however, this cannot be done as each action has more than one outcome. If actions are to be compared, some means has to be found of summarising the value of the various different outcomes, weighted in some appropriate way. The simplest way to carry this out would be to use expected monetary values, calculated according to the formula:

Expected monetary value $= \sum V_i P_i$ where:

V_i = the value of the i'th outcome
P_i = the probability of the i'th outcome

Expected monetary values involve weighting each outcome by its probability which seems intuitively plausible, at least at first sight. However, a simple example suffices to show the limitations of the EMV approach. If a fair coin is tossed for a bet of £1, the expected monetary value of taking part is equal to zero. If decisions are taken on the basis of expected values a rational decision-maker will be indifferent with respect to taking or refusing the bet, and a tiny inducement would be sufficient for them to accept the bet. A bribe of one penny would be enough to induce the decision-maker to take part. This analysis raises few problems if the size of the bet is small. Many people would be quite content to toss a coin for £1, £5 or perhaps £10. However, when the size of the bet becomes really substantial, the EMV approach begins to appear much less plausible. According to the arithmetic of EMVs, the expected value of tossing a fair coin for £1,000,000 is equal to zero, and a bribe of one penny would be enough to induce a rational decision-maker to take part. Intuition and casual observation suggest that this is clearly not a valid description of most people's behaviour. Few people would accept a fair 50/50 bet for £1,000,000 because the fear of losing is stronger than the prospect of gaining. In some sense, decision-makers 'care' more about losing £1,000,000 than they 'care' about winning £1,000,000.

Utility theory offers a framework within which to analyse this phenomenon. The example of the fair bet can be examined with the aid of Figure Solutions 12.1.

The example shows a relationship between the level of utility accruing to a decision-maker and its level of income. The curve becomes flatter as it rises, illustrating diminishing marginal utility of income. If the link between utility and income is of this form, and decision-makers make their choices on the basis of expected utility instead of expected monetary values, the example can be explained.

Consider the case of a fair bet for £1,000 for a household whose current income is £10,000. If the household wins the bet, its income will rise to £11,000. If it loses the bet, its income will fall to £9,000. The increase in utility arising from a win is shown by the distance AB on the diagram and the loss of utility is shown by the distance CA. Clearly, the potential loss is greater than the potential gain. The expected utility of the bet is given by:

$(0.5 \times \text{distance AB}) - (0.5 \times \text{distance CA})$

which is clearly negative.

If decision-makers behave in this way, they are said to be risk averse and the extent of their risk aversion will be reflected in the degree of curvature of their income/utility lines. If the line is almost straight, that implies a low degree of risk aversion. If the curve is highly curved, that implies a higher level of risk aversion.

Clearly, if the analysis is to be used to take decisions in practice, some method needs to be found to measure the extent of a particular decision-maker's aversion to risk. This

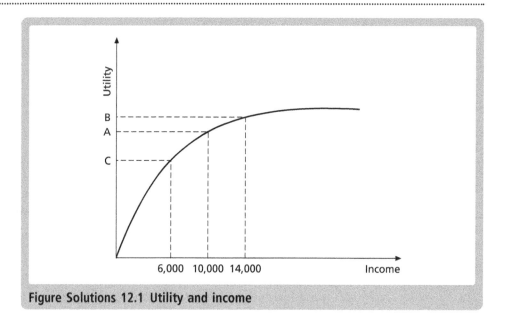

Figure Solutions 12.1 Utility and income

can be a difficult task, but it could be tackled in principle by offering the decision-maker a series of hypothetical gambles and asking which they would accept and which they would decline. Careful selection of the gambles offered would provide important information on the extent of risk aversion.

The usual assumption about decision-makers' attitude to risk is that they will be risk averse. Nevertheless, it should be recognised that there are other possible attitudes. A decision-maker could be risk neutral, having a linear income/utility line, in which case the expected monetary value criterion will be an acceptable way to evaluate decisions. Alternatively, a decision-maker could be a risk lover. In this case, the income/utility line becomes steeper at high levels of income, indicating that such a decision-maker places a higher incremental utility on a gain than on a loss of equal value. Clearly, such a decision-maker will always accept fair bets and will be willing to pay to take part in them. In summary, then, utility theory provides a means by which different attitudes to risk can be modelled, allowing for a more sophisticated approach to decision-making than that embodied in the expected monetary values approach.

Chapter 13

Self-test Questions

1 (a) A game in which the gains made by one player equal the losses made by the other
   (b) A game in which players move without knowing the move made by their rival
   (c) A common type of game in which both players could gain by cooperating but where they both defect
   (d) The situation where all players prefer the move they have made, given the moves made by the others
   (e) A strategy that will never be chosen because in every situation there is some other strategy that is preferred
   (f) A strategy where a player chooses a move with certainty, as opposed to a 'mixed' strategy where a player chooses to make a move with a given probability

2

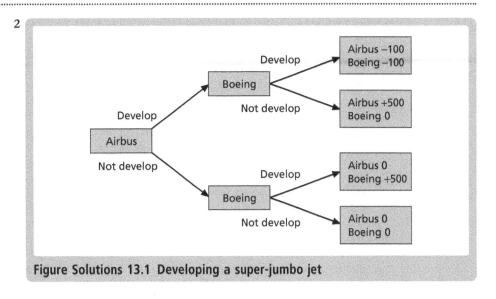

Figure Solutions 13.1 Developing a super-jumbo jet

Using rollback to solve the model, if Airbus moves first and develops, Boeing has a choice between developing (–100) and not developing (0). Hence Boeing would not develop and that branch of the model can be 'pruned'. If Airbus moves first and does not develop, Boeing has a choice between developing (+500) and not developing (0). Hence Boeing will develop and the 'not develop' branch can be pruned. Airbus is thus choosing between 'develop' (+500) and 'not develop' (0). Airbus will choose to develop and Boeing will stay out. However, that result depends entirely on Airbus being able to go first. If the situation is reversed, with Boeing acting first, the result is also reversed. Given the uncertainties associated with development, the analysis as it stands is not very helpful.

3 In Bertrand competition firms choose prices and the result is that price is forced down to marginal cost. In Cournot competition firms choose the level of output so that price need not fall to the same level. In von Stackelberg competition one firm sets the price and the other follows it. Hence the leader can set its own price, knowing how the follower will react.

4 If a game is repeated an infinite number of times, the incentive to cheat is much weaker. Hence when people know they will interact with the same other players for a long time into the future, they will behave in a trustworthy way.

5 Because it ensures that there is never any chance of restoring profitable cooperation if one player has defected just once.

Model answer to essay question

Game theory is a 'paradigm' – a set of concepts and the relationships among those concepts. It provides a means by which situations of interdependence can be analysed, and predictions made about the outcomes of those situations. For that reason it offers a formal and rigorous approach to the problems associated with oligopoly. Those problems were previously approached in a relatively informal way, simply assuming for instance that higher levels of concentration bring increasing levels of market power and increasing profits, which is difficult to justify without further analysis.

Game theory proceeds by formally stating the conditions that make up the game – the actions that the 'players' may take, the order in which they take them, and the extent of the knowledge they have. The game is then examined to see if a 'Nash equilibrium' can be identified – a situation that is preferred by each player, given what the other has done. The consequences of repeating the game and other variations are considered.

This approach has yielded important insights on issues like collusion and entry deterrence, and the economics of industrial organisation has become dominated by game theory. However, it remains problematical in a number of respects. The predicted outcome of a game can change very dramatically with small changes in the 'protocols' – the rules that determine the ways in which players 'move'. As the protocols are difficult to observe it can be almost impossible to decide which type of game is an appropriate model for a particular situation. Even if the protocols are known, a game may have many equilibria or none, which makes it difficult to predict which one (if any) will be reached. Furthermore, the situations examined (collude or not, enter or not) involve relatively limited decisions and yet they are often made extremely complex. Game theory assumes a kind of hyper-rationality on the part of players, in the sense that they calculate the very complex consequences of different moves, and yet common sense often suggests solutions to a game that the theory cannot find.

Overall, game theory has proved its value to academics by offering a means through which hitherto intractable issues could be modelled. However, its ability to predict important economic relationships, like that of a firm's actions to its environment and its performance, remain uncertain.

Chapter 14

Self-test questions

1 (a) Yes
  (b) No
  (c) No
  (d) Yes
  (e) No

2 $\dfrac{P - MC}{P} = \dfrac{s_i(1 + a)}{-E_d}$

3 Absolute cost advantages, scale economies, product differentiation. Limit price is the maximum price that can be set without inducing entry.

4 Markets must be separated, with no possibility of arbitrage between them, and elasticity of demand should be different in the different markets. First-degree price discrimination is where each customer is charged a different price, reflecting the amount they are willing to pay. Second-degree price discrimination is where the same customer is charged different prices for different amounts of the same product. Third-degree price discrimination is where buyers are divided into groups and each group is charged a different price.

5 Inelastic demand; a group of buyers who are willing to pay a higher price in order to have the product before others; uncertainty about the level of demand; limited cost penalties for low volume of production; limited possibility of entry being induced by the high price.

Model answer to essay question

Joel Dean introduced the terminology of 'skimming' versus 'penetration' pricing to describe two different approaches to setting the price of a new product. A strategy of 'skimming' involves setting a high price, at least initially, and then reducing the price if necessary, in order to serve other, lower-price, market segments. A policy of penetration pricing involves setting a relatively low price from the outset, in order to penetrate the market rapidly. Elementary economic theory suggests that in order to maximise profits, a firm should set the price in such a way that the following equation holds true:

$$\frac{P - MC}{P} = (-)\frac{1}{Ed} \quad \text{where:}$$

P = price
MC = marginal cost
Ed = elasticity of demand

This in turn suggests that a relatively high price should be set ('skim') when elasticity of demand is low, and a relatively low price should be set ('penetrate') when elasticity of demand is high. As the extent of elasticity is determined by the existence, price and performance of substitutes and by the proportion of buyers' total spending that is involved, these are the factors that determine the choice between the two different approaches to price. If the new product in question has no close substitutes and accounts for only a small proportion of buyers' total spending, its price should be set high, in order to skim. On the other hand, if there are close substitutes and buyers spend a large proportion of their income on the product in question, demand will be more highly elastic and a penetration price is indicated.

To this extent, the choice between the two different strategies may be seen as determined entirely by the extent of elasticity of demand. However, there are two other issues to be considered when choosing a pricing policy for new products. The first concerns the extent of uncertainty, and buyers' responses to changes in price. If the extent of the market is unknown, a firm may need to try both strategies, in order to find which is the most successful. In this case, if buyers respond in a hostile way to price increases, it may be appropriate to begin with a skimming price, reducing it later if necessary. The alternative of beginning with a low price and then raising it may be more difficult to implement.

The second consideration concerns the possibility of price discrimination through time. If the market for a product contains sub-markets in which buyers are prepared to pay more for a product in order to have it before others, it may be possible to maximise profits by first setting a skimming price, and selling at that price to the 'trend-setting' group of customers, and then gradually lowering the price over time to draw in other customers who are prepared to purchase the product at a lower price and are also prepared to wait for it. The market for books, for instance, would appear to conform to this pattern.

Chapter 15

Self-test questions

1 (a) False
  (b) False
  (c) True
  (d) True
2 (a) Yes
  (b) No
  (c) No
3 See Figure 13.3
4 (a) There will be a deficit
  (b) No deficit
  (c) No deficit

5 While a first-best optimal allocation of resources requires that all prices should be equal to marginal cost, if some prices are not set at that level there is no reason to suppose that setting others equal to marginal cost will lead to the second-best optimum.

Model answer to essay question

When a group of economists at Oxford first discovered, in the 1930s, that business pricing methods bore very little resemblance to the process described in the simple model of the firm, they were convinced that this showed the model to be inadequate. As business people showed no signs of even being aware of the vocabulary of marginal cost, marginal revenue and elasticity, preferring to describe their approach to pricing in terms of calculating the cost and then adding a margin, it was argued that the static, marginalist equilibrium model should be abandoned and replaced by some other form of model that bore a closer resemblance to reality as observed. However, fifty years later, the standard model remains at the centre of economic analysis and the consensus among mainstream economists is that the conclusions of the Oxford group were erroneous. This argument rests upon a number of foundations.

The first argument in favour of retaining the standard model is essentially methodological, or perhaps even philosophical. The question to be asked and answered is 'what is the purpose of a model, and what are the criteria for a good model?' The answer given is that the purpose of a model is to make predictions that are testable, and which are validated by the evidence. On those criteria, the descriptive realism or otherwise of a model is an entirely irrelevant issue. The standard model of the firm meets the criteria and is therefore perfectly acceptable. The Oxford economists made the mistake of assuming that the model was intended to be descriptive of firms' decision-making processes, rather than identifying the conditions that must hold if firms find some way of maximising profits.

The second foundation for the argument in favour of retaining the standard model of the firm lies in the evidence on the way in which firms go about the process of cost-plus pricing. At first sight, the procedure appears to be entirely mechanical, with a figure for cost per unit being calculated from cost accounting data, and a margin being added, in line with the custom within the industry. If that were actually the case it is clear that firms would be ignoring market conditions altogether. They would not be behaving like profit-maximisers, and the profit-maximising model would be unlikely to predict their behaviour with any accuracy. However, closer examination reveals that the calculation of both the cost per unit and the margin is a much less mechanical process than might have been thought and that both offer means by which market forces can influence the price eventually arrived at. In the case of calculating cost per unit, for instance, firms usually use some form of standard cost, which is set through a process of informal discussion during which market factors are taken into account. Firms often appear to have such factors in mind, as in the case of the firm that set prices on the basis of cost per unit at full capacity, even when it knew that it would not achieve full capacity. When asked why it used this apparently odd procedure, the firm explained that it did so for 'competitive reasons' – in other words it knew that if it calculated actual cost per unit and then added a conventional margin the resulting price would be higher than the one that was felt to yield maximum profit.

Just as the calculation of cost is actually very flexible, and is used as a vehicle for the introduction of market influences, so the addition of the margin provides an opportunity for firms to take account of buyers' response to different prices and competitors' pricing strategies. Firms are therefore able to make good, though rarely perfect, approximations to the profit-maximising price, through implicit adjustments rather than through explicit application of any economic model. The evidence on cost-plus pricing is therefore supportive of the standard model of pricing, rather than destructive of it.

Chapter 16

Self-test questions

1 Price – including discounts, allowances, payment terms and credit terms
   Product – attributes of goods offered; quality; packaging, service agreements, warranties
   Promotion – advertising, publicity, promotion, personal selling
   Place – locations and marketing channels

2 Price elasticity is likely to rise over all stages of the PLC. Advertising elasticity is more difficult to predict. In the introduction stage the product is a monopoly, which suggests relatively low advertising elasticity, but the newness of the product may offset that. In the growth stage the industry is an oligopoly, which suggests a high advertising elasticity, and then in maturity and decline both the age of the product and the large number of firms involved in production suggest a low advertising elasticity. Overall advertising intensity is likely to be high in the introduction and growth stages and low in maturity and decline.

3 (a) Information processing
   (b) Keyboard, screen, processor
   (c) Hardware, software, peripherals

4 Legal protection from copying, development of brand loyalty, assists segmentation and price discrimination, links and strengthens coroporate identity.

5 (a) Sold on a customised basis to a limited number of users, and there is value to be had from close links between the manufacturer and the buyer. The optimal marketing channel will therefore have a small number of levels and will often involve direct marketing.
   (b) Sold to a very widely dispersed group of buyers, which suggests a multi-level marketing channel. On the other hand, a small number of chain stores, which re-stock at very short intervals, are responsible for a very large portion of sales. There is likely to be at least two different channel configurations. One will be relatively direct, serving the main chain stores. The other will be multi-level, serving smaller and more dispersed shops and stores.

Model answer to essay question

There are various different rules-of-thumb that companies may use in order to set their advertising and promotion budgets, the best known of which are as follows:

- setting a percentage of sales
- spending all that the firm can afford
- matching the competition
- setting objectives and tasks.

If such rules are to be evaluated against the objective of profit maximisation, it is first necessary to consider what the profit-maximising model of the firm suggests with respect to the optimal level of advertising expenditure. This is to be found in the Dorfman–Steiner condition, which states that for profit maximisation the ratio of advertising spending to sales revenue should be equal to the ratio of the advertising elasticity of demand to the price elasticity. Each of the rules-of-thumb can thus be evaluated against that condition.

Setting a promotional budget by allocating a percentage of sales is a common approach in many companies. It has the advantage of being relatively simple and its form corresponds to the form suggested by the Dorfman–Steiner condition. However, it will only correspond to profit maximisation if the percentage chosen happens to coincide with the ratio of the advertising to the price elasticities. There is also a danger that if sales revenues fall for any reason, this leads to an automatic reduction in advertising, even if such a reduction is inappropriate.

One of the alternative approaches is known as the objective and task approach. A firm using this method establishes a number of objectives that advertising and promotion are intended to achieve, and then identifies the tasks that have to be carried out in order to meet those objectives. These tasks are then funded and the budget arrived at in that way. In itself, the objective and task approach is unlikely to achieve profit maximisation. However, if each task were evaluated in terms of the additional revenues it would create and the additional costs it would incur, and all those tasks that add more to revenues than to costs were undertaken, that process would provide a mechanism whereby maximum profit might be approximated. When considering the establishment of budgets for advertising and promotion it is important to recall that this is only one element of the marketing mix. Effective profit performance requires an appropriate balancing of the mix, as well as careful evaluation of each component independently.

Chapter 17

Self-test questions

1 (a) False
 (b) True
 (c) False
2 19 per cent
3 IRR can give multiple answers; IRR involves an implicit assumption about the reinvestment rate which is inappropriate; IRR ignores the absolute size of projects
4 (a) Linear programming
 (b) Integer programming
5 (a) If the stream of dividends is assumed to be a perpetuity, the cost of equity capital is given by:

$$K_e = \frac{d}{E}$$

 (b) According to the capital asset pricing model:

$$K_e = R_F + b[K_M + R_F]$$

Model answer to exercise

The 'traditional' view of the cost of capital is shown in Figure Solutions 17.1.

In the traditional view, the cost of debt is always lower than the cost of equity, as the holders of debt are exposed to less risk, having the first call on the firm's profits. As the gearing ratio increases both the cost of equity and the cost of debt increase because the holders of both types of capital face an increasing level of risk.

The weighted average cost of capital (WACC) which corresponds to these relationships has a U-shape. The WACC falls at first, as the higher proportion of lower-cost debt reduces the weighted average, and then rises as higher gearing ratios increase the risk held by holders of both debt and equity. As the curve has a U-shape there is an optimal capital structure where the cost of capital is minimised and the value of the firm maximised. This traditional view of the WACC has been challenged by Modigliani and Miller (M–M). They begin with the following set of assumptions:

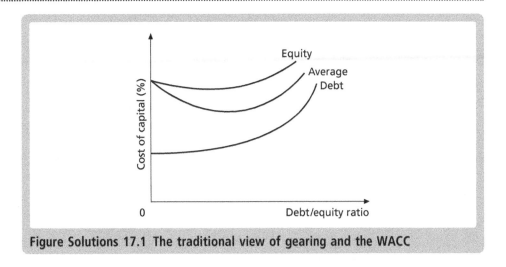

Figure Solutions 17.1 The traditional view of gearing and the WACC

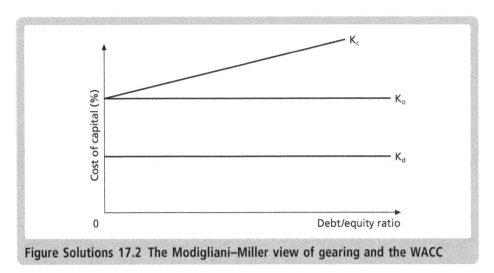

Figure Solutions 17.2 The Modigliani–Miller view of gearing and the WACC

- there are no taxes
- the capital market is efficient and competitive
- there are no transactions costs
- there are no costs associated with bankruptcy
- shareholders can borrow on the same terms as corporations
- the cost of debt is constant, whatever the level of gearing.

If these assumptions hold, M–M show that the cost of debt, the cost of equity and the WACC are as shown in Figure Solutions 17.2.

As the figure shows, the WACC remains constant, whatever the gearing ratio, and equal to the cost of equity in a firm that is entirely financed through equity. M–M argue that market forces must guarantee this result. If two firms are identical except for their gearing ratios they cannot have different costs of capital and different values because if they did there would be an incentive for shareholders to sell stock in the higher valued firm and buy it in the one with a lower value. This process of 'arbitrage' must even out

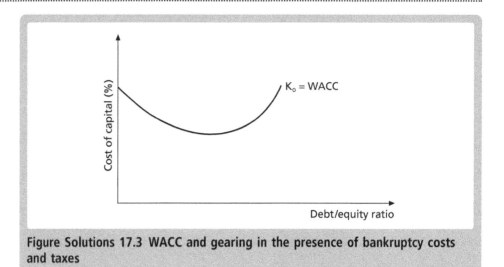

Figure Solutions 17.3 WACC and gearing in the presence of bankruptcy costs and taxes

the values of the two firms. In this case, the WACC is invariant with the gearing ratio and there is no optimal capital structure.

While the M–M conclusions may be valid under the assumptions they make, those assumptions are very restrictive and need to be relaxed if conclusions are to be drawn that are applicable to real-world firms. First of all, it is necessary to consider how the conclusions are altered if taxation is introduced. If there is taxation, and interest on debt is tax deductible while dividends are not, a firm can improve its net cash flow by having a higher gearing ratio. In this case, the WACC simply falls as gearing increases and the value of a firm would be maximised by having almost 100 per cent debt finance. The optimal capital structure involves virtually no equity. On the other hand, if bankruptcy costs are introduced, the cost of capital will tend to be higher at higher gearing ratios, as the risk of default increases. If these two effects are both introduced together, the result is a relationship between the WACC and the gearing ratio as shown in Figure Solutions 17.3.

At lower gearing ratios an increase in gearing leads to a lower WACC, because of the tax effect. However, as gearing increases, the risks and costs of bankruptcy begin to have an effect and eventually this is powerful enough to offset the tax effect. At higher gearing ratios the relationship between WACC and gearing becomes positive. As a result, the curve linking the WACC and gearing is U-shaped, as in the traditional view, though for different reasons. There is an optimal capital structure and the level of gearing is not irrelevant.

Chapter 18

Self-test questions

1 The terms 'competence' and 'capability' are often used interchangeably. However, 'core competence' may be interpreted as the unique and inimitable ability that may give a firm competitive advantage over its rivals. 'Organisational capability' may be interpreted as the ability to maintain and develop the core competence. 'Administrative heritage' is the structure, culture, routines and physical facilities that constrain the range of activities that are open to the firm.

2 System performance refers to the ability of the firm to maintain itself and to thrive in the long term as an organisation. Goal performance refers to the achievement of more specific lower-level objectives.

3 Entry barriers are advantages held by the incumbent firms in an *industry* that limit the ability of new firms to enter. Mobility barriers are barriers to the entry of new members to *strategic groups within the same industry* (barriers to adopting the same strategy). Isolating mechanisms are factors that prevent one firm from imitating the core competences and capabilities of another.

4 Heterogeneity; limited *ex post* competition (which may arise from inimitability and causal ambiguity); imperfect mobility; lack of *ex ante* competition.

5 Game theory has little to say about performance; its focus on interaction is inconsistent with the attention currently paid to firms' internal strengths as the key to performance; game theory focuses on a much narrower range of phenomena than strategy.

Model answer essay question

One of the earliest approaches to business strategy was the SWOT analysis framework – S for strengths, W for weaknesses, O for opportunities and T for threats. According to that framework the key task for the strategist is to carry out a careful internal appraisal of the firm's strengths and weaknesses, and an equally important external appraisal of the opportunities and threats.

As the analysis of strategy became more formal, drawing on economic analysis to a much greater extent, attention tended to focus much more heavily on external appraisal. Porter's work on the 'five forces' analysis, in particular, tended to emphasise the importance of the competitive structure in which a firm operates as the major determinant of performance. A firm that locates itself in an 'attractive' business environment, or one that is able to render its environment more attractive through its own actions, will be the firm that tends to make higher levels of profit. Hence the main task of the strategist was seen as the analysis of the environment, the identification of attractive product/market niches or the creation of such niches.

One implication of the 'five forces' analysis appears to be that firms operating in the same environment will earn the same level of profits. The idiosyncratic features of the individual firms become much less important. However, strategy analysts observed that firms in the same industry often behave and perform in different ways. Some empirical analyses seemed to show that profits varied much more significantly *within* industries than *across* industries. Hence attention shifted away from the external environment in which firms operate, and towards the differences in their competences, capabilities and resources – the resource-based perspective (RBP). In terms of the SWOT analysis, attention became much more focused on the firm's internal strengths and weaknesses.

While the RBP has yielded useful insights, there is no reason to suppose that the two different types of explanation are mutually exclusive. Indeed, the major insight arising from SWOT analysis is that both sets of dimensions need to be taken into account. More recent work on the variation in performance has confirmed that variation from firm to firm within industries is very important. However, it has also shown that industry effects do exist, returning the analysis to the original SWOT formulation. Both internal and external considerations need to be taken into account when examining the determinants of business performance.

Chapter 19

Self-test questions

1 (a) No

(b) Yes

(c) No

2 A network that has no owner will be subject to network externalities because the decision on how many participants will be left to individual decision-makers who decide on the basis of the cost and benefit to themselves. Hence the additional benefits that accrue to other users will not be taken into account by a potential user who is deciding on whether to join. The owner of a network would take such benefits into account, thereby internalising the externality. A perfectly competitive industry will produce too few network products for the same reason. Purchasers will only be willing to pay an amount equal to the benefit they themselves receive.

3 (a) Not proven

(b) True

(c) Not true

4 Marginal cost, which will be close to zero.

5 (a) Offer to lease your product with a cancellation option so that buyers can try it at no risk to themselves.

(b) Give the product free to an influential purchaser.

(c) Advertise heavily, emphasising the advantages of your product.

Model answer to essay question

It is often suggested that there are efficiency problems in the market for information products for a number of reasons. Most important, there are 'network' effects, because a product has more value to purchasers as its market share increases. A word-processor or spreadsheet program has more value to a potential purchaser as it is adopted by more users because the existence of a large 'installed base' provides compatibility and the ability to share, send and swap files.

Some analysts have suggested that network effects produce 'lock-in' whereby the market may select an inferior product because it comes first and its initially high market share ensures that subsequent users choose it, even if more efficient alternatives are available. However, the history of Lotus 1-2-3, Wordperfect and Microsoft Office provides evidence to counter this assertion. That is because both Lotus 1-2-3 and Wordperfect at one time had dominant shares of the market. If 'lock-in' were a major feature of these markets it would be expected that their early dominance would lead users to continue purchasing them, in order to ensure compatibility with their large installed base. However, in both cases Microsoft Office, containing Word and Excel, has come to dominate. Both of these products were rated superior to their predecessors by the computing community and both were available using the Windows graphical user interface, with the added benefit of compatibility between the two components. Critics of Microsoft have argued that Office succeeded because Windows gives the company monopoly power in the form of 'leverage'. However, that argument is also flawed because in other markets Microsoft products have not been so successful. In personal financial software, for instance, the market is dominated by Quicken from Intuit, not by Microsoft Money.

The argument over 'lock-in', 'increasing returns' market inefficiency and Microsoft will continue for a considerable time to come. For the moment, it is sufficient to note that it has not been firmly established that market economies do suffer significantly from these effects.

Chapter 20

Self-test questions

1 (a) True
  (b) True
  (c) Not true
2 Concentration: structure. Growth of demand: structure. Advertising intensity: structure or performance or conduct. Collusive agreements: conduct. Productivity growth: performance. Entry barriers: structure. Profitability: performance. Degree of diversification: structure. Company objectives: conduct.
3 Monopoly power, chance, entrepreneurial activity.
4 (a) No
  (b) Yes
  (c) Yes
5 Advantages: easily understood, inexpensive to administer, less prone to political manipulation, firms waste less resources trying to influence decision-makers. Disadvantages: inflexible, difficult to accommodate the circumstances of individual cases, the rules established may have little justification.

Model answer to essay question

In the conventional view, monopoly power is a common feature of industrial and commercial life, which reduces the efficiency of the resource allocation process in three different senses. First, it reduces static allocative efficiency, by leading to prices that are not equal to marginal cost. Second, it leads to X-inefficiency, as firms with monopoly power are not under pressure to keep their costs as low as possible. Third, it leads to dynamic inefficiency as the rate of innovation is less than would prevail in more competitive circumstances.

The cost of these inefficiencies is difficult to measure, but various attempts have been made to provide estimates. In most cases, these are based around the idea that profits arise from monopoly power, and that profits can therefore be used as the basis for estimating the costs of monopoly power. It is also suggested that firms waste resources in the process of attempting to secure monopoly positions, so that at least some of firms' spending on advertising and promotion should be included in the estimated costs of monopoly. The results of this process of measurement vary, as might be expected, but some suggest that the cost is very large indeed, so that considerable expense on anti-trust programmes would be worthwhile. This view can be attacked on a number of grounds, which centre around the view of competition that is adopted and the source of profits. In particular, the 'Austrian' view of competition suggests that the dangers and costs of monopoly may have been overestimated.

In the conventional view, on which the estimates for the cost of monopoly are based, profits can only arise, in the long run at least, from the ownership of monopoly power. In that case, profits are a direct reflection of monopoly power and can be the basis for such estimates. In the 'Austrian' view there are three possible sources of profit. The first is the ownership of monopoly power. The second is unexpected fluctuations in the environment, and the third is beneficial entrepreneurial activity. If a firm has a management team that 'clicks' better than others, or if it succeeds in finding a new market or creating a new product, it will enjoy a high level of profits, at least for a while. These are not monopoly profits in any meaningful sense of the term because the opportunities from which the profits have been made were open to all.

In this view, competition is not a state, but a continuous process of attempting to gain monopoly power or attempting to break into the monopoly positions established by others. Most monopoly profits are not the result of exploitative behaviour but the relatively short-lived reward for firms that have been able to develop new market opportunities creatively. As a result, it is argued that estimates of the cost of monopoly power are greatly exaggerated and most monopoly legislation is a waste of resources. There is some real and costly monopoly power in the economy, arising from the existence of barriers to entry, some of which are government induced, but its importance has been exaggerated and does not justify an expensive anti-trust effort.

It may also be argued that some anti-trust policy may be positively harmful. Anti-merger policy, for instance, is usually justified on the grounds that mergers may allow firms to establish dominant positions and use them to exploit consumers. However, if there is free entry to and exit from the industry, coupled with vigorous competition from firms attempting to break into the market, this power may be tightly constrained. The dominant firm will have little ability to exploit its position without attracting entry. There is therefore very little purpose served by having an anti-merger policy. Furthermore, a policy that prohibits mergers will insulate firms from an important aspect of competition, namely the threat of take-over and the market for corporate control. A firm whose managers know that they are safe from take-over because the monopoly legislation prevents it may indulge themselves in much more expensive X-inefficiencies. From this point of view, then, it may be argued that anti-monopoly policy is unnecessary and misguided.

Chapter 21

Self-test questions

1 'Public interest' theory assumes that regulation is put in place with the disinterested objective of serving the public interest. 'Capture' theories emphasise that regulators are economic actors with interests and that they may become 'captured' by the industries they are supposed to regulate. Regulation may even be demanded by industries as a means of protecting their profits.

2 Introduction of charges; contracting out; selling to the private sector; de-regulation and liberalisation.

3 Bidders cannot fully specify their obligations into the distant future; incomplete long-term or recurrent short-term contracts both have major difficulties; winning bidders may cheat on quality because it cannot be observed; it may not be realistically possible to transfer from one supplier to another because of asset specificities.

4 Monopoly power; externalities; public goods.

5 The demand side refers to the reasons that an industry may want to be regulated; the supply side refers to the conditions under which regulation is provided by vote-seeking legislators or rent-seeking bureaucrats.

Model answer to essay question

Rate-of-return regulation is a system whereby firms in a regulated industry are allowed to earn a specified return on capital. Prices are set in order to allow that rate of return to be earned. It has a number of weaknesses. First, it does not lead to allocative efficiency because price is unlikely to equal marginal cost. Second, it may encourage X-inefficiency and a waste of resources. Third, it encourages firms to over-invest in capacity in order to allow a higher absolute level of profit to be earned. Fourth, there are no incentives to innovate, and fifth, it shifts risk to the consumer, which is inappropriate. Finally, the governance process – the studies, legal hearings and appeals – uses up significant resources. However, there are some incentives to efficiency because regulators can disallow unnecessary expenditures, discouraging 'gold-plating'. Regulatory lag means that prices are set for a fixed period and firms can make extra profit if they are able to reduce costs (although prices will then be lowered in the next round of regulation).

Price-cap regulation is where a regulated industry is required to set prices according to a formula of the type RPI – X, where RPI is the change in the retail price index and X is an efficiency factor. If the RPI remains constant, firms are required to reduce prices each year by the percentage X. This approach should discourage X-inefficiency and over-investment in capacity. It is also easier to operate and less expensive in governance costs. However, it does have disadvantages. To be set appropriately, the X factor requires information on productivity gains, which is difficult to acquire. If it is set incorrectly, allocative inefficiency will arise. Companies will spend resources attempting to influence the X-factor, which is wasteful. As the method provides no long-term scheme for control, private investors may be hesitant to invest in price-cap regulated industries and hence there may be under-investment.

In practice, the two methods are not as independent as they seem. If firms in a price-cap industry earn very high levels of profit, there may be public pressure to lower their prices, as a means of limiting their rate of return. Overall, the most appropriate choice depends upon the balance between the various different aspects of efficiency and incentives in the economic and political environment of the individual industry.

Glossary of terms

Arc-elasticity of demand Elasticity of demand over a significant arc of the demand curve.

Asset-specificity The extent to which an asset's value is dependent upon its use in transacting with a specific other party.

Back-forecasting Checking the validity of a forecasting method by using it to make a 'forecast' for a period for which the outcome is already known.

Barriers to entry Advantages which incumbent firms in an industry have over potential entrants.

Bertrand competition A form of oligopolistic competition in which firms set prices for identical products, leading price to be forced down until it equals marginal cost.

Beta coefficient A measure of the extent to which the returns on security vary with the returns to the market as a whole.

Bounded rationality A form of behaviour associated with uncertainty where individuals do not examine every possible option open to them, but simply consider a number of alternatives which happen to occur to them.

Branding Attaching a brand mark or brand name to a product in order to distinguish it from other product variants.

Capital asset pricing model A model which attempts to measure the return which investors will require from a security, as a function of its riskiness.

Classical contracting Spot contracts between independent individuals, where the transaction is essentially 'in-out', the identity of the transactors is irrelevant and the transaction is self-liquidating.

Cobb-Douglas production function A mathematical function showing a particular form of relationship between inputs and outputs.

Cournot competition A form of oligopolistic competition in which each firm sets its own level of output, dependent upon the output of the other firm.

Certainty-equivalent The risk-free return on capital which gives the same level of satisfaction as other combinations of risk and return.

Concentration The extent to which industrial activity is in the hands of a small number of firms.

Conjectural variation A measure of a firm's belief with respect to the response which its rivals will make to its own actions.

Contestable markets Markets in which entry and exit are costless.

Contribution margin The difference between revenue per unit and variable cost per unit, in the framework of break-even analysis.

Control loss Cost increases attributable to management's inability to monitor and control the performance of subordinates.

Cost leadership A 'generic' form of corporate strategy which involves producing at lower cost than the competition.

Delphi technique A forecasting technique whereby individual experts anonymously give an opinion, and their reasons for it, and the opinions are then circulated and amended until a consensus is reached.

Differentiation A form of corporate strategy which involves producing products which differ from the competition in ways which buyers value.

Diversification Carrying on business in a range of industries.

Diversification discount A reduction in the market value of a diversified firm, in comparison with its value as a number of separate businesses.

Dividend valuation model A model which attempts to estimate the cost of equity capital by examining the relationship between that cost, the flow of dividends and the market value of the firm.

Dominant position A market structure in which a single firm has a very large market share.

Dorfman–Steiner condition The condition that, for profit-maximisation, the advertising to sales ratio should equal the ratio of advertising elasticity to price elasticity.

Duopoly An industry containing only two firms.

Econometrics The application of statistical methods to the estimation of economic models.

Economies of scale Reductions in cost which arise from the utilisation of larger sets of plant and equipment.

Economies of scope Reductions in cost which arise from producing a number of different goods together.

Engel curve A curve showing the relationship between a household's income and its consumption of a commodity.

Exit barriers Factors which make it expensive for a firm to leave an industry.

First-best optimum The absolutely optimal allocation of resources, where all prices are set equal to marginal social cost.

Focus A corporate strategy which involves serving the special needs of a narrow group of buyers.

Game theory A technique for predicting the actions which interdependent rivals may take in their relations with each other.

Governance structure The framework which governs a transaction.

Green mail A situation where a company buys shares in another and threatens to take it over, but is then 'bought off' by selling its shares back to the proposed 'victim' at a premium.

Group-think The process whereby the independent judgement of individuals is impaired by their desire to be seen as loyal and conforming members of the group.

Idiosyncratic investment Expenditure on assets which are specific to a particular transaction.

Incentive contracts Contracts which give an agent an incentive to behave in ways that meet the objectives of a principal.

Income effect The change in a basket of goods selected by a consumer which takes place when the consumer's real income increases but relative prices remain the same.

Indifference analysis A method of modelling consumer behaviour.

Information agreements Agreements between firms to share information on issues like price, in order to establish a tacit form of collusion.

Institutional investors Financial companies that own shares in other companies.

Internal rate of return The discount rate which reduces the net present value (NPV) of an investment project to zero.

Internalisation Making and coordinating transactions inside the managerial hierarchy of a firm, as opposed to making transactions between independent firms through contracts or spot markets.

Iso-sales line A line showing all the different combinations of two promotional media which yield the same level of sales.

Isoquant A curve showing all the different quantities of capital and labour which may be used to produce a given level of output.

Leading indicators Indicators whose behaviour is believed to be closely correlated with the future behaviour of a variable which is being forecast.

Learning effects Reductions in cost which arise as a result of experience in carrying out some activity.

Loss-leaders Products sold at below cost with the aim of inducing buyers to purchase other products as well.

Managerial diseconomies of scale Increases in cost per unit at larger scales of output attributable to the loss of control associated with attempting to manage larger organisations.

Managerial discretion The ability of senior managers to use a firm's resources to meet their own objectives, as opposed to maximising shareholder value.

Marginal product of labour The additional output arising from the use of an additional unit of labour.

Marginal rate of substitution The rate at which a consumer is willing to exchange one commodity for another, while achieving the same level of satisfaction.

Marginal sales response The change in the value or volume of sales arising from an additional unit of advertising or media exposure.

Minimum efficient scale (MES) The minimum scale of production at which all known scale economies have been achieved.

Nash equilibrium A central concept in game theory – the situation where each player has chosen the best 'move' for themselves, given that the other player has also chosen the move that they prefer in the circumstances.

Neo-classical economic model The standard economic model of the firm in which the objective is profit-maximisation and the firm has certain knowledge of its cost and demand conditions.

Neo-classical contracting Medium to long-term contracts between independent parties where the contract is understood to be incomplete and there are mechanisms for arbitration if the parties cannot agree in the event of an unspecified contingency.

Net present value The discounted value of a stream of cash outflows and inflows associated with an investment project.

Normative theories Theories concerned with 'what ought to be', as opposed to 'what is'.

OLI model Also known as the 'eclectic' model. Developed by Dunning as an explanation for the multinational enterprise (MNE).

Opportunism Guileful behaviour designed to take account of asymmetries of information between parties to a transaction.

Organisational slack Unnecessarily high costs due to lack of tight control.

Own price elasticity of demand A measure of the responsiveness of the demand for a product to changes in its own price.

Penetration pricing An approach to pricing new products which involves setting an initially low price.

Perfect competition A market structure in which there are a large number of small firms producing identical products and where there is free entry to the industry.

Poison pill A way to defend a company from take-over by imposing significant financial burdens on a successful bidder.

Positive theories Theories concerned with 'what is', rather than 'what ought to be'.

Price-cap regulation A form of regulation whereby government sets the prices that a company can charge, often on an RPI–X basis.

Price effect The change in the basket of goods selected by a consumer which takes place when the price of one of the goods changes.

Principal/Agent theory A branch of theory which examines the ways in which a principal may secure the behaviour he seeks from an agent, despite the fact that the agent is better informed than himself.

Principle of diminishing returns The generalisation that as more and more of a variable factor is added to a fixed factor, in order to produce more output, the additional output per unit of variable input must decline.

Prisoners' dilemma A type of game in which both players are best served if they cooperate but where the structure of the game leads them both to defect unless they can find some way to resolve the dilemma.

Proprietary technology Technological knowledge which can only be used with the permission of its owner.

Psychic costs of mobility The non-pecuniary costs of moving from place to place.

Pure monopoly A market structure in which there is only one firm and no possibility of entry.

Rate-of-return regulation Regulation of an industry based upon attempting to restrict its rate of return on capital to some target figure.

Resource-based perspective An approach to explaining business performance based upon the idea that superior performance requires the ownership of unique resources, often interpreted as 'competences' or 'capabilities'.

Restrictive agreements Agreements between firms which have the purpose of restricting competition.

Returns to scale The relationship between the unit cost of output and the scale at which the output is produced.

Revealed preference theory A theory of consumer behaviour.

Satisficing A form of behaviour where individuals seek to achieve a satisfactory target with respect to their goals, but do not seek more once that level has been achieved, at least in the short run.

Scope The range of activities, industries, markets and countries in which the firm is involved.

Second-best optimum The best allocation of resources available, given that a first-best optimum is not possible.

Skimming pricing An approach to the pricing of new products which involves setting an initially high price.

Span of control The number of individuals under the direct control of another individual.

Stochastic economies of scale Economies of scale which arise as a result of the properties of random variations.

Strategic Business Unit (SBU) A sub-unit of a corporation which is large enough, or different enough, to have its own strategy.

Structure–Conduct–Performance paradigm An approach to the economics of industrial organisation in which the structure of the industry – concentration, entry barriers and product differentiation – are seen as the determinants of performance.

Substitution effect The change in the basket of goods selected by a consumer that takes place when relative prices change but real income remains the same.

Super-majority amendments Amendments to a company's governance arrangements, requiring large majority votes for certain changes. May be used by senior managers to protect themselves against action by shareholders.

Time-series analysis A term applied to a number of different forecasting methods.

Vertical integration The extent to which a firm carries out activities at different stages of the production process from raw materials to the final purchaser.

Von Stackelberg competition A form of oligopolistic competition in which firms set output, with one acting as a leader and the other acting as a follower.

Weighted average cost of capital (WACC) The overall cost of capital to a firm, made up of a weighted average of the cost of debt and the cost of equity.

Workable competition The most desirable form of competition, selected from those which are actually possible.

X-inefficiency Where a firm incurs higher costs than are necessary, given the set of plant and equipment in use and its level of capacity utilisation.

Zero-sum game A game in which the gains to the winner are exactly equal to the losses to the loser.

Index